ENTERTAINMENT LAW

FUNDAMENTALS AND PRACTICE

REVISED FIRST EDITION

Corey Field

cognella®
SAN DIEGO

Bassim Hamadeh, CEO and Publisher
Mieka Portier, Field Acquisitions Editor
Carrie Montoya, Manager, Revisions and Author Care
Tony Paese, Project Editor
Alia Bales, Production Editor
Jess Estrella, Senior Graphic Designer
Trey Soto, Licensing Coordinator
Natalie Piccotti, Director of Marketing
Kassie Graves, Vice President of Editorial
Jamie Giganti, Director of Academic Publishing

This Treatise is a reference work of practical legal scholarship that presents all sides of the topics included. It does not constitute legal advice, nor do opinions expressed in this context foreclose the author, his law firm, or his clients from taking any position on current or future legal matters. The forms are provided solely as educational and illustrative examples and supplements to the main text.

Portions of this work were formerly available as a legal treatise under the title Entertainment Law: Forms and Analysis, published by Law Journal Press, a division of American Lawyer Media

Barry I. Slotnick, Advisory Editor

cognella® | ACADEMIC PUBLISHING
3970 Sorrento Valley Blvd., Ste. 500, San Diego, CA 92121

Brief Contents

Detailed Contents

CHAPTER 2   Television   167

CHAPTER 5   Live Theater   368

CHAPTER 8   Cyber Law   469

Acknowledgments

Entertainment Law Fundamentals and Practice is both a scholarly and a practical work. It is designed for comprehensive law school courses in all topics of entertainment law, and also as a practical "how to" guide for practicing lawyers. My enormous thanks to everyone at Cognella Academic Publishing for their expertise, professionalism, and enthusiasm in bringing this work to its readers.

Those readers include students in my entertainment law courses at USC Gould School of Law and at law schools nationwide that have, with my gratitude, adopted this book as their course textbook. "Be lawyers, think like lawyers" I have told my students, and this book is designed to achieve that goal. Those law students, and students in other courses are the future of the entertainment industry and this book is for them.

This publication is eminently practical thanks to my clients and colleagues who have put their faith and trust in me as an attorney in a broad range of entertainment law and intellectual property fields. Prior to becoming a lawyer I was a music publisher by profession, and many of those entertainment industry colleagues showed me how it works in the real world, an ideal preparation for the law which has made all the difference.

Law is a powerful and much needed force that protects and nurtures creativity, and the entertainment industry that depends on that divine spark. May this book help.

Corey Field

Preface

The definition of "entertainment law" expands in accordance with the needs of the companies and individuals that comprise the entertainment industry. "Entertainment law" can encompass vast areas of the law including contract law, corporate law, intellectual property, technology and regulatory law, and other areas that might intersect with an entertainment client's activities.

Chapter 1 discusses film, using the creative and business timeline for the film industry as the outline for a presentation of how projects are conceived, financed, produced, distributed, and accounted for, including the roles of talent and their representation. Also covered are legal issues encountered in productions ranging from depiction of characters and people in media, to financing.

Chapter 2 on television encompasses all the current business models, from traditional networks and affiliates, to cable and satellite Multichannel Video Program Distributors (MVPDs), to online and mobile "over the top" ("OTT") streaming apps and webisodes offering Subscription Video on Demand (SVOD).

Chapter 3 on book and magazine publishing includes a detailed description, along with the legal underpinnings, of publishing deal points and negotiation. The chapter also examines digital issues in the magazine and online database publishing industries.

Chapter 4 reviews all facets of the music industry, beginning with a presentation of copy right law as the "blueprint" of the music industry as an introduction to understanding the different creative aspects and business models such as recording, publishing, and live performance, licensing, royalties, digital and online formats, and the role of agents and managers. Music licensing, including performing rights, synchronization, mechanicals, and master licensing are all presented in detail. The current revision includes an introduction to the recently enacted Music Modernization Act and its initial impact on the music industry, which will evolve over the coming years.

Chapter 5 presents the major contractual, ownership, licensing and business models of live theatre, including the Broadway stage.

Chapter 6 discusses radio. The chapter provides a review of the regulatory background of the industry, the financial models, the complex world of Internet radio music licensing, and some of the leading issues regarding on-air formats and agreements with on-air personalities. As in Chapter 4, the current revision of this chapter includes an introduction to the recently enacted Music Modernization Act.

Chapter 7 on celebrity rights of publicity and privacy presents an in-depth history of the laws that affect celebrities, including the right of publicity, defamation, the right of privacy, and the so-called "anti paparazzi" laws, as well as negotiation points in celebrity endorsement agreements. It includes a summary of the leading case law on the myriad types of right of publicity cases, ranging from look-alike and sound-alike cases to computer games.

Chapter 8 reviews the evolving state of "cyber law," and the ways in which current high technology affects—and is affected by—the law, including summaries of domain name registration and litigation, trademark rights on the internet, open source software legal issues, and the Digital Millennium Copyright Act.

A varied collection of "real world" blank contract forms is available online from the publisher as a supplement to the text. The forms are essential for acquiring knowledge of potential deal points and business models, though the user is cautioned that as "real" contracts they may contain one-sided provisions and other customizations. Any adaptation of a form for practical use will require the practitioner's judgment, perspective, client needs, expertise, and edits, skills that will hopefully be greatly enhanced by this book.

CHAPTER 1

Film

§1.01   Introduction

As the Second Circuit has observed, "Filmmaking is a collaborative process typically involving artistic contributions from large numbers of people, including—in addition to producers, directors, and screen-writers—actors, designers, cinematographers, camera operators, and a host of skilled technical contributors."[1] Film is an enormously collaborative medium, more akin to a military general assembling and commanding an army than any other art form. Because filmmaking is a quasi-industrial endeavor, the creative vision of a few key people must be supported by a virtual army of technicians, craftspeople, marketers, financiers, and bookkeepers. An entertainment lawyer whose practice includes film may find a need to be conversant in several areas of the law, including:

- Intellectual Property Law: for the acquisition of underlying rights, and the protection of the IP embodied in the film, including copyright and trademarks;

- Business and Finance/Securities: for the successful acquisition of funding and investment for the project and the required accountings;

- Labor and Employment: for the personal services agreements for cast and crew, and for working with trade unions, guilds, and collective bargaining entities in the film industry;

- Agency: for dealing with the roles of agents and managers who represent actors, directors, and writers;

- Insurance: for advising on insurance coverage requirements in the film industry;

- Advertising: for advising on marketing and promotion, including celebrity rights of publicity, and product placement, tie-ins consisting of advertising the film in conjunction with other companies, and related advertising issues;

- Corporate Law: for dealing with formation of business entities;

---

1   See *16 Casa Duse, LLC v. Merkin*, 791 F.3d 247, 258 (2d Cir. 2015).

- Contract Law: for reducing all of the above to operative agreements.

This chapter will present a practical, chronological approach to the various tasks that an entertainment lawyer will likely encounter, from initial conception of a project to its completion, distribution, marketing, and financial accounting, both for motion pictures, and for television projects.

§1.02   The Life Cycle of a Film

[1]—Production

The life cycle of a film, from initial concept to completion and distribution, can span many years during which the producer will have many creative and business tasks to accomplish to complete a motion picture and achieve distribution to the public. A helpful visual aid describing the creative and business steps that must be climbed will be found as an Appendix to this Chapter (§1:15[1], "The Film Production Pyramid".

[a]—Development

The initial creative stages usually occur prior to obtaining a firm commitment for financing or production. During development, a writer will be commissioned to create the first draft of the screenplay. The project's producer will attempt to interest a lead actor and a director to "attach" themselves to the project. During this phase, the producer may obtain option rights on a preexisting story, and depending on how long development takes, may need to exercise those options in order to extend the period available to obtain either independent or studio financial backing. This phase will also include a draft budget for the project's finances, with a total amount represented by the "negative cost"[2] of the project.

Development may be underwritten by the studio that makes preliminary investments in the producer and the screenwriter. If the studio loses interest in the project, the project may go into "turnaround," whereby the studio allows the producer to shop the project to other studios. The original studio may retain certain rights in such turnaround scenarios, such as the right to be reimbursed for its prior development costs.

For a detailed insider's view of the development process, *Buchwald v. Paramount Pictures Corp.* recounts how an eight-page screen treatment took six years to be fully realized, in circumstances that ultimately led to a successful breach of contract

---

2   The "negative cost," or cost of production, culminates in the fully completed film's photographic negative from which positive prints can be made and shipped to theaters.

lawsuit.[3] The case describes in detail the long process of development of the film "Coming to America" and merits examination.

In *Buchwald,* Art Buchwald, a successful political satirist, used the real-life occasion of a visit by the Shah of Iran to the United States as the basis for a comedy in which an African leader travels to America where he becomes stranded by a coup back home, and ultimately finds happiness living in a Washington D.C. ghetto. Buchwald had submitted an eight-page "treatment"[4] to Paramount Pictures. At the time, Paramount was looking for a movie for comedy star Eddie Murphy.

Buchwald's treatment was one of many potential projects considered by Murphy and by Paramount. As part of the development process that took several years, Paramount engaged a producer, Bernheim, and engaged a director, and assigned a writer the task of creating a screenplay from the treatment. Paramount spent over $418,000 on screenwriting, option fees, and advances to the potential producer, director, and screenwriter.

Over the next three years, the studio extended its option to use the Buchwald treatment several times. By 1985, it appeared that the project would not happen. Paramount abandoned the treatment, and put it in "turnaround." Buchwald and Bernheim restarted the process at Warner Bros. Studios. In late 1987, Warner cancelled the project because it learned that Paramount was about to produce a film starring Eddie Murphy with a similar story line, titled "Coming to America." For Buchwald, six years had passed during which he received modest option extension fees from both Paramount and Warner, but to no avail.

When Paramount released "Coming to America" in 1988, Buchwald realized Paramount had, in essence, produced a film based on his original treatment. He and Bernheim successfully sued Paramount for Paramount's breach of its original agreement with Buchwald for a share of the film's net profits.[5]

---

3   See *Buchwald v. Paramount Pictures Corp.,* 1990 WL 357611 (Cal. Super. Jan. 31, 1990) ("Buchwald I") (Phase one of the proceedings found that Paramount breached its agreement with Buchwald. The court's finding on the unconscionability of the studio's net profit accountings was in the unpublished Phase Two opinion).

4   A treatment is a brief outline of the screenplay.

5   *Buchwald v. Paramount Pictures Corp.,* 13 U.S.P.Q.2d 1497 (Cal. Super. 1990) ("Buchwald II") (Phase two of the proceedings, unpublished). The Buchwald case also presents an accurate portrayal of the slow and uncertain path to production for many films, sometimes taking far more than the six years in the Buchwald case. It is also a good illustration of the "option", an important contractual mechanism. An option secures rights on a contingency basis, with the actual purchase of those rights postponed to a later time, triggered by events such as obtaining the financing to proceed with production. During the entire six-year saga of the Buchwald case, his only operative contract

[b]—Pre-Production

Once financing has been obtained and production is guaranteed, the project moves into the pre-production phase. During pre-production, the producers hire cast and crew and plan for production, which includes, for example, making arrangements for locations, soundstages, renting equipment, costumes, and music.

[c]—Principal Photography

Principal photography is the period during which the motion picture is shot, both on location and in the studio. Many last minute changes to the project can be made during the shoot, including changes to the script and even some of the cast members.

[d]— Post-Production

During post-production, the film's raw footage is edited, adding sound effects, special effects, and other technical matters, culminating with the completed final cut "negative." The film is now ready for the creation of prints for distribution to theaters for exhibition.

[e]—"Final Cut"

A studio-produced film will have a planned release date, which serves as incentive for the producer to deliver the final cut to the studio so preparations can be made for distribution and marketing. Given that studio films aim to create audience demand through widespread marketing campaigns, this "prints and advertising" expenditure[6] is typically enormous, sometimes approaching the entire cost of producing the film itself.

The project's financer, often the studio, reserves all rights to the finished and fully edited film, or "final cut" and can override the film's director with respect to editing, changes to the script, and even casting of actors.[7] The financer can decide to reshoot scenes or even change the ending, all in an effort to create a financially successful

---

with the studio was an option agreement that netted Buchwald a few thousand dollars. Ultimately, Buchwald was awarded $150,000, and Bernheim received $750,000.

6   The campaigns often consist of shipments of multiple prints of the film to theaters nationwide, along with the advertising campaigns.

7   See *Welch v. Metro-Goldwyn-Mayer Film Co.*, 207 Cal. App.3d 164, 254 Cal. Rptr. 645 (1988) (Actress Raquel Welch successfully sued studio that conspired to breach its contract with her by, *inter alia*, replacing her early in the production with no notice and fabricating claims that actress was uncooperative).

project. Such practices can lead to enormous tensions between the creative and business sides.[8]

[f]—Prints and Advertising

"Prints and advertising" is not actually a "phase" of production, but a description of the process surrounding the theatrical release of the film. Formerly, the distributor would order the manufacture of prints, which consist of several reels of film, for shipment to theaters around the world for the opening weekend. That process has been replaced by digital projection technologies, including secure digital distribution of films to theaters by specialist digital distribution companies. Increasingly gone are the large metal film canisters and the projectors used to exhibit the film.[9] It is at this point that the company plans the advertising campaign that will precede the release date. The initial publicity campaign can include television and radio ads, Internet ads, social networking, "grass roots" campaigns, print ads and billboards, interviews on talk shows, and tie-ins with other businesses. The advertising plans will start during post-production, if not earlier, and may include some marketing activities during principal photography.

[2]—Marketing Windows

Marketing and advertising for films are designed to create maximum audience demand on the opening weekend. The ability to "open" a film successfully is the goal of every filmmaker. This intense marketing means that most films make approximately 85% of their entire revenue in the first twenty-eight days after release.

This pressure continues, with several subsequent release "windows" over the next several years following the theatrical release, all designed to gradually "sell" the same movie to the consumer in different formats.

The above "windows" and rights may also be divided into territories of the world.

Changes in the traditional "release windows" continually occur. For example, in order to maximize DVD sales, studios ordinarily release home video formats for sale at least twenty-eight days before the same title is offered for rental. However, some studios have

---

8   See also, *TriStar Pictures, Inc. v. Directors Guild of America, Inc.*, 160 F.3d 537 (9th Cir. 1998) (under collective bargaining agreement between DGA and studio, director who was unhappy with studio's cuts to the TV version of his film had the right to request that his name not be used in the credits, and to have the request decided by arbitration).

9   See, e.g. *Stinky Love, Inc. v. Lacy*, 2004 Cal. App. Unpub. LEXIS 7497 (Cal. App. 2d Dist. Aug. 13, 2004) (company formed for sole purpose of financing prints and advertising).

Motion Picture Domestic Distribution Windows[10]		
Distribution Medium	Month Availability Begins Following Release Date	Duration in Months for the Window
Theatrical	1 (Release date)	4
Hospitality Industry (Airlines, hotels)	3	2
Home Entertainment – Physical Delivery:		
DVD/Blue Ray Sell Through	4	No limit
DVD/Blue Ray Rental	4	No limit
Netflix via mail/Red Box Kiosks	4 or 5 (per studio policy)	6
Home Entertainment – Digital Delivery:		
Premium Subscription Video on Demand (SVOD)	2 or 3	1
Electronic Sell-through (EST)	3.5 to 4	No limit
Internet Video on Demand (iVOD)	4 to 4.5	No limit
Cable Video on Demand (cVOD)	4 to 4.5	No limit
Premium Pay TV	9 to 10 (formerly 12)	15-18
Ad Supported TV	28 to 30	72 - 84

entered into deals with DVD rental companies in which the DVD rental is available the same day as the home video DVD release. In this case, the studio receives a portion of the rental revenue to make up for potentially lost DVD sales. [11]

The timing of release windows for DVD rentals has been a source of contention, and is still of interest as illustrative of studio distribution techniques despite DVD rentals being gradually replaced by online streaming.[12] Redbox is a company that offers DVD rentals at self-serve kiosks. Redbox had been obtaining the DVDs it rented from large DVD distributors, who, in turn, had obtained the DVDs directly from the studios. The distributors supplied the DVDs to Redbox prior to the official "DVD rental" release window. In response, certain studios enforced contractual provisions in their distribu-

---

10   See Ziffren, "Domestic Distribution Windows as of 06/30/12," Beverly Hills Bar Ass'n (Aug. 15, 2012). See *Redbox Automated Retail LLC v. Universal City Studios LLLP*, 2009 U.S. Dist. LEXIS 72700 (D. Del. Aug. 17, 2009) (DVD rental kiosk alleging antitrust violations against studios that refused to provide DVDs for rental because release windows allowed other retailers to exclusively sell DVDs for twenty-eight days following release of DVD for consumer purchase). See also, *Warner Bros. Entertainment, Inc. v. WTV Systems, Inc.*, 824 F. Supp.2d 1003 (C.D. Cal. 2011) (discussion of distribution windows).

11   See Marcus, "Reasons Not to Shorten Theatrical Windows," The Hollywood Reporter (July 19, 2010) ("Windowed release patterns are brilliant. Release a movie to different outlets over time so it can be sold to the same person multiple times. First see it in the theater, then buy or rent it, then catch it on cable or TV. Shorten the window and risk losing the ability to sell the product multiple times.").

12   See *Redbox Automated Retail LLC v. Universal City Studios LLLP*, 2009 U.S. Dist. LEXIS 72700, 2009 WL 2588748 (D. Del. Aug. 17, 2009).

tion agreements to force the distributors to stop supplying DVDs to RedBox prior to the DVD rental release window. Redbox alleged that these activities constituted a violation of the Sherman Antitrust Act. Such cases illustrate the value of an exclusive distribution window regardless of which technology represents the battle for exclusivity.

New technologies are becoming increasingly important. Several companies (Netflix, Hulu, Amazon, AppleTV, and broadcast and cable networks such as HBO, CBS, etc.) offer online streaming of films on subscription or purchase terms. The success of these business models has allowed online companies to produce new motion pictures and series outside the traditional broadcast and cable models.

§1.03   Project Inception

[1]—Idea Submission

Every film begins with an idea. The idea may be to adapt an existing work such as a novel into a motion picture, or it may be just a concept, such as a film about a historical event. Often, the person with the idea for a film does not have the financial resources to bring it to fruition. Instead, they must begin the classic Hollywood process of "pitching" the idea to a producer or studio or a financier, the one with the resources to turn a mere idea into a motion picture.

One of the most common client questions in the film industry is how to protect ideas as they begin the pitch process. Copyright law only protects the original creative expression of an underlying idea.[13] However, ideas *can* be protected under contract law, if the idea is disclosed in circumstances where there is an implied agreement that if the idea is used, the person disclosing the idea will be compensated.

[2]—Non-Disclosure Agreements and Releases Respecting Ideas

The ownership of "ideas" and alleged promises of compensation if those ideas are used as the basis of a film is a bitterly contested area of the industry. To protect themselves, production companies often will not accept unsolicited manuscripts or "take a meeting" with someone unfamiliar. Instead, they will only meet with prospective writers who are represented by a known and trusted agent or lawyer, and/or they will insist that prior to any meeting, the prospective writer sign a release or nondisclosure agreement ("NDA") that acknowledges there is no "deal" in place, no expectation of payment, and releases

---

13   17 U.S.C. §102(b).

the producer from any future causes of action based on any allegations that the producer "stole" the idea.[14]

Legal claims resulting from an unauthorized disclosure of confidential information may arise under state law where (1) the plaintiff disclosed confidential and novel information, and (2) the defendant knew it was supposed to be kept confidential.[15]

[3]—Protection of Ideas via Contract: *Desny v. Wilder*

[a]—California

While California does not recognize a property claim in a mere idea, courts will enforce express or implied contracts for payment in exchange for the use of an idea. The leading case is *Desny v. Wilder*.[16] Desny, a screenwriter, contacted the secretary of director Billy Wilder and described his screenplay. After reducing the screenplay to a short treatment at the secretary's suggestion, the plaintiff stated that "if anybody used it they would have to pay for it," to which the secretary replied "if Billy Wilder of Paramount uses the story, naturally we will pay you for it."[17] The court held this to be a valid oral agreement, and also noted that a contract in an idea submission may be implied when the recipient voluntarily accepts the idea, knowing that it is being tendered for a price.[18] The recipient's promise to pay may be made after the idea is submitted, the promise being supported by moral consideration.[19] Furthermore, because California idea submission claims are contract—as opposed to property—claims, the idea need not be novel to be protected.[20]

Although the practice of idea submission is common in the entertainment industry, California law will not recognize an implied contract solely on the assumption that

---

14   Submission of unsolicited scripts is an issue for talent agencies as well. See *Gable v. National Broadcasting Co.*, 727 F. Supp.2d 815 (C.D. Cal. 2010) (claims that "My Name is Earl" infringed work originally allegedly submitted via a talent agent, whose policy was not to accept unsolicited scripts). If the writer can get a meeting with a producer, the best he or she may be able to accomplish to protect his or her rights would be to verbally state that if the idea is actually used, he or she looks forward to discussing appropriate compensation terms. An example of such a Release and Covenant, and an NDA, is included in the forms accompanying this treatise.

15   *Montz v. Pilgrim Films & Television*, 649 F.3d 975, 981 (9th Cir. 2011) (citing *Entertainment Research Group, Inc. v. Genesis Creative Group, Inc.*, 122 F.3d 1211, 1227 (9th Cir. 1997)).

16   See *Desny v. Wilder*, 46 Cal.2d 715, 299 P.2d 257 (1956).

17   *Id.*, 299 P.2d at 261.

18   *Id.*, 299 P.2d at 267.

19   *Id.*, 299 P.2d at 269.

20   See *Donahue v. Ziv Television Programs, Inc.*, 245 Cal. App.2d 593, 54 Cal. Rptr. 130, 142 (1966) (implied contract for payment for idea for television series was enforceable, even though the idea was not novel).

the payment is expected.[21] The mere hope or expectation of payment does not create an inference that a defendant shared that expectation.[22] Further, the relationship of the parties must be considered when determining if an implied contract exists.[23]

Under the *Desny* rule, to show an implied-in-fact contract, the plaintiff must show that he or she "prepared the work, disclosed the work to the offeree for sale, and did so under the circumstances from which it could be concluded that the offeree voluntarily accepted the disclosure knowing the conditions on which it was tendered and the reasonable value of the work."[24] Note also, that the defense of independent creation may be asserted.[25]

Often, there is overlap between unauthorized use based on copyright infringement principles, and implied contract claims based on an implied promise to pay for an idea if used. Because copyright is governed by federal law, it would typically preempt state law claims where the state law rights are "equivalent to any of the exclusive rights within the general scope of copyright.[26] However, the Ninth Circuit held that a *Desny* claim for breach of implied contract is not preempted by the Copyright

---

21   See *Faris v. Enberg*, 97 Cal. App.3d 309, 158 Cal. Rptr. 704, 709 (1979) (where no intention to pay for a game show idea was established, "an obligation to pay could not be inferred from the mere fact of submission").

22   See *A Slice of Pie Productions, LLC v. Wayans Bros. Entertainment*, 487 F. Supp.2d 41 (D. Conn. 2007) (following *Desny* and *Grosso*). See also, *Benay v. Warner Bros. Entertainment, Inc.*, 607 F.3d 620 (9th Cir. 2010).

23   See *Blaustein v. Burton*, 9 Cal. App.3d 161, 88 Cal. Rptr. 319 (1970) (close relationship between parties, including sharing an attorney and constant invitations by defendant for plaintiff to disclose his idea, created a "joint venture," indicating an implied contract).

24   See *Desny v. Wilder at* 270 (stating "...if the idea purveyor has clearly conditioned his offer to convey the idea upon an obligation to pay for it if it is used by the offeree and the offeree, knowing the condition before he knows the idea, voluntarily accepts its disclosure (necessarily on the specified basis) and finds it valuable and uses it, the law will ... hold the parties have made an express (sometimes called implied-in-fact) contract, or under those circumstances, as some writers view it, the law itself, to prevent fraud and unjust enrichment, will imply a promise to compensate"). *Desny* also cautions the "idea man" from "blurting out" a pitch which would not imply any contract (the so-called "elevator pitch"): "The idea man who blurts out his idea without having first made his bargain has no one but himself to blame for the loss of his bargaining power." *Id.* at 269. See also the statement of the Desny rule quoted in the text in *Grosso v. Miramax*, 383 F.3d 965, 967 (9th Cir. 2004).

25   See *Hollywood Screentest of America, Inc. v. NBC Universal, Inc.*, 151 Cal. App.4th 631, 60 Cal. Rptr.3d 279 (2007) (Plaintiffs claimed their concept entitled "Hollywood Screentest" was infringed by defendant's reality show "Next Action Star." Summary judgment granted for defendant based partly on uncontroverted evidence of independent creation). See also, *Spinner v. American Broadcasting Companies, Inc.*, 215 Cal. App.4th 172, 155 Cal. Rptr.3d 32 (2013) (successful independent-creation defense to implied-in-fact contract claim over show "Lost").

26   See 17 U.S.C. § 301. See also, *Del Madera Properties v. Rhodes & Gardner, Inc.*, 820 F.2d 973, 976 (9th Cir. 1987).

Act, because a *Desny* claim is based not upon rights under copyright, but "upon the implied promise to pay the reasonable value of the materials disclosed."[27]

In 2011, the Ninth Circuit followed the preemption analysis of *Grosso*, holding in *Montz v. Pilgrim Film & Television, Inc.* that a *Desny* claim was not preempted by copyright law.[28] In the wake of *Grosso* and *Montz*, plaintiffs may theoretically bring claims based both on copyright and on a *Desny* "implied contract to pay" theory.[29]

[b]—New York

New York has two theories under which a claim in an idea submission case may be brought: (1) a contract claim, or (2) a property claim of misappropriation. New York courts have established that a novel idea can be protected as contract consideration.[30] However, the idea only needs to be novel to the recipient in order to give it the requisite value to constitute consideration.[31] Thus, New York contract-based idea submission claims require a fact-specific inquiry focusing on the perspective of the buyer.

Alternatively, an idea may be treated as property under a claim of misappropriation. Misappropriation claims arise when an idea is disclosed in confidence and then used in a manner that breaches that confidence.[32] The idea need not amount to a trade secret in order to be protected under the doctrine of misappropriation. Misappropriation claims require originality and novelty of the idea in absolute terms, because property law does not protect against the use of existing knowledge, which is free and available to everyone.[33]

In *Forest Park Pictures, Inc. v. Universal Television Network, Inc.*, the Second Circuit considered an idea submission/implied contact case, and by allowing the implied contract claim to survive preemption under copyright law, reached a result similar

---

27 See *Grosso v. Miramax*, 383 F.3d 965, 968 (9th Cir. 2004).

28 *Montz v. Pilgrim Films & Television, Inc.*, 649 F.3d 975 (9th Cir. 2011).

29 See *Benay v. Warner Bros. Entertainment, Inc.*, 607 F.3d 620 (9th Cir. 2010) ("The Last Samurai").

30 See *Murray v. National Broadcasting Co.*, 844 F.2d 988, 994 (2d Cir. 1988) (the idea of a non-stereotypical black family was not sufficiently novel to give rise to a breach of implied contract claim).

31 See *Nadel v. Play-By-Play Toys & Novelties, Inc.*, 208 F.3d 368, 376 (2d Cir. 2000) (abrogating *Murray* by holding that novelty to the buyer of the idea alone is sufficient to create contract consideration).

32 See *Lehman v. Dow Jones & Co.*, 783 F.2d 285, 299 (2d Cir. 1986).

33 See *AEB & Associates Design Group, Inc. v. Tonka Corp.*, 853 F. Supp. 724 (S.D.N.Y. 1994) (design for children's airbrush toy was not sufficiently novel to be protected because it was just an adaptation of commercial airbrushes).

to that of the Ninth Circuit in *Montz v. Pilgrim Films*.[34] In *Forest Park*, the plaintiffs (the actor Hayden Christensen and his brother) alleged they pitched an idea to a television network for a series about a concierge doctor for the residents of a wealthy community that was later developed by the defendant into a successful show, "Royal Pains." The Second Circuit held that the clear "promise to pay" in the pleadings was an extra element that avoided preemption under the Copyright Act. In applying California law to the breach of implied contact analysis, the Second Circuit noted that under California law, an implied-in-fact contract can have an open price term to be filled in by industry standards, while under New York law, price is an essential element of a contract.[35]

|4|—Projects Based on Preexisting Material: Book Option Agreements

Option agreements play a central role at the beginning stages of many film projects, because they put an exclusive "hold" on the rights to a novel or other property, sometimes for a relatively modest sum, for a specified period of time. Any subsequent actual purchase of the rights to the property, the exercise of the option, is deferred until such time as the holder of the option is ready to proceed. In many cases, an ambitious filmmaker may negotiate an option agreement, but never obtain financing, in which case the option is never exercised and all rights return to the owner of the property in question. Any option payments previously received are retained by the property owner. An option agreement must also specify the eventual purchase price in the event the option is exercised. The purchase price will be subject to negotiation, but is usually many multiples of the option fee.

For the filmmaker, a signed book option provides the ability to shop the project to potential financers or studios, and to attract commitments from actors, screenwriters, and directors.

Where a freelance producer options a book, the author may not have any control over the process or where it may lead, and the author may find that the copyrighted book becomes a mere "idea" for a film, pitched to studios as an "idea" instead of a book adaptation. In *Portman v. New Line Cinema Corp.*, a producer optioned the book "Party Crasher's Handbook," including not only the copyrighted book but also the right to develop a film based on the concept of the book. After unsuccessfully approaching a studio and a talent agency to package the film, the producer sued when the hit film "The Wedding Crashers" was released, allegedly based on his pitch and concept. The studio prevailed on statute of limitations grounds, but the decision is unclear as to whether the author

---

34   *Forest Park Pictures v. Universal Television Network, Inc.*, 683 F.3d 424 (2d Cir. 2012).

35   *Id.*, at 435.

of the book was a party to the suit or would have shared in any recovery. The suit was not based on any copyright principles.[36]

In cases where a novel may be a best seller and sought after, the agreement may be styled as a "purchase agreement" where the right to adapt the book is immediately conveyed, and not subject to exercise of options, while still qualifying for additional payments in the event a motion picture is ultimately produced and released.[37]

Premium properties carry with them premium option prices. For example, in *Siegel v. Warner Bros. Entertainment*, the court ruled on whether DC Comics had licensed the film rights to Superman to Warner Bros. at full market rates and conducted a survey of prices paid for high-value option agreements.[38]

---

36   *Portman v. New Line Cinema Corp.*, 2013 Cal. App. Unpub. LEXIS 1641, 2013 WL 820586 (Cal. App.2d Dist. March 6, 2013).

37   See *Terry T. Gerritsen v. Warner Bros. Entertainment, Inc.*, 112 F. Supp. 3d 1011 (C.D. Cal. 2015) (purchase agreement for film rights to novel "Gravity" sold for $1 million, with $500,000 production bonus, in suit over whether Warner Bros. hit film "Gravity" was subject to the purchase agreement. Because purchase agreement was not with Warner Bros., defendants' motion to dismiss granted).

38   See *Siegel v. Warner Bros. Entertainment, Inc.*, 2009 U.S. Dist. LEXIS 66115, 2009 WL 2014164 (C.D. Cal. July 8, 2009). The court relied on evidence of option and purchase prices for similar characters. For premium comic book character properties, the court noted that an agreement between Marvel Comics and Twentieth Century Fox for the "X-Men" characters was for an initial option payment of $150,000 against a purchase price of $1.5 million. *Id.*, 2009 U.S. Dist. LEXIS 66115 at *21. The terms for "Tarzan" were a two-year initial option period for $250,000 that could be extended for three years for another $750,000, with a purchase price of $1.75 million, for which the earlier option payments were made applicable. For "Iron Man", there was an eighteen-month option for $250,000, which could be extended one year for another payment of $650,000, with no purchase price payable upon exercise. However, there was also contingent compensation of 1.5% of first dollar gross escalating to 5% and a favorable merchandising component.

In another case opinion discussing the 1993 agreement between Twentieth Century Fox and Marvel Comics for film rights to the "X-Men" comic book series, the purchase price was determined to be $1.6 million, allocated as follows: $150,000 for the initial option period; $100,000 for subsequent extensions of the option period; $1,350,000 to exercise the option. See *Twentieth Century Fox Film Corp. v. Marvel Enterprises, Inc.*, 155 F. Supp.2d 1 (S.D.N.Y. 2001) (studio that had acquired motion picture rights to X-men franchise sued licensor over scope of rights vis-à-vis licensor's television exploitation).

These highly valued options and purchase prices are by way of example, and they apply to comic book characters. Best-selling novels may command greater prices, because their stories and characters are more defined and there may be greater audience anticipation in seeing a best selling story on the screen. Thus, the *Siegel* court's fact finding revealed that regarding the actual purchase prices, best sellers could command enormous sums. Clive Cussler's novel *Sahara* had a purchase price of $20 million plus 10% of producer's gross; Thomas Harris's *Hannibal* received $10 million with 10% of first dollar gross; the musical Annie had a purchase price of $9.5 million and 10% of first dollar gross escalating to 11.5%; and the Tom Clancy works *Rainbow Six* and *Red Rabbit* have a purchase price of $6 million and $7 million respectively and a profit participation of 10% of gross. *Siegel v. Warner Bros. Entertainment*,

Many option agreements are based on less well-known properties, and may be for more modest amounts. The producer pays for an option immediately, but the exercise of the option will not occur until and unless the producer obtains financing for the film. Thus, many producers who negotiate for options are very cautious about the initial option payment price, because the amount is paid directly by them. But when it comes to the purchase price, which would only be exercised in the event funding is obtained, any potential future purchase funds would come from the future investors in the film, not from the producer.

An option agreement contains all the terms and provisions that would be in effect should the option be exercised. Therefore, negotiation of an option agreement is also the negotiation of the full and final deal itself.[39] Some comments on the leading deal points are provided below:

- Property: Defines the work that is being optioned.

- Grant of Option: usually an initial option period of one year (or eighteen months), followed by an Extended Option Period for a similar amount of time, often for a greater amount. Given that options tie up the property and may not be for a large sum, most owners prefer to keep the time period as brief as possible as encouragement to move things along. The initial option fee is applicable against the purchase price (i.e., is an advance against the purchase price). The extended option fee is not applicable, in order to try and incentivize the Purchaser to move quickly.

- Authorized Pre-Production Activities: Purchaser has the right during the option period to create treatments, screenplays, etc. adapted from the Property, and to own them, whether or not option is exercised. Purchaser may not actually use those materials if the option expires without being exercised.

- Purchase Price/Contingent Compensation: Applies if the option is exercised. Often based on a percentage of the "going in" budget of the film, for example 2% of the approved budget, which shall not be less than $100,000 or more than $350,000.[40] The budget should be discussed, and the percentage and high/low numbers are part of the negotiation. Contingent compensation for a modest book option may be in the range of 3% to 5% of "producer's net profits" or "net proceeds" or some other defined term, often characterized as being no less advantageous than that calculation as used for Producer and all other profit participants. It may be difficult or impossible for someone with little "clout" to get a percentage based on some other more favorable

Inc., id., 2009 WL 2014164, at *9. See also, *Weisberg v. Smith*, 401 F. Supp.2d 359 (S.D.N.Y. 2005) (case involving dispute between novelist and agent over agent's commission where novelist Gregory John Smith received approximately $1 million from Warner Brothers for film rights to novel entitled "Shantaram.").

39   A Literary Option/Purchase Agreement is included in the forms accompanying this treatise.

40   This assumes a budget in the range of $5 million to $15 million.

definition of profits than "net profits," but it is a negotiating point.[41] The common understanding is that net profit participation only rarely results in receipt of funds, thus a higher option payment or guaranteed purchase price is sought.

- <u>Bonuses</u>: If possible, negotiate for a "Set up" bonus that pays a flat sum if the film is set up at a studio. Other possible bonuses that are more difficult to get may include a bonus based on gross box office.

- <u>Rights Granted</u>: This will be a comprehensive and extensive list of rights granted. Typically, financers want to see all rights to remakes, sequels, prequels, games, merchandise, television series, worldwide, etc.[42] Unless the book owner has negotiation leverage, it's difficult to limit the rights granted in connection with the film. However, there can be a negotiation for considerable compensation in connection with any sequels, prequels, or television adaptations.

- <u>Rights Reserved</u>: The print publication rights for the book are not conveyed, only the right to adapt the book for film. Other rights that may be expressly reserved include radio, live theater, and musical stage adaptation.[43]

- <u>Reversion</u>: In the event the option is exercised but the film is never completed or distributed, then all rights revert back to the original owner after a set number of years. The Purchaser may attempt to condition such a reversion on reimbursement of all their expenses. The right to produce any sequels or prequels or television adaptations can also be limited in time in order to incentivize the producer to move forward with those projects.[44]

- <u>Credit</u>: Separate card in main titles. Specify the specific language, for example "Based on the book _____ by _____." Specify inclusion in advertising of book title and author name.

---

41   For a fuller discussion of contingent compensation and profit participation, see § 1.04[4] *infra*.

42   See, e.g., *Jonesfilm v. Lion Gate International*, 299 F.3d 134 (2d Cir. 2002) (dispute over prequel/sequel rights to film "9½ Weeks" where holder of trademark in motion picture had reserved those rights).

43   See *Paramount Pictures Corp. v. Puzo*, 2012 WL 4465574 (S.D.N.Y. Sept. 26, 2012) (dispute over whether author's estate retained rights to create new prequel/sequel novels based on "The Godfather").

44   In *Siegel v. Warner Bros. Entertainment, Inc.*, the court conducted an analysis of various motion picture agreements in order to determine if the agreement between Warner Bros. and DC Comics was an arm's length transaction. In that opinion, the court focused heavily on reversion clauses as imparting important rights to the grantor because they gave the grantee an incentive to monetize the property as quickly as possible, and ensured that the grantor could reclaim the rights in the event the grantee did not deliver as promised. See *Siegel v. Warner Bros. Entertainment, Inc.*, 2009 WL 2014164, at *19 (C.D. Cal. July 8, 2009). See also, *Beatty v. Tribune Media Services, Inc.*, 2005 WL 6132339 (C.D. Cal. Aug. 10, 2005) (dispute over reversion of film rights for Dick Tracy character).

[5]—Life Story Rights and Depiction of Real Persons

Many films are based on real events. Individuals depicted in such films fall into two broad legal categories: (1) public figures whose lives and actions are legitimate subjects for public discourse, including films; and (2) private figures who have a reasonable expectation of privacy, an expectation that could be infringed by an unauthorized depiction in a film.[45] The torts that may be asserted by a private individual who finds themselves the subject of a film include defamation, libel, invasion of privacy, public disclosure of private facts, false light, and right of publicity.[46] In addition, plaintiffs who claim that an unauthorized depiction may also invoke the Lanham Act in connection with false endorsement or false advertising, and torts such as intentional infliction of emotional distress.[47]

However, assuming that the subject of a film is likely to be someone who is either a legitimate public figure, or at least someone whose story is a matter of legitimate public interest, and assuming that a film project does not defame the subject with damaging falsehoods, there may be few situations where "life rights" are a legal necessity. In *Sarver v. Chartier*, a former soldier whose story formed part of the basis for the lead character in the film *The Hurt Locker*, sued the filmmakers for defamation, false light, and intentional infliction of emotional distress.[48]

In affirming dismissal primarily under First Amendment principles, the Ninth Circuit noted that the film's protagonist, though only partly based on Sarver's own story, was sympathetic, the portrayal was not "highly offensive," and there was nothing outrageous or extreme in the way the character was depicted, stating "it is not outrageous that [a journalist's] factual account then led to a fictionalized screenplay and film."

Despite the holding in *Sarver* arguably making life rights unnecessary to obtain, film and television producers will in many cases continue to seek releases from actual persons discussed or depicted in their productions, or will attempt to avoid potential claims by transforming actual persons into composite or fictional characters. However, given the

---

45   See, e.g., *Seale v. Gramercy Pictures*, 949 F. Supp. 331 (E.D. Pa. 1996) (former leader of Black Panther party who was portrayed in historically accurate and partially fictionalized docudrama, "Panther," was a well-known public and historical figure. On summary judgment, the court dismissed plaintiff's claims including defamation, tortuous invasion upon private seclusion, right of publicity, and Lanham Act claims connected with the advertising of the film, while allowing Plaintiff's false light claim to go forward based upon one scene in the film that was wholly fabricated and involved assent to criminal acts.).

46   See Chapter 7 *infra* for an in-depth discussion of celebrity rights of publicity and privacy.

47   See generally, Chapter 7 *infra*.

48   See *Sarver v. Chartier*, 813 F. 3d 891 (9th Cir. 2016). See also *De Havilland v. FX Networks, LLC*, 21 Cal. App. 5th 845, 230 Cal. Rptr. 3d 625 (2018) (film depicting living actress protected by First Amendment from right of publicity and defamation claims).

broad protection of the First Amendment, there may also be many situations where such releases and consents are not in fact required, especially where the person depicted is a public figure or has been involved in matters of public interest.

There are however strong creative and commercial incentives for entering into agreements for life story rights, even where the subject is a public figure and thus consent is not required. The principal incentive falls into two categories: first, obtaining exclusive cooperation from the subject or his or her family allows the producer to market the film as the sole and exclusive "authorized" version of the person's story. Second, such agreements typically give the producer unique access to materials that are not otherwise available to the public or to competing filmmakers, including interviews with family and friends, and access to documents, diaries, photographs, and other materials and information not otherwise accessible.

In one recent case, the family of a deceased musician litigated against a documentary filmmaker because they alleged the filmmaker, whose rights were confined to a motion picture, improperly used their confidential materials for preparation of a book. In holding that the book did not use any substantial amount of the materials provided for the film, the court noted some of the exclusive cooperation provided by the musician's family as part of their agreement:

> "In reliance on the Margolis-Rhoads agreement, the Rhoads family contends it contributed access to Randy's musical equipment that had been in storage for 30 years; personal, private photographs of Randy and other members of the family; personal photographs and film footage of Randy obtained from Rhoads family friends and neighbors; access to Delores's home, access to Randy's automobile, costumes, jewelry and shoes; access to Delores's music school (now operated by Kelle); access to Randy's gravesite (including opening of the bars to the tomb); access to Randy's church and the 'meditation garden' dedicated to his memory; original music and a music school performance; photographs of Randy's deceased body; the autopsy report and introductions to Randy's family and friends, including Osbourne, his wife Sharon and Alice Cooper."[49]

[a]—Appearances by Actual Persons

Actual persons who are not actors may appear in a film under various circumstances.

---

49   See *Rhoads v. Margolis*, 2015 Cal. App. Unpub. LEXIS 585 (Cal. App.2d Dist. Jan. 26, 2015).

[i]—Documentary Films, Including Hidden Cameras

By their very nature, documentary films do not hire actors, using real people and events instead, often under the protection of First Amendment principles applicable to news reporting.[50] In some situations where the subject of a documentary film is being investigated, there is clearly no opportunity or likelihood of obtaining any consents or releases. Out of an abundance of caution, documentary filmmakers depicting a "friendly" subject may attempt to obtain consents and releases. While documentary films and television news reporting enjoy strong First Amendment protections, such a practice helps ensure that commercial distribution of the film can proceed with a reasonable expectation that those who appear in the film have provided releases and are therefore unlikely to come forward later with claims based on invasion of privacy or defamation.

Hidden camera techniques used in documentaries and investigative reporting on television, by definition, do not allow for a release or consent to be signed prior to filming. In theory, it is possible to obtain a consent and release after completion. However, assuming such consent is not obtained, hidden camera filming can violate a plaintiff's rights under several legal theories, including invasion of privacy (also known as the tort of intrusion), as well as under criminal "eavesdropping" statutes that prohibit the recording of confidential conversations.[51]

---

50 See *New York Times Co. v. Sullivan*, 376 U.S. 254, 84 S.Ct. 710, 11 L.Ed.2d 686 (1964) (reporting on public figures protected by First Amendment). See also: *Hustler Magazine, Inc. v. Falwell*, 485 U.S. 46, 108 S.Ct. 876, 99 L.Ed.2d 41 (1988) (standard of *New York Times Co. v. Sullivan* applies to claims of intentional infliction of emotional distress allegedly caused by parody advertisement ridiculing public figure); *Gertz v. Welch*, 418 U.S. 323, 94 S.Ct. 2997, 11 L.Ed.2d 789 (1974).

51 See *Candelaria v. Spurlock*, 2008 U.S. Dist. LEXIS 51595 (E.D.N.Y. July 3, 2008) (hidden camera in public restaurant did not violate plaintiff's privacy rights under New York Civil Rights Law § 51). In *Candelaria v. Spurlock*, the plaintiff was an employee at McDonald's whom the defendant, using a hidden camera, briefly depicted in the documentary film, "Supersize Me." The plaintiff sued the filmmaker under New York Civil Rights Law § 51 for the allegedly unlawful use of her image. In holding that the newsworthiness exception applied, the court noted:

> "plaintiff was not filmed in her home or any other location in which she could reasonably expect not to be filmed. She was at the counter of a McDonald's, meeting dozens if not hundred of members of the public in the course of her shift every day. She had no reasonable expectation of privacy while doing so."

Id., 2008 U.S. Dist. LEXIS 51595, at *16. Compare, J.P. *Turnbull v. American Broadcasting Cos., Inc.*, 2004 WL 2924590 (C.D. Cal. Aug. 19, 2004) (denying summary judgment to defendant "20/20" television producers on claims including invasion of privacy and intrusion where program surreptitiously recorded plaintiffs' casual conversations as part of hidden camera investigative report, where there was a reasonable expectation that such office conversation would not be covertly taped).

See also: *Sanders v. American Broadcasting Cos., Inc.*, 20 Cal.4th 907, 85 Cal. Rptr.2d 909, 978 P.2d 67 (1999) (covert video taping in workplace by television reporter was an intrusion because employees had an expectation of privacy); *Shulman v. Group W Productions Inc.*, 18 Cal.4th 200, 234-235, 74 Cal. Rptr.2d 843, 955 P.2d 469 (1998) (video

Under California law, several hidden camera cases have involved an action for intrusion, commonly referred to an "invasion of privacy," which has two elements: (1) intrusion into a private place, conversation or matter, (2) in a manner highly offensive to a reasonable person.[52] To prove actionable intrusion, the plaintiff must show the defendant penetrated some zone of physical or sensory privacy surroundings, or obtained unwanted access to data about the plaintiff. The standard for determining what constitutes a zone of physical or sensory privacy is whether the plaintiff had an objectively reasonable expectation of seclusion or solitude in the place, conversation, or data source.[53]

---

taping patient's conversations with medical rescuers is an invasion of privacy); *Wilkins v. National Broadcasting Co., Inc.*, 71 Cal. App.4th 1066, 1080, 84 Cal. Rptr.2d 329 (1999) (conversation in crowded restaurant not confidential).

Even members of the public who appear in the background or even featured briefly on screen may qualify as "private persons." Filmmakers who plan to shoot in a public location commonly post notices announcing that filming will occur on a particular day, so that members of the public are on notice that they may be filmed, and can choose to avoid the area on the day of shooting.

52   See *Wilkins v. National Broadcasting Co., Inc.*, 71 Cal. App.4th 1066, 1080, 84 Cal. Rptr.2d 329, 334 (1999) (conversation in crowded restaurant not confidential). California Penal Code Section 632 forbids electronic eavesdropping and states in relevant part:

> "Every person who, intentionally and without the consent of all parties to a confidential communication, by means of any electronic amplifying or recording device, eavesdrops upon or records the confidential communication, whether the communication is carried on among the parties in the presence of one another or by means of a telegraph, telephone, or other device, except a radio, shall be punished by a fine not exceeding two thousand five hundred dollars ($2,500), or imprisonment in the county jail not exceeding one year, or in the state prison, or by both that fine and imprisonment. If the person has previously been convicted of a violation of this section or Section 631, 631.5, 631.6, 631.7, or 636, the person shall be punished by a fine not exceeding ten thousand dollars ($10,000), by imprisonment in the county jail not exceeding one year, or in the state prison, or by both that fine and imprisonment.

*   *   *

> "The term 'confidential communication' includes any communication carried on in circumstances as may reasonably indicate that any party to the communication desires it to be confined to the parties thereto, but excludes a communication made in a public gathering or in any legislative, judicial, executive or administrative proceeding open to the public, or in any other circumstance in which the parties to the communication may reasonably expect that the communication may be overheard or recorded."

Cal. Penal Code §§ 632(a), 632(c).

53   See: *Medical Laboratory Management Consultants v. American Broadcasting Companies, Inc.*, 306 F.3d 806 (9th Cir. 2002) (Prime Time Live television show investigation of medical laboratory affirming judgment for defendants on claims including intrusion upon seclusion, trespass, and tortuous interference with contractual relations and prospective economic relations); *Deteresa v. American Broadcasting Companies, Inc.*, 121 F.3d 460 (9th Cir. 1997) (affirming judgment for defendants on claims including unlawful eavesdropping in violation of the California Penal Code, tortuous invasion of privacy, violate fraud, and violation of the federal eavesdropping statute, fraud, and

To enter upon another's property without consent constitutes trespass. The purpose of the law is to protect ownership or possession of real property. Subjects of hidden camera investigations have asserted claims based on several legal theories, including defamation, invasion of privacy, illegal wiretapping and other torts. They have also asserted claims based on trespass, including cases where consent to enter business premises was allegedly obtained fraudulently. Courts have been reluctant to include trespass as a tort that clearly arises from such situations, even in cases where the consent to enter onto premises was obtained by deceit. The rationale is that even fraudulently obtained consent to enter a premises does not interfere with the purposes of trespass law to protect ownership and possession of land. It might lead to other actionable torts, but it does not specifically interfere with ownership or possession.[54]

---

unfair business practices); *Baugh v. CBS, Inc.*, 828 F. Supp. 745 (N.D. Cal. 1993) (on motion to dismiss, dismissing plaintiff claims for appropriation of likeness, intrusion on seclusion, trespass, unfair competition and negligent infliction of emotional distress, and denying defendants' motion to dismiss claims including disclosure of private facts, fraud, and intentional infliction of emotional distress); *Shulman v. Group W Productions Inc.*, 18 Cal.4th 200, 231, 74 Cal. Rptr.2d 843, 955 P.2d 469 (1998) (videotaping patient's conversations with medical rescuers is an invasion of privacy). See also, Restatement (Second) of Torts, § 652B.

54   See *J.H. Desnick, M.D. Eye Services v. American Broadcasting Companies, Inc.*, 44 F.3d 1345, 1351-1353 (7th Cir. 1995). Judge Posner of the Seventh Circuit discussed the "surprising result" that entry to an optometrist's premises by journalists who concealed and misrepresented their true purpose was not a violation of trespass laws:

"To enter upon another's land without consent is a trespass. The force of this rule has, it is true, been diluted somewhat by concepts of privilege and of implied consent. But there is no journalists' privilege to trespass. And there can be no implied consent in any non-fictitious sense of the term when express consent is procured by a misrepresentation or a misleading omission. The Desnick Eye Center would not have agreed to the entry of the test patients into its offices had it known they wanted eye examinations only in order to gather material for a television exposé of the Center and that they were going to make secret videotapes of the examinations. Yet some cases deem consent effective even though it was procured by fraud. There must be something to this surprising result. Without it a restaurant critic could not conceal his identity when he ordered a meal, or a browser pretend to be interested in merchandise that he could not afford to buy. Dinner guests would be trespassers if they were false friends who never would have been invited had the host known their true character, and a consumer who in an effort to bargain down an automobile dealer falsely claimed to be able to buy the same car elsewhere at a lower price would be a trespasser in the dealer's showroom. Some of these might be classified as privileged trespasses, designed to promote competition. Others might be thought justified by some kind of implied consent—the restaurant critic for example might point by way of analogy to the use of the 'fair use' defense by book reviewers charged with copyright infringement and argue that the restaurant industry as a whole would be injured if restaurants could exclude critics. But most such efforts at rationalization would be little better than evasions. The fact is that consent to an entry is often given legal effect even though the entrant has intentions that if known to the owner of the property would cause him for perfectly understandable and generally ethical or at least lawful reasons to revoke his consent."

See also, *Food Lion, Inc. v. Capital Cities/ABC, Inc.*, 194 F.3d 505 (4th Cir. 1999).

[ii]—Feature Productions

Commercial, or "studio," productions may be very different with respect to their handling of the appearance of the general public in a film, sometimes going to great lengths to avoid depicting anyone who is not a cast member. Even street scenes shot on location usually have hired extras in the background.

The boundaries between the expectations surrounding a documentary film and a commercial film regarding depiction of members of the public were tested in the courts in connection with the 2006 "quasi documentary," *BORAT—Cultural Learnings of America for Make Benefit Glorious Nation of Kazakhstan* ("*Borat*").[55] *Borat* was a huge commercial success, and relied on techniques that presented an intensely satirical combination of comedy and documentary as the fictional title character's outrageous behavior was played off against the genuine reactions of shocked and bemused members of the public.

The Southern District of New York consolidated several cases brought by individuals who claimed that their written consent to appear in *Borat* was fraudulently induced, and the agreements themselves were ambiguous and unenforceable.[56] The plaintiffs claimed that they were approached by the film's producer

---

55   *Pseniscka v. Twentieth Century Fox Film Corp.*, 2008 WL 4185752 (S.D.N.Y. Sept. 3, 2008).

56   *Id.* In *Lemerond v. Twentieth Century Fox Film Corp.*, 2008 WL 918579 (S.D.N.Y. March 31, 2008), the plaintiff asserted claims under Section 51 of the New York Civil Rights Law, and under New York common law for the unlawful use of his image in Borat. One sequence in the film shows the fictional character Borat standing on the corner of 5th Avenue and 57th Street in Manhattan, greeting passers by who were all actual persons going about their day. As the plaintiff walked by, the Borat character (who appeared to be a "normal" person accompanied by a camera crew) extended his hand to the plaintiff and stated, "Hello, nice to meet you. I'm new in town. My name is Borat." Without further provocation, the plaintiff began to run away in apparent terror, screaming "Get away!" and "What are you doing?" The thirteen-second clip concludes as Borat responds, "What is the problem?" *Id.*

Although the plaintiff never signed any releases or consents, the court granted the defendants' motion to dismiss, holding that under the three-part test for Section 51 of the New York Civil Rights law, the film was not solely for advertising purposes or purposes of trade. The film come within the statute's exception for newsworthy events or matters of public interest, because it was at core "an ironic commentary of modern American culture, contrasting the backwardness of its protagonist with the social ills that afflict supposedly sophisticated society."

The plaintiff also sued based on the inclusion of a portion of the clip in the film's advertising trailer. In the trailer, the plaintiff's face was scrambled, rendering his likeness "blurry" and indiscernible. His face was not scrambled in the film itself. The court also noted that the trailer use did not overcome the newsworthiness exception, because "the mere fact that the defendants are spurred by the profit motive and engaged in the commercial exploitation of a motion picture does not negate their right to depict a matter of public interest or to advertise the picture by the showing of a trailer." *Id.*, 2008 WL 918579, at *3 (citing *Man v. Warner Bros., Inc.*, 317 F. Supp. 50, 52 (S.D.N.Y. 1970)). See also: *Walter v. NBC Television Networks, Inc.*, 27 A.D.3d 1069, 811 N.Y.S.2d 521 (2006) (use of plaintiff's image in "Headlines" segment of Jay Leno's "The Tonight Show" was not actionable because segment was newsworthy);

who represented that the film was a "documentary about the integration of foreign people into the American way of life." The plaintiffs were then asked to participate by providing their regular services.[57] All the plaintiffs were presented with a relatively short document entitled "Standard Consent Agreement," accompanied by several hundred dollars as payment. They signed the documents, allegedly having had no opportunity to review them before the cameras rolled. After filming, but before release of the film, one of the plaintiffs also signed an additional "Release of Liability" document for which they accepted an additional $4,450 to release the producers from any and all claims.

The plaintiffs arguably were made to look foolish in the film. However, the court held that the agreements were valid so they had no cause of action against the producers of the film.[58] Notable in the court's opinion were the following points:

- The Agreement contained an explicit waiver clause that on its face prevents plaintiffs from bringing a cause of action.

- The plaintiffs claimed that the term "documentary style" film was ambiguous: they thought it was a true documentary, but the court held that the operative word was "style" not "documentary." *Borat* was a fictional story told in the style of a true one.

- The Agreement had a merger clause stating that the plaintiff has not relied "upon any promises or statements made by anyone about the nature of the Film or the identity of any other Participants or persons involved in the Film." The court held that this merger clause overcame the charges of fraudulent inducement based on verbal assurances given by the film's producer prior to entering into the Agreement.

Consent can also be implied by the acts of the person who appears. In *Lane v. MRA Holdings, LLC*, the plaintiff, who was still a minor at the time of filming, was depicted in a "Girls Gone Wild" video.[59] She later sued under Florida state law claims for unauthorized publication, common-law commercial misappropriation of likeness, false light invasion of privacy, and fraud. In granting summary judgment for the defendants, the court noted the following dispositive facts:

Glickman v. Stern, 19 Med. L. Rptr. 1769, 1776 (N.Y. Sup. Oct. 15, 1991) (comedic skit on Howard Stern show "certainly presented a situation of interest to the public").

57   See generally, *id.*

58   The Borat Agreement is included in the forms accompanying this treatise, Form 1.006.

59   *Lane v. MRA Holdings, LLC*, 242 F. Supp.2d 1205 (M.D. Fla. 2002).

- The video was an expressive work and therefore there was no viable claim under the Florida right of publicity statute, which applies to direct promotion of a commercial product or service.[60]

- The facts show that plaintiff consented to be filmed: a cameraman, who was a total stranger to her, asked her to expose herself while he filmed; she did so in a public location while several pedestrians were in the vicinity; and her girlfriend who was with her stated on camera and prior to the plaintiff's exposing herself that she had once done the same thing and the photos wound up in a magazine. Given the facts and even the "warning" from her friend, the plaintiff proceeded to expose herself in front of the camera.[61]

The court held that the state statutes relating to the circumstances under which a minor could not consent as a matter of law, and which listed those instances specifically, did not apply to the ability to consent to publication of one's likeness. Therefore as a matter of statutory interpretation, the plaintiff had the legal capacity to consent.

While based on Florida law only, *Lane* is instructive, because in certain circumstances, filmmakers may not have any consent or release documents available at the moment they wish to film someone. Based on *Lane*, obtaining a clear express consent on camera could be sufficient, depending on the circumstances. The mere presence of a camera accompanied by willing participation in a public location may be sufficient. But as we have seen in the *Borat* case, even the existence of a legal document may not prevent a lawsuit being filed where the person who appears later regrets their decision.

[iii]—Persons Filmed in Public Places

As noted above, those out and about in public, in circumstances where there is no reasonable expectation of privacy, are "fair game" under state privacy laws to be photographed or filmed as they go about their activities, even if they become an incidental non-featured part of the background for a movie or television production.

Thus, for example, where a news or entertainment program or project may be filming in a public place (presumably having obtained any required permits or location permission), it is a highly recommended courtesy, but not a legal requirement, to post signs alerting the public to the filming. Those members of the public who do not wish to be filmed can then simply avoid the area.

---

60   Fla. Stat. § 540.08. See also: *Valentine v. CBS, Inc.*, 698 F.2d 430, 433 (11th Cir. 1983); *Tyne v. Time Warner Entertainment Co.*, LP, 204 F. Supp.2d 1338 (M.D. Fla. 2002).

61   *Lane v. MRA Holdings, LLC*, 242 F. Supp.2d 1205 (M.D. Fla. 2002).

Because there is no reasonable expectation of privacy in open public areas, and members of the public have no contractual privity with the happenstance of a nearby filmed production, attempts to create a binding release with passers-by members of the public via mere signage are not only legally unnecessary but probably not legally enforceable.

One recent example noticed by this author of a production company sign in a shopping mall in Los Angles where a TV entertainment news program was being filmed began with a courtesy notice, put into place hours before filming began, that filming would be taking place. That practice is recommended.

But the next portion of the sign purported to create a contractual agreement for "express consent" between passers-by in the mall and the production company, stating as follows, with the portion of the sign that is probably unenforceable highlighted here in italics:

Shooting Here Today

[Name of Show]

You may be photographed in connection with the program being filmed here today.

Your being in the vicinity of this production constitutes your express consent to use your likeness in connection with this production or any other productions or exhibition thereof in any and all media throughout the world.

There can however be differences of opinion as to whether what is or is not an area being filmed is "public." In the Seventh Circuit case *Bogie v. Rosenberg*, a fan of the comedian Joan Rivers went backstage after a performance in Wisconsin and spoke to the comedienne. The conversation was filmed by a documentary film crew. During the conversation, the fan made some comments that became part of the film, which the fan later regretted, and she sued the comedienne and the documentary producer for invasion of privacy and defamation.[62] While the location was a backstage area and not the public lobby or performance venue itself, the court held under Wisconsin right of privacy laws that the plaintiff had no reasonable expectation of privacy because it was a publicly accessible area, and there were several people present including the film crew with cameras. In addition, the claim failed based on the newsworthiness and public interest

---

62   See *Bogie v. Joan Alexandra Molinsky Sanger Rosenberg a/k/a Joan Rivers*, 705 F.3d 603 (7th Cir. 2013).

exception to Wisconsin right of publicity laws, as well as the "incidental use" exception.

[iv]—Depiction of Automobile License Plates in Documentary and Reality Productions

While it is a common practice for documentary style and reality television programs to obscure automobile license plates, federal law makes it illegal for any motor vehicle department, or any individual, to disclose personally identifying information connected to a license plate, except under specific circumstances.

The Driver's Privacy Protection Act of 1994 (DPPA), 18 U.S.C. § 2721—2725, regulates the disclosure of personal information contained in the records of state motor vehicle departments (DMVs).[63] The Act was passed following several incidents where crimes were facilitated by access to DMV records that disclosed the residence of drivers, which is now illegal for any DMV or person to disclose.

The limited exceptions include matters such as safety and theft notification, law enforcement, and legitimate business needs that do not invade privacy.

The constitutionality of the DPPA was upheld by the U.S. Supreme Court in *Reno v. Condon*.[64]

[b]—Portrayal of Real Persons by an Actor & Life Story Rights Agreements

Non-documentary productions can include "true life" stories. These so-called "docudramas" are based on actual persons or events, and in some cases, use real names.[65]

Where the subject of the film is a public figure such as politician or celebrity, or a private person who has become part of a public controversy, filmmakers may base their film on publicly available facts and news reports, or on unauthorized biographies. For such projects, First Amendment protections give filmmakers considerable leeway with respect to overcoming any potential claims of invasion of privacy or defamation.[66] However, where the film project depicts private persons who are not in the public eye, and uses their real names and otherwise private stories, it is

---

63   See 18 U.S.C. § 2721-2725.

64   See *Reno v. Condon*, 528 U.S. 141, 120 S.Ct. 666, 145 L.Ed.2d 587 (2000).

65   Examples include films such as *Erin Brockovich* (depicting the title character and based on her true life story); The *Blind Side* (based on a book depicting the Tuohy family); and *Friday Night Lights* (film and television series based on a book by Buzz Bissinger, which originally had been based on a magazine article).

66   See *New York Times Co. v. Sullivan*, 376 U.S. 254, 84 S.Ct. 710, 11 L.Ed.2d 686 (1964). See also: *Hustler Magazine, Inc. Falwell*, 485 U.S. 46, 108 S.Ct. 876, 99 L.Ed.2d 41 (1988) (standard of *New York Times Co. v. Sullivan* applies to

standard practice to obtain consents and releases, as well as other rights of access and information.

Where the film is based on a written work, the producers will need to obtain a complete release from those persons who appear therein, allowing the use of their name, and equally importantly, allowing the producer to dramatize and fictionalize the story in his or her sole discretion.[67] Often, producers will seek to obtain such releases only from the lead "characters" in the true-life story, and will rely on dramatized and fictionalized "composite" characters to move the story forward.

When the film is based on a book, the producer will enter into a standard book option agreement with the author, as well as a life story rights agreement with the book's subject. Where there is no book and the producer plans to commission a screenplay based on a public figure, the producer may decide to rely solely on news reports, interviews, and other generally known public facts about a public person. For films based on people who are not clearly public figures, or who have been thrust into the limelight but whose lives are not generally well known by the public, the producer will want to get access to the full story and background, and also secure the rights needed.[68]

Significant deal points in a life story rights agreement include the following:

- Exclusivity: Exclusive rights to the story for the motion picture and all other potential media and uses, including prequels, sequels, television, internet, books, games, etc.

- Dramatization: The producers will want the unfettered right to dramatize the life story.

- Approvals: The subject will want approvals over the script that depicts them. The producers may offer consultation rights, or "meaningful consultation" rights that still grant the producers sole discretion to dramatize. It is extremely rare for any producer to grant approval rights over the script, given that ultimately the financer or studio will typically only finance a project where they have the ultimate decision making power over all elements, including the script.

---

claims of intentional infliction of emotional distress allegedly caused by parody advertisement ridiculing public figure); *Gertz v. Welch*, 418 U.S. 323, 94 S.Ct. 2997, 11 L.Ed.2d 789 (1974).

67   Unless the person executing the release reserves the right to approve elements of the script, they will be foreclosed from bringing an action if the film ultimately casts them in a negative light. See *Marder v. Lopez*, 450 F.3d 445 (9th Cir. 2006) (release signed by dancer whose life story was basis for film "Flashdance"). See also *De Havilland v. FX Networks, LLC*, 21 Cal. App. 5th 845, 230 Cal. Rptr. 3d 625 (2018) (film depicting living actress protected by First Amendment from right of publicity and defamation claims).

68   A sample "life story rights" agreement is included in the forms accompanying this treatise.

- <u>Documents</u>: Access to all photos, letters memoirs, journals, etc. owned by the subject, especially any materials that were not previously the subject of press reports or common public knowledge. Access will include the right and license to use copyrighted materials such as photos and letters and to adapt them for the project. The subject will retain actual copyright ownership.

- <u>Interviews</u>: The subject will be available for interviews with the producers, screenwriters, director and others. The information given in the interviews will be part of the "Results and Proceeds" clause in the agreement, meaning that the producer has full rights to make use of the information and exclusively own it for the purposes of the film. The subject will want to limit the amount of time they are available in a reasonable way. For a subject who has a job, family, etc., the time demands of a production could turn out to be considerable. The subject may also be asked to provide access to others, such as family members and close friends, who in turn would likely be asked to sign some form of a consent and release.

- <u>Locations</u>: Where the subject's home or other premises are potentially of use in the film production, the agreement may also include a location agreement allowing filming to take place on the premises.

- <u>Consultation</u>: The subject may agree to generally serve as a consultant on the film, possibly for an additional fee based on daily or hourly rates, including paid transportation and accommodation costs as required, and pursuant to reasonable availability.

- <u>Credits</u>: Credits might include a notice such as "Based on a true story," or "With special thanks to [Subject]," or "Produced with the kind permission and agreement of [Subject]."

- <u>Use of name and likeness</u>: Permission to use the subject's name and likeness for any and all forms of advertising.

- <u>Attendance at premieres and awards</u>: Both the producer and the subject may see publicity benefits in the subject attending major premieres and awards shows. The agreement would provide for payment of travel and accommodations, and perhaps per diems and clothing/hair allowances.

- <u>Financial considerations</u>: As always, financial considerations will be subject to negotiation. Where the subject is not extremely famous, they may be presented with little in the way of guaranteed payments, however they could attempt to negotiate to share in the project's success, with, for example, bonuses based on box office performance or awards, net profit participation, and reservation of certain rights such as publication of autobiographical books.[69]

---

69   With respect to "profit participation" or deferred payments, see the discussion in § 1.04[4] *infra*.

[c]—Fictionalized or Composite Characters

When a film is based on a true story, there may still be a need to create fictional characters in the screenplay. Often, these fictionalized characters are composites of real life people in the original book or story. The potential liability for such fictionalized or composite characters may arise where a person who believes he or she is the basis for such a character also believes that the portrayal is defamatory, or constitutes an invasion of privacy.

For example, the film "Hardball" was based on a non-fiction work titled "Hardball: A Season in the Projects," which discussed baseball teams and coaches in inner-city Chicago.[70] In 1993, Paramount acquired the motion picture rights to the book. In 2001, the film "Hardball" was released. The film told the story of a fictional character, and it included a standard disclaimer that it was a "fictitious story and no actual persons, events or organizations have been portrayed." The main character was a composite of several real life coaches described in the original book, including the plaintiff. While the plaintiff believed the character in the film was a thinly veiled biography of himself, he also asserted that the character had been given undesirable characteristics. The plaintiff sued for defamation and invasion of privacy.[71]

The elements of a defamation claim include the requirement that the reputation of the defendant suffer harm, and that the defamatory statement be "of and concerning" the plaintiff. The Seventh Circuit noted that some viewers of the film who knew the plaintiff or had read the original book could reasonably conclude that the main character was based on the plaintiff. On the other hand, in the court's opinion, "the significant differences between [the main character and the plaintiff] could just as easily have led a reasonable viewer who knew about [the plaintiff] to conclude that [the main character] represented either a composite of the coaches described in Coyle's *Hardball*, or an amalgam of these real-life figures with a stock Hollywood leading man."[72] Because it was reasonable that the main character could be based on someone other than the plaintiff, he could not satisfy the "of and concerning" element of a defamation claim, and summary judgment on that claim was granted to defendants.[73]

---

70   *Muzikowski v. Paramount Pictures Corp.*, 477 F.3d 899 (7th Cir. 2007) ("*Muzikowski* 2007"). See also, *Muzikowski v. Paramount Pictures Corp.*, 322 F.3d 918 (7th Cir. 2003) ("*Muzikowski* 2003").

71   The litigation involved several decisions in favor of the defendants in the original case, on remand, and appeals up to the Seventh Circuit on two occasions in 2003 and 2007.

72   *Muzikowski* 2007, N. 45 *supra*, 477 F.3d at 907.

73   *Id.* Even if Paramount had been able to obtain a complete and full consent and release from Muzikowski including the right to use his name, and even the right to alter his character for dramatic purposes, the dramatic needs of the film would have likely still compelled them to include a coach with "problems" as part of the film's structure. Perhaps litigation could have been avoided if the screenplay somehow distanced the main character

[d]—Mere Mention of Persons

NBC Universal, Inc., released a film titled "American Gangster." The film depicts the life of a drug dealer, and includes references to corruption among some members of local police forces in New York City and New Jersey. As is common with films inspired by true events, there was a disclaimer in the end credits stating that a number of the incidents in the film are "fictionalized," and "some of the characters have been composited or invented."[74]

At the end of the film, a text "legend" stated that the cooperation of the drug dealer "led to the convictions of three quarters of New York City's Drug Enforcement Agency." There is no such agency. Several former United States Drug Enforcement Agency employees filed suit against the producers, claiming their group as a whole had been defamed because of the allegedly false disclaimer at the end of the film.[75]

In granting the defendant's motion to dismiss, the court held that because an allegedly defamatory statement must be "of and concerning" a particular individual, a defamation claim could not be sustained on behalf of a group. Under the group libel doctrine, no individual within that group can fairly say that the statement is about him, nor can the group as a whole state a claim for defamation.[76]

[e]—Libel-Proof Plaintiffs

In a case that involved the biographical film, "Donnie Brasco," the plaintiff sued the producers claiming that he was defamed by the depiction in the film of him engaging in criminal conduct while allegedly a member of an organized crime family.[77]

The film was based on a book by an undercover agent who infiltrated an organized crime family. In granting defendants' motion to dismiss, the court found that the depictions of the plaintiff in the film were based on the book, which was, in turn, based on actual criminal prosecution cases and testimony. Based on the record before it, including the plaintiff's criminal history, the court held that the plaintiff was "libel proof" because his reputation was already "badly tarnished," stating that "even assuming the pre-release and official versions of the film are defamatory, he

---

further from Muzikowski himself. Ultimately, combining real life stories and persons with fictional and composite characters based even loosely on real people carried some level of risk in this particular case.

74   *Diaz v. NBC Universal, Inc.*, 536 F. Supp.2d 337 (S.D.N.Y. 2008), aff'd 337 Fed. Appx. 94 (2d Cir. 2009).

75   *Id.*

76   *Id.*, 536 F. Supp.2d at 343.

77   *Cerasani v. Sony Corp.*, 991 F. Supp. 343 (S.D.N.Y. 1998).

can suffer no further harm and hence no reasonable jury could award him anything more than nominal damages."[78]

[f]—Disclaimers

In an effort to avoid the types of defamation and invasion of privacy cases discussed above, films typically include disclaimers in the end credits. Such disclaimers typically state that the characters in the film are not based on "any actual person, living or dead," and that "any resemblance to any living person is purely coincidental.[79]

Such disclaimers, especially in connection with films based on real events, have grown longer over the years.[80] 5 Courts have held that disclaimers will not overcome a legitimate defamation claim, but, at least in the context of printed materials, they are one of "many signals" a publisher may send to readers alerting them to the fact that a passage may be, for example, protected satire, not intended as a defamatory

---

78   *Id.*, 991 F. Supp. at 346. Note also that with respect to films based on literary efforts of convicted felons, some states may have statutes preventing convicted felons from profiting from stories of their crimes. See, e.g., *Keenan v. Superior Court*, 27 Cal.4th 413, 117 Cal. Rptr.2d 1, 40 P.3d 718 (2002) (discussing constitutionality of California's "Son of Sam" statute appropriating as compensation for crime victims all monies due to convicted felons based on story of their crimes. The case arose in connection with an action by Frank Sinatra, Jr. demanding that Columbia Pictures withhold a reported $1.5 million payment to his kidnappers for motion picture rights to their story of the crime.).

79   The use of such disclaimers is alleged to have begun in connection with a defamation lawsuit filed against MGM in 1931. In "Rasputin and the Empress," the plot included a scene in which Rasputin raped a member of the royal family, and the husband of the woman sued MGM claiming it was not true. Press reports indicate that the case settled, with MGM deleting the offending scenes from the film, and adding a disclaimer that became part of every motion picture end credit thereafter. See the review of "Rasputin and the Empress," available at http://movies.nytimes.com/movie/40349/Rasputin-and-the-Empress/overview.

80   For example, in the Muzikowski case, the following disclaimer appeared in the film's credits (although use of this disclaimer did not avoid a lawsuit):

"While this motion picture is in part inspired by actual events, persons and organizations, this is a fictitious story and no actual persons, events or organizations have been portrayed."

Muzikowski v. Paramount Pictures Corp. ("*Muzikowski 2003*"), 322 F.3d 918, 922 (7th Cir. 2003).

statement, or that a character is not based on any actual person.[81] Placement of the disclaimer is of paramount importance.[82]

Disclaimers may be of little value in avoiding lawsuits brought by determined plaintiffs. In *Moore v. The Weinstein Co.*, a musician sued the producers of the film "Soul Men," claiming the film was based on his life, notwithstanding the use by the filmmakers of the standard disclaimer "The persons and events in this motion picture are fictitious. Any similarity to actual persons or events is unintentional."[83]

[6]—Copyright in Characters

The Copyright Act does not include "characters" in the list of copyrightable subject matter. But books and films are replete with characters who reappear in a series of works, and whose value goes beyond and lives outside of one particular film or book.

In disputes involving rights to characters, courts in the Ninth Circuit and Second Circuits use different tests. In the Ninth Circuit, the seminal case involved the character of "Sam Spade," created by novelist Dashiell Hammett in his novel, *The Maltese Falcon*.[84] Hammett sold the book rights to Warner Bros. After the film's success, Hammett continued to write stories featuring Sam Spade, including projects with CBS. Warner Bros. sued, claiming they owned the character Sam Spade, and CBS could no longer use the character in new stories and productions.

---

81   See *New Times, Inc. v. Isaacks*, 146 S.W.3d 144, 160-161 (Tex. 2004), stating:

[W]hile a disclaimer would have aided the reasonable reader in determining the article was a satire, such a disclaimer is not necessarily dispositive. See, *e.g., Falwell v. Flynt*, 805 F.2d at 486-87 (Wilkinson, J., dissenting) (noting that, despite label proclaiming 'Ad Parody-Not to be Taken Seriously,' Flynt could have been subject to a libel judgment if the publication were found to be defamatory); *Pring v. Penthouse Int'l, Ltd.*, 695 F.2d 438 (10th Cir. 1982) ('The test is not whether the story is or is not characterized as "fiction," "humor," or anything else in the publication' but whether the story could reasonably be interpreted as stating actual fact). Rather, the presence of a disclaimer is one of many signals the reasonable reader may consider in evaluating a publication. *See, e.g., San Francisco Bay Guardian v. Superior Court*, 17 Cal. App.4th 655, 21 Cal. Rptr.2d 464, 466 (1993) (noting that '[t]he question of whether the average reader would have recognized the issue as a parody and the letter as a part of the joke depends upon a view of the entire issue, i.e., the "totality of circumstances"'; the fact that a phony letter to the editor was in a section of the newspaper labeled 'special parody section' was significant)."

82   See *Stanton v. Metro Corp.*, 438 F.3d 119 (1st Cir. 2006) (magazine disclaimer that persons in photo accompanying article were not actually the persons discussed in article was not sufficiently placed to be effective).

83   See *Moore v. The Weinstein Co.*, 2012 U.S. Dist. LEXIS 72929, 2012 WL 1884758 (M.D. Tenn. May 23, 2012), aff'd 545 Fed. Appx. 405 (6th Cir. 2013).

84   See *Warner Bros. Pictures, Inc. v. Columbia Broadcasting System*, 216 F.2d 945 (9th Cir. 1954).

In holding for the defendants, the court noted that the original agreement with Warner Bros. did not mention rights to any characters, and noted that such rights are "not customarily parted with by authors, but that characters which are depicted in one detective story together with their names are customarily retained and used in the intricacies of subsequent but different tales."[85]

The court declined to hold that characters, separate from the story, could be separately copyrighted. "The characters of an author's imagination and the art of his descriptive talent, like a painter's or like a person with his penmanship, are always limited and always fall into limited patterns."[86] However, the court went on to state that copyrightability could potentially be found where "the character really constitutes the story being told, but if the character is only the chessman in the game of telling the story he is not within the area of the protection afforded by the copyright."[87] Thus the "story being told" test made copyrightability of characters a high hurdle.[88]

Subsequent cases have found characters to be protectable apart from the story they appear in, often where they are part of a series of works, and where the characters have a distinct visual appearance (such as cartoons and television or movie characters that have a "constant set of traits that distinguishes him/her/it from other fictional characters."[89]). Thus, protection has been acknowledged for, among others, Mickey Mouse, Superman,[90]

---

85   *Id.*, 216 F.2d at 948.

86   *Id.*

87   *Id.*

88   The Second Circuit uses the "character delineation" test stemming from the 1930 Second Circuit case *Nichols v. Universal Pictures Corp.*, in which Judge Learned hand noted that "the less developed the characters, the less they can be copyrighted: that is the penalty an author must bear for marking them too indistinctly." See *Nichols v. Universal Pictures Corp.*, 45 F.2d 119, 121 (2d Cir. 1930).

89   See *Toho Co., Ltd. v. William Morrow & Co., Inc.*, 33 F. Supp.2d 1206, 1215 (C.D. Cal. 1998).

90   See *Warner Bros. Inc. v. American Broadcasting Cos., Inc.*, 720 F.2d 231, 240-245 (2d Cir.1983).

"Amos n' Andy,"[91] Godzilla,[92] "Star Wars" characters,[93] Rocky,[94] James Bond[95] and Betty Boop.[96]

The Ninth Circuit has evolved from the "story being told" test for character copyrightability, establishing a three-part test, described as follows in a case finding that the famous Batmobile is a copyrightable character that was infringed by a company selling replicas:

> "We read these precedents as establishing a three-part test for determining whether a character in a comic book, television program, or motion picture is entitled to copyright protection. First, the character must generally have "physical as well as conceptual qualities." Second, the character must be "sufficiently delineated" to be recognizable as the same character whenever it appears. Considering the character as it has appeared in different productions, it must display consistent, identifiable character traits and attributes, although the character need not have a consistent appearance. Third, the character must be "especially distinctive" and "contain some unique elements of expression." It cannot be a stock character such as a magician in standard magician garb. Even when a character lacks sentient attributes and does not speak (like a car), it can be a protectable character if it meets this standard.

> "We now apply this framework to this case. . . . First, because the Batmobile has appeared graphically in comic books, and as a three-dimensional car in television series and motion pictures, it has "physical as well as conceptual qualities," and is thus not a mere literary character.

> "Second, the Batmobile is "sufficiently delineated" to be recognizable as the same character whenever it appears. As the district court determined,

---

91   See *Silverman v. CBS, Inc.*, 632 F. Supp. 1344, 1355 (S.D.N.Y. 1986).

92   See *Toho Co., Ltd. v. William Morrow & Co., Inc.*, 33 F. Supp.2d 1206, 1215-1216 (C.D. Cal. 1998).

93   See *Ideal Toy Corp. v. Kenner Products Division of General Mills Fun Group, Inc.*, 443 F. Supp. 291, 301 (S.D.N.Y. 1977).

94   See *Anderson v. Stallone*, 1989 U.S. Dist. LEXIS 11109 (C.D. Cal. April 25, 1989).

95   See *Metro-Goldwyn-Mayer, Inc. v. American Honda Motor Co.*, 900 F. Supp. 1287 (C.D. Cal. 1995). See also: *Danjaq, LLC v. Universal City Studios, LLC*, 2014 U.S. Dist. LEXIC 180264 (C.D. Cal. Oct. 2, 2014) (denying motion to dismiss where complaint adequately stated copyright infringement claim against draft screenplay titled "Section 6" based on substantial similarities in character, theme, plot, sequence and dialogue related to James Bond character); *Halicki Films, LLC v. Sanderson Sales and Marketing*, 547 F.3d 1213 (9th Cir. 2008) (whether "Eleanor" car is copyrightable as a character is fact intensive and not decided on summary judgment).

96   *Fleisher Studios, Inc. v. A.V.E.L.A., Inc.*, 636 F.3d 1115 (9th Cir. 2011).

the Batmobile has maintained distinct physical and conceptual qualities since its first appearance in the comic books in 1941. In addition to its status as "a highly-interactive vehicle, equipped with high-tech gadgets and weaponry used to aid Batman in fighting crime," the Batmobile is almost always bat-like in appearance, with a bat-themed front end, bat wings extending from the top or back of the car, exaggerated fenders, a curved windshield, and bat emblems on the vehicle. This bat-like appearance has been a consistent theme throughout the comic books, television series, and motion picture, even though the precise nature of the bat-like characteristics have changed from time to time.

"The Batmobile also has consistent character traits and attributes. No matter its specific physical appearance, the Batmobile is a "crime-fighting" car with sleek and powerful characteristics that allow Batman to maneuver quickly while he fights villains. In the comic books, the Batmobile is described as waiting "[l]ike an impatient steed straining at the reins . . . shiver[ing] as its super-charged motor throbs with energy" before it "tears after the fleeing hoodlums" an instant later. Elsewhere, the Batmobile "leaps away and tears up the street like a cyclone," and at one point "twin jets of flame flash out with thunderclap force, and the miracle car of the dynamic duo literally flies through the air!" Like its comic book counterpart, the Batmobile depicted in both the 1966 television series and the 1989 motion picture possesses "jet engine[s]" and flame-shooting tubes that undoubtedly give the Batmobile far more power than an ordinary car. Furthermore, the Batmobile has an ability to maneuver that far exceeds that of an ordinary car. In the 1966 television series, the Batmobile can perform an "emergency bat turn" via reverse thrust rockets. Likewise, in the 1989 motion picture, the Batmobile can enter "Batmissile" mode, in which the Batmobile sheds "all material outside [the] central fuselage" and reconfigures its "wheels and axles to fit through narrow openings."

"Equally important, the Batmobile always contains the most up-to-date weaponry and technology. At various points in the comic book, the Batmobile contains a "hot-line phone . . . directly to Commissioner Gordon's office" maintained within the dashboard compartment, a "special alarm" that foils the Joker's attempt to steal the Batmobile, and even a complete "mobile crime lab" within the vehicle. Likewise, the Batmobile in the 1966 television series possesses a "Bing-Bong warning bell," a mobile Bat-phone, a "Batscope, complete with [a] TV-like viewing screen on the dash," and a "Bat-ray." Similarly, the Batmobile in the 1989 motion picture is equipped with a "pair of forward-facing Browning machine guns," "spherical bombs," "chassis-mounted shinbreakers," and "side-mounted disc launchers."

"Because the Batmobile, as it appears in the comic books as well as in the 1966 television show and 1989 motion picture, displays "consistent, identifiable character traits and attributes," the second prong of the character analysis is met here.

"Third, the Batmobile is "especially distinctive" and contains unique elements of expression. In addition to its status as Batman's loyal bat-themed sidekick complete with the character traits and physical characteristics described above, the Batmobile also has its unique and highly recognizable name. It is not merely a stock character.

"Accordingly, applying our three-part test, we conclude that the Batmobile is a character that qualifies for copyright protection."[97]

The Ninth Circuit's three-part test would appear to favor characters who appear repeatedly in different stories and thus consistently establish their appearance and/or traits, or animated or cartoon characters with consistent visual appearance, or characters featured in full length films that have the opportunity to "come alive" over several hours.[98]

Perhaps appropriate to the age of the YouTube video, a recent case in the Central District of California granted copyright protection to a "baseball announcer" character created by actor Hank Azaria, where the character appeared only once in a four-minute satirical "mockumentary" video released online on the "Funny or Die" web channel.[99] The fictional sportcaster Jim Brockmire's only appearance was in the video short "Jim Brockmire: A Legend in the Booth," but he made a huge impression on the court, which held that "[Brockmire's] personal history and physical appearance—down to his marital relationship, lucky pen, career arc, volatile temper, affinity for specific cultural trivia, plaid jacket, red tie, the rose on his lapel, and the classic sign off to his wife—are at least as individualized as several characters whose copyrights have been recognized in this District."[100]

---

97   See *DC Comics v. Towle*, 802 F.3d 1012 at *17 (9th Cir. 2015) (Internal citations omitted.).

98   See, e.g.: *Halicki Films, LLC v. Sanderson Sales and Marketing*, 547 F.3d 1213 (9th Cir. 2008) (car character "Eleanor" in "Gone In Sixty Seconds"); *Olson v. National Broadcasting Co.*, 855 F.2d 1446 (9th Cir. 1988) (characters in plaintiff's story "Cargo" drawn "thinly" and were not copyrightable and not infringed by defendant's "A Team" television series); *Toho Co., v. William Morrow & Co., Inc.*, 33 F. Supp.2d 1226 (C.D. Cal. 1998) (Godzilla).

99   See *Azaria v. Bierko*, 2013 U.S. Dist. LEXIS 25545 (C.D. Cal. Feb. 22, 2013).

100   *Id.*, at 7.

The Second Circuit's "character delineation" test led to a decision that Holden Caulfield, the central character in J.D. Salinger's novel, *The Catcher in the Rye*, was copyrightable.[101] In holding that an unauthorized sequel was not a fair use, the Second Circuit stated that Caulfield is "sufficiently delineated so that a claim for infringement will lie." Despite the fact that Caulfield appears in only one novel, and not a series of works, the court noted, "Holden Caulfield is quite delineated by words. It is a portrait by words. It is something that is obviously seen to be of value since the effort is made [by defendants] to recall everything that the character in the book does."[102]

Characters whose copyright protection arises in a film retain that protection despite their appearance in later media that might have become public domain under the strict rules of the former 1909 Copyright Act (now replaced by the 1976 Copyright Act). In an Eighth Circuit case, a defendant argued unsuccessfully that famous characters from The Wizard of Oz were unintentionally injected into the public domain because of their additional use in public domain theatre lobby cards and advertisements. In discussing the protectability of characters in this unusual context, the court noted:

> "Dorothy, Tin Man, Cowardly Lion, and Scarecrow from 'The Wizard of Oz,' Scarlett O'Hara and Rhett Butler from 'Gone with the Wind,' and 'Tom and Jerry' each exhibit 'consistent, widely identifiable traits' in the films that are sufficiently distinctive to merit character protection."[103]

Because the original films themselves were still protected under their copyrights, the existence of public domain publicity materials dating from the films' original release (such as production photographs and theatre lobby cards showing the characters in isolated poses) did not mean that the characters themselves had entered the public domain.

---

101   See *Salinger v. Colting*, 607 F.3d 68, 73 (2d Cir. 2010).

102   *Id.*

103   See *Warner Bros. Entertainment, Inc. v. X One X Productions, Inc.*, 644 F.3d 584 (8th Cir. 2011). See also:

Seventh Circuit: Gaiman v. McFarlane, 360 F.3d 644 (7th Cir. 2004) ("Spawn" comic book characters copyrightable as joint work).

Ninth Circuit: Rice v. Fox Broadcasting Co., 330 F.3d 1170, 1175-1176 (9th Cir. 2003) (magician character not sufficiently delineated to warrant copyright protection); *Walker v. Viacom International, Inc.*, 2008 U.S. Dist. LEXIS 38882 (N.D. Cal. May 13, 2008) (drawings of anthropomorphic sponge character not sufficiently consistent, distinctive, and identifiable to warrant copyright protection, therefore plaintiff's drawings were not infringed by famous Spongebob Squarepants cartoon character).

The copyright in Sir Arthur Canon Doyle's character Sherlock Holmes was not a mysterious "case" for the Seventh Circuit Court of Appeals.[104] Doyle's fifty-six stories and four novels featuring Holmes were published beginning in 1887 up until 1927. Any work published prior to 1923 in the United States has entered the public domain, but works published in 1923 and later enjoy 95 years of copyright protection in the United States, assuming all requirements were met under the former 1909 Copyright Act (such as publication with a copyright notice and renewal of the copyright).

The question before the Seventh Circuit was whether the public domain pre-1923 Holmes character was free for anyone to use in their own literary works, notwithstanding the existence of Holmes' copyright-protected doppelganger as published in the period 1923 to 1927. Based on the facts in the case, including that the accused infringer only used character elements from the pre-1923 period, the court held that the Holmes character has entered the public domain, even if Doyle's last published writings are still protected.

[7]—Screenplay Acquisition

It is also possible to provide a screenplay "on spec," which is then optioned or sold to a production company. The Writers Guild of America ("WGA") is a union that has negotiated fixed rates of compensation with production companies that are signatories to the WGA Theatrical and Television Basic Agreement (Master Bargaining Agreement or "MBA"). It is essential to determine if the production company is a WGA signatory, because its contractual relations with the author or authors of the screenplay will be guided by the MBA. The WGA also makes the final determination of screen credits for a film.

[a]—WGA "Blueprint" for Screenplay Acquisition

Typical issues in an agreement for a screenplay will include whether the deal covers only a story, or the story plus the screenplay.[105] With respect to the services to be performed, screenplay agreements typically include a number of "Steps" that track the creative process, and provide for payment when each step is delivered by the writer to the producer, with 50% due on commencement of each step, and 50% due upon delivery. Typical "steps" may include:

---

104   See *Leslie S. Klinger v. Conan Doyle Estate, Ltd.*, 755 F.3d 496 (7th Cir. 2014) (declaratory judgment plaintiff). See also, *Leslie S. Klinger v. Conan Doyle Estate, Ltd.*, 761 F.3d 789 (7th Cir 2014) (awarding attorneys' fees to prevailing declaratory judgment plaintiff).

105   A thorough and detailed description of the creative and contractual issues a screenwriter will encounter is available in the WGA online publication Creative Rights for Writers of Theatrical and Long-Form Television Motion Pictures, available at <http://www.wga.org/contracts/know-your-rights/creative-rights-for-writers>.

- Step 1: Story
- Step 2: First draft of screenplay
- Step 3: First rewrite
- Step 4: Second rewrite
- Step 5: Polish (final)

[b]—Writer Deal Memos

It is common to negotiate a short deal memo with a writer, with a long form agreement anticipated for completion in the future. Key deal points include the following:

- Working title.
- Confirmation whether is it adapted from preexisting material or treatments or original.
- Deadlines for treatment, notes from producer, first draft, first draft notes from producer, second draft, final delivery.
- Guaranteed compensation based on WGA minimums for proposed film budget and type of screenplay.
- Payment Schedule.
- Production bonus upon commencement of photography.
- Credits per WGA
- Net profit participation
- Work made for hire and copyright assignment to producer
- Travel if required
- Award bonuses for Academy Awards / Golden Globes
- Premiere invitation +1
- Producer right to assign (subject to WGA requirements)
- Miscellaneous (governing law, etc.)

[c]—Separated Rights: Publication and Theater Rights Retained by Screenwriters

Even where a writer has signed a work made for hire agreement with the producer for the screenplay, the writer may retain certain rights under the WGA MBA. The principle is similar to copyright law, which is premised on a "bundle of rights." Highlights of separated rights include the right of a screenplay author to create a novelization of her screenplay; as well as rights to theatrical stage versions of her work.

Entitlement to separated rights is subject to final WGA determination. In order to be qualified, a writer must meet a number of WGA criteria, governed by issues such as whether the writer has sole credit for the screenplay and whether the screenplay is entirely original with the writer including original characters, or is an adaptation based on preexisting material. Separated rights may be different for theatrical (motion picture) as opposed to television works.

In *Wagner v. Columbia Pictures Industries, Inc.*, actor Robert Wagner, who was one of the original owners of the "Charlie's Angels" television series, brought suit against Columbia Pictures, claiming that his original agreement with his co-producer, Aaron Spelling Productions, entitled him to a share of the profits of the theatrical motion picture versions produced years later by Columbia.[106] At issue in the case were the separated rights enjoyed by the original writers of the series pilot teleplay, because those separated rights included the right to create a motion picture version of the television series.

In the opinion, the court reviewed the nature of separated rights, and noted that despite a work made for hire agreement executed by the original authors of the teleplay in favor of the producer, under the WGA MBA, the authors' separated rights were held in trust by the producer until such time as the authors exercised those rights. Columbia Pictures purchased those separated rights directly from the heirs of the original teleplay authors. Therefore, Wagner was not entitled to any share in the profits from the motion picture versions.[107]

The specific nature of separated rights was at the heart of a dispute over the 2010 remake of the 1968 CBS television series "Hawaii Five-O." In a dispute between the estate of one of the writers of the original 1960s series and his talent agent and producing partner, the issue was the scope of rights the writer granted to his producing partner, and whether the term "reserved rights" in fact meant "separated rights" as defined under the WGA MBA. Holding that the grant had been of "reserved rights" as defined in the WGA MBA section on separated rights, the court noted that separated rights do not include episodic television, but rather *live* television (and other rights); thus the agent/producer did not hold any rights in the 2010 series remake, which was indeed episodic.[108]

---

106   See *Wagner v. Columbia Pictures Industries, Inc.*, 146 Cal. App.4th 586, 52 Cal. Rptr.3d 898 (2007).

107   *Id.*, 52 Cal. Rptr.3d at 904-905.

108   See George *Litto Productions, Inc. v. Robin Bernstein*, Case No. BC484021, Slip Op. (Cal. Sup. May 21, 2014). The court noted that the WGA MBA Separated Rights included the following: dramatic stage rights, theatrical rights, publication rights, merchandising rights, radio rights, *live* television rights and interactive rights. *Id.* at 5. All other rights, including *episodic* television, belonged to CBS.

For theatrical/motion picture works, and for television works, the WGA has published guides to separated rights. Separated rights, when exercised, are the subject of a separate negotiation, agreement, and consideration.[109]

[d]—Passive Income

Where a screenplay is original material and not an adaptation, and the writer qualifies for separated rights, that will also entitle the writer to what is commonly referred to as "passive income" on future projects based on the screenplay, whether or not the writer provides writing services on the future project, pursuant to Section 16(a)(5) of the WGA MBA. One example is that for future motion pictures based on the writer's original motion picture, the writer is entitled to 25% of their original fee.

Negotiations with writers or their representatives may include a demand for "passive income," but no such income applies unless the original screenplay qualifies for WGA separated rights by virtue of consisting of original characters and stories, and not being adapted from preexisting material.

[e]—Non-WGA Agreements

Where a production company is not a WGA signatory, as may be the case for independent production companies working on small budgets, and where the screenplay author is not a WGA member, the parties are free to work on any contractual basis, including the simplest type of copyright assignment. Student films, super low budget independent films, or films made abroad, may be typical situations where the parties are not members of, or signatories to, the standard entertainment industry guild and union collective bargaining agreements.

§1.04   Film Financing and Net Profits

Film production is a risky, highly speculative business. Producing even a modest-sized film requires a small army. Expenses are enormous and there are never guarantees of success. If audience response could be accurately quantified, then every film ever made would be a gigantic hit. The reality is that few films recoup their investment, and fewer still make large profits.

The overall concepts in film financing are simple: Capital investment is raised to pay the production costs of a film. Distributors of the film pass along much, but not all, of the box office revenues to the studio. These gross revenues flow initially to the financiers and the

---

109   See <http://www.wga.org/contracts/know-your-rights/creative-rights-for-writers>.

studio, who recoup their investments in the actual production or "negative costs" of the film, and also realize a profit on their investment, along with the opportunity to charge fees for general overhead and expenses.[110]

After the production costs, main investors and any deferrals are satisfied, what remains is the smaller pool of net profits. The net profits are split between the financers and/or studio, and the producers. The producer's half of the net profits will typically grant small percentages to other members of the main creative force behind the project, such as the individual producers, the director, the writers, actors, and the owners of any underlying book or life story rights.

The summary of the order of revenue distribution and deductions is:

- Gross Proceeds: the studio's gross revenues from all the distribution "windows," including theatrical, home video, television, etc.

- Distribution Fees: Typically 30% of the Gross Proceeds go to the distributor for domestic (United States) distribution, 35% in the U.K. and Canada, and 40% in all other territories.

- Distribution Costs: prints and advertising, including overhead charges on expenses of 10%.

- Production Costs: The "negative cost" of the film, plus interest, and plus an overhead charge of 15%.

- Deferrals: Monies due cast members who agreed to postpone much of their fee until the film was released and revenue was realized.

- Net Profits: Split 50/50 between the studio and the producer. Out of the producer's half, net profit deductions for "profit participants", typically the director, writer, stars, and owners of underlying rights, will be deducted. Where such a plan would reduce the producer's share of net profits to levels as low as 10%, the studio and director may agree that there is a "hard floor" for the producer's obligation to share their half of the net profit pool, in effect a guarantee of a 20% hard floor for the producer would mean that the studio would subsidize any net profit participation payments that would otherwise reduce the producer's share to less than 20%.

Complications arise when one considers how the "profit," is realized. The completed film is distributed throughout the range of "distribution windows,"[111] first to theaters, then to pay-per-view and home video, then to cable television and free television, and then online, and so on. For each distribution window, revenues are produced, and each distributor keeps a percentage of the revenues in exchange for their efforts. The distributors may also be entitled to reimbursement of certain costs and expenditures connected with their distribution efforts, for example advertising, shipping, and other costs.

---

110   "Deferrals" are contingent amounts owed talent who initially accept less than their normal fee or "quote," but defer the balance as a priority distribution if the film succeeds financially.

111   See § 2.13 infra.

[1]—Revenue Phases

The "gross" revenues received by the production company or studio are not truly the film's worldwide "gross box office" revenues. That is because the film industry trade publications report on gross box office sales; however, the theaters keep a portion of those revenues. The worldwide box office revenues are only the first stage in the journey of money paid by the consumer for a theater ticket. Beginning with the ticket sale, portions of the revenues are retained by participants at several stages in the process, including:

- the owners of the theaters where the films are shown;

- the distribution companies that produce the prints and ship them to the theaters, including P & A (prints and advertising) costs;

- the studio that produced the film and/or financiers;

- recipients of any deferred compensation;

- the producers;

- the net profit participants.

[a]—Box Office Revenue Retained by Theaters

Typically, theater owners will be entitled to deduct their fixed weekly operating expense from each week's gross ticket sales revenue. Then, the "rental fee," based on a percentage of box office revenues, will be remitted to the film's distributor. The rental fee formula may be based on gross ticket sales, net revenues after deduction of the weekly theater operating expenses, or a combination thereof. The percentages paid to the distributor may change from week to week during the engagement, with the distributor's percentage gradually decreasing if the film is successful. Generally, exhibiters may retain as much as 50% of the gross box office.

Theater owners are entitled to retain 100% of revenues from concessions, and from any third party advertising they run on their screens prior to the film being shown. Theater owners are not usually compensated for showing theatrical trailers, or previews of forthcoming releases, which are provided by the studios at no charge, either as part of the reel of film containing the actual released film, or as additional reels. During the course of a successful film run, studios may negotiate the showing of as many trailers as possible to a sizable "captive audience" in order to effectively promote future releases.[112]

Theatres compete with each other in order to obtain geographic exclusivity for popular films, known as "clearances." A clearance is "an exclusive right that a film dis-

---

112   See generally, National Association of Theater Owners Web site, www.nato.org.

tributor grants to a theater in connection with the licensing of a film."[113] It prohibits the distributor from licensing the film for exhibition at certain other theaters, either identified by name or located within a specified geographic region, while the film is being shown at the theater that obtained the clearance.[114] Theatres bid for clearances in a competitive process to obtain licenses to exhibit popular first-run films.[115]

[b]—Revenue Retained by the Distributor

The distributor may retain as much as 30% of the revenue received from the exhibiters, with the percentages increasing up to 40% for overseas distribution. In some cases, the studio that produced the film also has its own affiliated distribution subsidiary, so a studio that paid to produce a film, will at this early stage of revenue division, share in the fees retained by the studio's wholly owned distribution subsidiary. Prints and Advertising (P & A) costs are also deducted.

[c]— Gross Revenues Received by the Studio or Production Company

Revenue that makes its way from the theaters to the studio or production company is traditionally called "gross revenue." But it is actually only "gross" at this point in the process.[116] This somewhat inaccurate term is initially allocated to reimburse the financiers and investors for the costs of producing and advertising the film. In some rare cases, a major "star" attached to the project may be able to also share in these revenues. The gross revenues are also used to pay the studio's overhead charges, to reimburse specific expenses incurred, and to pay to the studio interest on the initial investment.

In the "waterfall" of allocation of revenues, first position will typically be allocated to any deferred compensation due above the line talent (star or director), then the bulk of the revenues will flow initially to the financiers (or studio), until they receive their investment plus an additional percentage, often between 10% and 20% above the amount invested.

---

113   See *Flagship Theatres of Palm Desert, LLC v. Century Theatres, Inc.*, 198 Cal. App.4th 1366, 1374, 131 Cal. Rptr.3d 519 (2011) (antitrust allegations by independent theater owner against large chain).

114   *Id.*

115   *Id.*, 198 Cal. App.4th at 1371.

116   As we have seen, a significant amount of the worldwide box office revenues has already been retained by the theater owners and the distributor.

[d]—Net Profits

If all the production and advertising costs are reimbursed in full, including deferrals and the priority return for the financiers, and if additional overhead and interest obligations are satisfied, the remaining revenues represent "net profits."

The net profits are divided up in order of priority: the original investors and financers (in many cases the studio) will typically be entitled to half of the net profits. The other half is claimed by the production company, designated the "producer share," and from the producer share, other "net profit participants" receive their "profit participation." This often includes the major creative forces behind the production, the "above the line" talent such as the individual producers, director, writer(s), and actors, and may also include the owner of the underlying book or life story rights. The agreements with the net profit participants will attempt to limit their shares to about half of the producer's share, for example:

- Director, 20% of producer's net share
- Writer, 15% of producer's net share
- Star, 15% of producer's net share
- Total commitments by producer: 50% of the producer net share

Where the net profit participants negotiated percentages are based on the entire net profit pool (the studio share and the producer share), the producers may find themselves with as little as 10% remaining. For example:

- Director, writer, two stars each receive 10% of the entire net profit pool, or 40% of the total
- Producer's share is 50% of the total net profit pool
- Producer must remit to the profit participants from producer's share (50% less 40%)
- Producer is left with only 10% of the net profits

In such cases, the studio and producer may agree that the producer's share of the net profits has a "hard floor," i.e., it will not be less than 20%, for example, of the total net profit pool. In such cases, the studio may agree to subsidize the profit participation payments, allowing the producer to retain at least 20%. Such subsidies would be chargeable as reimbursable costs to the studio. A "soft floor," on the other hand, would result in the studio only partially subsidizing the producer's obligation to remit profit participation payments.

Assume a film cost $20 million to produce, had $20 million in prints and advertising expenses, and grossed $140 million at the worldwide box office:[117]

Worldwide box office sales:	$140 million
Amount retained by theaters:	($40 million)
Amount received by distributor	$100 million
Amount retained by distributor	($30 million)
"Gross" received by studio	$70 million
Less gross revenue or deferrals due star	($5 million)
Less negative cost	($20 million)
Less prints and advertising	($20 million)
Less overhead and interest payable to studio	($10 million)
"Net profit" remaining	$15 million
Half of net profit to studio	($7.5 million)
Producer half share of net profit	$7.5 million
Less profit participants share paid from producer's half	($3.75 million)
Producer profit remaining and retained	$3.75 million

In this hypothetical, assuming the studio also owned the distributor, the studio's revenues above and beyond the negative costs, prints, and advertising were $47.5 million ($30 million fee received by wholly owned distribution subsidiary, plus overhead and interest fees of $10 million, plus half of net profits $7.5 million). The studio would have had considerable distribution costs to offset the revenues, and might argue that the distribution fee is entirely consumed by the distribution costs,

---

117   Overseas revenues are often equal to domestic, but overseas distributors may charge a higher percentage. For the purposes of this illustration, a hypothetical worldwide gross box office sales number has been used. Home video and television revenues would provide additional revenues, corresponding costs and distribution fees.

and the overhead fees are entirely consumed by overhead, leaving the studio with a few million in net profits.

The producer would net $3.75 million, and the net profit participants would share $3.75 million. The lead actor would receive $5 million in deferred compensation. The lead actor would have also received a smaller guaranteed fee to work on the picture. Depending on the type of agreement negotiated, that guaranteed fee may have been deducted from the deferred compensation.

Regardless of whether net profits ever accrue, everyone who worked on the film would have, during production, received whatever guaranteed "pay or play" fees they negotiated for their services, or union scale, which, in some cases, might have been sizable. Those fees would have been paid from the $20 million negative cost and production budget. If the film fails financially, the financiers will incur the loss.

[2]—Sources of Film Financing

Equity financing occurs when cash is invested in exchange for ownership of, and equity in, the film. Film financing can take many forms, ranging from a student filmmaker's overextended credit card to a major studio's deep pockets. Filmmakers must ensure that financing agreements are prepared by an attorney experienced in the areas of investment, SEC rules and regulations, perfection of security interests via UCC financing statements, formation of business entities such as corporations and LLCs, and related matters.

[a]—Studio Financing

[i]—Studio as Financier

Where a studio is the financier and owns all rights in the property from inception, it may fund a development phase. The project, if promising, will be "green lighted" to proceed to the production phase. If the project is not developing well—if a suitable screenplay has not been written or a suitable star has not attached to the project—the project may go into turnaround. In such cases, the original studio may have a claim to reimbursement of its development costs, and a claim to a share in the profits from the film produced by another studio.[118]

[ii]—Production-Financing-Distribution (PFD) Agreements

In a production-financing-distribution ("PFD") agreement, the project begins its life not as an internally developed studio project, but with an independent

---

118 See *Twentieth Century Fox Film Corp. v. Warner Bros. Entertainment, Inc.*, 630 F. Supp.2d 1140 (C.D. Cal. 2008) (dispute over distribution rights following "turnaround" phase at competing studio).

producer or production company that has acquired all rights in the underlying source material and arranged for or "attached" the key production team, including writer, director, and lead actors. The producer may work with a talent agency to "package" the project using talent from the agency's roster, and then present it to established studios with the goal of "setting up" the project at a studio, which will finance the production and distribute it when completed. In a PFD agreement, the studio is presented with a "turnkey" project that only requires financing to bring to completion.

[b]—Pre-Sales and Lender Financing

Based on factors like the talent attached to a project, the producer may be able to engage in "pre-sales" to distributors in the United States and abroad. This may involve cash or merely a written commitment to pay an advance upon completion of the film. Such a letter of commitment may serve as suitable collateral for a bank to provide lender financing.[119]

[c]—Negative Pick-Up

An independent producer may have an agreement with a studio to purchase the movie upon completion of the final negative. Written confirmation from the studio may be used by the producer as collateral for bank financing. The bank will look for a secure investment, such as existing production funding and involvement of a leading director and star.[120] Historically, this loan for production costs from a bank would be fully collateralized by the distributor's contractual obligation to make payment upon delivery of the film.[121]

[d]—Gap Financing

"Gap" financing refers to the difference between the costs of producing the film and the amount for which the film was pre-sold to distributors around the world.

---

119   See *Allianz Risk Transfer v. Paramount Pictures Corp.*, 2010 WL 1253957, at *3 (S.D.N.Y. March 31, 2010) (describing and comparing profitability to studio of international pre-sales compared to distribution by studio-affiliate).

120   See *General Star International Indemnity Ltd. v. The Chase Manhattan Bank*, 2002 U.S. Dist. LEXIS 7980, 2002 WL 850012 (S.D.N.Y. May 3, 2002) (insurance company insured loans made by Chase Manhattan Bank for a slate of films produced by Paramount. Insurer sued Chase for declaratory relief that the policies should be declared void based on allegations that Chase unlawfully concealed the fact that the scheme was virtually certain to result in substantial claims. Published opinion stayed state court actions pending resolution of the district court action.).

121   *Id.*

In *General Star International Indemnity Ltd. v. The Chase Manhattan Bank*,[122] Chase obtained insurance company commitments to insure the risk in its gap financing.[123] According to General Star, once the liability for the loans shifted from Chase to the insurer, Chase made increasingly risky loans on slates of films, and did not fully disclose the risk to the insurer.[124] The insurance coverage applied to an increasingly large "gap" between the pre-sales and the film's budget, and even at one point extended to insuring not distributor revenues, but actual box office revenues.[125]

Among other things, the plaintiff claimed that Chase misrepresented who would be "first in line" to recoup from gross revenues, and claimed that the "slate" concept of funding multiple films at one time would spread the risks adequately, so "overages" from more successful films would make up for the flops.[126] Despite those representations, the insurer suffered large losses on claims.[127]

[e]—Investor or "Equity" Financing

Film financing through wealthy individuals or groups may be regulated by the Securities and Exchange Commission ("SEC") where such investments appear to be equivalent to a public offering of securities, which are heavily regulated by the SEC. An offering prospectus or Private Placement Memorandum ("PPM") that contains suitable statements and risk disclosure should be prepared by an experienced attorney.[128]

---

122   *General Star International Indemnity Ltd. v. The Chase Manhattan Bank*, 2002 U.S. Dist. LEXIS 7980, 2002 WL 850012 (S.D.N.Y. May 3, 2002).

123   *Id.*

124   *Id.*

125   *Id.*

126   *Id.*

127   Losses included $4,421,740.47 for "A Simple Plan"; $12,900,110.70 for "A Civil Action"; and $21,227.568.82 for "Star Trek: Insurrection." Id., 2002 U.S. Dist. LEXIS 7980, at *10 n.6. See also, *Axa Corporate Solutions v. Underwriters Reinsurance Co.*, 2004 U.S. Dist. LEXIS 22609, 2004 WL 2534386 (N.D. Ill. Nov. 9, 2004).

128   However, under SEC Regulation D, certain types of investments that are offered to a close circle of friends and family are exempt from some, but not all, SEC securities requirements. See *SEC v. Platforms Wireless International Corp.*, 617 F.3d 1072 (9th Cir. 2010):

"Section 4(2) of the Securities Act, 15 U.S.C. § 77d(2), exempts from registration 'transactions by an issuer not involving any public offering.' '[T]he applicability of [Section 4(2)] should turn on whether the particular class of persons affected need the protection of the [Securities] Act. An offering to those who are shown to be able to fend for themselves is a transaction "not involving any public offering."' Stated another way, a limited distribution to highly sophisticated investors, rather than a general distribution to the public, is not a public offering.SEC-promulgated Regulation D creates a safe harbor within this exemption by defining

[i]—Private Placement Offerings Under SEC Regulation D

Under the Securities Act of 1933, a company that offers or sells investments in entertainment productions ("securities") must register the securities with the Securities Exchange Commission ("SEC"), or find an exemption from the registration requirements.[129] Section 4(2) of the Securities Act *exempts* transactions by an issuer not involving any "public offering," otherwise known as a "private placement."

The private placement exemption in Section 4(2) is regulated by SEC Regulation D. Section 506 of SEC Regulation D is often referred to as the "safe harbor" from SEC regulations for independent production companies, because companies using the Rule 506 exemption for private placement offerings can raise an unlimited amount of money without the cumbersome requirement of registering the securities with the SEC, by complying with the following standards:

1. The company cannot use general solicitation or advertising to market the securities. Instead, the investors must be from the company's "network" of prospects, friends of prospects, with whom the company has pre-existing relationships.[130]

---

certain transactions as non-public offerings. To qualify for Regulation D safe harbors, the issuer must comply with Rule 502(d) and 'exercise reasonable care to assure that the purchasers of the securities are not underwriters within the meaning of section 2(11) of the Act.' Rule 502(d) defines 'reasonable care' in this way: (1) Reasonable inquiry to determine if the purchaser is acquiring the securities for himself or for other persons; (2) Written disclosure to each purchaser prior to sale that the securities have not been registered under the Act and, therefore, cannot be resold unless they are registered under the Act or unless an exemption from registration is available; and (3) Placement of a legend on the certificate or other document that evidences the securities stating that the securities have not been registered under the Act and setting forth or referring to the restrictions on transferability and sale of the securities. While taking these actions will establish the requisite reasonable care, it is not the exclusive method to demonstrate such care.

"Stated another way, a limited distribution to highly sophisticated investors, rather than a general distribution to the public, is not a public offering."

Id., 617 F.3d at 1090-1091. (Footnotes and citations omitted.)

129   See: 15 U.S.C. §§ 77a *et seq.*, as amended. The private placement investment "safe harbor" is sometimes referred to variously as "Reg D" or "Section 506" or "Rule 506" or "Section 42." The California statutory equivalent is Cal. Corp. Code §25102(f).

130   See, e.g. *United States v. Lloyd*, 807 F.3d 1128 (9th Cir. 2015) (denial of appeal for conviction for selling unregistered securities to the public by telemarketing "boiler rooms" soliciting investments in partnerships to finance the production and distribution of motion pictures, noting "The defendants promised potential investors that the investments would return swift and large profits, with little to no risk. Approximately 650 individuals—including unsophisticated people who could not afford the financial loss—invested over $23 million. Most of the investors lost it all." Id. at 1136.

2. The company may sell its securities to an unlimited number of "accredited investors" defined as persons with a net worth over $1 million excluding the value of their primary residence and an annual income minimum over $200,000 per year as an individual, and $300,000 with a spouse, ideally with confirmation of that status via financial documents or accountant affidavits.[131]

3. The company may also sell securities to no more than thirty-five other "unaccredited investors." All non-accredited investors, either alone or with a purchaser representative, must be sophisticated—that is, they must have sufficient knowledge and experience in financial and business matters to make them capable of evaluating the merits and risks of the prospective investment.

4. Companies must decide what information to give to accredited investors, so long as it does not violate the antifraud prohibitions of the federal securities laws. But companies must give non-accredited investors disclosure documents that are generally the same as those used in registered offerings, for example certified accounting audits. If a company provides information to accredited investors, it must make this information available to non-accredited investors as well. As a practical matter, the enhanced disclosure requirements for non-accredited investors leads many companies to solely seek investments from accredited investors.

5. The company must be available to answer questions by prospective purchasers.

6. Purchasers receive "restricted" securities, meaning that the securities cannot be sold for at least a year without registering them.

7. While companies using the Rule 506 exemption do not have to register their securities and usually do not have to file reports with the SEC, they must electronically file what is known as a "Form D" after they first sell their securities. Form D is a brief notice that includes the names and addresses of the company's owners and stock promoters, but contains little other informa-

---

131 See Rule 501 of SEC Regulation D for a complete list of defined accredited investors.

tion about the company.[132] Investors should also confirm that the offerings comply with any state regulations.[133]

[ii]—Formation of a Production Corporation or Limited Liability Company

It may also be necessary to form a corporation or limited liability company ("LLC") for the purpose of production of the project. An LLC operating agreement, for example, will specify the capital contributions made by each member, and what their rights are to income distributions. Every precaution should be followed to comply with all laws designed to protect potential investors through disclosure of the project and the risks. Despite the known risks, investors lured by the glamour of the film business often resort to litigation when a project fails financially.[134]

---

132   See also, http://www.sec.gov/answers/rule506.htm. On April 5, 2012, Congress passed the Jumpstart Our Business Startups Act ("JOBS Act"), which included provisions directing the SEC to revise Rule 506 to allow general solicitation and general advertising of private offerings, but only for offerings to accredited investors. The SEC made the changes to Section 506, effective September 13, 2013. For a summary, see http://www.sec.gov/info/smallbus/secg/general-solicitation-small-entity-compliance-guide.htm#P9_40. For details on the revisions to Rule 506, see http://www.sec.gov/rules/final/2013/33-9415.pdf.

133   In addition to complying with SEC and state laws and regulations regarding entertainment industry investments, and in addition to taking advantage of state tax incentives, production companies seeking investors may potentially take advantage of Internal Revenue Service regulations such as Section 181, which allows producers to claim up to the first $15 million in production costs as deductible expense provided that 75% of the production takes place in the United States. Section 181is due to expire at the end of 2013, and in all such tax-related matters, a tax law specialist and certified public accountant must be consulted in advance, and appropriate disclaimers given.

134   See, *e.g., Streetscenes LLC v. ITC Entertainment Group, Inc.*, 103 Cal. App.4th 233, 126 Cal. Rptr.2d 754 (2003) (action for fraud involving independent film financing. When irate investors finally saw "dailies" from film production, it was of such poor quality that investors became concerned their investment was a scam). See also:

Second Circuit: Blue Angel Films v. First Look Studios, Inc., 2013 U.S. Dist. LEXIS 138594, 2013 WL 5405470 (S.D.N.Y. Sept. 25, 2013) (distributor failed to pay promised advance); Georgios Stamou, Debtor, 2013 Bankr. LEXIS 227, 2013 WL 209473 (Bankr. E.D.N.Y. Jan. 17, 2013) (purported film producer spent all of $328,000 for production on personal expenses; no film was ever made); *Allianz Risk Transfer v. Paramount Pictures Corp.*, 2010 U.S. Dist. LEXIS 32218, 2010 WL 1253957 (S.D.N.Y. March 31, 2010) (plaintiff alleged studio's overseas film pre-sale strategy changed, making investment risky); *Roer v. Oxbridge Inc.*, 198 F. Supp.2d 212 (E.D.N.Y. 2001) (film investors brought state law and federal securities claims against production company that omitted material facts and stated misleading fact in soliciting film financing investments from plaintiff). See also: In re IMAX Securities Litigation, 2012 U.S. Dist. LEXIS 108516, 2012 WL 2359653 (S.D.N.Y. June 20, 2012) (approving settlement and certifying class in case involving IMAX theaters offering large-format motion picture exhibition); *Carlone v. The Lion & Bull Films, Inc.*, 861 F. Supp.2d 312 (S.D.N.Y. 2012) (default judgment to lender who provided $115,000 "bridge loan" to production company, alleging breach of contract and fraudulent inducement); *Arrowhead Capital Finance, Ltd. v. Seven Arts Pictures PLC*, 36 Misc.3d 1205(A), 957 N.Y.S.2d 263 (N.Y. Sup. 2012) (action for repayment of $7,500,000 in loans incurred for production of two films).

On the other hand, producers occasionally need to be wary of unsavory financiers who fail to deliver on promises, especially those who demand upfront cash fees from the producer. *In re Stage Presence, Inc. v. Geneve International Trust* was a bankruptcy case in which a putative financier contracted to provide $5 million to finance two television music specials, in exchange for repayment of the loan, 50% of net profits, an Executive Producer credit, and VIP tickets to the star-packed event. The financier demanded and received from the eager producer advance cash fees of $80,000, characterized as a "bridge loan fee." When the production commenced and the loan was never received, the producer declared bankruptcy.[135]

In another case with the unusual fact pattern of a producer paying the financier, a putative Turkish financier of a $25 million animated film demanded a cash loan from the producer totaling $6.25 million, which amount would, it was claimed, be essential to securing the financing. The loan from the producer to the financier was secured by a letter of credit from a leading German bank, apparently making the loan repayment a sure thing, but it turned out that the letter of credit was allegedly not authorized by the bank itself, having been supplied by bank employees who were accused of being co-conspirators with the dubious financier. Notwithstanding that argument on behalf of the defense, the Central District of California denied the bank's motion to dismiss.[136]

The following is an example of the section of an independent film LLC operating agreement that provides for the distribution of income among the members of

---

Third Circuit: Shadowbox Pictures, LLC v. Global Enterprises, Inc., 2006 U.S. Dist. LEXIS 64943, 2006 WL 120030 (E.D. Pa. Jan. 11, 2006) (investors bring claims against producer including breach of contract, conversion, common law fraud, unjust enrichment, and violations of the Racketeer Influenced and Corrupt Organizations Act, 18 U.S.C. § 1962 (RICO)).

Fifth Circuit: Dykes v. Maverick Motion Picture Group, LLC, 2010 U.S. Dist. LEXIS 75436, 2010 WL 2985553 (M.D. La. May 11, 2010) (plaintiff invested in motion pictures to be produced by Madonna's company, and would receive a percentage of the profits and/or Producer credits. Plaintiff made several investments in increasingly large amounts without any returns.).

Ninth Circuit: Chimeza v. Turtle, 2011 WL 1950000 (Cal. App. May 23, 2011) (unpublished opinion) (Production company misrepresented actual funding obtained for film on life of boxer Sonny Liston; production shut down).

135   See *In re Stage Presence, Inc.*, 2013 Bankr. LEXIS 240 (Bankr. S.D.N.Y. Jan. 17, 2013). See also, *Doublevision Entertainment, LLC v. Navigators Specialty Insurance Co.*, 2015 U.S. Dist. LEXIS 83455 (N.D. Cal. June 25, 2015) (escrow company mismanaged bank letters of credit and corresponding payments for slate financing of independent films).

136   See *NFC Collections LLC v. Deutsche Bank Aktiengesellschaft*, 2013 U.S. Dist. LEXIS 61038 (C.D. Cal. April 29, 2013). See also, *Stinky Love, Inc. v. Lacy*, 2004 Cal. App. Unpub. LEXIS 7497 (Cal. App. 2d Dist. Aug. 13, 2004) (distributor whose claims of experience and financing were fraudulent never remitted purchase price or prints and advertising funding for film "Stinky Love").

the LLC, the so-called "Waterfall" of revenues. Note that the basic provisions dictate that any revenues go first to reimburse the financiers for the production costs, then to a priority return to the financiers with an interest return on their initial investment, then into an Adjusted Net Profits fund, 50% of which is distributed to the investors (the "Investor Adjusted Net Profits"), with the other 50% available to Net Profit Participants in the project (the "Production Adjusted Net Profits"). Note also that 10% of revenues are reserved to the LLC for operating expenses (bold highlights added).

"Distributions of Distributable Cash"

4.2 **Distributions of Distributable Cash.** Distributable Cash shall be distributed to the Members (other than the Managing Member unless the Managing Member has made a Contribution) in the following order of priority, as soon as practicable after receipt of the Company, subject to the terms contained herein:

4.2.1 **First**, to Members to the extent of the Member Contribution until such time as each such Member has received 100% of their Capital Contribution;

4.2.2 **Second**, in proportion to and to the extent of their Priority Returns (i.e., 10%) until each Member receives an aggregate amount equal to such Member's Priority Return;

4.2.3 **Third**, after each Member has received its pro-rata *pari passu* portion of 100% of their Capital Contribution and Priority Return, such remaining Distributable Cash, if any, shall be deemed "Adjusted Net Profits" of the Company and shall be applied and paid as follows:

4.2.3.1 **An amount equal to 50% of the Adjusted Net Profits shall be paid to the Members making Capital Contributions to the Company**, which amount shall be allocated to each Member in the same proportion as his or her Contribution to the Member Capital bears to the aggregate of the Contributions of all Members to the Member Capital ("Investor Adjusted Net Profits"); and

4.2.3.2 **An amount equal to 50% of the Adjusted Net Profits shall be reserved by the Managing Member to contract to and pay any person or entity that provides services to the Company, including but not limited to producers, writer/ director, actors, key crew members, the allocation of which shall be determined by the Managing Member and evidenced** in writing ("**Production Adjusted Net Profits**"). Prior to distributing any portion of the Adjusted Net Profits, the Managing Member shall have the right to reserve up to and pay $_____ in contingent cash deferment payments to any part(ies) providing production services to the Company, other than acting services ("<u>Production Deferments</u>"). Upon satisfaction of all Production Deferments, the remaining Production Adjusted Net Profits shall be distributed on a *pro-rata parri pasu* basis to those parties to whom the Managing Member has designated in writing to receive them. The Managing Member is entitled to retain for his own account any portion of the Production Adjusted Net Profits remaining after all contracted obligations have been satisfied. For avoidance of doubt, any obligation to provide profits of any kind related to the Picture contracted by the Managing Member for services contributed to the Company, the production of the Picture or retained for the benefit of the Managing Member for production services contributed to the Company shall be borne entirely by the Production Adjusted Net Profits and shall not effect the accounting, allocation or distribution of Investor Adjusted Net Profits.

4.2.4. **For purposes hereof, it is acknowledged and agreed that for the first twenty four (24) months after the initial domestic (i.e., North American) sale of the Picture, 90% of the Distributable Cash shall be distributed as set forth herein, and 10% of the Distributable Cash shall be retained by the Company for on-going operating purposes, including, but not limited to, legal, accounting, administrative and other customary operation.** After such 24-month period, 100% of the Distributable Cash shall be distributed as set forth herein).[137]

[iii]—[iii]—Crowdfunding

> For very small budget projects, organizations such as www.kickstarter.com offer a mechanism for soliciting donations from the public for virtually any type of creative project: film, music, art, literature, etc.[138] The producer is free to offer incentives such as "Thank you" credits or copies of the film on DVD when completed, but the contributions are gifts and not investments, and do not trigger any later profit shares or other financial rights in the production or the company. Those giving money to such project are in effect patrons of the arts.

---

137   See also, *Kroupa v. Garbus*, 583 F. Supp.2d 949, 950 (N.D. Ill. 2008) (film production LLC structure called for investor to contribute $1.3 million, to recover the investment plus 20%, after which any remaining profits would be split 60/40 in favor of the investor).

138   See www.kickstarter.com.

While such "donation" mechanisms are largely unregulated, with respect to public offerings of securities or private placements that are the traditional investment mechanisms and that come under SEC regulation, in 2012 Congress passed H.R. 3606, the Jumpstart Our Business Startups Act ("JOBS Act"). Title III of the JOBS Act addresses Crowdfunding, and directs the SEC to alter its regulations to allow issuers of securities who wish to use Crowdfunding techniques to raise up to $1,000,000 during a twelve-month period, with controls on the amounts that may be raised from individual investors. For example if either the annual income or net worth of an investor is less than $100,000, the amount of equity sold cannot exceed the greater of $2,000 or 5% of the annual income or net worth of the investor.

Under Title III, the issuer must also make financial and other disclosures. The SEC is currently considering how it will change its regulations to accommodate the Title III Crowdfunding legislation, and until the SEC does implement new regulations the Title III provisions are not yet in effect.

[f]—Co-Financing

Co-financing is a common way to spread the risk on a film project, or to fund a project that is too expensive for one studio or financer. Many films have multiple credits for multiple studios, cable television stations, and other financing sources. Agreements between the parties are sometimes referred to as Interparty agreements.

[g]—Slate Financing

Slate financing involves financing of a group of films. One of the advantages to slate financing is that the outside investors (i.e., outside the studio) spread their risk over several projects. One of the disadvantages is the large sum of money required for an investment in multiple films.[139]

[h]—Completion Guarantee

A completion guarantee provides financing to complete films in circumstances such as production stoppages or budget overruns. The guarantor will assess the project, including its artistic and financial chances of success, and if willing to guarantee completion, will charge a fee equal to a percentage of the film's overall budget. A

---

139   See, e.g., *Marathon Funding, LLC v. Paramount Pictures Corp.*, 2013 Cal. App. Unpub. LEXIS 1575 (Cal. App. 2d Dist. March 4, 2013) ($150 million in slate financing for fourteen films). See also, *Axa Corporate Solutions v. Underwriters Reinsurance Co.*, 2004 U.S. Dist. LEXIS 22609, 2004 WL 2534386 (N.D. Ill. Nov. 9, 2004) (insurance-backed gap financing for slate of five films).

completion guarantor may also seek insurance as financial backing.[140] The guarantor may become involved in the day-to-day production and post-production process in order to supervise their investment.

[i]—Assumption of Union and Guild Contractual Obligations

When copyright ownership rights in a motion picture or television show are transferred, or assigned to a distributor, and the production was by a union or guild signatory company, the future union and guild obligations such as SAG-AFTRA, WGA, and DGA residuals, and any arbitration awards, must be assumed by the transferee. Even if the transfer document neglects to specify those future guild obligations, 28 U.S.C. Section 4001 provides that, "Assumption of contractual obligations related to transfers of rights in motion pictures," states that any purchaser of the copyright in a motion picture is deemed to have constructive knowledge of their current and future obligations.[141]

Among the triggers of this "constructive knowledge" are recordation of the copyright assignment at the United States Copyright Office, or "from publication at a site available to the public on-line that is operated by the relevant union." For this purpose, the WGA Web site includes a "Signatory Project Confirmation" page, with a search tool by title.[142] SAG-AFTRA also offers a Web page with a signatory database search tool.[143]

Mere licenses to exhibit or broadcast the film are exempt, as are mortgages and security interests.[144]

[3]—State Tax Incentives

"Runaway production" describes productions that take place outside Los Angeles in order to take advantage of lower production costs in other parts of the country and

---

140 See *General Star International Indemnity Ltd. v. The Chase Manhattan Bank*, 2002 U.S. Dist. LEXIS 7980, 2002 WL 850012 (S.D.N.Y. May 3, 2002) (insurance company insured loans made by Chase Manhattan Bank for a slate of films produced by Paramount. Insurer sued Chase for declaratory relief that the policies should be declared void based on allegations that Chase unlawfully concealed the fact that the scheme was virtually certain to result in substantial claims.). See also, *Hoffman v. Chodos*, 2006 Cal. App. Unpub. LEXIS 1677, 2006 WL 457886 (Cal. App. Feb. 27, 2006) (description of cash flow insurance for film production companies). See also, *Axa Corporate Solutions v. Underwriters Reinsurance Co.*, N. 29 supra.

141 28 U.S.C. § 4001. Note that U.S. statutes do not apply outside the United States.

142 See WGA Signatory Project Confirmation, available at <https://apps.wga.org/coveredprojects/default.aspx>.

143 See http://www.sagaftra.org/search-signatory-database.

144 See: 28 U.S.C. §§ 4001(b), 4001(c).

the world. The advantages may include access to non-union labor in other states, or in countries such as Canada. In addition to offering lower labor costs, some states and countries have passed legislation offering tax incentives to production companies in order to entice them to spend their film budget dollars.[145]

Ordinarily, a state will grant a tax credit to the production company based on a percentage of the film's budget actually spent in-state. For a low budget independent production, and even for a major studio big budget film, that can amount to enormous savings. For example, in Pennsylvania, a project is eligible for a tax credit if at least 60% of the project's total production budget is spent "on the ground" in the state.[146]

Upon supplying proof of the budget and expenses and passing an audit, the production company will be awarded a transferable Pennsylvania state tax credit amounting to 25% of the budget. This transferable credit is in the form of a certificate for the 25% of budget amount. Most film companies from outside Pennsylvania will never have enough taxable income in the commonwealth to simply use the certificate themselves. Instead, the tax certificates can be sold to a Pennsylvania-based company with state tax liability, usually at a slightly discounted rate. There are companies that specialize in brokering the sale of such tax certificates, for a modest fee.

Here is an example of how a state tax credit for film production would work under the Pennsylvania initiative:

- Production budget: $1.5 million

- Amount spent in Pennsylvania on location: $1 million

- Percentage of budget spent in Pennsylvania: 66.66% (above the 60% required)

- 25% of total budget is the tax credit amount, or $375,000

- Broker sells tax credit certificate to a large Pennsylvania company at a 10% discount, or for $337,500

- Broker takes fee of 5% or $16,875

- Film production company receives check totaling $320,625

---

145   Such tax incentives are often passed based on studies demonstrating film productions provide significant economic stimulus to the location where they take place, filling up hotel rooms, renting location and studio space, and employing local labor.

146   Qualifying projects include the production of a feature film, a television talk or game show series, a television commercial, a television pilot, or each episode of a television series intended as programming for a national audience.

While state tax incentive programs are often successful, in some states they have led to concerns over whether reduction in tax revenue is adequately offset by the economic benefits of production companies coming to the state. Litigation against states that offer production tax incentives has occurred over issues including the deadlines to qualify for the tax breaks,[147] the types of productions eligible for the tax incentives,[148] and objections to public disclosure by states of confidential production budgets required by a state's "Open Records Law."[149]

Tax incentives are structured differently in each state that offers them. For example the California Film & TV Tax Credit Program 2.0, is a state program of the California Film Commission "which provides tax credits based on qualified expenditures for eligible productions that are produced in California. The $1.55 billion program runs for 5 years, with a sunset date of June 30, 2020. Each fiscal year – July 1 to June 30 – the $330-million funding is categorized

---

147   See *Red Stick Studio Development, LLC v. State of Louisiana*, 56 So.3d 181, 186-187 (La. 2011) (infrastructure development project budgeted at approximately $650,000,000 and designed to develop facilities for film production not eligible for tax credits because of missed deadline for completion. Supreme Court of Louisiana ruling described the motion picture investor tax credit program as created to "attract private investment for the production of motion pictures, videotape programs and television programs which contain substantial Louisiana content; develop a tax infrastructure which encourages private investment; develop a tax infrastructure utilizing tax credits which encourage investments in multiple state-certified production projects; encourage increased employment opportunities within the film sector and increase competition with other states in fully developing economic development options within the film and video industry; and encourage new education curricula in order to provide a labor force trained in all aspects of film productions.").

148   See *Michigan Film Coalition v. State of Michigan*, 2012 Mich. App. LEXIS 1637, 2012 WL 3590053 (Mich. App. Aug. 21, 2012) (only commercials that promote state certified qualified productions are eligible for the tax credit).

149   *Iowa Film Production Services v. Iowa Dep't of Economic Development*, 818 N.W.2d 207 (Iowa 2012). In this case, the Iowa Supreme Court refused to enjoin state from publicly releasing summaries of film production financial budgets under the state's Open Records Act, despite objections of film producers that film budget information is confidential. Among reasons cited by producers for the necessity of confidentiality was the example of "an actor who usually receives $10 million for a movie but may act in an independent film for $100,000, expecting this amount will be kept confidential." *Id.*, 818 N.W.2d at 216. The same concern was expressed over the director's salary. *Id.* Also cited as reasons for confidentiality was that "if the total cost of a movie became known, this could undermine the ability of the producer to make a substantial profit on it or could adversely affect audience reaction, because the public tends to believe a movie is worth what it cost to make." *Id.* The producer also testified that "the budget he submitted to [the Iowa film program] was artificially low. He wanted the guilds and unions to see a lower budget so they would not seek the premium that is associated with a higher-budget film." *Id.* The producer also testified that "Hollywood, our industry, is built on trust." *Id.*, 818 N.W.2d at 215. In denying the production companies' request to keep the budget information confidential, the court also noted that "[t]he record does not show that the Producers made reasonable efforts to preserve confidentiality of their financial data as against the outside world in general. There is no evidence that security measures were taken. The Producers failed to show, for instance, that individuals who worked for them and came into contact with this information were required not to disclose it." *Id.* at 225.

in: TV Projects, Relocating TV, Indie Features, and Non-Indie Features." Quoted from http://film.ca.gov/tax-credit/the-basics-2-0/ including the following summary:

[a] Relocating TV Series 25% Non-transferable Tax Credit: Relocating Television Series (any episode length) that filmed its most recent season (minimum 6 episodes) outside California. $1 million minimum budget per episode. Credit is reduced to 20% after the first season filmed in California.

[b] Independent Films 25% Transferable Tax Credit: Independent Films defined as $1 million minimum budget. Credits apply only to the first $10 million of qualified expenditures.

[c] Feature Film, Movie of the Week, Miniseries, New TV Series and Pilots 20% Non-transferable Tax Credit:

[i] Feature Film: $1 million minimum budget. Credit allocation applies only to the first $100 million in qualified expenditures, plus uplifts.

[ii] Movies-of-the-Week and Miniseries: $500,000 minimum budget.

[iii] New television series for any distribution outlet: $1 million minimum budget per episode (at least 40 minutes per episode, scripted only).

[iv] TV Pilots: $1 million minimum budget (at least 40 minutes).

[d] 5% Credit Uplift: Projects eligible for a 20% tax credit may receive an additional 5% credit for the following expenditures:

[i] Out-of-Zone Filming: Expenditures relating to original photography and incurred outside the 30-Mile Studio Zone (pre-production through strike). Eligible expenditures include qualified wages paid for services performed outside the Zone, and expenditures purchased or leased and used outside the Zone.

[ii] Music Scoring and Music Track Recording by musicians.

[iii] Visual Effects: To qualify, visual effects work must represent at least 75% of the VFX budget or a minimum of $10 million in qualified VFX expenditures incurred in California.

[4]—Profit Participation

Debate over the fundamental fairness of film industry accounting practices is more than academic. In 2010, a jury in *Celador International, Ltd. v. Walt Disney Co.* awarded the plaintiff $269 million in damages based on a claim that defendants failed to pay royalties due from them from the hit game show, "Who Wants to Be a Millionaire."[150] The plaintiff alleged that defendants concealed profits earned on the show to avoid paying licensing fees "through a complex web of self-dealing transactions" via "Hollywood accounting."[151]

The leading case to examine the accounting of net profits in film agreements is *Buchwald v. Paramount Pictures Corp.*[152] The court considered the production agreements entered into between the loan-out company and Paramount.[153] The court held that the net profit definition constituted a contract of adhesion and was unconscionable, as a matter of law and awarded damages totaling $900,000 to the plaintiffs.[154]

The court noted that while Paramount's definition of "net profits" was fairly standard in the motion picture industry, there was little evidence presented by the studio that it ever negotiated meaningful changes. Paramount countered by arguing that the level of risk in film production is immense:

> "'Coming to America' alone required script development costs of $500,000, $40 million in production costs, and $35 million for advertising and promotion, with no assurance that a single theater admission would

---

150   See *Celador International, Ltd. v. Walt Disney Co.*, 347 F. Supp.2d 846 (C.D. Cal. 2004).

151   *Celador International, Ltd. v. Walt Disney Co.*, Case no. 04-cv-3541 (C.D. Cal. July 16, 2010). See also, *Lee v. Marvel Enterprises, Inc.*, 386 F. Supp.2d 235 (S.D.N.Y. 2005) (recounting how Marvel comics, tired of "Hollywood accounting," make a strategic decision to achieve either "gross profit participation," "dollar one" participation," "real profit" participation," or "equity ownership interests in future films featuring Marvel comic book characters'").

State Courts:

California: Plaintiff actor Don Johnson was awarded $15 million plus interest in his suit over his co-ownership of his television series "Nash Bridges." The defendant production company had claimed that after two decades and successful international syndication, the show had still not earned a profit. *Don Johnson Productions, v. Rysher Entertainment, Inc.*, 209 Cal. App.4th 919; 147 Cal. Rptr.3d 590 (Cal. App. 2012). See also, *Paul Haggis, Inc. v. Persik Productions, Inc.*, 2014 Cal. App. Unpub. LEXIS 733, 2014 WL 346464 (Cal. App. 2d Dist. Jan. 31, 2014) (profit participation dispute between writer-director of film "Crash" and production company; writer-director awarded $12 million).

152   *Buchwald v. Paramount Pictures Corp.*, 1990 WL 357611 (Cal. Sup. Jan. 31, 1990) ("*Buchwald II*"). See § 2.02[1][b] *supra*, for a closer examination of *Buchwald v. Paramount Pictures Corp.*

153   At issue was a six-page deal memo between Paramount and Alma Productions, Inc., a three page "turn-around" agreement, six pages of additional terms and conditions; and Paramount's standard net profit participation agreement consisting of twenty-three pages, with two attachments relating to royalties.

154   *Buchwald v. Paramount Pictures Corp.*, 1992 WL 1462910 (Cal Sup. March 16, 1992) ("*Buchwald III*").

be sold. The level of return in the net profit formula was more than offset by these risks, and the hits must subsidize the flops, a status quo that was 'necessary for Paramount's survival.'"[155]

Based on that argument, the court appointed its own accounting expert to examine Paramount's books and records "to determine the accuracy of Paramount's representation with respect to its profitability, the number of films that make and lose money, and whether it was necessary for successful films to subsidize unsuccessful films."[156] Faced with the threat of a court ordered audit, Paramount quickly abandoned its argument.[157]

---

155   See Buchwald II, in passim.

156   *Id.*

157   *Id.* The court found that the plaintiffs did not persuasively present evidence that each and every one of the challenged provisions was "overly harsh" and "one sided" under the test for unconscionability. But it did find sufficient evidence on the following provisions:

"1. Fifteen Percent Overhead on Eddie Murphy Productions Operational Allowance. The court finds this provision unconscionable because an additional 15 percent charge is made for overhead 'on top of' this item. In effect, this results in charging overhead on overhead. The court is able to perceive no justification for this obviously one-sided double charge and Paramount has offered none.

"2. Ten Percent Advertising Overhead Not in Proportion to Actual Costs. This flat overhead charge, which has no relation to actual costs, adds significantly to the amount that must be recouped by Paramount before the picture will realize net profits. Again, the court is able to discern no justification for this flat charge and Paramount has offered none.

"3. Fifteen Percent Overhead Not in Proportion to Actual Costs. Paramount's charge of a flat 15 percent for overhead yields huge profits, even though the overhead charges do not even remotely correspond to the actual costs incurred by Paramount. In this connection it should be observed that although Paramount originally contended that this charge was justified because 'winners must pay for losers', this justification was abandoned by Paramount during the November 8, 1990 hearing held in this case.

"4. Charging Interest on Negative Cost Balance Without Credit for Distribution Fees. Paramount accounts for income on a cash basis, while simultaneously accounting for cost on an accrual basis. This slows down the recoupment of negative costs and inflates the amount of interest charged. The court finds this practice to be "one sided" in the absence of a justification for the practice.

"5. Charging Interest on Overhead. Paramount receives revenues in the form of distribution fees and overhead charges, neither of which are taken into account in determining whether costs have been recouped. This results in 'interest' becoming an additional source of unjustified profit. The court finds this practice to be 'overly harsh' and 'one sided,' and thus unconscionable.

"6. Charging Interest on Profit Participation Payments. Paramount charges the payments made to gross participants to negative costs. In fact, these payments are not paid until the film has derived receipts. Accordingly, Paramount has not in any real sense advanced this money. Nevertheless, Paramount charges interest on gross participation shares. This is unconscionable.

Not long after the *Buchwald* decision, however, a challenge to Warner Bros. accounting resulted in a determination that the agreements were not, in fact, unconscionable.[158]

[a]—Net Profit Definitions

Net profit formulas are lengthy lists of costs and expenses deductible from gross revenues. Definitions of terms are key because they will be reflected in the actual "Profit Participation" statements rendered by the studio.

Key deal points in a net profit definition are:

- <u>Gross Receipts</u>: All film rental revenue actually received in most categories of income, with the exception of home video (DVDs), where gross receipts represent an amount equal to 20% of the gross wholesale rental and sales income.[159]

- <u>Net Profits</u>: The order of deductions from gross receipts that arrives at net profits is:

- <u>Distribution fees</u>: Approximately 30% in the United States and Canada, 35% in the United Kingdom, and 40% in the rest of the world. Warner has its own distribution subsidiary, but these fees are treated as though they were paid to a separate entity in terms of profit distribution.

- <u>Distribution expenses</u>: This is typically a very long list including all production costs, advertising costs plus 10% overhead on same; all shipping costs; bank fees; attorneys' fees in connection with any disputes; royalties payable to technology providers and trade association dues; contingency reserves; payments to above the line personnel such as actors, writers, composers, including residuals; the costs of all insurance.

- <u>Negative costs</u>: The costs of production of the film plus interest thereon.

- <u>Contingent amounts</u>: Payments of gross profit participation or other profit payments.

"7. Charging an Interest Rate Not in Proportion to the Actual Cost of Funds. Paramount charges an interest rate which can be as much as 20 to 30 percent, even when no funds have been laid out by Paramount. This is a one-sided, and thus unconscionable, provision."

158   See *Batfilm Productions, Inc. v. Warner Bros. Inc.*, Nos. BC 051653 and BC 051654 (Cal. Super. March 14, 1994) (case regarding successful "Batman" film and studio's claim that no net profits had ever been generated. Court held that plaintiffs did not present evidence sufficient for a finding that overhead and interest fees assessed by studio were unconscionably higher than the actual production, advertising, and overhead costs.). See also, *Lee v. Marvel Enterprises, Inc.*, 386 F. Supp.2d 235 (S.D.N.Y. 2005) (in dispute over profit participation from licensing of Marvel comic book characters, court conducted an analysis of Lee's 10% profit participation).

159   Using the 20% figure instead of true gross home video receipts has been an area of intense scrutiny, given the important role of home video in the industry.

- <u>Allocations</u>: Where the studio licenses a "package" of films to television, the studio will determine how to allocate the overall revenue to each film in the package.[160]

- <u>Cost of Production</u>: Costs chargeable to production expense including deferred or accrued costs, where the liability may be included in the direct cost of the film at the time the liability is "incurred or contracted, regardless of whether actually paid out."[161]

- <u>Interest</u>: An overhead charge of 15% of the direct cost of production.[162]

- <u>Earnings Statements</u>: Some agreements may contain provisions allowing the studio to cease accounting for net profits at a point where the economic value of the film has already been maximized, for example when the last distribution "window," free television, has been reached, thus ignoring later revenue.

- <u>Audit Rights</u>: Audits often conclude in an out of court settlement. Key points in an audit provision include the right to review source books and records instead of mere summaries; the right to take sufficient time for the audit; and the right to have audit shortfalls immediately paid.

- <u>Music Publishing Income</u>: Where a film may contain music rights such as a hit song or popular soundtrack, music publishing revenues may be generated. The definitions specify the percentages that will be included in revenues. Where the profit participant is entitled to a direct share in separately paid music royalties, then music royalties are not included in that individual's profit participation statement.

---

160   See *Ladd v. Warner Bros. Entertainment, Inc.*, 184 Cal. App.4th 1298, 110 Cal. Rptr.3d 74 (2010) (awarding Ladd $3,190,625 in damages based on studio's failure to properly allocate television license fees for Ladd-owned films including "Bladerunner." Warner had practiced "straight lining" in which every film in the package is given the exact same value regardless of its value to the broadcaster. Evidence showed that in assembling its packages, Warner graded films A, B, and C, including a few "A" films along with several "C" films that might not otherwise be in demand. In one example, HBO licensed a package of films for a price of $141,475,000, of which only $400,000 was allocated to the highly desirable classic "Chariots of Fire." The evidence tended to show that the studio would allocate as much revenue as possible to films that were not profitable, thereby cutting or eliminating net profit payments to films that were popular.).

161   Critics contend that this allows the studio to charge contingent and future expense amounts against present cash revenues, thus slowing down recoupment. Similar "timing" issues arise where agreements state that revenues will be posted when "earned," which critics claim allows studios to interpret as allowing them to ignore payments such as advances against future income for purposes of posting revenue to the film's profit account, on the theory that such payments do not yet represent actual income received.

162   The issue is whether revenues that should reduce the negative costs, and the interest overhead charge, are applied against the negative cost balance.

- <u>Merchandising Income</u>: This specifies the percentages of merchandise income included in net profits.[163] Anyone who is entitled to a direct share of merchandise revenue will not have that revenue counted as part of their profit participation.

[b]—Alternatives to Net Profit Participation

Other, more advantageous types of profit participation exist. Examples include "first-dollar gross,"[164] adjusted gross receipts,[165] and "breakeven" profit participation.[166] Courts have described the terminology used in the motion picture industry for various types of profit participants and types of revenue, as follows, with the terms highlighted:

General Terms Used in Film Licensing Agreements.

"As testified to by numerous witnesses and confirmed by the various film licensing agreements in evidence, payment for the film rights to a literary property is the product of a fixed fee (in the form of a guaranteed advance, option payment and/or purchase price) and participation in contingent compensation derived from the later release of a film, expressed in a given percentage of some measure of the money received by the film at the box office and the surrounding activities from the exploitation of the film, including film-related merchandising and home video sales. Determining the amount of contingent compensation expressed as a percentage of the money thus generated is a complicated task.

"The money received by the film's distributor (typically the studio) is referred to as the '**distributor's gross**,' includes most, if not all, the money received at the box office, and typically serves as the largest pool of money available from which participation can be measured. From that, the mon-

---

163   In one series of protracted litigations, the author of the original Roger Rabbit books sued Disney over how royalties on merchandise were calculated. At issue was whether Disney had been properly including licensed merchandise manufactured by third parties in the gross revenues used to calculate net profits on merchandise. See *Wolf v. Walt Disney Pictures and Television*, 162 Cal. App.4th 1107, 76 Cal. Rptr.3d 585 (2008).

164   "First-dollar gross" is rarely given and reserved for superstars. As the name implies, it is based on gross revenues received by the studio from the distributor, before any further deductions are made.

165   "Adjusted gross receipts" may allow for some deductions from gross revenues but not as many as a net profit formula.

166   A contractually agreed-upon benchmark is set for reaching "breakeven," at which point a bonus is paid or gross profit participations kick in. See *Lee v. Marvel Enterprises, Inc.*, 386 F. Supp.2d 235, 242 (S.D.N.Y. 2005) (in dispute over profit participation from licensing of Marvel comic book characters, court conducted an analysis of Lee's 10% profit participation. Testifying expert discussed alternatives to net profit deal described as: defined proceeds; gross after breakeven; rolling breakeven; adjusted gross receipts).

ies paid to '**gross profit participants**' as well as the '**production costs**,' '**distribution costs**,' and '**distribution fees**' incurred by the distributor are deducted to arrive at a '**breakeven point**.'

"'**Gross profit participants**' are those participants (such as well-known directors and actors) who have negotiated and executed agreements providing them a share of the distributor's gross. '**Production costs**' are all the costs directly attributed to producing and shooting the film so as to put it on a final film negative (sometimes referred to as "negative costs"). '**Distribution costs**,' principally production of prints and advertising, are costs attributable to marketing and releasing a particular film; in contrast, '**distribution fees**' are not related directly to specific costs, but instead are assessed as a percentage of receipts, with the percentage varying based on the source (such as domestic box office or foreign box office).

"[The term '**breakeven point**'] is more fluid than it might appear, as the parties to a particular film agreement often decide that not all possible deductions should be made in determining the breakeven point, creating a contractually defined '**artificial breakeven point**' that differs from the standard formulation set forth above. Regardless, if the number that is arrived at after deducting from the distributor's gross some or all of those variables (depending upon the particular formulation used in the agreement) falls below the breakeven point, then no contingent compensation is owed thereunder.

"Thus, all participants' right to receive contingent compensation is dependent upon what amount of money comes into play after a breakeven point. It is in defining the breakeven point that distinguishes '**net profits**,' '**first dollar gross profits**' participants, and the various gradations of participation in between.

"The '**net profit participants**' normally must rely on the standard definition of a breakeven point noted earlier, that requires deductions for all the costs, fees, and expenses incurred in making and releasing the film before receiving any of their contingent compensation. For an obvious reason, and for perhaps one less obvious reason, this form of participation is less desirable than those held by other participants. The obvious reason is that a net profit participant collects compensation only if a film makes a profit after all the deductions identified earlier that could be made against the box office receipts are in fact made. The less obvious reason this position is less desirable relates to how other participants' share factors into the calculation of the breakeven point, which, in turn, triggers the net profits participants' right to compensation. The net profits participants stand in line behind the gross profits participants in that the gross profits participants' share of the box office receipts is deducted from the distributor's gross before the breakeven point, meaning that a film has to generate more revenue at the box office before a net profits participant is paid.

"In contrast, the so-called '**first-dollar gross**' participation is only set off against the participants' fixed fee (amounting to a non-refundable advance against the contingent compensation) with no other deductions taken; literally, the first dollar generated at the box office from the release of a film goes into the available pool from which the first dollar participant takes a percentage share. In this sense, the first-dollar gross participant has a fixed breakeven point-the fixed fee divided by the percentage sharing rate-that again is calculated on box office receipts, with no deductions for production costs, distribution fees and distribution expenses. In this sense, first dollar gross participation is the most desirable measure upon which to share in the box office receipts generated by a film's release.

"In between these two extremes in contingent compensation participation are gradations thereof, sometimes referred to as '**adjusted gross**' or '**defined gross**.' That compensation functions in some respects as a net profits deal in that, unlike with first dollar gross, deductions are taken against the distributor's gross before arriving at a breakeven point; however, the breakeven point is reached sooner than for a true net profits participation because certain of the cost variables are not deducted, or are deducted at lesser amounts than for their true full measure."[167]

[i]—Deferred Compensation

Where high priced talent desires to appear in a low budget production, talent compensation may sometimes be split: partly paid during production, and partly "deferred," paid after release as revenues are received. "Contractual breakeven" was employed in an agreement between actor Tommy Lee Jones and Paramount Pictures over deferred compensation payments for his appearance in the film, "No Country for Old Men."[168] Jones' usual "quote" to star in a film was $15 mil-

---

167   See *Siegel v. Warner Bros. Entertainment Inc.*, 2009 U.S. Dist. LEXIS 66115, at *3-*7, 2009 WL 2014164, at *1 (C.D. Cal. July 8, 2009).

168   See *Javelina Film Co. v. Paramount Pictures Corp.*, Ca. No. 2008CI15114 (Tex. Sept. 30, 2008). See also, *Marathon Funding, LLC v. Paramount Pictures Corp.*, 2013 Cal. App. Unpub. LEXIS 1575 (Cal. App. 2d Dist. March 4, 2013) (in dispute between financier and studio caused by same facts as Tommy Lee Jones compensation dispute, studio did not breach any fiduciary duty to investor).

lion, as well as first dollar gross profit participation. For "No Country for Old Men," Paramount offered $750,000 in up-front compensation, with a promise that "very favorable" back-end participation would bridge the gap between the up-front compensation and Jones' usual quote.[169] Jones signed an agreement with Paramount stating that his deferred compensation bonus would be payable "upon the earlier of the domestic box office receipts reaching an amount equal to the designated negative cost of the picture and/or the worldwide box office receipts multiplied by 2 reaching an amount equal to the designated negative cost."[170] Jones calculated that his profit participation, based on the success of the film, was at least $9 million. When Paramount contacted Jones claiming that the favorable "breakeven" formula was a mistake, Jones sued.[171] The matter was submitted to arbitration in which Jones was awarded $15 million.[172] Jones subsequently initiated proceedings against his talent agent, disputing the agency's commission on the proceeds from the film.[173] In subsequent litigation, the financier of the film sued the studio because the studio deducted the costs of the Tommy Lee Jones bonus from accountings to the financier.[174]

[ii]—Box Office Bonuses

While deferred compensation contemplates paying the talent's usual "quote" for flat fee compensation, contingent upon revenues reaching a specified benchmark, bonuses are "extra" amounts above and beyond any guaranteed or contingent fees. In the example below, an actor's box office bonus is determined by a formula based on "DBO" or daily box office, the theatrical box office receipts for the initial release of the picture as reported by industry trade publications such as Daily Variety, for the United States and Canada.

The thresholds are based on a multiple of "negative cost" (the production budget for the project), as well as "P&A" or "prints and advertising," the costs incurred for marketing and distribution which are separately reported. Items such as interest and overhead typically charged by the studio or financier are addressed as well in the formula, for example by basing the formula on a multiple of two

---

169 *Javelina Film Co. v. Paramount Pictures Corp.*, *id.* See also, *Wyler Summit Partnership v. Turner Broadcasting System, Inc.*, 135 F.3d 658 (9th Cir. 1998) (describing 3% of gross deal for director of "Ben Hur," beginning after studio broke even and earned the $20 million it invested in the picture).

170 *Javelina Film Co. v. Paramount Pictures Corp.*, *id.*

171 *Id.*

172 See *Jones v. William Morris Agency*, TAC No. 16396, slip op. (Cal. Lab. Comm. Oct. 1, 2012).

173 *Id.*

174 *Marathon Funding, LLC v. Paramount Pictures Corp.*, 2013 Cal. App. Unpub. LEXIS 1575 (Cal. App. 2d Dist. March 4, 2013).

times negative cost but with interest accounted for "once only" and "no overhead included." Note that in this example, the bonuses are triggered by multiples of the negative cost at the 2X, 2.5X, 3X, 4X, and 5X multiples, and thereafter continue until Lender (i.e. the loan out corporation for the actor) has received a maximum of 8 million dollars.

ACTOR BOX OFFICE BONUS:	
BO Bonus(es)	**DBO**
$150K	2x negative cost (with interest once only and no overhead included) + 1x P&A reported by the U.S. distributor of the Picture
$200K	2.5x negative cost (with interest once only and no overhead included) + 1x P&A reported by the U.S. distributor of the Picture
$250K	3x negative cost (with interest once only and no overhead included) + 1x P&A reported by the U.S. distributor of the Picture
$250K	4x negative cost (with interest once only and no overhead included) + 1x P&A reported by the U.S. distributor of the Picture
$250K	5x negative cost (with interest once only and no overhead included) + 1x P&A reported by the U.S. distributor of the Picture and at each addition 1x negative cost (with interest once only and no overhead included) + 1x P&A reported by the U.S. distributor for the Picture thereafter until Lender has received $8 million. For the avoidance of doubt the 1x P&A shall only be applied once and not in addition at each threshold

§1.05   Agreements with Talent

Those who play a creative role in the motion picture process are referred to as the "above-the-line" personnel, due to their positions on the standard film budget spreadsheet. All other crew members are "below-the-line."

Above-the-line talent is represented by several of the leading unions and guilds in the film industry. Above the line talent guilds include the Directors Guild of America (DGA);[175] SAG-AFTRA (formerly the Screen Actors Guild and the American Federation of Television and Radio Artists);[176] and the Writers Guild of America (WGA).[177] Production entities are represented by a voluntary membership organization (not a union) the Alliance of Motion Picture and Television Producers (AMPTP).[178] Producers are often members of the Producers Guild of America, a nonprofit trade group but not a union or guild, which promotes standards of professionalism for the producing industry (www.producersguild.org).

175   See www.dga.org.

176   See www.sagaftra.org.

177   See www.wga.org.

178   See www.amptp.org.

These organizations enter into collective bargaining agreements with production companies of all sizes, except the voluntary nonprofit PGA. The resulting union agreements govern the vast majority of contractual and employment relations between "talent" and "money," including the hours worked, the pay, and the conditions. Where talent is paid more than the basic union "scale," and has other perks such as special accommodations, those arrangements can be made in a deal memo, with the union provisions and approved contracts otherwise governing the relationship.

At the early stages of a project, talent may "attach" itself via a commitment to appear in the project, a commitment that may be reflected in a simple letter from the talent's representative. On occasion, not even a letter is exchanged, and plans are made based on verbal agreements.[179]

§1.06   Loan-Out Corporations and Letters of Inducement

In the entertainment industry, it is common for individuals to form a one-person corporation, or "loan-out corporation," for the purposes of entering into freelance agreements with production companies.[180] A loan-out corporation may be used by actors, directors, cinematographers, and any other individuals whose personal services may be the subject of an agreement, and who is not already a full-time employee of the production company. Doing business through such an entity not only provides possible "corporate shield" legal protections, but may also confer financial advantages with respect to tax treatment of income and expenses related to the talent's career, as well as retirement and health plan benefits.[181] The tax advantages of providing personal services through a loan-out corporation instead of as an individual, subject to compliance with all tax codes and laws, may include the following:

---

179   Such agreements can be binding. See *Main Line Pictures, Inc., v. Basinger*, 1994 WL·814244 at *1 (Cal. App. Sept. 22, 1994) (designated as not citable).

180   See *Caso v. Nimrod Productions, Inc.*, 163 Cal. App.4th 881, 77 Cal.Rptr.3d 313, 316-317 (2008):

"Loan-out corporations [are] a common practice in the entertainment industry. When an individual is hired by a producer to work on a production, the individual informs the producer he or she has a loan-out corporation. Then, three-way contracts are entered into in which the loan-out corporation agrees to furnish the services of its owner and sole employee to the producer; the producer agrees to pay the loan-out corporation for the owner/employee's services; and the owner/employee agrees to the arrangement. The loan-out corporation itself does not participate in any way in the production after the loan-out agreement is signed except to receive payment for its owner/employee's services."

See also, *Matthau v. Superior Court*, 151 Cal. App.4th 593, 60 Cal. Rptr.3d 93, 98-99 (2007).

181   A limited liability company ("LLC") may provide limitations on personal liability, but does not provide the same tax benefits that a corporation does.

- Avoiding the status of a direct employee of the production company thus avoiding employee withholding taxes. When the production company contracts with the loan-out corporation, payment is the full fee negotiated without deductions, as is customarily done in transactions between corporations.

- Potential deferral of tax obligations where the loan-out corporation operates on a fiscal year ending at some time other than December 31, thus potentially delaying year-end tax obligations as compared to filing an individual tax return.

- Greater ability to deduct expenses, for example corporations may be able to achieve a tax deduction for fees paid to lawyers and representatives, and for other expenses as compared to an individual.

- Opportunities to participate in employer health and retirement plans, and any tax advantages therein, as compared to a private individual.

Note that I.R.C. Section 269A allows the IRS to disregard the "legal fiction" of the personal services corporation where "substantially all the services of the corporation are performed for one other entity and the principal purpose of forming the corporation was to avoid federal income tax."[182]

Where talent enters into an agreement with a production company to provide their services through their loan-out corporation or LLC, the "loan-out agreement" is between the production company and the corporation. In a loan-out agreement, the talent's corporation is referred to as the "lender."

Because tax obligations for a loan-out corporation may be less than for an individual, the IRS has challenged the use of so-called personal services corporations in U.S. tax courts and

---

182   See also:

Second Circuit: Great Entertainment Merchandise, Inc. v. VN Merchandising, Inc., 1996 U.S. Dist. LEXIS 8973, 1996 WL 355377 (S.D.N.Y. June 27, 1996) (musician Vince Gill's loanout corporation granted merchandise rights licenses that called for return of portions of the advance paid if concert attendance was below the threshold amount. The Letter of Inducement arguably only obligated Gill personally to perform at the concerts, not to reimburse the plaintiff for any financial losses, thus on summary judgment, Gill was not personally liable for obligations of his loan-out corporation to reimburse plaintiff).

Ninth Circuit: Roddenberry v. Roddenberry, 44 Cal. App.4th 634, 51 Cal. Rptr.2d 907 (1996) (personal services corporation of deceased creator of Star Trek liable for fraudulent concealment of profits due under divorce settlement).

United States Tax Court: Charles Laughton, Petitioner, v. Commissioner of Internal Revenue, 40 B.T.A. 101 (1939) (upholding validity of Charles Laughton's personal services corporation "Motion Picture & Theatrical Industries, Ltd." Note that limited liability companies, or "LLCs" would not confer the corporate tax advantages of a true corporation.

in the federal courts, with decisions going both for and against the taxpayer depending on the circumstances.[183]

Where an author who creates copyrightable works has a personal loan out corporation, and complies with the IRS requirements to document "employee" status in the form of a written employee agreement, any works the individual creates are arguably works made for hire owned by the loan out corporation. Where the loan out corporation, in turn, assigns copyright in the work to a production company or publisher, it is unclear, and so far untested in the courts, as to whether that individual author would retain termination rights under the Copyright Act, because the right of termination does not apply to works made for hire. One course of action is to have a written agreement between the talent and their loan out corporation confirming that the works created are not works made for hire, but are owned by the talent, who, in turn, exclusively licenses the works to the loan out corporation, because authors retain termination rights in the context of copyright assignments and exclusive licenses. Whether the IRS would find the suitable level of corporate control in such an arrangement has not yet been determined in the courts.[184]

An essential addition to any loan-out agreement, usually in the form of an exhibit or schedule to the agreement, is the "letter of inducement," in which the talent personally affirms that their personal services are being provided to the loan-out corporation for the purposes of the agreement, which serves as a material inducement for the production company to enter into the agreement with the "lender."

A typical Letter of Inducement would state as follows (with "f/s/o" abbreviating "For the Services Of"):

---

183   See *Sargent v. Commisioner*, 929 F.2d 1252 (8th Cir. 1991) (loan out corporation valid where corporation acts as an employer in controlling the individual's actions, and where an agreement exists between corporation and the individual). But see, *Leavell v. Commissioner*, 104 T.C. 140 (1995) (the employment authority of National Basketball Association and Houston Rockets club indicated the true "employer" and therefore basketball player's earnings were attributable to him personally and not to his personal services corporation, notwithstanding player's written employment agreement with his own loan out corporation). See also, *Idaho Ambucare Centers, Inc. v. United States*, 57 F.3d 752 (9th Cir. 1995) (physician held to be employee of his personal services corporation despite absence of any written agreements confirming employee status).

184   See Moss and Basin, "Copyright Termination and Loan-Out Corporations: Reconciling Practice and Policy," 3 Harvard J. of Sports and Ent. L. 55 (2012).

LOANOUT CORPORATION NAME

f/s/o Talent Name

Dear _____:

As a material inducement to you to enter into the attached Agreement with Loanout Corporation ("Lender"), dated as of [date] (the "Agreement"), the undersigned hereby represents, warrants and agrees as follows:

I have heretofore entered into an agreement with Lender requiring me to render services to Lender for at least the full term of the Agreement and authorizing Lender to enter into the Agreement and to furnish my rights and services to you upon the terms, covenants and conditions thereof.

I am familiar with all of the terms, covenants and conditions of the Agreement and hereby consent to the execution thereof; I shall be bound by and will duly observe, perform and comply with all of the terms, covenants and conditions of the Agreement; I hereby confirm that there have been granted to Lender all of the rights granted by Lender to you under the Agreement; and I hereby join in and confirm all grants, representations, warranties and agreements made by Lender under the Agreement.

I am under no legal or other obligation or disability that would prevent or restrict me from performing and complying with any of the terms, covenants and conditions of the Agreement to be performed or complied with by me.

I will look solely to Lender and not to you for compensation for the services and rights I may render and grant to you under the Agreement and for the discharge of all other obligations of my employer with respect to my services under the Agreement.

If you serve Lender with any notices, demands or instruments relating to the Agreement or the rendition of my services thereunder, such service upon Lender shall constitute service upon me.

Signed,

Talent

As of date:

§1.07   Preliminary Verbal Agreements

The critical importance of timing in the entertainment industry makes verbal agreements particularly useful, despite the likelihood that they may lead to contract disputes.[185] Furthermore, while parties may intend to eventually reduce contracts to writing, this writing might not be created until after the parties have begun performance of the contract. Subsequent written contracts may include additional ancillary terms.

Verbal agreements are sufficient to constitute binding contracts when they involve a "manifestation of mutual assent to the exchange and consideration."[186] Assent may be demonstrated by acts or by written or spoken words.[187] Even if the parties agree that the contract will eventually be reduced to writing, until such writing is created, the terms of an oral contract will be binding if the parties so intended.**188** It is common for oral agreements in the entertainment industry to be performable within one year, thus avoiding the general statute of frauds applicable to contracts with a duration of more than a year.[189]

In *Main Line Pictures, Inc., v. Basinger*,[190] the actress Kim Basinger was party to a "handshake deal," a verbal agreement to appear in the film "Boxing Helena." In reliance on the initial oral agreement and subsequent negotiations between the filmmakers and Basinger's agent and lawyer, the producers pre-sold the foreign rights and made plans for the commencement of principal photography.[191]

---

185   Deal memos are unsigned documents outlining the material terms of a previously created oral agreement. See *Main Line Pictures, Inc., v. Basinger*, 1994 WL 814244 at *1 (Cal. App. Sept. 22, 1994) (describing certain industry practices giving rise to Basinger's alleged breach of oral contract with film studio). Examples include the use of deal memos in lieu of formal written contracts, or the verbal grant of authority to lawyers or agents to bind artists.

186   *Restatement (Second) of Contracts* § 17 (1981). California courts follow these sections of the Restatement (Second) of Contracts. See *Binder v. Aetna Life Insurance Co.*, 75 Cal. App.4th 832, 89 Cal. Rptr.2d 540, 551 (1999) (quoting §§ 17 and 19, noting that California courts look to the Restatement Second of Contracts for guidance).

187   Restatement (Second) of Contracts § 19 (1981).

188   *Columbia Pictures Corp. v. DeToth*, 87 Cal. App.2d 620, 197 P.2d 580 (1948) (director's oral seven-year contract with studio was binding, consistent with parties' intent, even though the agreement would eventually be reduced to writing); *Johnson v. Twentieth Century-Fox Film Corp.*, 82 Cal. App.2d 796, 187 P.2d 474 (1947) (author did not breach oral contract with filmmaker when author refused to sign subsequent written contract which contained a waiver of rights not agreed to orally).

189   See *Metro-Goldwyn-Mayer, Inc. v. Scheider*, 43 A.D.2d 922, 352 N.Y.S.2d 205 (1974) (looking to television industry practice to determine that actor's performance of oral contract would be complete within one year after agreement was made, thus avoiding statute of frauds). See also, *Jones v. William Morris Agency*, TAC No. 16396, slip. Op. (Cal. Lab. Comm. Oct. 1, 2012), appeal filed Case. No. BS 139747 (Oct. 12, 2012) (actor Tommy Lee Jones entered into an oral agreement with his talent agency, which would receive a 10% commission).

190   *Main Line Pictures, Inc., v. Basinger*, 1994 WL 814244 (Cal. App. Sept. 22, 1994).

191   *Id. at *1.

Before the finalized agreement could be signed, Basinger changed agents. Her new agent urged her not to make the film. Basinger's representatives ultimately informed the producers that she would not appear in the project. Basinger was replaced, and the producers filed suit for breach of contract. Following a jury verdict in favor of the plaintiff, judgment was entered against Basinger and/or her loan-out corporation for over $8 million.[192] Before retrial, the case settled.

§1.08   Written Agreements

Written agreements are the norm in the film industry, and in the case of productions by union and guild signatories, will be largely determined by the contracts approved in collective bargaining agreements. Deal memos that supplement such basis agreements will focus on the so-called "Three C's:" Compensation, Credits, and Creative control.[193]

[1]—Directors

In film, the director is often regarded as the true "author" of the work, because all elements of the film are the director's vision of the story. This contrasts with the role of the director in episodic television, which is a medium more driven by the creative vision of the writers.[194]

[a]—The DGA

The Directors Guild of America ("DGA") protects the rights of directors in the film industry. If the studio or production company is a signatory to the DGA Basic Agreement ("Basic Agreement"), it must abide by the minimum salary schedules set forth by the DGA for all types of productions.[195] The Basic Agreement has provisions relating to the director's rights and duties at every stage of production.[196] It applies to work in both film and television, and like all the guild collective bargaining agreements, its provisions reflect the actual production process and are essential to

---

192   *Id.*

193   Agreements with writers are discussed above in § 1.03.

194   However, authorship has its limits. Even though a director will deliver the "director's cut" of a film to the production company or studio, those same studios and production companies bear the ultimate financial risk for the project, and therefore may reserve the right to approve the "final cut" of a film, and to demand alterations and changes. See § 1.02[e] *supra*, for a discussion of the "final cut."

195   See DGA Basic Agreement, available at <https://www.dga.org/Contracts/Agreements.aspx>.

196   The following information, entitled "Summary of Directors' Creative Rights Under the DGA Basic Agreement of 2008," is excerpted from the DGA Creative Rights Handbook. See Director's Guild of America Creative Rights Handbook, available at <https://www.dga.org/Contracts/Creative-Rights.aspx>.

understand how to best represent a director and his or her rights. In any agreement with a DGA member director, a deal memo covering basic compensation and duties issues may supplement the Basic Agreement, and may also provide for additional compensation, perks, or other rights.

Under the standard "Results and Proceeds" provision, copyright in the film is owned solely by the studio. Moreover, the DGA's oversight of a project on behalf of its members requires detailed information on the budget for the production, the financers, and weekly reporting requirements during production.[197]

[b]—Leading Cases Involving Directors' Rights

As noted by the Ninth Circuit, "Cinephiles believe the director is the true author of a film: It's Coppola's *Godfather*, Spielberg's *Schindler's List* and Verhoeven's *Robocop*."[198] Often, the director's vision for the film will be realized, and not later changed or bowdlerized by the studio or others, because the director was initially hired with the expectation that his or her work would be both artistically satisfying and commercially viable, and the finished film reflects those expectations.

Because studios own the copyright in the completed film, this raises the question of what legal rights directors may still have, in cases where a director has had his or her creative and artistic vision compromised. Several cases are illustrative of the legal parameters of a director's creative control.

[i]—Authorship Rights Under the Copyright Act and the Lanham Act

A video company offered unauthorized edits of feature films to make them "family friendly"—removing what it deemed excessive violence, profanity, nudity, and sex. The studios and directors threatened legal action to enjoin the company from its activities.[199]

The defendant filed a declaratory judgment action in district court, asserting its edited versions did not violate the Copyright Act or any Lanham Act-based claims. To buttress its copyright claims, the defendants not only included a list of leading studios, but also a list of prominent of directors who, although they did not own the copyright in their films, might have claims based on false endorse-

---

197   See generally, www.dga.org. Copies of the DGA "Rate Cards" setting forth compensation.

198   See *TriStar Pictures, Inc. v. Directors Guild of America, Inc.*, 160 F.3d 537, 538 (9th Cir. 1998).

199   *Clean Flicks of Colorado, LLC v. Soderbergh*, 433 F. Supp.2d 1236 (D. Col. 2006). Clean Flicks had been offering two different types of technologies to its customers. One was the sale of videotapes containing unauthorized, edited versions of films. The other was a device designed for use in the home to electronically remove offending scenes from standard commercially purchased DVDs during playback, without actually altering the DVD itself.

ment and false designation or origin under the Lanham Act.[200] The Directors Guild of America intervened as well.

As the litigation progressed, Congress passed the Family Movie Act of 2005, which amended the Copyright Act to make in-home alterations of films for private use non-infringing.[201] The legislation rendered the issues in the case revolving around the in-home technology moot.[202] As for the other technology at issue, the commercially edited videocassettes, the court held for the copyright owners, the studios, and found that such alterations were not a fair use under § 107 of the Copyright Act.[203]

[ii]—The Ownership and Scope of Uses of a Director's Film

Stanley Donan directed the classic 1957 Paramount film, "Funny Face," which included a dance sequence featuring the movie's star, Audrey Hepburn. In 2006, Paramount licensed the sequence for use in television advertisements promoting ladies' pants sold by a clothing manufacturer. Donan filed a claim for copyright infringement, based on assertions that his work on the film was pursuant to an agreement in which MGM loaned his services to Paramount. While Donan had signed a standard "Results and Proceeds" agreement with MGM, he never exe-

---

200　The director defendants included Steven Soderbergh, Robert Altman, Michael Apted, Taylor Hackford, Curtis Hanson, Norman Jewison, John Landis, Michael Mann, Phillip Noyce, Brad Silberling, Betty Thomas, Irwin Winkler, Martin Scorsese, Steven Spielberg, Robert Redford, and Sydney Pollack.

201　See 17 U.S.C. § 110(11), stating:

"[T]he making imperceptible, by or at the direction of a member of a private household, of limited portions of audio or video content of a motion picture, during a performance in or transmitted to that household for private home viewing, from an authorized copy of the motion picture, or the creation or provision of a computer program or other technology that enables such making imperceptible and that is designed and marketed to be used, at the direction of a member of a private household, for such making imperceptible, if no fixed copy of the altered version of the motion picture is created by such computer program or other technology."

202　See *Huntsman v. Soderbergh*, 2005 WL 1993421 (D. Col. 2005). Note that "moral rights" retained by an author separate from ownership and economic rights under copyright are a legal concept recognized in Europe but not specifically addressed under United States law. For example, the heirs of director John Huston successfully obtain a judgment in French courts based on authorized colorization of Huston's iconic black and white film "Concrete Jungle" by its copyright owner, Turner Broadcasting. See *Gilliam v. American Broadcasting Cos.*, 538 F.2d 14 (2d Cir. 1976) (discussing Lanham Act equivalents to European "moral rights."). See also, *Turner Entertainment Co. v. Huston*, Court of Appeal of Versailles [France], Combined Civil Chambers, Decision No. 68, Roll No. 615/92 (French court decision awarding moral rights damages to heirs of director John Huston over unauthorized colorized version of film Blackboard Jungle, available in translation in 16 No. 10 Ent. L. Rep. 3).

203　*Clean Flicks of Colorado, LLC v. Soderbergh*, 433 F. Supp.2d 1236 (D. Col. 2006).

cuted a similar agreement with Paramount covering his work on "Funny Face," and therefore, allegedly retained a copyright interest in the film.[204]

Donan filed suit for a portion of the proceeds from the use of the clip in the ad, claiming that he never acquiesced in the use of the film by third parties for advertising purposes. The court partially granted the defendants' motion to dismiss, but found that several of Donan's claims survived dismissal. The case was reportedly settled out of court, but emphasizes the importance of signed "Results and Proceeds" agreements between the production company and the creative participants in a film project, expressly affirming work made for hire status of the copyrightable contributions.[205]

[iii]—Excessive Edits by a Studio and the Director's Screen Credits

Tristar Pictures, Inc. v. Directors Guild of America, Inc. involved edits and cuts made by a studio to the film "Thunderheart" to create a shortened version for commercial television broadcast.[206] The director, Michael Apted, objected to the extensive cuts, which involved 270 separate cuts totaling twenty-two minutes, as well as speeding up the credits, and compressing the rest of the film electronically to save an additional four minutes.

Apted requested that his name be removed from the edited version when it aired, and Tristar refused. Apted's relationship with Tristar was governed by the DGA collective bargaining agreement. The DGA went to arbitration, and won the right to have Apted's name removed from the edited version of the film. Tristar appealed the arbitration verdict. Both the district court and the Ninth Circuit affirmed, ruling that Tristar's cuts were so severe "as to breach Tristar's duty of good faith and fair dealing set forth in Section 7-1502 of the Basic Agreement."[207]

---

204   *Donen v. Paramount Pictures Corp.*, 2008 WL 5054340 (C.D. Cal. Nov. 20, 2008).

205   *Id.* See also, *Richlin v. Metro-Goldwyn-Mayer Pictures, Inc.*, 531 F.3d 962, 967 (9th Cir. 2008) (claim that a treatment for one of the Pink Panther films was still owned by plaintiff. Court held that any separate copyright in the treatment was included in defendant's overall copyright ownership of the film.).

206   *TriStar Pictures, Inc. v. Directors Guild of America, Inc.*, 160 F.3d 537 (9th Cir. 1998).

207   *Tristar Pictures*, Inc., 160 F.3d at 539. Additionally, under Section 8-211 of the DGA Bargaining Agreement, Apted could request a pseudonym in lieu of the removal of his name from the credits. As stated by the Ninth Circuit:

"In order to avail himself of this remedy, a director must first persuade the Director's Council of the DGA that he is entitled to a pseudonym. If the Council assents, the pseudonym question is presented to a joint panel composed of two representatives from the studio and two from the DGA. If a majority of the joint panel sides with the director, the film's directing credit goes to a fictitious director, typically 'Alan Smithee.' If not, the studio may continue to use the director's name."

Tristar argued that affirming the arbitrator's award would create a *per se* rule prohibiting studios from editing movies for television. The court did not agree, noting that any future arbitrations involving other films and other cuts would be governed by the specific facts at issue.[208]

[iv]—DGA Enforcement of the Bargaining Agreement

In *Directors Guild of America, Inc. v. Garrison Productions, Inc.*, the DGA successfully sued a producer to enforce an arbitration award in the DGA's favor.[209] The case involved the mishandling of financing and production of a film by inexperienced producers. The director refused to continue work on the project. In order to protect the rights of the DGA member involved and pursuant to the Basic Agreement, the DGA demanded that the producers place $50,000 into an escrow deposit to secure the salaries and health and welfare benefits of the project's DGA members.[210] When the producers refused to comply with the arbitration award, the DGA successfully filed suit to enforce its terms.[211]

Id. The arbitrator's award stated that Tristar must either allow the use of the pseudonym, or include the following disclaimer prior to the broadcast:

This film is not the version originally released. 22 minutes have been cut out. The director, Michael Apted, believes this alteration changes the narrative and characterization and is not associated with it. The film has also been electronically speeded up. The director believes that this alteration changes the pace of the performance and is not associated with it.

. . . This put Tristar in a box. If it used Apted's name, it would be forced to air the disclaimer, which would make it look as if the film had been butchered. If it used a pseudonym, it would lose the attraction of a respected director. Tristar chose what it saw as the lesser of the two evils, and when Thunderheart aired on Fox, sans disclaimer, it carried the label "An Adam Smithy Film."

Id.

208   *Id.*, 160 F.3d at 541.

209   *Directors Guild of America, Inc. v. Garrison Productions, Inc.*, 733 F. Supp. 755 (S.D.N.Y. 1990).

210   *Id.*, 733 F. Supp. at 757.

211   *DGA v. Garrison Productions* is notable for the fact that the DGA successfully "pierced the corporate veil" and obtained a judgment against the producer in his individual capacity. The court stated:

"[A]s the sole investor and as the sole director in control of the corporation's finances[, the producer] was in a control position as to [the production company]. That he failed to observe corporate formalities adequately . . . that he used his control over the company to further his personal interest; that he operated the company in such a way that it was often undercapitalized; this this manner of operating the company amounted to an unjust act with respect to DGA's members; and that Ginsberg's conduct is not consonant with fair dealing with employees."

Id., 733 F. Supp. at 762. The case is also a reminder that formation of a corporation or LLC for the purposes of producing an independent film may not act as a shield against the unions and guilds that have the resources to enforce the terms of their collective bargaining agreements.

[2]—Actors

Formerly, two separate unions represented actors—the Screen Actors Guild ("SAG") for motion pictures, and the American Federation of Television and Radio Artists ("AFTRA") for the television and radio industries. As of March 30, 2012, the two unions merged to form SAG-AFTRA.

For most actors, the terms of their employment will be determined by the collective bargaining agreements entered into between the SAG-AFTRA and the producer of a given project. The SAG-AFTRA agreement sets forth "scale" (minimum) rates of compensation and terms of employment covering things such as hours, overtime, meal breaks, wardrobe, access to scripts, and "residuals"—payments made for repeat broadcasts of films, television programs, and commercials.

Some actors may be in sufficient demand to be paid greater than scale, and to receive additional perks and benefits, all of which can be reflected in a written agreement that will incorporate by reference the terms and conditions of the basic SAG-AFTRA agreements.[212] For example, SAG-AFTRA has different negotiated terms for feature motion pictures, for small budget independent films, and for various forms of television.[213]

In addition to the SAG-AFTRA standard terms and conditions, actors[214] may also enter into deal memoranda with production companies that set forth much greater compensation than SAG-AFTRA scale, including details of perks such as luxury trailers on the studio lot, specific appearance of credits, first class travel accommodations, dressing facilities, and approvals over such matters as hairdresser and wardrobe personnel, outtakes and bloopers, and consultation rights regarding replacements of key cast. When an actor has endorsement or other agreements, the agreement may specify that the actor may refrain from appearing to endorse competing products, or that product placements shown in the film do not conflict with the actor's pre-existing obligations and commitments.

[a]—SAG-AFTRA Global Rule One

SAG-AFTRA's "Global Rule One" is that "No member shall work as a performer or make an agreement to work as a performer for any producer who has not executed a

---

212   Depending on the type of production, SAG-AFTRA agreements cover areas such as theatrical, television, commercials, new media, and industrial/educational films. For a full list of employment matters covered under the SAG-AFTRA agreement, see SAG-AFTRA Theatrical/Television Digest, available at http://www.sag.org/content/theatrical-film-contracts.

213   See www.sagaftra.org.

214   Typically via their loan-out corporations.

basic minimum agreement with the Guild which is in full force and effect."[215] For actors who are not SAG members, and for production companies that are not SAG-AFTRA signatories, agreements to appear in a film may be on any negotiated terms. In practice, SAG-AFTRA offers accommodations for even the lowest budget student films, which enables shoestring productions to use SAG-AFTRA members. SAG-AFTRA may also require a production company to guarantee payment to its SAG-AFTRA employees by depositing a SAG-AFTRA guaranty amount, held in escrow by SAG-AFTRA.

[b]—Taft Hartley Act

Under the provisions of the federal Taft Hartley Act, union power to prevent the hiring of non-union talent is not absolute.[216] Guild signatory producers may hire non-guild or union members for their productions, but doing so triggers an obligation for the performer to join the guild or union (usually within 30 days) in order for the employment to continue, if indeed the employment is of a continuing nature. Failure to join the guild within that time may result in the guild telling producers the talent may not be hired in the future even under the Taft Hartley exceptions.[217] Thus some actors and other talent may first be engaged under the guild's Taft Hartley rules (sometimes referred to as being "Taft Hartleyed"), which are a path to membership.

[c]—The Seven Year Rule

Disputes between actors and producers over employment matters have not halted since *de Haviland v. Warner Bros. Pictures* in 1945, in which actress Olivia de Haviland prevailed against Warner Bros. on the issue of whether her personal services agreement with the studio could be valid beyond the statutorily allowed seven years.[218] In the era of seven-year studio contracts and total studio control over actors, De Haviland had rebelled by refusing to take several roles she did not believe were right for her. As a result, she was suspended for twenty-five weeks, and Warner sought to have her contract term extended by twenty-five weeks beyond the statutorily sanctioned seven-year limit. In describing the facts, the court noted that "according to the contract the Producer was the

---

215   SAG-AFTRA Global Rule One, available at http://www.sag.org/content/global-rule-one.

216   See The Labor Management Relations Act of 1947 29 U.S.C. § 141-197 better known as the Taft–Hartley Act, (80 H.R. 3020, Pub.L. 80–101, 61 Stat. 136, enacted June 23, 1947).

217   See, e.g. http://www.sagaftra.org/what-taft-hartley report. Other guilds have similar Taft Hartley Act procedures and rules.

218   See *de Haviland v. Warner Bros. Pictures*, 67 Cal. App.2d 225, 153 P.2d 983 (1945). See also: West's Ann. Cal. Labor code § 2855 (limiting personal services agreements to seven years; note that in Section 2855(n), there are statutory requirements and limitations regarding Section 2855's applicability in the music industry); *MCA Records, Inc. v. Newton-John*, 90 Cal. App.3d 18, 153 Cal. Rptr. 153 (1979).

sole judge in such matters and she had to do as she was told."[219] Note that in addition to the de Haviland case confirming the Seven Year Rule, state statues also set forth similar laws, notably California Labor Code Section 2855, and Section 2855(n), which applies the Seven Year Rule to music recording agreements but with numerous requirements and *quid pro quo* terms.

[d]—Contractual Disputes With Talent

In 1989, the California Court of Appeals issued an opinion in a dispute between Raquel Welch and Metro-Goldwyn-Mayer and others over Welch's firing from the cast of the film "Cannery Row."[220] The claims arising from Welch's termination included breach of contract, conspiracy to induce breach of contract, slander, and breach of the implied covenant of good faith and fair dealing (bad faith). Welch recovered $2 million in compensatory damages and over $8 million in punitive damages. Although affirmed on appeal, the verdict was later vacated on other grounds, and the parties reportedly settled.[221]

[3]—Child Actors

Child actors are commonly employed in films and television. The conditions of their employment, including the requirement that a tutor be employed and a limit on their hours, are provided for under the labor laws of the state in which employment occurs.[222]

Article 35 of New York's Arts and Cultural Affairs statute, entitled "Child Performers and Models," provides similar statutory guidance on laws regarding minors in the entertainment industry.[223] Also, New York's Department of Labor has the Child Performer Education and Trust Act of 2003, which covers obtaining employer certificates and Child Performer Permits; establishing trust accounts; and maintaining satisfactory academic performance of child performers.[224]

---

219   *Id.*, 153 P.2d at 985. The *de Haviland* case is sometimes referred to as the beginning of the end of the "seven year contract" studio system. In later years, stars would gain independence, working on one project of their choosing at a time, and forming their own production companies, a relatively common practice in the current era.

220   *Welch v. Metro-Goldwyn-Mayer Film Co.*, 207 Cal. App.3d 164, 254 Cal. Rptr. 645 (1989) (vacated on other grounds, the case reportedly settled).

221   The opinion in the appeal phase describes in great detail contractual matters and studio politics, and provides a valuable insider's view of issues affecting actors.

222   California's child actor laws are codified in sections 6750-53 of the Family Code and section 1700.37 of the Labor Code. Cal. Family Code § 6750-6753.

223   N.Y. Arts & Cultural Affairs, Art. 35.

224   See N.Y. State Dept. of Labor Web site, "Child performer," available at http://www.labor.state.ny.us/worker-protection/laborstandards/secure/child_index.shtm.

[a]—Court Approval of Entertainment Contracts with Minors

Subject to each state's statutory prohibitions on the types of agreements that minors may enter into, minors may otherwise enter into contracts.[225] However, strong public policy reasons give minors the right to disaffirm such contracts prior to reaching the age of majority, or within a reasonable time thereafter.[226] Where disaffirmance occurs, the result is that the contract is rescinded.[227]

In the entertainment industry, great financial resources may be expended in promoting the acting or musical career of a minor, to the mutual benefit of the minor and the production company. In order to have such relationships governed by contractual certainty, without the looming threat of the minor disaffirming the agreement and "jumping" to a competitor, statutes in California and New York provide for court approval of contracts, eliminating the minor's right to disaffirm and making the contract enforceable against the minor including damages and injunctive relief.

Strong policy reasons favor the minor's right to disaffirm a contract. However, in some limited situations, such as agreements for the provision of the necessities of life, agreements with minors are enforceable.[228] In other limited situations, the parent's signature can legally bind the minor, but courts have limited such situations to cases where it is actually the parent who is entering into the agreement for the benefit of the child, for example a parent signing an agreement for medical services that binds the minor child to an arbitration clause, or a parent signing a liability release that allows the child to participate in a desirable activity.[229] Courts view such agreements as benefitting the child, as where, for example, because the parent

225   See *Lane v. MRA Holdings, LLC*, 242 F. Supp.2d 1205, 1216-1217 (M.D. Fla. 2002) (setting forth a long list of Florida statutory prohibitions on the types of activities in which minors may legally agree to participate).

226   See Cal. Fam. Code § 6710: "Except as otherwise provided by statute, a contract of a minor may be disaffirmed by the minor before majority or within a reasonable time afterwards." See also, *Ballard v. Anderson*, 4 Cal.3d 873, 878-879, 484 P.2d 1345, 95 Cal. Rptr. 1 (1971) ("The right of the infant to avoid his contracts is one conferred by law for his protection against his own improvidence and the designs of others. The policy of the law is to discourage adults from contracting with an infant and they cannot complain if as a consequence of violating the rule they are injured by the exercise of the right of disaffirmance vested in the infant").

227   See *NYC Management Group Inc. v. Brown-Miller*, 2004 WL 1077784 at *4 (S.D.N.Y. May 14, 2004) (Disavowal and rescission of modeling contract entered into by model Jessica Stam when model was sixteen years old. Case decided under California choice of law provisions.).

228   See *Lane v. MRA Holdings, LLC*, 242 F. Supp.2d 1205, 1216 (M.D. Fla. 2002) (various statutes and doctrines of common law remove the disability of nonage in specific instances such as borrowing money for educational expenses, blood donation, and contracting for necessities, including food, shelter, and in some cases automobiles).

229   See: *Doyle v. Giuliucci*, 62 Cal.2d 606, 401 P.2d 1, 43 Cal. Rptr. 697 (1965) (parent entering into health care contract for benefit of child); *Hohe v. San Diego Unified School District*, 224 Cal. App.3d 1559, 274 Cal. Rptr. 647 (1990) (parent can sign release of liability enabling child to participate in school activity, minor cannot disaffirm).

releases liability claims against a school, the child has the opportunity and benefit of participating in school activities.

Those contracting for entertainment services with minors may include in the agreement a signed affirmation, consent, and approval from the minor's parent or guardian, in the hopes that such a consent will make the agreement legally binding against the child. But because it is the minor performing the acting or musical services, not the parent, such signed affirmations will not make the contract enforceable against the minor. Parental approval or consent is not enough to override the right of the minor to disaffirm.[230]

Where the agreement goes beyond mere parental "consent" and makes the parent an additional contracting party, courts will allow the minor to disaffirm, but will hold the parent responsible for their separate contractual obligations.[231] In *Berg v. Traylor*, a manager entered into an agreement with a child actor giving the manager 15% of the child's acting and related income. The parent of the minor actor signed the agreement, promising to pay the commission to the manager. While the court allowed the minor to rescind the agreement and sever all ties with the manager, the court held the parent responsible for paying the commissions as promised.[232]

There are also some entertainment industry specific statutory exceptions to the minor's right to disaffirm, in cases where the parent or guardian has signed an agreement on behalf of the child. With respect to consents and releases for invoking the right of publicity, both the California Right of Publicity Statute § 3344 and the New York Civil Rights Law §§ 50 and 51 specify that the rights may be obtained via the prior written consent of the minor's parent or guardian.[233]

In a case involving actress Brooke Shields when she was a child model, a court in New York held that because the actress's mother consented to the widespread use of photos of the child actress, the actress herself could not disaffirm the grant of rights to the photographer.[234] While noting that normally the only way to overcome the

---

230   See also, *NYC Management Group Inc. v. Brown-Miller*, 2004 WL 1077784 at *5 (citing *Raden v. Laurie*, 120 Cal. App.2d 778, 262 P.2d 61, 65 (1953)).

231   See *Berg v. Traylor*, 148 Cal. App.4th 809, 56 Cal. Rptr.3d 140 (2007) (where minor actor and parent both signed an agreement with a manager promising to pay the manager 15% of child's acting earnings, child could disavow the agreement but parent remained liable for the 15% of the child's earning to be paid to manager).

232   *Id.*

233   See: *Cal. Civ. Code* § 3344; N.Y. CLS Civ. R. § 50.

234   See *Shields v. Gross*, 58 N.Y.2d 338, 448 N.E.2d 108, 461 N.Y.S.2d 254 (1983). See also, *Alvidrez v. Roberto Coin, Inc.*, 6 Misc.3d 742, 791 N.Y.S.2d 344 (2005) (minor model disaffirms modeling agreement photo use rights, claiming that parental signature on original agreement was forged by defendants).

minor's right to disaffirm is to seek court approval of entertainment contracts with minors, the court in *Shields* observed that the court approval process is lengthy and expensive, and best suited for agreements where the services are to be performed over an extended period, for example child actors or athletes. In the case of child models, most photo sessions are of short duration, and can be frequent, making court approval impractical for multiple different agreements of short duration. Therefore, the court held that parental consent can grant right of publicity releases for child model photos, without the threat of disaffirmance by the child models themselves.[235]

Shields v. Gross illustrates two different types of agreements involving the minor: first, there was the agreement to perform modeling services at the photo shoot. Second, was the agreement under New York Civil Rights law "right of publicity" provisions to allow the resulting photos to be used in any way in the future including for commercial advertising. As for the modeling services, there was no dispute: Shields provided the services at the appointed time as agreed upon in exchange for a fee. In many cases, agreements with minors for entertainment services may be similarly limited in scope, performed as agreed in a short time frame, perhaps a few hours, and completed, without incident or disagreement. It is the more extensive type of agreement, such as regular appearances for television programs over several years, that merits the time and expense required to obtain court approval of the agreement.

In California, Section 6751 of the California Family Code sets out the procedures for obtaining court approval of an entertainment contract with a minor, making it enforceable and eliminating the minor's right to disaffirm.[236] The policy behind al-

---

235   *Id.*

236   See Cal. Family Code §6751:

(a) A contract, otherwise valid, of a type described in Section 6750, entered into during minority, cannot be disaffirmed on that ground either during the minority of the person entering into the contract, or at any time thereafter, if the contract has been approved by the superior court in any county in which the minor resides or is employed or in which any party to the contract has its principal office in this state for the transaction of business.

(b) Approval of the court may be given on petition of any party to the contract, after such reasonable notice to all other parties to the contract as is fixed by the court, with opportunity to such other parties to appear and be heard.

(c) Approval of the court given under this section extends to the whole of the contract and all of its terms and provisions, including, but not limited to, any optional or conditional provisions contained in the contract for extension, prolongation, or termination of the term of the contract.

(d) For the purposes of any proceeding under this chapter, a parent or legal guardian, as the case may be, entitled to the physical custody, care, and control of the minor at the time of the proceeding shall be considered the minor's guardian ad litem for the proceeding, unless the court shall determine that appointment of a different individual as guardian ad litem is required in the best interests of the minor.

lowing such court approval is, in theory, to benefit the minor: without the certainty of court approval, and faced with the prospect that the minor could walk away at any time, production companies would be less inclined to invest in the minor's career, and less inclined to make substantial payments to the minor. Court approval provides certainty in the contractual agreement, which ideally is of benefit to both parties.

Like California, New York is also an active location for employment of child actors and offers a statutory process for obtaining court approval of contracts with minors.[237]

California and New York are unique in providing detailed statutory guidance on the process for obtaining court approval of entertainment industry contracts with minors, and for having a judiciary with experience in such petitions. In other jurisdictions, there may not be any statutory guidance, and the process will have to be carefully investigated to determine which court has jurisdiction, and the procedures for submitting a petition to the court.

[b]—Coogan Accounts

Jackie Coogan was a child star during the silent film era. He appeared in films with Charlie Chaplin and earned millions of dollars. Coogan's parents squandered the funds. In response, the California legislature passed "Coogan laws" in 1939.[238] Other states, including New York, Louisiana, and New Mexico, have similar laws requiring the handling of trust accounts for child actors.

Under Coogan laws, 15% of funds payable to a child actor must be placed in a trust account, preserved for the child's benefit upon reaching the age of majority. Most entertainment industry employers are experienced in ensuring that 15% of any funds for the services of a child actor are paid solely into a Coogan account.

Coogan accounts may be opened at a number of institutions that are experienced in offering them. Organizations such as the Screen Actors Guild have information on which financial institutions are experienced with the requirements of Coogan accounts.

---

237   See N.Y. Arts & Cultural Affairs Laws, Art. 35. Article 35.03 sets forth the process for obtaining court approval of agreements with minors. For a comprehensive summary of New York State Department of Labor regulations governing child performers, see https://labor.ny.gov/workerprotection/laborstandards/secure/child_index.shtm.

238   See: Cal. Family Code, §§ 6750-6753.

[c]—Child Labor Laws Applicable to the Film Industry

Labor laws govern the conditions of employment of minors, in addition to laws governing contracts with minors and deposit of funds into Coogan accounts. Such laws may require that an application for a work permit be filed, and approved, before the minor can begin employment in the entertainment industry.[239] They will also govern the hours worked, supervision by parents and guardians, and the presence of a studio teacher.

As an example, the State of California Department of Industrial Relations Division of Labor Standards Enforcement publishes the Summary Chart regarding labor requirements for the employment of minors, including work time when school is in session, work time when school is not in session, and concurrent requirements such as the types of work permits required and whether parents or guardians, and/ or a studio teacher, must be present.[240] For infants, the requirements also severely limit the amount of on-camera time, and even the amount of intense film lighting to which the infant is exposed.[241]

[4]—Animals

The exploits of star animal actors such as Lassie, Toto, Benji, and Rin Tin Tin echo as if with a halo through the misty decades of motion picture history. Even animal actors with brief careers can make a memorable impression such as Shasta, the dog who communicates telepathically with a Martian in the film "K-Pax". And who would deny the importance to John "Duke" Wayne of his trusty horse? Animals in films are usually supplied by a professional animal trainer or "wrangler," who may own the animals, and who may assist in coaching the animals through filming.

For production companies shooting scripts that include animals, the American Humane Association's Film & TV Unit provides guidelines on the use of animals, as well as monitoring of animals' safety during production.[242] The Film & TV Unit is the only

---

239   See Cal. Labor Code § 1700. See also, N.Y. State Dept. of Labor website, "Child Performer," available at http://www.labor.ny.gov/workerprotection/laborstandards/secure/child_index.shtm.

240   See, e.g. California Labor Commissioner Child Labor Law Pamphlet including section on minors in the entertainment industry, available at <https://www.dir.ca.gov/dlse/ChildLaborLawPamphlet.pdf>. See also SAG-AF-TRA Young Performers Handbook, available via links at https://www.sagaftra.org/content/young-performers.

241   In at least one example, television producers decided to employ identical twins playing one role, in order to maximize the amount of time each child actor could be available to fulfill the demanding needs of a weekly situation comedy. Mary-Kate Olsen and Ashley Olsen are twins, who alternated in portraying one character in the television series "Full House."

242   See Humane Association Film & TV Unit, available at http://www.americanhumane.org/animals/programs/no-animals-were-harmed/. Animal actors sometimes appear under their own names in the credits, such as "Gra-

organization authorized to provide the end credit stating that "No animals were harmed during the course of this production," and publishes Guidelines for the Safe Use of Animals in Filmed Media.[243] They also provide Certified Animal Safety Representatives to be present on set during filming, and to monitor compliance with the Guidelines. Any animal handler engaged by a production company should be familiar with these guidelines, and abide by them.

[5]—Screen Credits

Screen credit is an essential part of professional development and compensation. In some cases, a credit will be determined by the production company. In other cases, the applicable guild, such as the Writers Guild of America, will have strict procedures and rules for determining who is entitled to credits and dispute resolution proceedings that signatory production companies must abide by. Where guilds or unions have final authority over on-screen credits, written agreements with talent will state that the final determination of the on-screen credit will be subject to the guild rules.

Courts have held that monetary damages in connection with omitted credits may be difficult to establish and speculative, and may not fully compensate a plaintiff, in which case specific performance may be granted as a remedy, i.e., the credits must be restored. As noted by one court, "it has been held that failure to give an artist screen credit would constitute irreparable injury."[244]

Contractual provisions for credits may distinguish between "single card" and "shared card." In *Sobini Films v. Clear Skies Nevada, LLC*, a producer sued over a mistake in which his name appeared on a shared card below two other names. The producer's contract had the following provision:

> "[Producer] shall be entitled to: one (1) individual producer credit on screen, in no less than third position of all 'Produced by' credits, on a single card, which credit shall appear in the main titles of the Picture. . . .

---

ham the dog was played by Cleo," or under character names, often with several animals of similar appearance contributing, such as "Marina the dog was played by Freya, Leonora, and Pierre." Even aquatic creatures, such as the moon betta fish in "Rumblefish" may require the services of a professional "fish wrangler."

243   The Guidelines are available at http://www.americanhumane.org/animals/professional-resources/for-producers-filmmakers/guidelines.html.

244   See *Poe v. Michael Todd Co.*, 151 F. Supp. 801 (S.D.N.Y. 1957), quoted in Tamarind Litho. *Workshop v. Sanders*, 143 Cal. App. 3d 571, 577 (Cal. App. 2 Dist. 1983). See also, *Sobini Films, Inc. v. Clear Skies Nevada, LLC*, 2016 Cal. App. Unpub. LEXIS 7246 (Cal App. 2 Dist. Oct. 4, 2016).

"No casual or inadvertent failure of [Distributor] to comply with the credit requirements, nor any failure of any third party to comply therewith, shall constitute a breach of this Agreement. If [Distributor] or a third party fails to accord [Producer] credit pursuant to the terms of this Agreement, [Distributor] agrees to use reasonable good faith efforts to prospectively cure such failure following receipt of written notice from [Producer] setting forth in detail such failure, but nothing shall require [Distributor] to cease using or to replace prints, negative, advertisements or other materials then in existence."[245]

Based on the above language that did not require any "correction" by the distributor, and testimony that the mistake in providing a shared credit did not in fact harm the producer's reputation (partly because the film was not a success thus not seen by many people), the court dismissed the claim.

The crucial importance of credits in the entertainment industry is evident from the extensive credit guidelines and dispute resolution procedures published by the trade guilds, discussed below.

[a]—"Written by" (Writer Credits)

As noted by the Ninth Circuit, "In Hollywood, a screenwriter's name is his most coveted asset."[246] The Writers Guild of America governs all motion picture, television, and new media screen credits for productions by Guild signatory companies, with the WGA having sole final authority, exceeding that of the production company itself, over screen credits for its members. Therefore, agreements with writers may have a provisional credit indicated but a statement that the final credit is subject to the WGA rules.

Navigating that process requires that the writer, and the writer's representatives, be well informed about how the WGA makes its credit determinations, especially in situations where there may be co-writers, or where a writer may be entitled to a "Story by" credit instead of "Written by." Among the documents that are part of the process is the WGA "Notice of Tentative Writing Credit" or NTWC form, copies of which for film and television productions are included in the Forms for this Chapter.

---

245   *Sobini Films, Inc. v. Clear Skies Nevada, LLC*, 2016 Cal. App. Unpub. LEXIS 7246 (Cal App. 2 Dist. Oct. 4, 2016) at *4.

246   See *Wellman v. Writers Guild of America West*, 146 F.3d 666 (9th Cir. 1998) (denying screenwriter's appeal of WGA arbitration award denying him credit for motion picture screenplay entitled "Fair Game"). The fact section of the Ninth Circuit opinion in Wellman describes the process of screenplay credit and the WGA's role as arbitrator as it functioned circa 1998.

The WGA publishes several online resources for writers including the "Credits Survival Guide," full details of which can be found in the WGA's "Minimum Basic Agreement" or MBA. As is always the case with union and guild rules and guidelines, they are a helpful guide to how the entertainment industry actually works on a day-to-day basis and are essential information for attorneys representing clients in the industry.

[b]— "Directed by" (Director Credit)

The Directors Guild Master Agreement ("MA") Article 8 governs the guild rules and procedures for the "Directed by" credit, including dispute resolution procedures.[247] The following is an excerpt from Article 8, Section 100, setting forth the basic credit principles:

"8-101 Guild to Determine Controversy Over Credits

"Should more than one Director do work on a motion picture, the Guild and all such Directors (other than Directors of second units) shall be notified in writing as to the directorial credit intended to be given.

"Should any such Director be dissatisfied with such determination, he or she may immediately appeal to the Guild and likewise notify the Employer in writing that he or she is so doing. The Guild may then determine the issue. Except as herein provided, the Employer agrees to be bound by such determination as to credits. If the Guild should fail to reach a decision and notify the Employer within fourteen (14) days in the case of a theatrical motion picture, and seven (7) days in the case of a television motion picture (such time to run from receipt by the Guild of the print of the film), the Employer shall determine the issue and its determination shall be final. In the event that the Guild's determination as to credit is given at too late a date to permit the giving of screen or advertising credit as indicated by the Guild, then credit shall be given in such manner as may have been designated by the Employer, but appropriate credit shall be given in any bulletin to be issued by the Guild or in such other bulletin as may be mutually agreed upon. In no event shall an Employer be obligated to delay the preparation or issuance of advertising matter or the release of any motion picture pending proceedings for the determination of credits.

"8-102 Form of Director's Credit

---

247 See Directors Guild 2014-2017 Basic Agreement, available at https://www.dga.org/Contracts/Agreements.aspx.

"The form of the Director's credit on screen, paid advertising, phonograph records, books, tapes, videodiscs, videocassettes and the containers thereof, when and as required, shall be 'Directed by. . . .' The words 'Directed by' on screen shall be at least one-half the size of type used to accord credit to the Director's name.

"Should a Director other than the Director, or one of the Directors, receiving credit on the motion picture have the same first and last name, the Guild shall determine whether or not such Director's credit must include his or her middle name, if any, or middle initial. The Directors involved shall be bound by such determination and the Employer shall also be bound, if notified thereof by the Guild in writing within a reasonable time before prints with the main titles are prepared but shall not be bound with respect to advertising, publicity or other material prepared prior to such notice.

"8-103 Restriction on Use of Word 'Director'

"(a) The Employer will not hereafter and during the term hereof enter into any agreement with any guild, craft, union, or labor organization in which it agrees to accord members thereof credit on screen, paid advertising, phonograph records, books, tapes (including the cover of the book, record or tape as well as any album, envelope, box or other container in which such record or tape is contained) which includes the word 'Director,' 'Direction' or any derivation thereof, but the foregoing shall not apply to a guild or craft with which the Employer heretofore entered into an agreement requiring such credit.

"(b) Except as required by agreements heretofore executed by the Employer, and agreements permitted by subparagraph (a) above to be hereafter executed, Employer will not grant to any individual, other than a Director, any credit which includes the word 'Director,' 'Direction' or any derivation thereof."

[c]—"Produced by" (Producer Credit)

The Producers Guild of America does not have the same final authority to determine "Produced By" credits as the WGA, but it actively encourages the voluntary use of PGA standards for determining credits, and offers an arbitration system for disputes.

The PGA website includes detailed descriptions of what duties a producer may be expected to perform in theatrical and television productions. The PGA has entered into agreements with the six largest studios to us the "p.g.a." designation after the name of members in the screen credits.

Academy Award eligibility rules of the Academy of Motion Picture Arts and Sciences ("AMPAS") limit the number of "Produced By" credits for a motion picture, and Oscar statuette eligibility, to three names.[248]

"Executive Producer" credits have no AMPAS numerical limitation because Executive Producers, who may be financiers or others not part of the day-to-day production process, are not eligible for Best Picture Award statuettes.[249]

[d]—"Executive Producer" Credits

Under the PGA's non-binding guidelines, the credit of Executive Producer shall apply only to an individual who has made a significant contribution to the motion picture and who additionally qualifies under at least one of two categories:

- Having secured an essential and proportionally significant part (no less than 25%) of the financing for the motion picture; or

- Having made a significant contribution to the development of the literary property, typically including the securement of the underlying rights to the material on which the motion picture is based.

[e]—Actor Credits

SAG-AFTRA's basic provisions for billing and credit are summarized in the SAG-AFTRA Contract Summary included in the Appendices to this chapter. "Billing" addresses prominence and size of the actor's name, subject to negotiated agreement with the Producer:[250]

Billing: (Television & Theatrical) The Producer is required to honor individually negotiated billing as described and agreed upon in the performer's individual contract.

Credit:

---

248   See Rule Sixteen Special Rules for the Best Picture of the Year Award, available at http://www.oscars.org/awards/academyawards/rules/86/rule16.html.

249   See Producers Guild of America, Code of Credits, available at http://www.producersguild.org/?page=code_of_credits.

250   See SAG-AFTRA Contract Summary Theatrical Motion Pictures and Television, available at <http://www.sagaftra.org/2017-tvtheatrical-contract-deal-summary>.

(Television) One card in the end credits is required. If credit not negotiated, then it is at Producer's discretion.

(Theatrical) Films with a cast of 50 or less, all performers shall receive screen credit. All other films, not less than 50 performers shall be listed at the end of the film. Stunt performers need not be identified by role.

Should the Producer fail to meet the requirements of either the billing or credit provisions, and the facts are not in dispute, liquidated damages in the amount of the performer's day, 3-day (TV), or weekly contract will be paid. However, such payment will not exceed $4,800 (television) or $6,200 (theatrical).

If there is a dispute as to the facts, the matter may be submitted for arbitration. All other performers should contact the Guild. Note: Any such claim must be filed within one year after the first theatrical release or within one year of the first broadcast of a television film.

§1.09   Residuals and Foreign Levies

[1]—Residuals

Residuals are guild-mandated compensation paid to actors, writers, and directors for use of a motion picture or television program after its initial use. For television work, residuals begin once a show starts re-airing or is released to video/DVD, pay television, broadcast television or basic cable. For film work, residuals begin once the movie appears on video/DVD, basic cable and free or pay television.[251]

Residuals are based on formulas that take into account factors including the collective bargaining agreement in place during the specific year, time spent on the production, the production type and the market where the product appears (e.g., broadcast television, video/DVD, pay television, basic cable). The collective bargaining agreements specify what type of employment qualifies to receive residuals,[252] and set forth the specific future payments, often in a formula that gradually declines over time, but continues as long as the production earns revenue.

Residual payments, unlike "net profit participation," are not dependent on the profitability of the venture. They are a production cost—compensation made under a future

---

251   See http://www.sag.org/content/residuals-faq.

252   For example, background actors without lines, or "extras," do not qualify for residuals under bargaining agreements.

payments schedule regardless of whether the producer believes the project is profitable or has "broken even." Residuals are also payable to those entitled to receive them, regardless of whether or not those individuals are also entitled to any profit participation. Residuals may be received by the estate after the recipient's death.

The main guilds have detailed schedules of residuals payments included in their collective bargaining agreements. Those terms may include the right of the guild to have a security interest in the copyright of the production in order to ensure future compliance with payments of residuals and other obligations.[253]

[2]—Foreign Levies and Foreign Royalties Payable Directly to Creators

In some European countries, societies that represent the rights of creators collect monies from the entertainment industry (and from the technology industry for goods such as blank DVD discs), and remit payments to creators of literary and artistic works, including screenwriters, directors, and actors. In Europe, copyright laws directly enforce "author's rights" or "droit moral," a legal concept that, under United States law, is addressed by provisions in the Lanham Act protecting against false endorsement and false designation of origin.[254]

In concept, the payments made directly to authors by these European collectives are similar to the way performing rights organizations operate in the music industry in that some of the license monies collected from businesses that use music are remitted directly to the creators. Such European levies are sometimes referred to as "EEC" rights, or rights that originate in the countries of the European Economic Community ("EEC").

Such levies may include royalty payments designated as payable directly to creators (and not via the production company) for home video rentals, cable transmissions, and as compensation for illegal copying and piracy. The European collectives then remit the monies to the respective guilds that represent creators in the United States, which in turn remit those monies to their members. Royalties based on foreign levies are not the same as residuals.

Distribution of foreign levies to the ultimate recipients is done through the leading guilds. Several class actions in Los Angeles Superior Court brought on behalf of individual creators reached settlements in which the formulas for remittance of foreign levies

---

253   See *The Kindred Limited Partnership v. The Screen Actors Guild, Inc.*, 2009 WL 279080 (C.D. Cal. Feb. 3, 2009) (SAG action to foreclose on security interest in film "The Kindred" due to producer's failure to make SAG payments including health, pension, and residuals).

254   See *Gilliam v. American Broadcasting Companies, Inc.*, 538 F.2d 14, 21 (2d Cir. 1976).

to actors, directors, and writers by SAG (the predecessor to SAG-AFTRA), the DGA, and the WGA were agreed upon by the parties.[255]

§1.10   Agreements with Production Crew

So-called below-the-line unions include the International Alliance of Theatrical and Stage Employees and Motion Picture Operators ("IATSE"), the labor union representing technicians, artisans and craftspersons in the entertainment industry. IATSE members include employees in live theater, motion picture and television production, and trade shows.[256] The Teamsters Union represents film industry transportation workers. National Association of Broadcast Employees and Technicians ("NABET") represents the broadcasting and cable television workers, as is a subsidiary of the Communication Workers of America ("CWA").[257]

Where the production crews are members of the applicable unions, the collective bargaining agreement will control many of the employment arrangements. There will still be a written agreement specifying terms such as compensation and ensuring that all "Results and Proceeds" of the creative work, including copyright, are the property of the Producer.[258]

§1.11   Music in Film and Television

[1]—Licensing

Licensing music from third parties for films[259] will involve many details on the planned use, for example:

- Title of work

- Duration of excerpt used

- Nature of the use: background, or featured (for example a song sung by a cast member)

- Exhibition type: film festivals, theatrical exhibition, public television, commercial television, Internet streaming, etc.

---

255   See *Richert v. Writers Guild of America*, BC 339972 (L.A. Sup. June 1, 2010). See also: *Webb v. Directors Guild of America*, No. BC 352621 (Sup. Sept. 10, 2008); *Osmond v. Screen Actors Guild*, No. BC 377780 (L.A. Sup. Sept. 13, 2010). See also, *Screen Actors Guild, Inc. v. Federal Insurance Co.*, 957 F. Supp.2d 1157 (C.D. Cal. 2013) (holding for insurer in dispute with SAG over foreign levy litigation costs).

256   See http://www.iatse-intl.org/home.html.

257   See http://www.nabetcwa.org/.

258   A sample crew member agreement is included in the forms accompanying this treatise.

259   See Chapter 4 *infra* for an in-depth discussion of licensing in the music industry.

- Distribution media; DVDs, Internet, mobile phones, etc.
- Territory: United States only, other countries, the entire world
- Term: number of years; options to renew; perpetuity
- Responsibility for public performance royalties payments

The licensor will use all of the above factors to arrive at a fee. It is often possible to have a less expensive, limited rights license than pay additional fees for additional rights.

Most commercially viable projects such as motion pictures and most television projects will need unlimited, worldwide rights in perpetuity, so that the production company never has to be concerned with the license expiring in the future.

Licenses are granted on a non-exclusive basis, meaning that the licensor can license the same music to another film or television project.[260]

[a]—Master License for Sound Recordings

A license to use the sound recording is called a "master" license, referring to the historical process whereby an original, high quality "master" tape recording was used to manufacture vinyl records. In the digital era, every CD or high quality audio file can serve as a "master."

[b]—Synchronization or "Sync" License for the Musical Composition

A license to use a musical composition in a film or television production is called a synchronization, or "sync" license (also commonly referred to via the abbreviation "synch"), because music used in a film is referred to as "synchronized" with the visual images.

[c]—Production Libraries

Companies called music libraries offer a wide selection of pre-composed background music, referred to as "production" music. In the past, vinyl LPs of production music samples were sent to producers, who could sample the tracks by dropping the phonograph needle on various tracks and listening.[261]

---

260 In an unusual case, a producer's alleged failure to license a song in a film was used by the producer as a reason to block release of the film in the course of a dispute with the financier. See *Future Films USA, LLC V. Sriram Das,* 2013 Cal. App. Unpub. LEXIS 552 (Cal. App. 2 Dist. Jan. 24, 2013).

261 The term "drop the needle" licensing is still occasionally used in connection with production music libraries.

Today, production music is often stored on a Web site for inspection, or provided on a CD. Production music has the advantage of being easy to obtain, and often competitively priced, but may carry the disadvantage of being generic in sound and impact. In order to license the music, the production library will have essentially the same list of questions as a music publisher granting a sync license or a record company granting a master license. This is because the production company is granting both licenses as a package.[262]

[2]— Commissioned Scores

Film composers can bring tremendous artistic and commercial cachet and success to a film. Unlike other elements of a film, a music score may have an independent commercial life.[263] It is common for large studios that own film soundtracks and songs to have a separate music publishing division in order to manage those rights. A studio may also arrange for a third party publisher to administer the revenue on the studio's behalf.

When a composer is commissioned to create a score for a movie, the question as to who owns and handles the music publishing rights once the film is completed will arise. Independent, low budget production companies with little or no expertise in this area may be inclined to let the composer retain the publishing rights, so long as the production company has the worldwide, perpetual and exclusive right to the score as used in the film. In other words, the composer could manage and benefit from any future music publishing rights, but could not license the same music to another film.

Another approach the production company or studio may take is to retain the publishing rights. Revenues from the film score and the publishing rights will be included in the gross revenues and net profit calculations made by the studio in connection with profit participation statements.[264]

The major deal points in a commission agreement for a film score are:

- Employment: A description of the project and the services to be performed in delivering the original score and, usually, all required sound recordings. Some rare projects

---

262   Examples of production company licenses are included in the forms accompanying this treatise.

263   For example, a hit score may generate revenue in the form of soundtrack recordings, or live concert performances, or licensing of a popular movie theme in connection with commercials, greeting cards, mobile phone ringtones, etc.

264   Some music publishers may seek to obtain publishing rights in the film score by subsidizing the producer's costs of the composition of the score and the studio recording in exchange for the publishing ownership. See, e.g. *Ennio Morricone Music Inc. v. Bixio Music Grp. LTD*, 2017 U.S. Dist. LEXIS 177643 (S.D.N.Y. 2017) (composer sought to terminate film score copyrights owned by Italian music publisher, because composer had been hired on a work for hire basis composer did not have termination rights under U.S. Copyright Act).

may hire a composer to only write the score with the studio or production company responsible for the recording sessions, but a "package" deal including composition and all recordings is increasingly the norm. Where composers hire assistants to create some of the music or to perform tasks such as orchestration, care should be taken to secure all rights from all such assistants.[265]

- Package: This confirms that the amount paid is "all in" and includes both the film score compositions and the sound recording, including the hiring of all musicians, score copyists, orchestrators, other personnel, payroll taxes, editing, equipment, instruments, studio time, engineering and recording costs, mixing, etc. In essence, the film composer is required to also be a recording studio.

- Delivery: Delivery materials may include a copy of the score and all instrumental and vocal parts (the performing materials used by the musicians and conductor during the recording session), and the original recording masters in a pre-agreed upon technical format.

- Term: The Term ends with full delivery, including any re-takes or other needs to revise the score.

- Compensation: The all-in fee may be split with 50% payable upon signing, 35% payable upon commencement of scoring of the film (which may not occur for some time until the film is edited and the director and composer have discussed where music should be used in the film); and 15% upon completion of all services and delivery of all materials.

- Music Publishing: This may involve several different approaches, most typically the studio will retain the right to administer the publishing rights and retain the "publisher's share" of all revenue, while the composer remains entitled to the full "author share" of all royalties.[266]

- Film Soundtrack: This portion of the agreement relates to the composer's rights for purposes of a potential commercial release of a soundtrack CD or digitally. Therefore, it may include provisions that are related to both aspects of the composer's work: music publishing royalties for the composition of the score, and recording royalties for the production of the sound recording. Thus, on the composition side, the agreement may specify that for a film soundtrack released on CD or as digital files, the mechanicals royalty rate (the royalty attributable to the music publishing of the film score composition) can be 75% of the statutory rate. On the "sound recording" side, the agreement may provide an artist royalty to the composer for the sound recordings,

---

265   See *Kolton v. Universal Studios, Inc.*, 2004 WL 3242338 (C.D. Cal. Dec. 14, 2004) (where composer who created music scores for network had hired an assistant who composed some portions of the scores, and assistant later sued studio for additional compensation).

266   For a more detailed introduction to the music publishing business, please see Chapter 4.

for example 8% artist royalty, and 4% producer royalty, based on sales of the sound recording of the film score.

- Accounting: The accounting portion is akin to such provisions as found in music publishing and recording agreements.

- EEC Payments: In the European Economic Community ("EEC") there may be royalty streams not available in the United States, for example broadcast royalties for sound recordings, or other payments made directly to authors under the European "moral rights' principles. The studio may ask the composer to assign all such rights to the studio.

- Travel and Expenses: There may be provisions for reimbursement of travel expenses incurred by composer, or by musicians who perform on the recordings.

- Name and Likeness: A grant of the composer's right of publicity in her name, image, and likeness for purposes of advertising throughout the world in perpetuity in connection with the film, including commercial tie-ins, merchandising, by products, etc.[267]

- Results and Proceeds: A grant of all rights in the work product to the production company, including confirmation that copyright in the work is on a "work made for hire" basis, along with backup assignment of all rights under copyright, including rights under other areas of intellectual property law, such as rental and lending rights, neighboring rights under European (EEC) laws, and all possible derivations and adaptations of the film, including videogames, all digital formats, etc.

- Union and Guild Membership: This will state whether the project is union or non-union, and confirm that any musicians engaged fall into the correct category, for example whether all musicians engaged must be members of the American Federation of Musicians ("AFM"), which sets minimum compensation rates for its members. It may also include provisions that if the composer must join a guild or union for purposes of the film, she will do so.

- Credit: Usually a screen credit on a separate "card" in the main titles, stating "Music by [composer]." There may be a condition precedent to get screen credit, for example that at least 50% of the score must be embodied in the film upon initial release. There should be a guarantee that where there is a "billing block' used in advertising (the condensed list of credits that typically appears at the bottom of the movie poster, for example), the composer's name will be included.

- Credit Exclusions: There may be a long list of situations where the production company is not obligated to include a credit for the composer, so-called "Excluded ads," which may include teaser and announcement advertising; advertising focused on other participants in the film; "award" or "congratulatory" ads; publicity and promotional items, etc.

---

267   For a more detailed discussion of the right of publicity, see Chapter 7.

§1.12   Production Issues

[1]—Budgeting

The budget for a film is crucial to the production process. Many of the sources of financing, for example, look to the film's "going in"—or initial—budget, to see the amount required to complete the film. Trade unions and guilds also often demand budget information for the film as part of their collective bargaining agreements in order to ensure that proper financing is in place. Those whose compensation is tied to the budget also have an interest in the actual amount. For example, the purchase price paid for the underlying rights to a book or story may be based on a range determined by the film's budget. The budget or negative cost will also be a key figure in accounting for profit participation in the future.

The budget serves another function, which is to monitor and control the weekly expenditures during filming. Accounting is an important part of the filmmaking process, and one of the producers may be assigned to spend much of their time during the production working with accountants to update and maintain the weekly budget numbers as compared to actual expenditures. Should the weekly tracking indicate the film is going over budget, for example, that can trigger not only contractual penalties, but can set in motion new requests for financing or completion guarantees.

The budget may break down the production phases into pre-production, principal photography, and post-production:

1.   The "above-the-line" items will include acquisition of the rights to the underlying story; screenplay costs; director fees; and fees for the leading actor or actors.

2.   The "below-the-line" line items will include the entire remaining cast and crew, including studio costs, transportation, location costs, etc.[268]

Public disclosure of film budgets can be a sensitive topic, where the budget may be the benchmark that drives negotiations for advances from a distributor, or where the budget may disclose that cast and crew are working substantially below their customary "quote," for example. In *Iowa Film Production Services v. Iowa Dep't of Economic Development*, a dispute arose between independent production companies and the State of Iowa's film tax incentive program over whether the state had the right to publicly disclose budgets for films that received state tax credits under the state's Open Records Act.[269] The Iowa Supreme Court refused to enjoin state from publicly releasing summaries of film production financial budgets, despite objections of film producers that film budget information

---

268   A sample film budget is included in the forms accompanying this treatise.

269   *Iowa Film Production Services v. Iowa Dep't of Economic Development*, 818 N.W.2d 207 (Iowa 2012).

is confidential. Among reasons cited by producers for the necessity of confidentiality was the example of "an actor who usually receives $10 million for a movie but may act in an independent film for $100,000, expecting this amount will be kept confidential."[270]

The same concern was expressed over the director's salary. Also cited as reasons for confidentiality was that "if the total cost of a movie became known, this could undermine the ability of the producer to make a substantial profit on it or could adversely affect audience reaction, because the public tends to believe a movie is worth what it cost to make."[271] The producer testified that "the budget he submitted to [the Iowa film program] was artificially low. He wanted the guilds and unions to see a lower budget so they would not seek the premium that is associated with a higher-budget film."[272] Despite those disclosures, the producer also testified that "Hollywood, our industry, is built on trust."[273] In denying the production companies' request to keep the budget information confidential, the court also noted that "[t]he record does not show that the Producers made reasonable efforts to preserve confidentiality of their financial data as against the outside world in general. There is no evidence that security measures were taken. The Producers failed to show, for instance, that individuals who worked for them and came into contact with this information were required not to disclose it."[274]

[2]—Errors and Omissions Insurance

Various types of insurance coverage may be required for a film. In addition to standard general liability insurance covering the production against claims relating to accidents, damages, and injuries, special coverage may be needed for films including stunts, driving sequences, rented equipment, owned equipment, props, sets and wardrobe, negative and faulty stock, and even injury or death of lead cast members.[275]

Virtually all film projects intended for the commercial market must carry Errors and Omissions ("E&O") insurance. E&O coverage applies to risks such as intellectual property infringement and other rights involved in the filmmaking process, including rights

---

270   *Id.*, 818 N.W.2d at 216.

271   *Id.*

272   *Id.*

273   *Id.*

274   *Id.*, 818 N.W.2d at 225.

275   See *Alta Vista Productions, LLC v. St. Paul Fire & Marine Insurance Co.*, 796 F. Supp.2d 782 (E.D. La. 2011) (dispute over insurance coverage for two week delay in shooting film "The Expendables" arising from illness of lead actor).

of publicity and privacy. E&O coverage will be required as one of the terms of any distribution agreement for the project.[276]

[3]—Location Agreements

Under basic principles of trespass law, property owners have full rights to decide what activities to allow on their premises, and under what terms and conditions. Similarly, municipal, state, and federal authorities can decide when and where, and under what terms, they will issue permits allowing film production companies access to locations. Many cities and states have film offices, whose functions include facilitating the issuance of filming permits from local governments. Such permits may be necessary in order to ensure the safety of the public.

For owners of private locations, allowing a production company to film on the premises is often accompanied by a written agreement setting forth issues such as the dates and locations, responsibility for cleanup and repairs, and fees paid.

Unless a building's design has achieved trademark status, there is little to prevent a production company from filming the exterior from a public location.[277] Only where a building of unique design is used in a way that serves a source-identifying function, thus creating trademark rights, can the owner of that trademark protest if the building is depicted in a way that violates its trademark rights.[278] Even where such rights in a building's image may exist, depiction of the building merely as part of its public location setting is protected by the First Amendment, and is unlikely to violate any trademark

---

276 See *Barris/Fraser Enterprises v. Goodson-Todman Enterprises, Ltd.*, 638 F. Supp. 292, 293 (S.D.N.Y. 1986) (dispute between game show formats involving "To Tell the Truth" and proposed new competing show "Bamboozle," with opinion noting that "all payment for the pilot and the series, however, is contingent upon plaintiff's obtaining 'errors and omissions' insurance for each, naming ABC as an insured").

277 See *Sherwood 48 Associates v. Sony Corp. of America*, 213 F. Supp.2d 376 (S.D.N.Y. 2002) (Where Times Square building depicted in "Spider-Man" film without permission as part of digitally altered futuristic Times Square, no trademark or trade dress rights in the building were violated, and photography of building did not constitute trespass, noting "Light beams bounce off plaintiff's three buildings day and night in the city that never sleeps."). See also, *Sherwood 48 Associates v. Sony Corp. of America*, 76 Fed. Appx. 389 (2d Cir. 2003) (Building in Times Square in New York depicted in Spider-Man film sued studio for trade dress infringement, unfair competition, deceptive trade practices, dilution, and trespass claims under New York law. The court affirmed summary judgment for defendant, noting that the mere fact that a building allegedly has "unique configuration and ornamentation" does not entitle the building to trade dress protection.).

278 See *The Rock and Roll Hall of Fame and Museum, Inc. v. Gentile Productions*, 134 F.3d 749 (6th Cir. 1998) (Poster depicting uniquely designed building was not a trademark infringement because the owners of the building had not established actual trademark rights in the building design).

rights, which depend entirely on whether consumers are likely to be confused as to source, affiliation, or endorsement.[279]

The leading deal points in a location agreement include the following:

- <u>Right to Enter</u>: The owner will grant the right to enter the premises on dates and times set forth in detail.

- <u>Authorization to Photograph</u>: The production company is authorized to photograph the production, including bringing to the location personnel and equipment. The production company shall have unlimited rights in the footage created.

- <u>Fee</u>: A daily or lump sum fee will be paid to the premises owner, and there will be reimbursement for all costs associated with use of the premises, including any staff, guards, and utilities used. The fee will include rights for depicting the premises solely in connection the specific scenes filmed there. If, as a result of the location agreement and production on the premises, the premises are repeatedly used in a featured way, for example an establishing shot used in every episode of a television series, the owner may request a premium fee for repeated uses.

- <u>Alterations and Damages</u>: The production company will alter the premises only by prior agreement and be responsible for all costs, including restoring the premises to their original condition, and will be responsible for any damages.

- <u>Name and Likeness</u>: The production company will refrain from using the owner's name, or the name of the property, in any commercial advertising in connection with the film.

- <u>Subject Matter</u>: The production company must fully disclose the nature of the production overall, and the nature of the scenes to be shot at the location, so as to ensure that the location is not used in a way that is scandalous or repugnant, or that will subject the owner or the location to future ridicule.

- <u>Permits and Licenses</u>: Production company shall be responsible for obtaining all required permits and licenses from city and state authorities, including all arrangements for parking of production vehicles and cars.[280]

- <u>Security</u>: Production company will be responsible for engaging adequate security personnel.

---

279   See *New York Racing Ass'n, Inc. v. Perlmutter Publishing, Inc.*, 959 F. Supp. 578 (N.D.N.Y. 1997) (owner of race course possessed no trademark rights in images of race course on defendant's souvenir items, and first amendment protected defendant's use of alleged marks in paintings and t-shirts depicting scenes in which marks actually appeared).

280   See *Klein v. City of Los Angeles*, 2011 Cal. App. Unpub. LEXIS 3685 (Cal. App. May 18, 2011) (dispute involving police officer providing traffic and crowd control at movie and television film locations in Los Angeles, where police department revoked retired officer's work permit).

- <u>Owner's Use of Premises</u>: The agreement will carefully define what specific areas may be used by the production company, and what areas are off limits and reserved to the owner. If the owner continues to live on or near the premises during the location shoot, adequate rights must be reserved to the owner to protect their privacy.

- <u>Insurance</u>: producer shall provide proof of adequate insurance.

[4]— Film Clearances: Titles, Depiction of Third-Party Copyrights and Trademarks

"Clearance" for films involves obtaining licenses from third parties for their intellectual property depicted in a film. It may include clearances for music and/or from individuals who appear in the film. It may also involve clearance of the title of the film with respect to any trademark or other claims, as well as copyrighted works such as background artwork, or for trademarked products that appear in the film. Clearance also can involve "chain of title" issues, especially with older copyrights.[281]

Most parties dealing with the production company will request to be added to the policy as a named insured.[282] With respect to E&O policies that insure against intellectual property infringement claims, the distributor will ask to be a named insured under the policy to eliminate their risk in distributing the film.

[a]—Film Titles

[i]—The MPAA Title Registration Bureau

The Motion Picture Association of America ("MPAA") describes itself as:

"the voice and advocate of the American motion picture, home video and television industries, domestically and, through our subsidiaries and affiliates, internationally. We champion a healthy, thriving film and television industry by engaging in a variety of legislative, policy, education, technology and law enforcement initiatives. These efforts range from safeguarding intellectual property rights to using technology to expand

---

281   See, e.g., *Paramount Pictures Corp. v. International Media Films, Inc.*, 2013 U.S. Dist. LEXIS 92345 (C.D. Cal. June 12, 2013) (dispute over copyright ownership of classic Fellini film "La Dolce Vita"). See also, *Dunlap v. Starz Home Entertainment, LLC*, 2013 Cal. App. Unpub. LEXIS 4101 (Cal. App.2d Dist. June 12, 2013) (affirming breach of contract and fraud claims against purported owner of rights to "The Man From U.N.C.L.E.").

282   See *American Casualty Co. of Reading, Pa. v. General Star Indemnity Co.*, 125 Cal App.4th 1510, 24 Cal. Rptr.3d 34 (2005) (dispute between two insurers of film "The Crow" with respect to liability for on-set injury to crew member, noting that production company was required to carry liability insurance that made production facilities a named insured).

consumer entertainment choices, to championing fair trade agreements and a secure future for artistic freedom of expression."[283]

The MPAA Title Registration Bureau is a voluntary central registration entity for titles of movies intended for American theatrical distribution, and it is intended to prevent public confusion over films with similar titles.[284] In order to register titles, filmmakers must subscribe to the Bureau's registry. There are currently almost 400 subscribers, including all of the major motion picture studios. Subscribers are bound by the Bureau's rules, which prescribe procedures for registering titles and handling any related disputes, including submitting disputes to binding arbitration. Non-subscribers are not bound by the MPAA's TRB.[285]

[ii]—Trademark Protection for Titles

Some titles are purely a matter of artistic expression, and where a single title of a single artistic work functions primarily as no more than a title, without strong consumer impressions that create commercial value in the title itself, First Amendment concerns may prevent a single title being eligible for trademark protection.[286]9 But where titles have established the trademark requirement of

---

283   See www.mpaa.org. The MPAA ratings system for films is also a film industry service of the organization, administered by the Classification and Rating Administration ("CARA"). For complete rules on the MPAA rating process, see http://www.filmratings.com/filmRatings_Cara/#/ratings/rules/.

284   See *Guichard v. Mandalay Pictures, LLC*, 2005 U.S. Dist. LEXIS 45410, 2005 WL 2007883 (N.D. Cal. Aug. 22, 2005) (discussing the MPAA's Title Registration Bureau).

285   See *Tri-Star Pictures, Inc. v. Leisure Time Productions*, B.V., 749 F. Supp. 1243, 1245 (S.D.N.Y. 1990) (dispute over trademark rights with respect to sequel to film "Bridge on the River Kwai," including description of MPAA Title Registration service, stating "when a prospective title for a movie is filed, the MPAA is then charged with the duty of notifying interested members of the MPAA of the prospective title. Under the MPAA's rules, any member of the MPAA with a complaint has seven days to protest the title.").

286   See *Rogers v. Grimaldi*, 875 F.2d 994 (2d Cir. 1989). The Rogers court set forth the "Rogers" test for determining whether a title is infringing, holding that the title in question was not infringing where it was (1) artistically relevant; and (2) did not explicitly mislead. In discussing the "artistic vs. commercial" circumstances under which a title may be eligible for trademark protection, the Rogers court noted:

"The District Court ruled that because of First Amendment concerns, the Lanham Act cannot apply to the title of a motion picture where the title is 'within the realm of artistic expression,' and is not 'primarily intended to serve a commercial purpose.' Use of the title 'Ginger and Fred' did not violate the Act, the Court concluded, because of the undisputed artistic relevance of the title to the content of the film. . . . In effect, the District Court's ruling would create a nearly absolute privilege for movie titles, insulating them from Lanham Act claims as long as the film itself is an artistic work, and the title is relevant to the film's content. We think that approach unduly narrows the scope of the Act.

"Movies, plays, books, and songs are all indisputably works of artistic expression and deserve protection. Nonetheless, they are also sold in the commercial marketplace like other more utilitarian products, making

"secondary meaning" in the mind of consumers, and signify a specific commercial product source, they are eligible for trademark protection.

Where titles of entertainment properties such as motion pictures and television shows are also used for ongoing commercial purposes they may also qualify for trademark or service mark protection as a service mark, for example a title that signifies the commercial source for the ongoing production of television episodes or a series of motion pictures.

Motion picture and television producers use trademark law to enforce their rights in titles. Warner Bros., owners of exclusive rights to make films based on J.R.R. Tolkien's "The Hobbit" and "The Lord of the Rings" books, and owners of trademarks for various uses of the word "Hobbit" in connection with entertainment products, successfully brought an action against a production company that was held to have created a likelihood of confusion by advertising a film entitled "Age of Hobbits" just prior to Warner's release of "The Hobbit."[287]

---

the danger of consumer deception a legitimate concern that warrants some government regulation. Poetic license is not without limits. The purchaser of a book, like the purchaser of a can of peas, has a right not to be misled as to the source of the product. Thus, it is well established that where the title of a movie or a book has acquired secondary meaning—that is, where the title is sufficiently well-known that consumers associate it with a particular author's work—the holder of the rights to that title may prevent the use of the same or confusingly similar titles by other authors. Indeed, it would be ironic if, in the name of the First Amendment, courts did not recognize the right of authors to protect titles of their creative work against infringement by other authors.

"Though First Amendment concerns do not insulate titles of artistic works from all Lanham Act claims, such concerns must nonetheless inform our consideration of the scope of the Act as applied to claims involving such titles. Titles, like the artistic works they identify, are of a hybrid nature, combining artistic expression and commercial promotion. The title of a movie may be both an integral element of the filmmaker's expression as well as a significant means of marketing the film to the public. The artistic and commercial elements of titles are inextricably intertwined. Filmmakers and authors frequently rely on word-play, ambiguity, irony, and allusion in titling their works. Furthermore, their interest in freedom of artistic expression is shared by t heir audience. The subtleties of a title can enrich a reader's or a viewer's understanding of a work. Consumers of artistic works thus have a dual interest: They have an interest in not being misled and they also have an interest in enjoying the results of the author's freedom of expression. For all these reasons, the expressive element of titles requires more protection than the labeling of ordinary commercial products."

Id., 875 F.2d at 998. (Citations omitted.)

287   See *Warner Bros. Entertainment v. The Global Asylum, Inc.*, 2012 U.S. Dist. LEXIS 185695 (C.D. Cal. Dec. 10, 2012). See also, *TriStar Pictures, Inc. v. Unger*, 14 F. Supp.2d 339 (S.D.N.Y. 1998) (unauthorized sequel "Return to the River Kwai" infringed trademark rights in original film "Bridge on the River Kwai").

Owners of service marks for entertainment properties can also find themselves on the receiving end of infringement claims. Fox Television successfully defended a claim that its fantasy police procedural involving supernatural beings, "The Gates," infringed trademark rights in a local television religious program focused on music, "The Gate."[288]

Lionsgate Entertainment, producers of the film "50/50," successfully defended a trademark infringement action brought by a rap duo "Phifty-50," with the court making an easy decision that the phonetically altered rapper's name, despite sounding like "50/50," would not create any consumer confusion with an unrelated film based on the main character surviving cancer.[289]

[b]—Third-Party Copyrights

Experienced film clearance lawyers will scan film sets for anything that might require clearance. If a copyrighted work is depicted in a film, that constitutes reproduction of the work, and reproduction is one of the copyright owner's exclusive rights.[290] Whether a copyrighted work such as an artwork or photograph that is included in a film arises to the level of a copyright infringement is highly fact dependent.

In *Ringgold v. Black Entertainment Television, Inc.*,[291] the producers of a situation comedy filmed an episode that involved the central characters, an African American family, participating in a music recital set in a church. The church set, created by the show's art department, included a published poster of a work by the plaintiff entitled "Church Picnic" hanging on a wall in the background. The poster was shown a total of nine times during the "church concert" sequence, totaling 26.75 seconds. The poster was never discussed or highlighted by the characters in the episode. The show was first televised in 1992, and in 1994, the episode was shown on cable television. In 1995, the plaintiff happened to watch the episode on BET and saw her poster. She sued for copyright infringement.

The defendants asserted that the use in the background was either *de minimis*, or a fair use under copyright law. The Second Circuit determined that with several repeated showings, some of them in relative close up next to an actor, the use was in fact not *de minimis*. The *de minimis* analysis looks to the amount of the copyrighted

---

288 *Scorpiniti v. Fox Television Studios, Inc.*, 2013 U.S. Dist. LEXIS 8758 (N.D. Iowa Jan. 23, 2013).

289 *Eastland Music Group, LLC v. Lionsgate Entertainment, Inc.*, 707 F.3d 869 (7th Cir. 2013).

290 See 17 U.S.C. §106.

291 *Ringgold v. Black Entertainment Television, Inc.*, 126 F.3d 70 (2d Cir. 1997).

work that was copied, as well as the observability of the copyrighted work in the allegedly infringing work. Observability is determined by the length of time the copyrighted work appears in the allegedly infringing work, and its prominence in that work as revealed by the lighting and positioning of the work. With regard to the fair use defense, the court noted that artwork is sold for its decorative value that, when used as part of a television set, did not qualify as a fair use.[292]

In 2008, the Southern District of New York applied the *de minimis* copyright infringement test to a work depicted in the background of a movie set. In *Gottlieb Development, LLC v. Paramount Pictures Corp.*, the manufacturer of a pinball machine sued for copyright and trademark infringement, based on a pinball machine appearing in the background of a set in the film "What Women Want."[293]

In granting defendant's motion to dismiss because the use was *de minimis*, the *Gottlieb* court noted that the "Silver Slugger" pinball machine appeared only sporadically in a scene lasting three and a half minutes, and was always in the background. It was never mentioned and, unlike the poster in *Ringgold* that reinforced the plot, it

---

292   *Id.*, 126 F.3d at 79-80. In support of its analysis, the court stated:

"[I]t must be recognized that visual works are created, in significant part, for their decorative value, and, just as members of the public expect to pay to obtain a painting or a poster to decorate their homes, producers of plays, films, and television programs should generally expect to pay a license fee when they conclude that a particular work of copyrighted art is an appropriate component of the decoration of the set."

However, an entirely different result was reached in *Sandoval v. New Line Cinema Corp.*, 147 F.3d 215 (2d Cir. 1998). The plaintiff was a photographer, and transparencies of ten of his photographic self-portraits were briefly shown in a scene from the movie "Seven," as two characters searched an apartment for evidence. The photos were "briefly visible" in eleven different camera shots. The photographs never appeared in focus, and except for two shots are seen in the distant background, often obstructed from view by the two actors. In one shot, the photos are completely obstructed by a prop. In the district court proceedings, the court held that the use of the photos in the background was a fair use.

On appeal, the Second Circuit noted that where an infringement is arguably *de minimis*, the court should first make that determination before conducting a fair use analysis. The court then proceeded to find the use was *de minimis* as a matter of law, because it was "so trivial as to fall below the quantitative threshold of substantial similarity, which is always a required element of actionable copying." *Id.*, 147 F.3d at 217.

In conducting the above analysis, the *Sandoval* court held that the plaintiff's photographs as used in the movie were not displayed with sufficient detail for the average lay observer to identify even the subject matter of the photographs. The photos were displayed in poor lighting and at great distance, and were out of focus. Unlike *Ringgold*, where the court found that brief but repeated shots of the poster at issue reinforced its prominence, the eleven shots in the Sandoval case had no cumulative effect because the images contained in the photographs were not distinguishable. The court found the uses to be de minimis as a matter of law and not actionable. *Id.*, 147 F.3d at 218.

293   *Gottlieb Development, LLC v. Paramount Pictures Corp.*, 590 F. Supp.2d 625 (S.D.N.Y. 2008).

played no role in the plot. It was almost always partially obscured by the actor and by furniture, and was fully visible for only a few seconds during the entire scene. The court in *Gottlieb* pointed out that in *Ringgold*, there was a "qualitative connection between the poster and the show" entirely missing in the *Gottlieb* case.

In a rare holding granting a preliminary injunction against a major studio, an artist's drawing of a "Neomechanical Tower" was reproduced as a stage set in the film "12 Monkeys," with the court finding that the movie copied the drawing "in striking detail," in a scene that lasted approximately five minutes.[294]

In each of the above cases, the copyrighted works were displayed on a set for significant amounts of time. The differing results arise from the prominence the copyrighted works played in the scene. Thus, the mere presence of a copyrighted work on a film set does not necessarily constitute infringement. "Rights clearance" review is often strongly emphasized, because the goal is to avoid being sued in the first place.

Even where third-party copyrights have been cleared, over-zealous plaintiffs may still bring suit. In *Krupnik v. NBC Universal, Inc.*, a bikini model signed a comprehensive release in connection with photographs she licensed to a stock photography company.[295] When Universal Studios released the film "Couples Retreat," a scene in the film showed the model as part of a brochure that elicited suggestive comments from one of the characters in the film. The studio had paid a $500 fee to license the photo, which appeared on screen for a total of nine seconds. The court held that the model's unlimited release applied to the studio's use and that it included any defamation claims arising from the allegedly "vulgar" scene.

In a notable fair use holding involving Woody Allen's film "Midnight in Paris," the estate of novelist William Faulkner sued the studio over its use of a nine-word quote from the Faulkner novel "Requiem for a Nun": "The past is never dead. It's not even past." In the film, a character makes the following statement: "The past is not dead. Actually, it's not even past. You know who said that? Faulkner, and he was right. I met him too. I ran into him at a dinner party." As the court noted: "At issue in this case is whether a single line from a full-length novel singly paraphrased and attributed to the original author in a full-length Hollywood film can be considered a copyright infringement. In this case, it cannot."[296]

---

294   See *Woods v. Universal City Studios, Inc.*, 920 F. Supp. 62 (S.D.N.Y. 1996).

295   *Krupnik v. NBC Universal, Inc.*, 37 Misc.3d 1219(A), 964 N.Y.S.2d 60 (N.Y. Sup. 2010).

296   See *Faulkner Literary Rights, LLC v. Sony Pictures Classics, Inc.*, 953 F. Supp.2d 701, 704 (N.D. Miss. 2013).

[c]—Third-Party Trademarks

While the mere reproduction of a copyrighted work raises the possibility of infringement, trademarks function differently. The standard for trademark infringement is based on whether or not consumers are confused regarding the source or origin of goods, including matters of endorsement and affiliation. Mere depiction of a trademark is not actionable unless the plaintiff can show that consumers were likely to be confused, or that the use was such that the trademark itself was, in the eyes of the average consumer, maligned and damaged in its value.

In the entertainment industry, "artistic" works may have first amendment protections against trademark claims under freedom of speech principles. In *Rogers v. Grimaldi*, Ginger Rogers (of the Rogers and Astaire famed dance team) sued Italian filmmaker Federico Fellini, alleging that the title of his film "Ginger and Fred" implied that Rogers had endorsed or was affiliated with the film. The Second Circuit held that under first amendment principles, the Lanham Act is inapplicable to "artistic works" as long as the defendant's use of the mark is (1) "artistically relevant" to the work, and (2) not "explicitly misleading" as to the source or content of the work.[297]

In *Rogers*, the threshold for what constitutes "artistic relevance" is purposely low and will be satisfied unless the use "has no artistic relevance to the underlying work whatsoever."[298] A work will be "explicitly misleading" only where the defendant's use of the mark induces members of the public to believe the work was prepared or otherwise authorized by the plaintiff.[299] Only a "particularly compelling" finding of likelihood of confusion can overcome the First Amendment interests. The *Rogers* test has subsequently been applied to all aspects of "artistic" works, not just the title, including depiction of trademarked goods within a film, and to artistic works other than motion pictures.[300]

---

297   See *Rogers v. Grimaldi*, 875 F.2d 994 (2d Cir. 1989) (title of Fellini film "Ginger and Fred" not misleading because it was relevant to Fellini film's artistic statement and did not explicitly assert the film was sponsored or approved by Ginger Rogers and Fred Astaire). See also: *Twin Peaks Productions, Inc. v. Publications International Ltd.*, 996 F.2d 1366 (2d Cir. 1993); *Louis Vuitton Mallatier S.A. v. Warner Bros. Entertainment, Inc.*, 868 F. Supp.2d 172 (S.D.N.Y. 2012) (depiction of knock-off Louis Vuitton luggage in film "The Hangover: Part II" not infringing under Rogers test for works such as films protected by the First Amendment).

298   See *Rogers v. Grimaldi*, id., 875 F.2d at 999. See also, *E.S.S. Entertainment 2000 Inc. v. Rock Star Videos, Inc.*, 547 F.3d 1095, 1100 (9th Cir. 2008) ("the level of relevance merely must be above zero").

299   See *Twin Peaks Productions, Inc. v. Publications International Ltd.*, N. 27 supra, 996 F.2d at 1379.

300   See *Louis Vuitton Mallatier S.A. v. Warner Bros. Entertainment, Inc.*, 868 F. Supp.2d 172 (S.D.N.Y. 2012) (depiction of knock-off Louis Vuitton luggage in film "The Hangover: Part II" not infringing under *Rogers* test for works such as films protected by the First Amendment). See also:

Second Circuit: Twin Peaks Productions, Inc. v. Publications International Ltd., 996 F.2d 1366 (2d Cir. 1993) (book).

Note, however, that the *Rogers* test requires that the defendant not "explicitly mislead" as to the source or content of the work, and not all defendants prevail under the *Rogers* test despite the low threshold for artistic relevance. To determine whether a defendant has explicitly misled, courts apply the relevant "likelihood of confusion" tests for trademarks in their jurisdiction. In a case in the Central District of California pitting Warner Bros. against a studio that released a film using Warner's proprietary "Hobbit" title apparently to take advantage of the timing of Warner's worldwide publicity for all things Hobbit, the Court applied the Ninth Circuit's likelihood of confusion test under *Sleekcraft*, holding that the defendants explicitly mislead by using "Hobbit" in the title of their film.[301]

A case decided prior to *Rogers*, *Dallas Cowboys Cheerleaders, Inc. v. Pussycat Cinema, Ltd.*, did affirm the lower court's injunction against a pornographic film that made unauthorized use of a football team's trademark cheerleader outfits, based on a pre-*Rogers* analysis that emphasized damage to the plaintiff's reputation over First Amendment principles, and subsequent courts have noted that *Rogers* expressly declined to follow the First Amendment approach of that earlier case, which has subsequently been criticized by other courts.[302]

In another case alleging trademark infringement arising from the content of a motion picture, Caterpillar, the manufacturer of bulldozers and other heavy earth-moving equipment, sued Disney over the depiction of its bulldozers in the film "George of the Jungle 2."[303] During three scenes of approximately ten seconds each, the

Fifth Circuit: *Westchester Media v. PRL USA Holdings, Inc.*, 214 F.3d 658 (5th Cir. 2000) (magazine).

Seventh Circuit: *Fortres Grand Corp. v. Warner Bros. Entertainment, Inc.*, 2013 U.S. Dist. LEXIS 70283 (N.D. Ind. May 16, 2013) (fictional software program "clean slate" in film "The Dark Knight Rises" did not infringe trademark of real product with same name); *Dillinger, LLC v. Electronic Arts Inc.*, 2011 U.S. Dist. LEXIS 64006, 101 U.S.P.Q.2d 1612 (S.D. Ind. June 16, 2011) (video games).

Ninth Circuit: *Mattel, Inc. v. Walking Mountain Productions*, 353 F.3d 792 (9th Cir. 2003) (photographs).

301   See *Warner Brothers Entertainment v. The Global Asylum, Inc.*, 2012 U.S. Dist. LEXIS 185695 (C.D. Cal. Dec. 10, 2012).

302   See *Dallas Cowboys Cheerleaders, Inc. v. Pussycat Cinema, Ltd.*, 604 F.2d 200, 205 (2d Cir. 1979) (affirming injunction and finding virtually no artistic relevance in the pornographic film's depiction of the plaintiff's trademark cheerleading uniforms, stating "[p]laintiff expects to establish on trial that the public may associate it with defendants' movie and be confused into believing that plaintiff sponsored the movie, provided some of the actors, licensed defendants to use the uniform, or was in some other way connected with the production. The trademark laws are designed not only to prevent consumer confusion but also to protect the synonymous right of a trademark owner to control his product's reputation"), discussed in *Louis Vuitton Mallatier S.A. v. Warner Bros. Entertainment, Inc.*, 868 F. Supp.2d 172, 181 (S.D.N.Y. June 15, 2012).

303   *Caterpillar Inc. v. The Walt Disney Co.*, 287 F. Supp.2d 913 (C.D. Ill. 2003). In the film, the villain attempts to destroy the hero's jungle habitat by calling in a fleet of bulldozers to flatten everything in sight. The earth-moving

narrator disparagingly refers to the machinery as "deleterious dozers" and "maniacal machines."[304] Caterpillar sued, claiming that Disney infringed its trademarks, engaged in unfair competition, diluted its trademarks, and engaged in deceptive trade practices. Caterpillar claimed that the mere appearance of its products and trademarks was likely to confuse consumers into believing that the film was somehow sponsored by, associated with, or otherwise affiliated with Caterpillar.

In denying Caterpillar's motion for a temporary restraining order on the trademark infringement claim, the court noted that the appearance of products bearing well-known trademarks in cinema and television is a common phenomenon. The court further noted that "trademarks help consumers select goods . . . it appears unlikely to the Court . . . that any consumer would be more likely to buy or watch [the film] because of any mistaken belief that Caterpillar sponsored this movie."[305]

With regard to the trademark dilution claim, the court focused the enquiry on whether the depictions would tarnish the reputation of Caterpillar's business and products—reducing the trademark's reputation and standing in the eyes of consumers.[306] In this context, the court noted that "Caterpillar is perhaps rightfully disturbed to see its products associated with the embodiment of evil that is Lyle, although the Court notes that Lyle's evil is of a spectacularly incompetent sort."[307]

The court did explain why this case was different from cases that did find trademark infringement in fact patterns that involved motion pictures. In *MGM-Pathe Communications Co. v. Pink Panther Patrol*,[308] a gay rights organization used the plaintiff's

---

equipment clearly bore the Caterpillar and "Cat" trademarks. The hero and his simian friends "manage to decommission these bulldozers in several different ways, generally involving instances of combustible ape flatulence and projectile coconuts."

304   *Id.*, 287 F. Supp.2d at 917.

305   The court stated: "For example, action movies frequently feature automobiles in a variety of situations. Is the mere appearance of a Ford Taurus in a garden variety car chase scene is insufficient by itself to constitute unfair competition?" *Id.*, 287 F. Supp.2d at 919-920.

306   *Id.*, 287 F. Supp.2d at 922.

307   *Id.*, 287 F. Supp.2d at 921. However, the court concluded that:

"[t]here is nothing in [the film] to even remotely suggest that Caterpillar products are shoddy or of low quality. As for Caterpillar's argument that the film cast their products in an unwholesome or unsavory light, it noted the overall context: George of the Jungle 2 was a children's comedy that is really a live action cartoon. . . . It is clear to even the most credulous viewer or child that the bulldozers in the movie are operated by humans and are merely inanimate implements of Lyle's environmentally unfriendly schemes."

Id., 287 F. Supp.2d at 922.

308   *MGM-Pathe Communications Co. v. Pink Panther Patrol*, 774 F. Supp. 869 (S.D.N.Y. 1991).

"Pink Panther" mark as a part of its name, a situation where "[f]or obscure groups with no mark on the public consciousness, there is a clear incentive to free ride on the fame of a well-known trademark as a shortcut to raising awareness and publicity for their causes."

In a similar fashion, "the defendant's adoption of the distinctive trade dress of the Dallas Cowboy cheerleaders and the advertising campaign insinuating that the actress in the pornographic film "Debbie does Dallas" was employed by the team was a clear attempt to capitalize on the fame of the Dallas cowboy cheerleaders' trademark to drive the sales and awareness of the movie in *Dallas Cowboys Cheerleaders, Inc. v. Pussycat Cinema, Ltd.*"[309]

[d]—Documentary Films

Documentary films often invoke special rights clearance difficulties, because by their very nature, documentaries capture real experiences on film. As the subjects of a documentary film go about their lives, they, like anyone else in modern society, are subjected to a constant barrage of media: music, images, and trademarks. When proprietary media find their way into a documentary film, the question of whether the producer must clear all those third party rights arises, the same way that the producer of an entirely commercial film would.

The rights-clearance problems inherent in documentary films are compounded by two opposing forces: the sheer amount of third party intellectual property that may be captured, even inadvertently, versus the typically low production budget of such films. In theory, a documentary filmmaker who obtained licenses for all third party works that appear in the film, even fleetingly, would need to devote an enormous percentage of the film's budget to such license fees, if he or she could afford them at all.

[i]—Leading Documentary Film Fair Use Cases

Documentary films by their nature often emphasize the First Amendment principles that lie at the heart of fair use, such as educational and scholarly use of copyrighted materials in historical context and in discussion of historical figures and events, as well as criticism and commentary on matters affecting society as a whole.[310] As noted in one judicial opinion: "[H]istory has its demands. There is a public interest in receiving information concerning the world in which we

---

309   *Dallas Cowboys Cheerleaders, Inc. v. Pussycat Cinema, Ltd.*, 604 F.2d 400 (2d Cir. 1979).

310   See Appendix 1:15[2] for a detailed discussion of fair use..

live."[311] A string of important cases has held such uses to be "transformative use" under the test applied by the Supreme Court in *Campbell v. Acuff-Rose Music, Inc.*[312]

In a trilogy of fair use cases applying the doctrine to documentary films, the widow of horror movie mogul James Nicholson sued three broadcast media companies for copyright infringement, claiming that their television and film biographies and documentaries using clips from her late husband's films without authorization constituted copyright infringement.[313] In all three cases, the court found that the uses constituted a transformative fair use. In *Hofheinz v. AMC Productions, Inc.*, the defendant produced a documentary on the history of Nicholson's studio entitled "It Conquered Hollywood! The Story of American International Pictures."[314] Initially a television production obtained licenses for the clips used, but a later version for theatrical release did not have a license for

---

311   See *Monster Communications, Inc. v. Turner Broadcasting System, Inc.*, 935 F. Supp. 490, 494 (S.D.N.Y. 1996) (fair use for television documentary to use short clips of boxer Muhammed Ali taken from motion picture).

312   See *Campbell v. Acuff-Rose Music, Inc.*, 510 U.S. 569, 114 S.Ct. 1164, 127 L.Ed.2d 500 (1991) (parody lyrics of song "Pretty Woman" a transformative fair use). Under *Campbell*, the key question underpinning the four "fair use factors" in 17 U.S.C. § 107 is whether the copyrighted material is used in the allegedly infringing work for a transformative purpose. The four "fair use" factors are stated in 17 U.S.C. § 107, entitled "Limitations on exclusive rights: Fair use:"

Notwithstanding the provisions of sections 106 and 106A, the fair use of a copyrighted work, including such use by reproduction in copies or phonorecords or by any other means specified by that section, for purposes such as criticism, comment, news reporting, teaching (including multiple copies for classroom use), scholarship, or research, is not an infringement of copyright. In determining whether the use made of a work in any particular case is a fair use the factors to be considered shall include—

(1) the purpose and character of the use, including whether such use is of a commercial nature or is for nonprofit educational purposes;

(2) the nature of the copyrighted work;

(3) the amount and substantiality of the portion used in relation to the copyrighted work as a whole; and

(4) the effect of the use upon the potential market for or value of the copyrighted work.

The fact that a work is unpublished shall not itself bar a finding of fair use if such finding is made upon consideration of all the above factors.

313   See *Hofheinz v. AMC Productions, Inc.*, 147 F. Supp.2d 127 (E.D.N.Y. 2001). Nicholson had been one of the driving forces behind American International Pictures, which from 1954 through 1980 released more than five hundred films that helped establish the "monster" and "teenage" motion picture genres. The titles included "I Was a Teenage Frankenstein," "I Was a Teenage Werewolf," "The Amazing Colossal Man," "The Invasion of the Saucermen," "It Conquered the World," and many others.

314   *Id.*, 147 F. Supp.2d at 129.

certain of the clips. In denying the plaintiff's motion for a preliminary injunction, the court held that the use of the clips was transformative, in part because

"[D]efendants' documentary aims to educate the viewing public of the impact that Arkoff and Nicholson had on the movie industry. The Documentary appears intended to add something of value rather than simply copying the copyrighted expression that it documents. Indeed, it seems likely to stimulate a market for the original rather than replace it."[315]

In *Hofheinz v. A&E Television Networks*, the allegedly infringing work was a biography on the actor Peter Graves, which used short clips from his early appearance in the film "It Conquered the World."[316] In granting summary judgment for the defendant and holding that the uses were a fair use, the court noted that "biographies in general and critical biographies in particular, fit comfortably within [the] statutory guidelines of uses illustrative of uses that can be fair."[317] Moreover,

"[A]ppearing in 'It Conquered The World' was a fact of Graves' life. The 20 seconds of footage shown of that appearance in defendants' biography was not shown to recreate the creative expression reposing in plaintiff's film, it was for the transformative purpose of enabling the viewer to understand the actor's modest beginnings in the film business."[318]

In *Hofheinz v. Discovery Communications, Inc.*, the documentary at issue was titled "100 Years of Horror."[319] In finding fair use, the court noted that "defendant used the clips from "Invasion of the Saucermen" in a documentary-style program that identified the common themes and political contexts of alien visitation films."[320] In describing how the uses in the documentary were transformative and not merely exploitation of the original films, the court noted that the defendant used the clips

"for various purposes, including: (1) to illustrate the theme of the government cover-up; (2) to demonstrate how, and with what special effects technology, aliens have been represented in film; and (3) to provide contrasts

---

315   *Id.*, 147 F. Supp.2d at 137.

316   See *Hofheinz v. A&E Television Networks*, 146 F. Supp.2d 442 (S.D.N.Y. 2001).

317   *Hofheinz*, 146 F. Supp.2d at 446.

318   *Id.*, 146 F. Supp.2d at 446-447.

319   See *Hofheinz v. Discovery Communications, Inc.*, 2001 WL 1111970 (S.D.N.Y. Sept. 20, 2001).

320   *Id.* at *4.

between the early science fiction films like 'Saucermen' and more recent films. The fleeting clips betray little of 'Saucermen's' plot . . . Discovery had no interest in 'Saucermen' in its own right, the story, characters, etc.; its interest was confined to 'Saucermen' as an early example of a common theme in alien visitation films."[321]

Not all published opinions regarding fair use in documentary films result in a holding for the defendant. The Ninth Circuit affirmed the grant of a preliminary injunction against a sixteen-hour documentary about the life of Elvis Presley[322]

---

321   *Id.* The holdings of the *Hofheinz* trilogy of cases were echoed in *Video-Cinema Films, Inc. v. Cable News Network*. See *Video-Cinema Films, Inc. v. Cable News Network, Inc.*, 2001 WL 1518264 (S.D.N.Y. Nov. 28, 2001). The plaintiff owned the copyright in a 1945 World War II movie entitled "G.I. Joe," starring actor Robert Mitchum. When Mitchum died in 1997, several television news organizations, including defendants CNN, ABC News, and CBS News, ran obituaries that included a seventeen-second clip from the film. In ruling that the uses were a transformative fair use, the court pointed out the clips did not supercede "G.I. Joe," the use was for:

> "an entirely new purpose and character than the original film. While Plaintiff's copyrighted work intended to entertain its audience, as well as to inform them of the reality that American infantrymen faced in World War II, Defendants' obituaries aimed to inform the viewing public of Mitchum's death and educate them regarding his impact on the arts. Moreover, defendants' clips were used because of their relevance to Mitchum and not to convey a synopsis of the original film. Just as parody must mimic the original work to make its point, and biographers are permitted to quote their subjects, so too should obituaries about actors be allowed to show reasonable clips of their work."

Id. at *6. In *Lennon v. Premise Media Corp.*, LP, at issue was the use of a fifteen-second clip from John Lennon's song "Imagine" in a documentary about the debate between proponents of intelligent design and the scientific theory of evolution. *Lennon v. Premise Media Corp.*, 556 F. Supp. 2d 310 (S.D.N.Y. 2008). The clip from the song included lyrics that were also shown on-screen, including the line "Nothing to kill or die for/And no religion too." *Id.* at *3. In holding in favor of fair use, the court found the clip to be a transformative examination of John Lennon's views, because the defendants "selected an excerpt containing the ideas they wished to critique, paired the music and lyrics with images that contrast with the song's utopian expression, and placed the excerpt in the context of a debate regarding the role of religion in public life." *Id.* at *8.

322   See *Elvis Presley Enterprises, Inc. v. Passport Video*, 349 F.3d 622 (9th Cir. 2003). The plaintiffs included the copyright owners of television shows of the 1950s in which Elvis appeared, such as the Ed Sullivan Show and the Steve Allen Show. The court noted "some of the clips are played without much interruption, if any. The purpose of showing these clips likely goes beyond merely making a reference for a biography, but instead serves the same intrinsic entertainment value that is protected by Plaintiffs' copyrights." *Id.*, 349 F.3d at 629. In addition, the court stated:

> "[w]e think Passport's use of significant portions of The Steve Allen Show is especially troubling. While showing a clip from these television shows is permissible to note their historical value, Passport crosses the line by making more than mere references to these events and instead shows significant portions of these copyrighted materials."

Id.

The court did not find the uses to be fair, citing as a principal rationale the sheer length of the excerpts used without permission, far beyond what would have been necessary to make a historical point, with one clip playing for over a minute, offering virtually "the heart" of the performance and using the "inherent entertainment value" in a way that was not historical or scholarly, but instead exploited the commercial appeal of the performances.[323]

[ii]—Documentary Filmmakers' Statement of Best Practices in Fair Use

The practical problem for documentary filmmakers is that the distributor that licenses and exhibits their films has no interest in participating in litigation, even where a fair use victory is assured. Thus, like all other film distribution agreements, an agreement for documentary film distribution will include provisions requiring that every instance of third party material in the film has been duly licensed, and requiring that copies of all such licenses be delivered along with the film. In addition, the distributor will require representations and warranties that the film contains no unlicensed material, and an indemnification in the event of any third party claims.

In response to this impasse, documentary filmmakers have attempted to educate rights holders and film distributors regarding copyright law's fair use principles, in an effort to arrive at an acknowledgement that some uses are likely to be regarded by courts as fair use, and do not need to be pre-cleared and licensed. The main effort in this regard is the publication entitled "Documentary Filmmakers' Statement of Best Practices in Fair Use."[324]

In addition to the Statement, a group representing documentary filmmakers, the International Documentary Association ("IDA"), has negotiated a "Fair Use Rider" for Errors and Omissions Insurance with one leading media industry

---

323   *Id.*

324   Published by the Center for Social Media of the School of Communications at American University in Washington, D.C., and available online. See Documentary Filmmakers' Statement of Best Practices in Fair Use, available at http://www.centerforsocialmedia.org/sites/default/files/fair_use_final.pdf. The Statement includes descriptions of documentary film uses that, in view of the authors, courts are likely to consider constituting "fair use," focusing on four types of uses:

- Employing copyrighted material as the object of social, political, or cultural critique;
- Quoting copyrighted works of popular culture to illustrate an argument or point;
- Capturing copyrighted media content in the process of filming something else (for example a radio playing music in the background);
- Using copyrighted material in a historical sequence.

Id.

insurance provider, thus allowing the E&O policy (which is a requirement for distribution agreements) to be issued even in the absence of a license from the third party rights holder. The rider requires that the filmmaker first arrange for an attorney who is on a list of "approved clearance counsel" to submit an opinion letter to the insurer, analyzing the fair use, in order to qualify.[325]

[5]—Product Placement and Brand Integration

[a]—In General

Agencies that specialize in product placement are also part of the entertainment industry landscape. Many manufacturers seek to have their trademarked goods appear in motion pictures to serve as a dramatically integrated advertisement woven into the plot of the film. According to Nielsen Media Research, many television programs include brand integration and product placement an industry that generates millions of dollars annually for production companies.[326] Many manufacturers are happy to pay for such depictions that rise to the level of "brand integration" into the film.[327]

---

325   See "IDA Helps Put Some Fair in Fair Use," available at http://www.documentary.org/magazine/ida-helps-put-some-fair-fair-use.

326   See www.nielsenmedia.com. Similar statistics are not available for the motion picture industry, but press reports of large product placement deals are common.

327   Second Circuit: *American Express Marketing and Development Corp. v. Black Card LLC*, 2011 WL 5825146 at *2 (S.D.N.Y. Nov. 17, 2011) (discussing "active pursuit" of product placement in films for American Express "Centurion" card); *The Gap, Inc. v. G.A.P. Adventures, Inc.*, 2011 WL 2946384 at *1 (S.D.N.Y. June 24, 2011) (in addition to spending tens of millions of dollars on advertising in the United States each year, The Gap "receives unsolicited coverage and product placement on television shows and in motion pictures"); *Montblanc-Simplo GmgH v. Aurora Due* S.R.I., 363 F. Supp.2d 467, 472 (E.D.N.Y. 2005) (luxury pen known as the Meisterstück appeared in "numerous television shows" through product placement).

Eighth Circuit: 3M Co. v. Mohan, 2010 WL 5095676 at *4 (D. Minn. Nov. 24, 2010) (plaintiff's stethoscopes "are frequently seen on television shows and in movies featuring doctors, nurses or hospital settings. 3M has never paid for these product placements; instead, prop masters have requested Littman stethoscopes. For example, many of the actors on the medical drama 'Grey's Anatomy' have a Littmann brand stethoscope engraved with their name. Littmann stethoscopes have also appeared in the television shows 'General Hospital,' 'ER,' 'Chicago Hope,' 'Touched by an Angel,' 'NYPD Blue,' and others. Littman stethoscopes have appeared in the movies 'Multiplicity,' 'Thinner,' 'Mars Attacks,' and others over the years."); *Bebe Stores, Inc. v. The May Department Stores International, Inc.*, 230 F. Supp.2d 980, 983 (E.D. Mo. 2002) ("Bebe's garments have appeared in television shows (and were recently worn and mentioned by a character on the hit show 'The Sopranos'), and various celebrities have worn them and spoken about them. Bebe was also a sponsor of this year's Miss America pageant.").

Ninth Circuit: New Line Productions, Inc. v. Little Caesar Enterprises, Inc., 9 Fed. Appx. 658, 2001 WL 537776 (9th Cir. 2001) (promotional tie-ins and product placement connected with film "Lost in Space"); *Signeo USA, LLC v. Sol Republic, Inc.*, 2012 WL 2050412 at *1 (N.D. Cal. June 6, 2012) (audio headphones marketed via "print, radio, television, and product placement in movies, music videos, and through its well-publicized association with recording

What is generically referred to as "product placement" or a "trade out agreement" consists of two categories:

1. <u>Product placement</u>: the mere depiction of a product in a film, without any guarantee the scene will be included in the final cut, but perhaps with a promise that competing products will not be shown. The agreement may be a short one-page memo, and the compensation may be merely free product.

2. <u>Brand integration</u>: This involves the prominent use by a lead character. It will involve compensation paid by the manufacturer to the film production company, and it will include a marketing or "brand activation" component that uses the film to help sell the product, either via ads for the product mentioning the film or using stills from the film. A company paying a large fee for brand integration might seek assurances regarding the scope of the film's release and the studio's advertising commitment, in order to ensure that the fee paid results in appropriate exposure. The parties may also enter into a confidentiality agreement that forbids disclosure of the fact that payments were made for the brand's feature as a prominent plot device. Filmmakers will not offer a brand a "final cut" guarantee that the product will ultimately appear in the film, but the brand can attempt to ensure the usage by have a representative on the set. In some cases, the brand depiction can still be added in post-production if it is not actually depicted during principal photography.[328]

[b]—Government Regulation

For television productions, Section 317 of the Communications Act of 1934 requires television broadcasters to disclose to their listeners or viewers if any material has been aired in exchange for money, services or other valuable consideration.[329] Section

---

artist Christopher Bridges, aka Ludacris."); *Fiji Water Co., LLC v. Fiji Mineral Water USA, LLC*, 741 F. Supp.2d 1165, 1171 (C.D. Cal. 2010) ("Fiji water was been the subject of articles in major U.S. publications and has been placed on many popular TV shows and in major motion pictures."); *The Aspect Group v. Movietickets.com, Inc.*, 2006 WL 5894608 (C.D. Cal. Jan. 24, 2006) (in dispute between producer of short motion picture theatre "trailers" promoting online ticket service and the ticket service, noting that the parties planned to obtain $500,000 in net revenue from "third party sponsors in exchange for product placement and branding integrated into the [trailers].").

328 By way of example, a famous example of brand integration was the appearance of Reese's Pieces candy as the preferred snack of the alien in "E.T. The Extra-Terrestrial." According to press reports, the makers of M&Ms candy turned down the studio's request. Reese's Pieces, a competitor, said yes. There was reportedly no payment made, but the studio and the candy manufacturer did agree to a "tie-in": Reese's would run $1 million worth ads for the film, including mention of its candy as well; in effect, ads for both the film and the product.

329 47 U.S.C. § 317. The announcement must be aired when the subject matter is broadcast. The Commission has adopted a rule, 47 C.F.R. § 73.1212, which sets forth the broadcasters' responsibilities to make this sponsorship

508 governs disclosure of receipt of any payments to any persons.[330] However, this requirement does not apply to motion pictures broadcast on television, even where the motion picture arguably contains product placements or brand integration.

---

identification.

330   47 U.S.C. § 508:

"(a) Payments to station employees

"Subject to subsection (d) of this section, any employee of a radio station who accepts or agrees to accept from any person (other than such station), or any person (other than such station) who pays or agrees to pay such employee, any money, service or other valuable consideration for the broadcast of any matter over such station shall, in advance of such broadcast, disclose the fact of such acceptance or agreement to such station.

"(b) Production or preparation of programs

"Subject to subsection (d) of this section, any person who, in connection with the production or preparation of any program or program matter which is intended for broadcasting over any radio station, accepts or agrees to accept, or pays or agrees to pay, any money, service or other valuable consideration for the inclusion of any matter as a part of such program or program matter, shall, in advance of such broadcast, disclose the fact of such acceptance or payment or agreement to the payee's employer, or to the person for whom such program or program matter is being produced, or to the licensee of such station over which such program is broadcast.

"(c) Supplying of program or program matter

"Subject to subsection (d) of this section, any person who supplies to any other person any program or program matter which is intended for broadcasting over any radio station shall, in advance of such broadcast, disclose to such other person any information of which he has knowledge, or which has been disclosed to him, as to any money, service or other valuable consideration which any person has paid or accepted, or has agreed to pay or accept, for the inclusion of any matter as a part of such program or program matter.

"(d) Waiver of announcements under section 317(d)

"The provisions of this section requiring the disclosure of information shall not apply in any case where, because of a waiver made by the Commission under section 317(d) of this title, an announcement is not required to be made under section 317 of this title.

"(e) Announcement under section 317 as sufficient disclosure

"The inclusion in the program of the announcement required by section 317 of this title shall constitute the disclosure required by this section.

"(f) 'Service or other valuable consideration' defined

"The term 'service or other valuable consideration' as used in this section shall not include any service or property furnished without charge or at a nominal charge for use on, or in connection with, a broadcast, or for use on a program which is intended for broadcasting over any radio station, unless it is so furnished in consideration for an identification in such broadcast or in such program of any person, product, service, trademark, or brand name beyond an identification which is reasonably related to the use of such service or property in such broadcast or such program.

"(g) Penalties

The Federal Trade Commission ("FTC") is the government agency tasked with protecting consumers from false or misleading advertising. In 2009, it released updated guidelines concerning the use of endorsements and testimonials in advertising.[331] Those guidelines include requirements that celebrities disclose their affiliation with product sponsors in any context in which they discuss or mention the product, including during interviews.[332]

[c]—Depiction of Tobacco Products

As a result of suits filed by the attorneys general of forty states over deceitful tobacco advertising, including advertising aimed at children, the major tobacco companies entered into a Master Settlement Agreement ("MSA") with those states.[333] The terms of the settlement included financial payments to the states, as well as changes in how tobacco products are advertised and promoted.

Under Section III(e) of the MSA, no Participating Manufacturer may make any payment or other consideration to a production company to use, display, make reference to or use as a prop any tobacco product in any motion picture, television show, theatrical production or other live performance, live or recorded performance of music, commercial film or video, or video game. There are a very few and very limited exceptions to this ban on paid product placement for tobacco products in the entertainment industry.

As a result, some productions that depict characters using tobacco have added a disclaimer similar to the following to the end credits of the production: "No person or entity involved in this motion picture accepted anything from any tobacco company or its representatives."

[6]—Film Ratings

The Motion Picture Association of America ("MPAA") is a non-profit organization whose members are the leading film studios. The MPAA ratings system for films is a film industry service of the organization, administered by the Classification and Rating Administration ("CARA"). Ratings act as a guide to parents and the public regarding

---

"Any person who violates any provision of this section shall, for each such violation, be fined not more than $10,000 or imprisoned not more than one year, or both."

331   16 C.F.R. Part 255.

332   *Id.*

333   See Master Settlement Agreement, available at http://oag.ca.gov/tobacco/msa. See also, *Freedom Holdings, Inc. v. Spitzer*, 447 F. Supp.2d 230, 233 (S.D.N.Y. 2004) (describing the MSA).

the type of content the film contains. Prior to release, films may be submitted to CARA for one of the following ratings:

G—General Audiences: No restrictions on admittance

PG—Parental Guidance Suggested: Some material may not be suitable for children under 10

PG-13—Parents Strongly Cautioned: Some material may be inappropriate for children under 13

R—Restricted: Under 17 requires accompanying parent or legal guardian

NC-17—No One 17 and Under Admitted

There is also the unofficial category "Not yet rated" for films that have not yet completed the ratings process.[334]

Distribution agreements may require that the film not have a rating that could adversely affect ticket sales, because the rating a film receives can have a strong impact on its chances of box office success. For example, an "NC-17" or "R" rating means that much of the movie-going public, such as children and families, will not be admitted, drastically affecting potential ticket sales. On the other hand, a "PG" rating for a film intended for savvy teenagers could also adversely affect ticket sales, if the target audience perceives the film as being for "children."

The MPAA's CARA ratings process includes an appeal procedure, and in some cases, production companies have challenged MPAA ratings in the courts.[335] In *Forsyth v. MPAA*, a member of the public attempted to force the MPAA to grant a rating of not less than "R" for films that depicted tobacco use, in order to protect children. The court struck the claims under California's anti-SLAPP statute on First Amendment grounds, noting the connection between freedom of speech in motion pictures and the MPAA ratings of those films:

> "Undoubtedly, movie ratings are made 'in connection with an issue of public interest.' Movies are produced and released for public consumption, and movie ratings speak generally to the content of movies and

---

334   For complete rules on the MPAA rating process, see http://www.filmratings.com/filmRatings_Cara/#/ratings/rules/.

335   See *Maljack v. Motion Picture Ass'n of America*, 52 F.3d 373 (D.C. Cir. 1995); see also, *Miramax v. MPAA*, 148 Misc.2d 1, 560 N.Y.S.2d 730 (1990) (cases under former ratings system that used "X" designation).

their suitability for different audiences. See Time Warner Entertainment Co., L.P. v. FCC, 93 F.3d 957, 982, 320 U.S. App. D.C. 294 (D.C. Cir. 1996) ('[T]here is . . . no doubt that [movie] ratings supply useful and important information to parents, and to their children, about what to expect [in a movie].') Movie ratings are also 'in furtherance of free speech,' because movies themselves are a form of free speech, and the ratings help advance that free speech by giving potential audiences an indication of a movie's content or suitability. See Greater Los Angeles Agency on Deafness, 742 F.3d at 423 (holding that 'CNN's decision to publish and its publication of online news videos without closed captions' was in furtherance of free speech)."[336]

§1.13   Distribution Agreements

Distribution is the financial heart of the film and television industries. No matter how artistically successful a production is, it needs to be distributed through the channels that create revenue. Distribution agreements may encompass all of the distribution "windows."[337] Increasingly, digital technology is changing what types of distribution are available online, with Internet and mobile services making products available across technological platforms, and leading to new types of rights, for example, "stacking" or the ability for consumers to have an entire season of a show available at any time.

Some projects have the distribution rights handled or sub-licensed by the financing studio. Other independent film productions will attempt to place the film with the most advantageous distributor, in consideration for payment of cash advances against future distribution revenues, if possible. In some cases, such pre-sales to a distributor may finance the production, or at least enable the production company to obtain production financing from banks or other lenders based on the distributor's commitment.[338] The name and logo of the distributor are featured prominently in the credits and advertising.

Distribution rights can be divided up in various ways. They can be granted to separate distributors for various territories and countries throughout the world, or they can be granted separately for a sequel as compared to the original film,[339] or can be granted to one studio, while another studio produces the film. In *Twentieth Century Fox Film Corp. v. Warner Bros. En-*

---

336   See *Forsyth v. Motion Picture Ass'n of America*, 2016 U.S. Dist. LEXIS 156719 (N.D. Cal. Nov. 10, 2016).

337   See generally, discussion at § 1.02[2] supra.

338   See discussion at § 1.04[2] supra.

339   See *AGV Productions, Inc. v. Metro-Goldwyn-Mayer Pictures, Inc.*, 115 F. Supp.2d 378 (S.D.N.Y. 2000) (dispute involving distribution rights to the sequels for "The Terminator" motion pictures).

tertainment, Inc., two major studios litigated over distribution rights to the film "The Watchmen."[340] The film's complicated and lengthy development history included a "turnaround" phase in which the original producer took the film from one studio to another in an attempt to revive the project. Fox claimed that as part of its turnaround deal with the producer, Fox retained distribution rights notwithstanding the film's ultimate production by Warner Bros. The court granted summary judgment to Fox, stating that "Fox owns a copyright interest consisting of, at the very least, the right to distribute the 'Watchmen' motion picture."[341]

There are many different types of film distribution companies designed to address various types of markets. In addition to theatrical exhibition and television, there may be for example specialist distributors who handle mostly documentary films, and who may focus their efforts on suitable channels, for example educational use in schools, public broadcasting, and home video.

[1]—Independent Films and the Role of Film Festivals

Independent films produced outside the studio system may rely on exposure via film festivals in order to attract a distributor.[342] There are hundreds of festivals around the world. The leading festivals also serve as important film industry marketplaces, where deals are made for all types of distribution.

A film is submitted to the festival by the production company. The festival selects those films to be shown, and a jury grants awards to the films deemed most outstanding. Major studio productions already assured of distribution may be premiered at some of the leading festivals, but for independent filmmakers, inclusion at a festival where the worldwide film industry has gathered represents an important opportunity to interest a distributor in the film. Ideally, an independent film that generates interest in both the audience and jury at a leading film festival will have several distributors actively bidding on distribution rights during the festival itself.[343]

---

340   See *Twentieth Century Fox Film Corp. v. Warner Bros. Entertainment, Inc.*, 630 F. Supp.2d 1140 (C.D. Cal. 2008).

341   *Id.*, 630 F. Supp.2d at 1144. See also, *Richard Feiner and Co., Inc. v. Paramount Picture Corp.*, 95 A.D.3d 232, 941 N.Y.S.2d 157 (2012) (dismissal of claim that producer retained exclusive television rights in New York City to seventeen films sold to defendant).

342   Other prominent film industry events include the annual American Film Market in Santa Monica, California.

343   See *The Weinstein Company v. Smokewood Entertainment Group, LLC*, 664 F. Supp.2d 332 (S.D.N.Y. 2009). In *The Weinstein Company v. Smokewood Entertainment Group*, that "behind the scenes" bidding process for a "hot" film was the subject of a lawsuit. The case involved the critically acclaimed independent film "Push: Based on the Novel by Sapphire", which was premiered at the 2009 Sundance Film Festival in Park City, Utah, where it won both the prestigious grand jury prize and audience award in the U.S. dramatic competition (only the third film in the history of the festival to do so).

While a theatrical distribution agreement is still much sought after by aspiring film-makers whose work is accepted into the leading film festivals including, The Sundance Film Festival; Tribeca Film Festival; The Toronto International Film Festival; and the Cannes Film Festival; distribution via specialist cable television channels and online distributors such as Netflix and Amazon and iTunes is increasingly the fallback position that at least makes the work available worldwide, though without any substantial financial guarantees.

[2]—Theatrical Distribution

A comprehensive distribution agreement, such as those offered by major studios, will include theatrical distribution with supporting advertising and marketing, and may also cover most if not all of the distribution windows, including home video, pay per view, cable television, and broadcast television. Such comprehensive agreements may or may not include territories outside the United States. For example, a production company may prefer to reserve foreign rights and offer those separately, for example as "pre sales" that help finance a film.[344]

Typical distribution fees are 30% domestic, 35% in Canada and the United Kingdom, and 40% in the rest of the world, though these are always subject to negotiation and can vary. In addition, the distributor will have the right to be reimbursed for expenses including prints, marketing, and advertising.

The leading issues to consider are:

The success of the film led to intense negotiations between the distributor, The Weinstein Company, and the lawyers who represented the production company, beginning shortly after the film's screening at the festival. Several meetings and email exchanges took place, leading Weinstein to believe they were about to sign a written agreement to distribute the film. But by the following week, it was announced that Lions Gate Entertainment Corp., not The Weinstein Company, had acquired distribution rights to the film. Two days later, The Weinstein Company filed suit, alleging that the producers had breached a contract entered into in the prior weeks. The court granted the defendants' motion to dismiss, holding that despite the negotiations and emails, the lack of a signed distribution agreement meant that the plaintiff never acquired the rights they were in the process of negotiating for. In addition, the court found that there was no breach of a binding preliminary commitment to negotiate in good faith, partly because the email exchanges were, in the court's view, "decidedly non-committal." The court also noted that because the agreement was for exclusive rights under copyright to distribute the film, a signed writing was required under Section 204(a) of the Copyright Act. But see *Sisyphus Touring, Inc. v. TMZ Prods.*, 2016 U.S. Dist. LEXIS 130746 (C.D. Cal. Sept. 23, 2016) (email response "I agree" to email copyright assignment offer satisfied Section 204(a) of the Copyright Act).

Id., 664 F. Supp.2d at 348.

344   Sample film distribution agreements are included in the forms accompanying this treatise.

- <u>Grant of Rights</u>: This will include confirmation of the exclusivity of the agreement, including the right to have the film dubbed in foreign languages, to edit the film for various purposes including for television broadcast, and to collect revenues generated by the film.

- <u>Licensed Territory</u>: This will set forth the territories that are exclusive to the distributor. As noted, many producers reserve various territories and sell the distribution rights separately.[345]

- <u>Term</u>: The agreement may include different terms for different territories or media channels.

- <u>Media</u>: This will grant rights in various media, including many of the distribution "windows" such as pay television, on-demand television, free television, home video, etc.

- <u>Acquisition Price</u>: This represents an advance against future revenues paid upon delivery of the film to the distributor.

- <u>Distribution Fees</u>: This sets forth the percentage of gross revenues the distributor will retain for its services.

- <u>Distribution Expenses</u>: This clause will include expenses of making copies of the film, advertising, promotion and publicity costs, taxes, collection costs, etc. This requires careful negotiation, for example a cap on advertising expenses.

- <u>Interest</u>: There may be a requirement for interest payments on the acquisition price/advance.

---

345   Examples of legal disputes involving overseas film distribution include:

Second Circuit: Troma Entertainment, Inc. v. Centennial Pictures, Inc., 729 F.3d 215 (2d Cir. 2013) (on allegations that sales agent fraudulently sold two films to a German distributor without authorization and retained all proceeds, case dismissed on jurisdictional grounds).

Ninth Circuit: LatinAmerican Theatrical Group LLC v. Swen International Holding, 2013 U.S. Dist. LEXIS 110745 (C.D. Cal. Aug. 5, 2013) (dispute over $292,800 minimum guarantee distribution fee for film "13" triggered by failure of film to achieve theatrical release).

State Courts:

California: Toho-Towa Co., Ltd. v. Morgan Creek Productions, Inc., 217 Cal. App.4th 1096, 159 Cal. Rptr.3d 469 (2013) (in dispute over alleged non-payment of $4.5 million in reimbursable distribution expenses to Japanese distributor of film "The Good Shepherd," court granted plaintiff's motion to add defendant's affiliate as judgment debtor); E1 *Films Canada Inc. v. Syndicate Films International*, 2013 Cal. App. Unpub. LEXIS 332 (Cal. App.2d Dist. Jan. 15, 2013) ("Output Agreement" for four films required that produced films would be theatrically released in the United States on at least 500 screens to qualify for Canadian distribution, otherwise distributor would qualify for partial reimbursement of minimum guarantees already paid to producer. Canadian distributor was entitled to reimbursement of $1.39 million when films were released direct to video instead of to wide theatrical release in the United States.).

- <u>Accounting Statements and Audit</u>: Remittance of detailed statements and audit rights.[346]

- <u>Cross-collateralization</u>: All expenses and revenue will be "mixed" among all the relevant territories and media. For example, if pay television produces enormous revenues but theatrical exhibition produces losses, the two categories of revenue will balance each other out.

- <u>Delivery</u>: The delivery requirements such as prints and master copies, and deadlines can be enormously expensive to comply with. If possible there should be a portion of the advance available to fund these costs, and the producer must carefully consult with their suppliers to confirm the costs and feasibility of complying with the requested deadlines. The delivery requirements may also include advertising materials such as trailers, which can be expensive to produce. Delivery may also include chain of title documents, including documentation of all underlying rights, and U.S. copyright registrations for the screenplay and motion picture.

- <u>Security Interest</u>: The distributor will be granted a security interest in the film, such that the distributor would be "first in line" in the event the distributor is owed money from the producer. Such security interests will typically also be filed with the state under the Uniform Commercial Code, and may also be recorded at the Copyright Office as a security interest against the copyright.

- <u>Foreign Language Versions</u>: Where appropriate, the distributor will have the right to create dubbed or subtitled versions of the film.

- <u>Windows</u>: The agreement may have a chart of windows, time frames within which the film will be available for the various steps of distribution windows, including the exact date each window begins and ends.

- <u>Assignment</u>: An exhibit to the agreement may have an assignment agreement, assigning to the distributor exclusive rights under copyright for the term and territory in the agreement. This assignment document can be recorded by the distributor with the U.S. Copyright Office, thereby making the distributor the copyright owner of public record of the exclusive rights conveyed.

- <u>Errors and Omissions Insurance</u>: the producer will be required to maintain E&O insurance during the entire term of distribution, making the distributor a named insured, and providing a certificate of insurance.

---

346   Accounting disputes are common. See, e.g., *Animal Film, LLC v. D.E.J. Productions, Inc.*, 193 Cal. App.4th 466, 123 Cal. Rptr.3d 72 (2011). See also *Napoleon Pictures v. Fox Searchlight Pictures*, 2015 Cal. App. Unpub. LEXIS 2420 (Cal. App. 2 Dist. April 9, 2015) (dispute over home video royalties for "Napoleon Dynamite", including audit matters and dispute over written terms and alleged verbal agreement to the contrary. Referee's judgment for defendant studio affirmed).

- <u>Arbitration</u>: The agreement may include an arbitration provision, and arbitration in film industry disputes is often favored by the party with greater bargaining power, in the hope that the result would be more favorable to them as compared to a jury verdict in civil litigation. In addition to arbitration provisions under the rules of the American Arbitration Association, film industry agreements often prefer to use the arbitration services provided by the American Film Market Association ("AFMA").

[3]—Sales Agency

A sales agency may act as a middleman or broker to promote a film to distributors in various territories of the world, both for theatrical exhibition and television.[347] A motion picture sales agency will attend the leading festivals and markets where representatives of distributors from across the world can learn about the films available, and negotiate agreements for their territories.[348]

A sales agency will not undertake the actual distribution or marketing, but will enter into agreements with third parties to perform those services in each territory. Therefore, a sales agency's commission will be approximately 15% domestic, 20% foreign. In each territory in which the film is licensed, the relevant distributor will remit payments minus distribution fees and expenses.

Sales agency agreements include a chart of license fee minimums in the various major territories in which the film will possibly be licensed, including asking prices, and minimum acceptable amount.[349]

[4]—Overseas Television Distribution of Independent Films

For many independent productions that do not achieve widespread theatrical distribution, there may still be a potentially lucrative market for foreign television rights. There is an appetite for American films on television throughout the world. Usually, a requirement of such agreements is that the film has already been broadcast at least on domestic cable, to establish its credentials as a released (at least on television) and marketable film.

One of the hallmarks of an overseas television distribution agreement is the requirement that the film be dubbed into foreign languages as necessary. Overseas television

---

347   See *Cinezeta Internationale Filmproduktionsgesellschaft MBH & Co. 1 Beteiligungs KG v. Inferno Distribution, LLC*, 2012 WL 255539 (C.D. Cal. Jan. 26, 2012) (dispute over sales agency agreement for film).

348   Where a broader distribution agreement has not been secured, considerable results can be obtained through a sales agent that can still cover much of the word, albeit on a "country by country" basis.

349   See, e.g., *McCombs v. Confidential Report, LLC*, 2013 Cal. App. Unpub. LEXIS 2129, 2013 WL 1208573 (Cal. App.2d Dist. March 26, 2013) (international sales agency dispute with producer).

agreements include a chart of license fee minimums in the various major territories in which the film will possibly be licensed, including asking prices, and minimum acceptable amount.

§1.14   Representation of Talent

Talent agents in the film industry are a major creative and business force. The employment opportunities they obtain can potentially "make or break" an actor's career, at least in the short term.[350] Personal managers play a different role in representing talent. Personal managers primarily advise, counsel, direct, and coordinate the development of the artist's career, advising on both business and personal matters.

As described by the California Supreme Court, the lines between the roles of a talent agent and a manager can become blurred:

> "In Hollywood, talent-the actors, directors, and writers, the Jimmy Stewarts, Frank Capras, and Billy Wilders who enrich our daily cultural lives—is represented by two groups of people: agents and managers. Agents procure roles; they put artists on the screen, on the stage, behind the camera; indeed, by law, only they may do so. Managers coordinate everything else; they counsel and advise, take care of business arrangements, and chart the course of an artist's career. This division largely exists only in theory. The reality is not nearly so neat. The line dividing the functions of agents, who must be licensed, and of managers, who need not be, is often blurred and sometimes crossed. In Hollywood, talent agents act as intermediaries between the buyers and sellers of talent. Generally speaking, an agent's focus is on the deal: on negotiating numerous short-term, project-specific engagements between buyers and sellers. Personal managers primarily advise, counsel, direct, and coordinate the development of the artist's

---

350   See *Main Line Pictures, Inc., v. Basinger*, 1994 WL 814244, at *1 (Cal. App. Sept. 22, 1994), discussed in § 1.07 supra.

In *Grigson v. Creative Artists Agency, LLC*, producers of the film "Return of the Texas Chain Saw Massacre" sued actor Matthew McConaughey and his agency based on allegations that the agency tortuously interfered with the distribution contract for the film by pressuring the distributor to limit release of an allegedly inferior film made before the actor became a star. See *Grigson v. Creative Artists Agency, LLC*, 210 F.3d 524 (5th Cir. 2000) (quoting from the complaint which alleged, among other things, that the distributor, TriStar, "had planned to distribute Chainsaw movie posters prominently featuring the likeness and name of McConaughey and, in fact, had printed posters reflecting this plan. Creative Artists, acting for McConaughey, contacted Columbia Tristar and successfully pressured it to retreat from its plan for the posters on the grounds that McConaughey's fame should not be exploited in such a manner in connection with the Chainsaw movie."). *Id.*, 210 F.3d at 529.

career. They advise in both business and personal matters, frequently lend money to young artists, and serve as spokespersons for the artists.

"Agents sometimes counsel and advise; managers sometimes procure work. Indeed, the occasional procurement of employment opportunities may be standard operating procedure for many managers and an understood goal when not-yet-established talents, lacking access to the few licensed agents in Hollywood, hire managers to promote their careers."[351]

Under Section 1700.4(b) of California's Talent Agencies Act, an "artist" is defined as follows:

"Artists means actors and actresses rendering services on the legitimate stage and in the production of motion pictures, radio artists, musical artists, musical organizations, directors of legitimate stage, motion picture and radio productions, musical directors, writers, cinematographers, composers, lyricists, arrangers, models, and other artists and persons rendering professional services in motion picture, theatrical, radio, television and other entertainment enterprises."[352]

The California Labor Commissioner interprets what constitutes an "artist" as someone rendering professional services that are "creative" in nature. Thus, a producer can be an "artist," and is typically represented by a talent agent, where the producer's services are "artistic or creative in nature, as opposed to services of an exclusively business or managerial nature."[353]

---

351   See *Blanks v. Seyfarth Shaw*, 171 Cal. App.4th 336, 89 Cal. Rptr.3d 710, 726 (2009) (quoting *Marathon v. Blasi*, 42 Cal.4th 974, 70 Cal. Rptr.2d 727, 730, 174 P.3d 741 (2008)).

352   See Calif. Labor Code § 1700.4. See also Nat'l Conf. of Pers. *Managers, Inc. v. Brown*, 2017 U.S. App. LEXIS 7287 (9th Cir. Cal. Apr. 25, 2017) (affirming dismissal of constitutional challenge to Talent Agencies Act).

353   See *James Mark Burnett v. Conrad Riggs*, TAC No. 10192 (Slip Op.), (Cal. Lab. Com'n May 10, 2011) (stating "although Labor Code § 1700.4(b) does not expressly list producers or production companies as a category within the definition of 'artist,' the broadly worded definition includes 'other artists and persons rendering professional services in . . . television and other entertainment enterprises.' Despite this seemingly open ended formulation, we believe the legislature intended to limit the term 'artists' to those individuals who perform creative services in connection with an entertainment enterprise. Without such limitation, virtually every 'person rendering professional services' connected with an entertainment project—including the production company's accountants, lawyers and studio teachers . . . would fall within the definition of 'artists.' We do not believe that the Legislature intended such a radically far reaching result . . . In order to qualify as an 'artist,' there must be some showing that producer's services are artistic or creative in nature, as opposed to services of an exclusively business or managerial nature." *Id.*, at *7, quoting from *American First Run dba American First Run Studios, Max Keller, Micheline Keller v. OMNI Entertainment Group*, A Corporation; Sheryl Hardy, Steven Maier, TAC 32-95.

[1]—Talent Agents

Talent agents procure employment for their clients, and in some states are subject to regulation as an employment agency. For example, the licensure application process for agents under the California Talent Agencies Act requires a written application for a license that includes a background character investigation, if warranted, a license fee, and the posting of a $50,000 surety bond.[354] The proposed agency contracts and fee schedules must be submitted for approval and to ensure the agreement is not "unfair, unjust, and oppressive to the artist."[355] The agreement must also include the following statement:

> "THIS TALENT AGENCY IS LICENSED BY THE LABOR COMMIS-SIONER OF THE STATE OF CALIFORNIA. The form of this contract has been approved by the State Labor Commissioner on the __ day of _____, 20__."[356]

Under the TAA, agency agreements must specify the term or duration, and must contain a provision whereby if the artist does not obtain employment or *bona fide* offers of employment for a period of time in excess of four consecutive months, the agreement may be terminated by either party.[357] The agreement must also refer any controversy between the artist and the agent to the Labor Commissioner. The agent must also file a schedule of fees, and set up a trust fund account for receipt of any monies due to the artist, while maintaining all records pertaining not only to the fund, but also to the agent's general books and records of employment history, all of which are subject to state inspection.

Talent agency advertising is also regulated as to truthfulness, and the agency may not send any artist to any place where "the health, safety, or welfare of the artist could be adversely affected," or send any minor to any saloon or place where liquor is sold or consumed on the premises. Also, no talent agency shall knowingly permit any persons of bad character, prostitutes, gamblers, intoxicated persons, or procurers to frequent, or be employed in, the place of business of the talent agency.[358] Agencies may not charge a registration fee, and if they charge expenses to procure employment, the expenses must be reimbursed if the employment or the employment fee does not materialize.[359] State regulations may limit the percentage fee the agent can charge to 10% or 15%, and in some cases require that the agent's overall agreement and fee schedule be submitted

---

354   Talent Agencies Act (TAA), Cal. Labor Code, §§ 1700 et seq.

355   TAA, Cal. Labor Code, § 1700.23.

356   Title 8. Cal. Code of Regulations, § 12003.1.

357   Title 8. Cal. Code of Regulations, §§ 12001 et seq.

358   TAA, Cal. Labor Code, §§ 1700.32 to 1700.35.

359   TAA, Cal. Labor Code, § 1700.40.

to the state for prior approval.[360] Note that under Section 1700.4(a) the act of procuring recording agreements for musicians is exempt from the TAA, while procuring music publishing agreements is not an exempt activity.

Under California's Advance Fee Talent Services Act ("AFTSA"), agents may not charge advance fees of any kind, may not have any direct relationship with third parties that may offer training, photography, costumes, or other services, and may only be reimbursed for specific expenses on behalf of clients in limited situations.[361]

---

360   Among the state labor and employment statutes relating to agents, New York theatrical employment agencies are governed by the New York General Business Law, §§ 170 et seq., and the New York Arts and Cultural Affairs Statutes, §§ 37.01 to 37.11. See also, *Friedkin v. Harry Walker, Inc.*, 90 Misc.2d 680, 395 N.Y.S.2d 611 (Civ. Ct. N.Y. Cty. 1977) (New York's employment agency laws apply to theatrical agents).

361   See Advance Fee Talent Services Act, Cal. Labor Code §§ 1701 et seq. See also, *Dufour v. Be LLC*, 2010 U.S. Dist. LEXIS 62518, 2010 WL 2560409 (N.D. Cal. June 22, 2010). The AFTSA defines the activities that would constitute an Advance Fee Talent Agency, which is in turn a prohibited entity. Under Section 1701.12 of the AFTSA, the following types of activities and advance fees are prohibited:

"(a) Make, or cause to be made, any false, misleading, or deceptive advertisement or representation concerning the services the artist will receive or the costs the artist will incur.

"(b) Publish or cause to be published any false, fraudulent, or misleading information, representation, notice, or advertisement.

"(c) Give an artist any false information or make any false promise or misrepresentation concerning any engagement or employment, or make any false or misleading verbal or written promise or guarantee of any job or employment to an artist.

"(d) Make any false promise or representation, by choice of name or otherwise, that the advance-fee talent service is a talent agency or will procure or attempt to procure employment or engagements for the artist as an artist.

"(e) Charge or attempt to charge, directly or indirectly, an artist for registering or listing the artist for employment in the entertainment industry or as a customer of the advance-fee talent service.

"(f) Charge or attempt to charge, directly or indirectly, an artist for creating or providing photographs, filmstrips, videotapes, audition tapes, demonstration reels, or other reproductions of the artist, casting or talent brochures, or other promotional materials for the artist.

"(g) Charge or attempt to charge, directly or indirectly, an artist for creating or providing costumes for the artist.

"(h) Charge or attempt to charge, directly or indirectly, an artist for providing lessons, coaching, or similar training for the artist.

"(i) Charge or attempt to charge, directly or indirectly, an artist for providing auditions for the artist.

"(j) Refer an artist to any person who charges the artist a fee for the services described in subdivisions (e) to (i), inclusive, in which the advance-fee talent service has a direct or indirect financial interest.

The basic provisions of an agency agreement will track the relevant state statutes, and in the case of California agencies, the agreement will state on it that it has been approved by the Labor Commissioner. The main agreement points will be:

- Duration of the agreement: often year-to-year with either part able to decline to renew.

- The agent will exclusively represent the artist in the specified territory. The artist may want to reserve the right to use a different agent overseas, for example.

- The scope of the entertainment services and industries covered by the agreement.

- Commissions percentages for various types of engagements, payable only when monies are actually received.

- Provisions clarifying "post-term commissions" whereby commissions may be collected on engagements contracted by the agent, but performed after the termination or expiration of the agreement, as well as any substitutions or replacements of the agreement. Conversely, the talent will seek a "sunset" provision that gradually ends post-term commissions.

- Provisions clarifying cases where a performer's employment agreement may be expanded or renewed or replaced by a new document yet still subject to a commission as a "substitution" agreement.[362]

"(k) Accept any compensation for referring an artist to any person charging the artist a fee for the services described in subdivisions (e) to (i), inclusive."

362   Truly "new deals" would not be subject to a continuing commission. See *William Morris Agency, LLC v. Dan O'Shannon*, TAC No. 06-05, Slip. Op. (Cal. Labor Com'n Sept. 26, 2007) (under Cal. Code of Regulations, Title 8, Section 12002, a talent agency is entitled to receive a commission from an extension or renewals of an agreement it originally procured, and agency agreements typically ensure that any attempt to "replace" or "substitute" the original employment agreement is also commissionable). See also, *The Endeavor Agency, LLC v. Alyssa Milano*, TAC No. 10-05, Slip. Op. (Cal. Labor Com'n Aug. 6, 2007) (where actress fired her agent she was still liable for the agent's post-term commission, noting "Certainly, Milano may terminate a personal services agreement if she feels that her agent is not providing the services contracted for. But she may not unilaterally determine that she has no further obligation to pay for work already performed."). *Id.* at p. 8; *The Stein Agency v. James Tripp Haith*, TAC No. 46-05 (Cal. Labor Com'n Oct. 30, 2006) (awarding post-term commissions to agent); J.K.A. *Talent and Literary Agency, Inc. v. Sheila Rivera*, TAC No. 27-05, Slip. Op. (Cal. Labor Com'n Feb. 28, 2006) (awarding post-term commissions to agent); *Natural Talent, Inc. v. Gavin Dell*, TAC No. 48-02 (Cal. Labor Com'n Aug. 18, 2004) (awarding post-term commissions to agent); *Doug Apatow v. John Tintori*, TAC No. 75-92 (Cal. Labor Com'n Nov. 19, 1993) (awarding post-term commissions to agent).

But see, *William Morris Agency, LLC v. Dan O'Shannon*, TAC 06-05, Slip Op. (Cal. Labor Com'n Sept. 26, 2007) (holding also that deal "improvements" achieved by a later agency were commissionable by that later agency, but only with respect to the increased amount realized. For example, if Agency 2 improved Agency 1's $1 million agreement to $2 million, then Agency 1 would be entitled to continue its post-term commission on the original $1 million amount, while Agency 2 would be entitled to receive its commission based on the additional $1 million "improvement" it negotiated.).

- Expenses provisions clarifying what agency expenses, if any, are reimbursable.

- Termination provisions in the event no work or offers of work are obtained over four consecutive months or other circumstances.

- Talent must approve and sign all agreements.

- Trust fund accounts and statements: where an agent has the right to receive the client's fees; ideally, those funds are segregated and not comingled with monies of other clients.

- A statement that the agent is free to represent other persons.

- Procedures and jurisdiction for disputes, referred to either the appropriate state agency, or pursuant to union mandated arbitration, in which case the Labor Commissioner will reserve the right to attend any arbitration.

[a]—Agency Packaging

In the film industry, talent agencies play an expanded role, including creation of "package" deals where several of the agency's clients, such as a director, screenwriter, and actors, are presented to a studio as one unit for a new project. The agency will be entitled to an additional "packaging fee" above and beyond the commission it earns from the individual clients.[363] Packaging fees paid by the network or studio to the agency are typically on a "3-3-10" percentage basis, as follows: (1) 3% of 100% of the final production budget or cost of production, whichever is greater; (2) 3% of such production budget or cost of production payable out of 50% of 100% of net proceeds (i.e., the network's half of the net proceeds, where the net proceeds are divided equally between the network and the production company); and (3) 10% of the back-end proceeds based on the network's most favorable definition (back end proceeds may include merchandise, foreign licensing of the program, and other ancillary revenues).

[b]—California Labor Commissioner Jurisdiction for Disputes Under the TAA

Disputes between an artist and his or her agency under the Talent Agencies Act fall under the exclusive jurisdiction of the Labor Commissioner.[364] Filing of a petition

---

363   See *Bernal v. Paradigm Talent and Literary Agency*, 788 F. Supp.2d 1043, 1054 (C.D. Cal. 2010) (agency "packaged" the "Desperate Housewives" show because it represented the writer, two lead actors, and the executive producer). See also, *Hyperion Animation Co., Inc. v. Toltec Artists, Inc.* (Cal. Lab. Com. Dec. 27, 1999), TAC No. 7-99, at pp. 16-17 (where packaging agreements are in the nature of an agency being compensated for the "idea or concept" of a project including which talent should participate, and that packaging fees call for direct payments to an agency from a production company for packaging services, thus such payments are separate from the agency's commission on the talent's direct compensation and the Labor Commissioner does not have jurisdiction).

364   See: Cal. Lab. Code §§ 1700 et seq.

must occur within the one-year statute of limitations.[365] In some cases, disputes may come before an arbitrator, via provisions contained within union and guild collective bargaining agreements that are also contained within the artist's agreement with the agency.[366]

[c]—SAG-AFTRA and Agency Agreements

Until 2002, the "Legacy SAG" (before the merger with AFTRA) had agreed with members of the Association of Talent Agencies (ATA) to abide by SAG Rule 16g which put certain restrictions on talent agencies and made numerous suggestions as regards fairness in talent agency agreements with actors. Subsequently, the ATA objected to continuing to abide by SAG's Rule 16g format, and SAG ultimately allowed its Rule 16g agency guidelines to expire with respect to its ability to bind members of the ATA.[367]

Whether talent agencies' packaging fees and role as a producer in some cases (several large agencies also own production companies) constitute a conflict of interest for the talent represented by those same agencies is the subject of ongoing litigation between the WGA and several large agencies.

[d]—New York Regulation of Talent Agents

New York General Business Law § 171(8) defines a "theatrical employment agency" that must be licensed under General Business Law § 172, as follows:

---

365 See *Blanks v. Seyfarth Shaw*, 171 Cal. App.4th 336, 89 Cal. Rptr.3d 710 (2009) (celebrity client allegations that law firm did not file petition with Labor Commissioner within one year statute of limitations). For a different example of a dispute between talent and their attorney, see *Solis v. Blancarte* (Cal. Lab. Com. Sept. 30, 2013), TAC No. 27089 (lawyer who negotiated agreements or television reporter under 5% commission agreement was acting as unlicensed agent under TAA).

366 See *Grammer v. The Artists Agency*, 2000 U.S. Dist. LEXIS 20462 (C.D. Cal. Nov. 6, 2000) (dispute between actor and agency in which court confirmed arbitrator's award of over $2 million to agency, based on entitlement to agency commission on actor's 5% of the adjusted gross receipts derived from television series "Frasier"). See also, *Matthau v. Superior Court*, 151 Cal. App.4th 593, 60 Cal. Rptr.3d 93 (2007) (dispute between heirs of actor Walter Matthau and The William Morris Agency regarding whether agency commission was payable by heirs on income received after actor's death).

367 For a history of Legacy SAG Rule 16g, see *Lenhoff Enters. V. United Talent Agency, Inc.*, 2016 U.S. Dist. LEXIS (C.D. Cal. April 20, 2016) (dismissing anti trust suit by small talent agency against the "Big 4" agencies, alleging inter alia that the large agencies conspired to not renew the ATA/SAG Rule 16g thereby easing restrictions on talent agencies). See also, "Member Update on Talent Agents" https://www.sagaftra.org/member-update-talent-agents.

8. "Theatrical employment agency" means any person (as defined in subdivision seven of this section) who procures or attempts to procure employment or engagements for an artist, but such term does not include the business of managing entertainments, exhibitions or performances, or the artists or attractions constituting the same, where such business only incidentally involves the seeking of employment therefor."[368]

The definition contains the "manager exception" where the person or company either solely manages, or where seeking employment is only incidental to the management activities. Accordingly, under New York law there is a similar cause of action as compared to California, where talent may accuse their manager of procuring employment without a license in violation of General Business Law section 172.[369]

New York's General Business Law section 181 also requires that every licensed agency give each client a copy of the agency contract.[370]

[2]—Personal Managers

Talent agents solicit and procure employment on behalf of their clients. Managers advise their clients on how to develop and grow all aspects of their talent and careers, including which specific engagements, as offered via talent agents, to accept.

The rights and duties of managers are a matter of contractual agreements between managers and their clients. Managers perform broad advisory functions, for which they receive a percentage of the client's overall income, typically 10% to 15%.

In California, the TAA is a powerful statutory protection, and sometimes a sword, for clients who can allege a violation of the Act by their agent or manager by filing a petition

---

368   N.Y. Gen. Bus. L. § 171(8).

369   See *Washington v. Excobar*, 2009 NY Slip Op 32008(U), No. 103027/09 (Supreme Ct, N.Y. Cty Aug. 28, 2009) (holding that manager did not act as an employment agency and did not need to be licensed, and noting that the agreement between talent and manager stated "Artist acknowledges that Manager is not an employment agency, theatrical agent, or licensed artist's manager. In this connection, Manager has not promised to procure employment or engagements for Artist, and shall not be obligated to do so hereunder"). *Id.*, at 6. See also, *Karaszek v. Blonsky*, 2008 N.Y. Misc. LEXIS 9460 (N.Y. Sup. Ct. 2008) (Sup. Ct. N.Y. May 30, 2008) (dispute between unlicensed personal manager and minor who appeared in musical "Hairspray").

370   See *William Morris Endeavor Entertainment, LLC v. Geraldo Rivera*, 2014 NY Slip Op 50458(U), No. 653301/2013 (Sup. Ct. New York Cty. March 26, 2014) (holding that agency did not have an enforceable contract with television host).

with the Division of Labor Standards Enforcement. Such petitions are adjudicated and ruled on by the Labor Commissioner in the form of a Determination of Controversy.[371]

The Labor Commissioner has the power to declare agreements between talent and agents or managers void *ab initio* in their entirety, or under the doctrine of severability, void as to the specific illegal acts complained of.[372] The Commissioner can also require disgorgement of commissions earned in violation of the TAA during the one-year statute of limitations prior to filing of the petition. Appeal can be taken from a Determination of Controversy to the state superior court for trial *de novo*, with subsequent rights of appeal up to the state supreme court.[373]

Managers can receive a percentage based commission fee based on virtually all of a client's gross income. This fee is not subject to statutory percentage limitations. Therefore, managers will generally avoid becoming licensed talent agents and subject themselves to the limitations on earnings and regulatory requirements that apply to agents. Managers can also more freely take an ownership interest in or act as producers for businesses that hire their clients, because in so doing, they are not "procuring" employment. Instead, they are directly providing employment without acting as an intermediary agent.[374]

---

371   See *Styne v. Stevens* 26 Cal.4th 42, 109 Cal. Rptr.2d 14, 26 P.3d 343 (2001) (when the Talent Agencies Act is invoked in the course of a contract dispute, the Labor Commissioner has exclusive jurisdiction to determine his jurisdiction over the matter, including whether the contract involved the services of a talent agency as defined in the TAA).

372   See *Marathon Entertainment, Inc. v. Rosa Blasi*, 42 Cal.4th 974, 743, 70 Cal. Rptr.3d 727, 174 P.3d 741 (2008) (the Talent Agencies Act applied to an unlicensed personal manager who performed the duties of a talent agent, and that the doctrine of severance applied to contracts partially illegal under the TAA).

373   See TAA, Cal. Labor Code § 1700.44(a); see also, *Buchwald v. Katz*, 8 Cal.3d 493, 500-501, 503 P.2d 1376, 105 Cal. Rptr. 568 (1972). Because of the thorough nature of the TAA, and the body of judicial rulings related to the TAA, most of the comments here will be with reference to California's TAA. But a practitioner in a given state should check the regulations that apply in that jurisdiction.

374   See *Chinn v. Tobin*, Cal. Lab. Comm'r Case No. TAC 17-96 at *7 (March 26, 1997) (Slip Op.) (The TAA deals with the role an agent plays when acting as an intermediary between the artist and the employer. Managers who have a role in an entity that employs an artist are not acting as an agent/intermediary. The court also stated "[concluding otherwise] would mean that every television or film production company that directly hires an actor would itself need to be licensed."). Note however, that the TAA has "safe harbor" carve-outs that acknowledge some of the special roles managers play in the music industry. See Ch. 4 infra for an in-depth discussion of music managers. Procurement of recording and publishing agreements by managers, for example, is not a violation of the TAA, nor is a situation where a manager, working together with a licensed agent, negotiates agreements for employment. Recording contracts are exempted under Cal. Labor Code § 1700.4. Music publishing contracts have been held by the Labor Commissioner as not constituting "employment" under the TAA, because licensing of an artist's musical compositions does not involve the artist undertaking an affirmative duty to render present or future services. See *Kilcher v. Vainshtein*, 2001 WL 35678880 (Cal. Lab. Com., May 30, 2001), Slip Op. at 22-23. See also, Talent Agencies Act, Cal. Labor Code § 1700.44.

In California, enforcement is predicated on an artist filing a petition with the Department of Industrial Relations Division of Labor Standards Enforcement *within one year*.[375]

As a result of such complaints by artists against the manager, the manager may find that their client has successfully had the entire agreement between the client and the manager declared void *ab initio*, and the manager may also be subject to disgorgement of commissions earned by the manager during the one-year period prior to the petition.[376] Given that management agreements may require fees to continue long after the agreement ends, voiding of a contract by the Labor Commissioner would also cut off the manager's future income.

Under rulings by the California Supreme Court however, the doctrine of severability may be applied by the Labor Commissioner, who may now declare void only the specific portions of a management agreement that violate the TAA, leaving the rest of the agreement in place and valid.[377]

The Labor Commissioner's power to sever selected portions of a challenged agreement also extends to changing commission percentages. In *Sebert v. Das Communications, Ltd.*, the singer known as "KE$HA" brought an action against her Personal Manager under the Talent Agencies Act.[378]2 FN The Labor Commissioner determined that the manager

---

375   See Lab. Code, § 1700.44, subd. (c). See also, *Blanks v. Seyfarth Shaw*, 171 Cal. App.4th 336, 89 Cal. Rptr.3d 710 (2009) (celebrity client allegations that law firm did not file petition with Labor Commissioner within one year statute of limitations).

376   Note, however, the decision in *Kilcher v. Vainshtein*, N. 18 supra. Although the court declared the management agreement void ab initio, the court noted that the manager had in fact helped Jewel's career reach considerable heights in other respects, therefore the Labor Commissioner declined to order any disgorgement of the manager's commissions for the year prior to the Petition.

377   *Marathon v. Blasi*, 42 Cal.4th 974, 70 Cal. Rptr.3d 727, 174 P.3d 741 (2008). The Court in *Marathon v. Blasi* also called for the legislature to consider revisiting the TAA, noting that although the TAA was "adopted with the best of intentions, the Act and guild regulations aimed at protecting artists evidently have resulted in a limited pool of licensed talent agencies and, in combination with high demand for talent agency services, created the right conditions for a black market for unlicensed talent agency services." *Id.*, 70 Cal. Rptr.3d at 756.

For a summary of agreement deal points in management agreements, please see the discussion in Chapter 4 on the Music Industry.

378   See *Sebert, p/k/a KE$HA v. Das Communications, Ltd.*, Cal. Lab. Comm'r Case No. TAC 19800 (2012). The services performed by several staff at the management company that the Labor Commissioner deemed of great help to the singer's career, and which were adjudged as legal management services that did not procure employment, were described as follows:

"The evidence establishes that McAvenna provided Sebert with an extensive range of strictly managerial services that were quite beneficial. She connected Sebert with writers and producers so she could co-write songs, produce recordings, and build up her catalogue. She sought to further Sebert's career by regularly in-

performed very helpful, and legal, services 55% of the time and illegal services (procuring employment) 45% of the time. The ruling was that the illegal portions of the agreement (procuring employment) were severed and nullified, leaving the legal portions, the management services, intact. However, the ruling determined that the commission for the remaining legal management services performed in the past would be 11%, not 20% (based on the legal services being 55% of the overall agreement). Presumably, after the litigation, the parties may indeed have parted ways with respect to any continuing future relationship.

Reported cases involving disputes between talent and their personal manager demonstrate a variety of business and commission arrangements. In *Howard Entertainment, Inc. v. Kudrow*, the actress and star of the long-running television sitcom "Friends," Lisa Kudrow, entered into an oral agreement with her personal manager, under which his commission on her income was originally 10%, then later lowered to 5%.[379] Kudrow's income from "Friends" in its final 2004 season reached $1 million per episode and 1.25% of "back end" revenues. In 2007 Kudrow terminated the manager and stopped paying the commission. The manager subsequently sued Kudrow, alleging that the commissions should continue in perpetuity. In holding for the manager on appeal over whether testimony regarding post-termination commissions would be admissible, the court relied on expert testimony that post-termination commissions are standard in the entertainment industry. Notably, there were no allegations in the case that the personal manager procured employment in violation of the Talent Agencies Act, thus the jurisdiction of the California Labor Commissioner was never invoked.[380]

---

troducing her to influential people in the music industry. She encouraged Sebert to explore various musical ideas and concepts, and provided feedback and direction on the material she developed. She provided advice on Sebert's appearance, attire, fashion, and health, and arranged for a stylist and fitness instructor. In addition, she provided Sebert with personal advice, guided her on establishing her presence on the web, and brought her into contact with visual artists and photographers.

"The evidence establishes that Sonenberg also provided Sebert with many strictly managerial services. He set up meetings and contacts with record companies with an eye toward obtaining a recording contract for Sebert. He assisted Sebert in selecting songs, and regularly provided evaluation and feedback on the songs and arrangements that she created. He assisted Sebert in her difficult dealings with her prior manager, and provided advice on her health, fitness, and attire. Sonenberg maintained regular contact with McAvenna to keep abreast of the day to day activities affecting Sebert and to provide overall guidance and direction to [the management company's] efforts on Sebert's behalf."

Id. at 15.

379   *Howard Entertainment, Inc. v. Kudrow*, 208 Cal. App.4th 1102, 146 Cal. Rptr.3d 154 (2012).

380   *Id.* Note the holding addressed allowing testimony on post-term commissions, but did not specifically rule on whether a right to perpetual post-term commissions should have to be reduced to a writing in order to be enforceable.

A similar holding in the Southern District of New York, in the classical music industry, was reached in *Columbia Artists Management, LLC v. Alvarez*, holding that even under an oral agreement, a group of opera singers owed a commission to their former management company for performances arising from engagements obtained prior to the artists and their manager parting ways. [381] In sharp contrast to California's Talent Agencies Act, which prohibits unlicensed managers from acting as agents by procuring employment in the form of musical engagements, the New York court noted, but did not comment on, the fact that the management company was not licensed with the State of New York. [382]

A similar result occurred in *Columbia Artists Management, LLC v. Swenson & Burnakus, Inc.*, where the opera singer Ruth Ann Swenson paid her manager 10% from opera performances and 20% from concert performances. Upon Swenson's terminating the manager and refusing to pay any future commission, the manager sued and was awarded post-termination commissions, notwithstanding the manager's unlicensed status. [383] In stark contrast to the provisions of California's Talent Agencies Act, the New York court found that "[p]laintiff's lack of a license did not render the contract unenforceable." [384]

Under California's Talent Agencies Act, "procurement" of employment is defined broadly and includes negotiation of employment agreements. [385] In *Solis v. Blancarte*, a television newscaster successfully brought an action against his attorney, who agreed to act as both attorney and representative, and proceeded to negotiate television employment agreements in exchange for 5% of the client's revenue from those agreements. By negotiating the agreement without a talent agent participating as well, a common practice in the entertainment industry (especially in the common scenario where a fledgling artist does not yet have a talent agent), the Labor Commissioner found, in a controversial decision, that the attorney violated the TAA. Had the attorney been part

---

381   *Columbia Artists Management, LLC v. Alvarez*, 2011 U.S. Dist. LEXIS 22509, 2011 WL 781179 (S.D.N.Y. March 3, 2011).

382   Id., 2011 WL 78119 at *2.

383   *Columbia Artists Management, LLC v. Swenson & Burnakus, Inc.*, 2010 U.S. Dist. LEXIS 32879 (S.D.N.Y. March 3, 2010).

384   Id., 2010 U.S. Dist. LEXIS 32879 at *2.

385   See *Solis v. Blancarte*, Cal. Lab. Comm'r Case No. TAC 27089 (2013), stating:

"The Labor Commissioner has long held that 'procurement' includes the process of negotiating an agreement for an artist's services. Significantly, the Talent Agencies Act specifically provides that an unlicensed person may nevertheless participate in negotiating an employment contract for an artist, provided that he or she does so in conjunction with or at the request of a licensed talent agent. Labor Code § 1700.44(d). This limited exception to the licensing requirement would be unnecessary if negotiating an employment contract for an artist did not require a license in the first place."

Id. at pp. 6-7.

of the artist's "team," including a licensed talent agent under the TAA, there would have presumably been no violation.

Solis v. Blancarte is controversial, but it is also clearly limited to its facts, which included a finding "according to the petitioner" that "in addition" to providing legal services, the attorney agreed to provide "management type" services, specifically, to look for opportunities for work as a television broadcaster.[386] Thus the case, according to its findings of fact, is based on a dual role of one individual providing both attorney services and management services, and its applicability to a pure attorney-client relationship is a question not clearly decided.

Managers may position themselves as producers of their client's projects, thereby potentially achieving producer fees and equity in projects that employ their clients, a potential conflict. In such cases the talent should be aware of the financial details, including assurances that no part of any compensation paid to a manager by a production company under the title "Producer" is taken from compensation otherwise due talent. Talent may insist that where a manager is employed as a producer, the talent's compensation on the same project not be commissioned by the manager, to avoid so-called "double dipping."[387]

[a]— Personal Management Agreement Deal Points

Unlike agency agreements in California, which are regulated under the Talent Agencies Act and must be approved by the Labor Commissioner, management agreements in all states are entirely unregulated. Although management agreements may have a recital of the manager's services in the nature of "advice and counsel in the entertainment industry," and may even have a disclaimer that the manager is not a licensed talent agent and is not acting as one, such agreements generally have very similar provisions as compared to an agency agreement, as follows.

---

386   Id., at p. 2.

387   See, e.g. *Thomas Gibson v. Frontline Entertainment Management, Inc.*, Case No. TAC 36861 (Ca. Lab. Comm Mar. 23, 2017) (describing the evolution of an actor's agent from agent, to manager, to producer as follows "When "Dharma & Greg" ended, Mr. Dorfman and Mr. Gibson agreed Mr. Dorfman would be Mr. Gibson's manager (and no longer his agent) and would help him produce his own television series. If this venture succeeded, Mr. Dorfman would be a producer and be paid in that capacity. As Mr. Gibson's manager, Mr. Dorfman, pursuant to an oral agreement, would be paid a 10% commission (with the definition of what was "commissionable" being defined by a Screen Actors Guild-approved talent agency contract) and Mr. Gibson would hire another person as his agent." Id. at 4-5. See also Moodform Mission v Campbell, 2011 N.Y. Misc. LEXIS 3197, 2011 NY Slip Op 31787(U) (N.Y. Sup. Ct. June 29, 2011) (dispute between model and her agency regarding agency's alleged "double dipping" in project involving development of perfume fragrance products and allegedly excessive commissions. Model's claims included breach of fiduciary duty and fraud).

Services to Be Performed by the Manager: This may be a list of general services in the nature of advising on the entertainment industry and related publicity and career matters, and using the manager's network to further the talent's career. To the extent the parties have discussed any specific services, such as representation at specific events or inclusion of the talent's name in advertising and on websites, or regular e-mail or telephone communications, reports, and updates, those specifics should be included. Personal managers, especially those active in California and aware of the Talent Agencies Act, will typically not make any specific mention of obtaining employment for the talent and/or will include a disclaimer that they do not obtain employment and are not licensed agents, although such disclaimers will not protect managers who actually procure employment for their clients.

Term of the Agreement: Given that personal managers do not typically guarantee results or propose concrete career benchmarks in written agreements, the artist may not want to be legally bound for more than one year at a time, in the event the manager's services prove to be lacking. Conversely, a dedicated manager may need considerable time to help establish a career and leverage the artist's network toward ambitious goals. A good compromise is a one-year term that automatically renews unless either party gives notice in advance that he or she will not renew. The period of required notice would be reasonable at thirty days, but people often forget to calendar such things, so if possible, the agreement should only be renewable if both parties agree to do so in writing.

Scope and Geography of Career Areas: Talent with interests in different entertainment industry areas, for example broadcasting on the one hand, and fashion on the other, may feel they are best served by more than one manager who has expertise in each area. Managers, however, prefer to have the talent be exclusively contracted to them so as not to miss out on commissions in one area that may have arisen via the manager's efforts in a different field of endeavor. The same calculus applies to geography since the talent's needs may be different in Japan as compared to the United States.

Commission: Unlike licensed agents who typically receive a 10% commission, managers (who are not restricted by state approval of their agreements) often seek a 15% to 20% commission on gross earnings from all sources. Where the talent also has an agent, the manager may agree to lower his or her commission further in acknowledgment of the "double commission" paid by the talent. In some cases where the talent has a lucrative career, managers reportedly accept commissions as low as 5%. To the extent the talent cannot find an agent, and the manager is his or her only option, talent who is new to the industry has been known to accept commission rates of 20% or more on the premise that a manager who brings in revenue has earned the commission (and only gets paid if in fact revenue is received).

Post-Term Commissions: Managers will demand that their commission continues for the life of any revenues that originate during the Term, including any extensions or substitutions. Agreements will typically state that with respect to any "negotiations" begun before the expiration of the term, the managers are entitled to a full commission, as well as for any post-term agreements entered into by talent within six months of the end of the term, provided the manager had "approached" the other party during the term. It is in the talent's best interest to carefully define "negotiations" or "approached" to be actual deal point and term sheet written negotiations, something more concrete than a claim that a phone call was made, or an e-mail blast went out, and polite but noncommittal interest was expressed. Talent should always propose a "sunset" provision for post-term commissions, for example, a commission that over three years post-term diminishes from 15%, to 10%, to 5%, to zero. Sunset provisions are a matter of negotiation "power"; in the vast majority of cases, managers will strongly resist such clauses as deal breakers.

Approval: Talent should have the full and final approval, and signature power, over any agreements entered into. The manager may ask for a power of attorney to sign documents on behalf of the talent, which in some situations would expedite business dealings, but which is ultimately a matter of trust as to whether talent should grant that power to the manager and risk being bound by an agreement signed by the manager.

Expenses: There should be clarity as regards whether the manager may be reimbursed for any expenses and under what circumstances. Some agreements may state that the talent must pay a share of the manager's promotional and/or travel expenses along with other clients. Others will state that the manager may be automatically reimbursed for minor expenses (such as taxis, FedEx), but must seek approval for any expenses over $50.

Handling of Funds: The manager may ask that all funds payable to the talent during the term be paid to the manager (via provisions in any employment agreements), whereupon the manager will deduct his or her commission and any approved expenses before forwarding the balance to the client on an expedited basis, within three to five business days. Other agreements allow the client to receive all funds, subject to the client's obligation to remit the commission fee to the manager. Should the client agree to the manager controlling the incoming funds, the client may demand that the manager establish a separate bank account in trust for the client, so that the client's funds are not comingled with the general funds of the manager's business and/or those of other clients. Where the talent has a separate business manager, the personal manager may be more agreeable to the funds being sent to the business manager for disbursement.

<u>Planning and Communications</u>: Although few management agreements specify planning, communications, and reporting, talent may seek to arrange for at least an annual or semi-annual planning meeting with written minutes or notes, and monthly or bi-weekly regular telephone or e-mail updates and reports on progress on the plans for his or her career and the steps taken to achieve the agreed-upon goals. Any agreement to foster regular communications and clear goals benefits both parties.

<u>Dispute Resolution</u>: Both parties should have the opportunity to put any alleged breaches into writing, and give the other party a reasonable time to cure the alleged breach before any further action is taken. Further action may consist of an agreement to mediate via a mutually agreed-upon neutral party, or to enter into binding arbitration under the rules of the American Arbitration Association or JAMS, or to resort to the court system. Whatever choices are considered should provide for maximum possibility of a quick and inexpensive resolution. Note that where the dispute invokes the provisions of the California Talent Agencies Act because it is related to securing employment, unlicensed personal managers will not be able to avoid the jurisdiction of the Labor Commissioner.[388]

---

388   See Cal. Civ. Code § 1700.45, entitled "Contract provision for arbitration; Provisions prerequisite to validity," which only recognizes arbitration provisions that are included in authorized licensed agency agreements and that give the Labor Commissioner the opportunity to attend all hearings:

"Notwithstanding Section 1700.44, a provision in a contract providing for the decision by arbitration of any controversy under the contract or as to its existence, validity, construction, performance, nonperformance, breach, operation, continuance, or termination, shall be valid:

"(a) If the provision is contained in a contract between a talent agency and a person for whom the talent agency under the contract undertakes to endeavor to secure employment, or

"(b) If the provision is inserted in the contract pursuant to any rule, regulation, or contract of a bona fide labor union regulating the relations of its members to a talent agency, and

"(c) If the contract provides for reasonable notice to the Labor Commissioner of the time and place of all arbitration hearings, and

"(d) If the contract provides that the Labor Commissioner or his or her authorized representative has the right to attend all arbitration hearings.

"Except as otherwise provided in this section, any arbitration shall be governed by the provisions of Title 9 (commencing with Section 1280) of Part 3 of the Code of Civil Procedure.

"If there is an arbitration provision in a contract, the contract need not provide that the talent agency agrees to refer any controversy between the applicant and the talent agency regarding the terms of the contract to the Labor Commissioner for adjustment, and Section 1700.44 shall not apply to controversies pertaining to the contract.

[b]—The SAG-AFTRA Personal Manager Code of Ethics and Conduct

Although personal managers are unregulated by any state, SAG-AFTRA has drafted a Personal Manager Code of Ethics and Conduct. Those managers who agree to be bound by its provisions can be listed on SAG-AFTRA's list of approved personal managers.[389]

SAG-AFTRA also publishes a "top ten" list of things to look out for in personal manager agreements, reproduced below:

"1: <u>Listed with SAG-AFTRA</u>: Wherever possible, you should enter into personal management relationships with professional and ethical representatives that are vetted by your union. Always ask your personal manager, 'Are you listed with SAG-AFTRA? If not, why [not]?' Listen very carefully to the answer. Remember, you are on your own if you enter into a personal management contract with an entity that is not listed with the union. All the information your manager will need to list with SAG-AFTRA can be found on the SAG-AFTRA website at sagaftra. org/managers. Your first stop for information should be your union's website. We are here to protect you. Questions? Call the SAG-AFTRA Professional Representatives Department directly at (323) 549-6745 in Los Angeles or (212) 863-4305 in New York.

"2: <u>Payment Timeline</u>: If your personal manager is going to be collecting and distributing your compensation, make sure the contract reflects that when your money is received by the personal manager, it will be held in a non-interest-bearing trust account separate from the manager's business operating account and that you establish a timeline for payment—both from you to the personal manager and from the personal manager to you. For your reference, SAG-AFTRA franchised agents must distribute checks to performers within a three-, five- or seven-day period, depending on the circumstances. Whenever possible, build these requirements into your personal management contract.

"3: <u>No Advance Fees</u>: No personal management contract should expect or require advance fees for any service. The personal manager should get paid when you are, just like an agent.

"4: <u>No Third Parties</u>: Ensure that your personal management contract does not require you to enter into any business relationship with any third-party business-

---

"A provision in a contract providing for the decision by arbitration of any controversy arising under this chapter which does not meet the requirements of this section is not made valid by Section 1281 of the Code of Civil Procedure."

389   The SAG-AFRA list of approved personal managers is available at http://www.sagaftra.org/sagaftramanagers. The SAG-AFTRA's Personal Manager Code of Ethics and Conduct is available at http://www.sagafra.org/managers/code-ethics-conduct.

es, such as photography studios, acting teachers, etc. It is entirely possible that an unregulated personal manager will have either direct or indirect financial interest in these entities, so you should ensure that representation is not contingent on you purchasing these services. At the very least, keep them out of your contract. If your personal manager wants to recommend industry professionals, he or she should have a working list in each area that you can investigate before using. Do your own Internet search on everyone that is recommended to you.

"5: <u>Dispute Resolution</u>: Ensure your management contract has a dispute resolution provision—failure to do so could result in expensive court fees. If you are with a SAG-AFTRA-listed manager, you will automatically default to the comparatively inexpensive SAG-AFTRA arbitration process. However, if your manager is not listed with SAG-AFTRA, you should ensure that you preserve access to the State Labor Commissioner (in California) or the Department of Consumer Affairs (New York) for your dispute resolution whenever possible. In other locales, performers should contemplate an arbitration provision that protects their dispute resolution choices. You should consult with an attorney with regard to whether an arbitration provision for dispute resolution through a legitimate arbitration provider is in your best legal interests in such relationships.

"6: <u>Commission Rate</u>: Managers generally take, on average, 10-15 percent commission. Fifteen percent is considered higher-end compensation in the industry. This should be clearly spelled out in your agreement with your personal manager.

"7: <u>No Self-Renewing Provisions</u>: Beware of any contract with provisions such as: 'If the performer earns $5,000 or greater in the last year of the contract, the term of representation will automatically renew for an additional three-year period' or 'If the parties fail to terminate this agreement 30 days prior to its expiration, the contract will automatically renew for three years.' If the personal manager wants to sign you to an additional contract term, you should be asked to sign a new contract.

"8: <u>Get an Agent</u>: Since managers are not permitted to legally procure employment in California, New York, and some other states unless [they are] under the control and direction of a licensed agent, the contract should clearly spell out that the manager will secure you an agent (or work with a licensed agent to procure you work opportunities). Otherwise, what will the personal manager get paid for doing?

"9: <u>Personal Manager, not Agent</u>: Whenever possible, be sure your management contract clearly spells out what role the manager is going to fill. Because personal managers are largely unregulated, you should, contractually, ensure [that] you both agree on what the personal manager's job functions will entail. As a reminder, personal managers cannot legally procure employment for you under California law (with a very similar provision under New York law) unless he or she does so under the control and direction of a licensed agent. If you are a SAG-AF-TRA member, that agent must also be franchised by the union. This should be spelled out in your agreement.

"10: <u>Length of Contract</u>: Be sure your management contract closely mirrors any potential agency contract that you may sign. The initial term should be no more than 18 months, with renewals to be no longer than three years. Never commit for any longer period than that, especially with an entity that you do not know well, regardless of how great you think [that management] is today. Also, handshake or hip pocket (i.e., verbal) agreements are common in the personal management world. With that kind of relationship, you are generally free to terminate the contract and move on at your discretion."[390]

§1.15   [1] Appendix: The Film Production Pyramid

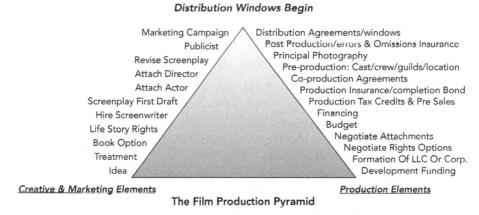

Fig. 1.1: Corey Field, "The Film Production Pyramid." Copyright © by Corey Field Law Group, P.C. Reprinted with permission

§1.16   [2] Appendix: Copyright Fair Use Fundamentals for the Film Industry

Fair use is the mechanism by which copyright law's exclusive rights are tempered by First Amendment freedom of speech concerns.[391] While courts often characterize fair use as a

---

390   See SAG-AFTRA "Do's and Don'ts" (2014), available at http://www.sagaftra.org/professional-representatives/managers-section/dos-and-donts.

391   See *Eldred v. Ashcroft*, 537 U.S. 186, 219-221, 123 S.Ct. 769, 154 L.Ed.2d 683 (2003), discussing the relationship between copyright law, the First Amendment, and fair use:

"The Copyright Clause and First Amendment were adopted close in time. This proximity indicates that, in the Framers' view, copyright's limited monopolies are compatible with free speech principles. Indeed, copyright's purpose is to promote the creation and publication of free expression. As Harper & Row observed: '[T]

defense to an infringement allegation, both the Ninth and Eleventh Circuits have made clear pronouncements that fair use is one of the inherent affirmative rights under copyright, fully authorized by the law, and not merely a defense to an infringement claim.[392] Although the statute and case law provide guidelines and tests for how courts determine whether an alleged infringement is a fair use, ultimately every case is decided on a *sui generis* basis. Fair use is not a matter of bright lines, but of evolving case law and educated guesses about how a court might rule.

Strong First Amendment concerns are a highlight of fair use, including where works are used without authorization in connection with criticism, comment, news reporting, teaching, scholarship, and research. As the Supreme Court has noted, there is a balance between copyright law's monopoly for the author and owner, and the First Amendment.[393] By establishing a marketable right to the use of one's artistic expression, copyright supplies the economic incentive to create and disseminate original works. Balancing First Amendment rights against copyright owners' exclusive rights requires judgment as to how strongly to apply the First Amendment in a given instance. As noted by the Supreme Court, the First

---

he Framers intended copyright itself to be the engine of free expression. By establishing a marketable right to the use of one's expression, copyright supplies the economic incentive to create and disseminate ideas.'

"In addition to spurring the creation and publication of new expression, copyright law contains built-in First Amendment accommodations. First, it distinguishes between ideas and expression and makes only the latter eligible for copyright protection. Specifically, 17 U.S.C. § 102(b) provides: 'In no case does copyright protection for an original work of authorship extend to any idea, procedure, process, system, method of operation, concept, principle, or discovery, regardless of the form in which it is described, explained, illustrated, or embodied in such work.' As we said in Harper & Row, this 'idea/expression dichotomy strike[s] a definitional balance between the First Amendment and the Copyright Act by permitting free communication of facts while still protecting an author's expression.' Due to this distinction, every idea, theory, and fact in a copyrighted work becomes instantly available for public exploitation at the moment of publication.

"Second, the 'fair use' defense allows the public to use not only facts and ideas contained in a copyrighted work, but also expression itself in certain circumstances. Codified at 17 U.S.C. § 107, the defense provides: '[T]he fair use of a copyrighted work, including such use by reproduction in copies . . . , for purposes such as criticism, comment, news reporting, teaching (including multiple copies for classroom use), scholarship, or research, is not an infringement of copyright.' The fair use defense affords considerable 'latitude for scholarship and comment,' and even for parody."

Id. (Footnotes and citations omitted.)

392   See *Lenz v. Universal Music Corp.*, 815 F. 3d 1145, 1153 (9th Cir. 2016) (stating "[e]ven if, as Universal urges, fair use is classified as an "affirmative defense," we hold—for the purposes of the DMCA—fair use is uniquely situated in copyright law so as to be treated differently than traditional affirmative defenses. We conclude that because U.S.C. § 107 created a type of non-infringing use, fair use is "authorized by the law" and a copyright holder must consider the existence of fair use before sending a takedown notification under § 512(c)). See also *Bateman v. Mnemonics, Inc.*, 79 F. 3d 1532, 1542 n. 22 (11th Cir. 1996) (Birch. J.).

393   Id.

Amendment "securely protects the freedom to make or decline to make one's own speech: it bears less heavily when speakers assert the right to make other people's speeches."[394]

Section 107 sets forth the four factors courts use to determine fair use:

> "Notwithstanding the provisions of sections 106 and 106A, the fair use of a copyrighted work, including such use by reproduction in copies or pho-norecords or by any other means specified by that section, for purposes such as criticism, comment, news reporting, teaching (including multiple copies for classroom use), scholarship, or research, is not an infringement of copyright. In determining whether the use made of a work in any particular case is a fair use the factors to be considered shall include—
>
> "(1) the purpose and character of the use, including whether such use is of a commercial nature or is for nonprofit educational purposes;
>
> "(2) the nature of the copyrighted work;
>
> "(3) the amount and substantiality of the portion used in relation to the copyrighted work as a whole; and
>
> "(4) the effect of the use upon the potential market for or value of the copyrighted work."

The fact that a work is unpublished shall not itself bar a finding of fair use if such finding is made upon consideration of all the above factors.[395] In the leading Supreme Court opinion on fair use, the Court examined a musical parody of the song "Pretty Woman," finding that it was a fair use commentary on, and criticism of, the original song.[396] Parody of a work is a classic

---

394   See *Eldred v. Ashcroft*, 537 U.S. 186, 221, 123 S.Ct. 769, 154 L.Ed.2d 683 (2002). Note that copyright protection in some works with minimal original authorship is deemed "thin," for example databases of otherwise unprotectable facts are "thin" copyrights where infringement would only arise as a result of virtually exact copying. *Feist Publications, Inc. v. Rural Telephone Services Co.*, 499 U.S. 340, 348, 111 S.Ct. 1282, 113 L.Ed.2d 358 (1991). More creative works are deserving of stronger copyright protection. Thus in this element of the fair use test, where a compilation of facts is at issue, this factor may favor the defendant. However where a highly original work is at issue, this factor may favor the plaintiff. While short excerpts from a longer work may often be more indicative of a fair use, note that in *Sony v. Universal Studios*, 464 U.S. 417, 104 S.Ct. 774, 78 L.Ed.2d 574 (1984), the Betamax video recorder at issue usually recorded entire programs, not excerpts. Nevertheless the time-shifting of those entire programs by the user was considered to be a fair use.

395   See 17 U.S.C. § 107. See also, *Harper & Row, Publishers, Inc. v. Nation Enterprises*, 471 U.S. 539, 105 S.Ct. 2218, 85 L.Ed.2d 588 (1985).

396   See *Campbell v. Acuff-Rose Music, Inc.*, 510 U.S. 569, 114 S.Ct. 1164, 127 L.Ed.2d 500 (1994).

fair use, providing that no more of the target work is used than is necessary to make the point. In *Campbell*, the court noted that parody is more likely to be a fair use, as compared to satire:

> "Parody needs to mimic an original to make its point, and so has some claim to use the creation of its victim's (or collective victims') imagination, whereas satire can stand on its own two feet and so requires justification for the very act of borrowing."[397]

In conducting its analysis, the court considered each of the four statutory elements in turn. The court considered whether the use was "transformative."[398] The *Campbell* court described transformative fair use:

> "The central purpose of this investigation is to see, in Justice Story's words, whether the new work merely 'supersede[s] the objects of the original creation' ('supplanting' the original), or instead adds something new, with a further purpose or different character, altering the first with new expression, meaning, or message; it asks, in other words, whether and to what extent the new work is 'transformative.' Although such transformative use is not absolutely necessary for a finding of fair use, the goal of copyright, to promote science and the arts, is generally furthered by the creation of transformative works. Such works thus lie at the heart of the fair use doctrine's guarantee of breathing space within the confines of copyright, and the more transformative the new work, the less will be the significance of other factors, like commercialism, that may weigh against a finding of fair use."[399]

Where a parody work created under fair use principles otherwise qualifies for copyright protection, the author of the parody work may claim copyright protection, notwithstanding that the parody may contain elements of the original work used without authorization.[400]

---

397   *Id.*, 510 U.S. at 580-581. See also, *Bourne v. Twentieth Century Fox*, 602 F. Supp.2d 499 (S.D.N.Y. 2009). Compare, *Dr. Seuss Enterprises, LP v. Penguin Books USA, Inc.*, 109 F.3d 1394 (9th Cir. 1997) (satire of O.J. Simpson trial based on "The Cat in the Hat" not a fair use).

398   Transformative fair use has become a term of art, and while fair use can be found where the use is not transformative (for example using copies of excerpts of works for classroom use is not transformative, but is likely to be a fair use), determining whether a use is transformative plays an important role in any fair use analysis.

399   See *Campbell v. Acuff-Rose Music, Inc.*, N. 5 *supra*, 510 U.S. at 578-579.

400   See *Keeling v. Hars*, 809 F.3d 43 (2d Cir. 2015) (parody stage adaptation of film *Point Break*, using dialogue from the film but adding for parody effect jokes, props, exaggerated staging, and humorous theatrical devices "to transform the dramatic plot and dialogue of the film into an irreverent, interactive theatrical experience").

In *Cariou v. Prince*, a Second Circuit fair use case pitting a photographer against an "appropriation" artist who used the photographs in out-of-context collages, the Second Circuit confirmed that in order to be a fair use, the accused work need not comment directly on the original work in establishing fair use's "new expression, meaning, or message."[401] It is sufficient that the new work employ the original "in the creation of new information, new aesthetics, news insights and understandings."[402] Thus, where the new works manifested "an entirely different aesthetic," transforming the "serene" original photographs into "crude and jarring works" that were "hectic and provocative," fair use was found.[403]

In support of its holding that twenty-five of thirty works at issue were fair use (and remanding on the remaining five works), the court conducted an analysis of the fourth prong of the statutory test, the "effect on the market" test. The Second Circuit noted the entirely different "market space" inhabited by the defendant's collages, which sold for millions of dollars to a celebrity clientele, compared to the plaintiff's modestly selling original book of photographs. By emphasizing that the plaintiff's photographs were re-purposed to the defendant's enormous financial advantage, the court arguably raised a question of basic fairness that was not further examined amidst the following recitation of the many celebrities that constituted a new "market space" for the appropriation art:

> "Prince's work appeals to an entirely different sort of collector than Cariou's. Certain of the *Canal Zone* artworks have sold for two million or more dollars. The invitation list for a dinner that Gagosian hosted in conjunction with the opening of the *Canal Zone* show included a number of the wealthy and famous such as the musicians Jay-Z and Beyonce Knowles, artists Damien Hirst and Jeff Koons, professional football player Tom Brady, model Gisele Bundchen, *Vanity Fair* editor Graydon Carter, *Vogue* editor Anna Wintour, authors Jonathan Franzen and Candace Bushnell, and actors Robert DeNiro, Angelina Jolie, and Brad Pitt. Prince sold eight artworks for a total of $10,480,000, and exchanged seven others for works by painter Larry Rivers and by sculptor Richard Serra. Cariou on the other hand has not actively marketed his work or sold work for significant sums, and nothing in the record suggests that anyone will not now purchase Cariou's work, or derivative non-transformative works (whether Cariou's own or licensed by him) as a result of the market space that Prince's work has taken up. This fair use factor therefore weighs in Prince's favor."[404]

---

401   *Cariou v. Prince*, 714 F.3d 694, 705 (2d Cir. 2013).

402   *Id.*, 714 F.3d at 706 (quoting *Blanch v. Koons*, 467 F.3d 244, 253 (2d Cir. 2004)).

403   *Id.*

404   *Id.*, 714 F.3d at 709.

Fair use also comes into play with respect to whether new technological developments aid and abet copyright infringement. For example, the Supreme Court issued two seminal opinions on the impact of new technology and copyright infringement. In 1984, the Court found that Sony's Betamax videocassette recorder was capable of substantial non-infringing uses, because its primary use, private at-home "time shifting" recording of television programs, constituted fair use.[405] Therefore, Sony's sale of the technology to consumers did not constitute contributory copyright infringement.

In a 2005 case, the Supreme Court considered whether peer-to-peer online software, which was also accused of contributing to copyright infringement online, like the videocassette recorder, constituted a fair use.[406] In *Metro-Goldwyn-Mayer Studios, Inc. v. Grokster*, however, there was evidence that the defendants knew their technology was being used for mass copying of music and film files online, and not in a bona fide fair use context. The court announced a new "inducement" doctrine, stating, "one who distributes a device with the object of promoting its use to infringe copyright, as shown by clear expression or otherwise affirmative steps taken to foster infringement, is liable for the resulting acts of infringement by third persons."[407]

In *Authors Guild, Inc. v. Google*, a significant digital online book publishing fair use decision, the Second Circuit held that the Google Book Project, which had scanned millions of books into a searchable database without permission from the copyright owners, was a fair use, "which augments public knowledge by making available information about Plaintiffs' books without providing the public with a substantial substitute for matter protected by the Plaintiffs' copyright interests in the original works or derivatives of them."[408]

Notably, the "Google Books" holding discussed the tension between the use of the term "transformative" in the fair use analysis which connotes fair use, and the use of the same term in the Copyright Act's definition of a derivative work, which can only be created with the authority of the copyright owner:[409]

---

405   See *Sony Corp. of America v. Universal City Studios, Inc.*, 464 U.S. 417, 104 S.Ct. 774, 78 L.Ed.2d 574 (1984).

406   See *Metro-Goldwyn-Mayer Studios, Inc. v. Grokster, Ltd.*, 545 U.S. 913, 125 S.Ct. 2764, 162 L.Ed.2d 781 (2005).

407   *Id.*

408   See *Authors Guild v. Google, Inc.*, 804 F.3d 202, 2015 U.S. App. LEXIS 17988 at *3 (2d Cir. 2015).

409   See 17 U.S.C. § 101 definition of a derivative work, stating:

"A 'derivative work' is a work based upon one or more preexisting works, such as a translation, musical arrangement, dramatization, fictionalization, motion picture version, sound recording, art reproduction, abridgment, condensation, or any other form in which a work may be recast, transformed, or adapted. A work consisting of editorial revisions, annotations, elaborations, or other modifications, which, as a whole, represent an original work of authorship, is a 'derivative work.'" (Emphasis added.).

"A further complication that can result from oversimplified reliance on whether the copying involves transformation is that the word 'transform' also plays a role in defining 'derivative works,' over which the original rights holder retains exclusive control. Section 106 of the Act specifies the 'exclusive right[]' of the copyright owner 'to prepare derivative works based upon the copyrighted work.' See 17 U.S.C. § 106. The statute defines derivative works largely by example, rather than explanation. The examples include 'translation, musical arrangement, dramatization, fictionalization, motion picture version, sound recording, art reproduction, abridgement, condensation,' to which list the statute adds 'any other form in which a work may be . . . transformed.' 17 U.S.C. § 101 (emphasis added). As we noted in **Authors Guild, Inc. v. Hathi Trust**, '[p]aradigmatic examples of derivative works include the translation of a novel into another language, the adaptation of a novel into a movie or play, or the recasting of a novel as an e-book or an audiobook.' 755 F.3d 87, 95 (2d Cir. 2014). While such changes can be described as transformations, they do not involve the kind of transformative purpose that favors a fair use finding. The statutory definition suggests that derivative works generally involve transformations in the nature of changes of form. 17 U.S.C. § 101. By contrast, copying from an original for the purpose of criticism or commentary on the original or provision of information about it, tends most clearly to satisfy *Campbell's* notion of the 'transformative' purpose involved in the analysis of Factor One."[410]

Every fair use case revolves around its facts as applied to the four-factor test, and whether the use is transformative.[411]

---

410   *Authors Guild v. Google, Inc.*, N. 16 supra at *27.

411   See:

Second Circuit: Cariou v. Prince, 714 F.3d 694 (2d Cir. 2013) (appropriation of art partly fair use, partly not); *Blanch v. Koons*, 467 F.3d 244 (2d Cir. 2006) (photo used in collage fair use); *Bill Graham Archives v. Dorling Kindersley Ltd.*, 448 F.3d 605 (2d Cir. 2006) (Grateful Dead concert posters reproduced in reduced size in book on the band fair use); *Leibovitz v. Paramount Pictures Corp.*, 137 F.3d 109 (2d Cir. 1998) (parody of photo used to promote film "Naked Gun 33 1/3" fair use); *Lennon v. Premise Media Corp. LP*, 556 F. Supp.2d 210 (S.D.N.Y. 2008) (John Lennon song "Imagine" excerpted in documentary film about role of religion in society a fair use).

See also, *Authors Guild, Inc. v. Hathi Trust*, 755 F.3d 87 (2d Cir. 2014) (scan of library books to enable digital search deemed a fair use).

Ninth Circuit: Seltzer v. GreenDay, Inc., 725 F.3d 1170 (9th Cir. 2013) (poster art used as part of live concert background projections a fair use); *Sofa Entertainment, Inc. v. Dodger Productions, Inc.*, 709 F.3d 1273, 1279 (9th Cir. 2013) (use of seven-second video clip from "Ed Sullivan Show" in stage musical "Jersey Boys" a fair use. Notwithstanding the impact of Ed Sullivan's "charismatic personality" in the video clip, court noted "charisma, however, is not copy-

§1.17   [3] Appendix: Copyright Ownership Fundamentals Including Works Made for Hire and Co-ownership

[1]—Ownership by the Author or Authors is Automatic upon Creation

Initial ownership of a work vests automatically in the author or authors of a work.[412] Registration or other formalities are not required to establish ownership, only the creation of an original work fixed in a tangible medium of expression as required under Section 102 for copyrightability.

[2]—Works Made for Hire

Under the "work made for hire" doctrine, if work is created by an employee, authorship and ownership of the work vest not in the employee, but in the employer.[413]

There are two ways that work made for hire status arises: (1) a bona fide employee creating a work for the employer within the scope of employment; or (2) a commissioned work, where an independent contractor and the commissioning party agree in writing

---

rightable"); *Perfect 10, Inc. v. Google, Inc.*, 487 F.3d 701 (9th Cir. 2007) (thumbnail images on Internet search engine a fair use); *Mattel Inc. v. Walking Mountain Productions, Inc.*, 353 F.3d 792 (9th Cir. 2003) (photos of Barbie doll in bizarre poses fair use commentary); *Kelly v. Arriba Soft Corp.*, 336 F.3d 811 (9th Cir. 2003) (image thumbnails on Web search engine fair use); *Paramount Pictures Corp. v. Axanar Prods.*, 2017 U.S. Dist. LEXIS 19670 (C.D. Cal. Jan. 3, 2017) (Star Trek fan film with large budget not fair use).

Eleventh Circuit: *Suntrust v. Houghton Mifflin Co.*, 268 F.3d 1257 (11th Cir. 2001) (unauthorized sequel to "Gone With the Wind" held to be transformative parody of original).

But see:

Second Circuit: *Salinger v. Colting*, 607 F.3d 68, 73 (2d Cir. 2010) (unauthorized sequel to novel Catcher in the Rye not a fair use); *Castle Rock Entertainment, Inc. v. Carol Publishing Group, Inc.*, 150 F.3d 132 (2d Cir. 1998) (book containing trivia on Seinfeld television series not fair use); *Rogers v. Koons*, 960 F.2d 301 (2d Cir. 1992) (sculpture based on copyrighted photo not fair use); *Warner Bros. Entertainment, Inc. v. RDR Books*, 575 F. Supp.2d 513 (S.D.N.Y. 2008) (lexicon based on Harry Potter novels not fair use).

Ninth Circuit: *Monge v. Maya Magazines, Inc.*, 688 F.3d 1164 (9th Cir. 2012) (publication in magazine of unpublished personal photos that were allegedly stolen from owner not a newsworthy fair use); *Dr. Seuss Enterprises, LP v. Penguin Books USA, Inc.*, 109 F.3d 1394 (9th Cir. 1997) (cartoon book on murder trial written in style of Dr. Seuss ruled an infringing satire that inappropriately used Dr. Seuss's style for its inherent entertainment value and not to transformatively comment on Dr. Seuss books themselves).

412   See 17 U.S.C. § 201(a).

413   See 17 U.S.C. § 201(b): "Works Made for Hire.—In the case of a work made for hire, the employer or other person for whom the work was prepared is considered the author for purposes of this title, and, unless the parties have expressly agreed otherwise in a written instrument signed by them, owns all of the rights comprised in the copyright."

that the work shall be considered a work made for hire, and where the type of work being created fits within the statutory definition of a work made for hire.[414]

[a]—Works by an Employee

Where an employee creates a work within the scope of their employment, the work will automatically be considered a work made for hire. Where an employee is on the payroll of a business engaged in the creation of works, e.g., a motion picture studio, the status is not in doubt. In such cases the employer may also ask the employee to acknowledge work made for hire status in a written agreement. Technically, it is unnecessary, since the employer's ownership vests automatically under the Copyright Act.

However, in the event of a dispute over the author's employment status, and by extension, the ownership status of the work created, the Supreme Court has held that the law of agency is used to determine whether someone is an actual employee, or an independent contractor.[415] The factors in the test, none of which are exclusive, include:

(1) the skill required;

(2) the source of the tools and instrumentalities used to create the work;

(3) the location of the work;

(4) the duration of the relationship between the parties;

(5) whether the hiring party has the right to assign work;

(6) the extent of the hired party's right to determine when and how long to work;

(7) the method of payment;

(8) the hired party's role in hiring and paying assistants;

(9) whether the work is part of the regular business of the hiring party;

(10) whether the hiring party is in business;

(11) the provision of employee benefits; and

(12) the tax treatment of the hired party.[416]

---

414   *Id.* See also, *Schiller & Schmidt, Inc. v. Nordisco Corp.*, 969 F.2d 410, 412 (7th Cir. 1992) (a work made for hire agreement with a freelancer "must precede the creation of the property").

415   See *Community for Creative Non-Violence v. Reid*, 490 U.S. 730, 751-752, 109 S.Ct. 2166, 104 L.Ed.2d 811 (1989).

416   *Id.*

[b]—Specialty Ordered or Commissioned Works

Where an independent contractor has been engaged to create a copyrightable work, two types of ownership may arise. Either the independent contractor will be the initial owner of the work who then assigns or licenses rights to the hiring party, or the work will come within the statutory definition of a work made for hire, in which case the parties may both sign a agreement that must comply with statutory requirements, including that the agreement state it is a work made for hire, and that the agreement be signed by *both* parties.[417]

The statutory definition of a work made for hire lists nine types of creations. The list was determined by Congress and includes categories or works that commonly require creative contributions from more than one person:

(1) a contribution to a collective work;

(2) a motion picture or other audiovisual work;

(3) a translation;

(4) a supplementary work;

(5) a compilation;

(6) an instructional text;

(7) a test;

(8) answer material for a test;

(9) an atlas.[418]

---

417   See 17 U.S.C. § 101, stating in relevant part:

"A 'work made for hire' is—

"(1) a work prepared by an employee within the scope of his or her employment; or

"(2) a work specially ordered or commissioned for use as a contribution to a collective work, as a part of a motion picture or other audiovisual work, as a translation, as a supplementary work, as a compilation, as an instructional text, as a test, as answer material for a test, or as an atlas, if the parties expressly agree in a written instrument signed by them that the work shall be considered a work made for hire. For the purpose of the foregoing sentence, a 'supplementary work' is a work prepared for publication as a secondary adjunct to a work by another author for the purpose of introducing, concluding, illustrating, explaining, revising, commenting upon, or assisting in the use of the other work, such as forewords, afterwords, pictorial illustrations, maps, charts, tables, editorial notes, musical arrangements, answer material for tests, bibliographies, appendixes, and indexes, and an "instructional text" is a literary, pictorial, or graphic work prepared for publication and with the purpose of use in systematic instructional activities."

418   See 17 U.S.C. § 101. A collective work is defined in Section 101 as a periodical issue, anthology, or encyclopedia. For a brief period in 1999, sound recordings were added as a tenth item on the list, but that amendment was repealed, leaving the statute with unusual disclaimer language that the addition or deletion of sound recordings

[i]—Agreements for Specially Commissioned Works Made for Hire

We have noted that work made for hire agreements must use the words "work made for hire" and be signed by both parties. But when must such agreements be signed?

Nunc pro tunc or later-executed copyright assignment and work made for hire agreements executed after a work is created are common, but several jurisdictions that have ruled on the issue require that work made for hire agreements for specially ordered or commissioned works be executed *prior* to the creation of the work.

The Seventh Circuit in *Schiller & Schmidt, Inc. v. Nordisco Corp.* held that the written agreement "must precede the creation of the property in order to serve its purpose to identify the (noncreator) owner unequivocally."[419]

The Ninth Circuit, citing to the Seventh Circuit and also to a Second Circuit case, reached a similar conclusion, noting that the definition of a work made for hire in Section 101 of the Copyright Act refers to commissioned works as works that "shall" exist in the future, upon execution of the required writing:

---

from the list of works that can be specially ordered or commissioned as works made for hire shall not be considered in any future litigation disputes over the status of sound recordings as works made for hire. See Intellectual Property and Communications Omnibus Reform Act of 1999, as enacted by section 1000(a)(9) of Public Law 106-113, adding sound recordings, which addition was subsequently deleted by Congress in the Work Made for Hire and Copyright Corrections Act of 2000. See also, Field, "Their Master's Voice? Recording Artists, Bright Lines, and Bowie Bonds: The Debate Over Sound Recordings as Works Made for Hire," 48 J. Copyright Society 145 (2000) (discussing sound recordings as works made for hire). See also, the relevant addition to the definition of works made for hire in Section 101 of the Copyright Act:

"In determining whether any work is eligible to be considered a work made for hire under paragraph (2), neither the amendment contained in section 1011(d) of the Intellectual Property and Communications Omnibus Reform Act of 1999, as enacted by section 1000(a)(9) of Public Law 106-113, nor the deletion of the words added by that amendment—

"(A) shall be considered or otherwise given any legal significance, or

"(B) shall be interpreted to indicate congressional approval or disapproval of, or acquiescence in, any judicial determination, by the courts or the Copyright Office. Paragraph (2) shall be interpreted as if both section 2(a)(1) of the Work Made For Hire and Copyright Corrections Act of 2000 and section 1011(d) of the Intellectual Property and Communications Omnibus Reform Act of 1999, as enacted by section 1000(a)(9) of Public Law 106-113, were never enacted, and without regard to any inaction or awareness by the Congress at any time of any judicial determinations."

419   See *Schiller & Schmidt, Inc. v. Nordisco Corp.*, 969 F.2d 410, 413 (7th Cir. 1992).

"Section 101 of the Copyright Act defines a 'work made for hire' as 'a work specially ordered or commissioned . . . if the parties expressly agree in a written instrument signed by them that the work shall be considered a work made for hire . . . .' 17 U.S.C. § 101(2). The plain language of the statute indicates that a work-for-hire agreement cannot apply to works that are already in existence. Works 'specially ordered or commissioned' can only be made after the execution of an express agreement between the parties. See *Playboy Enters., Inc. v. Dumas*, 53 F.3d 549, 558-559 (2d Cir. 1995); *Schiller & Schmidt, Inc. v. Nordisco Corp.*, 969 F.2d 410, 412-13 (7th Cir. 1992) ('The writing must precede the creation of the property' to qualify as a work-for-hire agreement). Accordingly, Marin could not acquire copyright ownership in Gladwell's Pre-Existing Materials through a work-for-hire agreement."[420]

[ii]—California Labor Code § 3351.5

Work made for hire agreements entered into with freelance contractors under California law theoretically come within the little-known Section 3351.5 of the California Labor Code, which creates statutory "employee" status for any freelancer who signs a work made for hire agreement under the Copyright Act.[421].3 California Labor Code Section 3351.5 would then require the employer to have workers' compensation insurance for their statutory "employee." The provision appears to have been enacted to benefit large entertainment employers such as studios, which would have the benefit of keeping any freelance contractor injury lawsuits within the judgment-limiting confines of the state's workers' compensation rules for employees, but it would clearly be a burden on any individual who engaged a freelance contractor to create a work made for hire.

Commentators have suggested that such agreements could avoid triggering the statutory employee status by omitting any "work made for hire" language, and instead use a simple assignment of copyright. But for works with multiple copyrightable contributions, such as motion pictures, that is problematic: copyright

---

420   See *Gladwell Government Services, Inc. v. County of Marin*, 265 Fed. Appx. 624, Copy. L. Rep. (CCH) ¶ 29,510 (9th Cir. 2008). See also, *Andreas Carlsson Productions, AB v. Barnes*, 2012 U.S. Dist. LEXIS 86308 (C.D. Cal. June 18, 2012); *Sisyphus Touring, Inc. v. TMZ Productions, Inc.*, 2016 U.S. Dist. LEXIS 111695 (C.D. Cal. Aug. 22, 2016) (stating "Allowing the writing instrument to be executed after the work is created would defeat the purpose of the statute in requiring a written instrument altogether."). *Id.*, at *14.

421   See Calif. Labor Code, § 3351.5(c), which states:

"Any person while engaged by contract for the creation of a specially ordered or commissioned work of authorship in which the parties expressly agree in a written instrument signed by them that the work shall be considered a work made for hire, as defined in Section 101 of Title 17 of the United States Code, and the ordering or commissioning party obtains ownership of all the rights comprised in the copyright in the work."

assignments, unlike works made for hire, can be terminated after thirty-five years under Section 203 of the Copyright Act, an untenable situation which could theoretically lead to multiple termination claims for different facets of the motion picture.

A perhaps more workable solution would be to ensure that any freelance work made for hire agreements are signed with the freelancer's loan out corporation acting on behalf of the individual author, because corporations would be exempt from the Labor Code provision.[422]

The one case to discuss Section 3351.5(c), a personal injury suit brought by a cinematographer on the remake of "Flight of the Phoenix" against Twentieth Century Fox, concluded that the statute fails to supersede "the common law distinction between employee and independent contractor" and declined to apply the statute based on the facts and procedure in that case.[423] In addition to the courts being apparently reluctant to enforce it, Labor Code Section 3351.5(c) also seems unlikely to survive any statutory constitutional challenge based on preemption by federal copyright law.

[c]— Work Made for Hire Status for Freelance Contractors Under the 1909 Copyright Act Compared to Under the 1976 Act

Under the 1976 Copyright Act's Section 101, for freelance contractors there must be a written agreement with the words "work made for hire" signed by both parties. However that provision was not part of the prior 1909 Act applicable to works created prior to January 1, 1978. Therefore, disputes over the work made for hire status of freelance contractor works made for hire created prior to January 1, 1978, where there is no clear writing, are determined by an analysis of whether the work was created at the "instance and expense" of the hiring party.[424]

---

422   See the discussion on loan out corporations in the entertainment industry in § 1.06 *infra*.

423   See *Barry v. Twentieth Century Fox Film Corp.*, 2011 Cal. App. Unpub. LEXIS 7132, at *17, 2011 WL 4360994, at *6 (Cal. App.2d Dist. Sept. 20, 2011) (noting that the trial court "rejected appellants' argument because they cited no authority that section 3351.5, subdivision (c) supersedes the common law distinction between employee and independent contractor").

424   See *Gary Friedrich Enterprises, LLC v. Marvel Characters, Inc.*, 716 F.3d 302, 320 (2d Cir. 2013) (reversing district court's denial of summary judgment to author on ownership, work made for hire, and copyright renewal claims under 1909 Copyright Act regarding "Ghost Rider" comic books).

A work is made at the hiring party's "instance and expense" when the employer induces the creation of the work and has the right to direct and supervise the manner in which the work is carried out, even if that right is never exercised.[425]

[3]—Co-Ownership

The Copyright Act defines a "joint work" as "a work prepared by two or more authors with the intention that their contributions be merged into inseparable or interdependent parts of a unitary whole."[426] The touchstone of the statutory definition "is the intention at the time the writing is done that the parts be absorbed or combined into an integrated unit."[427]

In most cases, the joint authors/owners will enter into an agreement that defines their respective duties and rights, including matters such as who can issue licenses, and the receipt of royalties or share of reve-nues. Where no such writing exists, copyright law's joint authorship default provisions entitle each co-authors to equal undivided interests in the whole work. As further described in the leading cases, each joint author has the right to use or to nonexclusively license the work as he or she wishes, subject only to the obligation to account to the other joint owner for any profits made.[428] Joint owners cannot sue each other for copyright infringement, but may sue each other for an accounting.[429] Any third party who nonexclusively licenses from either co-owner is insulated from any threat of copyright infringement, and from any demand for payment from the nonlicensing co-owner.

With respect to the "profits" to be accounted, while no court has extensively analyzed how such profits are to be determined, in the context of the Copyright Act's definition of

---

425   *Gary Friedrich Enterprises, LLC v. Marvel Characters, Inc.*, 716 F.3d 302, 320 (2d Cir. 2013). See also:

Supreme Court: Community for Creative Non-Violence v. Reid, 490 U.S. 730, 109 S.Ct. 2166, 104 L.Ed.2d 811 (1989).

Second Circuit: Martha Graham School & Dance Foundation, Inc. v. Martha Graham Center of Contemporary Dance, Inc., 380 F.3d 624 (2d Cir. 2004); *Marvel Characters, Inc. v. Simon*, 310 F.3d 280 (2d Cir. 2002).

See also, *Urbont v. Sony Music Entm't*, 100 F. Supp. 3d 342 (S.D.N.Y. 2015), setting forth the tests for a work made for hire under the 1909 Act.

426   See: 17 U.S.C. §§ 101, 201(a). See also, *Thomson v. Larson*, 147 F.3d 195 (2d Cir. 1998).

427   See H.R. Rep. No. 94-1476, 94th Cong., 2d Sess. 120, 121 (1976), reprinted in 1976 U.S. Code Cong. & Admin. News 5659, 5735.

428   See *Community for Creative Non-Violence v. Reid*, 846 F.2d 1485, 1498 (D.C. Cir. 1988), aff'd without consideration 490 U.S. 730, 109 S.Ct. 2166, 104 L.Ed.2d 811 (1989) ("Joint authors co-owning copyright in a work are deemed to be tenants in common, with each having an independent right to use or license the copyright, subject only to a duty to account to the other co-owner for any profits earned thereby.").

429   See *Oddo v. Ries*, 743 F.2d 630 (9th Cir. 1984). See also *Davis v. Blige*, 505 F.3d 90 (2d Cir. 2007).

profits for the purposes of infringement damages in Section 504(b), note that the formula is to start with gross revenues, then consider "deductible expenses and the elements of profit attributable to factors other than the copyrighted work," which deductions would presumably apply to any co-owner accountings.[430]

Joint authorship can also be established in a written contract, but where no such writing exists and there is a dispute over co-authorship, the test for joint authorship is that (1) the joint author made a copyrightable contribution to the work;[431] and (2) evidence of intent to treat the plaintiff as a co-author.[432]

One Second Circuit case dealt with a dispute over co-authorship of the musical *Rent*.[433] The court applied tests of intent, including decision-making authority, creative billing and credits, written agreements with third parties regarding authorship of the work, and any additional evidence of the intent of the author to grant co-author status to the plaintiff, holding that the late author of the work did not have the requisite intent to grant co-author status to the "dramaturg" who made copyrightable revisions to the work.[434]

In the Ninth Circuit, a work must be (1) copyrightable, (2) have two or more authors, who (3) must intend their contributions be merged into inseparable or interdependent parts of a unitary whole" in order to qualify as a "joint work."[435] In the absence of a contract, the Ninth Circuit uses three criteria for determining whether a contributor should be considered an "author" for the purpose of joint authorship: (1) whether the purported author controls the work and is "the inventive or master mind" who "creates, or gives effect to the idea," (2) whether the "putative coauthors make objective manifestations of shared intent to be coauthors; and (3) whether the audience appeal of the work turns on both contributions and the share of each in its success cannot be appraised.[436]

---

430   See 17 U.S.C. § 504(b). See also, *Corbello v. DeVito*, 832 F. Supp.2d 1231, 1249 (D. Nev. 2011), stating that the calculation of profits to a co-owner can take into consideration factors including what percentage of royalties are attributable to the work, and what percentage "is attributable to other works or assistance . . . provided under the license." See also, 1-6 Nimmer on Copyright, § 6.12, n.3.2 stating "In the sphere of copyright infringement, the word 'profits' has a well-defined meaning — gross receipts less expenses incurred in earning them." See also, *Corbello v. DeVito*, 777 F.3d 1058 (9th Cir. 2015).

431   In other words, the contribution was not mere editing or commentary, but consisted of actual copyrightable creative contributions.

432   See *Thomson v. Larson*, 147 F.3d 195, 203-204 (2d Cir. 1998) (citing *Childress v. Taylor*, 945 F.2d 500 (2d Cir. 1991)).

433   *Thomson v. Larson, id.*

434   Id., 147 F.3d at 203-204.

435   See *Aalmuhammed v. Lee*, 202 F.3d 1227, 1231 (9th Cir. 2000).

436   Id., 202 F.3d at 1234. (Internal citations omitted.)

Note that while under United States co-ownership case precedent, co-owners may unilaterally grant a non-exclusive license subject to their duty to account, a co-owner cannot unilaterally grant an exclusive license, because to do so would limit the other co-owners' independent rights to exploit the copyright.[437]

Note that United States case precedent on co-ownership may differ from the law in other countries that require the consent of all co-owners for any license.[438]

§1.18   [4] Appendix - Duration of Copyright

Duration of copyright protection is complex because there are two different schemes of protection: counting years from publication under the 1909 Act, and counting years from the death of the author under the 1976 Act. In addition, the duration of protection under both schemes has been subject to statutory extensions.[439]

[1]—Works Published Prior to January 1, 1978 That Are Not Works Made for Hire

[a]—The First Term and the Renewal Terms Totaling Fifty-Six Years

Works in their first or renewal terms prior to January 1, 1978 have a duration of protection derived under the 1909 Copyright Act,[440] based on the date that copyright was "secured." Under the 1909 Act, federal copyright was secured on the date a work was published, or, for unpublished works, the date of registration. There was a first term of twenty-eight years, followed by a renewal term of twenty-eight years, for a potential total of fifty-six years, assuming the work was properly renewed.[441]

---

437   See:

Second Circuit: Davis v. Blige, 505 F.3d 90, 101 (2d Cir. 2007).

Ninth Circuit: Sybersound Records, Inc. v. UAV Corp., 517 F.3d 1137, 1143 (9th Cir. 2008).

438   See, e.g. 1 Nimmer on Copyright § 6.10[D] (stating that in many "foreign jurisdictions, a license will not be valid unless all joint owners are party to it"). Note however that non-exclusive license agreements may specify governing law and jurisdiction in the United States.

439   See 17 U.S.C. § 305. Pursuant to Section 305, all terms of protection run to the end of the calendar year in which they expire.

440   See: 17 U.S.C. § 304(a) (works in their first term as of January 1, 1978); § 304(b) (works in their renewal term as of January 1, 1978). The distinction between works in their first or renewal term was necessary in 1978, but is no longer applicable to the question of duration of term.

441   See: 17 U.S.C. §§ 304(a)(3), 304(a)(4). See also, *Gary Friedrich Enterprises, LLC v. Marvel Characters, Inc.*, 716 F.3d 302, 312 (2d Cir. 2013) (discussing renewal term of copyright).

Public Law 102-307, enacted in 1992, made renewal automatic and renewal registration optional for works originally copyrighted between January 1, 1964 and December 31, 1977. Although no longer required, the optional renewal registration may be made at any time during the extended renewal term, and provides a public record of the ownership of the renewal term.[442]

There have been two extensions to this fifty-six-year term, the nineteen-year extension, and the twenty-year extension.

[b]—The Nineteen-Year Extension

Legislative planning for what would become the 1976 Copyright Act began as early as 1962. During this preparatory period, Congress did not want to let protection for existing works expire, and passed a series of term extensions over the years. By the time the 1976 Copyright Act was enacted, the extensions of duration totaled nineteen years, giving a total of seventy-five years of protection to works that would have otherwise expired after fifty-six years.[443]

[c]—The Twenty-Year Extension

Under the Copyright Term Extension Act of 1998 ("CTEA"), the term of protection was extended for an additional twenty years for all works. Thus, so-called "Pre-'78" works had their term of protection extended from seventy-five years to ninety-five years.[444]

As of the effective date of the CTEA:

---

442   17 U.S.C. §§ 304(a)(3), 304(a)(4).

443   See Duration of Copyright, Copyright Office Circular 15A.

444   See 17 U.S.C. § 304(a). The Copyright Term Extension Act ("CTEA") became law on January 27, 1998. It extended the term of copyright for works that were still under copyright protection. To summarize: for pre-1978 works, the total term of ninety five years is the result of the following, in sequence:

1. The first term of twenty-eight years;

2. The renewal term of twenty-eight years;

3. The nineteen-year extension;

4. The twenty-year extension,

For a total of ninety-five years.

(1) Works published in 1922 or earlier had already entered the public domain, because a 1922 work with seventy-five years of copyright protection expired at the end of 1997. The CTEA did not retroactively change the status of those works.

(2) As of January 27, 1998, works published in 1923 were in their last seventy-fifth year of copyright protection. But under the CTEA, instead of the copyright expiring at the end of 1998, the copyright in those works, and all other works protected by copyright, was extended another twenty years.

Accordingly, since passage of the CTEA in 1998, no works have gone into the public domain because of expiration of copyright. Beginning after 2018, works published in 1923 or later will gradually enter the public domain.

[d]—Works Created but Not Published as of January 1, 1978

Under Section 303(a), works that were created before January 1, 1978, but were unpublished and unregistered, have a term of protection as set forth in Section 302, which is life plus seventy years.[445]

[2]—Works Created On or After January 1, 1978 Other Than Works Made for Hire

Under the 1976 Act, the term of copyright was not a matter of calculating the date of publication. Instead, it was based on the life of the author plus fifty years, a scheme used widely in other countries that do not require complex registration and renewal procedures as formerly mandated under the 1909 Act.

Under the CTEA, the term was extended by twenty years, to life plus seventy.[446] In the case of works by one or more authors, the expiration is the date of the last surviving author's life, plus seventy years.[447]

---

445   See 17 U.S.C. § 303(a):

"(a) Copyright in a work created before January 1, 1978, but not theretofore in the public domain or copyrighted, subsists from January 1, 1978, and endures for the term provided by section 302. In no case, however, shall the term of copyright in such a work expire before December 31, 2002; and, if the work is published on or before December 31, 2002, the term of copyright shall not expire before December 31, 2047."

446   See 17 U.S.C. § 302(a).

447   See 17 U.S.C. § 302(b).

[3]—Works Made for Hire

Works made for hire have a term of ninety-five years from the year of first publication, or 120 years from creation, whichever expires first.[448]

[4]—Renewal

For pre-1978 works, Congress made renewal automatic and renewal registration optional for works originally copyrighted between January 1, 1964 and December 31, 1977.[449] For post-1978 works (works created on or after January 1, 1978, the effective date of the 1976 Copyright Act), renewal is not required because the term of copyright protection changed from the system counting from the publication date, to the "life plus" system. Although no longer required, the optional renewal registration may be made at any time during the extended renewal term, and provides a public record of the ownership of the renewal term.[450]

Under the several copyright term extensions passed since 1962, the term of the renewal period increased. Originally, renewal registration added a second renewal term of twenty-eight years to the first term of twenty-eight years for a total of fifty-six years of protection. Under the so-called "nineteen-year extensions," the total renewal term duration became forty-seven years, thus the first term of twenty-eight years plus the forty-seven-year renewal term totaled seventy-five years. Under the CTEA, the renewal term increased by twenty years to sixty-seven years, which when added to the initial term of twenty-eight years, totaled ninety-five years of protection.

[5]—The Public Domain

A work that is not under copyright protection is deemed to be in the public domain, free for anyone to use in any manner. Public domain status for a work that was at one time protected by copyright can occur in several ways, including expiration of the term, forfeiture due to publication without notice during the period when a notice was required, and forfeiture due to a failure to timely renew the copyright, during the period when renewal was mandatory.

Thus, investigation into the copyright status of a work requires information on the publication and registration history of the work. In some cases, it may be difficult to discover sufficient facts to determine whether, for example, a work was, at some time, published without notice over the course of several decades.

---

448   See 17 U.S.C. § 302(c).

449   See The Copyright Renewal Act of 1992, Pub. L. No. 102-307, 106 Stat. 264, 266 (June 26, 1992).

450   See: 17 U.S.C. §§ 304(a)(3), 304(a)(4).

[a]—Expiration of Copyright Protection

The Copyright Clause of the Constitution allows Congress to protect works for "limited times," after which the work enters the public domain. All works published in the United States in 1922 or earlier have now entered the public domain in the United States.[451] Passage of the Copyright Term Extension Act in 1998 created a pause in expiration of the term of pre-1978 works, which will begin to enter the public domain again via expiration of their extended ninety five-year term beginning after 2018.

[i]—Post-1978 Works

Under the "life plus 70" regime for post-1978 works, the earliest date that any works will enter the public domain is after the end of 2048. For example, if an author died in 1978, and created several works in 1978 prior to her death, that author's works created on or after January 1, 1978 will enter the public domain seventy years after her death in 1978, after the end of 2048, or as of January 1, 2049.

[ii]—Pre-1978 Works

Conversely, and perhaps somewhat paradoxically, any earlier works by the same author published prior to January 1, 1978 would have a longer term of copyright protection. The author's pre-1978 works are protected for ninety-five years from the date of publication. So in the above example of an author who died in 1978, protection of her work published in 1977 would be protected for ninety-five years, or up until 2072. But her works created in 1978 would come under the "life plus" scheme for Post-1978 works, and would enter the public domain after the end of 2048.

[b]—Publication Without Notice Prior to 1989

In 1989, the United States signed an international copyright treaty, the Berne Convention, which led to a reduction of "formalities" under American law, such as the requirement of a copyright notice on published copies.[452]

---

451   The term of protection is different in foreign territories. It is possible for a pre-1978 work that has entered the public domain in the United States to still be under copyright in another country. For example if a German composer had a work published in the United States in 1920, and died in 1950, the status would be that the work's copyright protection in the United States expired seventy-five years later after the end of 1995, but because copyright protection in Germany is life plus seventy, all the composer's works will be protected in Germany (and in other countries with copyright treaties) through the end of 2020.

452   See the Berne Convention Implementation Act of 1988, Pub. L. No. 100-568, 102 Stat. 2853, effective as of March 1, 1989.

Prior to the Berne Convention, publication in the United States without notice resulted in a forfeiture of copyright, and the work was forced into the public domain.[453] No official notices or announcements would be made in such event, nor would the records of the Copyright Office reflect that publication without notice had occurred. Thus, for someone seeking to use a work that purportedly entered the public domain because of lack of notice, they would be well advised to have evidence in order to avoid any infringement claims.

In some cases, whether "publication" had in fact occurred was disputed. For example, a private distribution to a limited amount of personal contacts has been held to not constitute "publication" as defined in the statute.[454]

---

453   See Estate of *Martin Luther King v. CBS, Inc.*, 194 F.3d 1211, 1214 (11th Cir. 1999):

"Under the regime created by the 1909 Act, an author received state common law protection automatically at the time of creation of a work. This state common law protection persisted until the moment of a general publication. When a general publication occurred, the author either forfeited his work to the public domain, or, if he had therebefore complied with federal statutory requirements, converted his common law copyright into a federal statutory copyright."

(Internal citations omitted.) Under the 1909 Act, copyright protection subsisted for a first term of twenty-eight years, which could then be renewed for an additional renewal term. The renewal had to be made during the final year of the first term, or else it was not timely, and the work was ejected into the public domain. See *Rose v. Bourne, Inc.*, 176 F. Supp. 605, 610 (S.D.N.Y. 1959), *aff'd* 279 F.2d 79 (2d Cir. 1960) (cited in *Barris v. Hamilton*, 1999 WL 311813 at *4 (S.D.N.Y. 1999) (discussing renewal of works under the 1909 Act)).

454   *See Estate of King*, N. 17 *supra*, 194 F.3d at 1214–1215:

"In order to soften the hardship of the rule that publication destroys common law rights, courts developed a distinction between a 'general publication' and a 'limited publication.' Only a general publication divested a common law copyright. See id. A general publication occurred 'when a work was made available to members of the public at large without regard to their identity or what they intended to do with the work.' Conversely, a non-divesting limited publication was one that communicated the contents of a work to a select group and for a limited purpose, and without the right of diffusion, reproduction, distribution or sale."

(Internal citations omitted.)

See also, *Penguin Books U.S.A., Inc. v. New Christian Church of Full Endeavor, Ltd.*, 288 F. Supp.2d 544 (S.D.N.Y. 2003) (holding copyright registration in book "A Course in Miracles" invalid because of publication without notice).

[c]—Copyright Restoration for Certain Foreign Works

The Uruguay Round Agreements Act ("URAA") of 1994 implemented the provisions agreed upon at the Uruguay Round of negotiations of the General Agreement on Tariffs and Trade ("GATT").[455]

Congress enacted the URAA on December 8, 1994, to bring the United States into compliance with the Berne Convention's Rule of Retroactivity. The URAA restored copyright protection for foreign works that had fallen into the public domain for technical reasons unrelated to expiration of the copyright term.[456] Congress's intention in restoring such protection to foreign copyrights was to secure similar protection for American copyright holders abroad.[457]

Section 104A of the Copyright Act contains the provisions for restoration of copyright for so-called "GATT works." By definition, the copyright owners of GATT works will be based overseas, however, in many cases the copyright restoration benefits the exclusive United States agents for those overseas copyright owners. The provisions for restoration of GATT works include accommodations for those who had previously relied on the public domain status of the foreign works, by granting them reasonable licenses to continue their use.[458]

---

455   See:

Supreme Court: Golan v. Holder, 565 U.S. 302 (2012).

Second Circuit: Troll Co. v. Uneeda Doll Co., 483 F.3d 150, 156–157 (2d Cir. 2007).

Third Circuit: Dam Things from Denmark v. Russ Berrie & Co., Inc., 290 F.3d 548, 554-555 (3d Cir. 2002) (discussing copyright restoration for foreign works).

456   E.g., failure to adhere to United States copyright "formalities" such as publication with notice, and renewal of copyright registrations.

457   See 17 U.S.C. § 104A.

458   See 17 U.S.C. § 104A(d)(3). The URAA restores copyrights for original works that (1) are not in the public domain of their source countries through expiration of their copyright terms, (2) are in the public domain in the United States because of noncompliance with legal formalities, (3) have at least one author who was a national or domiciliary of an eligible country, and (4) were first published in an eligible country and were not published in the United States within thirty days of first publication. See also, *Golan v. Holder*, 565 U.S. 302 (2012) (holding URAA constitutional).

CHAPTER 2

Television

§2.01　Television: Introduction and Overview

The word "Television" means "far vision," from the Greek *tèle* (far) and French *vision* (vision). It is a word invented in the early 20th century to describe a technology that transmits images from one location to another. Like telegraph ("far writing") and telephone ("far sounds") that preceded it, and "internet," a word invented towards the end of the 20th century, it has come to symbolize a category of entertainment whose hallmark is to deliver sound and vision across distances increasingly unlimited by technological constraints to cover the entire earth, moon, solar system, and beyond.[1]

The technology is capable of transmitting sound and vision instantaneously, and it can do so originating from any place the technology can reach. Thus the content of television is as broad and varied as its users dictate, including virtually any activity from any location. A short list of the scope of what television can deliver would include preexisting productions such as films and entertainment, prerecorded productions and sports events, news reporting, live discussion, special events, advertising and marketing, live events of virtually any kind, and even "slow TV" showing the natural world at its own slow and beautiful pace.

However, as noted by one court, "Production for television is a highly risky undertaking, like wildcat drilling for gas and oil."[2] Thus, imbued with high risk, the television industry has developed business models that balance risks and benefits, but those business models vary depending on the type of "television" involved.

1　See, e.g. http://www.dictionary.com/browse/television. As of December 24, 1968, the first television transmission "live from the moon" (Apollo 8 in lunar orbit, reading Genesis) symbolized the expansion of television to the universe. See https://www.nasa.gov/topics/history/features/apollo_8.html.

2　See *Schurz Communs. v. FCC*, 982 F. 2d 1043, 1046 (7th Cir. 1992).

The television industry has three predominant technological distribution methods that have historically led to three overall business models: terrestrial over the air broadcast, cable and satellite closed circuit systems (including cable production networks such as HBO and CNN), and the more recent internet and mobile software and application platforms (including "Over the Top" (OTT) online-only distributors and producers such as Amazon, Hulu, and Netflix).

§2.02 Terrestrial Broadcast and The Original Big Three Networks

[1]—Network Technology Platforms

The primary original technology remains broadcast transmitters via antenna towers, with TV stations broadcasting in a geographical area limited by the electrical wattage of their transmitters, typically covering one city or region. Due to the limitations of the technology, all TV stations are "local" in their reach and market area, and with respect to ownership are either affiliated with a network, thus privileged to carry network programming, or independent. The original "Big Three" networks are ABC, CBS, and NBC. The Federal Communications Commission (FCC) regulates broadcasters by requiring licenses to use the public airwaves.[3]

[2]—Network Business Models

The traditional network business model is to sell advertising and for the revenue to exceed production and distribution costs. Local stations were either owned by or affiliated with one of the big three networks (ABC, CBS, NBC) in which case the local affiliate offered 1) exclusive network broadcasts in prime time hours (received by local stations via a private distribution network); and 2) other content (local news, locally produced programs, reruns of old network shows in syndication, sports). Independent local stations offered all the above except for network programming in prime time, which was reserved to network-owned affiliates. The exception are public broadcasting stations that are funded partly by the government and partly as nonprofits receiving donations, grants, and underwriting of programming.[4]

[3]—Network Production Business Model

The traditional production model for network programming, prior to 1970, was that network productions in prime time were produced either by the network, or by independent

---

3   See FCC publication "The Public and Broadcasting," available at https://www.fcc.gov/media/radio/public-and-broadcasting#ACT.

4   See generally *Schurz Communs. v. FCC*, 982 F. 2d 1043, 1046 (7th Cir. 1992) (discussing structure of network broadcast television industry).

production companies whose programs were carried by the network. Independent producers complained that in exchange for accepting the programming, networks insisted on ownership of the programs (financial interest) and future syndication distribution rights, thereby creating a so-called "fin-syn" monopoly in programming and distribution, including favoring network owned affiliate local stations over independent local stations when it came to syndication licensing of hit shows in public demand. Networks measure success of a production, and corresponding advertising rates via ratings services such as Nielsen. Successful programming may result in several seasons of shows, and once the show has run its course, the old episodes are available for lucrative syndication via distribution to local stations nationwide and worldwide. More details on the network production business model are below.

§2.03   Cable and Satellite: Multichannel Video Program Distributors (MVPD)[5]

[1]—MVPD Technology Platforms

Cable systems arose originally to serve customers in remote and rural areas that broadcast transmissions through the air did not reach. Cable systems would obtain network and local television broadcast signals then retransmit those signals over a cable system to subscribers, who paid a monthly subscription fee for the service.[6] Satellite systems offer a similar platform via satellite instead of cables.

[2]—MVPD Business Models

MVPD distributors such as Comcast and Time Warner Cable include on their systems cable-only distribution and production networks such as HBO, ESPN, AMC, CNN, as well as carrying and retransmitting broadcast network and local station transmissions. Under FCC and Copyright Act laws and regulations described below, where MVPDs retransmit broadcast programming, cable system providers compensate the original broadcasters and production companies by negotiation of retransmission consent fees under FCC regulations. Thus the financial model for cable (and later satellite services) is based on subscriber fees to the cable company, then fees and payments made by the

---

5   Section 602 (13) of The Communications Act of 1934 (as amended by the Telecommunications Act of 1996) defines an MVPD as "a person such as, but not limited to, a cable operator, a multichannel multipoint distribution service, a direct broadcast satellite service, or a television receive-only satellite program distributor, who makes available for purchase, by subscribers or customers, multiple channels of video programming."

6   See, e.g. *Fortnightly Corp. v. United Artists Television*, 392 U.S. 390 (describing early origins of cable television industry). Abrogated by later 1976 Copyright Act Section 111.

cable system to broadcasters and content owners for carrying the content and broadcasts on the cable system.

The statutory basis is Section 111 of the Copyright Act, which provides for a compulsory licensing regime setting forth statutory royalties payable by Multichannel Video Programming Distributors (MVPD's, or "cable companies" as they are commonly referred to) to copyright owners of the television programs for the right to provide "secondary transmissions" via cable of the broadcast network's "primary transmissions."[7] Section 119 of the Copyright Act has similar retransmission provisions for satellite television providers.[8]

In addition to the statutory licensing of copyrighted programming in the retransmission context under copyright law, the Federal Communications Commission in Section 325(b) of the Communications Act, requires that broadcasters who so elect are entitled to negotiated "retransmission consent" fees for their broadcast signals when retransmitted by MVPDs.[9]

In addition, the cable networks carried by MVPDs generate revenue from the subscription fees received from MVPD customers, and also in most cases from advertising carried on their networks. A few cable networks such as HBO rely only on subscription revenues and do not carry commercial advertising.

[3]—MVPD Broadband Services

MVPD's often also provide broadband internet access and sometimes voice telephone services in additional to cable television programming. For consumers who "cut the cord" and choose to solely use broadband and WiFi internet connections for television entertainment, the MVPD remains a crucial service provider and realizes revenues even from those who don't subscribe to any cable television services or bundles.

[4]—MVPD Production Business Models for Cable Networks

Exclusively cable and satellite based production networks such as HBO, AMC, and other arose that do not use traditional over the air broadcast technologies. Such cable

---

7   See 17 U.S.C. § 111.

8   See 17 U.S.C. § 119.

9   See 47 U.S.C. §325(a). Note that, while large broadcasters may demand a retransmission consent fee, smaller broadcasters with little leverage in such negotiations may at least ensure that their signals are carried by the MVPDs, by asserting a mandatory "right to carriage" under Section 534(b) of the Communications Act, the "must carry" regulations. See, e.g., *Cablevision Systems Development Co. v. Motion Picture Association of America, Inc.*, 836 F.2d 599 (D.C. Cir. 1988) (explaining basis for Section 111 retransmission fees under the Copyright Act).

networks license motion pictures and other content from traditional studios and network production companies, carry sports (ESPN), news (CNN), special interest content (HGTV), and virtually any type of niche content for which there may be potential subscribers. Some are "premium cable" networks funded exclusively by subscriber fees received via the cable system without commercial advertising (e.g. HBO). The majority of cable networks are funded by a combination of subscriber fees received through the MVPD that carries their network, and traditional advertising.

§2.04   Internet and Mobile Platforms Offering Subscription Video On Demand (SVOD)

[1]— SVOD Technology Platforms

Web sites, mobile applications, and other server and software application based web platforms

[2]— SVOD Internet Platform Business Models

Internet only platforms have a financial model based on user subscription fees, online advertising, and ad-share revenue. Leading content providers include Netflix, Amazon, and Hulu. "Over the Top" or "OTT" services are accessed by consumers without MVPD subscriptions, thus going "over the top" of MVPDs. OTT services either license or acquire third party content from studios, production, companies, and networks, or finance and produce their own content and original programming.

For low-cost Webisode production, ad-share revenue is the model on web platforms such as YouTube and Vimeo.

[3]— SVOD Internet Production Business Models

"Over The Top" ("OTT") broadband and internet based platforms increasingly rely on Subscription Video On Demand (SVOD) services via Netflix; Amazon; Hulu, where consumers can stream content at any time including "binge watching" entire seasons of a series without waiting for each week's premiere date. OTT SVOD has led to the emergence of original programming produced on a "buy out" or "cost plus" basis (where the producer simply sells the content to the platform instead of the network model of co-ownership and participation in a potential syndication back end.

Reported examples of current business models allowing OTT services to acquire content include purchasing content for 25% over actual production costs. This would provide

certainly as regards guaranteed 25% return on investment for the producer or studio, but does not includeany potential for a lucrative syndication downstream profit.

OTT platforms whose business model is based on acquiring subscribers and not advertisers thus cutting the traditional direct connection between a show's ratings success and its advertising revenue. Online platforms traditionally do not share viewing statistics for specific shows, as the goal is to have shows that viewers demand leading to increased long term viewer monthly subscriptions, not increased sales of products advertised during shows, which is the traditional network model.

Webisode low cost production and distribution models have emerged, with initial crowd-sourced funding via IndieGogo, Kickstarter, and other crowd-sourced financing models aimed at initially achieving distribution and ad-share revenue on platforms such as YouTube and Vimeo, then ideally repurposing content for other platforms with greater financial gain including SVOD, broadcast, and long form motion pictures.

§2.05   The Traditional Network Prime Time Pilot to Series to Syndication Model

The traditional network prime time program life-cycle has three main components, the pilot, the series order(s) with network license fees, and post-network syndication distribution benefiting the studio or producer, not the network.

The traditional business model is that a studio or production company produces and owns the show, but initially licenses exclusive network exhibition for a license fee that is less than the cost of production, requiring "deficit financing" via loans during the initial network exhibition over the first few years. Only if the show is successful, after several years, does the producer reap the main financial reward of syndication license fees "off-network" to third party local stations and cable networks.

[1]—Pilot Episode

A show concept is produced as one sample episode to allow a network to make the decision on its potential for acquisition. All talent involved will be asked to sign option agreements, giving the producer the option for continuing their services up to the statutory limit of seven years for personal services contracts under California law.

[2]—Series Order and License Fees

The traditional network season runs from September to June each year, traditionally resulting in orders for 13 show episodes to cover half a season, or a full season of 22 or more episodes. In a traditional agreement between the production company and the network, the network only licenses the right to premiere the episodes, and to show reruns, for several years. The network also holds options on future seasons, typically 4 years of additional seasons after the premiere season, for a total of 5 years. The production company retains ownership of the show outside the bounds of the network license agreement. Therefore the network license fees to the producer are less than the full cost of production, as the network is only obtaining a limited license and not full ownership.

The gap between the production costs and the network license fee is referred to as "deficit financing," discussed in more detail below. Note that if a show runs for more than 5 years, the producer will be able to negotiate a new agreement with the network at a higher license fee. Note also that the talent on the show, e.g. writers, directors, and actors, will have contracts with options that continue for no more than seven years under the "seven year rule." Therefore for exceptionally successful shows that run for more than seven years, there are usually highly publicized negotiations with the primary cast who, after seven years, are contractually free and can negotiate for increases of salary and other compensation.

[3]—Imputed License Fees

Where the production company and the network are affiliated companies, the license fee the production company charges to the network will not be the result of an open market "arm's length" transaction, but will be instead a co-called "imputed" license fee set between affiliates. Where possible, co-producers and those entitled to profit participation are likely to demand contractual language stating that any such imputed license fee between affiliates be the same as an otherwise arm's length transaction between unrelated companies that achieves the highest possible price.

[4]—Syndication

Where a show is successful and runs for several seasons on the network, the producer will then own 100 or more episodes, which can then be syndicated by distribution to local television stations and cable systems and overseas. Such syndication fees are lucrative and allow for any deficit funding or loans to be paid back. For the producer or studio that provides a series to a network, the true financial reward for a traditional network series comes after several years, via the syndication distribution. Long running hits may begin syndication of old shows after several years, when the network's exclusive exhibition rights expire, while at the same time still producing new episodes for the network under extensions or renewals of the original agreement.

§2.06   The Financial Interest and Syndication ("Fin-Syn") Consent Decrees Era 1970–1995

Prior to 1970 Network productions in prime time were predominantly owned by the network in conjunction with independent production companies, but independent producers complained that in exchange for accepting the programming, networks insisted on ownership of the programs (a financial interest) and future syndication distribution rights, thereby creating a monopoly in programming and distribution, including favoring network owned affiliate local stations over independent local stations when it came to syndication licensing of hit shows in public demand.

This monopoly power violated the Sherman Antitrust Act,[10] and led to FCC regulations and Department of Justice action in the courts, resulting in consent decrees issued by the Federal Court for the Central District of California governing ABC, CBS, and NBC with respect to television production, making the networks subject to financial interest and syndication rules (known as the "Financial Interest Rule" or "Fin-Syn" rules).

The FCC regulations included Prime Time Access Rules, limiting how many weekly hours of prime time programming could be owned by networks, and forbade direct network control over subsequent syndication. The intent was that the consent decrees would encourage more independent production of television content, which would benefit the public by increased diversity of program content.

The FCC regulations dated from 1970, and the Consent Decrees from the period 1978 to 1980, when the original Big Three networks were still the major forces in the television industry.[11] However, developments in the television industry over those years subsequently lessened the need for government oversight of network programming. Chief among those developments was the rise of the cable industry and new cable networks providing an increasing variety of programming, and the emergence for the first time of a fourth network, Fox Network owned by 20th Century Fox studios.

All of these developments had the effect of lowering the power and market share of the original Big Three networks, who could also claim they were at a disadvantage because the Financial Interest Rule did not apply to these new competitors. By 1990, the Consent

---

10   15 U.S.C. §§ 1 – 7.

11   The FCC rules were enacted in 1970 pursuant to 47 C.F.R. §73.658(j), and were eventually repealed and amended in 1995 pursuant to 60 Fed. Reg. 48, 907 (1995). The Department of Justice Consent Decrees against ABC, CBS, and NBC under the Sherman Antitrust Act were enacted between 1978 and 1980 by the U.S. District Court for the Central District of California as follows: *United States v. National Broadcasting Co.*, 449 F. Supp. 1127 (C.D. Cal. 1978); *United States v. CBS, Inc.*, 1980 U.S. Dist. LEXIS 14679 (C.D. Cal. July 3, 1980); *United States v. American Broadcasting Cos.*, 1980 U.S. Dist. LEXIS 16787 (C.D. Cal. Nov. 14, 1980).

Decrees had expired, and by 1992, the Seventh Circuit abrogated the FCC regulations of network production.[12] Finally, in 1995, the FCC regulations of network production came to an official end.

The television industry quickly responded to the lifting of regulatory and court limitations, with several production studios acquiring television networks (e.g. Disney Studios acquired ABC, 20th Century Fox had already started the Fox Network, Warner Bros. launched "The WB," etc.) and becoming vertically integrated, with production (studio) and distribution (network) under unified control.

§2.07   Traditional Network Production Agreements

The outline of traditional network production and license agreements for prime time content may include some of the following highlights in production agreements between a network and a producer, or "packager:"

Series Order: As described and in the pilot as to content and duration (30 or 60 minutes total, less commercial breaks).

Term: Five years or the date as of which network orders the last season (or "cycle") of shows. The five year term may be divided into as many as 16 broadcast "cycles," with each cycle containing a set number of shows and reruns. The network will have the right to stop production or simply decline to order additional seasons or cycles, or to continue for all five years, depending on ratings and popularity.

First Negotiation and First Refusal Rights: Should the show be a hit, with respect to additional seasons or cycles after five years, the network has first negotiation and first refusal rights as compared to any third party.

License Fees: Per season or cycle, with increases on the assumption that additional cycles indicate the show is profitable for the network. Where the production company and the network are affiliated, there will be an "imputed license fee" that will likely come with contractual requirements that it be no less than a comparable arm's length transaction.

Deficit Financing: The producer (sometimes designated as "Packager") will negotiate to have as low a deficit as possible, and hope to achieve off-network syndication, overseas and foreign licensing, and ancillary rights (spinoff books, music, etc.) to recoup the deficit. Producer may

---

12   See *Schurz Communs. v. FCC*, 982 F. 2d 1043 (7th Cir. 1992) (Posner, J.) (vacating subsequent 1991 version of the relevant FCC regulations). See also *United States v. NBC*, ABC, CBS, 842 F. Supp. 402 (C.D. Cal. 1993) (following Schurz in modifying the Consent Decrees).

seek to limit producer's share of the deficit in the range of 20% to 40% and share the deficit with the studio. The network may be willing to treat some of the deficit amount as a loan subject to first priority return from syndication revenues. Producer may seek to build in increases caused by union or guild increases or studio and facilities rental costs.

<u>Creative, Location, and Budget Approvals</u>: While the network will have ultimate approval and power to broadcast or not, some reasonable creative approval power may be achievable, perhaps as much as final cut for delivery to network. Budget approvals are important should there be any penalties for going over budget, the producer can allocate a budget surplus against a budget deficit to avoid such penalties. Location approvals can be key with respect to taking advantage of state or foreign tax credits.

<u>Breakage</u>: "Breakage" provisions apply to talent costs over budget and may be subject to studio approval and cost sharing.

> <u>Advances and Timing of Payments</u>: May include pre-production advances, and provisions whereby 80% of budgeted per episode cost is paid upon beginning of production and 20% upon final delivery. Separate repeat fees will be included.

> <u>Format Rights</u>: In addition to retaining ownership of the "ready mades" (i.e. deliverable episodes) the format or concept rights may be retained by the producer for exploitation in other territories and other languages, generating format license fees from other territories as well as producer services fees for guiding and consulting on new versions of the producer's existing format.

> <u>Production Facilities</u>: Network may require use of network production facilities.

> <u>Broadcast Territory</u>: The United States. This leaves the producer free to monetize the show overseas, thought there may be blackout requirements in Canadian territories that overlap with the United States.

> <u>Exclusivity</u>: Negotiation of ancillary revenues to be retained by producer, as well as rights to spinoffs, sequels, prequels, and adaptations.

> <u>Talent Exclusivity</u>: Cast shall be exclusive to network in television to maximum extent permitted by SAG-AFTRA. Producer shall have the obligation to secure cast services via option that cover the entire term. Note that a hit show can enter syndication after year five, even if the producer and network come to a new agreement for additional network seasons, with the show available on network for new episodes and in syndication for repeats. Note that personal services agreements with cast may contain options for up to seven years, the maximum under California law for personal services agreements, and two years beyond the five year network license agreement. Thus the producer may be

able to negotiate years six and seven with the network, and may also begin to syndicate the show, prior to having to renegotiate with the cast after year seven of cast agreements.

<u>Pay or Play</u>: Beyond the network's obligation to pay for shows delivered, it is not obligated to exhibit.

§2.08   SVOD Business Models

Online SVOD services include licensed studio content as well as original productions. Netflix, Amazon, and Hulu pioneered this creative outlet which will expand to traditional cable and broadcast networks online, as they pursue the consumer's preference for OTT SVOD, which is "over the top" i.e. direct to the consumer online going "over the heads" of the cable or satellite service, and offering subscription video on demand any time including binge watching of an entire season at once enabled by the release of entire seasons on one premiere date, or simply the luxury of catching up with a series that has premiered gradually over time but has all episodes available for streaming at any time.

SVOD services may often be purely subscriber funded and not beholden to the demands of television advertisers whose need to reach maximum customers, and whose products become identified with a show. Such sponsorship, can create limitations on creativity and content, for example where an ad supported show must be careful not to have content that may offend its advertiser or its customers.

SVOD services are more concerned with attracting subscribers, and currently do not share actual viewer data for their programs. They rely instead on having compelling and original content that drives subscriptions. The current SVOD production business model is different from the traditional network model for several reasons, including the lack of a broadcast schedule, the ability for consumers to view at will, the tendency to have shorter seasons of ten or less episodes, and the initial reliance on superstar movie talent that is willing to be in ten episodes but no more. Thus the traditional syndication distribution producer payout is not an option, nor does the producer have to rely on deficit financing, which is a mechanism of the network license fee, multiyear series, and syndication.[13]

Thus a studio or producer of SVOD content will have less up front risk because all of the production costs are immediately paid, with the "profit" being the producer's negotiated markup over the full cost of production, reportedly often around 25%, the "cost plus" scenario

---

13   See generally Green Hasson Janks Fall 2016 Entertainment Report Whitepaper "The Evolution of New Media: Making Money in a World Where Digital Streaming Rules," available at https://www.greenhassonjanks.com/publications/whitepapers/2016-entertainment-media-whitepaper-evolution-new-media/.

for a buyout. Traditional "profit participation" points may still be offered, but in the form of "bonus points" with fixed economic value, not true profit percentages.

With respect to full length motion pictures produced on this platform, the lack of a "qualifying run" of theatrical exhibitions at the correct time of year means the film will not qualify for nominations for Academy Awards given by the Academy of Motion Picture Arts and Sciences.[14]

Within this business model, producers may still be able to negotiate for the following:

- Additional territories where the SVOD service does not or cannot operate.

- A term that expires instead of a buyout in perpetuity (five or ten years).

- Where the SVOD service will not provide viewer data, attempt to mine social media to determine the show's popularity either for bonus payments or the next project.

- Structure the budget to include both a producer's markup and overhead so the "cost" already has built in profitability, even prior to the negotiation of the "cost plus" additional revenues.

- Reserve ancillary income from merchandise, soundtracks, etc.

- Reserve theatrical exhibition rights.

- Guarantee additional seasons or minimum number of episodes.

- Lock the producer for the life of the series, including budget approval.

- Include use of producer-owned equipment and facilities for industry standard fees.

- Series production bonuses in lieu of ratings bonus.

- Control over brand integration (product placement) that may provide financing or additional revenue.

§2.09   SVOD Production and Talent Guilds

While shorter seasons and closed loop story lines may create consumer success, and the overall success of SVOD original content has led to an explosion of television content production, and major stars reportedly enjoy tremendous salaries for SVOD original content, for other talent this represents both good and bad news. The good news is the explosion of employment opportunities as SVOD original content production gains in popularity. The bad news is that each shorter project translates into less work on an annual basis, especially compared to the network model of up to 26 episodes per full season.   Budgets may also be leaner in

---

14   See http://www.oscars.org/oscars/rules-eligibility (AMPAS rules for eligibility).

order to attract buyout interest, which has to cover 100% of production costs. Adding to this downward pressure on talent compensation (other than the much sought after "movie stars") is the lack of any lucrative syndication or net profit future payday, and the lack of traditional residuals payments generated by network and cable broadcasts.

In response, guilds such as the Directors Guild of America (DGA) and Writers Guild of America have negotiated salary increases for members applicable to SVOD. For example, the DGA has a High Budget Subscription Video on Demand agreement and rate card tailored for SVOD.[15]

§2.10 Public Broadcasting

The Corporation for Public Broadcasting ("CPB") is a private, nonprofit corporation created by Congress in 1967. The mission of CPB is outlined in the Public Broadcasting Act of 1967.[16] CPB's mission is to facilitate the development of, and ensure universal access to, non-commercial high-quality programming. It is a major funder of the nonprofit stations that are members of the Public Broadcasting Service ("PBS"). PBS stations offer commercial-free programming, which may be licensed, or produced by a PBS-affiliated station. Many of the programs are underwritten by corporate sponsorship.

§2.11 FCC Regulation of Broadcasters

The airwaves over which television and radio are transmitted belong to the public. As noted above, the Federal Communications Commission ("FCC") is the government agency that administers all uses of the public airwaves. The FCC issues licenses authorizing the operation of local television stations, regulates the extent to which media conglomerates can own multiple radio and television stations as well as print media such as newspapers, and also regulates aspects of the cable television industry.[17]

---

15   See DGA High Budget SVOD Package, available at <https://www.dga.org/Contracts/~/link.aspx?_id=FD-6319734D884947A5F2115A0867B68B&_z=z >, and a corresponding Rate Card, available at <https://www.dga.org/Contracts/Rates-2017-to-2018.aspx >. See also WGA High Budget SVOD Minimums, available as part of the WGA Digital New Media guidelines at <http://www.wga.org/the-guild/going-guild/get-involved/digital-new-media/guide#15plus >.

16   47 U.S.C. § 396, as amended.

17   See *Prometheus Radio Project v. FCC*, 373 F.3d 372 (3d Cir. 2004) (reviewing FCC revisions of regulations regarding broadcast media ownership, including review of the history of FCC regulation over station ownership in the 1934 Telecommunications Act and The Telecommunications Act of 1996. Held that FCC deregulatory acts permitting broader scope of conglomerate ownership of radio, television, and newspaper print media came within FCC's power to regulate media ownership.).

The FCC also has authority to regulate purportedly indecent content on over-the-air broadcast television and radio stations. Under Section 1464 of Title 18 of the United States Code, "[w]hoever utters any obscene, indecent, or profane language by means of radio communication shall be fined under this title or imprisoned not more than two years, or both."[18]

In the years since passage of Section 1464, the FCC's approach to enforcement was restrained. In 2001, the FCC issued guidelines regarding how it would use its powers of censorship.[19] The guidelines stated that "fleeting and isolated" expletives were not actionably indecent. However, during a 2003 Golden Globe Awards broadcast, a member of the popular rock band, U2, gave an impromptu acceptance speech that included an expletive. This incident, and other similar outbursts on awards shows, triggered complaints to the FCC, and resulted in FCC actions against the broadcasters. In addition, the level of fines that could be levied was increased dramatically from $32,500 to $325,000 per broadcast, meaning that a national broadcast carried by hundred of local stations could result in millions of dollars in fines.[20]

In 2010, the broadcasters filed a Petition for Review of the FCC enforcement actions based on the on-air outbursts. In *Fox Television Stations, Inc. v. FCC*, the Second Circuit struck down the FCC's current indecency policy as impermissibly vague in its description of what is "patently offensive," stating "[t]o place any discussion of these vast topics at the broadcaster's peril has the effect of promoting wide self-censorship of valuable material which should be completely protected under the First Amendment."[21] The Court noted that the FCC could revise its guidelines to comport with constitutional guidelines.

The Second Circuit holding issued between two Supreme Court rulings on whether the FCC indecency standards were (1) arbitrary and capricious under administrative law principles;[22] and (2) constitutional under First Amendment principles.[23] In deciding the case, however,

---

18   This authority was the subject of the landmark 1978 *Supreme Court case, FCC v. Pacifica Foundation*, 438 U.S. 726, 98 S.Ct. 3026, 57 L.Ed.2d 1073 (1978). *Pacifica* dealt with comedian George Carlin's "Filthy Words" monologue, a twelve-minute string of expletives broadcast on the radio at 2:00 p.m. Based on the specific facts in the case, and noting that such censorship must be exercised with restraint, the Supreme Court held that the FCC could restrict indecent speech in the broadcast context. The court's rationale was based on its findings that broadcast media has "a uniquely pervasive presence in the lives of all Americans," and the nature of broadcast television—as opposed to printed materials—made it "uniquely accessible to children, even those too young to read."

19   See Industry Guidance on the Commission's Case Law Interpreting 18 U.S.C. § 1464, 16 F.C.C. Rcd. 7999, at ¶ 1 (2001).

20   See 47 U.S.C. § 503(b)(2)(c)(iii). See also, *Fox Television Stations, Inc. v. FCC*, 613 F.3d 317 (2d Cir. 2010) (reviewing history of FCC indecency actions and holding that FCC policy was impermissibly vague and violated freedom of speech).

21   *Fox Television Stations, Inc. v. FCC, id.*, 613 F.3d at 335.

22   See *FCC v. Fox Television Stations, Inc.*, 556 U.S. 502, 129 S.Ct. 1800, 173 L.Ed.2d 738 (2009) (*Fox I*).

23   See *FCC v. Fox Television Stations, Inc.* 567 U.S. __, 132 S.Ct. 2307, 183 L.Ed.2d 234 (2012) (*Fox II*).

the Court did not settle whether the FCC policy violated the First Amendment. Instead, it held only that broadcasters had a constitutional right to be warned in advance of what the new policy prohibited, and the FCC had imposed its changed policy after the broadcasts had aired, rather than before. The FCC has the option now of reconsidering its policy, or keeping it as is, and awaiting a new constitutional challenge in court.

FCC regulation of obscenity is not applicable to subscription-based services such as cable television, satellite television, and pay-per-view, where subscribers who are offended can, in theory, simply cancel their subscriptions, unlike over-the-air broadcasts, which courts have held are more "pervasive" in our society.

§2.12   Advertising and Ratings

Network television and much of cable television are built upon an advertising revenue model. Information on a program's audience, including its composition and size, is essential in order to determine the popularity of a program, and in order to charge advertisers a premium rate. Nielsen Media is the private organization that profiles and measures audiences. Nielsen Media meters viewership of television programming, and publishes ratings with details of the number of viewers, the percentage of households watching, and the demographics or "market segment" represented by the viewership.[24] The statistics are published as "ratings points" and audience "share."

A ratings point represents one percent of the total number of U.S. households with a television. If there are 100 million households with a television, one point equals one million households. A "share" is the percentage of households actually watching television that are tuned in to the program. The difference between rating and share is that a rating reflects the percentage of the total population of televisions tuned to a particular program, while share reflects the percentage of televisions actually in use. Where there are 100 million households with a television, a Nielsen rating of 10/20 means that 10 million households were watching the program, representing 20% of all viewers who were actually watching television at that time.

The "share" figure is also broken down into market segment, which divides up the population into gender and age groups. This aids advertisers that are trying to reach particular groups of consumers when they purchase time slots for their commercials.

   The Nielsen Ratings are then used by the broadcaster to set the per-minute advertising rates for the program.

---

24   See www.nielsenmedia.com.

§2.13   Liability Review

Broadcasters are potentially liable for regulatory violations related to truth in advertising, such as those promulgated by the Federal Trade Commission ("FTC"), and for advertising-based torts such as violation of the Lanham Act related to false advertising. Networks therefore commonly screen advertising before it is broadcast to ensure it is not false or misleading. In the case of long-form commercial advertising, or "infomercials," broadcasters commonly precede such programs with a disclaimer that the "program" is paid commercial programming, and that the advertiser, and not the broadcaster or cable station, is solely responsible for the content.

Broadcasters may also pre-screen programs such as news reporting, and hour-long "news magazine" programs for issues such as defamation, invasion of privacy, and indecency.[25] Even fictional scripted programming is not immune to charges of defamation based on allegations that fictional characters were modeled on real individuals.[26]

§2.14   Episodic Television Business Models

The variety of television programming is wide, ranging from high-budget films to low-budget public-access talk shows. Each type of show may have its own particular nuances with respect to legal agreements with producers, cast, and crew.[27]

---

25   See *Conradt v. NBC Universal, Inc.*, 536 F. Supp.2d 380 (S.D.N.Y. 2008) (case involving NBC Dateline news magazine segment entitled "To Catch a Predator," in which sister of suicide victim alleged that network's intrusion into law enforcement and its broadcast of pursuit of her brother caused his suicide. Court denied defendant's motions to dismiss, stating that a reasonable jury could find that "[r]ather than merely report on law enforcement's efforts to combat crime, NBC purportedly instigated and then placed itself squarely in the middle of a police operation, pushing the police to engage in tactics that were unnecessary and unwise, solely to generate more dramatic footage for a television show." *Id.*, 536 F. Supp.2d at 383.).

26   See *Tamkin v. CBS Broadcasting, Inc.*, 193 Cal. App.4th 133, 122 Cal. Rptr.3d 264 (2011) (defamation claim based on characters in "CSI").

27   Some of the leading types of programming include:

Dramatic Series
Comedy Series (single or multiple camera)
Reality Shows
Broadcast Network News
Cable News Networks
Weather
Business news
Local news
News magazines

Episodic television series production is often financed by the television division of one of the major motion pictures studios or by a production division of a large network. The series is then licensed to the broadcast or cable network at a per-episode license fee. The fee charged is usually less than the actual cost of production. If a broadcaster pays full production costs, it may make more financial sense to own all rights in the show as a work made for hire instead of licensing the exclusive broadcast rights for a limited term. The licensing rights do not extend more than five years. After the five years have expired, if the series is still successful, the production company can greatly increase the per-program license fee by renegotiating the license agreement. Alternatively, it can exercise its "right of first refusal" provisions with the original network, and leave to strike a more lucrative deal with a new network.

When the license fee generated is less than the cost of production, this creates a short-term deficit that needs to be bridged with "deficit financing." Deficit financing leaves all ownership in the series in the hands of the production company. This means that if a series is successful and runs for several years, the producer can license the show into syndication, where local stations and cable networks may broadcast old episodes of the series on a nightly basis. This usually requires that at least 100 shows have been produced to ensure syndication on a nightly basis will be able to stretch over about twenty weeks before any episodes are repeated. Another syndication "rule of thumb" model requires at least sixty-five episodes, enabling a licensee to broadcast the show every weekday night (the "strip" format, like a comic strip that runs in a daily newspaper) for thirteen weeks, equivalent to a calendar quarter, before any episodes have to be repeated.

Such syndication, multiplied by the number of local stations in the United States and throughout the world, can be enormously profitable, more than making up for any deficit financing that was required during the series' initial network broadcasts.[28] The tremendous

---

Documentaries

Sports

Talk Shows

Game Shows

Awards Shows

Variety Shows

Special Interest Programs

Concerts and performances

Music video

Children's television

Children's animation

Television pilots and series

Even renowned newscasters can find themselves in litigation with the network. See *Rather v. CBS Corp.*, 68 A.D.3d 49, 886 N.Y.S.2d 121 (2009) (television anchor suit for unfair dismissal, defendant's motion to dismiss granted).

28   See *Ivy Street Productions, Inc. v. Sony Pictures Entertainment, Inc.*, 2005 WL 1484035 (Cal. App. June 23, 2005) (suit over profit participation in long running series "Married With Children," stating that gross revenues including

financial gains from a long-term series that goes into syndication also help finance the development of new projects, including pilot episodes, and the deficits incurred by even a successful series in its first few years before it goes into syndication.

Other business models exist. For example, reality television productions may have little "back end" economic potential because they are not usually popular as syndicated reruns.[29] Therefore, the license fee per episode must cover the entire production costs. In such an event, the network may insist on full ownership of the series, since they are paying the full price for producing it. Other types of programming with little "back end," such as how-to shows, may also simply be purchased by the network as a work made for hire. In such cases, the production company must build any profits into the per-episode fee.

Because of the expense of producing a series, the project begins with a "pilot" episode that is audience-tested to determine whether it will have sufficient appeal for the network to place an order with the production company for a season's worth shows (usually with an initial order of thirteen shows, with the option for a total of twenty-two shows).

§2.15   Pilot Episode Agreements

The hallmark of an agreement for a pilot and potential series is that the future services of the creative team and the cast must be secured in the initial agreements.[30] In the event the pilot is "picked up" and the network places an order for a series, the initial agreement must extend to several future seasons via exercisable options. The production company's agreement with the lead actors may include options to extend up to the statutorily allowed maximum of seven years, even though the license agreement with the network is for a maximum of five years.

The basic terms of a pilot agreement with series option for a series creator/writer/producer are:

- <u>Pilot Writing Fee</u>: This will be no less than WGA scale.

- <u>Pilot Delivery</u>: Production of the pilot with costs reimbursed by the network.

- <u>Series Option</u>: Options for the network to order series episodes, giving deadlines, for example May 1 for a series beginning in the Fall, and December 1 for a Midseason start.

- <u>Series Term</u>: From the date of first broadcast, with annual renewal options totaling no more than five years.

---

syndication were $851,800,000).

29   See § 2.15[7][b] *infra*, for an in-depth discussion of reality television programming.

30 ˙ A series pilot and series option agreement is included in the forms accompanying this treatise.

- <u>License Fees</u>: License fees for seasons one through five, and where the production company and the network are affiliated, there will be an "imputed" license fee in the absence of genuine arm's length transactions between producer and network.

- <u>Minimum Order Commitment</u>: for the first Fall or Midseason start, thirteen episodes, with an option to increase the order to twenty-two episodes, and possibly with an option to order up to thirty episodes.

- <u>Approvals</u>: including approval of the writer/creator as executive producer.

- <u>Broadcast Rights</u>: the right to broadcast and use in other media (online), including limitations on the number of broadcasts allowed for each episode. First run episodes are often repeated once as a "rerun," perhaps during the summer between seasons.

- <u>First Negotiation and First Refusal on Series Term Extension</u>: The agreement is for no more than five years total, but at the end of five years the original network has the right to negotiate for an extension beyond five years, include a right of first refusal.[31]

- <u>Broadcast Territory</u>: Typically limited to the United States and possessions, and Canada.

- <u>Exclusivity</u>: The exclusive right to the series during the term belong to the network in the territory, however the producer has the right to exploit the series outside the territory, and the right to exploit ancillary rights such as recordings, publications, and merchandise.[32]

- <u>Spin Offs</u>: A series may have non-continuing characters who become the basis for a new and separate series or "spin off," in which event the network may be given a right of first refusal on the spin-off rights.

- <u>Exclusivity of Series Actors</u>: This provision will obligate the producer, to the extent possible under SAG agreements, to guarantee that the series star or stars are exclusive to the series, limiting their appearances on other programs to one-off "guest appearances" for example, and limiting the type of appearance so as not to detract from the success of the series. There may also be restrictions on the actor performing other duties in the television industry. There will also be an undertaking by the producer that "continuing performers" in the series shall sign agreements covering the full series term and all extensions. The network will also want the producer to ensure that the continuing stars are available for promotional duties, and that they consent to the use of their name and likeness for advertising purposes.[33]

---

31   If the producer obtains an offer from a third party, the producer must give the original network the opportunity to match the offer, thus obtaining an extension on those new terms.

32   See *Scholastic Entertainment, Inc. v. Fox Entertainment Group, Inc.*, 336 F.3d 982 (9th Cir. 2003) (production company alleged that network licensing its series improperly allowed a network affiliate to broadcast the series without payment of additional license fees).

33   See *Touchstone Television Productions v. The Superior Court*, Sheridan, 208 Cal. App.4th 676, 145 Cal. Rptr.3d 766 (2012) (where actress had one-year contract with up to six additional option years, and studio declined to exercise option for season 6, actor could not claim she was unfairly terminated).

- <u>Writer/Producer Considerations</u>: Unlike the director's paramount creative role in motion pictures, in episodic television, the lead "auteur" is the head writer, who also serves as a producer or "show runner." Thus for a traditional network television pilot, the main writer/producer deal points will include detailed writing and producer fees and credits, and a "lock" (i.e., guarantee) that may tie writing credits to producing fees and credits. For example, if the writer is granted sole "written by" credit on the pilot, then he may be "locked" as an Executive Producer for Year 1 and Year 2, but contingent on not being "pay or played" by a benchmark episode (perhaps halfway through the season) in Year 1 ("pay or played" meaning paid, but not providing any actual services).

Other writer/producer deal points may include a bonus if the pilot is sold (which may be tied to the actual number of episodes subsequently produced); a per episode royalty in a fixed amount; a percentage of net profit participation (after deduction of 10% to 20% distribution fees and 12.5% to 15% overhead) that gradually vests over time (e.g., 25% vested on signing the agreement, 25% on pilot production, 25% upon completion of services in Year 1, and 25% upon completion of services in Year 2); and passive payments if the series is spun off.

Further "perks" may include guaranteed on-screen credit position and size, on-screen credit for the writer's own production company, reversion of rights if the pilot is not sold, a guarantee as regards the number of screenplays to be written, added as an additional insured on E&O insurance policies, free DVDs, and travel, and a future paid and credited (even if "fired" and not providing actual services) consulting position.

- <u>Profit Participation</u>: The formulas may be very similar to motion picture profit participation deals, but a successful long running series that goes into worldwide syndication may produce more revenues than even the biggest hit motion pictures

In *Sander/Moses Productions, Inc. v. NBC Studios, Inc.*,[34] two producers engaged by NBC to produce a pilot and a series later sued the network, claiming they were due profit participation payments. The reported case factual background section, reproduced in the footnotes, provides an excellent example of how series agreements are negotiated. Note that this case is from the post-consent decree era and demonstrates the vertical integration between the network and its wholly owned production studios, with the suit brought by producers but not an independent production company (the production company was the network's wholly owned affiliate). Compare with the *CBS Broadcasting Inc. v. The Carsey-Werner Co.* case discussed infra which is from the consent decree era and pits an independent production company against a network that did not have its own production entity. [35]

---

34   See *Sander/Moses Productions, Inc. v. NBC Studios, Inc.*, 142 Cal. App.4th 1086, 48 Cal. Rptr.3d 525 (2006).

35   See *id.* The fact portion of the reported opinion is reproduced below as it is instructive on the details of television financing:

FACTUAL AND PROCEDURAL BACKGROUND

The Agreement Between NBC Studios and Sander/Moses for the Services of Sander and Moses As Executive Producers of the Profiler Series

In 1996, NBC Studios was a production company that produced television programs and sold them to the NBC television network, among others. The network paid NBC Studios a licensing fee for the right to broadcast the programs NBC Studios developed.

Ian Sander (Sander) and Kim Moses (Moses) were experienced executive producers. [FN1] They were the principals in Sander/Moses, a loan-out company that made the executive production services of Sander and Moses available to production companies.

Production companies such as NBC Studios hire executive producers to manage the day-to-day production of television programs. In 1996, NBC Studios purchased a script for a television pilot entitled Insight from its author, Cynthia Saunders. NBC Studios renamed the pilot Profiler. At the time NBC Studios acquired the rights to Profiler, the NBC television network was planning a Saturday night program lineup of 'spooky' programs that the network referred to as 'thrillogy night.' The NBC television network had expressed an interest in airing Profiler as part of thrillogy night, along with two other new one-hour programs entitled The Pretender and Dark Skies.

NBC Studios began searching for an executive producer for the Profiler pilot and ultimately entered into negotiations with Sander/Moses for the services of Sander and Moses as executive producers for the Profiler pilot and proposed series. NBC Studios expected Sander and Moses to render the types of services customarily rendered by executive producers in the television industry. An experienced entertainment attorney and an agent from Creative Artists Agency (CAA) represented Sander/Moses in the negotiations, and NBC Studios was represented by an in-house attorney from its business affairs department.

On February 29, 1996, Sander/Moses entered into an agreement with NBC Studios with respect to production of a one-hour pilot script for Profiler and a proposed one-hour series based on the pilot. The agreement provided that if the pilot was produced, NBC Studios would pay Sander/Moses $95,000 and would engage Sander and Moses as the executive producers for the first year at $37,500 per episode. The agreement also gave NBC Studios an option to retain the services of Sander and Moses for the second and third years of production at $40,000 and $45,000 per episode, respectively. In addition, the agreement provided that if NBC Studios retained Sander and Moses for the second year of the series, but did not retain them as executive producers for the third year, they would be engaged as executive consultants for the third year at $20,000 per episode.

In addition to the fixed compensation, the agreement specified that Sander/Moses was entitled to contingent compensation. For executive producing the pilot, Sander/Moses was to receive 2.5 percent of NBC Studios's 'adjusted gross' from the series. Sander/Moses was also entitled to an additional 2.5 percent of the 'adjusted gross' for executive producing the first year of the series and another 2.5 percent for executive producing the second year of the series.

The term 'adjusted gross' was defined in Appendix I to the agreement as the amount of 'gross receipts' that remained after certain deductions, such as distribution expenses. The term 'gross receipts' had a traditional definition in the Appendix, but then was further defined to be the same as the license fees that the NBC television network paid to NBC Studios for the rights to broadcast Profiler. The provision equating gross receipts to license fees further required NBC Studios to use '[a]n amount equal to ninety-five percent (95%) of the published final pattern budget for the applicable broadcast year approved by [NBC Studios] for programs produced for the first four (4) full broadcast years' (Budget Formula) for purposes of calculating gross receipts for the first three years of the series. That Budget Formula, however, was subject to an overriding limitation: '[P]rovided, however, that the total license fee . . . shall in no event exceed the license fee . . . paid by [the] NBC [television network] during the applicable broadcast year to suppliers of programs comparable to the Program [Profiler] in a similar broadcast year. . . .' The 'programs comparable' limitation did not apply to the fourth year of the series.

According to the attorney who negotiated the agreement on behalf of NBC Studios, Appendix I was based on a form that had been developed through prior negotiations between other CAA agents and NBC Studios. The compensation scheme described in Appendix I was the 'top' definition of adjusted gross that NBC Studios had negotiated in the past with CAA agents, i.e., it had the most favorable terms of the agreements negotiated between NBC Studios and CAA on behalf of its other clients.

The 'published final pattern budget' is the budget for each episode of the program that is approved by NBC Studios and the NBC television network before shooting commences. The final pattern budget per episode for Profiler for the first season was $1,336,182.

The entire provision reads as follows: 'Company [NBC Studios] and Participant [Sander/Moses] have agreed that for purposes of computing Gross Receipts arising out of Company's authorization of the broadcast of the Program [Profiler] over the facilities of the NBC television network ('NBC'), the network license agreement between NBC and Company with respect to such broadcast shall be deemed to provide for the payment by NBC to Company of the following applicable license fees, which license fees shall be deemed to be in lieu of all actual Gross Receipts, if any, accruing to Company from the authorization of such broadcast:

(i) for the initial network broadcast by NBC of the Program, the following amounts: [REDACTED].

In the case of a series, an amount equal to ninety-five (95%) of the published final pattern budget for the applicable broadcast year) [sic] approved by Company for Programs produced for the first four (4) full broadcast years (five (5) broadcast years if a Midseason broadcast start), and in the fifth (sixth if a Midseason start) and succeeding broadcast years, for programs produced subsequent to the first four (4) full broadcast years (five (5) broadcast years if a Midseason start), one hundred percent (100%) of the published final pattern budget, plus, in any event, such additional cast protection allowances or other 'breakage,' if any, which NBC shall pay Company in connection with the Program (the foregoing is not meant to guarantee that NBC shall agree to pay any such 'breakage' fees), provided, however, that the total license fee including 'breakage' shall in no event exceed the license fee including customary 'breakage,' if any, paid by NBC during the applicable broadcast year to suppliers of programs comparable to the Program [Profiler] in a similar broadcast year. . . .

Under the agreement, NBC Studios retained all ownership rights to Profiler, including any copyrights. [FN5] NBC Studios also controlled the production, distribution, and exploitation of Profiler. It had the right to make the 'final and controlling' determination 'in all matters respecting the performance of [Sander and Moses's] services (including without limitation matters involving creative judgment and financial controls).' The agreement further provided that '[NBC Studios] shall have no obligation to produce, complete, release, distribute, advertise, or exploit any television program or series . . .' and that '[n]othing contained in this Agreement shall constitute a partnership or joint venture by the parties hereto. . . .'

Specifically, the agreement provided that '[a]ll results and proceeds of [Sander and Moses's] services under this Agreement shall be and become the property of [NBC Studios], and [NBC Studios] shall own all rights of every kind and character therein throughout the universe in any and all languages in perpetuity.'

The Parties' Performance Under the Agreement

§2.16   Deficit Financing of Episodic Television

As noted above, the license fee a network pays to the production company will not typically cover 100% of the production costs. The expectation is that a successful series will generate profits in syndication, thus allowing the loans that bridge the gap to be repaid.

In *CBS Broadcasting, Inc. v. The Carsey-Werner Co.*, the network had provided the deficit financing for a television series in the form of a loan to the production company.[36] The production company and the network were not affiliates thus there was a genuine license fee and not an "imputed" license fee.

The loan was to be paid back solely from any profits realized by the production company from syndication. After four years on the air with eighty-seven episodes available for syndication, the production company owed the network $53 million in debt financing loans. The network alleged that the production company failed to pursue any syndication rights at all, allegedly because any profits from syndication would have had to be used to pay back the deficit funding loans from the studio. The appeal court reversed the lower court's grant of demurrer to the defendants. Note that this case is from the consent decree era pitting an independent production company against the network, in a context where the network did not have its own wholly owned production company. Compare with the *Sander/Moses Productions v. NBC* case discussed above which was from the post-consent decree era where the studio had a wholly owned production entity. [37]

Sander and Moses provided executive production services for the Profiler pilot, which, in May of 1996, the NBC television network 'picked up'—i.e., opted to have produced for exhibition or distribution-as a series for an initial season on the NBC television network. Pursuant to the agreement, they also provided executive production services for the first and second years of Profiler. The NBC television network broadcast Profiler on Saturday night, back-to-back with another thrillogy series, The Pretender.

Although Profiler was picked up by the NBC television network for a third season, NBC Studios did not retain Sander and Moses as executive producers that year. Instead, pursuant to the agreement, they were paid $20,000 per episode as executive consultants for the third season, but were not asked to perform any services. They did not perform any services or receive any compensation for the fourth and last season of Profiler. In total, NBC Studios paid Sander/Moses over $2,122,500 for Sander and Moses's work on Profiler.

36   See *CBS Broadcasting, Inc. v. The Carsey-Werner Co.*, 2003 WL 139986 (Cal. App. Jan. 21, 2003).

37   *Id.* The background section of the opinion describes in detail the deficit funding arrangements and the fees paid to the production company. It is reproduced below:

Plaintiff and appellant CBS Broadcasting, Inc. appeals from a judgment of dismissal following the sustaining of a demurrer without leave to amend in favor of defendants and respondents The Carsey-Werner Company, LLC (the Production Company), YBYL Productions, Inc., and Carsey-Werner Distribution, Inc. (the Distribution Company). CBS and the Production Company entered into a written agreement for the production of a television series starring *Cybill* Shepherd. The Production Company was to create the series and license it to CBS to broadcast for a license fee. In addition to payment of the license fee, CBS was to loan the Production

Company the costs of production. The loan was to be repaid by the Production Company solely from the cash flow of the Production Company generated by syndication of the series. The series was never syndicated. CBS contends the implied covenant of good faith and fair dealing in the written agreement required defendants to make reasonable commercial efforts to syndicate the television series in order to repay the CBS loan, which they did not do. CBS further contends defendants negligently performed the contract. We reverse.

PROCEDURAL BACKGROUND

On January 19, 2001, CBS filed a complaint against defendants for breach of the implied covenant of good faith and fair dealing and negligence. Defendants demurred on the ground that the contract did not obligate the Production Company to syndicate the television series, and therefore, a covenant to exercise good faith efforts to syndicate the series could not be implied. After a hearing, the trial court sustained the demurrer without leave to amend. The trial court entered a judgment of dismissal on May 15, 2001. CBS filed a timely notice of appeal.

FACTS

The Production Company has produced several successful television series. It has also successfully promoted and sold several television series into syndication through the Distribution Company. The Production Company, the Distribution Company, and YBYL are agents of one another. They are also alter-egos of one another, in that they are owned by the same interests, operate in the same business from the same offices, and employ the same employees.

In December 1993, CBS and the Production Company entered into a letter agreement prepared by the Production Company. CBS ordered a minimum of 13 episodes of the television series *Cybill* for the 1994/1995 season. The 13 episodes could, at CBS's election, include a pilot episode. The agreement also provided CBS with renewal options for succeeding seasons.

Paragraph 2, subdivision (a) of the agreement provided that the per-episode license fee for the 1994/1995 season was $550,000. Paragraph 2, subdivision (c) provided that CBS would loan the Production Company on a non-recourse basis an amount equal to the difference between the actual final cost of production incurred by the Production Company and the amount of the license fee.

Paragraph 3 of the agreement set forth the terms of the non-recourse loan. The Production Company's obligation to repay the loan was contingent upon, and did not arise until, the Production Company had completed production of, delivered to CBS, and received payment for 67 episodes. This was the number of episodes required to sell the series in syndication. Paragraph 3 of the agreement provided: '[The Production Company] shall repay such loan, plus accrued interest, in two installments [on specified dates]; provided, however, that in no event shall the amount of any loan payment plus accrued interest . . . be in excess of [the Production Company's] cash flow from the net proceeds received by [the Production Company] from the Series prior to the date such payment becomes due (i.e., [the Production Company] shall only be obligated to make a loan (plus accrued interest) payment to the extent that [the Production Company's] cash flow from the net proceeds received by [the Production Company] up to the point that such payment falls due equals or exceeds the amount of the payment, plus the prior loan payment, if applicable). In the event that the cash flow is not equal to or greater than the amount of the loan (plus interest) payments that would otherwise be due in accordance with this provision, then CBS and [the Production Company] shall negotiate in good faith to extend the time by which the full amount of such payment or payments shall be made, but in no event shall [the Production Company] be required to make any loan and/or accrued interest payment(s) which would exceed the cash flow

§2.17   Unscripted "Reality Television"

Reality television relies on the inherent drama (or comedy) of placing "real" people in challenging situations, and filming the result. Reality television is less expensive to produce than scripted programming. It does not require the creation of the minimum number of scripts or any writers, nor the hiring of actors, nor even necessarily the construction of sets. Nevertheless, it results in far less "back end" revenue potential because there is no market for syndicated old shows as compared to scripted television.

Reality shows also must attempt (1) to have contestants who are interesting to viewers, and (2) to be dramatic. In *SEG, Inc. v. Stillman*,[38] a contestant on the first season of the popular "Survivor" show had made public statements containing allegations that the producers of the show manipulated the contest which was the central premise of the show. The contestant had undergone screening, and had signed a confidentiality agreement with the producers. When the contestant sued the producers and posted her complaint on the Internet, as well as making statements to the press, the producers of the show filed an action against her claiming, *inter alia*, that she breached the confidentiality agreement, and defamed the producers.

---

from the net proceeds theretofore received by [the Production Company] from the Series. For the purposes of this Paragraph 3, in determining cash flow [to the Production Company] from net proceeds from the Series, the distribution fee and expenses attributable to the Series shall be the actual distribution fee and expenses charged by the Series distributor, except that if [the Distribution Company] is the distributor, then [the expenses and distribution fees are as set forth in the agreement].' In conclusion, the agreement provided, '[a]ll other terms and conditions shall be negotiated in good faith between us.' On October 5, 1994, the Production Company assigned its rights and obligations under the agreement to YBYL.

CBS broadcast *Cybill* for four seasons. The Production Company produced 87 episodes, and CBS loaned the Production Company a total of $53,325,000 for production costs. The marketing of a broadcast series for sale into syndication typically begins during or shortly after the initial network run. In 1996, the Production Company and YBYL, through the Distribution Company, undertook to market the series for distribution rather than hire a third party distribution company. However, the Production Company failed to undertake the customary efforts to market and sell *Cybill* into syndication. Instead, the Production Company, YBYL, and the Distribution Company abandoned efforts to syndicate *Cybill* and concentrated on obtaining syndication for other projects whose profits would not have to be paid to CBS.

The Production Company, YBYL, and the Distribution Company failed to make good faith, commercially reasonable efforts to market and sell the series into syndication. The Production Company's, YBYL's, and the Distribution Company's negligent handling of the marketing of the series into syndication breached their duty to perform their distribution services in a reasonable and competent manner and resulted in their failure to sell the series in any form of second run distribution and failure to generate any proceeds to repay CBS. The Production Company has not repaid any portion of the CBS loan.

Id.

38   See *SEG, Inc. v. Stillman*, 2003 WL 21197133 (Cal. App. May 22, 2003).

The court found that the elements of a defamation claim were met. The opinion in the *Stillman* case includes a description of Stillman's alleged experiences as a contestant on the show, and the confidentiality document she signed.[39]

---

39 Id. The fact portion of the above opinion is instructive and reproduced below:

FACTUAL AND PROCEDURAL BACKGROUND

In December 1999, Stillman applied to be a contestant on a new television 'reality' show that was being produced for CBS by SEG. The name of the new show was 'Survivor' and it involved 16 contestants who would be 'marooned' on a remote island in the South China Sea, divided into two 'tribes,' required to engage in multiple contests between the tribes and then, on a regular periodic basis, asked to vote on which member to evict from the tribe. A majority vote of the then existing members of the tribe that had lost the most recent contest with the other tribe would be sufficient to evict a member of that tribe. This process would go on over several weeks until there was only one surviving contestant who would win $1 million. All of these activities would be recorded by television cameras for broadcast by CBS during the period May to August 2000.

The tribal contests in which the participants engaged (so-called 'immunity challenges') tested, and placed . . . a premium on, the team work of each tribe and the physical and mental stamina of each of its members. Each of the non-surviving contestants accepted for the show would receive some compensation for their participation. More than 6000 people applied to become contestants. In January and February of 2000, Stillman went through an extended screening process that included multiple personal interviews in San Francisco and Los Angeles and medical and psychological testing. As a part of her application process, Stillman entered into several written agreements including an Applicant Agreement. In that agreement, Stillman promised not to disclose, without SEG's consent, any information concerning the show and its production. The record leaves little doubt that Stillman was aware of and understood this obligation.

In section 19 of that agreement, clearly entitled 'Confidentiality and Life Story Rights,' it was provided, in relevant part: 'I understand any appearance I may make on the Series is strictly for the purpose of participating in the Series as a contestant. Except as specifically provided herein or as otherwise authorized by Producer and/or CBS, I will not myself, and I will not authorize others to, publicize, advertise or promote my appearance on the Series, receive or generate any monetary advantage from my appearance on the Series, or use or disclose to any party any information or trade secrets obtained or learned as a result of my participation in the Series, including without limitation any information concerning or relating to the Series, the contestants, the events contained in the Series or the outcome of the Series, for a period from the date of this agreement until three (3) years after the initial broadcast of the last episode of the Series. Without limiting the foregoing, I acknowledge that the initial broadcast of the episodes in which I may participate will occur, if at all, after the contest is completed and that any information revealed or disclosed prior to broadcast will cause irreparable harm to Producer and CBS. In that connection, I specifically agree that any information regarding the elimination of contestants and the selection of any winner is to be held in strict confidence by me and cannot be disclosed by me to any third parties. . . . I agree that disclosure by me in violation of the foregoing shall constitute and be treated as a material breach of this agreement which will cause irreparable harm to Producer and/or CBS and will cause substantial damage in excess of $5,000,000, entitling Producer to seek, among other things, (a) injunctive relief, without posting any bond, to prevent and/or cure any breach of threatened breach of this paragraph by me, (b) return or recovery of the value of any prize received or to be received in connection with the Series, (c) recovery or disgorgement of the monies or other consideration received in connection with such disclosure, if any, and (d) recovery of Producer's attorneys' fees incurred to enforce this paragraph.'

Other reported cases involving reality television have involved disgruntled contestants who

---

At the time she signed the Applicant Agreement, Stillman was a practicing lawyer. She was an associate in the San Francisco offices of Brobeck, Phleger & Harrison. She negotiated certain modifications to the Applicant Agreement. Finally, the agreement itself provided (just above her signature) that Stillman (1) had had ample opportunity to read the agreement and had done so, (2) fully understood its provisions and (3) had reviewed them with her own legal counsel prior to signing.

After being accepted as one of the 16 contestants, Stillman, along with the others, traveled to Malaysia in March of 2000. She was assigned to the tribe designated 'Tagi.' The Survivor series was shot over a 39-day period (for later broadcast on CBS from May 31, 2000 to August 23, 2000). Every three days during the shooting, one of the two tribes (i.e., the one that had lost the most recent immunity challenge contest) was required to vote to evict one of its members. The first contest was lost by the Tagi tribe and participant Sonja Christopher was voted off. This left Tagi with seven members, including Stillman. Tagi won the second contest, but lost the third. As a result, on the 9th day of shooting, the Tagi tribe was again required to vote off another member. The tribe voted 5-2 to evict Stillman.

According to her declaration, filed in this matter in support of her motion under section 425.16, Stillman states that she was informed on August 23, 2000 and again in October 2000, by another Tagi tribe member, Dirk Been, that he and one other member (Sean Kenniff) had been told by the show's executive producer, Mark Burnett (an officer of SEG), to vote to evict Stillman. As a result of these conversations, Stillman came to believe that the producer had manipulated the votes of at least two of the members of the Tagi tribe. It was her view that such actions were not only unfair, and contrary to the free competition theme of the 'Survivor' show, but also constituted a violation of federal laws prohibiting the 'rigging' of game shows. During October 2000, Stillman had exchanged written and oral conversations with one Peter Lance who was then in the process of researching a book about the 'Survivor' show (later published in November 2000 under the title 'Stingray'). In these exchanges, she discussed this information with him.

For example, she is quoted in Lance's book as stating (in an e-mail addressed to him explaining why CBS would not object to her sale of several pictures she took during the filming of the show): 'Boo hoo, CBS. If they go after me, I have info that establishes a nice federal offense they wouldn't want disclosed and could undermine SII.' In his book, Lance states that she later explained what she meant by repeating the information she had received from Dirk Been.

Thereafter, Stillman hired an attorney who sent a demand letter to CBS and Mark Burnett in which Stillman's concerns about how the 'Survivor' show had been manipulated were discussed.

...

SEG's complaint alleges that Stillman applied to be a contestant on the "Survivor" show and agreed, in writing, as a part of the application process, that she would not use or disclose any information or trade secrets learned as a result of her participation in the show. SEG alleged that Stillman breached that agreement and disclosed information and trade secrets to a writer (Peter Lance) knowing that he intended to write a book about the program. SEG's defamation claim is based on allegations that (1) Stillman orally and in writing stated that SEG and its officers and employees rigged the outcome of the program by coaching and manipulating the participants voting choices, (2) Lance published his book and included the falsehoods by Stillman, and (3) Stillman repeated these falsehoods in numerous public appearances beginning February 5, 2001.

thought their appearance on the show defamed them;[40] and copyright infringement suits based on alleged unauthorized adaption of a show treatment.[41] Even the owners of successful shows such as "Survivor" have filed suit against competitors based on allegations that copyrightable elements in the show were infringed.[42] Reality shows have also been the target of employment and union-related litigation.[43] Paradoxically, the stars of reality television have filed suit to protect their privacy.[44] Perhaps because reality television is produced out in the "real world" and features participants eager for fame yet inexperienced in the entertainment industry, it has attracted a wide variety of legal disputes.[45]

---

40   See *Christakis v. Mark Burnett Productions*, 2009 U.S. Dist. LEXIS 60751, 2009 WL 1248947 (C.D. Cal. April 27, 2009) (waiver and release signed by contestant on "The Apprentice" barred suit for claim including defamation).

41   See *Milano v. NBC Universal, Inc.*, 584 F. Supp.2d 1288 (C.D. Cal. 2008) (author of treatment for weight loss show "From Fat to Phat" alleged infringement by producers of "The Biggest Loser"). See also:

Second Circuit: *Rodriguez v. Heidi Klum Co.*, LLC, 2008 U.S. Dist. LEXIS 80805, 2008 WL 4449416 (S.D.N.Y. Sept. 30, 2008) (author of treatment entitled "American Runway" sued producers of "Project Runway").

Ninth Circuit: *Bethea v. Burnett*, 2005 WL 1720631 (C.D. Cal. June 28, 2005) (author of treatment for show entitled "C.E.O." sued producers of "The Apprentice").

42   See *Survivor Productions LLC v. Fox Broadcasting Co.*, 2001 U.S. Dist. LEXIS 25512, 2001 WL 35829270 (C.D. Cal. June 12, 2001) (claim that program "Boot Camp" infringed copyright in "Survivor").

43   See *Sharp v. Next Entertainment*, 163 Cal. App.4th 410, 78 Cal. Rptr.3d 37 (2008) (non-union writers brought wage and labor law class action lawsuits against reality television production); see also, *Pelloni v. Women's Entertainment Network*, 2008 U.S. Dist. LEXIS 89201, 2008 WL 4501845 (C.D. Cal. Oct. 5, 2008) (employment related suit against producers of reality show "Bridezillas").

44   See *Chapman v. Krutonog*, 2010 WL 727577 (D. Haw. Feb. 26, 2010) ("Dog the Bounty Hunter" star filing motion to seal in dispute with former manager. Reality star did not want per episode salary of $100,000 for twenty-six episodes publicly revealed, but court found that the information had already been publicized.). See also, *A&E Television Networks, LLC v. Pivot Point Entertainment*, LLC, 2013 U.S. Dist. LEXIS 43775, 2013 WL 1245453 (S.D.N.Y. March 27, 2013) (dispute over producer's share of payments for show "Dog the Bounty Hunter").

45   See, e.g.:

First Circuit: *United States v. Hatch*, 514 F.3d 145 (1st Cir. 2008) (affirming conviction of taxpayer based on taxpayer's failure to pay taxes on $1 million prize for winning first season of CBS reality television show "Survivor").

Second Circuit: *Paul Thayil v. Fox Corp.*, 2012 U.S. Dist. LEXIS 13669, 2012 WL 364034 (S.D.N.Y. Feb. 2, 2012) (dismissal of copyright, trade secret, unfair competition, fraud, and other claims brought by plaintiff who alleged that "American Idol" was based on plaintiff's marketing plan for a television show "that would air selected tapes of participants dancing in their own households, free of inhibition"); *Hard Rock Cafe International (USA), Inc. v. Hard Rock Hotel Holdings, LLC*, 808 F. Supp.2d 552 (S.D.N.Y. 2011) (trademark dispute over reality show "Rehab: Party at the Hard Rock Hotel"); *Benardo v. American Idol Productions, Inc.*, 2010 U.S. Dist. LEXIS 129184, 2010 WL 4968177 (S.D.N.Y. Dec. 6, 2010) (dismissing allegations of employment discrimination based on sexual orientation brought by American Idol contestant); *Olaes Enterprises, Inc. v. A.D. Sutton & Sons, Inc.*, 2010 WL 3260064 (S.D.N.Y. Aug. 6, 2010) (trademark dispute involving "American Choppers" reality television show); *A&E Television Networks v. Gen-*

[1]—Format Rights and Production Issues in "Reality Television"

Production of a reality television show can begin with an idea or concept, or it can be an adaptation of a successful show already being produced in another country. Where a reality series is a contest or competition-based show that changes each week, the intellectual property that can be licensed when the show's format is licensed may be a combination of a title, trademark rights in a title, copyrightable characters, and other elements.

In *Endemol Entertainment B.V. v. Twentieth Television, Inc.*, the plaintiff was a Dutch producer that had considerable success on European television with a popular game show series called "Forgive Me."[46] Plaintiff had negotiated with the defendant regarding the United States television rights to the series format, based on the "format, expression, and concepts of "Forgive Me."[47] Plaintiff also had a United States copyright registration for the show, registered as a motion picture.

---

uine Entertainment, Inc., 2010 WL 2308092 (S.D.N.Y. June 10, 2010) (breach of implied contract claim brought by plaintiff alleging they conceived and successfully pitched reality show entitled "Steven Seagal: Lawman").

Third Circuit: Goodson v. Kardashian, 413 Fed. Appx. 417 (3d Cir. 2011) (affirming dismissal of complaint by pro se plaintiff against reality television stars Kim and Kourtney Kardashian alleging their programs caused plaintiff "intense emotional and psychological strain").

Fourth Circuit: Trademark Properties Inc. v. A&E Television Networks, 422 Fed. Appx. 199 (4th Cir. 2011) (oral agreement over revenue sharing for reality show "Flip This House" found valid).

Sixth Circuit: Clark v. Viacom International, Inc., 2014 WL 1934028 (M.D. Tenn. May 13, 2014) (American Idol contestant defamation claim); *Riches v. Wilkinson*, 2011 WL 452982 (E.D. Ky. Feb. 4, 2011) (pro se prison inmate making "bizarre and implausible . . . patently delusional, factually frivolous" allegations against reality television show star Kendra Wilkinson, action dismissed by court sua sponte).

Seventh Circuit: Annie Oakley Enterprises, Inc. v. Sunset Tan Corporate & Consulting, LLC, 703 F. Supp.2d 881 (N.D. Ind. 2010) (trademark allegations arising from reality show "Sunset Tan").

Ninth Circuit: Petersen v. Fox Entertainment Group, Inc., 2010 WL 2089304 (Cal. App. May 26, 2010) (dismissal of tort allegations stemming from reality show "Deadbeat Dads"); *Arenas v. Shed Media US Inc.*, 2011 WL 8427612 (C.D. Cal. Aug. 22, 2011), aff'd 462 Fed. Appx. 709 (9th Cir. 2011) (NBA player denied injunction against "Basketball Wives" reality show); *Greenstein v. The Greif Co.*, 2009 WL 117368 (Cal. App. Jan. 20, 2009) (affirming dismissal of claims of misappropriation of persona arising from plaintiff's consent to appear in episodes of "Gene Simmons Family Jewels" reality program).

46   See *Endemol Entertainment B.V. v. Twentieth Television, Inc.*, 48 U.S.P.Q.2d 1524, 1998 WL 785300 (C.D. Cal. 1998). See also, *Scottish American Media, LLC v. NBC Universal, Inc.*, 2009 WL 1124942 (Cal. App. April 28, 2009) (affirming summary judgment for defendants in suit alleging that American adaptation of "Eurovision" singing competition format was a breach of implied contract with plaintiff, who pitched allegedly similar format to network).

47   Id. (*Endemol Entertainment B.V. v. Twentieth Television, Inc.*), 48 U.S.P.Q.2d at *1525.

Negotiations for the United States version of the format broke down, but when plaintiff learned that the defendant was allegedly still proceeding with the development of an American version, entitled, "Forgive and Forget," plaintiff filed suit with claims including copyright infringement, and breach of implied contract. The published opinion is a dismissal of the contract claim, leaving the copyright claim intact.48

In *Endemol*, the claim to own a "format" was backed up by a copyright registration for the original show. An attempt to support a format claim with trademark principles however failed in *RDF Media Limited v. Fox Broadcasting*.49 In *RDF Media*, the plaintiff was the producer of the popular reality show "Wife Swap," and had entered into negotiations with ABC network for a United States version of the format entitled "Wife Swap US." The plaintiff then learned that Fox was developing a reality show entitled "Trading Spouses," and filed suit based on multiple claims, including copyright and trade dress protection for the format of its UK show.

In its complaint, the plaintiff alleged that its show format was entitled to trade dress protection under the Lanham Act, described as follows:

> "The total image and appearance of 'Wife Swap US,' as defined by the selection, compilation, arrangement, sequence, and combination of the cast of characters, the structure of each airing of a complete swap, the sequence of events, the plot, the tone, the theme, the pace, the scene set-ups, the narration, the dialogue that arises from constructed situations, the contrasting settings, the structured before-and-after dialogue, the topics explored, the dramatic and comedic effect created by music, and the introductory segment, constitutes the trade dress of 'Wife Swap US.' The unique images, scenes, themes, and artistic choices employed by RDF Media in 'Wife Swap US' serve to identify the source of the program."50

The court declined this invitation to "recognize the reality show itself as the trade dress subject to protection," noting that:

> "[A]lthough titles of books, plays, films, and songs, distinctive elements of a television series, and distinctive comic book characters have qualified as marks entitled to protection under section 1127 of the Lanham Act,

---

48   The parties later settled.

49   See *RDF Media Limited v. Fox Broadcasting Co.*, 372 F. Supp.2d 556 (C.D. Cal. 2005).

50   *Id.*, 372 F. Supp.2d at 563.

the scope of section 1127 does not extend to the corpus of the book, play, film, song, television show, or comic book."[51]

The court further pointed out intellectual property rights in the "corpus" of the work, its expressive content as described in the plaintiff's attempt to invoke trade dress protection, was a matter of copyright law, not trademark law.[52]

In *RDF Media*, the court dismissed the trade dress claim and other claims, but allowed the copyright infringement claim to proceed based on the plaintiff's registrations. While a format might be something that is arguably recognizable, the total look and feel of a program, the intellectual property law basis for "format" claims, at least in the *Endemol* and *RDF Media* cases, appears to be based entirely on traditional principles of copyright ownership.

While unscripted television programming will not have the same mix of copyrightable dramatic and character elements as scripted teleplays, courts have been willing to apply traditional substantial similarity copyright analyses to reality television in disputes over format and copyright rights. In *Dillon v. NBC Universal Media LLC*, the creator of a reality competition show built on the exploits of Navy SEAL team members called "Celebrity SEALS" sued the producers of a network reality show entitled "Stars Earn Stripes."[53] On a motion to dismiss, the court conducted an analysis of the reality show copyrightable elements, determining that the complaint adequately stated a copyright infringement claim in the context of an unscripted reality television format and program. The court's consideration of all the elements illustrates how courts primarily assess "format" disputes as copyright matters.[54]

---

51   *Id.* (quoting *Whitehead v. CBS/Viacom, Inc.*, 315 F. Supp.2d 1, 13 (D.D.C. 2004)).

52   *Id.* See also, *EMI Catalogue Partnership v. Hill, Holliday, Connors, Cosmopulos, Inc.*, 228 F.3d 56 (2d Cir. 2000) (in the context of a dispute claiming trademark rights in a song, a musical composition could not be protected as its own trademark under the Lanham Act, and noting the "[t]he Supreme Court has stressed that there are fundamental differences between copyright law and trademark law. Copyright law has its roots in the Constitution. It protects fruits of intellectual labor, such as literary or dramatic works, musical compositions, motion pictures, sound recordings, architectural works, and other similar original works of authorship. A trademark, by way of contrast, grows out of the adoption and use of a distinctive symbol by the party using it. Its function is simply to designate the goods as the product of a particular trader and to protect his good will against the sale of another's product as his."). *Id.*, 228 F.3d at 63-64. (Internal citations omitted.)

53   *Dillon v. NBC Universal Media LLC*, 2013 U.S. Dist. LEXIS 100733, 2013 WL 3581938 (C.D. Cal. June 18, 2013).

54   "a. Theme and Mood

"The theme and mood of the Program is one of appreciation and respect for military personnel, law enforcement, and first responders and the sacrifices they make in the line of duty. As stated by Defendants, the Program is 'an unabashedly positive tribute to military personnel, law enforcement, and first responders.' Similarly, the Treatment provides that '[w]hen the President of the Unite[d] States calls on the military to execute the most dangerous

When a network does want to import a format into the United States, the network will

---

assignments, . . . he sends in the military's most physically powerful, courageous, and mentally strong men and women. Spending over a year in specialized training, which many cannot complete, these people, the toughest of the tough, become SEALs.' Thus, both works are generally reverential of the men and women of the armed forces and the service they perform, and both the Treatment and the Program highlight the dedication required to become proficient in fulfilling these important duties.

"b. Plot and Sequence of Events

"The respective plots of the Treatment and the Program also share similarities. Both works pair a celebrity contestant with a coach who is in the military. In both shows, the celebrity contestants compete in skill-based competitions based on military scenarios. For example, the Treatment describes such potential tasks as 'heavy weapon qualification,' 'over-the-beach scenarios and ambush techniques,' and 'sniper lessons.' The first episode of the Program, entitled 'Amphibious Assault,' has the contestants dropping from a helicopter into water, taking a boat onto shore, and demolishing buildings with explosives. The second episode features a sniper duel between two of the celebrity contestants. These 'missions' are similar to the tasks described in the Treatment.

"Defendants observe that there are some differences between the works in terms of plot. For instance, Defendants note that, unlike the Treatment, there is no panel of experts in the Program, and the other contestants do not vote on who is eliminated. As already discussed, however, these elements are stock elements of the reality television genre that play no role in the substantial similarity analysis.

"c. Dialogue

"Both Plaintiff and Defendants agree that because the works are both unscripted reality television programs, dialogue is not relevant to the Court's analysis.

"d. Setting

"As noted by Plaintiff, both works feature 'military exercises at a training facility.' There is a distinction between the Program and the Treatment, though, in that the Treatment contemplates that the celebrity contestants would live together in a military barracks, and they would be depicted performing 'menial tasks.' The Program, by contrast, does not feature the contestants living together, nor does it depict them performing daily activities. Nevertheless, this distinction by itself is insufficient for the Court to hold as a matter of law that the works are not substantially similar.

"e. Characters

"The Treatment's list of proposed celebrity contestants is uncannily similar to the contestants chosen to participate in the Program. For example, the Treatment proposes as a contestant Drew Lachey, a former member of the music group 98 Degrees. The Program features as a contestant Drew Lachey's brother, Nick Lachey, who was also a member of 98 Degrees. The Treatment also proposes WWE professional wrestling stars Steve Austin and Chris Jericho; the Program features Eve Torres, a former WWE professional wrestling star. Similarly, the Treatment proposes Brooke Burke, a model and former Dancing with the Stars contestant and host, as a celebrity contestant. The Program features Samantha Harris, a model and former Dancing with the Stars host, as a co-host. Further, the Treatment proposes a list of 'retired seals . . . who have the "it" factor' who could serve as host of Celebrity SEALs. One of these is Jesse Ventura, a retired SEAL who was a professional wrestler for a time before entering politics and being elected governor of Minnesota. One of the Program's hosts is General Wesley Clark, a former general in the United States Army who later entered politics. Other similarities abound.

consider various approaches to how to proceed with production and ownership issues, including the following:

- Should the network license the format and produce shows itself, or pay a license fee to a production company for completed episodes.

- The license fee will be based on the production budget, and not use deficit financing as is commonly done for scripted television. The reason is that there is little back end revenue for a reality show, thus the producers will need to have 100% of production costs paid for in the license fee.

- The production or license fee per episode will include 10% of the total representing the producer's fee, and 5% representing the format fee for the underlying intellectual property rights.

- The agreement would include "bumps" or increases in the fee in successive years.

- The term could be for a term or years, or perpetual.

- Ancillary income from merchandise would be considered. The network might insist on revenue sharing, if not part ownership, of any products or merchandise connected with the show, for example a show about a hair salon might launch a line of hair products.

- Distribution Rights: U.S. & Canada, potentially international as well.

- Distribution Rights in the format

- Distribution fees

- Back End: share of revenue above the per program productions costs; any third party revenue shares such as packaging fees from an agency?

- Digital Rights: The network will want digital rights, for example online streaming, for a period of time after the initial broadcast. Since there is typically little or no revenue for this service the network will not want to offer any share.

- Other Digital Rights: videogames

- Ratings Bonus: the production company will want to negotiate a bonus payable if a ratings threshold is reached.

"Viewing the protectable elements of the works as a whole, the Court cannot conclude that they are not substantially similar on the pleadings. This is especially true in light of the high degree of access alleged by Plaintiff—that Plaintiff and Moss provided a copy of the Treatment to Hurwitz. In such situations, courts 'require a lower standard of proof of substantial similarity.'"

Id., 2013 U.S. Dist. LEXIS 100733, at *14-*19. (Internal citations omitted.)

- <u>Product Integration</u>: if the producer wants to integrate a product into a reality show, the network's ad sales division will insist that the product manufacturer also make a media buy, i.e. buy ad time on the network.

[2]—Unscripted Television Participant Agreements

Agreements for participants in reality shows are surprisingly similar to agreements with actors, with several important exceptions, for example there is no SAG-AFTRA involvement because the "real people" are not members of any actor's guild or union. And there may be extensive requirements for background checks, in an effort to keep unstable people, or people with criminal records, off the show. But otherwise, the agreement will address some of the following issues, some or all of which might be found in an actor's agreement to provide services:

- <u>Services</u>: the description might be "On-camera personalities," and the participant would have to be available for all phases of the production, including on-camera, voiceover, promo spots, as well as marketing and public appearances.

- <u>Location</u>: Where filming might take place in the home or business location, permission for that will be included.

- <u>Options</u>: These are the extension of term options that production company will exercise in the event the network carrying the show renews for additional seasons.

- <u>Compensation</u>: the compensation for reality television stars can be considerable, comparable with that paid to actors. The rates payable will vary depending on whether they are for half-hour or hour episodes.

- <u>Contingent Compensation</u>: This will include a percentage share in the shows net profits or adjusted gross profits depending on the definitions used, as well as a share of revenue from merchandise or publications arising from the show.

- <u>Personal Appearances</u>: there may be compensation for making personal appearances.

- <u>Travel & Accommodation</u>: designating the type of accommodations and travel, and any per diems supplied by the production company.

- <u>Right of First Negotiation/Last Refusal</u>: Because television programs can continue for years, or lead to spin offs, the production company will want to be in a priority position as regarding obtaining any future rights.

- <u>Exclusivity</u>: the participants will not be able to provide their services to any other production, but the agreement may specify activities that are allowed without special permission, such as being a guest on a talk show or news program, or endorsement agreements that pre-existed or are excluded for other reasons.

With respect to any purported restrictions on employment post-term, for example provisions stating that the participant will not be involved in any other competing reality television production for a period of time after the current production ends, in California such restrictions after the term of employment are likely unenforceable under California Business and Professions code Section 16600, which states: "[e]xcept as provided in this chapter, every contract by which anyone is restrained from engaging in a lawful profession, trade, or business of any kind is to that extent void."[55]

[3]—The Scope and Enforceability of Participant Releases in Reality Television

Filmed productions that depict ordinary people—non-actors—can rely on several strategies for obtaining valid releases and consents for the depiction of those persons. Depending on the circumstances, consent can be validly obtained verbally, or by written releases knowingly entered into, and in some cases inferred from the surrounding circumstances and conduct.[56] Even the "mockumentary" film, "Borat," was found to have obtained valid consents by relying on standard contract terms such as an integration clause stating that the individual was not granting the release based on any representations other than the document itself.[57]

Reality television productions however may go a step further if they intentionally manipulate the participants in order to create a compelling entertainment experience for the viewer. In the quest to create drama and spectacle from otherwise often mundane real life, reality television shows may place contestants in physically dangerous circumstances, manipulate the story arc by use of deception and surprise, create intimate social and personal situations between participants, and conduct extensive and probing background checks including personal finances, job history, and criminal records, and

---

55   See Cal. Bus. & Prof. Code § 16600 (narrow exceptions include protection for bona fide trade secrets of the former employer).

56   See:

Ninth Circuit: *Newton v. Thomason*, 22 F.3d 1455 (9th Cir. 1994) (consent to use of name for character in television series in circumstances where consent arising from plaintiff's involvement in production was "obvious").

Eleventh Circuit: *Lane v. MRA Holdings, LLC*, 242 F. Supp.2d 1205 (M.D. Fla. 2002) (consent to be photographed in public location clear from circumstances and conduct including willingness to pose semi-nude for video camera).

State Courts:

California: *Greenstein v. The Greif Co.*, 2009 WL 117368 (Cal. App. Jan. 20, 2009) (unpublished opinion) (consent to be depicted in "Gene Simmons Family Jewels" television reality show established by plaintiff's conduct, including plaintiff's role as a segment producer responsible for signage notifying public that their presence at production location constituted consent to be depicted in program); *Aisenson v. American Broadcasting Co.*, 220 Cal. App.3d 146, 269 Cal. Rptr. 379 (1990) (plaintiff cannot prove invasion of privacy where he "voluntarily entered into the public sphere" and "was photographed only while in public view").

57   See *Lemerond v. Twentieth Century Fox Film Corp.*, 2008 U.S. Dist. LEXIS 26947, 2008 WL 918579 (S.D.N.Y. March 31, 2008).

make such information public. In theory, such intentional acts could lead to a host of civil complaints including tort claims based on intrusion into private affairs, false light, defamation, intentional infliction of emotional distress, and battery.

In order to avoid liability, reality television production companies use increasingly elaborate release of claims agreements that participants are required to sign.[58] Such "participant releases" may include acknowledgment that there could be a host of physically and psychologically intentionally dangerous and harmful activities aimed at the participant, including dangers created by other show participants and contestants. Such agreements may include acknowledgment that the producers may engage in intentional acts that would otherwise constitute torts, including unwelcome physical contact, and that to the extent the participant may engage in intimate encounters with other contestants, the participant may be exposed to harmful physical consequences.

The legal principles underlying all release of claim agreements are based on contract: an individual may expressly agree to accept a risk of harm arising from another's negligent conduct, and cannot recover for such harm, unless the agreement is invalid as contrary to public policy.[59] No public policy opposes private, voluntary transactions in which one party, for a consideration, agrees to shoulder a risk which the law would otherwise have placed upon the other party.[60] A written release extinguishes any obligation covered by the release's terms, provided it was not obtained by fraud, deception, misrepresentation, duress, or undue influence.[61] The interpretation of a release is governed by the same principles applicable to any other contractual agreement, giving effect to the parties' mutual intent as it existed when they contracted. The parties' intent should be

---

58   Sample participant releases are included in the forms for this chapter.

59   See *Restatement* (Second) of Torts, § 496B. See also, *Cal. Civ. Code* § 1668:

"All contracts which have for their object, directly or indirectly, to exempt anyone from responsibility for his own fraud, or willful injury to the person or property of another, or violation of law, whether willful or negligent, are against the policy of law."

60   See *Tunkl v. Regents of University of California*, 60 Cal.2d 92, 101, 32 Cal. Rptr. 33, 383 P.2d 441 (1963). Where valid releases were signed, heirs of participants killed or injured during dangerous sporting and recreational activities were foreclosed from bringing liability claims under assumption of the risk principles. See: *Randas v. YMCA of Metropolitan Los Angeles*, 17 Cal. App.4th 158, 161-162, 21 Cal. Rptr.2d 245 (1993) (swim class); *Paralift, Inc. v. Superior Court*, 23 Cal. App.4th 748, 756, 29 Cal. Rptr.2d 177 (1993) (skydiving); *Buchan v. United States Cycling Federation, Inc.*, 227 Cal. App.3d 134, 277 Cal. Rptr. 887 (1991) (cycle racing); *Saenz v. Whitewater Voyages, Inc.*, 226 Cal. App.3d 758, 764, 276 Cal. Rptr. 672 (1990) (river rafting); *Madison v. Superior Court*, 203 Cal. App.3d 589, 597-599, 250 Cal. Rptr. 299 (1988) (scuba diving); *Kurashige v. Indian Dunes, Inc.*, 200 Cal.App.3d 606, 611-612, 246 Cal. Rptr. 310 (1988) (motorcycle dirtbike); *Coates v. Newhall Land & Farming, Inc.*, 191 Cal. App.3d 1, 8, 236 Cal. Rptr. 181 (1987) (riding dirtbike).

61   See *Marder v. Lopez*, 450 F.3d 445, 449 (9th Cir. 2006) (release given by subject of film "Flashdance" barred later claims for additional compensation).

inferred from the language of the release, so long as that language is not ambiguous or uncertain.[62] The language used must be clear, explicit and comprehensible in each of its essential details, and the agreement read as a whole must clearly notify the prospective releaser of the effect of signing the agreement.[63]

But there are limits to this power to contract away liability: contracts that violate public policy are unenforceable. California Civil Code Section 1668 states that:

> "All contracts which have for their object, directly or indirectly, to exempt anyone from responsibility for his own fraud, or willful injury to the person or property of another, or violation of law, whether willful or negligent, are against the policy of the law."[64]

Reported cases on the validity and enforceability of releases in reality television focus primarily on traditional contract formation principles such as: (1) was the release willingly given; (2) was there an opportunity to negotiate, or was it a contract of adhesion with no opportunity to negotiate; (3) were the terms of the agreement unconscionable and against public policy.

In *Higgins v. The Superior Court*, five orphaned siblings sued, among others, the producers of the reality television show Extreme Makeover, claiming that an arbitration provision in a release signed for the show was unenforceable.[65] In finding the arbitration provision unenforceable, the court's analysis first considered whether the contract was one

---

62   *Id.* (Internal citations omitted.)

63   *Madison v. Superior Court*, 203 Cal. App.3d 589, 597–598, 250 Cal. Rptr. 299 (1988). Under California Civil Code Section 1542, a release of claims does not apply to future claims unknown at the time of release, however the protections of that statutory provision may be waived. See Cal. Civ. Code § 1542:

"A general release does not extend to claims which the creditor does not know or suspect to exist in his or her favor at the time of executing the release, which if known by him or her must have materially affected his or her settlement with the debtor."

See also: *Larsen v. Johannes*, 7 Cal. App.3d 491, 502, 86 Cal. Rptr. 744 (1970) (the protections of Cal. Civ. Code § 1542 may be waived); *Mesmer v. White*, 121 Cal. App.2d 665, 674–667, 264 P.2d 60 (1953) (Section 1542 only applicable to debtor/creditor transactions).

64   See *Cal. Civ. Code* § 1668. See also: *City of Santa Barbara v. Superior Court*, 41 Cal.4th 747, 62 Cal. Rptr.3d 527, 161 P.3d 1095 (2007) (liability for future gross negligence cannot be released); *Capri v. L.A. Fitness International, LLC*, 136 Cal. App.4th 1078, 39 Cal. Rptr. 425 (2006) (release of all future unknown claims invalid where purported to apply to violation of statutory law); *Dieu v. McGraw*, 2011 Cal. App. Unpub. LEXIS 87 (Cal. App. Jan. 6, 2011) (*under Cal. Civ. Code* § 1668 while releases may bar actions based on ordinary negligence, they cannot bar claims for fraud, intentional acts, and negligent violation of statutory law).

65   See *Higgins II v. Superior Court*, 140 Cal. App.4th 1238, 45 Cal. Rptr.3d 293 (2006).

of adhesion, and then considered whether the contract was unconscionable, which was the dispositive factor in the analysis.

A contract of adhesion is a standardized contract that is imposed and drafted by the party of superior bargaining strength and relegates to the other party only the opportunity to adhere to the contract or reject it.[66] In *Higgins*, the court noted that "adhesion contracts are routine in modern day commerce. If a court finds a contract to be adhesive, it must then determine whether other factors are present which, under established legal rules legislative or judicial, operate to render it unenforceable."[67] A court need not enforce an adhesion contract that is unconscionable.[68] However, adhesion is not a prerequisite for unconscionability.[69]

Unconscionability has both a procedural and a substantive element, the former focusing on "oppression" or "surprise" due to unequal bargaining power, the latter on "overly harsh" or "one-sided" results. Both must be present for a court to find a contractual provision unenforceable.[70]

The *Higgins II* court found that the arbitration provision was unenforceable because (1) the contract was lengthy, standardized with no customization, drafted by the more powerful party, and presented in a few minutes on a "take it or leave it" basis thus was held to be adhesive; (2) the arbitration provision was procedurally unconscionable, based on the "surprise or oppression" standard because the Higgins children were young and unsophisticated and vulnerable, the provision was buried in a larger "miscellaneous" section of the overall agreement, was not highlighted or printed in bold or capitol letters or larger font; and (3) the provision was substantively unconscionable because it was unfairly one-sided. It only required the Higgins children to submit their claims to arbitration, while the production company was not limited with respect to remedies,

---

66   *Id.*, 140 Cal. App.4th at 1248.

67   *Id.*

68   See *Armendariz v. Foundation Health Psychcare Services, Inc.*, 24 Cal.4th 83, 99 Cal. Rptr.2d 745, 6 P.3d 669 (2000).

69   See *Harper v. Ultimo*, 113 Cal. App.4th 1402, 1409, 7 Cal. Rptr.3d 418 (2003).

70   *Higgins II*, 140 Cal. App.4th at 1249. See also, *Cal. Civ. Code* § 1670.5:

"(a) If the court as a matter of law finds the contract or any clause of the contract to have been unconscionable at the time it was made the court may refuse to enforce the contract, or it may enforce the remainder of the contract without the unconscionable clause, or it may so limit the application of any unconscionable clause as to avoid any unconscionable result.

"(b) When it is claimed or appears to the court that the contract or any clause thereof may be unconscionable the parties shall be afforded a reasonable opportunity to present evidence as to its commercial setting, purpose, and effect to aid the court in making the determination."

being free to seek injunctive or equitable relief, which the court held to be harsh and one-sided.[71]

[4]—Child Labor Laws in the Reality Television Industry

As noted earlier, labor laws regulating the employment of minors in entertainment productions may require work permits, control the number of hours that minors may work, require that education and schooling not be interrupted, and require that a portion of the minor's compensation be placed into trust accounts for the future benefit of the minor.

Reality television productions that depict minors as part of the featured "cast" have historically not come under state "entertainment industry" employment regulations for minors due to their inherent "documentary" nature which does not have scripts or employ professional actors. In addition, most reality television productions are non-union, thus the "cast" are not subject to SAG-AFTRA regulations.[72]

In 2012, the Pennsylvania legislature enacted a prospectively effective revision to the state's child labor laws specifically addressing the participation of minors in reality television productions.[73]

---

71   *Higgins II*, 140 Cal. App.4th at 1253-1254. See also:

Second Circuit: Klapper v. Graziano, 970 N.Y.S.2d 355 (N.Y. Sup. 2013) (plastic surgeon accused of negligence signed a valid release and could not sue producers of "Mob Wives").

Seventh Circuit: Malec v. MTV Networks, 2010 U.S. Dist. LEXIS 134559, 2010 WL 5313817 (N.D. Ill. Dec. 20, 2010) (release signed by background participant in "Jersey Shore" show valid).

Ninth Circuit: Doe v. Gangland Productions, Inc., 2013 WL 5066826 (9th Cir. Sept. 16, 2013) (former gang member prisoner claimed reality television production release that allowed use of his real name and identity to his detriment was fraudulently procured and therefore void, where prisoner had informed producer that prisoner had "extreme difficulty reading" and was told the release was "just a receipt" for a payment of $300); *Christakis v. Mark Burnett Productions*, 2009 U.S. Dist. LEXIS 60751 (C.D. Cal. April 27, 2009) (release and waiver signed by participant in "The Apprentice" show valid).

District of Columbia Circuit: Amirmotazedi v. Viacom, Inc., 768 F. Supp.2d 256 (D.D.C. 2011) (triable issue as to whether release signed by participant in "Real World" reality show was valid where participant signed while intoxicated).

72   See, e.g., *Harmon T. Sharp III v. Next Entertainment, Inc.*, 163 Cal. App.4th 410, 78 Cal Rptr.3d 37 (2008) (non-union writers brought wage and labor law class action lawsuits against reality television production companies and television networks; appeal affirmed denial of defendants' motion to disqualify plaintiff's counsel).

73   See Pennsylvania Child Labor Act, House Bill 1548, Regular Session 2011-2012, effective Jan. 18, 2013, replacing 34 Pa. Code § 11 "Employment of Minors."

Notable provisions in the Pennsylvania statute include definitions of "Documentary Program" and "Reality Program," thereby unequivocally including such productions within the state's child labor laws:

"'Documentary program.' A genre of motion picture program, including programming for television, that depicts or portrays a nonfiction story and may present an opinion or a specific message along with factual material.

"'Reality program.' A genre of program that principally presents actual events and generally features ordinary people and not professional actors."[74]

The Pennsylvania statute also specifically states that participation in a reality television program or documentary for compensation qualifies as a "performance" subject to regulation, where the minor's participation is "substantial" and the production depends on the minor's participation, and where anyone receives remuneration for the minor's participation:

Section 5. Employment of minors in a performance.

(a) General rule—For purposes of this section, a minor is engaged in a performance if:

(1) The minor models or renders artistic or creative expression in a live performance, on the radio, on television, in a movie, over the Internet, in a publication or via any other broadcast medium that may be transmitted to an audience and any person receives remuneration for the performance. Rehearsal for this activity is part of the performance.

(2) The minor participates in a reality or documentary program that expressly depends upon the minor's participation, the minor's participation is substantial and any person receives remuneration for the minor's participation. For the purposes of this subsection:

(i) Remuneration shall include one or more monetary payments, but shall not include reimbursement for expenses incurred by the minor or the minor's family, any prize or goods or services received in connection with the program with a value of less than $2,500.

---

74   *Id.*

(ii) 'Substantial' shall mean the minor is a principal subject of the reality or documentary program or the minor participates in the filming of the reality or documentary program for ten or more days in a 30-day period.[75]

The regulatory provisions of the Pennsylvania statute are similar to those in California that apply to "professional" child actors, including a required work permit, limitations on the numbers of hours worked, educational provisions, monitoring of compliance, and a requirement that 15% of the compensation be placed into a trust account for the minor's benefit.

Production companies that wish to avoid the regulatory effect of the statute may presumably do so by structuring their productions to avoid the remuneration or filming day "triggers."

§2.18   Event Programming

Event programming includes high profile annual entertainment industry award shows such as the Academy Awards for motion pictures, the Grammy Awards for sound recordings, the Emmy awards for television, MTV Awards, Golden Globes, beauty competitions, and many others. The organization presenting the award typically enters into a direct production and broadcast agreement with a broadcast or cable network. But in at least two well-known cases, The Academy of Country Music Awards and the Golden Globe Awards, the presenters have an agreement with an independent production company that specializes in such spectacles, Dick Clark Productions, which in turn licenses the broadcast to a network, sharing the revenue with the presenting organization.

In *Hollywood Foreign Press Association v. Red Zone Capital Partners II*, the presenters of the Golden Globes Awards Show, the Hollywood Foreign Press Association, had a dispute with their contractual partner, Dick Clark Productions, over the scope of Clark's rights to produce the telecast in the future.[76]

For years the show had been produced by Clark and licensed to NBC for network broadcast, with annual license fees averaging 21.5 million dollars.[77] On the one hand, Clark's contractual option periods to produce the show expired in 2005. But on the other hand, the agreement had language stating that Clark's future rights would nonetheless continue so long as the

---

75   *Id.*

76   See *Hollywood Foreign Press Ass'n v. Red Zone Capital Partners II*, 870 F. Supp.2d 881 (C.D. Cal. 2012) (Dick Clark Productions had a contractual right to license the Golden Globes Award Show to NBC so long as NBC commits to broadcast that show).

77   *Id.*, 870 F. Supp.2d at 911.

underlying license between Clark and NBC was renewed or extended in the future, an arrangement the court referred to as "end-of-deal protection" for Clark.[78]

In holding in favor of Clark's interpretation of the agreement, the court conducted a detailed historical review of the agreement negotiations and amendments over two decades, noting instances where the agreement's provisions comported with testimony on entertainment industry practice, and instances where Clark had apparently bargained for rights that were normally difficult to obtain.[79]

The case well illustrates the imperative of seeking contractual protection for production companies that "devote substantial resources to the development, promotion and exploitation of a property" and their desire to obtain contractual protection against being cut out of the deal at a later point in time, when the property may have increased in value.[80] As the court noted, "[t]his may take various forms, including rights of first negotiation and first or last refusal, perpetual options or a grant of rights in perpetuity."[81]

§2.19   Time-Buy Programming

Broadcast and cable networks may, in effect, "rent" time to third party producers who supply the programs and the advertising for the time slots purchased. The content can be anything from an "infomercial" (a.k.a. "long form advertising") to elaborate productions that may appear to viewers to be network productions. The producer recoups its investment by selling the advertising that is inserted into the program, and must deliver a ready-to-broadcast program to the network, which may also add a few minutes of promotion for its own programming. The producer is required to submit the program, commercials, and advertisements to the networks standards departments seventy-two hours prior to the broadcast.[82]

§2.20   Online Fan Fiction Video Productions

With the advent of inexpensive video production technology and distribution via YouTube and other platforms, the literary phenomenon known as "Fan Fiction" has expanded to video productions that use characters, costumes, sets, and stories in new adventures. Whether fan

---

78   *Id.*, 870 F. Supp.2d at 920.

79   *Id.*

80   *Id.*, 870 F. Supp.2d at 899.

81   *Id.*

82   See *Baiul v. NBCUniversal Media, LLC*, 2014 U.S. Dist. LEXIS 57474 (S.D.N.Y. April 24, 2014) (describing Time-Buy process for figure skating productions).

"Fan Films," Startrek.com. Copyright © by CBS Interactive, Inc

fiction is fair use or copyright infringement has not been established in the courts, but its increasing popularity, and a certain reluctance of some copyright owners to sue their fans, has led one copyright owner to publish Fan Fiction guidelines. CBS and Paramount, the owners of the Star Trek franchise, recently published the following guidelines in an attempt to keep fan fiction on a non-commercial amateur basis. The success of this program has not yet been determined, but as an acknowledgment of fair use rights and an attempt to encourage fans without harming revenue, it may be a precursor of further attempts to, in essence, license and control the scope of fair use:

> "CBS and Paramount Pictures are big believers in reasonable fan fiction and fan creativity, and, in particular, want amateur fan filmmakers to showcase their passion for *Star Trek*. Therefore, CBS and Paramount Pictures will not object to, or take legal action against, *Star Trek* fan productions that are non-professional and amateur and meet the following guidelines.

Guidelines for Avoiding Objections:

1. The fan production must be less than 15 minutes for a single self-contained story, or no more than 2 segments, episodes or parts, not to exceed 30 minutes total, with no additional seasons, episodes, parts, sequels or remakes.

2. The title of the fan production or any parts cannot include the name "*Star Trek*." However, the title must contain a subtitle with the phrase: "A *STAR TREK* FAN PRODUCTION" in plain typeface. The fan production cannot use the term "official" in either its title or subtitle or in any marketing, promotions or social media for the fan production.

3. The content in the fan production must be original, not reproductions, recreations or clips from any *Star Trek* production. If non-*Star Trek* third party content is used, all necessary permissions for any third party content should be obtained in writing.

4. If the fan production uses commercially-available *Star Trek* uniforms, accessories, toys and props, these items must be official merchandise and not bootleg items or imitations of such commercially available products.

5. The fan production must be a real "fan" production, i.e., creators, actors and all other participants must be amateurs, cannot be compensated for their services, and cannot be currently or previously employed on any *Star Trek* series, films, production of DVDs or with any of CBS or Paramount Pictures' licensees.

6. The fan production must be non-commercial:

CBS and Paramount Pictures do not object to limited fundraising for the creation of a fan production, whether 1 or 2 segments and consistent with these guidelines, so long as the total amount does not exceed $50,000, including all platform fees, and when the $50,000 goal is reached, all fundraising must cease.

The fan production must only be exhibited or distributed on a no-charge basis and/or shared via streaming services without generating revenue.

The fan production cannot be distributed in a physical format such as DVD or Blu-ray.

The fan production cannot be used to derive advertising revenue including, but not limited to, through for example, the use of pre or post-roll advertising, click-through advertising banners, that is associated with the fan production.

No unlicensed *Star Trek*-related or fan production-related merchandise or services can be offered for sale or given away as premiums, perks or rewards or in connection with the fan production fundraising.

The fan production cannot derive revenue by selling or licensing fan-created production sets, props or costumes.

7. The fan production must be family friendly and suitable for public presentation. Videos must not include profanity, nudity, obscenity, pornography, depictions of drugs, alcohol, tobacco, or any harmful or illegal activity, or any material that is offensive, fraudulent, defamatory, libelous, disparaging, sexually explicit, threatening, hateful, or any other inappropriate content. The content of the fan production cannot violate any individual's right of privacy.

8. The fan production must display the following disclaimer in the on-screen credits of the fan productions and on any marketing material including the fan production website or page hosting the fan production:

    "Star Trek and all related marks, logos and characters are solely owned by CBS Studios Inc. This fan production is not endorsed by, sponsored by, nor affiliated with CBS, Paramount Pictures, or any other Star Trek franchise, and is a non-commercial fan-made film intended for recreational use. No commercial exhibition or distribution is permitted. No alleged independent rights will be asserted against CBS or Paramount Pictures."

9. Creators of fan productions must not seek to register their works, nor any elements of the works, under copyright or trademark law.

10. Fan productions cannot create or imply any association or endorsement by CBS or Paramount Pictures.

CBS and Paramount Pictures reserve the right to revise, revoke and/or withdraw these guidelines at any time in their own discretion. These guidelines are not a license and do not constitute approval or authorization of any fan productions or a waiver of any rights that CBS or Paramount Pictures may have with respect to fan fiction created outside of these guidelines.[83]

§2.21   Television Series Showrunner Agreements

While the primary creative author and driving force behind a motion picture is often the director, television series are controlled and dominated by the writer who created the series, wrote the pilot, and continues to act as the lead writer and executive producer, and possibly as a director also, making creative decisions and executing the series arch for the story line and characters that keep the series vibrant over the course of multiple seasons. This creative force is the "showrunner."

Agreements between production companies and showrunners will combine those job descriptions and include duties such as writing the pilot episode (if there is one), providing executive producer functions, supervising other writers and writing additional episodes, and directing.

Notable in such agreements is that the different job descriptions fall under different unions and guilds, for example the writing and writing credits come under the jurisdiction of the Writers Guild of America, including granting of a "created by" credit that generates separate royalties as compared to fees for writing scripts. Directing services and fees are governed by the master bargaining agreement with the Directors Guild of America which, like the WGA Master Bargaining Agreement, sets the minimum "scale" compensation.

Key deal points in a television series showrunner agreement may include the following, presented here as a showrunner-favorable agreement:

---

83   Available at, http://www.startrek.com/fan-films . See also *Paramount Pictures Corp. v. Axanar Prods.*, 2017 U.S. Dist. LEXIS 19670 (C.D. Cal. Jan. 3, 2017) (large budget fan film not a fair use).

Pilot Script: Creation of the pilot script (if there is a pilot), including the fee and a timetable for the writing steps beginning with the commencement of writing, for example allowing six weeks for the first draft rewrite, four weeks for a set of further revisions, and two weeks for the final polish. The negotiated fee will typically be more than the WGA minimums.

Pilot Producing: Contingent on the showrunner receiving sole "written by" credit, Executive Producer status and fee for the pilot episode. Such producer fees are not governed by the WGA or DGA and are subject to free negotiation.

Series Producing: If the series is produced based on the pilot, Executive Producer duties and fees for the entire seasons one and two on a "pay or play" guaranteed basis, including increases for subsequent seasons should the producers want to engage the showrunner as an executive producer for season three and beyond. The production company may reserve the right to have showrunner and production duties shared with any other key writers on the series.

Series Production Bonus: If the showrunner writes the pilot, receives "created by" credit, and the series is actually produced for season one, a bonus payment may be negotiated based on a benchmark number of episodes ordered, or a pro rata share thereof.

Directing Services: This provision will reference fees and credits for directing episodes, and may include a bonus for directing the pilot if it results in season one. Directing the pilot may also result in a royalty (i.e. a payment by right and not as a result of providing services) for all future episodes produced, whether or not the showrunner provides the directing services.

Consultant Services: Contingent upon the executive producer services being successfully provided in seasons one and two (and potentially beyond), the production company shall engage the showrunner as a consultant for as many future seasons as the showrunner served as executive producer. Or, if the showrunner received sole "created by" credit for the series, the consulting services may continue for the life of the series.

Series Royalty: Under the WGA Master Bargaining Agreement, sole "created by" credit for a series results in WGA mandated royalty payment for every series produced without the requirement of doing any actual writing (thus termed a "royalty"). The parties may negotiate royalty fees higher than the WGA minimums.

Future Assignments: The showrunner may be assigned writing and directing duties on future episodes, with the rates and fees subject to negotiation but locked in at production company's so-called "top of show" rates.

Separation of Rights: If the showrunner is entitled to WGA separated rights, for example reserving future rights to adapt the series for the live stage or motion pictures, the agreement may include a specific fee for which the showrunner grants those future rights to the production company.

Exclusivity: The showrunners services may be exclusive to the production company during the production of the pilot, and thereafter on a non-exclusive but first priority basis during each subsequent production season, and a non-exclusive but no material interference basis at all other times while the series is being produced. "First priority" may be defined as the showrunner being not contractually exclusive on an outside project, and available to consult with the production company in person or by phone on the same day as a consultation request is received.

Screen Credits: Many of the different types of credits a showrunner may receive are contingent upon qualifying by receiving sole credit for writing the pilot episode or being granted "created by" credit or providing executive producer services for the first two seasons:

Writing Credit: pursuant to WGA credit determination.

Directing Credit: pursuant to DGA credit determination.

Executive Producing Credit: Based on providing the services as agreed, with specification of separate or shared card in the main titles.

Company Credit: For a showrunner with sole "created by" and "executive producer" credits, the showrunner's loan out corporation or production company name may receive a separate card or animated logo credit at the close of each episode.

Consulting Credit: Where a consulting credit is used, this provision may provide for the showrunner sharing a credit card with other consultants.

Contingent Participation: Profit participation based on a percentage of Modified Adjusted Gross Receipts ("MAGR") as defined in the agreement, which rights may vest ¼ each at the following benchmarks: 1) delivery of Pilot rewrite; 2) delivery of Pilot episode; 3) conclusion of first season; 4) conclusion of second season (in both seasons contingent upon providing executive producer services for the entire season). Where the production company and the network are affiliated thus there will not be a market-establish highest possible rate, the license fee between affiliated companies will be an "imputed license fee" which should be no less than a comparable arm's length transaction on the open market.

First Negotiation: A period of good faith negotiation for the first derivative "spin off" production based on the series, for the showrunner to provide similar writing, executive producer, and directing services.

Passive Payments: For spin-offs where the showrunner does not actually render writing or executive producing services, the showrunner may still be entitled to passive payments based on a percentage of the contingent compensation and royalties earned from the original series.

Theatrical Release Bonus: In the event the pilot is theatrically released, this provides for additional payments based on the original fee for writing the pilot script, with additional fees payable if the showrunner directed the pilot.

Awards Bonus: Cash bonus amounts based on nominations and wins for leading television industry awards (Emmy, Golden Globe, and other prominent awards in the television industry).

"Created By" Condition: Where a pilot is based on underlying material, the WGA may not award a "Created By" credit to the showrunner, in which event a "developed by" credit may be granted, or at least a "most favored nations" type promise made that in such situations, nobody will receive a "created by" credit, i.e. if the showrunner can't receive that credit, then nobody else will.

Consultation: An undertaking by the production company to meaningfully consult with the showrunner on key creative development and production matters.

Travel and Expenses: May specify first or business class air travel as required, may include privileges such as designated studio parking spaces where not mandated by WGA, etc.

Assistant and Other Personnel: May specify the hiring of a specific personal assistant and co-producers.

Standard Terms and Conditions: This may include specifics of employment including guild-mandated work rules, standard "work made for hire" copyright provisions, details of visa and immigration matters, suspension and termination, and specifics regarding guild mandated payments such as residuals. Other matters typically includes address right of publicity, independent contractor status, insurance policies and physical examinations, and tax withholding.

Letter of Inducement: As the agreement will be between the production company and the showrunner's personal services or "loan out" corporation, a standard Letter of Inducement will be included in which the individual acknowledges they will perform the services being contracted for with their personal services corporation.

CHAPTER 3

Book and Magazine Publishing

---

§3.01   Introduction: Publishing, Technology, and the Law

Modern "publishing"[1] is the use of technology to capture creative works in a fixed format, so the works can be owned, reproduced and sold as widely as the market will bear. In the broadest sense, all facets of the entertainment industry are about publishing some form of creative work, whether it be literature, motion pictures, art, or music.

Copyright and technology have continued to evolve together, and publishing's legal basis goes far beyond copyright to include the law of contracts, First Amendment freedom of speech, the law of libel and defamation, and evolving business models. Even with the advent of new digital publishing technologies such as online publishing and downloads, and book-like electronic display devices such as the "Kindle," the legal fundamentals of publishing remain the same, and fall into three broad areas:

(1) the acquisition of rights and the act of publication;

(2) legal issues arising from publication such as libel and defamation, invasion of privacy, and First Amendment freedom of speech; and

---

1   The publishing business as we know it began with Johannes Gutenberg's invention of the printing press in Mainz, Germany in 1455, and the printing of the "Gutenberg Bible." In a technology-driven leap similar to the advent of the Internet in our own time, it has been estimated that within fifty years of the invention of the printing press, the number of books in Europe increased from a few thousand hand-copied and largely inaccessible volumes to more than nine million published volumes, with a corresponding surge in literacy and an exchange of ideas that mankind had not previously experienced. The format and technology of the printed book was so successful that its basic contours—words printed on sheets of paper bound in a volume that can be easily held and transported—represent a 500-year-old technology still in daily use today.

(3) the further types of entertainment media that can arise from the creative work being published, such as production of a motion picture based on a book.

§3.02   Book Publishing Agreements

[1]—Introduction

Because publishing can encompass many different types of works, from fiction to college textbooks, publishing agreements may vary widely in appearance, terms, and length. But the fundamentals of any publishing agreement remain the same:

- Creation of the work
- Scope and duration of rights granted
- Delivery
- Publication format and timing
- Royalties, including any advances against royalties

[2]—The Operative Grant

[a]—Exclusive License or Assignment of Copyright

The default position of copyright law is that upon creation of a work by an author, the author is the copyright owner of that work.[2] For most literary genres, the publishing agreement will proceed on that basis, granting either:

(1) an exclusive license from author to publisher in which the author retains actual copyright ownership but the publisher obtains the exclusive right to print the work; or

(2) an assignment (i.e., transfer) of copyright from the author to the publisher, where the author sells the copyright to the publisher.

Whether the operative copyright function is an exclusive license or an assignment will depend on the bargaining positions of the parties, but in the world of book publishing, it is common for an author to retain copyright ownership while granting exclusive licenses to the publisher.

In both of the above scenarios, the author will, however, still retain his or her right under Section 203 of the Copyright Act to terminate the license or transfer thir-

---

2   17 U.S.C. § 201(a). See Chapter 1 for a full discussion of copyright ownership principles.

ty-five years after the initial assignment.[3] If the author initially granted "worldwide" rights, the termination of those rights thirty-five years later would only apply under U.S. law and in the United States, and not in other territories of the world. Nevertheless, the right of termination can be a powerful right for an author or his/her heirs, enabling them to reclaim the United States rights, especially where the work has proved to be commercially viable.

[b]—Works Made for Hire

Another type of commonly published work falls into another copyright category and creates a different relationship between authors and publishers: the "work made for hire."[4] Under the Copyright Act, works made for hire include the following types of works when they are created by an independent contractor, pursuant to an agreement signed by both parties that the work will be considered one "made for hire":

- A contribution to a collective work (e.g., an encyclopedia or magazine type format);

- A translation;

- A supplementary work, defined as a work that is an adjunct to another author's work in the way of introducing, concluding, illustrating, explaining, revising, commenting upon, or assisting in the use of the other work, such as forewords, afterwords, pictorial illustrations, maps, charts, tables, editorial notes, bibliographies, appendices, and indexes;

- An instructional text, defined as a literary, pictorial, or graphic work prepared for publication and with the purpose of use in systematic instructional activities.[5]

An author whose work falls within the above categories presented with a publishing agreement may find that the agreement calls for "work made for hire" status for his or her contribution. Conversely, if the work does not fit within the above publishing categories, under the law the work cannot be a work made for hire. Section 101 of the Copyright Act precisely defines the situations in which works made for hire can be created. They are:

"(a) works created by employees within the scope of their employment (without the need for any written agreement); and

---

3　17 U.S.C. § 203. See also, Chapter 1 for a discussion of termination rights.

4　See *Community for Creative Non-Violence v. Reid*, 490 U.S. 730, 109 S.Ct. 2166, 104 L.Ed.2d 811 (1989) (discussing and defining commissioned works made for hire). See also, Chapter 1.

5　17 U.S.C. §§ 101, 201(b).

"(b) works specially ordered or commissioned for creation by independent contractors, if and only if the works—

"(i) fall in the nine categories enumerated in section 101; and

"(ii) there is a written agreement signed by the commissioning party as well as by the independent contractor saying that the work will be one 'made for hire.'"[6]

The distinction is of some consequence, because "works made for hire" are the only types of works for which there is no right of termination.[7] The author of a work made for hire will thus never be able to terminate the publisher's rights in the United States or recapture the rights for herself or her heirs.

Publishers and others who commission works will often mistakenly assert that such works are "works made for hire," perhaps appreciating that such status is advantageous to them, but merely calling a work one for hire will not make it so. The work must fit in the nine categories enumerated in the statute, and there must be a written agreement to that effect. An invalid "work for hire" agreement will typically be considered by a court to merely grant the publisher a license to publish the work and will not effect a transfer of the copyright to the publisher.[8] In either event—whether a license or a transfer is deemed to have occurred—the work will be subject to the inalienable right of termination enjoyed by the author and her heirs.

Accordingly, authors, illustrators, editors, and others who enter into publishing agreements should first determine what type of work is at issue, and be prepared where necessary to negotiate an appropriate grant of rights under the copyright.

[c]—Book Formats

The printing and binding of books typically falls into three general categories: hard cover; trade paperbacks;[9] and "mass market" paperbacks,[10] usually released within a year of the hard cover publication. Trade paperbacks are usually released within a year as well, unless the original publication is in that format from the beginning.

---

6   *Id.*

7   17 U.S.C. § 203(a) (termination rights apply "[i]n the case of any work other than a work made for hire. . . .").

8   See *Effects Associates, Inc. v. Cohen*, 908 F.2d 555 (9th Cir. 1990).

9   Trade paperbacks are usually the same size as a hard cover but have paper bindings.

10   Mass market paperbacks are smaller in size and lower in price, compared to the corresponding hard cover edition.

The choice of format depends on a variety of factors, including the marketability of the book and the type of publication, the expectations of the purchaser, and the estimation as to whether a book may initially qualify for the more expensive, "premium" hard cover edition, which can produce higher revenue, with the less expensive paperback edition following only after the publisher believes the original, and higher-priced, hard cover edition has run its course.[11]

The publisher will typically seek rights in all formats of any kind. Ideally, the publisher will position and market the book, including the timing and choice of format, in the most effective manner. However, there may be situations where an author can limit the grant of rights to a specific format, reserving the right to license other formats to third parties, typically after a "hold back" period that allows the original publisher time to recoup its investment. This may be especially true of foreign rights agreements, or reprints of older works no longer controlled by the original publisher.

Publishers will also typically seek "electronic" or digital rights to the work, now a standard format included in publishing agreements. With respect to older agreements from the "pre-digital" era, at least one prominent case, *Random House, Inc. v. Rosetta Books, LLC*, found that digital or electronic book rights were not included in the contractual language in a license that was granted to publish a work "in book form."[12]

Random House, Inc. v. Rosetta Books, LLC was a "new technologies" case that depended on contract language, not copyright. In *Peter Mayer Publishers, Inc. v. Shilovskaya*, the issue was whether an e-book version of an already published translation constituted a new derivative work under copyright law principles.[13] In examining the definition of a derivative work under Section 101 of the Copyright Act, the court held that merely taking an existing printed translation and digitizing it as an e-book lacked the requisite originality to constitute a derivative work. Therefore, under the facts of that case, the translator could continue to offer the existing translation as a digitized e-book and did not need a new license.

Note that while there has been extensive litigation concerning the respective rights of freelance journalists and their publishers in digital database versions of the jour-

---

11   See *United States Naval Institute v. Charter Communications*, 936 F.2d 692 (2d Cir. 1991) (dispute over when sub-licensee of paperback rights could exercise right to distribute mass-market paperback of hardcover bestseller).

12   *Random House, Inc. v. Rosetta Books*, LLC, 282 F.3d 490 (2d Cir. 2002).

13   See *Peter Mayer Publishers, Inc. v. Shilovskaya*, 11 F. Supp.3d 421 (S.D.N.Y. 2014).

nalists' contributions to collective works such as magazine and newspaper articles,[14] book authors typically do not fall within the Copyright Act's relevant statutory provisions.[15]

[3]—The Work Defined

Publishing agreements will have a description of the "Work" that is the subject of the agreement, either a work to be written and delivered in the future, or an existing manuscript being accepted by the publisher.

As noted above, the description of the work to be published can have copyright ownership consequences.[16] Notwithstanding the importance of the work description, it may be surprisingly brief.[17] Because the publisher may include in the agreement a form of non-compete clause requiring the author to forego similar projects for other publishers,[18] it will typically be in the author's interest to define the work narrowly, especially in the case of non-fiction works, so that the work for which rights are being granted will not encumber the author's future publishing projects for other publishers.

In one case involving publishing agreements dating from the 1960s, where the operative grant language was to "print, publish and sell the work in book form," a court in 2001 found that the grant was limited to books printed on paper, and the author had never granted digital and electronic rights, which had been later licensed to a third party.[19]

---

14   See:

Supreme Court: *New York Times Co. v. Tasini*, 533 U.S. 483, 121 S.Ct. 2381, 150 L.Ed.2d 500 (2001).

Second Circuit: *Faulkner v. National Geographic Enterprises, Inc.*, 409 F.3d 26 (2d Cir. 2005) (publication of digital archive was privileged "revision" of publisher's previously authorized print product under 17 U.S.C. § 201(c)).

Eleventh Circuit: *Greenberg v. National Geographic Society*, 244 F.3d 1244 (11th Cir.), cert. denied 555 U.S. 1070 (2008).

15   See § 3.05 *infra*, for a discussion of magazine and newspaper publishing.

16   For example, does a non-fiction "how to" book constitute an "instructional text," for purposes of defining "works made for hire"? If the publisher chooses to describe the book as an instructional text in the agreement, supports the conclusions that the operative copyright agreement should be a work made for hire.

17   For example, the description can consist of the general type of work to be written or created (text, or as appropriate photographs or illustrations), an approximate word count and page count, and a provisional title.

18   See § 3.02[18] *infra*.

19   See *Random House, Inc. v. Rosetta Books LLC*, 150 F. Supp.2d 613 (S.D.N.Y. 2001), *aff'd* 282 F.3d 490 (2d Cir. 2002).

[4]—Territories

The designation of applicable territories is a crucial negotiation point. While a typical agreement will seek to grant worldwide rights in the work, it's to the author's advantage to limit the territorial grant to the United States and its territories and Canada, so that the author can negotiate separate licenses, including translation rights, with publishers in various territories around the world, with their additional advances. This strategy also allows the author and his or her agent to attempt to identify the best publisher available in various territories of the world, rather than relying on the overseas offices or affiliates of the publisher located in the United States.

Conversely, granting broad territories, or even worldwide rights, to one publisher, particularly one that has significant operations throughout the world, may be advantageous where the work is unlikely to generate sufficient overseas interest to attract publishers on a country-by-country basis. In that scenario, the publisher will, ideally, have an established worldwide distribution network and the incentive to use that network to publish the book as broadly as possible, or at least have the distribution capacity wherewithal to fill orders for the book worldwide.

A third course is to grant exclusive rights in certain territories, and non-exclusive rights in others. However, it may not be realistic to expect much marketing and promotional effort from a publisher that does not have exclusive rights in a territory where, by definition, the publisher could face competition from other non-exclusive licensees for the same work.

[5]—Term

In the case of exclusive licenses and assignments of copyright, the publisher will typically propose that the agreement, whether an exclusive license or assignment of copyright, endure for the full term of copyright, including all extensions thereof, which, for works by a living author is currently seventy years after death, or in the case of joint works, seventy years after the death of the last surviving author.[20] Note that an agreement in the form of a work made for hire would automatically make the publisher the statutory author and owner for the full term for a work made for hire, which is ninety-five years from publication or 120 years from the date of creation, whichever expires first.[21]

Whether the author seeks a shorter term is part of the overall negotiation strategy. Shortening the term of an agreement can have an adverse effect on other deal points. For example, the size of the royalty advance or the royalty percentages may be lower where a shorter term lessens the publisher's long-term revenue expectations.

---

20   17 U.S.C. §101 etc.

21   17 U.S.C. § 302(c).

There are pros and cons to such a strategy, but authors generally prefer to have the ability to reclaim their rights in their work. Balanced against that is the possibility that when the term expires, the author will regain the rights to a book that nobody wants to publish. Where a publisher plans to invest heavily in production and promotion, a shorter term may be extremely difficult to achieve.

[6]—Advance Against Royalties

An advance against future royalties is an upfront payment designed to entice an author to enter into an agreement, including providing funds for the author to live on while the work is created. It is typically split into three payments: one-third upon signing of the agreement; one-third upon publisher's acceptance of the complete manuscript; and one-third upon publication of the work (but no later than a specified time after acceptance of the manuscript). The advance is deducted from subsequent royalty statements until it is recouped, at which time the author will receive additional royalties. Here is an example based on two hypothetical royalty accountings for a book where the author received a $20,000 advance:

Accounting 1:	
Royalty amount per book sold:	$2.00
Advance paid to author:	$20,000.00
First Royalty Statement:	10,000 books sold, therefore $20,000 in royalties credited to author
First Royalty Check:	$0.00 (no check issued with the statement), because the author already received $20,000 in the form of an advance against future royalties. The debit (advance) and credits (sales) to the royalty account balance each other out to zero.

Accounting 2:	
Royalty amount per book sold:	$2.00
Second Royalty Statement:	15,000 books sold; therefore $30,000.00 in royalties credited to author's royalty account.
Second Royalty Check:	$30,000.00. The advance was previously recouped in the first royalty accounting, so now there is no debit to the author's royalty account, and the author receives all royalties for each book sold.

Many factors affect the negotiations over an advance. Because the advance is a cash outlay for the publisher, the publisher will want to recoup it as soon as possible via sales of the book. The payment of an advance gives the publisher an incentive to make the project a success.[22] An author who has long-term faith in his or her work may reap the greatest rewards by foregoing some of the advance in exchange for larger royalty percentages.

Note that in the event royalties credited to the author's account from sales of the book never equal the amount advanced to the author, the author is not required to repay any portion of the advance to the publisher.

However, should the author fail to deliver an "acceptable" manuscript or otherwise default under the agreement, any advances received by the author prior to the default may indeed have to be repaid to the publisher, depending on how such "default" provisions are negotiated.[23] It is often possible to obtain the right for the author to delay repayment until he or she has succeeded in placing the manuscript with another publisher, in which case he or she will repay the advance from the "first proceeds" of that subsequent placement, i.e., the author's income arising from resale of the book to the third-party publisher.

Such a "first proceeds" repayment provision can be triggered in the event the author delivers the manuscript and the publisher later rejects it pursuant to the terms of the agreement. In that scenario, the author may be free to license or sell the rejected work to a third-party publisher, but any such third-party sale would be subject to a "first proceeds" clause. Some publishers may attempt to go a step further and claim that the author must arrange for such re-sale within a specified time. If the deadline to reimburse on a "first proceeds" basis is not met by the author, the agreement may require the author to actually repay the advance in cash from whatever source the author has available.[24]

---

22   In the case of a large advance totaling $2,000,000, a publisher took out a life insurance policy on the author's life in the event the author died before the author could fulfill their obligations under the agreement. *Helprin v. Harcourt, Inc.*, 277 F. Supp.2d 327, 329 (S.D.N.Y. 2003).

23   See, e.g., *Melodrama Publishing, LLC v. Santiago*, 2013 U.S. Dist. LEXIS 56988 (S.D.N.Y. April 11, 2013) (Agreement terminated where ghostwriter failed to deliver book, and agreed to return the advance. Court held that ghostwriter's subsequent attempt to trademark their pseudonym was fraudulent).

24   Such provisions should be strenuously resisted. Note that the applicable state law statute of limitations applies with respect to breach of contract actions. See *G.P. Putnam's Sons v. Owens*, 51 A.D.2d 527, 378 N.Y.S.2d 637 (1976) (where the publisher brought an action for return of an advance seven years after the manuscript due date, the claim was time barred by the six-year statute of limitations, which began to run when author missed the agreed-upon deadline).

[7]—Delivery and Acceptance of Manuscript

The agreement will have delivery deadlines for a complete manuscript, and provisions whereby the publisher may accept or reject the manuscript. Ideally, the publisher will agree to give written notice of the reasons for any proposed rejection, and the author will be given sufficient time to cure or otherwise address the claimed deficiency. No publisher can be forced to publish a work that they determine is not of sufficient quality; however, it may be possible to negotiate a provision whereby if the publisher rejects the manuscript, only 50% of the advance previously received would have to be repaid.[25]

A publisher may also submit the manuscript to a legal review for issues such as libel and defamation, and may request that the author make changes aimed at eliminating any passages that are identified as problematic, or may negotiate for the right to make such changes without the author's involvement. The publisher may also seek a provision that allows the publisher to terminate the agreement in the event the author fails to cooperate in making such changes. In the event of such termination, the publisher will typically require reimbursement for any advance—either immediately, or on a "first proceeds" basis, as discussed above.

[8]—Proofreading and Corrections

Authors, understandably, take great care in their choice of words in the work. The agreement should provide that, upon acceptance of the manuscript, the publisher will make no changes other than copyediting (corrections of grammar, for example) without the author's consent. The author will also cooperate in making any mutually agreed-upon alterations, and in promptly reading and marking proof copies in the form of galley

---

25   Cases go both ways depending on the facts, with some finding that a publisher has an unfettered right to reject a submitted manuscript, while others find that the publisher has an obligation to work assist with a revision. See: *Dell Publishing Co., Inc. v. Whedon*, 577 F. Supp. 1459 (S.D.N.Y. 1984) (before rejecting manuscript publisher had an implied good-faith obligation to offer author the opportunity to revise the manuscript with publisher's editorial assistance, and because publisher failed to meet that obligation, it could not recover from author the advance payments made pursuant to the contract); *Harcourt Brace Jovanovich, Inc. v. Goldwater*, 542 F. Supp. 619 (S.D.N.Y. 1982) ("there is an implied obligation in a contract of this kind for the publisher to engage in appropriate editorial work with the author of a book . . . allowing unfettered license to publishers to reject a manuscript submitted under contract would permit "overreaching by publishers attempting to extricate themselves from bad deals."); *Gregory v. Simon & Schuster, Inc.*, 1994 U.S. Dist. LEXIS 9833, 1994 WL 381481 (S.D.N.Y. July 14, 1994), *aff'd* 60 F.3d 812 (2d Cir. 1995) (no opinion) (publisher terminated contract for book by former ballerina after three versions and author sued to recover balance of the advance. Publisher motion for summary judgment denied). But compare, *Nance v. Random House, Inc.*, 212 F. Supp.2d 268 (S.D.N.Y. 2002) (after two rewrites done collaboratively by author and editors, and ultimate rejection of revised manuscript, rejection was not in bad faith, and author had to return $350,000 advance to publisher. Author had subsequently sold rejected work to third party publisher for $550,000 advance.). See also, *Little Brown & Co. v. Klein*, 1993 WL 643380 (N.Y. Sup. 1993) (when White House withdrew author's access to President, purpose of book was frustrated and publisher could terminate agreement and demand return of advance).

proofs.[26] In the event the author wishes to make substantive changes based on the galley proofs other than mere correction of errors, the agreement would ideally allow such changes at no cost to the author, assuming the changes are minimal. One formula is for the publisher to absorb such costs if they do not exceed 10% of the total typesetting fees paid by the publisher, and for any amounts above that cap to be charged against the author's royalty account. There may also be provisions whereby the author commits to assist with any reasonable and topical updates or revisions that may be required for future reprints of non-fiction works.[27]

[9]—Publication

The agreement should confirm that all production costs shall be borne by the publisher, and possibly, though not necessarily, give the author a consultation right regarding the cover art. There must be a deadline by which the book will be published following the publisher's acceptance of the manuscript, including provisions for an extension of time if publication is delayed. Ultimately, in the event of a failure to publish that is not attributable to a *force majeure* event, the agreement will terminate, and the author should be entitled to retain any advances received. The publisher may claim reimbursement of any advances on a first proceeds basis.

[10]—Promotion

While retaining a broad right to determine the nature and amount of promotion and advertising, the publisher may also seek confirmation that it can use the author's name, image, and likeness in connection with promotion of the book, and confirm that it can use substantial excerpts from the work for promotional purposes, including excerpts on the publisher's Web site, and in any media such as television, radio, print, etc. There may also be provisions whereby the author, on reasonable notice, will make himself or herself available for personal appearances in media such as television and radio, with the publisher responsible for reasonable travel expenses incurred.

Typically, there will not be any specific commitments by the publisher regarding promotion, with the exception of a "commercially reasonable efforts" statement. Given that many if not most authors feel (rightly or wrongly as the case may be) their works are not being adequately promoted by their publishers, it is recommended to seek at least a

---

26   Galleys are the fully typeset pre-publication sheets.

27   See *Windt v. Shepard's/McGraw Hill, Inc.*, 1997 WL 698182 (E.D. Pa. Nov. 5, 1997) (publisher's failure to proofread manuscript before publication was not a breach of contract); see also, *Kirschten v. Research Institutes of America, Inc.*, 1997 WL 739587 (S.D.N.Y. Sept. 24, 1997) (summary judgment for publisher on breach of contract claims relating to alleged failure regarding editorial and marketing functions including review of galley proofs, incorporating edits, confirming acknowledgments, and marketing plans).

commitment by the publisher to hold an annual promotion meeting with the author or the author's representatives, in order to review the current promotion activities and to plan activities for the future. In many cases, simply formalizing the obligation to communicate in this way at least once per year on promotion and advertising matters can improve the long-term working relationship between publisher and author.[28]

[11]—Author Copies

The author is entitled to a reasonable supply of free copies upon publication, perhaps a dozen such copies, and is granted the right to purchase additional copies at an author's discount of typically 40% to 50% off the retail selling price, plus shipping. The publisher may place restrictions on re-sale of books so purchased by the author to ensure that the author is making personal use of such books for gifts and promotion, and not acting as a bookseller at discounted prices. Additionally, the publisher may be willing to have any monies owed by the author for such purposes to be debited to the author's royalty account rather than paid in cash.[29]

[12]—Copyright and Credits

In the case of an agreement on an exclusive license basis, the publisher will undertake to publish the book with a copyright notice in the name of the author, and to file a copyright registration application with the Copyright Office in the name of the author, and indicating publication under the publisher's imprint. In the case of an assignment of copyright from the author to the publisher, or in the case of a work made for hire agreement, the copyright notice will be in the name of the publisher, and the copyright registration application will list the publisher as the claimant. In either case, in order to get the maximum protection under the copyright laws, the publisher should agree to register the copyright within three months of first publication of the work. The publisher should reserve the sole and exclusive right to file any copyright registration applications.

---

28 See *Perry v. McGraw-Hill, Inc.*, 966 F. Supp. 233 (S.D.N.Y. 1997) ("in the absence of specific contractual provisions, it is common sense and trade practice that as between an author and a publisher, the publisher controls marketing and promotion."). *Id.*, 966 F. Supp. at 237. See also: *Zilg v. Prentice-Hall, Inc.*, 515 F. Supp. 716 (S.D.N.Y. 1981) (summary judgment for author in suit alleging publisher failed to act in good faith with respect to promoting book when subject of book, a corporation, complained about book); *Van Valkenburgh, Nooger & Neville v. Hayden Publishing Co.*, 30 N.Y.2d 34, 330 N.Y.S.2d 329, 281 N.E.2d 142 (1972) (publisher breached obligation to use "best efforts" to promote book where efforts ceased following a royalty dispute with author).

29 See *Gard v. Pelican Publishing Co.*, 230 Neb. 656, 433 N.W.2d 175 (1988) (dispute between author and publisher included terms under which author, who was public speaker, could purchase copies of his book from publisher for the purpose of reselling or giving away at his public speaking engagements).

The agreement may also specify specific credits on the cover and title page of the book, including type size and location, for example, in the case of a co-written work by two authors or in the case of an editor who receives prominent acknowledgment for work on a compilation.[30]

[13]—Royalties

[a]—Domestic Royalties

Perhaps the single most important economic aspect of a publishing agreement is whether or not the royalty paid to the author for the sale of each copy of the book is based on the cover price (or suggested list price). Where royalties are based on the cover price, there is certainty in the amount of royalty due on each book. It will always be the negotiated percentage of the current cover price. If a book has a cover price of $25.00 and the royalty is 10% of the cover price, the royalty per book sold, paid for, and not returned, will always be $2.50.[31]

Compare this with the formula some publishers use, in which the royalty calculation formula is based on "net amounts actually received" by the publisher. This "net amount" can vary widely, and where retail book dealers have been given discounts as high as 55% or even 60% for special promotions, a 10% royalty based on "net amounts" would look very different than the "cover price" example. For example, a book with a cover price of $25.00, in which the book dealer received a 50% discount, would net the publisher $12.50, and the 10% royalty would amount to $1.25, half of what the 10% royalty produced using the "cover price" formula. Because publishers sell virtually all books through retailers who receive discounts for their labors, virtually no sales under this formula will result in royalties that compare with the "cover price" formula.

---

30 See *Columbus Rose, Ltd. v. New Millennium Press*, 2002 WL 1033560 (S.D.N.Y. May 20, 2002) (claims under Lanham Act and Copyright Act in dispute over anthology cover credited author's contribution, such that author claimed that anthology that included works by other authors falsely appeared to be his next full length novel). See also:

Second Circuit: *Kwan v. Schlein*, 246 F.R.D. 447 (S.D.N.Y. 2007) (editor of book claims to have been offered co-author credit and royalties).

Fourth Circuit: *Zim v. Western Publishing Co.*, 573 F.2d 1318 (4th Cir. 1978) (use of author's name on unapproved revised version of book stated cause of action for unlawful appropriation of author's name).

Seventh Circuit: *Flynn v. AK Peters, Ltd.*, 377 F.3d 13 (7th Cir. 2004) (unsuccessful suit by author against publisher for accepting book revisions from her co-author without her consent and for giving a third individual co-authorship credit, when author felt that his effort did not merit such credit).

31 See *Williamson v. Simon & Schuster*, 735 F. Supp. 565 (S.D.N.Y. 1990) (dispute over whether royalties were calculated based on publisher net revenue or on retail sales price of book).

The 10% royalty offered by the publisher who uses the "net amount" formula is, when compared to the "cover price" formula, only a 5% royalty. Even where the publisher using the "net revenue" formula increases it to 15%, that would still compare unfavorably to a "cover price" formula at 10%.

The royalty percentage for hard cover books ideally starts at no less than 10%, and should have "bumps" or increases triggered by total unit sales, for example increasing to 12.5% at the 10,000 copies sold plateau, and up to 15% at the 15,000 copies plateau and thereafter. As more copies are sold, the publisher amortizes its initial investment in production and manufacturing. It is reasonable for the author to share in the increased profit margins resulting from higher sales, and potentially less expensive reprints.

Trade paperback royalties are typically lower, usually 7.5% of the cover price, and mass-market paperback royalties may start at 8% of the cover price for the first 150,000 copies sold, and 10% thereafter.

These are all general guidelines, subject to negotiation, which will tend to play off higher royalty percentages against smaller advances, or vice versa. The royalty provisions will typically go into considerable detail concerning other types of non-standard sales and distribution by the publisher, on the theory that the author accepts lower royalties in scenarios where the publisher has extra distribution costs or grants higher discounts to customers. Examples include special editions such as large-type editions for the visually impaired, or copies sold at extra discount in connection with book clubs or other special mail order promotions.

Electronic Books or "e-books" don't require the investment a publisher makes in printing and warehousing physical books, although they do require considerable upfront investment in technology—an investment the publisher may already have made, however. Royalties for e-books fall generally in the 15% to 25% range. Online sales of physical books may be in a separate category, but there should not be any royalty reduction for such sales.[32]

---

32   See *Bovee & Thill LLC v. Pearson Education, Inc.*, 564 F. Supp.2d 199 (S.D.N.Y. 2008) (dispute over royalties including royalties for electronic versions of textbook); see also: *Postlewaite v. McGraw Hill, Inc.*, 333 F.3d 42 (2d Cir. 2003) (dispute over royalties from CD-ROM version of treatise); *Keiler v. Harlequin Enterprises Ltd.*, 751 F.3d 64 (2d Cir. 2014) (book authors' class action survived motion to dismiss, alleged that when authors were forced to sign publishing agreement with Swiss subsidiary of New York publisher, authors' expectation of 50% royalty on United States e-book revenues was drastically reduced because subsidiary licensed e-book rights back to parent company at drastic discount).

Failure to pay royalties is regarded by courts as a serious breach of the agreement, and can lead to rescission of a publishing agreement.[33]

[b]—Foreign Royalties

With respect to overseas sales, the publisher will lower royalties anywhere from 25% to 50%, on the theory that the overseas distributor charges a hefty distribution fee, and shipping costs are higher, thus lowering the revenue. This is an incentive to withhold overseas rights wherever possible in order to strike deals without reduced royalties. One possible negotiation technique is to insist on full royalty percentages (or close to full) in territories where the publisher has wholly owned affiliates instead of a third-party distributor, because a wholly owned affiliate relationship is very different from an arm's length transaction with a third party overseas distributor.

Other issues with overseas sales include whether the royalties are calculated "at source"—at the full cover price in the local currency, and under what circumstances and when the amounts are converted to U.S. dollars. As noted below, taxes withheld from foreign payments can and should be minimized wherever possible.

In *Cordell v. The McGraw-Hill Companies, Inc.*, a class of authors brought suit against a publisher over the lowering of royalty percentages in connection with overseas sales, sales which were handled by the publisher's own international book division.[34] The royalty provision at issue stated:

Foreign Sales: 10.00 percent of the Publisher's net receipts for each copy of the Work (hardcover or paperback) sold by the Publisher to the McGraw-Hill international book division or to third parties for use outside the United States.[35]

---

33   See *Alexander v. Chesapeake, Potomac, and Tidewater Books, Inc.*, 60 F. Supp.2d 544 (E.D. Va. 1999) (author's letter of termination to publisher valid where last royalty payment was fifteen and one-half months previous, and publisher withheld royalties during sell-off period of existing inventory); see also, *Sperber v. Lawrence Freundlich Publishers*, 1987 N.Y. Misc. LEXIS 2846 (N.Y. Sup. Sept. 4, 1987) (substantial and willful failure to pay royalties is a fundamental breach and author is entitled to terminate the agreement). *But cf., Nolan v. Williamson Music, Inc.*, 300 F. Supp. 1311, (S.D.N.Y. 1969), aff'd sub nom. *Nolan v. Sam Fox Publishing Co., Inc.*, 499 F.2d 1394 (2d Cir. 1974) (where failure to pay royalties due to oversight, negligence and bad bookkeeping and where only 26% of royalties due over six year period had been paid, rescission denied where breach of contract not material and willful).

34   See *Cordell v. The McGraw-Hill Companies, Inc.*, 2012 U.S. Dist. LEXIS 152398, 2012 WL 5264844 (S.D.N.Y. Oct. 23, 2012).

35   *Id.*, 2012 WL 5264844, at *1. "Net receipts" were defined in the agreement "as the Publisher's selling price less discounts, credits, actual returns and a reasonable reserve for anticipated returns of 20%." *Id.* at n.3.

In addition, the agreement provided that the publisher "shall publish the Work at its own expense at such time and in such style and manner . . . and sell the Work at such prices, as it shall deem suitable."[36]

The authors asserted that the lower royalties arising from the publisher's sales to its international subsidiary constituted self-dealing at artificially low prices, constituting a breach of the implied duty of good faith and fair dealing under New York law. In granting the publisher's motion to dismiss, the court noted that the contract as signed accurately described exactly what the publisher's international distribution practice was, therefore there was no breach in following those procedures. Furthermore, the contractual provision giving the publisher the sole right to determine what constituted suitable pricing, along with the express right to deal with its own subsidiary, also meant that the plaintiffs could not complain about rights they had expressly granted.

[14]—Subsidiary Rights

The above royalty scenarios are based primarily on sales of the book as printed. The publisher will also want access to several revenue streams that arise from sub-licensing rights in the book.

[a]—Rights Granted to the Publisher

- First serialization of condensations, excerpts, digests, etc. in newspapers or magazines or other periodicals prior to publication of the work in book form[37]

- Second serialization after publication of the work in book form

- Book club custom printings

- Permissions (licensing of excerpts to third parties)

- Trade or mass-market paperback (sub-licensed)

- Anthology excerpts

[b]—Rights Reserved by Author

Foremost among the rights ideally reserved to authors in a "Reserved Rights" clause, are the following:

- Translations

---

36   *Id.*, 2012 WL 5264844, at *3. (Emphasis in original.)

37   Such licenses cannot only produce revenue, but can dramatically promote the book if timed to appear shortly before publication.

- Merchandise

- Sequels

- Dramatization

- Performance rights (television, radio, dramatic, musical, motion picture, video)

- Audio books

- Commercial endorsement

- Interactive media

- The characters and the right to future stories featuring the characters

[15]—Audio Rights

An audio book consists of a sound recording of the text. Where possible, audio rights should be reserved by the author, and excluded from the book publishing agreement. This can allow the author to execute an audio rights agreement with a separate company that may be more experienced at producing audio books, or that may have better access to suitable talent for the recording.

In a separate audio rights deal, there will also be a different advance payment, which is to the author's advantage. Audio book royalties range from 7% to 10% of the publisher's net revenue or are based on marked list price. Typical deal points would include understandings regarding whether any cuts in the original text are proposed, approvals thereof, and selection of the talent for the reading. Moreover, there may be an opportunity for approval over the package art or additional information. Care should be taken to not infringe on any packaging rights held by the original publisher.

Audio books are, technically, sound recordings, and as such they may be distributed and marketed in appropriate ways online. The agreement should seek a higher royalty percentage for digital uses. One thing for authors to consider is making the recording themselves, if that results in the most marketable project.[38]

[16]—Use of Third-Party Materials

Where the work requires the use of copyrighted material from third parties, such as illustrations, photographs, or extensive quotes, it will usually be the responsibility of the author to obtain such licenses, including the expense of the licenses. However, the publisher may offer assistance with the licensing process, and be willing to remit the

---

38 As is the case with motion pictures produced from books, audio recordings can provide unexpected promotional boosts. They may also be eligible for a Grammy Award in the category of Best Spoken Word Album.

license fees on behalf of the author, with the amounts remitted then debited against the author's royalty account.

Where copyrighted photographs are licensed for the publication and the license is limited in scope—for example for a specific term of years or only for the initial print run—photographers have been known to file copyright infringement lawsuits based on the license being exceeded. Where possible, it is to the publisher's advantage to obtain "all in" clearance for photographs, covering all territories, print runs, translations, and the life of copyright and, if such rights cannot be obtained, to consider a different photograph.[39]

[17]—Statements of Account and Audit Rights

Publishers will typically remit statements of the author's royalty account semi-annually as of June 30 and December 31 each year, with the statements and any amounts due calculated and mailed to the author within three or four months thereafter. There will be provisions regarding royalties arising from foreign territories, if any, including in most cases a disclaimer that such payments may reflect deductions for foreign taxes and bank charges. Note that some foreign countries may have tax treaties with the United States such that, upon filing the correct notices and tax forms, foreign governments will not deduct taxes before the payments are remitted to the United States. Where possible, such forms should be filed prior to publication to avoid any unnecessary deductions.

Audit rights for the author are essential in any publishing agreement, and there will typically be a provision allowing for an audit of publisher's books and records upon reasonable notice and during regular business hours at the author's own expense, typically no more than once per year, and no longer than two or three years after receipt of the disputed royalty statement. A standard provision, but one that must be requested, provides that where such an audit uncovers a shortfall in payments due to the author of 5% or more, the publisher will reimburse the author for the expense of the audit, and will remit any sums owing within thirty days.

---

39   See, e.g.:

Second Circuit: Cole v. John Wiley & Sons, Inc., 2012 U.S. Dist. LEXIS 108612 (S.D.N.Y. Aug. 1, 2012) (action for exceeding print-run limitations of photo license and for using photos in types of publications not licensed); *Palmer Kane LLC v. Scholastic Corp.*, 2012 U.S. Dist. LEXIS 100812, 103 U.S.P.Q.2d 1632 (S.D.N.Y. July 16, 2012) (denying class certification in action alleging publisher (1) printed more copies of books containing plaintiff photographs than allowed under the license and (2) published prior to obtaining a license).

Third Circuit: Grant Heilman Photography, Inc. v. The McGraw-Hill Companies, Inc., 2012 U.S. Dist. LEXIS 168550 (E.D. Pa. Nov. 28, 2012) (contractual print run quantity limit exceeded under photo licenses).

[18]—Competitive Works

Provisions attempting to limit the author's right to produce potentially competitive works may be unenforceable in certain circumstances, especially where they are not sufficiently delineated or defined in scope or time. For example, provisions that forbid an author from writing additional future books on "similar" subjects that may in the publisher's sole judgment "directly compete" with the work or "injure the sales" of the work are problematic. Such potential restrictions on an author's future work should be negotiated very carefully, and any restrictions compensated for by other incentives offered to the author. If the author needs carve outs for various projects that are in progress or contemplated, they should be discussed in detail.

It may be advisable to protect the author's own right to use excerpts from the work on the author's own Web site, or to quote from the work in articles or in other ways that advance the author's work but do not impinge on the publisher's sales.[40]

[19]—Next Publication Option

There are various mechanisms by which the publisher may seek to have an option to publish any subsequent work by the author, including any future installments or revisions of the initial publication. These range from the vague and probably unenforceable commitment to negotiate rights to the author's next work "in good faith"; to the:

- Right of first negotiation whereby the publisher must tender an acceptable offer in a specific amount of time;

- Right of first refusal that obligates the author to show the next work to the publisher first; or

- "Matching right" where the author must bring to the publisher any third party offers for the next work, and give the publisher a set amount of time in which to match the offer.

All scenarios require as much specificity as possible in order to be enforceable; otherwise, courts have held such agreements to be nothing more than an unenforceable "agreement to agree."[41]

---

40   See *Frederick Fell Publishers, Inc. v. Lorayne*, 422 F. Supp. 808 (S.D.N.Y. 1976) (alleged breach of non-compete clause); see also, *Harlequin Enterprises Ltd. v. Warner Books, Inc.*, 639 F. Supp. 1081 (S.D.N.Y. 1986) (non-compete clause in contract did not forbid author of action/adventure novels from entering into new agreement with publisher of mystery/mystical books).

41   See *Pinnacle Books, Inc. v. Harlequin Enterprises, Ltd*, 519 F. Supp. 118 (S.D.N.Y. 1981) (a clause stating that with respect to an option on future publications, the author and the publisher would use their "best efforts" to reach an agreement. In the event no agreement was reached the author would be free to offer the future book to third parties. In finding the provision unenforceable, the court stated "[W]here the parties agreed only to negotiate and

[20]—Inserts, Back-of-Book Advertising

The parties may agree that the work as published in hard cover will not include any advertising for the publisher's other books, with the possible exception of a listing of books by the same author. With respect to paperback editions, whether advertising of books by other authors is permitted may be subject to the author's approval, which may not be unreasonably withheld.

[21]—Remainders

After one year following publication has passed, the publisher may reserve the right to discontinue sale of the book if it is deemed "no longer profitable," and sell off the remaining inventory at sharp discounts as "remainders." In such event, the author shall be entitled to a greatly reduced royalty, usually 10% of the net revenue from the sale of the remainders, minus costs. The author will usually also be offered the opportunity to purchase some or all of the remaining inventory at the remainder price, plus shipping, without any restrictions on resale.

In the event the printed stock is remaindered, the agreement should include a statement that the agreement is terminated and all rights revert to the author, while the publisher remains liable for paying any remaining royalties to the author until all such income ceases.[42] Note, however, in at least one case, an author sued the publisher on a theory that the entire inventory of books was intentionally remaindered with the intention of resale at full price, and that such a scheme deprived the author of her rightful royalties.[43] Therefore, any remainder sale of the existing inventory should include provisions whereby such book may only be sold on a remainder reduced price basis, and also trigger a reversion of all rights to the author.

---

failed to state the standards by which their negotiation efforts were to be measured, it is impossible to determine whether [they] used their "best efforts" to negotiate a new agreement . . . in short, the option clause is unenforceable due to the indefiniteness of its terms."). *Id.*, 519 F. Supp. at 122.

See also: *Dorchester Publishing Co. v. Lanier*, 2007 U.S. Dist. LEXIS 23103 (S.D.N.Y. March 19, 2007) (myriad breach of contract and other issues including dispute over right of first refusal to author's future novel); *McLoone v. Funk & Wagnalls Corp.*, 1996 U.S. Dist. LEXIS 7615 (S.D.N.Y. June 4, 1996) (issues include whether publisher's future rights and right of first refusal included a "revision" of original work); *Candid Productions, Inc. v. International Skating Union*, 530 F. Supp. 1330 (S.D.N.Y. 1982) (option clause uncertain and unenforceable because no length of time for the proposed exclusive negotiation was defined); Harcourt, *Brace Jovanovich, Inc. v. Farrar, Straus & Giroux, Inc.*, 4 Med. L. Rep. 2625 (N.Y. Sup. 1979) (among reasons option clause was an unenforceable agreement to agree was lack of a method to ascertain the option price, and lack of a specific provision calling for a right to match terms that may be offered by other publishers).

42   See *Lifetime Books, Inc. v. Thomas Nelson Publishers, Inc.*, 1998 Tenn. App. LEXIS 696 (Tenn. App. Oct. 16, 1998) (dispute over author's right of first refusal to purchase remainder copies).

43   See *Summer Rain v. The Donning Co.*, 964 F.2d 1455 (4th Cir. 1992).

[22]—Out of Print and Reversion

If the publisher's inventory of a book is depleted, the book is deemed to be "out of print." Such inventory depletion may be only temporary, with the publisher fully intending to reprint the work. It may also represent an opportunity for the publisher to assess the commercial viability of the book, and to consider leaving the work out of print permanently.

Agreements should include a mechanism whereby if a work goes out of print, the author may give written notice to the publisher,[44] and the publisher will have a period of time in which to either reprint the book, or to terminate the publishing agreement, with all rights reverting to the author. In such event, the publisher may offer to the author the production materials for the book at a discounted price, so that the author can hope to interest another publisher in the work.[45]

If the agreement is for a limited period of time, at the conclusion of the term, the publisher will have a sell-off period to dispose of old inventory, while still having an obligation to pay applicable royalties. In the event the author seeks out a new publisher, it is in the author's best interests to have any sell-off period as short as possible, ideally no more than six months.

Given the advent of electronic or digital books, the issue has arisen as to whether a book can ever truly be out of print, if there is always a copy available electronically, via "print on demand," or as a download or via some proprietary technology device. Accordingly, some agreements now specify that the electronic availability of a book means it is not out of print, assuring the publisher of ongoing rights even if not a single printed copy is ever manufactured again.

Authors, on the other hand, still see great value in actual printed editions, and believe it is the publisher's obligation to ensure that books are available in physical format. Solutions to this impasse may be offered by new printing technologies that can produce small quantities of printed books indistinguishable in appearance from traditional large print run editions manufactured on an offset printing press.

In addition, publishers may be willing to use a revenue threshold for the "in print" versus "out-of-print" determination instead of a physical inventory requirement—for

---

44   The author must first be apprised of the status of the book's inventory.

45   See *Hauser v. Harcourt Brace Jonanovich, Inc.*, 140 Misc.2d 82, 530 N.Y.S.2d 431 (N.Y. Sup. 1988) (allowing book to go out of print following libel action by subject of book breached publisher's duty of good faith, and publisher did not have right to refuse to revert rights to author under publishing agreement); see also, *Gard v. Pelican Publishing Co.*, 230 Neb. 656, 433 N.W.2d 175, 178 (1988) (discussing meaning of "out of print" in publishing agreement as being when "book is unavailable from the publisher").

example, a provision that specifies that so long as the book is available electronically, and it sells at least 300 copies per year, it shall be considered "in print." By so doing, the publisher at least ensures that any electronic editions are finding significant consumer acceptance as well. But if an author believes that his or her book must always be available in printed format, the agreement must include a provision stating "the Work shall not be considered in print if the only available edition is an electronic or digital book."

[23]—Warranties and Indemnification

Although authors are not typically experts in copyright or publishing law, they are required in virtually all publishing agreements to warrant that their work is wholly original, that they have the right to enter into the publishing agreement, and that their work does not infringe on the rights of anyone, whether it be on the basis of copyright infringement, invasion of privacy, libel, defamation, trademark, right of publicity, or any other tort.[46] In addition, the author may be asked to warrant that any recipe, formula, or instruction contained in the book is accurate and will not cause injury.[47] Publishers want assurances that "by buying the work they are not also buying a lawsuit." The justification for demanding such assurances is that the author is in a position to know what went into the writing of the book and the publisher is not.

In addition to the above representations and warranties by the author, publishers demand indemnification against any and all costs, expenses, and damages, including legal fees and costs, that the publisher may incur based on any violation of the author's warranties, and in many cases based on any alleged violation of the author's warranties brought by third parties. Publishers may also claim the right to withhold royalties from

---

46   See the discussion on privacy torts in Chapter 6.

47   Suits against publishers on product liability, "negligent publication" and other grounds have included *Lacoff v. Buena Vista Publishing, Inc.*, 183 Misc.2d 600, 705 N.Y.S.2d 183 (N.Y. Sup. 2000) (no cause of action against publisher of "how to" investment book that falsely claimed authors had 23.4% annual returns, holding that the First Amendment protects even erroneous statements on the book's cover, and publisher had no duty to investigate or confirm prior to publication).

See also:

Fourth Circuit: *Rice v. Palladin Enterprises*, 128 F.3d 233 (4th Cir. 1997) (family of murder victim brought wrongful death claim against publisher of "how to" book entitled "Hit Man: A Technical Manual for Independent Contractors").

Ninth Circuit: *Winter v. G.P. Putnam's Sons*, 938 F.2d 1033 (9th Cir. 1991) (claim that book on wild mushrooms injured readers who relied on erroneous information in the guide, held that publisher does not have a duty to investigate the accuracy of the contents unless it offers an express warranty).

the author in the event of any claim, and to deduct indemnification claims against royalties due to the author.[48]

Such sweeping indemnification provisions are problematic for authors who, realistically, usually do not have the financial wherewithal to fund expensive litigation that might be based on mere "allegations," on behalf of a publisher that may be a large and well-funded international corporation.[49]

Another potential solution is to limit the author's indemnification obligation to the royalty amounts actually paid to and/or due the author, or to seek release from any indemnification obligation where the publisher's attorneys have reviewed the work prior to publication and given the "all clear" to proceed. Authors may also consider forming a business entity such as a corporation or Limited Liability Company ("LLC") that will be the signatory and responsible party, with the author asked to sign a letter of inducement guaranteeing his or her personal performance on behalf of the business entity. Whether such a procedure would insulate the author personally from any potential indemnification liability would depend on the facts of each case.

[24]—Agency

Where the author has a literary agent, agreements will confirm that payment due to the author can be made to the author's authorized literary agent, and such payment will constitute a discharge of the publisher's payment obligations to the author. In addition, there may be a statement confirming the literary agent has a right to an agreed-upon percentage of the author's income arising from the agreement. Such statements may in fact have been drafted by the literary agent in order to protect the right to a commission, but given that the author and the literary agent's agreement may be terminable, may expire, or may be revocable in some way in the future, an attorney who represents the author—not the literary agent—should take care that the "agency" statement is not crafted as an irrevocable, permanent, or perpetual right. Instead, the literary agent's rights should be more accurately characterized as being subject to a separate agreement

---

48   See In re "A Million Little Pieces" Litigation, 435 F. Supp.2d 1336 (Judicial Panel on Multidistrict Litigation, June 14, 2006) (multiple lawsuits brought by individuals against author James Frey and his publisher for claims including negligence, consumer fraud, breach of contract, and unjust enrichment arising from revelations that purported non-fiction best-selling book was largely fabricated). See also, *Stutzman v. Armstrong*, 2013 U.S. Dist. LEXIS 129204 (E.D. Cal. Sept. 10, 2013) (suit against Lance Armstrong for books allegedly violating false advertising and other laws after revelations of performance-enhancing-drug use by athlete, but action dismissed under California anti-SLAPP statute).

49   In practice, as alluded to above, publishers are often very reluctant to soften harsh warranty and indemnification provisions, although they are sometimes willing to include the author as a named insured on the publishing liability insurance carried by the publisher.

between the agent and the author, and subject to change at the sole discretion of the author in accordance with that separate agreement.

[25]—Ghostwriters

While some authors may use a pseudonym for various reasons, for example for a book that is outside their normal genre, a ghostwriter is someone who writes a book that appears under someone else's name. The circumstances are often where a publisher desires to publish a "true story" book by a celebrity with a sellable story, but where the celebrity lacks the talent or time to actually write an engaging and sellable book.[50]

Ghostwriter agreements can have the same provisions as standard author agreements including advances and royalties, or a one-time buyout fee. They may also have confidentiality provisions prohibiting the ghostwriter from revealing their authorship, which can be enforced by liquidated damages penalties, or, in the case of an ongoing royalty, by the publisher's right to terminate the royalty payments if the ghostwriter breaches the confidentiality provisions.

Another ghostwriter scenario is similar to using a "pseudonym," where the publisher has created a fictional author, with a fictional name, for genre books such as teen novel series or adventure story series, perhaps choosing a name that evokes the adventure or mystery of the book better than the author's true name.

In such cases, the publisher may use trademark law to claim rights in the pseudonym. In *Melodrama Publishing, LLC v. Santiago*, the publisher of a fictional series of teen adventure novels entered into an agreement with a writer to ghostwrite a series of short novels under the pseudonym "Nisa Santiago."[51]

---

50   See, e.g., In re Lorraine Brooke Associates, Inc., 2007 Bankr. LEXIS 2668 (Bankr. S.D. Fla. Aug. 2, 2007) (bankruptcy action over rights to "If I Did It" book by Orenthal James Simpson, noting that book was ghostwritten by Pablo Fenjves). See also, http://en.wikipedia.org/wiki/Pablo_Fenjves (Mr. Fenjves has ghostwritten over a dozen books, including several best sellers).

51   See *Melodrama Publishing, LLC v. Santiago*, 2013 U.S. Dist. LEXIS 56988 (S.D.N.Y. April 11, 2013). Notwithstanding the court opinion confirming that Nisa Santiago books are ghostwritten by several "third-party ghostwriters", the publisher's website includes a biography of Nisa Santiago, stating "The author was born and raised in Brooklyn and is now living in Harlem, and she is moving at full speed with her writing endeavors. Coined the Duchess of Hip-Hop lit, Nisa humbly admits, 'I'm just grateful to be doing what I love as a career and not just a hobby.'" See http://melodramapublishing.com/authors.php .

See also:

Second Circuit: *Penn Group, LLC v. Slater*, 2007 U.S. Dist. LEXIS 50651 (S.D.N.Y. June 14, 2007) (dispute over ghostwriting services); *Follett v. New American Library, Inc.*, 497 F. Supp. 304 (S.D.N.Y. 1980) (Lanham Act suit to prohibit use of author's name).

The agreement contained standard provisions for an advance and a delivery deadline, along with a provision confirming that the publisher retained all trademark rights associated with the series of books, including any "trademark, trade name, logo, imprint or other identification now or hereafter used by publisher, nor shall [ghostwriter] use any such identification during the term of this agreement or thereafter."[52]

When the author failed to deliver the book on schedule despite the submission of two sample chapters, the publisher terminated the agreement and demanded the return of the advance. When the publisher proceeded to engage new ghostwriters and publish the planned series of books, the ghostwriter sued for copyright infringement, a suit that was dismissed.[53]

The ghostwriter then took two of the publisher's book covers with the "Nisa Santiago" author name, and proceeded to file a trademark registration application with the United States Patent and Trademark Office, claiming to own the trademark "Nisa Santiago" for "a series of books and written articles in the field of fiction" despite the fact that it was the publisher that used the pseudonym "Nisa Santiago" in commerce and not the ghostwriter. The publisher sued, with the result that the court cancelled the ghostwriter's trademark registration on the grounds of fraud, because the publisher, and not the ghostwriter, was the true owner of the "Nisa Santiago" name and trademark rights therein.[54]

§3.03   Self-Publishing and "Vanity Press" Agreements

Self-published projects have become increasingly common.[55] "Self publishing" agreements differ considerably from a traditional publishing agreement because the author contracts and pays for the services a traditional publisher normally provides as part of its business operations: typesetting, editorial support, cover design, printing, advertising and marketing, warehousing, and shipping. In particular, distribution costs charged to the self-published

---

Fourth Circuit: Estate of Andrews v. United States, 850 F. Supp. 1279 (E.D. Va. 1994) (publisher and surviving family used ghostwriter to continue publishing best-selling books after author's death).

52   *Melodrama Publishing, LLC v. Santiago*, N. 44 supra, 2013 U.S. Dist. LEXIS 56988 at *3.

53   *Id.*, 2013 U.S. Dist. LEXIS 56988, at *3-*4.

54   *Id.*, 2013 U.S. Dist. LEXIS 56988, at *14.

55   Self-publishing is particularly convenient for business speakers and/or consultants who wish to have a book to offer during presentations. Vanity press publishing is most common for an aspiring author who wants to see his or her work in print.

author, which include charges for warehouse storage, and for processing any returned books, can result in additional and financial obligations of the author.[56]

§3.04   Acquisition of Author Rights in Magazine and Newspaper Publishing

The creation of a book is an act of some consequence, both creatively and economically. Most books, however, are works by one freelance author who is not an employee of the publisher. The book author expects to share in the long-term income produced by the book in the form of royalties and other payments, such as shares of the revenues generated through the sale of subsidiary rights. In order to grant exclusive rights to the publisher in exchange for royalties and other consideration, the book author and the publisher enter into a written agreement, which agreement may be the subject of much negotiation.

By contrast, the publication of newspapers and magazines[57] is based on much greater publishing volume with multiple contributing authors, and is much faster-paced, giving rise to different economic and copyright ownership principles. Even a monthly magazine or a quarterly journal represents a shorter life cycle compared to the average book.[58] The total number of words and pages published in a year is enormous, and in some cases, the number of pages and words in just one edition of a large daily newspaper or its Sunday edition may easily rival or exceed that of many books.

Where the contributors are employees of the publisher, then the output is considered "work for hire." But what about freelance contributors to a periodical? In contrast with books that sell and produce revenue for years, the economic life of a single issue of a periodical does not extend beyond a one-time newsstand or subscription sale. There usually will be no future sales to generate future income in which the author can share in the form of royalties. In addition, each individual author's contribution to a periodical typically represents a smaller percentage of the entire publication compared to that of the sole author, or even co-author, of the average book.

Given these facts, it is no wonder that the magazine and newspaper industry has traditionally placed less emphasis on written agreements with freelancers. Even the most well-known magazines have been known to rely on notices stamped on the back of the checks issued to

---

56   See *Stellema v. Vantage Press, Inc.*, 109 A.D.2d 423, 492 N.Y.S.2d 390 (1985) (class action suit alleging fraudulent misrepresentation against "subsidy" publisher).

57   Newspapers are also referred to as "serials," and magazines as "periodicals."

58   See, e.g., *Anderson News, L.L.C. v. American Media, Inc.*, 2012 WL 1085948 (2d Cir. April 3, 2012) (describing detailed distribution and financial models for retail magazine distribution).

freelancers—notices that can serve as effective transfers of copyright ownership once the freelancer endorses and deposits the check.[59]

Where there is no agreement transferring copyright ownership or granting exclusive licenses at all, the understanding, as reflected in section 201(c) of the Copyright Act,[60] is that while the publisher owns the copyright in the collective work as a whole, including the compilation of contributions, and all contributions created by the publisher's employees, the freelance author retains the copyright in her individual contribution.[61] In that case, the publisher enjoys two overall rights in the form of a non-exclusive license: (1) the right to publish the contribution in the periodical or, in copyright parlance, the "collective work;" and (2) the publisher's privilege to include the contribution in any future republication or reprinting of the collective work, providing that the republication preserves the original context and placement of the contribution, or providing that the contribution appears in a later issue of the same periodical.

Section 201(c) reads:

> "In the absence of an express transfer of the copyright or of any rights under it, the owner of copyright in the collective work is presumed to have acquired only the privilege of reproducing and distributing the contribution as part of that particular collective work, any revision of that collective work, and any later collective work in the same series."[62]

The onset of the digital era led to hotly contested litigation over the scope of the publisher's privilege to reproduce contributions in digital online "revisions" of collective works.[63] Licensing periodicals to online databases has grown into a considerable revenue source for publishers. Authors who thought they had struck a deal for essentially one-time publication in a periodical felt shut out of the new digital database revenue stream.

---

59 See *Playboy Enterprises, Inc. v. Dumas*, 53 F.3d 549, 552 (2d Cir. 1995) (long-time freelance contributor of artwork to Playboy magazine never executed a written agreement, but checks tendered by Playboy and cashed by freelancer bore stamped legends on the reverse containing purported work for hire and assignment clauses).

60 17 U.S.C. § 201(c).

61 Section 201(c) embodies in the Copyright Act the holding in *Goodis v. United Artists Television, Inc.*, 425 F.2d 397 (1970). Prior to the Goodis case, and under the 1909 Copyright Act, publication by a magazine of a freelance contribution, without any copyright notice in the name of the author, was potentially a publication without notice that injected the contribution into the public domain. Goodis was a dispute over rights arising from the David Goodis noir novel Dark Passage.

62 17 U.S.C. § 201(c).

63 See *Faulkner v. National Geographic Enterprises, Inc.*, 409 F.3d 26 (2d Cir. 2005) (publication of digital archive was privileged "revision" of publisher's previously authorized print product under 17 U.S.C. § 201(c)). See also, *Greenberg v. National Geographic Society*, 244 F.3d 1244 (11th Cir.), cert. *denied* 555 U.S. 1070 (2008).

In *New York Times Co. v. Tasini*, the Supreme Court held that the publisher's re-use privilege does *not* extend to searchable digital databases that allow the contribution to be retrieved on its own, completely out of the original context of the collective work.[64] The decision highlighted the need for publishers who license their periodicals to searchable databases to ensure they have obtained written agreements from authors that expressly include such searchable database rights.

However, lower courts have held that National Geographic magazine's reproduction of a comprehensive set of historic issues in an omnibus digital format that preserved the original context and layout constituted privileged "revisions" of the original publication under Section 201(c), and the authors of photographs in the magazine were not entitled to any further compensation.[65]

The provisions of Section 201(c) regarding privileged re-uses apply only in "the absence of an express transfer of copyright or of any rights under it." Where a freelance author signs a work made for hire agreement or unlimited assignment of copyright without reservation of rights, digital or otherwise, the publisher controls all the exclusive rights of a copyright owner and is free to publish the work digitally or in any other format.

However, because the history of author/publisher dealings in the world of periodicals was often based on the freelance author retaining copyright in the contribution while the publisher had the right of first publication and privileged revisions under Section 201(c), some freelance authors may be reluctant to assign copyright ownership to a periodical publisher. In such cases, if the publisher needs online searchable database rights beyond the default rights, it should seek confirmation from the freelance author that the publisher has all Section 201(c) rights and is also granted a perpetual non-exclusive license to include the contribution in searchable online electronic databases licensed to third parties.

An exclusive license or copyright assignment agreement granted by an author to a periodical will usually be much shorter than a book publishing agreement, as it will not typically include royalty provisions. The agreement will include the basics of consideration, delivery, and the operative transfer language. Because collective works fall within the statutory definition of works made for hire that can be commissioned from a freelancer, such agreements will typically be on a work made for hire basis.

---

64   See *New York Times Co. v. Tasini*, 533 U.S. 483, 121 S.Ct. 2381,150 L.Ed.2d 500 (2001).

65   See *Faulkner v. National Geographic Enterprises, Inc.*, 409 F.3d 26 (2d Cir. 2005) (publication of digital archive was privileged "revision" of publisher's previously authorized print product under 17 U.S.C. § 201(c)). See also, *Greenberg v. National Geographic Society*, 244 F.3d 1244 (11th Cir. 2008).

§3.05   Translations and Other Overseas Rights

Agreements for rights outside the United States typically involve either a specific country or territory for the original English language edition,[66] or they may involve a translation and the worldwide right to publish and sell the book in that language.

To illustrate the latter scenario, if a publisher in Spain wants to print a Spanish language translation of the work, it requests worldwide rights to the Spanish translation. Given the number of countries where Spanish is spoken, it may still be desirable to limit the agreement to specific territories—the world excluding the Western Hemisphere, for example. Such a grant would still allow the author to separately license Spanish language rights in Central and South America, granting the rights to local publishers who may be in the best position to market the work and to achieve the strongest possible sales in that region.

The major difference in the approach of a territorial license or translation agreement as compared to the comprehensive publishing agreement discussed is that the work may already be in existence, or at least the commitment to write and deliver the work in English are part of the original publishing agreement, and not germane to the translation or overseas rights agreements. Therefore, such overseas rights or translation agreements tend to look more like limited licenses to a pre-existing copyrighted book, focusing less on delivery and editorial matters, and more on the mechanics of distribution and royalty payments.

The duration of the agreement will normally be for shorter periods of time, with options to extend the term. The same issues pertaining to advances will be present. There is some truth to the philosophy that advances should play a greater role in such agreements because of the potential difficulties in conducting audits overseas in the case of a dispute over royalty payments.

A key point will be approval of the translation by the author, who will need access to someone who can provide a reliable assessment of the quality of the translation. While the author will retain all copyright in the original English language work, the publisher of the translation will typically retain copyright in the translation, but will have to cease publication of the translation after the agreement expires. It may be possible, however, for the author to insist that the translation become the author's copyright as well, and such a provision or at least the request for such a provision may give the author some bargaining leverage vis-a-vis the royalty percentages and the advance.

Another major point will be how and if foreign taxes are deducted from payments remitted to the author. Many countries are signatories to international treaties that provide for the filing of tax documents that exempt royalties from tax deductions at source.

---

66   English language rights in Australia, or in the United Kingdom, for example.

Rights such as audio, dramatization, etc. should be reserved to the author.

If the original English language edition included third-party materials such as licensed photographs, illustrations, or licensed excerpts used by permission, the author may be asked to confirm that the underlying licenses extend to the territories and translations being licensed. This is a reminder to the author that when such permission licenses are originally obtained, they should be applicable in all languages and territories worldwide.

§3.06   Agreements Between Authors and Literary Agents

For authors, literary agents provide contacts with and access to publishers. They create opportunities. Indeed, a good agent can also provide overall career and publishing guidance. In many cases, leading publishers will only seriously consider submissions that come in through known and trusted agents.

In exchange for his or her services, the agent retains a commission[67] on the author's income from the publishing agreement and possibly from sales of subsidiary rights. An agent does not, however, act as an attorney, but may have pre-negotiated key aspects of a publishing agreement before the author submits the draft to his or her attorney for review.

An agent has considerable power because he or she will typically have the right to receive advances and royalty income on behalf of an author, to retain his or her commission, and to deduct certain of his/her expenses. Significantly, an agent who brings a publishing deal to an author may have a right to collect the commission for the entire duration of that deal, which can amount to a significant amount of money over the entire lifetime of the author.[68]

Key items in an agreement between an author and a literary agent include the following:

[1]—Scope of Representation

> A literary agent's representation should be limited to either a specific publishing project, or to the field of literary publishing. It should not extend to subsidiary rights areas such as film, television, or stage rights where other agents with a better understanding of the market and better contacts can provide better services to the author.

---

67   The typical commission is 15%.

68   Samples of literary agency agreements are included in the forms accompanying this treatise.

[2]—Term

The duration of an agency agreement may include an initial period of six months to one year, followed by automatic renewals either for the same term, or on a month-to-month basis, with either party given the right to terminate upon thirty or sixty days' notice. Note, however, that expiration of the term does not necessarily end the agent's right to collect a commission on agreements entered into during the term, which right can continue for the full duration of copyright.

Typically, the agent will also retain the right to a commission for agreements substantially negotiated prior to the end of the term. There should be specific language in the agreement requiring the agent to demonstrate the substantiality of such negotiations for purposes of establishing his right to such commissions (and setting some standards for such substantiation such as written correspondence, for example,) in order to avoid conflicts with any new agent engaged by the author after termination or expiration of the prior agreement.

[3]—Commission

A 15% commission is standard, but there may be flexibility to lower the percentage depending on the circumstances.[69] In situations where a co-agent needs to be involved,[70] the commission may be increased to 20% to cover the sub-agent's commission as well. In such a case the agent would be responsible for paying the commission for the overseas sub-agent.

[4]—Disbursements

The agent will be authorized to receive funds on behalf of the author. He or she should be required to use a separate trust account for the author rather than co-mingling the author/client's funds with the funds of the agent's other clients. The agent should pay the client the funds, less the agent's commission, within ten days of receipt, or within five days of the funds clearing the agent's bank account. There should also be provisions especially relevant for situations where the agent is a sole proprietorship and not part of a larger corporation in the event of the agent's disability or death, the funds held for the client can be released to the client or otherwise freed from encumbrances.

[5]—Expenses

There should be an agreement regarding what expenses the agent will absorb as part of the commission, and what expenses will be charged against the client's account for

---

69   If the author comes to the agent with a deal that is already in place or under discussion, for example.

70   Selling overseas rights where the services of an agent in the foreign territory are needed, for example.

reimbursement. Any such reimbursable expenses should be capped at an amount above which the client's pre-approval is required.

[6]—Powers of the Agent and Communications

The agent should not be authorized to sign any agreements on behalf of the client. The agent should be required to immediately forward to the client copies of all important correspondence, and to keep the client regularly informed of potential opportunities.

[7]—Accounting, Statements, and Audits

The agent should provide semi-annual or annual statements summarizing all revenue, commissions, expenses, and reimbursement, along with any required tax forms such as the IRS Form 1099. The client should have the right to audit the agent's books and records at regular intervals.

[8]—Termination

The termination provisions should be clearly set forth, including any thirty-day notices required, and the author should have the right to terminate immediately in the event that the agent files for bankruptcy or in the event of insolvency, liquidation, death, or disability of the agent. Notwithstanding the prevalence of provisions permitting termination when a bankruptcy filing is made, such clauses may not be enforceable against the bankruptcy estate that, under bankruptcy laws, takes over the affairs of the entity.

[9]—Dispute Resolution

Given the fiduciary relationship between agent and client, it is especially important to have a dispute resolution mechanism in the agreement that requires things such as face-to-face settlement meetings and mediation, with deadlines, before the parties turn to more formal mechanisms, such as arbitration or other types of legal action.

§3.07   Copyright in Quotes and Journalistic Interviews

Copyright ownership can only be claimed where the author has created an original work. In the case of works that quote from others, or works such as interviews that consist substantially of the words of someone other than the author, what is the copyright ownership status of the interview quotes?

The author of a factual work may not, without an assignment of copyright, claim copyright in statements made by others and reported in the work, because the author may not claim originality as to those statements.[71] Journalists may seek such an assignment and claim ownership of the words spoken in an interview they report.[72] Whether interview subjects for a print publication or television show would consent to assign copyright in their words would be case-specific, but journalists who seek such an assignment prior to the interview may run the risk of "chilling" the willingness of the subject to be interviewed and to speak candidly.

Should later works by third parties draw upon quotes from the interviewee, absent an assignment of copyright from the interviewee as discussed above, the journalist who first reported the interview, including the quotations, cannot object to the use of the interview words themselves by others. In *Rokeach v. Avco Embassy Pictures Corp.*, the author of "The Three Christs of Ypsilanti," a psychiatrist, based his book on accurately transcribed interviews with and quotes from his mental patients. When the author later sued over a play and a film that in various ways used the original source material quotes from the patients themselves, the court held that the playwright "had every right as a creative dramatist to draw upon social science source material of the kind represented by plaintiff's work and in doing so made "fair use" of such materials."[73]

For most interviews, the subject retains copyright in the words spoken during the interview, but by granting the interview for eventual publication, the subject also grants an implied non-exclusive license to the journalist and their publisher to publish the interview.[74] This analysis assumes that the interview is recorded or transcribed or otherwise reduced to a tangible medium of expression, thus meeting the "fixation" requirement for a work to be copyrightable.[75]

---

71   *Suid v. Newsweek Magazine*, 503 F. Supp. 146, 148 (D.D.C. 1980). See also:

Second Circuit: Maxtone Graham v. Burtchaell, 803 F. 2d 1253 (2d Cir. 1986) (use of quotations in book fair use).

Tenth Circuit: Russell v. Turnbaugh, 1991 WL 283837 (D. Col. Feb. 7, 1991) ("an author may not claim copyright violations in statements made by others and reported or quoted in their work"). See also *Jacobsen v. Deseret Book Company*, 287 F. 3d 936, 947 (10th Cir. 2002) ("quotations may be freely copied if the quotation is recorded contemporaneously or taken directly from a written source").

District of Columbia Circuit: Quinto v. Legal Times of Washington, Inc., 506 F. Supp. 554 (D.D.C. 1981) (journalistic compilation of facts or data is copyrightable).

72   *Id.*

73   See *Rokeach v. Avco Embassy Pictures Corp.*, 1978 WL 23519 (S.D.N.Y. Jan. 17, 1978). See also, *Hoehling v. Universal City Studios, Inc.*, 618 F.2d 972 (2d Cir. 1980) (where author of book presented his historical theories as facts, author had no claim against studio that used those facts in the plot of a motion picture).

74   See *Estate of Ernest Hemingway v. Random House, Inc.*, 23 N.Y.2d 341, 244 N.E.2d 250, 296 N.Y.S.2d 771 (1968) (Hemingway's words and conduct "left no doubt of his willingness to permit [the journalist] to draw freely on their conversation in writing about him and to publish such material").

75   See 17 U.S.C. § 102.

With respect to short quotes that may appear in later articles and books, the fair use principles of copyright law would apply in most cases. For longer quotes, publishers may decide to seek permission, depending on their own view of industry custom and risk assessment. Fair use is completely fact specific on a case-by-case basis.

CHAPTER 4

Music

---

§4.01   Introduction

The music business is "an industry heavily regulated by copyright law."[1] The key to any music-related client need is to find the intersection between two coordinates: First, with *whom* must you deal? In the music industry, knowing who the copyright owners are is not always an easy question to answer. Second, conduct an analysis of *how* the music is being used, which, in turn, will tell you *which* of the six exclusive rights under copyright is invoked by that use. Once it is determined *who* the copyright owners are, and *how* the music is being used, we can then "triangulate the coordinates" and build the foundation for a successful music transaction.

§4.02   Copyright Ownership in the Music Industry

Any music transaction involving sound recordings requires the lawyer to peel back the layers of copyright ownership in the sound recording and to identify its two main components: first, the underlying musical composition; and second, the recording based on that underlying composition.[2]

---

1   See *EMI Entertainment World, Inc. v. Karen Records, Inc.*, 806 F. Supp.2d 697, 703 (S.D.N.Y. 2011) (copyright infringement based on failure to pay mechanical royalties).

2   See *Newton v. Diamond*, 204 F. Supp.2d 1244 (C.D. Cal. 2002), aff'd 388 F.3d 1189 (9th Cir. 2004) ("[s]ound recordings and their underlying musical compositions are separate works with their own distinct copyrights"). See also: 17 U.S.C. § 102(1)(a)(2), (7) (setting forth separate copyrightable subject matter for musical compositions and sound recordings); *Jarvis v. A&M Records*, 827 F. Supp. 282, 292 (D.N.J. 1993) ("[u]nder the Copyright Act, there is a well-established distinction between sound recordings and musical compositions . . . [p]ursuant to this distinction, the rights of a copyright in a sound recording do not extend to the song itself . . . and vice versa") (citations omitted); *T.B. Harms Co. v. Jem Records, Inc.*, 655 F. Supp. 1575, 1577 n.1 (D.N.J. 1987).

The copyright ownership of the two main components is usually quite different. The underlying musical compositions are originally created by songwriters, composers, and lyricists. Those creators, in turn, typically assign or license their copyright ownership to a music publisher. The sound recording, however, is originally created by performing artists ("artists"), who, in turn, typically assign or license their copyright ownership to a record company.

These two components co-exist quite closely in some respects. The recording and the song comprise one overall unit. But from the perspective of copyright ownership, the two main copyright components of a typical recording can represent an uneasy alliance of copyright owners with divergent goals, interests, and licensing requirements.

Precision of terminology is paramount in the music industry. Terms such as "musical composition," "composer," "artist," "sound recording," and "phonorecord," "performance," "reproduction," "synchronization license," "master license," and "mechanical license" all have specific meanings that carry very different copyright ownership and licensing requirements.

[1]—The Underlying Musical Composition

Copyright ownership exists immediately upon creation of an original work, expressed in a tangible medium of expression.[3] Copyright law regards the underlying musical composition, including music and lyrics, as the original and first act of copyright creation.

The authors are the original copyright owners of the musical composition, and may consist of one or more composers of the music, and one or more authors of the words or lyrics (or "lyricists"), who become co-authors and co-owners of the entire work, the undivided whole.[4] Those authors will typically enter into a contractual relationship with a business entity whose main function is to commercially exploit the song through various types of licensing activities, in order to maximize the income from that musical composition.

The name of that business entity is the music publisher, and by virtue of an agreement, with the songwriters, the music publisher becomes the copyright owner or exclusive licensee of rights in the musical composition, including any lyrics it may contain. The rights granted to the music publisher may range from complete copyright ownership

---

3   17 U.S.C. § 102.

4   17 U.S.C. § 101. Definition of joint work as "a work prepared by two or more authors with the intention that their contributions be merged into inseparable or interdependent parts of a unitary whole." Songwriting teams can be the "classic" combination of the Beatles' John Lennon and Paul McCartney, who both contributed words and music, or Broadway musical writers like Tim Rice (words) and Andrew Lloyd Webber (music).

to only a subset of the potential overall copyright rights, e.g., a percentage ownership of selected income streams in selected territories for a limited time.[5]

[2]—The Sound Recording

Unlike the underlying musical composition, which is created by composers and lyricists, the original authors and owners of the copyright in a sound recording are the artists who perform on that sound recording. The copyright arises from capturing the performances the artists create in a "tangible medium of expression. There may also be additional creative contributions by a producer whose job it is to oversee the musical performances and recording techniques in order to achieve the best sound recording possible.

The artists typically enter into a contractual relationship with a business entity whose main function is to commercially exploit the sound recording featuring the artists, and to maximize income from that sound recording. The business entity that acquires copyright ownership or exclusive rights in the sound recording is ordinarily the record company. The main product of the traditional record company is the "phonorecord."[6]

Thus, a "song"[7] consists of two entirely separate copyrights, often owned by two entirely separate business entities:

(1) The underlying musical composition, created by the composer and lyricist, who typically assign copyright ownership to a music publisher.

(2) The sound recording, created by the performing artists, who typically assign their copyright to the record company, which then manufactures a traditional phonorecord or a digital phonorecord.

---

5   See § 4.13 *infra* for a discussion on music publishing.

6   Under the Copyright Act, "Sound recordings" are works that result from the fixation of a series of musical, spoken, or other sounds, but not including the sounds accompanying a motion picture or other audiovisual work, regardless of the nature of the material objects, such as disks, tapes, or other phonorecords, in which they are embodied. "Phonorecords" are "material objects in which sounds, other than those accompanying a motion picture or other audiovisual work, are fixed by any method now known or later developed, and from which the sounds can be perceived, reproduced, or otherwise communicated, either directly or with the aid of a machine or device. The term "phonorecords" includes the material object in which the sounds are first fixed." 17. U.S.C. § 101. The definition also includes the physical or digital embodiment of the sound recording, the CD, or in the case of a digital file, a digital phonorecord.

7   Although the term "song" is used throughout to indicate an underlying musical composition, there are other types of copyrighted musical compositions, such as orchestral, chamber, and electronic works for which the same principles apply. In addition, note that that literary and dramatic works (plays) are also included the section 106(4) exclusive rights of public performance, and can of course also be the subject of sound recordings.

There is an inherent tension in the duality of copyright ownership contained within every phonorecord: if the music publisher owns the copyright in the musical composition, doesn't the record company need a license from the music publisher to "use" the underlying song for the purposes of creating the sound recording, reproducing copies as phonorecords, and distributing those copies? The answer, in short, is "yes," and the licensing mechanism that facilitates this is called a "mechanical license"—a license for the mechanical reproduction of a musical composition on a phonorecord.[8]

§4.03   The Six Exclusive Rights Under Copyright

There are six exclusive rights accorded by the Copyright Act to copyright owners, and these rights correspond to specific licensing procedures and organizations in the music industry. All of these rights can be negotiated, licensed, bought and sold in virtually unlimited ways, because copyright is "infinitely divisible" with respect to exclusive rights, time, and territory.[9] However, the music industry is a special case because there are categories of exclusive rights where the license rates and fees are not freely negotiated by the owner, but are instead set by Congress, the Copyright Office, or collective licensing organizations that handle licensing on behalf of copyright owners.

Those collective licensing organizations closely track the different exclusive rights. For example, the performing rights organizations ASCAP, BMI, and SESAC were established by the music publishing industry to administer the licensing for public performance. Likewise, many music publishers use the Harry Fox Agency, a collective that administers mechanical licensing. Sound Exchange is a collective organized by the recording industry and authorized under the Copyright Act to administer digital performance rights in sound recordings for the Internet and satellite radio.

The following chart summarizes the six rights, and the leading music industry organizations that administer those rights:

---

8   The license is referred to as "mechanical" in the sense that CD players and computers and MP3 players are machines that mechanically reproduce music. A mechanical license is a fee that a record company pays to a music publisher for the right to use the music publisher's song in the record company's sound recording. See generally, 17 U.S.C. § 115, the mechanical licensing provisions of the Copyright Act. The mechanical license will be discussed in greater detail in § 4.05 *infra*.

9   17 U.S.C. § 201(d)(2). "Any of the exclusive rights comprised in a copyright, including any sub-division of any of the rights specified by section 106, may be transferred as provided by clause (1) and owned separately. The owner of any particular exclusive right is entitled, to the extent of that right, to all of the protection and remedies accorded to the copyright owner by this title."

Exclusive Rights under 17 U.S.C. § 106	Collective Licensing Organization Involved	Situations where copyright owner licenses without using a collective
Reproduction § 106(1)	For phonorecords and "mechanical" licensing: Harry Fox Agency	Where publisher is not a member of Harry Fox and issues their own mechanical licenses, and situations other than phonorecords (e.g., sync and master licenses for film/tv)
Derivative Works § 106(2)	For phonorecords and "mechanical" licensing: Harry Fox Agency	Other than phonorecords: copyright owner (e.g., an arrangement of a musical work or a change in the lyrics).
Distribution § 106(3)	For phonorecords and "mechanical" licensing: Harry Fox Agency	Other than phonorecords: copyright owner
Public Performance § 106(4)	For nondramatic musical works—performing rights organizations: ASCAP, BMI, SESAC	For dramatic musical works: copyright owner (or where copyright owner chooses to license public performance themselves)
Display § 106(5)	Copyright owner	Copyright owner
Digital Performance of Sound Recordings § 106(6)	SoundExchange for streamed performances	Copyright owner for downloads.

It is *how* music is *used* that determines which of the six exclusive rights are in play; the key to understanding what type of licensing regime and organization will be involved.

[1]—Reproduction

The first exclusive right given copyright owners is the right to reproduce a work. The "how" of the reproduction right is the physical act of making copies.[10] This right applies to the reproduction of even a portion of the copyrighted work, and may apply to the creation of only one copy.[11]

---

10   Whether the copies are physical or digital copies also comes into play. The Copyright Act defines "copies" as "material objects, other than phonorecords, in which a work is fixed by any method now known or later developed, and from which the work can be perceived, reproduced, or otherwise communicated, either directly or with the aid of a machine or device. The term 'copies' includes the material object, other than a phonorecord, in which the work is first fixed." 17 U.S.C. § 101.

11   Typical examples in the music industry would include the act of making copies of a sound recording and the musical composition it contains on a compact disc, or as a digital file, or as part of an audiovisual work on a DVD or other digital media or transmission. There are other types as well: copies made as part of printed music editions; copies of song lyrics that might be made as part of CD packaging or on merchandise; and copies of works for ring tones on mobile phone devices.

[2]—Derivative Works

[a]—Derivative Works in the Music Industry

Copyright owners are also granted the right to control the creation of derivative works.[12] To illustrate: a musical composition exists prior to any sound recording of that composition. The sound recording is a derivative work based on the composition.[13]

Similarly, an arrangement of a musical composition is a derivative work based on the original underlying musical composition. The creator of the derivative work will be entitled to copyright ownership, but only with respect to the new material added, so long as the work meets originality thresholds in the form of some "substantial" variation from the underlying work, and has a license from the owner of the underlying work.[14]

With respect to song lyrics, altering the lyrics in any substantive way creates a derivative work that requires the permission of the copyright owner. Note that altering song lyrics for purposes of legitimate criticism or commentary may rise to the level of a "transformative" fair use.[15] Courts ultimately make such determinations, however, on a *sui generis* basis.

[b]—Creating Derivative Work Musical Arrangements in Connection with Sound Recordings

Mechanical licensing accords the recording artists a special privilege—the right to create derivative works in the form of arrangements of the underlying musical composition, subject to the following limitations:

- the musical arrangement may be made "to the extent necessary to conform it to the style or manner of interpretation of the performance involved; but

---

12   A derivative work is defined in the Copyright Act as "a work based upon one or more preexisting works, such as a translation, musical arrangement, dramatization, fictionalization, motion picture version, sound recording, art reproduction, abridgment, condensation, or any other form in which a work may be recast, transformed, or adapted. A work consisting of editorial revisions, annotations, elaborations, or other modifications, which, as a whole, represent an original work of authorship, is a "derivative work." 17 U.S.C. § 101. See also, *Woods v. Bourne*, 60 F.2d 978, 989 (2d Cir. 1995). "[S]ound recordings are clearly derivative works." *Id.*, 60 F.3d at 989.

13   The sound recording will typically have a different copyright owner (the record company) as compared to the underlying musical composition (owned by the music publisher).

14   See L. *Batlin & Son, Inc. v. Snyder*, 536 F.2d 486, 491 (2d Cir.) (*en banc*), *cert. denied* 429 U.S. 857 (1976).

15   See *Campbell v. Acuff-Rose Music, Inc.*, 510 U.S. 569, 114 S.Ct. 1164, 127 L.Ed.2d 500 (1994) (rap group's parody of song "Pretty Woman" may be a transformative fair use within the meaning of Section 107 of the Copyright Act). See also, 17 U.S.C. § 107, the fair use provisions of the Copyright Act, discussed in greater detail in Chapter 1, *supra*.

- the arrangement shall not change the basic melody or fundamental character of the work; and

- shall not be subject to protection as a derivative work, except with the express consent of the copyright owner. This means that, for example, the privilege would allow an arranger to score a song for an ensemble for the purposes of making a recording, but the arranger would not then have any further copyright ownership of that arrangement, and could not, for example, sell or rent copies of the arrangement without a license from the copyright owner of the underlying musical composition.[16]

[3]—Distribution

The Act also gives copyright owners the exclusive right to distribute copies of their works.[17] The distribution right is tied to the concept of publication, as

> "the distribution of copies or phonorecords of a work to the public by sale or other transfer of ownership, or by rental, lease, or lending. The offering to distribute copies or phonorecords to a group of persons for purposes of further distribution, public performance, or public display, constitutes

---

16   17 U.S.C. § 114(a)(2). In the event a recording artist wanted to perform the arrangement live in concert or record it as part of an audiovisual work requiring a sync license, the copyright owner could demand that the arrangement, as used outside the context of a sound recording, be licensed. The public performance licenses that would cover any live performances do not include any right to make arrangements, and in the case of ASCAP licenses, there is a provision expressly disclaiming any valid license with respect to unauthorized orchestral arrangements.

Musical arrangements are one of the types of works that can be works made for hire under the definition of a commissioned work made for hire in Section 101 of the Copyright Act. The owner of the underlying composition, if they are willing to authorize an arrangement even for one specific performance, typically insists on becoming the work made for hire author and owner of the arrangement. It may still be possible for the arranger to receive some sort of royalty in that case, depending on the approach favored by the copyright owner.

In order for a work to qualify as a derivative work, it must be independently copyrightable. See *Woods v. Bourne*, supra at 990. To be copyrightable, a derivative arrangement must contain sufficient originality of expression, such that there is "at least some substantial variation from the underlying work, not merely a trivial variation." See *L. Batlin & Son, Inc. v. Snyder*, 536 F.2d 486, 491 (2d Cir.) (*en banc*), *cert. denied* 429 U.S. 857 (1976). While many musical arrangements may indeed meet that standard, in at least one case, courts have held that even a well executed, but standard, piano/vocal arrangement of a popular song such as those provided with sheet music, did not contain sufficient originality under copyright law to rise to the level of an independently copyrightable arrangement. See *Woods v. Bourne, id.*, 60 F.3d at 992-993.

17   See, e.g., *A&M Records v. Napster*, 239 F.3d 1004, 1014 (1991) (stating the distinction between reproduction and distribution rights as follows: "plaintiffs have shown that Napster users infringe at least two of the copyright holders' exclusive rights: the rights of reproduction, § 106(1); and distribution, § 106(3). Napster users who upload file names to the search index for others to copy violate plaintiffs' distribution rights. Napster users who download files containing copyrighted music violate plaintiffs' reproduction rights.").

publication. A public performance or display of a work does not of itself constitute publication."[18]

Under copyright law, a business that seeks to reproduce and distribute copies of a work must be certain to obtain *both* reproduction and distribution rights. The mechanical license paid by a record company to a music publisher for the right to include a musical composition on a phonorecord encompasses all three of the rights considered so far: the right to reproduce copies of the phonorecord; the right to create a derivative work (a sound recording) based on the musical composition; and the right to distribute the phonorecord.

[4]—Public Performance

The public performance of a musical composition (for profit) is the right most closely allied with the musical experience itself, because it is based on the performance of a musical composition for an audience. It is different from rights such as reproduction and distribution that depend on tangible physical or digital "manifestations."

The Copyright Act defines a public performance as follows:

To perform or display a work "publicly" means—

(1) to perform or display it at a place open to the public or at any place where a substantial number of persons outside of a normal circle of a family and its social acquaintances is gathered; or

(2) to transmit or otherwise communicate a performance or display of the work to a place specified by clause (1) or to the public, by means of any device or process, whether the members of the public capable of receiving the performance or display receive it in the same place or in separate places and at the same time or at different times.[19]

The public performances and transmissions referred to cover a very broad range of means by which that music can be heard, including radio and television broadcasts, live performances in concert halls and clubs, "on hold" music for phone systems, background music in shopping malls and music on the Internet.[20]

---

18   17 U.S.C. § 101.

19   17 U.S.C. § 101.

20   See generally, www.ascap.com; www.bmi.com; www.sesac.com. The Web sites for each PRO discuss the many different types of licenses available for different public performance scenarios.

[a]—Performing Rights Societies

The genesis of the nondramatic performance right was recognized in the courts in the case involving Victor Herbert, the American composer and one of the founders of the American Society of Composers, Authors and Publishers ("ASCAP"). In the early years of the twentieth century, Herbert enjoyed the exclusive "grand right" to present staged productions of his works. However, the right to publicly perform nondramatic excerpts, such as individual songs, was not clearly protected.[21] While Herbert was out to dinner one evening, he heard one of his compositions being performed for the clientele. Realizing that the restaurant was profiting from music that attracted customers, and that he, the composer of the work, was not being compensated, Herbert and his publisher brought suit against the restaurant.

The lower courts held that although Herbert had exclusive dramatic performance rights with respect to the staged "grand rights," there was no exclusive right of public performance with respect to song excerpts sold as sheet music and performed in a nondramatic setting, without any admission charge. Supreme Court Justice Oliver Wendell Holmes reversed, and memorably explained how the public performance of nondramatic works had value, and contributed to profits, in a commercial setting such as a restaurant, where music provided "a luxurious pleasure not to be had from eating a silent meal."[22]

At this point, music publishers and songwriters recognized that no single composer or music publisher had the resources to monitor music performances in every venue and in every available medium. Herbert helped to create a "performing rights soci-

---

21 *Herbert v. Shanley Co.*, 229 F. 340 (2d Cir. 1916), *rev'd Herbert v. Shanley Co.*, 242 U.S. 591, 593, 37 S.Ct. 232, 61 L.Ed. 511 (1917). Among the rationales was that there was no admission charge for the music, and hence it was presented "for free" for the enjoyment of diners. The lower courts held that the hotel did not infringe Herbert's public performance rights.

22 *Herbert v. Shanley Co.*, 242 U.S. 591, 37 S.Ct. 232, 61 L.Ed. 511 (1917).

"If the rights under the copyright are infringed only by a performance where money is taken at the door, they are very imperfectly protected. Performances not different in kind from those of the defendants could be given that might compete with and even destroy the success of the monopoly that the law intends the plaintiffs to have. It is enough to say that there is no need to construe the statute so narrowly. The defendants' performances are not eleemosynary. They are part of a total for which the public pays, and the fact that the price of the whole is attributed to a particular item which those present are expected to order is not important. It is true that the music is not the sole object, but neither is the food, which probably could be got cheaper elsewhere. The object is a repast in surroundings that to people having limited powers of conversation, or disliking the rival noise, give a luxurious pleasure not to be had from eating a silent meal. If music did not pay, it would be given up. If it pays, it pays out of the public's pocket. Whether it pays or not, the purpose of employing it is profit, and that is enough."

Id., 242 U.S. at 593.

ety" ("PRS") that could represent all music publishers and songwriters, and through strength in numbers, have the business, accounting, and administrative resources to monitor public performances, issue licenses, collect license fees, and distribute those license fees to its publisher and songwriter members.[23] While the Copyright Act uses the name "Performing Rights Society," the name "Performing Rights Organization" and the corresponding acronym "PRO" are also commonly used.

ASCAP is an unincorporated membership association, formed in 1914 by and for the benefit of its composer, lyricist, and music publisher members, who also comprise the board of directors. ASCAP licenses public performing rights to users wherever and via the myriad technological methods by which music is publicly performed.[24]

In 1939, a second performing rights society, Broadcast Music, Inc. ("BMI"), was founded. BMI is a New York corporation formed by broadcasters, whose shareholders and board of directors are comprised of current or former broadcasters.[25]

ASCAP and BMI initially held an exclusive monopoly over the licensing of performing rights, which was challenged in the courts. As a result of antitrust litigation brought by the government against both ASCAP and BMI, ASCAP now operates under a consent decree.[26] Anyone requesting a blanket license for public performances will be granted the license subject to payment of a fee. Should the user object to the license fee, they have the right to petition the district court for a ruling. The court

---

23   The Copyright Act defines a performing rights society "an association, corporation, or other entity that licenses the public performance of nondramatic musical works on behalf of copyright owners of such works, such as the American Society of Composers, Authors and Publishers (ASCAP), Broadcast Music, Inc. (BMI), and SESAC, Inc." 17 U.S.C. § 101. The PRS's retain a small percentage of the gross licensing revenue to cover their administrative costs.

24   Venues include local television and radio stations, broadcast and cable/satellite television networks, Internet service providers, cable systems operators and direct broadcast satellite services, restaurants, night clubs, universities and colleges, hotels, concert promoters, sports arenas, roller skating rinks and other businesses. See *United States v. ASCAP*, 562 F. Supp.2d 413, 423-425 (S.D.N.Y. 2008), determining license fees for performances of music online, and also describing the activities of ASCAP.

25   See www.bmi.com. See also, *United States v. ASCAP*, N. 16 supra, at 425 (describing BMI and noting the differences between BMI and ASCAP).

26   See: *United States v. ASCAP*, 1940-43 Trade Cas. (CCH) ¶ 56,104 (S.D.N.Y. 1941; *United States v. BMI*, 1940-43 Trade Cas. (CCH) ¶ 56,098 (S.D.N.Y. 1941). In 1941, the United States brought a civil action against ASCAP and BMI for alleged violations of the Sherman Antitrust Act. The actions were settled by the entry of a consent decree. The 1941 ASCAP consent decree was amended on March 14, 1950 to form the Amended Final Judgment, and again on January 7, 1960. The terms of those orders regulated the manner in which ASCAP could operate within the music industry and gave the Southern District of New York exclusive oversight jurisdiction. The Amended Final Judgment was again amended on June 11, 2001. See *United States v. ASCAP*, 2001 U.S. Dist. LEXIS 23707, 2001 WL 158999 (S.D.N.Y. June 11, 2001).

issues a determination of fees after a bench trial.[27] Moreover, ASCAP's rights are non-exclusive; ASCAP members retain the right to license performing rights directly to users.[28] BMI is also subject to consent decrees, and licenses non-exclusively.[29]

In 2016, at the request of ASCAP and BMI who proposed changes that would lessen the impact of the Consent Decrees, the Department of Justice reviewed their respective Consent Decrees, and issued a report declining to make any of the changes requested by ASCAP and BMI.[30] The DOJ did however propose that the PROs engage in so-called "100% licensing" or "full-work licensing" for co-owned works, using the established principles of U.S. copyright law that a co-owner may grant nonexclusive licenses subject only to a duty to account to the other owner(s). This would represent a change from the music industry's current practice of fractional licensing whereby each rights holder agrees to only license their percentage of ownership. It would also simplify licensing for licensees. The PROs are currently seeking judicial determination in their respective rate courts as regards whether they should be compelled to engage in full-work licensing.[31]

While ASCAP and BMI are the leading performing rights organizations (or "PRO") with respect to the number of songwriters, songs, and publishers they represent, a third, smaller performing rights organization exists. SESAC, which was originally the "Society of European State Authors and Composers," is now a purely United States-based entity. While SESAC is not subject to a Department of Justice consent decree, it has been the subject of antitrust challenges and in settlement of litigation has agreed to arbitration of disputed license fee rates, which one court has described as equivalent to court oversight.[32]

---

27   Thus, there is continual "rate court" litigation in the Southern District of New York. See *United States v. ASCAP*, N. 18 supra.

28   *Id.* at 14.

29   See *United States v. BMI*, 1940-43 Trade Cas. (CCH) ¶ 56,098 (S.D.N.Y. 1941).

30   See DOJ, "Statement of the Department of Justice on the Closing of the Antitrust Division's Review of the ASCAP and BMI Consent Decrees," (Aug. 4, 2016), available at *https://www.justice.gov/atr/file/882101/download*.

31   See *United States v. Broadcast Music, Inc.*, 2016 U.S. Dist. LEXIS 126588 (S.D.N.Y. Sept. 16, 2016) (holding that the Consent Decree for BMI "neither bars fractional licensing nor requires full-work licensing"). On appeal.

32   See *Meredith Corp. v. SESAC LLC*, 2014 U.S. Dist. LEXIS 26992 (S.D.N.Y. March 3, 2014). The case, brought by a group of local television stations, reportedly settled on terms including SESAC's agreement to negotiate via the Television Music License Committee (TMLC) that represents local TV stations in blanket license negotiations with ASCAP and BMI. See http://tvmlc.com/.

A fourth PRO was founded in 2013, Global Music Rights (GMR) which is a privately held for profit company representing what it describes as a small elite group of successful songwriters represented by invitation only.[33]

Composers and songwriters can belong to only one performing rights society at a time, but their music publishers typically join each society to which their composers belong. Publishers must use different business names for each society to avoid confusion, but need not actually form separate corporations for their membership in each PRO.

Performing rights societies operate on a non-exclusive basis, meaning that publisher members can choose to license performing rights directly to a user for a specific usage, which is known as "source" or "program" licensing.[34]

[b]—Types of Licenses

[i]—Blanket Licensing

Most of the licenses issued by PRO's are "blanket" licenses, because payment of the fee results in a license to all the copyrighted works in the repertoire of that PRO.[35] In order to be completely licensed for all copyrighted nondramatic songs, and be free to perform any music it chooses, a radio station, for example, will enter into blanket licenses with all three PRO's. By virtue of agreements with similar performing rights societies in other countries, licenses with the three American PRO's ultimately cover most of the copyrighted music in the world today.

While blanket licensing is the most comprehensive for the licensee, it may also be the most expensive. Therefore, radio and television broadcasters may seek a

---

33   GMR is currently in litigation with the Radio Music License Committee, which represents radio broadcasters. In the litigation, GMR describes itself as representing less than 1% of the songwriting market share as compared to ASCAP, BMI, and SESAC. See, e.g. *Global Music Rights, LLC v. Radio Music License Committee*, Case No. 16-cv-09051 (C.D. Cal. Docket #23 First Amended Compl. Filed Jan. 7, 2017 at p. 12).

34   See *Buffalo Broadcasting Co., Inc. v. ASCAP*, 744 F.2d 917 (2d Cir. 1984) (blanket licensing of local television stations was not an unreasonable restraint of trade where, because ASCAP's rights to license music are non-exclusive, stations also had opportunity to acquire the necessary broadcast performance rights directly from copyright owners via "program" license, "direct" license, or "source" license was realistically available to the local stations). See also, *Broadcast Music, Inc. v. DMX, Inc.*, 683 F.3d 32 (2d Cir. 2012) (blanket license fees are subject to adjustable carve-outs to account for direct licensing).

35   See *Buffalo Broadcasting Co., Inc. v. ASCAP*, N. 22 *supra*, 744 F.2d at 920-923 (discussing performance licensing including blanket licensing, source licensing, and direct licensing in the context of local television broadcasts, also noting that usage of music on television programming is categorized as "theme," "background," or "feature.").

less expensive alternative by licensing public performance rights directly from copyright owners of the music (a "direct license") or from producers of television programs who, in effect, pass through the music licensing to their program because they have obtained the right to do so from the owner of the music copyright (a "source license").

[ii]—Direct Licenses

A direct license is a license for performance rights granted directly to the licensee, without anyone acting as an intermediary, by the copyright owner of the music. Under their consent decrees, ASCAP and BMI are required to permit stations to obtain direct licenses from the music publishers that own the copyrights. The music publisher and songwriter members of ASCAP and BMI, in turn, only grant nonexclusive license rights to ASCAP and BMI, and thus have the right to grant direct licenses at their discretion.

[iii]—Source Licenses

A source license in effect uses a producer of a television program as a licensing middleman between the music copyright owner and the television station. For example, the producer of a television program that includes music can obtain from the music copyright owner the right to publicly perform the music in the program and to license that right to others whenever the producer licenses the entire production. In that case, a television station that pays the producer to broadcast the program will also have a license to publicly perform the music, i.e., the television station will have obtained the music license from the source of the program, the producer, instead of from the PRO.

[iv]—Per-Program Licenses

Where a television station has engaged in either direct licensing or source licensing, the station will have obtained some of the public performance rights it needs without going through a PRO. But that may leave a lot of music being broadcast that is not included in the direct or source licenses. The television station can then go to the PRO to license any remaining programs, on a "per-program license" ("PPL") basis.

[c]—Direct Royalty Payments: Author Share and Publisher Share

Performing rights societies distribute the royalties in two halves, or "shares." One half goes to the music publishers and copyright owners of the compositions (the "publisher share"), and the other half goes directly to the composers and songwriters (the "author share").[36] This is an important distinction to bear in mind. All categories of music publishing income, other than performing rights royalties, are "filtered" through the publisher, who then remits to the author the contractual share of the revenue in the form of author's royalties.

[d]—Exceptions for Grand Rights

Performing rights societies license only "small rights" non-dramatic works such as typical popular songs. Dramatic and staged works, such as operas, musical theatre, and ballet are licensed directly by the music publisher, not by ASCAP, BMI, or SESAC. This holds true with respect to, for example, radio broadcasts of operas, which would not be licensed by any of the PRO's. Instead, a radio station wishing to broadcast the copyrighted opera would have to obtain a grand rights performance license directly from the music publisher.[37]

[e]—Registration of Works with Performing Rights Societies

The PRO can pay royalties only if the work is registered with its database.[38] In order to participate in the PRO's licensing efforts and receive income from performances, the music publisher must first apply to the PRO to become a publisher member or affiliate. After establishing membership or affiliation, the publisher must then register with the PRO every work the publisher represents, and every new work the publisher acquires.

The registration of the "title" must indicate the names of all authors of the work, and their percentage of the "writer's" share. For example, if there are two songwriters, the title registration will indicate both as authors and will indicate they each receive 50% of the author's share of royalties. As for the other half of royalties, the "publisher share," that also can be divided between more than one publisher.

Total royalty	$200
Composer (entire author share)	$100
Publisher share	$100

---

36 Writer members may assign their "writer share" of royalties to third parties in exchange for a cash advance or other consideration and, if they do so, must comply with notice and other requirements of their membership agreement with their PRO. See, e.g., *Stewart v. First California Bank*, 2013 Cal. App. Unpub. LEXIS 3829 (Cal. App. 2d Dist. May 30, 2013) (detailing various dealings of performer and songwriter Sly Stone, including his assignment of the writer share of his performing rights royalties).

37 Music publishers may sometimes differ with presenting organizations as to whether a "revue" or "cabaret" with a story line is a dramatic or non-dramatic use of the musical compositions, and thus whether it would be covered by a license from a PRS.

38 Registration can be accomplished via written forms or online.

Two authors, a composer and lyricist, split the author share:

Total royalty	$200
Composer (half of author share)	$50
Lyricist (half of author share)	$50
Publisher	$100

Two authors, each with a different publisher, split royalties:

Total royalty	$200
Composer (half of author share)	$50
Lyricist (half of author share)	$50
Composer's publisher (half of publisher share)	$50
Lyricist's publisher (half of publisher share)	$50

[f]—Limitations to the Public Performance Right

The exclusive rights of a copyright owner under Section 106 of the Copyright Act are subject to limitations set forth in Sections 107 through 122, which contain the Act's fair use guidelines, the first sale doctrine, and various exemptions and compulsory licensing schemes in which Congress sets license rates.[39]

The limitations on the right of public performance are concentrated in Section 110, which contains an extensive list of situations where no performance licenses are required.[40] The exemptions must be reviewed closely, however, to confirm if a given performance meets exemption requirements.

Places of worship are exempt from obtaining performance licenses for music performed in the course of religious services, provided that the music is either non-dra-

---

[39] 17 U.S.C. §§ 107-122. One example of licensing schemes is the compulsory mechanical royalty for sound recordings.

[40] 17 U.S.C. § 110(5). The exemptions that affect the largest portions of society include performance of non-dramatic music and literary works (including song lyrics) in schools, in places of worship in the course of religious services, and radio and television transmissions in restaurants of limited size. The exemptions for smaller eating establishments were enacted as part of the hotly contested "Fairness in Music Licensing Act of 1998" sought by the restaurant lobby. Pub. L. No. 106-44, Title II, 113 Stat. 221 (Oct. 28, 1998).

matic, or a dramatic work of a religious nature.[41] That exemption does not apply to commercial performances held in a place of worship.[42]

Section 110 also exempts performances of non-dramatic works in the course of face-to-face teaching at nonprofit educational institutions, including some related television transmissions.[43] There are also exemptions for nonprofit and fundraising performances at any location, provided that none of the presenters or participants receive compensation, and provided that any proceeds, after deduction of reasonable production costs, are used exclusively for educational, religious, or charitable purposes.[44]

Other notable exemptions include performance of music at retail music establishments where the performances are meant to promote the sale of the recordings,[45] and performances of non-dramatic musical works by a governmental body or nonprofit agricultural or horticultural organization in connection with an agricultural or horticultural fair. This latter exemption does not extend to for-profit performances by concessionaires or businesses at the event.[46]

[g]—Movie Theatres

In the United States, movie theatres are not licensed by the performing rights societies.[47] Movie producers obtain the performing rights for movies when they obtain synchronization licenses from the copyright owners.[48]

[h]—Foreign Performances

Performing rights societies exist in most countries, and have cooperative agreements to remit royalties from their respective territory to their fellow societies.

---

41   17 U.S.C. § 110(3).

42   If a concert promoter presents a concert that is not part of a church service and charges admission, then the usual performance licenses would be required in the event the concert included nondramatic copyrighted works.

43   17 U.S.C. §§ 110(1), 110(2).

44   17 U.S.C. § 110(4).

45   17. U.S.C. § 110(7).

46   17 U.S.C. § 110(6). Exemptions also are included for transmissions intended for the blind and other handicapped persons, see 17 U.S.C. § 110(8), and for social events organized by veterans' groups to which the general public is not invited. 17 U.S.C. § 110(10).

47   See *Alden-Rochelle, Inc. v. ASCAP*, 80 F. Supp. 900 (S.D.N.Y. 1948). However, outside the United States, performing rights societies do license movie theatres.

48   See § 4.06 *infra*, for a discussion of synchronization licenses.

ASCAP, BMI, and SESAC will receive and forward to their members foreign accountings. Many publishers have "sub-publishers" in foreign territories whose job is to collect monies from all sources in that territory. The sub-publisher will belong to the local PRO in its territory. It collects and forwards to the U.S. publisher any publisher-share royalties earned in the foreign territories. The author's share, however, will usually be transferred from the foreign PRO to the PRO in the United States, and then to the authors, without going through the publishing company.[49]

[i]—ASCAP and BMI Rate Court Rulings on Digital Media Rights and Pandora Radio

The advent of new digital music industry business models, such as digital radio streaming via Pandora and limited downloads via other types of services, led to several important new digital licensing models with overlapping interests: music publishers license digital mechanicals and digital performing rights simultaneously but through different mechanisms, while coexisting with sound recording digital performance licensing by record companies to the same digital services.

From the perspective of music publishers, their share of the new digital royalties, as compared to the record companies, was tightly constrained by the Copyright Act setting mechanical royalty rates and by the court-governed Consent Decrees that regulate public performance royalties charged by ASCAP and BMI. In an attempt to negotiate "market" rates not subject to regulatory and court restrictions, some large music publishers sought to withdraw from the PROs and privately negotiate with Pandora for only a subset of their overall rights, the so-called "Digital Media" performance rights.

Ultimately, the ASCAP and BMI rate courts determined that publishers could not withdraw the "digital rights subset" of their repertoire, which led to a different

---

49   Because other countries do not have the same antitrust laws as the United States, in other countries there is usually only one performing rights society for that territory, and the PRS's in other countries may also handle mechanical licensing as well as performing rights. Some of the leading foreign performing rights societies, all of whom have reciprocal agreements with the United States based PRS's, include the following, listed by their commonly used acronyms. For more information, see the Web site of the International Confederation of Societies of Authors and Composers ("CISAC"), at www.cisac.org:

Argentina: SADAIC; Australia: APRA; Austria: AKM; Belgium: SABAM; Brazil: UBC, ECAD; Canada: SOCAN; China: MCSC; Denmark: KODA; Finland: TEOSTO; Greece: AE; France: SACEM; Germany: GEMA; Hong Kong: CASH; Hungary: Artisjus; Iceland: STEF; India: IPRS; Ireland: IMRO; Israel: ACUM; Italy: SIAE; Japan: JASRAC; Lithuania: LATGA-A; Malaysia: MACP; Mexico: SACM; Netherlands: BUMA; New Zealand: APRA; Norway: TONO; Poland: ZAIKS; Portugal: SPA; Russia: RAO; Singapore: COMPASS; South Africa: SAMRO; Spain: SGAE; Sweden: STIM; Switzerland: SUISA; Turkey: MESAM; United Kingdom: PRS.

strategy, a request to the Department of Justice to review and update the ASCAP and BMI Consent Decrees supervised by the Southern District of New York courts.

In 2016, the Department of Justice issued a report declining to make any of the changes requested by ASCAP and BMI.[50] The DOJ did however propose that the PROs engage in so-called "100% licensing" or "full-work licensing" for co-owned works, using the established principles of U.S. copyright law that a co-owner may grant nonexclusive licenses subject only to a duty to account to the other owner(s). The Second Circuit subsequently upheld the fractional licensing status quo, holding that the BMI Consent Decree allowed it. [51]

[j]—Assignment of the Writer Share of Performing Rights Royalties

Writers or their heirs have the right to assign their writer share of public performance royalties from ASCAP, BMI, and SESAC to others, provided they give proper written notice to the PROs, who will then remit the royalty amounts to the assignee. Typically, where the writer has a relatively steady and predictable annual revenue, assigning that income is done in order to convert the revenue stream into a large lump sum for whatever financial reasons apply (pay off debts, purchase real estate, etc.). The assignment may be tied to repayment of the lump sum plus interest, or even become a permanent assignment, depending on the deal structure. The royalties paid by the PROs can continue for a considerable time, as they are tied to the duration of copyright of the musical works claimed by the writer.

Although such financial decisions may work well, two cases demonstrate the perils that can accompany these transactions.

In *Currency Corporation v. Wertheim, LLC*, two companies in the business of acquiring royalty revenue streams had a dispute revolving around acquisition of the writer share controlled by an elderly widow of a successful songwriter. Both companies had entered into agreements with the widow, in circumstances the court found "unconscionable," in dealings the court described as with "an unsuspecting elderly widow with short term memory loss, who had been institutionalized for mental illness."[52]

Dealing with legally unsophisticated writers and their heirs (who apparently did not consult an attorney) can also backfire. In *Gold Forever Music, Inc. v. Structured Asset Sales, LLC*, a writer sold his writer share of ASCAP royalties to one such company in

---

50   See Statement of the Department of Justice on the Closing of the Antitrust Division's Review of the ASCAP and BMI Consent Decrees, August 4, 2016, available at <*https://www.justice.gov/atr/file/882101/download*>.

51   See *United States v. Broad. Music, Inc.*, 720 F. App'x 14 (2d Cir. 2017)

52   See *Currency Corp. v. Wertheim, LLC,* No. B240444, 2013 WL 5434631 (Cal. App. Sept. 30, 2013).

2004, but apparently neglected to advise that he had previously parted with all rights and revenue in the subject songs decades previously.[53] As a result, the true owner of the royalties successfully brought suit.

In such cases where the recipient of the writer share is in dispute, and during the litigation, the PROs remain neutral pending the court's adjudication, and typically pay the royalties as they arise to the court via filing an interpleader, with the funds ultimately released by the court to the prevailing party when the matter is completed.

[5]—The Display Right

Another exclusive right given copyright owners is the right to publicly display a work. In the pre-Internet era, the display right had less relevance to the music industry. However, in the digital age, the display of song lyrics on the Internet and via technology such as karaoke machines has greatly enhanced the importance of the display right.[54]

[6]—Digital Performance Rights in Sound Recordings

The first five rights in Section 106 of the Copyright Act apply "across the board" in all technologies and distribution channels. The sixth right—the "digital performance right in sound recordings"—is more limited in scope.[55] It is a public performance right that is enjoyed not by songwriters and music publishers, but by performing artists and their record companies. Instead of being broadly applicable across all media such as television, terrestrial radio broadcasts (the traditional technology of through-the-air broadcast of radio signals), and the Internet, it is limited to so-called "digital performance" that takes place on the Internet, such as on Web sites that stream sound recordings, and on satellite radio.

---

53   See *Gold Forever Music, Inc. v. Structured Asset Sales*, LLC, No. B221921, (Cal. App. May 23, 2012). Not all writer royalty transactions are with corporations. See *Sepe v. Sepe-Wiesenfeld*, 2013 Cal. App. Unpub. LEXIS 3109 (Cal. App.2d Dist. May 2, 2013) (songwriter of "You're the First, the Last, My Everything" granted his brother half of his future royalties in exchange for $10,000, after songwriter's death his heirs ceased remitting payments to their uncle resulting in litigation).

54   See *Leadsinger, Inc. v. BMG Music Publishing*, 512 F.3d 522 (9th Cir. 2007). The display of lyrics on a karaoke machine screen, where the lyrics move across the screen in sync with the music, must be licensed separately in the nature of a sync license, and is not covered by compulsory mechanical license for reproducing sound recordings.

55   17 U.S.C. § 106(6). Note that the works subject to performance rights in Section 106(4) do not include sound recordings. Under Section 106(6), the performance right for sound recordings is limited because it is granted only with respect to the right "to perform the copyrighted work publicly by means of a digital transmission."

Sound recordings were not protected under the Copyright Act until 1972.[56] Thus, when sound recordings first achieved statutory protection in 1972, it was limited and did not include public performance. When new digital technologies, including the Internet, emerged in the 1990s, Congress granted copyright owners of sound recordings a limited public performance right limited to the new digital media of the Internet and satellite broadcasting with the Digital Performance Right in Sound Recordings Act of 1995,[57] and the closely related Digital Millennium Copyright Act of 1998 ("DMCA").[58] The tradeoff for the new right is that under certain conditions, in particular where a recording is streamed on the Internet, the license fees are compulsory, not subject to negotiation by the copyright owners, and set by the Copyright Royalty Judges at the Copyright Office. Although most other countries have a performance right for sound recording copyright owners on terrestrial radio, the United States limits the right to digital, online and satellite technology.[59]

Prior to the passage of the Music Modernization Act on October 11, 2018, sound recordings created prior to February, 1972 were protected under arcane state copyright laws and not the federal Copyright Act. This led to disputes over whether online digital services had to pay any performance rights at all for pre-1972 sound recordings under the untested state laws. FN 60. However, the MMA included provisions that granted limited

---

56 Sound Recording Act of 1971, Pub. L. No. 92-140, 85 Stat. 391 (Oct. 15, 1971). Prior to 1972, their protection arose under common law copyright. See *Capitol Records, Inc. v. Naxos of America Inc.*, 4 N.Y.3d 540, 797 N.Y.S.2d 352, 830 N.E.2d 250 (2005).

57 Pub. L. No. 104-39, 109 Stat. 336 (Nov. 1, 1995).

58 Pub. L. No. 105-304, 112 Stat. 2860 (Oct. 28, 1998).

59 SoundExchange is the collective licensing organization responsible for administering the rights, including collection of payments from Webcasters and the payment of royalties to record companies and recording artists. Just as the collective licensing organizations ASCAP and the Harry Fox Agency were initially formed by music publishers, SoundExchange has its origins in the trade organization for record companies, the Recording Industry Association of America ("RIAA"). Like the performing rights societies that pay separate "publisher share" and "author share" royalties, SoundExchange makes direct payments to performing artists and to the record company copyright owners as follows: 50% to record company; 45% to featured artists on the sound recording; 2.5% to backup musicians; and 2.5% to non-featured vocalists. 17 U.S.C. § 114(g). The digital performance right for sound recordings applies to commercially released audio recordings, and is codified in Section 114 of the Copyright Act, which sets out the statutory licensing scheme and the rates that have been established by a panel of Copyright Royalty Judges and published in the Code of Federal Regulations. See generally: 37 C.F.R. §§ 260-270 for current licensing fees. See also, www.soundexchange.com. The digital performing rights are for commercially released audio recordings, but do not extend to situations where an audio recording is included in an audiovisual work. If for example a sound recording is licensed for inclusion in a television program, and that television program is digitally streamed on the Internet, the digital performance right in sound recordings would not apply.

federal copyright protection for pre-1972 sound recordings such that they subsequently come within the licensing provisions for digital music services. [60]

[a]—Types of Webcasters[61]

[i]—Commercial Webcaster/Broadcast Simulcaster

A "commercial webcaster/broadcast simulcaster" is a "radio station that provides pure streams of musical works in a noninteractive, nonsubscription digital audio transmission service, including retransmissions on the Internet of terrestrial radio broadcast transmissions."[62] The primary purpose of the service must be to provide audio or other entertainment programming and not to sell, advertise, or promote particular products or services other than sound recordings, live concerts, or other music-related events.[63]

To be "noninteractive," a service may not offer "on-demand" access to individual sound recordings or offer programs that are "specially created for the recipient." Playing requests does not make a service interactive, provided that the service does not substantially consist of sound recordings that are performed within one hour of the time they are requested or at a designated time.[64]

[ii]—Noncommercial Webcaster

A "noncommercial webcaster/broadcast simulcaster" is any webcaster/simulcaster that (1) is exempt from taxation under Section 501 of the Internal Revenue Code of 1986;[65] (2) has applied in good faith to the Internal Revenue Service for exemption from taxation under Section 501 of the Internal Revenue Code and has a commercially reasonable expectation that such exemption shall be granted; or (3) is operated by a State or possession or any governmental entity or subordinate thereof, or by the United States or District of Columbia, for exclusively public purposes.

---

60   See MMA Title II Classics Protection and Access Act, Pub. L. No. 115-264. See also 17 U.S.C. §1401 Unauthorized use of pre-1972 sound recordings.

61   See also, the discussion of Internet radio music licensing in Chapter 5 *infra*.

62   See *Bonneville International Corp. v. Peters*, 347 F.3d 485 (3d Cir. 2003). Web streams of terrestrial radio signals come within Section 114 statutory licensing for performance of sound recordings.

63   17 U.S.C. § 114(j)(6).

64   17 U.S.C. §§ 114(j)(7), 114(j)(13).

65   28 U.S.C. § 501.

[iii]—Preexisting Subscription Service

A "preexisting subscription service" offers sound recordings by means of non-interactive, audio-only subscription digital transmissions that existed and offered such transmissions to the public for a fee on or prior to July 31, 1998.[66]

[iv]—Preexisting Satellite Digital Radio Service

A "preexisting satellite digital audio radio service" ("SDAR") is a subscription satellite digital audio radio service provided pursuant to a license issued by the FCC on or before July 31, 1998, and any renewal of such license to the extent of the scope of the original license.[67] The rates and terms applicable to the SDARS are the subject of a license agreement entered into between SoundExchange and the two SDAR services.[68]

[v]—Business Establishment Service

A "business establishment service" is a background music service that digitally delivers music to businesses to be played in stores, restaurants, offices, or retail locations.[69] The services are exempt from sound recording performance royalties under Section 114(d)(1)(C)(iv) of the Copyright Act, providing they do not exceed the sound recording performance complement. However, business establishment services must obtain a compulsory license under section 112(e) to make ephemeral recordings for the sole purpose of facilitating its exempt transmissions.[70]

[b]—Types of Uses for Digital Performing Rights for Sound Recordings

[i]—Non-Interactive Streaming

"Streaming" means that listeners can access and hear music on their computers without the storage of data files on the users' hard drives. It is similar to the terrestrial radio experience.[71] A terrestrial radio station that streams its signal on the Web falls into this category, for example. If a Web site or satellite sta-

---

66   17 U.S.C. § 114(j)(11). The three subscription services in this category are Music Choice, Muzak, and DMX Music, Inc.

67   The two SDARs are XM Satellite Radio, Inc. and SIRIUS.

68   17 U.S.C. § 114(j)(10).

69   "Business establishment service" is also referred to as "background" or "elevator" music.

70   17 U.S.C. § 114(d)(1)(C)(iv).

71   See *United States v. ASCAP*, 485 F. Supp.2d 438, 442 (S.D.N.Y. 2007). "[S]treaming . . . allows the real-time (or near real-time) playing of the song and does not result in the creation of a permanent audio file on the client computer." Note that streaming may invoke some temporary memory retention of the song file sufficient for the playing of the music, but no "permanent audio file" as noted by the court.

tion streams music, and the user is passive, i.e., cannot "interact" by selecting specific musical selections, a compulsory license scheme allows the Web site to obtain a statutory license for performing the sound recordings at a rate set by the Copyright Royalty Board.[72]

Streaming is subject to the Sound Recording Performance Complement, which is a set of restrictions aimed at keeping the streamed music random enough so that listeners do not have advance notice of particular songs to be played.[73] Non-interactive streaming of sound recordings is subject to compulsory licensing under Section 114(d)(2), administered by SoundExchange, with license fees determined by the Copyright Royalty Board, and published in the Federal Register.[74]

Pure streams constitute a public performance and must be licensed by ASCAP, BMI, and SESAC. Because pure streams do not involve a download other than the ephemeral copies made to facilitate transmission under Section 112(e), pure non-interactive streams are not currently subject to mechanical licensing of the underlying musical composition.

A Web site that streams sound recordings for listeners on a non-interactive basis needs two types of "blanket" licenses: (1) the traditional ASCAP/BMI/SESAC blanket licenses for the public performance of the underlying musical compositions on the Web site; and (2) a statutory license administered by SoundExchange for the digital performance of the sound recordings themselves.

[ii]—Interactive or On-Demand Streaming

To the extent a Web site offering streamed music allows the user to select specific musical works, the experience is deemed to be "interactive" or "on-demand."

---

72   See: 37 C.F.R. §§ 260-270 for fee schedules in all categories.

73   17 U.S.C. § 114(j)(13). The "sound recording performance complement" is the transmission during any three-hour period, on a particular channel used by a transmitting entity, of no more than—

"(A) 3 different selections of sound recordings from any one phonorecord lawfully distributed for public performance or sale in the United States, if no more than 2 such selections are transmitted consecutively; or (B) 4 different selections of sound recordings—(i) by the same featured recording artist; or (ii) from any set or compilation of phonorecords lawfully distributed together as a unit for public performance or sale in the United States, if no more than three such selections are transmitted consecutively: Provided, That the transmission of selections in excess of the numerical limits provided for in clauses (A) and (B) from multiple phonorecords shall nonetheless qualify as a sound recording performance complement if the programming of the multiple phonorecords was not willfully intended to avoid the numerical limitations prescribed in such clauses."

74   See: 37 C.F.R. §§ 260-270, setting out the current statutory licensing fees. See also, www.soundexchange.com.

On-demand streams of sound recordings fall outside the statutory licensing scheme of Section 114(d)(2) which is limited to noninteractive "pure" streaming. Web sites offering interactive or on-demand streams are subject to negotiated licenses with the sound recording copyright owners[75] and must be licensed by ASCAP, BMI, and SESAC in order to obtain the performance rights for the underlying musical composition.

With respect to the reproduction and distribution licensing of the underlying musical compositions embodied in the sound recordings, on-demand streams and so-called "limited" or "tethered" downloads (downloads that are for limited periods of time, then expire, sometimes called "conditional downloads") are licensed pursuant to a ruling by the Copyright Office's Copyright Royalty Board, which set the royalty rate per each stream via a complex formula based on 10.5% of the online service's revenues.[76]

[iii]—Digital Phonorecord Deliveries

Where the user can download and retain a file, through, for example, iTunes and other online digital music retailers, a digital phonorecord delivery occurs, and no compulsory licensing scheme applies.[77] The license is discretionary with the copyright owner and not represented by any collective licensing organization.

As for the underlying musical composition, the mechanical royalty is a Digital Phonorecord Download mechanical royalty that must be paid by the record company to the music publisher with respect to each recording digitally delivered. The DPD rate is the same as the rate for "physical" recordings.[78]

---

75   See 17 U.S.C. § 114(d)(3).

76   See 37 C.F.R. § 385. See also Melissa Ferrick, et al. v Spotify USA, Inc., Case 1:16-cv-08412-AJN (S.D.N.Y.) Class Action Settlement - $43.45 Million Dollars for unpaid interactive streaming mechanicals.

77   See 17 U.S.C. § 115(d), definition of a digital phonorecord delivery:

"(d) Definition.—As used in this section, the following term has the following meaning: A 'digital phonorecord delivery' is each individual delivery of a phonorecord by digital transmission of a sound recording which results in a specifically identifiable reproduction by or for any transmission recipient of a phonorecord of that sound recording, regardless of whether the digital transmission is also a public performance of the sound recording or any nondramatic musical work embodied therein. A digital phonorecord delivery does not result from a real-time, non-interactive subscription transmission of a sound recording where no reproduction of the sound recording or the musical work embodied therein is made from the inception of the transmission through to its receipt by the transmission recipient in order to make the sound recording audible."

78   See 37 C.F.R. § 385.

As regards the performance rights, courts have held that a digital download of a musical work is not a performance of that work and therefore does not invoke the performance right.[79]

[7]—Licensing Procedures

[a]—Filing of Notice

An online service that intends to offer non-interactive streamed Webcasts pursuant to the statutory licensing under Section 114 must first file a Notice of Use of Sound Recordings Under Statutory License.[80] The notice requests the Web site to identify the type of service they are: either a new subscription service or one of the preexisting services under the Copyright Act.

[b]—Reporting Requirements

The online service may report usage of sound recordings on either a per-performance basis, or an aggregate tuning hour basis.[81] The online service must file regular reports of use in the form of electronic data files. The reports must include specific identifying information that will enable SoundExchange to distribute royalties to those copyright owners and performers entitled to such royalties:

- name of the service making transmissions;

- identification of the transmission category from one of eleven choices;

- name of the featured artist;

- sound recording title;

- album title and marketing label OR International Standard Recording Code ("ISRC"); and

- aggregate tuning hours, channel or program name, and play frequency OR actual total performances.

---

79 See *United States v. ASCAP*, 627 F.3d 64 (2d Cir. 2010) (digital downloads of musical works do not constitute a public performance of that work).

80 37 C.F.R. § 270.1. For a copy of the notice, see http://www.copyright.gov/forms/form112-114nou.pdf.

81 See generally, www.soundexchange.com.

§4.04 Mapping the Copyright Coordinates

The following chart illustrates the types of licensing for recordings and broadcasts invoked by various uses, both analog and digital:

CHART: MUSIC COPYRIGHT BASICS FOR RECORDINGS AND BROADCASTS				
Type of Work & Format	Type of Use	Reproduction & Distribution Rights § 106(1)(3)	Musical Works Performing Rights § 106(4)	Digital Performance Rights in Sound Recordings § 106(6)
Nondramatic Musical Works (Physical)	Phonorecord of a sound recording, distributed in physical format (CD)	Mechanical License	ASCAP, BMI, SESAC blanket licenses for performances of the composition on radio	N/A
Nondramatic Musical Works (Digital)	Sound recording, distributed digitally or streamed online	Statutory mechanical license for DPDs, for tethered downloads, and on-demand streams 10.5% of service revenue. No mechanical license for pure streaming in compliance with § 114.	For online streams: ASCAP, BMI, SESAC blanket licenses for Web sites & satellite uses. For pure DPDs, currently no performance occurs so no PRS licenses	SoundExchange compulsory licenses for pure streaming of sound recordings. For on-demand streams or DPDs, negotiated licenses with copyright owners.
Nondramatic Musical Works (Sync)	Used in an audiovisual production (film/TV/commercial)	Sync license from copyright owner of underlying musical composition	ASCAP, BMI, SESAC for television broadcasts and webcasts. Movie theatre licenses in United States granted with sync license	N/A
Nondramatic Musical Works (PBS)	Used in an audiovisual production on Public Broadcasting Service (PBS)	Either special PBS sync license some publishers administer through Harry Fox Agency, or Section 118 sync license with rates under Copyright Act.	PBS blanket licenses from ASCAP, BMI, SESAC	N/A
Dramatic Musical Works, e.g. Opera or Musical (Physical & Digital)	Phonorecord of a sound recording, distributed in physical format (CD); and digital streaming or DPDs	Grand rights mechanical license must be negotiated with copyright owner. No compulsory license for grand rights works.	Dramatic works not covered by ASCAP, BMI, SESAC. Publisher must issue grand rights license for radio broadcasts.	SoundExchange compulsory licenses for pure streaming of sound recordings. Negotiated licenses with sound recording copyright owners for on-demand streams or DPDs.
Sound Recordings (Physical)	Phonorecord, for example, a sound recording used under license for a new CD compilation); and digital streaming or DPDs	Master License from sound recording copyright owner/record company will cover CDs and other physical formats.	N/A	For pure Web streaming, statutory licenses administered by SoundExchange. For on-demand streams and DPDs, negotiated license from the sound recording copyright owner.
Sound recordings (Digital)	Used in an audiovisual production (film/TV/commercial)	Master License from copyright owner/record company for audiovisual uses	N/A	N/A. Digital performance rights for sound recordings do not extend to sound recordings included within audiovisual works.

Ringtones		Master license from record company, mechanical license from music publisher	ASCAP, BMI, SESAC wireless music licenses	N/A

§4.05 Mechanical Licensing

Record companies and music publishers are two separate copyright owners, with the record company owning the copyright in the sound recording, and the music publisher owning the copyright in the underlying musical composition embodied in the sound recording.[82] Therefore, when a record company sells its sound recordings, it needs a license from the music publisher to also include the underlying musical composition. The name of this license is a "mechanical license," a somewhat arcane term from the early days of the music industry, described at the time as the inclusion of a musical composition in a "mechanical device" for reproducing sounds, such as a player piano or early Gramophone records.[83]

However, the valuable right to issue the first commercial release of a recording is still reserved by the music publisher.[84] Therefore, a recording artist needs the music publisher's

---

82   See: *EMI Entertainment World, Inc. v. Karen Records, Inc.*, 806 F. Supp.2d 697 (S.D.N.Y. 2011) (failure to obtain a mechanical license is copyright infringement); *Peer International Corp. v. Luna Records, Inc.*, 887 F. Supp. 560 (S.D.N.Y. 1995) (licenses terminated where no payment received); *Cherry River Music Co. v. Simitar Entertainment, Inc.*, 38 F. Supp.2d 310 (S.D.N.Y. 1999).

83   Mechanical licenses are required for recordings "made and distributed." 17 U.S.C. § 115(a). See *Apple Records, Inc. v. Capitol Records, Inc.*, 137 A.D.2d 50, 529 N.Y.S.2d 279 (1988). This case discusses the music industry practice of "drilling" holes in CDs that are intended for promotional use only. Drilling makes it impossible for a retailer to use free promotional CDs as the basis of any returns for credit. It may also form the basis of a record company claim or contractual provision with a recording artist that such promotional copies fall outside the need for payment of a mechanical license. In this case, the court stated "[p]laintiffs also allege that defendants distributed an excessive amount of promotional copies of Beatles' recordings, aimed not at gaining any needed publicity for the Beatles, but instead with the design to benefit defendant Capitol Records, who allegedly used the promotional copies as currency to gain promotional advantages for other of its artists. As many of these promotional records were, contrary to the normal practice, not 'drilled,' i.e., marked, to prevent retail sale and/or subsequent return to Capitol Records for credit, it is argued that this practice also served to dilute the legitimate market for sale of Beatles' recordings." *Id.*, 137 A.D.2d at 56-57.

It is unnecessary to distinguish between distributions arising from sales to consumers, and distribution arising from free or promotional copies. Note that while a record company may not be able to avoid paying mechanicals even on promotional copies, there may be contractual provisions with the recording artist stating that the record company is not responsible for payment of mechanicals for promotional copies. Under such provisions, an artist may find themselves responsible for mechanicals. See *Cafferty v. Scotti Brothers Records, Inc.*, 696 F. Supp. 193, 201-202 (S.D.N.Y. 1997) (noting a contractual provision whereby a record company could distribute a limited number of "free goods" without paying a mechanical license to the copyright owner of the musical compositions embodied in the sound recordings).

84   17 U.S.C. § 115(a)(1). See generally, *Cherry River Music Co. v. Simitar Entertainment, Inc.*, 38 F. Supp.2d 310 (S.D.N.Y. 1999). Note that mechanical licenses are issued for specific commercial releases and specific catalog

express consent to release the first commercial recording of a song, but does not need explicit permission from a music publisher to make a cover record of a nondramatic musical composition that has previously been commercially released.

As part of the statutory provisions for such cover recordings, artists can also create and perform their own musical arrangements of the song, so long as the new recording does not alter the lyrics or the fundamental character of the composition.[85] While the record company owns the copyright in the subsequent "cover" sound recording, the ability to make arrangements for the recording sessions does not grant to the record company any further copyright interests in any such arrangements, beyond their use for the recording itself.[86]

In exchange for the compulsory license, record companies pay to publishers a guaranteed royalty amount as set by Congress for each phonorecord distributed (the "statutory mechanical license" fee).[87] Because the compulsory mechanical license is for non-dramatic musical works only, the record company must negotiate the right to make recordings of dramatic works such as operas and musicals with the music publisher. As a practical matter, the music publisher will, in many cases, use the same rate schedule as that for non-dramatic works.[88]

Larger record companies will account for and pay mechanical royalties via quarterly statements remitted to either the music publisher, or, if the music publisher is a member, to the Harry Fox Agency.[89] Smaller companies that may plan to manufacture small quantities of CDs

---

number and format, of a sound recording. Where a sound recording that originally appeared on an artist's album is later released on a different product, for example a later "greatest hits" compilation, a new mechanical license must be obtained. See generally, *Fred Ahlert Music Corp. v. Warner/Chappell Music, Inc.*, 155 F.3d 17, 24-25 (2d Cir. 1998). The court in Ahlert ruled on issues relating to future royalties in the context of copyright terminations, but also confirmed the scope of a mechanical license is limited to a specific release.

85   17 U.S.C. § 115(a)(2).

86   17 U.S.C. § 115(a)(2). If a record company were to commission a full orchestral arrangement of a song for a recording session, for example, it would not need the publisher's permission. But after the recording session is concluded, the record company cannot sell or rent the orchestral arrangement without a license from the publisher. Similarly, should the performers desire to change the lyrics of the song in any substantive way, they would need the publisher's permission and cannot rely on the compulsory mechanical license.

87   37 C.F.R. § 255.

88   Mechanical licensing also applies to the Internet, where the term of art is "digital phonorecord deliveries" or "DPDs." 17 U.S.C. § 115(c)(3). Note that in both physical media such as CDs, and in online delivery of DPDs, the record company is responsible for accounting and remitting mechanical license fees to the music publishers or their agents, so-called "pass through" mechanical licensing.

89   The Harry Fox Agency is a mechanical licensing clearinghouse created by the National Music Publishers Association. The agency charges its member publishers a varying percentage of revenue collected for its services in acting as an agency for the administration of mechanical licenses. Whether the publisher or the songwriter, or both, pay for the Fox Agency commission can be a matter of dispute.

have the option of simply paying the entire mechanical royalty for the print run in advance. While the upfront costs may be a bit higher, the obligation to produce quarterly accounting statements of copies distributed and sold can be avoided.

Although Section 115 of the Copyright Act contains detailed provisions for obtaining a statutory compulsory mechanical license under the Act, most mechanical licensing is done on a routine "negotiated" licensing basis whereby the copyright owners waive some of the statutory formalities.[90] However, the granting of such negotiated mechanical licenses is a matter of transactional convenience for both parties. Nothing in that choice requires the copyright owner to alter any terms other than those that may be expressly altered. For example, a copyright owner using a negotiated mechanical license is under no obligation to license at a rate less than the full statutory rate.

The current mechanical royalty rates under the Copyright Act, effective as of January 1, 2006, are:

9.10 Cents for songs 5 minutes or less or 1.75 Cents per minute or fraction thereof over 5 minutes.[91]

For example for "long song" licensing:

5:01 to 6:00 = $.105 (6 x $.0175 = $.105)

6:01 to 7:00 = $.1225 (7 x $.0175 = $.1225)

7:01 to 8:00 = $.14 (8 x $.0175 = $.14)[92]

Another collective licensing organization for mechanical licensing in the United States is the American Mechanical Rights Agency, Inc. ("AMRA"). See www.amermechrights.com.

90   See 17 U.S.C. § 115(b)(2) (either a negotiated license, or a compulsory license under the statute, is required). See also, *The Rodgers and Hammerstein Organization v. UMG Recordings, Inc. and The Farm Club Online, Inc.*, 2001 WL 1135811 (S.D.N.Y. Sept. 26, 2001) (noting the difference between the statutory license and the negotiated license as stated in 17 U.S.C. § 115(b)(2), stating "[t]hus Congress clearly recognized that those like Defendants who wished to obtain a license to include a copyrighted work in a phonorecord had a choice either to serve the notice required to obtain a compulsory license or to obtain a 'negotiated license.' Congress manifested no preference for either of these licensing methods. By choosing to submit a license application to Harry Fox rather than serve the statutorily required notice, Defendants exercised the option Congress granted them to obtain a "negotiated license." They are, therefore, bound by the terms they negotiated."). *Id.*, 2001 WL 1135811, at *5.

91   37 C.F.R. § 255.1.

92   Since 1978, the rate has gradually increased from 2¢ to 9.10¢, the current rate, as published in the Code of Federal Regulations. 37 C.F.R. § 250. There are no legislative increases pending from the current 9.10¢ rate.

The statutory mechanical license is a maximum rate. It is therefore common for record companies to seek a reduction in the rate directly from the music publisher. A common request is 75% of the current statutory rate, or "75% of stat."

Ultimately, unless there is some contractual obligation to provide a reduced rate,[93] the music publisher can freely grant or deny the record company's request for a mechanical license rate discount. The publisher will then either issue a written license at the reduced rate, or provide written authorization for the Harry Fox Agency to issue the license at a reduced rate. The record company will be responsible for sending quarterly accountings, and payments, to the music publisher, or to the Harry Fox Agency if the publisher uses its administrative services.[94]

As noted above, compulsory mechanical licenses are only available after the song copyright owner has authorized the first commercial release of their song, as described in Section 115(a)(1) limiting compulsory licenses to "[w]hen phonorecords of a nondramatic musical work have been distributed to the public in the United States under the authority of the copyright owner."[95]

While the above provision protects the right of the copyright owner of the song to determine the first release, there are two other statutory prohibitions against compulsory mechanical licenses that protect the rights of the sound recording copyright owner, preventing licensing from occurring in circumstances including unauthorized bootleg recordings, and unauthorized distribution of the sound recording itself. Thus, in Section 115(a)(1) of the Copyright Act:

> "[a] person may not obtain a compulsory license for use of the work in the making of phonorecords duplicating a sound recording fixed by another unless:
>
> "(i) such sound recording was fixed lawfully; and
>
> "(ii) the making of the phonorecord was authorized by the owner of copyright in the sound recording. . . ."[96]

[1]—Digital Distribution and Mechanicals

Digital distribution of recordings is also covered by mechanical licenses. Under the Orrin G. Hatch – Bob Goodlatte Music Modernization Act passed on October 11, 2018

---

93   In some songwriter publishing contracts, it is acknowledged that the songwriter will make records and the record company will insist on paying 75% of the full statutory rate.

94   In one case, a recording artist who claimed that record sales were under-reported by her record company sought copies of the record company's mechanical license accountings to third party music publishers as evidence of actual sales. See *Connie Franconero v. Universal Music Corp.*, 2002 WL 31682648 (S.D.N.Y. Nov. 27, 2002).

95   See 17 U.S.C. § 115(a)(1).

96   See: 17 U.S.C. §§ 115(a)(1)(i), 115(a)(1)(ii).

(Pub. L. No. 115-264), mechanical licensing for interactive streaming services will in the future be managed by the Mechanical Licensing Collective ("MLC") which, instead of individual mechanical licenses, will offer blanket licensing services between digital music providers and music publishers.

[a]—Digital Phonorecord Deliveries

A Digital Phonorecord Delivery ("DPD") is a complete download with the computer file retained by the user, currently licensed at the same statutory rates as for physical phonorecords.[97] Because downloading a DPD does not invoke an audible performance of the work, courts have held that a DPD is not a "performance" under the Copyright Act; therefore, performing rights licenses are not required for businesses that offer downloads without audible performances of the complete musical works.[98]

As noted above, record companies often include a "controlled compositions" clause in their recording agreements with artists, providing that for compositions written by the artist and recorded by them the record company is granted a discount from the full statutory mechanical licensing rate.[99] A typical controlled compositions mechanical royalty clause provides for the record company to pay 75% of the statutory mechanical license rate.

While controlled composition clauses continue to apply to "physical" phonorecords such as CDs, the Digital Performance Rights in Sound Recordings Act of 1995, which set royalty rates for DPDs, has a provision that preserves the full 100% statutory mechanical license rate for DPDs, but only with respect to recording agreements entered into after June 22, 1995.[100] While this may ensure that music publishers issue DPD mechanical licenses to record companies at the full DPD statutory rate, it may be that the recording artist's agreement with the record label still preserves some right of the record label to recoup against the artist's royalties the difference between the 100% mechanical license rate and a reduced "controlled compositions" license rate.

---

97 See *Tufamerica, Inc. v. The Orchard Enterprises, Inc.*, 2011 WL 4946663 (S.D.N.Y. Oct. 14, 2011) (dispute over DPD mechanical license payments between copyright owner and digital online music service). See also, *Napster, LLC v. Rounder Records Corp.*, 761 F. Supp.2d 200 (S.D.N.Y. 2011) (describing agreement whereby digital online music service was responsible for paying DPD mechanical royalties).

98 *United States v. ASCAP*, 485 F. Supp.2d 438 (S.D.N.Y. 2007), *aff'd* 627 F.3d 64 (2d Cir. 2010) (downloading a digital file does not constitute a performance of the song embodied in the file).

99 See § 4.12[1][m] infra.

100 See 17 U.S.C. § 115(c)(3)(E) (1995), codifying the Digital Performance Right in Sound Recordings Act of 1995, Pub. L. No. 104-39, 109 Stat. 336 (amending, *inter alia*, 17 U.S.C. §§ 114, 115) (enacted Nov. 1, 1995).

[b]—Limited or "Tethered" Downloads

Limited—or "tethered"—downloads occur where a file is downloaded for a fixed period of time,[101] or as a "limited use download," which governs the number of times a song may be played. Limited downloads are subject to a mechanical licensing rate based on 10.5% of the online service's revenues.[102] Under the Music Modernization Act, the Mechanical Licensing Collective will offer blanket licenses at rates to be determined.

[c]—Streaming

Streamed files are not fully downloaded, but merely stored on the recipient's computer for the length of the song.[103] Streamed files constitute a performance and must be licensed by a PRS. They are not currently licensed as mechanicals because there is no download beyond the temporary file in the computer's memory for the purposes of streaming. Any copies of such streamed recordings made by the transmitting entity fall within the ephemeral recordings exceptions under § 12(e).[104]

[d]—On-Demand or Interactive Streaming

On-demand or interactive streams are songs that the user may select and listen to at their discretion, but are not downloaded and retained. Mechanicals for on-demand streams are licensed at a rate based on 10.5% of the online service's revenues.[105] Under the Music Modernization Act, the Mechanical Licensing Collective will offer blanket licenses at rates to be determined.

[e]—Ringtones

Ringtones are musical snippets played on a mobile phone in lieu of the traditional telephone "ring." The two types of ringtones are (1) "phonic," which is the song rendered as a MIDI file, using the sounds available on the phone itself, and (2) "pre-recorded," which uses actual clips from a sound recording.[106] The mechanical license royalty rate for ringtones is currently 24¢ per ringtone.[107]

---

101   Either as a "limited-time download" for a fixed number of days.

102   See 37 C.F.R. § 385.

103   Typically in the case of webcasting "online radio" services.

104   17 U.S.C. § 112(e).

105   See 37 C.F.R. § 385. See also Melissa Ferrick, et al. v Spotify USA, Inc., Case 1:16-cv-08412-AJN (S.D.N.Y.) Class Action Settlement - $43.45 Million for unpaid interactive streaming mechanicals.

106   The sound recording would be licensed from the record company that holds the copyright.

107   See 37 C.F.R. § 385.3.

[f]—New Categories of Online Services

Under industry negotiated revisions to Section 115 of the Copyright Act that take effect on January 1, 2013, mechanical royalty rates for several newly recognized types of online digital music services include:

- Paid locker services: subscription-based locker services providing on-demand streaming and downloads;

- Purchased content lockers: a free locker functionally provided to a purchaser of a permanent digital download, ringtone, or CD where the music provider and locker have an agreement;

- Limited offerings: subscription-based service offering limited genres of music or specialized playlists;

- Mixed service bundles: for example, a locker service, limited interactive service, downloads or ringtones combined with a non-music product such as a mobile phone, consumer electronics device or Internet service; and

- Music bundles: bundling music products such as CDs, ringtones and permanent digital downloads.[108]

[2]—Licensing Procedures

Even though the NMPA created the Harry Fox Agency as an administration clearinghouse to process compulsory mechanical licenses and collect payments from record companies on behalf of publishers, not all music publishers use it to administer mechanical licenses. Because the Fox Agency charges its publisher members for its mechanical license administration services, some publishers instead issue their own licenses as a standard licensing transaction.[109]

Of course, the first step in any licensing transaction is to identify and locate the copyright owner of a musical composition. Online searches by song title can be conducted at the following Web sites.

Performing Rights Societies Database:

---

108   See Copyright Royalty Board ("CRB") Section 115 Settlement Fact Sheet, available at http://www.nmpa.org/pdf/whats_new/CRBSection115SettlementFactSheet.docx.pdf. Under the announced Section 115 settlement, the permitted length of promotional sound recording clips that online download services such as iTunes, Amazon, and Google may provide to their potential customers will be extended from thirty seconds to ninety seconds. See 7 C.F.R. § 385.14(d), "Promotional Royalty Rate."

109   A search of the Harry Fox Agency Web site or a phone call to the publisher of record will quickly determine whether a publisher uses the Harry Fox Agency to administer mechanical licenses or handles the licenses itself.

www.ascap.com

www.bmi.com

www.sesac.com

Harry Fox Agency Database:

www.songfile.com

U.S. Copyright Office Database:

www.copyright.gov/records

However, where the composition has never been recorded before, the publisher can refuse a request for the first commercial release. Exceptions to the general rule include situations in which the composition is a dramatic musical work subject to a negotiated grand rights recording license, or where the performers seek to change the lyrics or alter the character of the composition beyond the scope of the compulsory mechanical license.[110]

Once contacted, publishers issue mechanical licenses as a routine matter. If the publisher cannot be located or does not respond, there are formal procedures to follow to obtain the statutory "compulsory" license. A statutory notice must be served on the copyright owner within thirty days of making the recording, and prior to release.[111] In the event the owner cannot be located, notice may be served on the Copyright Office. If a statutory notice is used, it must comply with the format set out in the Code of Federal Regulations.[112] If the copyright owner cannot be located, the notice can be served on the Copyright Office.[113] Failure to comply fully with the statutory license requirements for timely service and filing makes it impossible to obtain a compulsory license, and unless

---

110   17 U.S.C. § 115(a)(2). But see, *Campbell v. Acuff-Rose Music, Inc.*, 510 U.S. 569, 114 S.Ct. 1164, 127 L.Ed.2d 500 (1994) (parody lyrics of song "Pretty Woman," though unlicensed, held to be a noninfringing transformative fair use). For small quantities of recordings, mechanical licenses paid for in full in advance can be obtained online at www.harryfox.com.

111   17 U.S.C. § 115(b).

112   38 C.F.R. §§ 201.18(c) and 201.18(d). The Code of Federal Regulations ("C.F.R.") also establishes the requirements for reporting royalties.

113   17 U.S.C. § 115(b)(1).

the copyright owner is willing to negotiate a license, the recording will constitute an infringement.[114]

In the event the record company wants to pay a reduced mechanical license rate, it must seek the publisher's written permission and confirmation of any rate reduction before the Harry Fox Agency will process a mechanical license.

[3]—Importation

Under Section 602(2)(a) of the Copyright Act, recordings imported from overseas must be licensed upon import into the United States.[115] The import license is in addition to the mechanical license. Currently, the Henry Fox Agency's import license fee is the same as the statutory mechanical license fee.[116]

[4]—Broadcast Mechanicals Paid Outside the United States

Outside the United States, performing rights societies in other countries, or their equivalents that specialize in collecting mechanical royalties, may collect from broadcasters "broadcast mechanical royalties" based on television broadcasts of motion pictures and television programming containing music. Such broadcast mechanicals are separate from public performance rights royalties. This is an additional economic benefit for composers as compared to U.S.-based mechanicals which are limited to sound recording distribution or interactive streaming, but do not include broadcasts of music recordings embedded in the audiovisual soundtrack.[117]

The United States based PROs (ASCAP, BMI, SESAC, GMR) deal only in the public performance right, thus payments from PROs in the UK or Europe designated as broadcast mechanicals may not ultimately reach U.S.-based composers and lyricists, unless they

---

114   17 U.S.C. § 115(b)(2). See also, *Cherry River Music Co. v. Simitar Entertainment, Inc.*, 38 F. Supp.2d 310 (S.D.N.Y. 1999) (failure to obtain compulsory license in required time frame is fatal to obtaining compulsory license).

115   See the Harry Fox Agency import licensing form in the forms accompanying this treatise. See also, *T.B. Harms Co. v. Jem Records, Inc.*, 655 F. Supp. 1575 (D.N.J. 1987) (recordings of song "Ol' Man River" manufactured in New Zealand, where mechanical royalties were duly paid to copyright owners of underlying musical composition, were also subject to importation license and fees upon import into the United States under Section 602 of the Copyright Act).

116   See *T.B. Harms Co. v. Jem Records, Inc.*, 655 F. Supp. 1575 (D.N.J. 1987) (recording of "Ol' Man River" lawfully manufactured in New Zealand, where compulsory mechanical licenses were obtained, still subject to § 602 importation license).

117   See, e.g. the web site of the UK's PRS (Performing Rights Society) and MCPS (Mechanical Copyright Protection Society), noting that the MCPS collects and pays royalties to its members including "TV, film, or radio:" <https://www.prsformusic.com/what-we-do/prs-and-mcps>.

have a sub-publisher or agent based in those territories who can ensure the broadcast mechanicals are collected and remitted overseas back to the composer or lyricist based in the United States. Where a composer is a direct member of an overseas PRO or mechanical collection organization, the composer may be entitled to directly collect their share of such broadcast mechanicals, similar to the way the U.S.-based PROs pay the writer share directly to the writer.

Film and television score agreements, including any exhibit thereto such as a "Certificate of Authorship," may contain provisions referring to "EEC" or European Economic Community rights the producer asks the composer to assign to the production company. It should be confirmed whether such rights include some direct writer share of overseas broadcast mechanicals that should be reserved to the composer, similar to the writer share of PROs royalties, which are paid directly to the composer even where the background score is a work made for hire owned by the production company.

[5]—The Music Moderation Act of 2018

Several of the complex music industry licensing practices and applicable Copyright Act provisions changed significantly with the passage of the Orrin G. Hatch and Bob Goodlatte Music Modernization Act on October 11, 2018, Pub. L. No. 115-264 ("MMA"). The MMA addressed several areas of the music industry that needed updating as a result of the increasing role of changing digital technologies, especially the popularity of online streaming as the main music delivery technology.

The MMA is divided into three sections summarized as follows, with the highlight being the creation of a new collective licensing organization, the Mechanical Licensing Collective or MLC, for blanket licensing of interactive online streaming royalties payable from digital music services to music publishers, the so-called "streamed mechanicals." As of this writing, the MLC is in the early stages of being organized and will become operational over time, adding a new and important licensing collective to the group including for performing rights ASCAP, BMI, SESAC and GMR, and for digital sound recording non-interactive performing rights SoundExchange.

Title I: Title I of the MMA created the MLC, and changed the streamed mechanical license rate setting process at the Copyright Royalty Board to a "willing buyer willing seller" basis for future licensing rate determinations. It also changed the Department of Justice Consent Decrees for the two regulated PROs, ASCAP and BMI, to replace designated judges in the Southern District of New York with the standard random assignment of judges to each rate court litigation.

Title II: Title II of the MMA, also known as the Classics Protection and Access Act, granted pree-1972 sound recordings partial protections under the Copyright Act.

For example, pre-1972 recordings are now including in digital performing rights for sound recordings. However some federal Copyright Act provisions still do not apply to pre-1972 sound recordings, for example termination rights. In practice, this means that digital music service providers will include all pre-1972 sound recordings in their licensing, either via SoundExchange for noninteractive services, or in voluntary private agreements for interactive digital music services.

Title III: Also known as the Allocation for Music Producers Act, Title III confirms that for noninteractive digital sound recording performances administered by SoundExchange, the royalty due to the producer of the recording will be paid by SoundExchange pursuant to a letter of direction instructing SoundExchange to make the payments. Previously, the statute allowed only for payments to the featured artist and to side-musicians, and now producers are statutorily included as well.

§4.06 Synchronization ("Sync") License

What rights are invoked when the producer of a film or television production decides to include a musical recording on the soundtrack?[118]

The sound recording will contain two different copyrights: the underlying musical composition owned by a music publisher, and the sound recording, owned by the record company. The license to include the musical composition[119] in the film is called a synchronization license, commonly referred to as a "synch" or "sync" license.[120]

---

118   Under the Copyright Act, audiovisual works are

"works that consist of a series of related images which are intrinsically intended to be shown by the use of machines or devices such as projectors, viewers, or electronic equipment, together with accompanying sounds, if any, regardless of the nature of the material objects, such as films or tapes, in which the works are embodied."

17 U.S.C. § 101.

119   The license to include the sound recording in the film is a "master" license, discussed *infra*.

120   The term "synchronization" comes from using music in a timed sequence with visual images. See *Freeplay Music, Inc. v. Cox Radio, Inc.*, 404 F. Supp.2d 548 (S.D.N.Y. 2005). The opinion in Freeplay Music provides not only a description of what a synchronization license is, but an explanation of the differences between the synchronization right which arises from the copyright owner's exclusive right of reproduction, and performance rights, which arise from the exclusive right of public performance:

  The Copyright Act does not explicitly define or confer any separately-labeled "synchronization" right. It does, however, give the copyright holder the exclusive right (among others) "to reproduce the copyrighted work in copies or phonorecords." 17 U.S.C. § 106(1). As the Second Circuit has described it, "the so-called synchronization right, or 'synch' right . . . [is] the right to reproduce the music onto the soundtrack of a film or a videotape in synchronization with the action. The 'synch' right is a form of the reproduction right also created by statute as one of the exclusive

There are no collective licensing organizations in the United States that currently grant sync licenses. Unlike mechanical license rates, which are set by Congress, and unlike ASCAP/BMI/SESAC blanket license rates that are subject to court approval, the price of a license is a matter of negotiation between the parties. Sync fees can be in the form of a one-time flat fee, or in the case of media available for sale or download, in the form of a per-unit or percentage of sales royalty. Therefore, the television or film producer will have to go directly to the music publisher to negotiate the license.

[1]—Synchronization Licensing Steps

[a]—Identify the Publisher

The online title databases of ASCAP, BMI, and SESAC are essential tools to identify and approach the publisher of a song.[121] All three performing rights societies have search engines for their repertory of works. A typical search will indicate the names of the publishers, including the contact information. Administration rights

---

rights enjoyed by the copyright owner." *Buffalo Broadcasting Co., Inc. v. Am. Soc'y of Composers*, Authors & Publishers, 744 F.2d 917, 920 (2d Cir. 1984). The court went on to note, "When [a] producer wishes to use outside music in a film or videotape program, it must obtain from the copyright proprietor the 'synch' right in order to record the music on the soundtrack of the film or tape." Id. at 921. Such a license is necessary because "incorporating a copyrighted sound recording into the soundtrack of a taped commercial television production infringes the copyright owner's exclusive right of reproduction." *Agee v. Paramount Communications, Inc.*, 59 F.3d 317, 319 (2d Cir. 1995).

The exclusive right to reproduce a copyrighted composition or recording, of which the synchronization right is an aspect or subdivision, is distinct from the right, separately granted to a copyright holder by 17 U.S.C. § 106(4), to perform a copyrighted musical work publicly. The distinction, at least in its most common applications, is straightforward: performing a copyrighted musical composition (say, singing Bob Dylan's song "Blowin' in the Wind") on a radio show constitutes a performance of the work; incorporating a tape of a copyrighted recording into a television commercial or the soundtrack of a movie (say, copying the recording of Mr. Dylan singing "Blowin' in the Wind" onto the soundtrack of a commercial for a store selling kites or a fiction film about hang-gliders) constitutes a reproduction of the work (specifically, in the form of synchronization).

Rights to perform and reproduce copyrighted works are separately granted and may be separately licensed. For example, both musical compositions such as songs, 17 U.S.C. § 102(a)(2), and particular sound recordings embodying versions of those compositions, id. § 102(a)(7), may be copyrighted, but different rights attach to each. Thus, any copyright confers on its owner the exclusive right to reproduce the copyrighted work. Id. § 106(1). However, while a copyright in a musical work confers the exclusive right to perform the copyrighted work publicly, id. § 106(4), a copyright in a sound recording does not. Id. §§ 106(4), 114(a). Although the owner of a copyright in the musical composition holds the exclusive right both to reproduce and to perform the composition, he or she may license, or decline to license, either right separately.

Id. at 551–552. See also, *Bourne v. The Walt Disney Co.*, 68 F.3d 621 (2d Cir. 1995) (discussing sync licensing in contexts including motion pictures and television advertising). See also, *Leadsinger, Inc. v. BMG Music Publishing*, 512 F.3d 522 (9th Cir. 2008) (karaoke featuring lyrics on screen requires sync license).

121   See: www.ascap.com; www.bmi.com; www.sesac.com.

and ownership do change regularly for some catalogs, so contacting the publisher to confirm current ownership is a good idea. Virtually all publishers will ask for the details of the sync request in writing, and most have forms for supplying information of the proposed use.[122]

Where more than one publisher is listed, the general rule of thumb is to contact the first publisher listed and confirm which of the publishers administers the rights and actually negotiates the agreement on behalf of all the other publishers. Where there may be multiple publishers of a song, most of the music industry practices "fractional licensing," i.e. licensing only their proportional fraction of ownership, notwithstanding copyright law's well established principle that any co-owner of a copyright may independently grant non exclusive licenses, subject to a duty to account to the other owners. In practice, while any co-owner could proceed this way, few if any music publishers want to have any responsibility or duty to account to other co-owners.[123]

[b]—Sync Licensing Concepts from the Publisher's Perspective

Use of music in an audiovisual work creates immediate associations in the public's mind. This can increase public interest in a song, or potentially harm it. The publisher will therefore have two perspectives about a proposed usage; the "micro" perspective relative to the exact license usage proposed, and the "macro" perspective relative to the long-term value of the copyright. The publisher must assess whether the audiovisual work is objectionable in any way.[124-125]

[i]—Promotional Value

When music is used in a film or television production, it can bring great value to that production by evoking moods and emotions that give the story depth. But such usage may also turn out to be valuable advertising for the music publisher, not only for the song itself, but potentially for other songs by the same songwriter. A well-placed sync license can "break" a new song or artist, and it can revive interest in older works that comprise the "catalog" portion of a music publisher's holdings. There are more immediate, concrete benefits as well. The performing

---

122   Samples of sync license forms are included in the forms accompanying this book.

123   See *Oddo v. Ries*, 743 F.2d 630 (9th Cir. 1984). Each co-owner of a copyright has an independent right to use or license use of the copyright, subject to a duty to account to other co-owners for any profits.

124-126   For example, a highly violent film, or an extremist political association, or an ad for products might subject the song to ridicule and lower its long-term value.

rights royalties that will be generated if and when the production is shown on various forms of television or cable licensed by performing rights societies.[126]

[ii]—Related Performing Rights Income

It is important that a sync license require that the producers of the film submit to the publisher the production cue sheet, which lists all the copyrighted music in the film (the music "cues") to the relevant performing rights societies. The license should require the producer to warrant that the producer will only authorize broadcasts of the film for media such as television, satellite, cable, or the Internet, where those distribution channels in turn are properly licensed for performing rights. Every time the film is shown on television, the performing rights societies can refer to the cue sheet to confirm which songs are included in the broadcast. They can then apportion a percentage of the broadcaster's blanket performing rights royalties to the publisher and authors of that song.

The same provisions will apply to television broadcasts worldwide, by virtue of performing rights societies abroad that collect and forward the royalties to the appropriate United States performing rights society.

[iii]—Scope of Use

As we have seen, not all uses of a musical work in a television or film production are the same. In order to determine a sync license fee, the music publisher will want considerable detail regarding the amount of music used, and how it is used, either background usage, or feature/foreground usage, which involves the performers in the film performing the work—for example, where a character in a film sings the song. Greater duration and foreground use will command a higher license fee than shorter, background uses.

[iv]—Step Deals

Although film and television makers should try to obtain all rights in perpetuity, in many cases music publishers will offer quotes for a "menu" of uses, a so-called "step" deal, in which the price escalates in proportion to the scope of the use. The producer must then decide what rights are most immediately required and how that fits within the budget.

Publishers divide potential distribution of the audiovisual work into several categories, including:

---

126   For example, a successful motion picture will be shown on television for decades after its initial release, where it will earn public performance royalties for the publisher and songwriters for years.

Limited Theatrical: Film festivals, usually with a limited number of screens to distinguish from broader releases

Theatrical: broad commercial release

Video: including DVD, on demand, downloads, and digital streaming on the Internet or mobile devices such as phones

Television: including broadcast, cable, and satellite, and noncommercial services such as PBS

Computer Games: the use of music in computer games as part of the musical score invokes a sync license[127]

New Media: new platforms for distribution, such as online streaming of programs, streaming to mobile phones, downloads, electronic and computer games including online live gaming, etc.[128]

[v]—Author Approvals

The music publisher may be contractually obligated to seek the approval of the songwriter or her heirs, or obligated to refuse a license in certain circumstances based on the content of the production. In many cases, although the publisher will have to go through the potentially time-consuming process of contacting the artist or her representatives for the necessary approvals, it may be that the artist has a contractually limited time in which to grant approval, after which the publisher is free to grant approval. Always ask if there is a time limit on the artist's right to approve.

[vi]—Most Favored Nations

A copyright owner is free to negotiate any fee that the market will bear. In the case of a production requiring multiple sync licenses from different owners, only the producer will know the full scope of the number of licenses needed and the fees quoted. In order to protect themselves financially, copyright owners issue sync licenses on a "most favored nations" ("MFN") basis, meaning the copyright owner will not accept a license fee less than the fee paid to other copyright owners for comparable uses. It then becomes the obligation of the producer to carefully assemble all the sync license quotes before accepting the fees, and to

---

127   Where the game software package also includes the full track as a "bonus," apart from visual elements, a mechanical license right may be invoked as well.

128   Each technology represents another business entity that may be seeking a license to support its business model. Therefore, each format will have to be carefully considered to assess its likely economic impact, the security of digital delivery, longevity, etc. Producers will want all conceivable technological rights for their program so they have the freedom to distribute on any platform now known or invented in the future. Such digital rights will typically come at a premium from the music publisher.

negotiate everyone down to approximately the same amount. Otherwise, a high license fee granted to one owner may effectively require the producer to give all other owners the same amount.

Because sync license requests are usually based on uses of varying duration, the producer is well-advised to analyze the license fee quotes and uses to arrive at the actual "per minute" average rate for each owner. With this information, the producer may be able to achieve some level of MFN parity between varying license fees. If that can be accomplished, it may be easier to negotiate by telling all copyright owners that they are getting the same "per minute" rate, pro-rated for the duration of their particular usage.

[vii]—Cue Sheets

The producer is obligated to supply to the music publisher a "cue sheet," a chart listing each segment of music used in the production, known as a music "cue," including its duration, publisher, composer, and performing rights society affiliation. The music publisher will send a copy of the cue sheet to the relevant PRS so that it can log the performance of the music publisher's song whenever the production is shown on television or cable, or exhibited in movie theaters outside the United States, where public performances are also licensed.[129]

[viii]—Non-Exclusivity

Sync licenses are always non-exclusive. The music publisher can therefore also license the musical composition to other filmmakers at any time.

The typical grant of rights in a sync license will specify the scope of the license, as in the following example of a "grant of rights" summary section, including initially limited rights for theatrical and festival screenings, and a "step up" option for more comprehensive rights in the future for DVD ("Video Option"), and for worldwide television ("TV Option"):

PRODUCTION:	FILM TITLE
CREDIT INFORMATION:	Motion Picture
COMPOSITION:	SONG TITLE
WRITER(S):	SONG AUTHORS

---

129   ASCAP has a sample cue sheet, which is included in the forms accompanying this treatise. It is also available at http://www.ascap.com/musicbiz/cue_sheet_corner/pdf/SampleCueSheet.pdf.

PUBLISHER(S):	Used by Permission of PUBLISHER NAME. All rights reserved.
% OWNED/CONTROLLED:	Fifty Percent (50%)
THERE MAY BE A CO-PUBLISHER WITH THE OTHER 50% U.S. SOCIETY(IES):	ASCAP
MFN:	With Co-Publishers and Master Initial
TERRITORY:	United States and Canada
PRODUCTION:	FILM TITLE
TERM:	Three (3) year(s)
USE/TIMING:	Background Vocal/1:00
RIGHTS GRANTED:	Limited Theatrical (up to 25 screens), Non-theatrical (excluding Common Carriers, Military Bases and Oil Rigs)
FEE:	_____
Video Option:	
TERRITORY:	World
TERM:	Perpetuity
USE/TIMING:	Background Vocal/1:00
RIGHTS GRANTED:	All Video NKHD ("Now Known or Hereafter Discovered")
FEE:	_____
TV Option:	
TERRITORY:	World
TERM:	Perpetuity
USE/TIMING:	Background Vocal/1:00
RIGHTS GRANTED:	All TV Media (Free, Basic, and Pay TV w/DBS, PPV, VOD, Internet, Wireless, Non-Theatrical—which includes Common Carriers)
FEE:	_____
SUPPLEMENTAL PROVISIONS:	None[131]

[ix]—Credits

The publisher will provide information for end credit in the films, stating the title of the work, and acknowledgment of the music publisher's name or other

---

130   See the Sync License Forms included in the online forms.

information. This credit line is important for the producer because it signifies that the music rights were indeed cleared, information the producer will need in any event when it enters into distribution or broadcast agreements.[131]

[x]—License Fees

Sync license fees for incorporating the composition into the audiovisual production are typically on a flat fee basis, depending on the scope of rights granted. In a "step" deal, there may be an initially lower fee for a narrow scope of rights, with a "menu" for broader rights and increased fees available at a later time.

There are at least two ways of arriving at a license fee where usage also includes the sale or licensing of media such as DVDs or paid downloads. One way is to arrive at a "per unit" formula, similar to the concept of a mechanical license fee, in which a set amount is due for every copy manufactured.[132] The publisher may negotiate whatever per unit royalty license fee it wishes. Although there is no statutory reason that such sync license fees be similar to compulsory mechanical license fees, in some cases, the music publisher may arrive at a per-unit royalty that may be similar to what the compulsory mechanical rate would have been. In the case of a per-unit royalty, the publisher may also negotiate advances against future sales, or license only one manufacturing run at a time.

The second licensing technique is based on a percentage of revenue. Typically this would be a pro rata calculation that takes into account the retail selling price, then estimates a pro rata share of an overall royalty for the music. For example, if a DVD sells at retail for $20.00, and if the royalty for music is 15%, or $3.00, a publisher whose copyrights represent 10% of the total music in the DVD might charge $.30 per unit ($3.00 × 10% = $.30).

§4.07   Ephemeral Rights

When a copyrighted musical work is performed in a live performance, the only license needed is a public performance license, because there has been no usage that implicates other protected rights.[133]

---

131   See Chapter 1 for an in-depth discussion of the agreements producers must make with broadcasters and distributors, pursuant to which the producer must warrant they have cleared all rights.

132   Note that under 17 U.S.C. § 115(a), compulsory mechanical royalties for phonorecords are payable on every unit made and distributed. There is no distinction between distribution arising from sale, or from copies given away without charge.

133   See the discussion of Section 112 ephemeral licensing infra.

Once the line is crossed between a live performance and a permanent copy that can be viewed at any future time, the copyright licensing scheme expands from the section 106(4) performance right, to implicating additional rights based on section 106(1) reproduction rights and section 106(3) distribution rights.[134]

[1]—Television Broadcasts

To facilitate network transmissions, there is a limited reproduction right for broadcasters known as the "ephemeral recordings exception."[135] This exception allows television and radio entities ("transmitting organizations") the right to make one copy of an otherwise live or tape delay program containing copyrighted music for later broadcast or transmission.[136] These copies are "ephemeral" because of the requirement that they be used for no more than six months, after which they must either be destroyed or kept for archival purposes only.[137] The ephemeral recording must be "retained and used solely by the transmitting organization that made it," and must be used solely for that organization's own transmission within its "local service area."[138] The most important requirement is that the music in the program be otherwise licensed for public performance, either directly from the copyright owner (in the case of Pre-cleared music), or via the performing rights clearinghouses ASCAP, BMI, and SESAC.[139]

Section 112 carves out a narrow exception to permit broadcasters to make copies of live or tape delay programs for distribution purposes, without the need for a sync license. If the usage is "live," only a performing rights blanket license is required. If copies of the

---

134   See *Angel Music Inc. v. ABC Sports, Inc.*, 631 F. Supp. 429 (S.D.N.Y. 1986). In *Angel Music*, the broadcaster's BMI public performance license included language that allowed for "incidental" copying of music by the broadcaster for purposes of "delayed and supplemental" broadcasts, file, reference, audition and "sales purposes." However, the broadcaster, ABC, used plaintiff's music in a pre-produced segment on ski-jumping broadcast as part of the live coverage. The copyright owner of the music claimed that the produced-in-advance "segment," as opposed to a live broadcast, represented a reproduction of the music that required a sync license. ABC claimed the "incidental" copying allowed under the BMI license covered the use of the music in the segment, thus a sync license from the publisher for the "segment" that included music was not necessary. The court denied both parties' summary judgment motions, stating that whether a license was required in "this highly sophisticated and intricate industry is a question of fact properly reserved for a trial on the merits." The parties settled. See also, *Agee v. Paramount Communications, Inc.*, 59 F.3d 317 (2d Cir. 1995) (discussing the rights implicated in a pre-produced segment broadcast as part of an otherwise live broadcast).

135   17 U.S.C. § 112(a).

136   *Id.* Otherwise, making even that one "ephemeral" temporary copy, even for technical purposes, would require permission of the copyright owner of any music contained in the program in the form of a sync license.

137   17 U.S.C. § 112(a)(1)(C).

138   17 U.S.C. § 112(a)(1)(A-B).

139   17 U.S.C.§ 112(a)(1).

program with any music are made for later transmission, for different time zones or for distribution to affiliated stations, a sync license is not required, even though the usage has shifted from live performance[140] to reproducing[141] and distributing[142] the work.

Section 112 does not serve as a substitute for producers who normally need sync licenses for use in a television production, or in a pre-produced segment of an otherwise live show.[143] It applies purely to facilitate distribution by the broadcast or cable network.

[2]—Digital Transmission of Music

Section 112(e) addresses similar statutory "ephemeral" licenses in the context of entities that use the statutory licenses under section 114(d) for digital transmission of sound recordings. Such transmitting organizations need to make a copy of a sound recording on their computer servers that, in turn, stream the sound recording to listeners via satellite or the Internet. These organizations are entitled to make no more than one phonorecord of the sound recording if the following conditions are satisfied:

---

140   17 U.S.C. § 106(4).

141   17 U.S. C. § 106(1).

142   17 U.S.C. § 106(3).

143   See *Agee v. Paramount Communications, Inc.*, 59 F.3d 317 (2d Cir. 1995). In Agee, the plaintiff owned the copyright in sound recordings containing underlying compositions in the form of themes from Laurel and Hardy movies. The television show "Hard Copy" produced a three-minute segment featuring inept criminals, and used a portion of the music without obtaining a license. Agee sued Paramount, producers of "Hard Copy", and 125 Paramount affiliates that broadcast the show. Paramount argued that its ASCAP and BMI blanket licenses for performing rights covered such "incidental" uses.

On appeal to the Second Circuit Court of Appeals, the Court ruled that fixing copyright works to film footage created an audiovisual work, and involved making a reproduction that was not covered by the ASCAP/BMI blanket licenses, which covered only performance, not reproduction. Therefore Paramount infringed because it did not obtain a master license from Agee for his sound recordings.

In considering the respective liabilities of Paramount on the one hand and the Paramount affiliates on the other, the Court had occasion to clarify the are two "levels" or "stages" in the television production and distribution process. At the first level, Paramount was the supplier of the program because it produced the program, and as the producer, Paramount was also the infringer because it did not obtain a master license for the sound recording used in the pre-edited segment at issue in the case (the segment being a short pre-edited film shown during the course of an otherwise live or tape-delay program).

Paramount was not, however, the transmitting organization. It was the 125 Paramount affiliate TV stations that were the transmitting organizations at the second level. Because each TV station complied with Section 112 (they each made one copy, each did not use it for over six months), each TV station came within the section 112 exemption and therefore had no liability arising as a result of the fact they carried the programming produced by Paramount.

- The phonorecord is retained and used solely by the transmitting organization.

- The phonorecord is used solely for the transmitting organization's own transmissions originating in the United States under the § 114 statutory license.

- Unless preserved for archival purposes, the phonorecord is destroyed within six months from the date of first transmission.

- The source phonorecord must be an authorized copy to begin with.[144]

§4.08   Master License for the Sound Recording

The corresponding license to include a sound recording in an audiovisual work is called a "master license."[145] The process for negotiating and obtaining a master license from a record company is very similar to the sync license process: the same basic deal points will arise, the same approvals will be required, the same most-favored nation ("MFN") status will be demanded.

The essential grant of rights for a master license will be similar to the following sample of a basic grant, which includes broad television and Internet/mobile phone rights, but has limited theatrical exhibition rights:

GRANT OF LICENSE. Subject to all of the terms of this Agreement, Licensor hereby grants to Licensee the non-exclusive right worldwide ("Territory") in perpetuity ("Term") to synchronize, rerecord and reproduce the Licensed Portion of the Master Recording in timed relation with the Film for all forms of television, including but not limited to free television, basic cable/satellite, subscription and pay television, and on no more than 5,000 units of audio-visual DVDs intended primarily for "home use," and for all forms of streaming via the Internet or mobile devices, including mobile phones ("Licensed Use"). Licensor also grants Licensee the non-exclusive right in the Territory for a period of one (1) year commencing on [date], and terminating on [date], to show the Film non-commercially at educational institutions and at film festivals ("Additional Licensed Use"). No other use may be made of the Licensed Portion of the Master Recording except the Licensed Use and Additional Licensed Use. Licensor reserves exclusively to itself all rights and uses of the Master Recording, whether now or hereafter in existence, other than the Licensed Use and Additional Licensed Use.

---

144   17 U.S.C. § 112(e)(A-D).

145   The term "master" stems from the days of vinyl records. A filmmaker would obtain from the record company a copy of the "master" magnetic tape, in order to get the best possible sound into the production's soundtrack. Note that recording agreements may commonly refer to licensing their master recordings for film and television somewhat incorrectly by the generic term "synch" licensing. With respect to licensing to film and television producers, technically, a "synch" license is a term that is only applicable to the right in the underlying musical composition, and a "master" license is the term only applicable to the sound recording.

§4.09   Noncommercial Broadcasting

The Public Broadcasting Service ("PBS") and National Public Radio, as well as noncommercial college radio stations, perform services in the public good, and are entitled to special consideration in the form of lower royalty rates. These organizations pay lower rates to AS-CAP, BMI, and SESAC as determined by the Copyright Royalty Board, and published in the Code of Federal Regulations.[146] It is the rare television production that aspires to be broadcast solely on PBS. But for those productions aimed at a PBS broadcast only, Section 118 of the Copyright Act provides the closest thing to a "compulsory" synchronization license under United States law.[147]

Subject to those statutory license fees, a public broadcasting entity may perform or display a published nondramatic musical work by or in the course of a transmission and may reproduce copies or phonorecords of the program to the extent necessary for the broadcasts.[148]

If the producers plan other uses in addition to the PBS broadcast, they must contact the publishers for a sync license for those other uses. Such standard sync licenses will typically charge fees based on the "menu" of non-PBS uses, e.g., theatrical exhibition, commercial domestic broadcast, overseas broadcast, DVDs and downloads, or Internet transmissions. But while such licenses may indeed refer to the PBS broadcast as being licensed via Section 118,[149] the sync licenses should not assess any additional fees for the PBS usage. The publisher will receive amounts based on the license fees published in the Federal Register.

§4.10   Production Music for Film and Television

While obtaining sync and master licenses may give a film or television producer the additional impact of famous or up-and-coming musical talent, the licensing process is time-consuming, and can be expensive. Even with the increasing availability of "one stop" licensing where

---

146   37 C.F.R. §§ 253 *et seq.*

147   Unlike musical compositions, sound recordings are not specifically included in Section 118. Under its provisions, copyright owners of published nondramatic musical works and published pictorial, graphic, and sculptural works must make those works available for PBS broadcast (i.e. as part of audiovisual works that would normally require a negotiated sync license) at rates fixed either by the Copyright Royalty Judges, or as a result of a license negotiated by a collective agent representing music publishers, the Harry Fox Agency, and approved by the Librarian of Congress. 17 U.S.C. § 118(b). In this limited scenario, these are the equivalent of sync licenses at either a fixed rate published in the Federal Register, or at a rate negotiated between the Harry Fox Agency and PBS (applicable only to Fox member publishers) and not subject to further licensing or most favored nations requirements. See 37 C.F.R. §§ 253.1 *et seq.*, specifying PBS broadcast fees for music.

148   17 U.S.C. § 118(d).

149   Or via the Harry Fox Agency/PBS-negotiated agreement, if the publisher is a Harry Fox Agency member.

a publisher and record company may join forces to offer the convenience of both sync and master license components at one price, producers may want other alternatives, or may even have a production in which simple, atmospheric background music is all that is required or appropriate. This type of "off the shelf" music is called "production music," and companies that offer it for licensing are called "production music libraries."

Production music might be described as pre-composed and pre-recorded music serviceable for many purposes, and less expensive than a chart-topping hit. The music is often provided in either CD or MP3 format online so they can be previewed before use.[150]

Production music libraries operate in a similar way to music publishers and record companies. They use a questionnaire that asks for all the uses the producer will make, the duration of the usage, and the territories, and the quantity and duration of the tracks to be used. Based on the proposed usage, a license fee is assessed. The producer, or the music supervisor, then selects the music they want for the production.

The licensing does not normally include the performing rights. Thus, all future broadcasts can be authorized only for broadcasters or Web sites that have valid performing rights licenses from ASCAP, BMI, or SESAC.

In addition to collecting a combined sync and master license fee, the production music library will, like the traditional music publisher, count on future performance royalties when the production is shown on television. Note that production libraries sometimes engage in the practice of "retitling" existing works, where a pre-existing song's title is changed only for the production library's licensing exploitation. Thus, it is possible that one song could be listed in the PRS's database under two completely different titles.

§4.11   Commissioned Music

The alternative to all sync and master licensing for audiovisual productions is to engage a composer to write an original musical score, and to hire musicians and producers to create the soundtrack.[151] The primary benefit of this arrangement must be weighed against the

---

150   This harkens back to the days of vinyl records as the exclusive media, turntables and "drop the needle" licensing (referring to the record player stylus, and the habit of dropping the tone arm onto the spinning vinyl record to hear, evaluate, and select different tracks).

151   See *Buffalo Broadcasting Co., Inc. v. ASCAP*, 744 F.2d 917, 921 (2d Cir. 1984) (stating in the context of syndicated television productions that "[s]yndicators wishing to include music in their programs may either select pre-existing music (sometimes called 'outside' music) or hire a composer to compose original music (sometimes called 'inside' music). Most music on syndicated programs, up to 90% by plaintiff's estimate, is inside music commissioned

drawbacks: the extra costs involved in commissioning music, and in paying for musicians, engineers, and recording studio time.[152]

Because films and television productions fall into the works made for hire category of the Copyright Act,[153] the vast majority of agreements to create original music for those productions are categorized as work made for hire agreements vesting copyright authorship and ownership in the production company.

---

through the use of composer-for-hire agreements between the producer and either the composer alone or the composer and a corporation entitled to contract for a loan of the composer's services.").

152   On the other hand, some film composers have their own one-person studios with an array of synthesizers and other technology capable of economically generating the equivalent of virtually any type of instrumental or vocal soundtrack, including full orchestral and choral scores.

153   See 17 U.S.C. § 101. The definition of a work made for hire in the Copyright Act includes two scenarios: works by an employee, and works commissioned from freelancers. See also, *Community for Creative Non-Violence v. Reid*, 490 U.S. 730, 109 S.Ct. 2166, 104 L.Ed. 2d 811 (1989), discussing the works made for hire doctrine in the context of an analysis for determining whether a work is created by an employee or a freelance contractor. The definition of a work made for hire in the Copyright Act follows:

(1) a work prepared by an employee within the scope of his or her employment; or

(2) a work specially ordered or commissioned for use as a contribution to a collective work, as a part of a motion picture or other audiovisual work, as a translation, as a supplementary work, as a compilation, as an instructional text, as a test, as answer material for a test, or as an atlas, if the parties expressly agree in a written instrument signed by them that the work shall be considered a work made for hire. For the purpose of the foregoing sentence, a "supplementary work" is a work prepared for publication as a secondary adjunct to a work by another author for the purpose of introducing, concluding, illustrating, explaining, revising, commenting upon, or assisting in the use of the other work, such as forewords, afterwords, pictorial illustrations, maps, charts, tables, editorial notes, musical arrangements, answer material for tests, bibliographies, appendixes, and indexes, and an "instructional text" is a literary, pictorial, or graphic work prepared for publication and with the purpose of use in systematic instructional activities.

17 U.S.C. § 101. (Emphasis added.)

Some music publishers may seek to obtain publishing rights in the film score by subsidizing the producer's costs of the composition of the score and the studio recording in exchange for the publishing ownership. See, e.g. *Ennio Morricone Music Inc. v. Bixio Music Grp. LTD*, 2017 U.S. Dist. LEXIS 177643 (S.D.N.Y. 2017) (composer sought to terminate film score copyrights owned by Italian music publisher, because composer had been hired on a work for hire basis composer did not have termination rights under U.S. Copyright Act).

Some music publishers may seek to obtain publishing rights in the film score by subsidizing the producer's costs of the composition of the score and the studio recording in exchange for the publishing ownership. See, e.g. Ennio Morricone Music Inc. v. Bixio Music Grp. LTD, 2017 U.S. Dist. LEXIS 177643 (S.D.N.Y. 2017) (composer sought to terminate film score copyrights owned by Italian music publisher, because composer had been hired on a work for hire basis composer did not have termination rights under U.S. Copyright Act).

While the composer of a custom score for television, film, or advertising will rarely if ever be able to retain her copyright, she can often retain publishing rights in other areas. For example, if the film is shown on television, the composer can receive the composer's share of performing rights income arising from the broadcast. If the soundtrack appears on a recording, the composer can receive mechanical royalties. The composer may also seek to enter into a co-publishing agreement with the studio's own music publishing subsidiary.[154]

Thus, an agreement for a composer to write a score for a motion picture looks very similar to a publishing agreement, with the additional provisions that the score is being written on commission, with delivery deadlines, and fees for the composition itself.[155]

§4.12   Recording Agreements

The fundamental legal principle in any agreement between a recording artist and a record company is a simple copyright transaction: the recording artist who provides the talent and marketability, conveys his or her rights in the sound recording of his or her performance to the record company, which provides the production, distribution, and marketing resources and expertise.[156] As a result, the record company owns the copyright in the sound recording, manufactures the resulting "phonorecord" for sale, sells and licenses the phonorecord, and in return shares income with the artist in the form of future royalties.[157]

However, unlike other entertainment transactions that trade copyright ownership for future royalties, in the record business a practice has evolved in which many of the record compa-

---

154   Note that in the case of very low or no payments to the composer (who may be willing to work for a modest fee in order to enter the profession), composers may negotiate to retain the copyright in their score and the publishing rights, granting the producer an irrevocable non-exclusive license.

155   See § 2.18[50] *supra*.

156   See The *Gordy Co. v. Mary Jane Girls, Inc.*, 1989 U.S. Dist. LEXIS 14581, 1989 WL 149290 (S.D.N.Y. Dec. 6, 1989) (extensive summary judgment opinion in a dispute over recording and publishing royalties between artist Rick James and Motown Records, containing detailed information on recording industry practices as well as contractual and royalty analysis). The case was amended one year later. The *Gordy Co. v. Mary Jane Girls, Inc.*, 1990 WL 47684 (S.D.N.Y. April 12, 1990) ("[a]n inherent tension exists between the creative talent and drive of a [recording artist] under exclusive contract and the administrative, legal, and commercial requirements of a record distribution company such as Motown. The artist seeks promotion from the distributor, and the distributor seeks to bring the disciplines of business to the creative process. The vagaries of the public's taste for music and the economics of the record business in the United States heighten these inherent tensions."). *Id.*, 1990 WL 47684, at *3.

157   Given the overall decrease in CD sales since the advent of the Internet and online copyright infringement, the record company also seeks participation in the artist's other income-producing areas such as live performances, endorsements, and advertising revenue.

ny's expenditures and investments do not come from overhead. Instead, they are treated as advances to the artist against future royalties. As a result, a recording artist often discovers that after receiving an initial advance, years may go by without any actual cash receipt of royalty payments. In the event that the artist's royalty account succeeds in recouping the "advances" and costs charged by the record company, the artist will receive royalties as cash payments. Conversely, in the event that the artist never sees recouped earnings from the recording, he or she never has to repay advances to the record company. Ultimately, the financial risk lies with the record company.

In addition to the overall issue of recoupment, key recording agreement issues include:

- The scope of exclusive services the artist must provide to the record company

- The number of projects or "albums" that must be delivered by the artist pursuant to "options" held by the record company

- The advances payable to the artist for each album

- The royalty costs for the producer of the recordings

- The types and amounts of record company's "recoupable" costs to be legitimately be charged against the artist's royalty account

- Limitations on the amount of music publishing mechanical royalties the record company is willing to pay

- So-called "360 deals," in which the record company is entitled to a share of the artist's earnings from other sources, such as live concerts

[1]—Recording Agreement Overview[158]

[a]—Exclusive Services

The agreement will require that the artist make recordings, including live concerts, exclusively for the record company during the life of the agreement.[159] There will also be prohibitions against making re-recordings of previously released material, even

---

158   Several recording agreements are included in the forms accompanying this treatise.

159   See *TVT Records v. The Island Def Jam Music Group*, 412 F.3d 82 (2d Cir. 2005) (record label that wanted to reunite soloist with his former group needed permission and a license, including financial participation, from soloist's current record label). See also:

Second Circuit: Radioactive, J.V. v. Manson, 153 F. Supp.2d 462 (S.D.N.Y. 2001) (dispute arising from solo artist Shirley Manson being signed to first label and later recording, with permission, with group "Garbage" on second label, resulting in complex contractual claims).

Seventh Circuit: Westbound Productions, Inc. v. Phonogram, Inc., 76 Ill. App.3d 359, 394 N.E.2d 1315 (1979) (on summary judgment facts supported claims by first label that efforts by second label to sign artists already signed to first

for a time after the term expires. There may be prohibitions against performing musical services as part of any audiovisual motion picture or television production without the record company's approval, though such restrictions would not normally include live television performances.

In the event of a dispute, courts may refuse to compel an individual to perform a contract for personal services, based in part on the Thirteenth Amendment's prohibition of involuntary servitude.[160]

For example, under Civil Code Section 3423, California courts will not enjoin the breach of a personal service contract unless the service is unique in nature, the performer is guaranteed, and actually receives annual compensation as specified in the statute.[161] In such cases a remedy may have to be sought against the third party

---

label constituted tortious interference with a contractual relationship by interfering with or inducing a breach of a valid contract).

160   See *American Broadcasting Co., Inc. v. Wolf*, 52 N.Y.2d 394, 438 N.Y.S.2d 482, 420 N.E.2d 363 (1981). See also:

California: *Beverly Glen Music, Inc. v. Warner Communications, Inc.*, 178 Cal. App.3d 1142, 224 Cal. Rptr. 260 (1986) (refusing to grant an injunction against singer Anita Baker who had allegedly breached her contract by recording for Warner, stating that "[d]enying someone his [sic] livelihood is a harsh remedy. The Legislature has forbidden it but for one exception. . . . Yet if Warner's behavior has actually been predatory, plaintiff has an adequate remedy by way of damages.").

New York: *Zomba Recording LLC v. Williams*, 15 Misc.3d 1118(A) (Slip Op.), 839 N.Y.S.2d 438, 2007 WL 1063869, at *10 (N.Y. Sup. Feb. 19, 2007) (recording artist "Tonbx" enjoined from recording for other in violation of Zomba agreement, while court notes that "this court cannot force defendant Williams back to the studio to record for plaintiff.").

161   See Cal. Code Section 3423, specifying the value of the contract and payments that must be at issue before an injunction can issue against an individual as follows:

"An injunction may not be granted:

"(a) To stay a judicial proceeding pending at the commencement of the action in which the injunction is demanded, unless this restraint is necessary to prevent a multiplicity of proceedings.

"(b) To stay proceedings in a court of the United States.

"(c) To stay proceedings in another state upon a judgment of a court of that state.

"(d) To prevent the execution of a public statute, by officers of the law, for the public benefit.

"(e) To prevent the breach of a contract the performance of which would not be specifically enforced, other than a contract in writing for the rendition of personal services from one to another where the promised service is of a special, unique, unusual, extraordinary, or intellectual character, which gives it peculiar value, the loss of which cannot be reasonably or adequately compensated in damages in an action at law, and where the compensation for the personal services is as follows:

employing the artist in breach of the agreement.[162] If the state with jurisdiction has no statutory bar to an injunction, courts may be willing to grant the record company an injunction prohibiting the artist from providing such services to others, assuming such acts violate an exclusive services agreement with the recording company.[163]

In a traditional record company agreement, the artist is otherwise free to engage in non-recording activities such as concerts, touring, television appearances, so long as those activities do not result in a recording intended for commercial sale. More

---

"(1) As to contracts entered into on or before December 31, 1993, the minimum compensation provided in the contract for the personal services shall be at the rate of six thousand dollars ($6,000) per annum.

"(2) As to contracts entered into on or after January 1, 1994, the criteria of subparagraph (A) or (B), as follows, are satisfied:

"(A) The compensation is as follows:

"(i) The minimum compensation provided in the contract shall be at the rate of nine thousand dollars ($9,000) per annum for the first year of the contract, twelve thousand dollars ($12,000) per annum for the second year of the contract, and fifteen thousand dollars ($15,000) per annum for the third to seventh years, inclusive, of the contract.

"(ii) In addition, after the third year of the contract, there shall actually have been paid for the services through and including the contract year during which the injunctive relief is sought, over and above the minimum contractual compensation specified in clause (i), the amount of fifteen thousand dollars ($15,000) per annum during the fourth and fifth years of the contract, and thirty thousand dollars ($30,000) per annum during the sixth and seventh years of the contract. As a condition to petitioning for an injunction, amounts payable under this clause may be paid at any time prior to seeking injunctive relief.

"(B) The aggregate compensation actually received for the services provided under a contract that does not meet the criteria of subparagraph (A), is at least 10 times the applicable aggregate minimum amount specified in clauses (i) and (ii) of subparagraph (A) through and including the contract year during which the injunctive relief is sought. As a condition to petitioning for an injunction, amounts payable under this subparagraph may be paid at any time prior to seeking injunctive relief.

"(3) Compensation paid in any contract year in excess of the minimums specified in subparagraphs (A) and (B) of paragraph (2) shall apply to reduce the compensation otherwise required to be paid under those provisions in any subsequent contract years."

See also, *Motown Record Corp. v. Tina Marie Brockert*, 160 Cal. App.3d 123, 207 Cal. Rptr. 574 (1984) (a mere "option" to pay the minimum under the statute is insufficient, the amount must be actually received by the artist).

162   See *Beverly Glen Music, Inc. v. Warner Communications, Inc.*, 178 Cal. App.3d 1142, 224 Cal. Rptr. 260, 262 (1986) (refusing to grant an injunction against an artist who started to record for another record company, but pointing out that "[i]f [other record company's] behavior has actually been predatory, plaintiff has an adequate remedy by way of damages.").

163   *American Broadcasting Co., Inc. v. Wolf*, 52 N.Y.2d 394, 438 N.Y.S.2d 482, 420 N.E.2d 363, 367 (1981).

recent types of recording company agreements, "360 deals,"[164] expand the contract-ed services, and the record company's entitlement to a share of revenues, to include virtually all of an artist's activities and revenue streams, including, but not limited to, live touring, endorsements, branding, merchandise, and acting.[165]

[b]—Copyright

Except for unusual circumstances where an artist may be able to retain copyright ownership of the sound recordings and grant an exclusive license for a term of years, virtually all recording agreements will seek to on a works made for hire basis, with an accompanying "backup" assignment of all rights under copyright.

[i]—Work Made for Hire Status of Sound Recordings

There has been controversy in the entertainment industry over whether sound recordings qualify as "works made for hire."[166] The central issue is that agree-

---

164 Because they encompass the entire 360 degrees of the musical "world."

165 Such global business arrangements are no longer the exclusive domain of record companies, for example leading concert promotion companies have begun to enter into such "360" agreements, as part of which they take on, or at least sublicense, the functions traditionally performed by record companies.

166 See 17 U.S.C. § 101(2) definition of a commissioned work made for hire; see also, the detailed discussion on copyright principles in Chapter 1 *supra*; see also:

Supreme Court: Community for Creative Non-Violence v. Reid, 490 U.S. 730, 109 S.Ct. 2166, 104 L.Ed.2d 811 (1989) (discussing requirements for a work made for hire under the Copyright Act).

Second Circuit: Fifty-Six Hope Road Music Ltd. v. UMG Recordings, Inc., 2010 WL 3564258 (S.D.N.Y. Sept. 10, 2010) (finding sound recordings made prior to the 1976 Copyright Act to be works made for hire under the 1909 Copyright Act).

Third Circuit: *Ballas v. Tedesco*, 41 F. Supp.2d 531 (D.N.J. 1999) (sound recordings are not in the definition of a work made for hire in the Copyright Act).

Fifth Circuit: Lulirama Ltd, Inc. v. Axcess Broadcast Services, Inc., 128 F.3d 872 (5th Cir. 1997) (commissioned sound recordings do not come within the definition of a work made for hire in the Copyright Act).

District of Columbia Circuit: Staggers v. Real Authentic Sound, 77 F. Supp.2d 57 (D.D.C. 1999).

Compare, UMG Recordings, Inc. v. MP3.com, Inc., 109 F. Supp.2d 223, 225 (S.D.N.Y. 2000) (for the purposes of calculation of damages under 17 U.S.C. 504(c)(1) that "each CD that defendant copied is a 'compilation' under § 504(c)(1)." The significance of the statement is that a compilation is one of the specified works that can be a work made for hire in the Copyright Act.). See also: Field, "Their Master's Voice? Recording Artists, Bright Lines, and Bowie Bonds: The Debate Over Sound Recordings as Works Made for Hire," 48 J. Copyright Soc'y 145 (2000); Field, "Corporation and Copyright in Cyberspace: 'Hidden' Internet Regulation and the Corporate Director's Duty to Monitor—*UMG Recordings, Inc. v. MP3.com, Inc.* Seen from the Perspective of In Re Caremark Derivative Litigation," 27 Del. J. of Corp. Law 99 (2002).

ments that are copyright "assignments" are subject to a statutory right of termination after thirty-five years, while agreements that are deemed a "work made for hire" are not subject to any future termination rights.[167]

Business entities, including record companies, prefer, and usually insist on obtaining ownership on a work made for hire basis. There is a catch, however. The Copyright Act only allows work made for hire status to exist in two limited situations: either the work must have been created by a bona fide employee of the business entity as part of the normal job duties; or the work, if commissioned from an independent artist, must fit within one of nine categories in the Copyright Act.[168] Those categories do not specifically include "sound recordings."[169]

---

167   See 17 U.S.C. § 203(a) stating that the termination provisions do not apply to a work made for hire. Under the Copyright Act, there are two basic types of ownership that can be obtained by a business entity from an individual: (1) a work made for hire where the business entity's ownership cannot be terminated at any time; and (2) assignment of copyright where the individual retains a right to terminate the grant of ownership thirty-five years later. See 17 U.S.C. § 203(a) stating that works made for hire are excluded from the right of termination. See also, 17 U.S.C. § 201(b) (in the case of commissioned works made for hire, there must be a written instrument signed by both parties). Compare, 17 U.S.C. § 204(1) (in the case of a transfer of copyright, the required writing need only be signed by the owner of the rights conveyed. Work made for hire agreements must therefore not only state it is a work made for hire, but must be signed by both parties.). See the forms accompanying this treatise.

168   17 U.S.C. § 101.

169   For a brief time in 1999, "sound recordings" were added to the statutory definition of works made for hire in Section 101 of the Copyright Act as part of the Intellectual Property and Communications Omnibus Reform Act of 1999, then were quickly removed after a flurry of objections from recording artists that the amendment to the Copyright Act had not been duly considered before the change was made. As a result, the definition in section 101 contains a provision stating that the addition of "sound recordings" to the list of commissioned works made for hire, and the later removal of "sound recordings" from that list, shall not "be considered or otherwise given any legal significance" in determining whether any work is eligible to be considered a work made for hire:

"In determining whether any work is eligible to be considered a work made for hire under paragraph (2), neither the amendment contained in section 1011(d) of the Intellectual Property and Communications Omnibus Reform Act of 1999, as enacted by section 1000(a)(9) of Public Law 106-113, nor the deletion of the words added by that amendment—

"(A) shall be considered or otherwise given any legal significance, or

"(B) shall be interpreted to indicate congressional approval or disapproval of, or acquiescence in, any judicial determination, by the courts or the Copyright Office. Paragraph (2) shall be interpreted as if both section 2(a)(1) of the Work Made For Hire and Copyright Corrections Act of 2000 and section 1011(d) of the Intellectual Property and Communications Omnibus Reform Act of 1999, as enacted by section 1000(a)(9) of Public Law 106-113, were never enacted, and without regard to any inaction or awareness by the Congress at any time of any judicial determinations."

17 U.S.C. § 101. See also, Field, "Their Master's Voice? Recording Artists, Bright Lines, and Bowie Bonds: The Debate Over Sound Recordings as Works Made for Hire," 48 J. Copyright Soc'y 145 (2000).

Because recording agreements traditionally seek work made for hire ownership, record companies assert that a sound recording qualifies as a work made for hire.[170]

If future litigation should decide that sound recordings do not qualify as works made for hire, then the operative transfer will be the "backup" assignment language in the agreement, in which case recording artists would have a statutory right of termination thirty-five years after the agreement is signed. The statutory right of termination is not the same as any contractual rights to termination that may arise. The statutory right of termination cannot be waived regardless of any language in the agreement stating otherwise.[171]

[ii]—New Technologies and Digital Rights

In the music industry, platforms for reproducing music have evolved from player piano rolls to digital delivery. Where creators have conveyed their rights in broad grants, courts have held that they include new technological platforms, including platforms and technologies not known at the time of the original grant.[172] Agreements typically include language stating that the grant is made without reservation, and includes all technologies, media, or formats now known or hereafter invented.

---

170   See Field, id.

171   17 U.S.C. § 203(a)(5) ("[t]ermination of the grant may be effected notwithstanding any agreement to the contrary, including an agreement to make a will or to make any future grant"). See also, the discussion of copyright termination rights in Chapter 1.

172   See *Greenfield v. Phillies Records, Inc.*, 98 N.Y.2d 562, 750 N.Y.S.2d 565, 780 N.E.2d 166 (2002) (in the absence of an explicit contractual reservation of rights by the artists, the artists' transfer of full ownership rights to the master recordings of musical performances carried with it the unconditional right of the producer to redistribute those performances in any technological format"). See also:

Second Circuit: *Boosey & Hawkes Music Publishers, Ltd. v. Walt Disney Co.*, 145 F.3d 481 (2d Cir. 1998) (use of Stravinsky's music in film "Fantasia" did not exceed original grant when released on video cassettes); *Chambers v. Time Warner, Inc.*, 123 F. Supp.2d 198, 200-201 (S.D.N.Y. 2000) (agreements permitted the conversion of master recordings to digital format), vacated on other grounds 282 F.3d 147 (2d Cir. 2002); *Silvester v. Time Warner, Inc.*, 1 Misc.3d 250, 763 N.Y.S.2d 912 (N.Y. Sup. 2003) (a transfer of all rights without reservation allowed the record company to use any new digital technological formats).

Fifth Circuit: *Batiste v. Island Records, Inc.*, 179 F.3d 217, 223 (5th Cir. 1999) (grant of unconditional rights to a musical composition included the licensing of a record containing a digital sample of the song).

Ninth Circuit: *Maljack Productions, Inc. v. Goodtimes Home Video Corp.*, 81 F.3d 881, 885 (9th Cir. 1996) (unconditional grant of motion picture music rights included right to synchronize music in videocassette format).

Because most agreements are drafted with these broad grants of rights, cases excluding new technologies were not included in the original grant are relatively rare. In *Cohen v. Paramount Pictures Corp.*, a license to exhibit a film "by means of television" did not include distribution of videocassettes.[173] Although a successful action by singer Peggy Lee against the Walt Disney Co. for royalties earned as a result of subsequent videocassette sales of "Lady and the Tramp" garnered much attention, that case was unique to its facts.[174]

New technologies may also affect royalty rates paid to artists, because most agreements apply one type of calculation for actual sale of physical recordings (typically in the 5% to 15% range); and another where the copyright is licensed without a physical sale.[175] In several cases, a group brought suit against their record company, claiming that digital deliveries should be accounted for as licenses of the masters garnering a 50% royalty, not as sales of physical recordings where the group was entitled to only a royalty based on 5% of the list price.[176]

Digital distribution of music no longer qualifies as a new technology, and contractual agreements have specific language addressing how royalties are to be allocated for digital licensing. However, courts still must address disputes arising from agreements drafted prior to the rise of digital distribution, where contractual language may not have transparently defined the royalty provisions that apply to sales of physical media versus online "sales" of permanent downloads.

In *F.B.T. Productions, LLC v. Aftermath*, contractual language in a 1998 agreement regarding recordings by the artist Eminem was at the center of the dispute.[177]

---

173   See *Cohen v. Paramount Pictures Corp.*, 845 F.2d 851 (9th Cir. 1988) (license granting right to exhibit film "by means of television" did not include right to distribute videocassettes of the film for home viewing).

174   See *Lee v. Walt Disney Co.*, No. B058897 (Cal. App. Sept. 30, 1992) (unpublished opinion), cert. denied 1992 Cal. LEXIS 6172 (Cal. Dec. 16, 1992) (singer Peggy Lee successfully asserted that a contract prohibiting "transcriptions sold to the public" of the film "Lady and the Tramp" applied to the later invention of video cassettes).

175   One example is the case of master licenses to film or television production companies where the average royalty is 50%.

176   See *The Youngbloods v. BMG Music*, 2008 U.S. Dist. LEXIS 30600, 2008 WL 919617 (S.D.N.Y. March 28, 2008) (partly granting and partly denying defendant's motion to dismiss, and giving plaintiff leave to amend the complaint). The case settled as part of a class action on October 4, 2012. See also: *James v. UMG Recordings*, 2011 U.S. Dist. LEXIS 126221, 2011 WL 5192476 (C.D. Cal. Nov. 1, 2011) (class action suit over royalty rate for digital downloads of sound recordings); *Clifford v. Concord Music Group, Inc.*, 2012 U.S. Dist. LEXIS 14084, 2012 WL 380744 (N.D. Cal. Feb. 6, 2012) (suit by members of Creedence Clearwater Revival seeking 50% royalty instead of 13.5% for digital sales of recordings). See also, *Davis v. Capital Records, Inc.*, 2013 U.S. Dist. LEXIS 55917, 2013 WL 1701746 (N.D. Cal. April 18, 2013) (class action concerning digital royalties).

177   *F.B.T. Productions, LLC v. Aftermath Records*, 621 F.3d 958 (9th Cir. 2010).

With respect to sales of physical media, in that agreement the plaintiff was entitled to a royalty between 12% and 20% for "full price records sold in the United States . . . through normal retail channels."[178] With respect to licensed uses of the masters, the plaintiff was entitled to 50% of the defendant record label's net receipts, "on masters licensed by us . . . to others for their manufacture and sale of records or for any other uses."[179] Basing its holding on principles of contract law, the plain meaning of the agreement, and defining digital distribution as a license and not a sale, the Ninth Circuit held that permanent downloads available via Apple's iTunes digital service and telephone "mastertones," were licensed uses that fell within the higher 50% royalty provisions of the agreement.[180]

The result in such pre-digital era contract disputes is heavily dependent on the specific language in each contract. Thus the opposite result was reached in a dispute between Yngwie Malmsteen and his record label, with the court holding that "[i]n today's market, the phrase 'Normal Retail Channels' comfortably encompasses digital downloads sold through Apple's iTunes store and similar platforms—brick-and-mortar record shops have gone the way of the 8-track, the phonograph, and the mastodon."[181]

Litigation by other recording artists based on digital royalty rate claims included a class action against Sony Music Entertainment that settled in 2012 with reported terms including a payment of $7.95 million to the members of the class and their attorneys, and a 3% royalty increase on future digital downloads.[182]

The question whether online uses of recordings are "transmissions" with higher royalty rates, or "sales" with lower royalty rates on digital radio services such as Spotify, was the issue in litigation between 19 Recordings Ltd. and Sony Music Entertainment. 19 Recordings Ltd had exclusive rights to the recording services of the winners of the popular "American Idol" television competition, and entered into distribution agreements with Sony Records, which in turn licensed Spotify and other digital music services. Even with parties of this high level of

---

178   *Id.*, 621 F.3d at 961.

179   *Id.*

180   *Id.* See also, *Young v. Wideawake Death Row Entertainment, LLC*, 2011 U.S. Dist. LEXIS 54631 (C.D. Cal. May 16, 2011) (Slip Op.) (granting summary judgment to plaintiff, upholding reservation of digital distribution rights for sound recordings to plaintiff based on 1996 agreement).

181   *Malmsteen v. Universal Music Group, Inc.*, 940 F. Supp.2d 123 (S.D.N.Y. 2013).

182   See settlement terms in consolidated class actions *The Youngbloods v. BMG Music*, 1:07-cv-02394, and *Shropshire v. Sony Music Entertainment*, 1:06-cv-03252, both in the Southern District of New York (case closed Oct. 4, 2012). See also, *Clifford v. Concord Music Group, Inc.*, 2012 U.S. Dist. LEXIS 14084, 2012 WL 380744 (N.D. Cal. Feb. 6 2012) (claim by Creedence Clearwater for 50% of digital revenue).

sophistication, in ruling on preliminary motions for judgment on the pleadings, the court could only conclude that the various agreements with Spotify and others were ambiguous as regards the category of the uses for royalty purposes.[183]

[c]—Term

The term of the exclusive services provided by an artist in a recording agreement is not based on a number of years. It is based on the delivery of a specified number of recordings. Where each album must be composed, recorded, released, and promoted via touring, the amount of time between album deliveries can easily be two to three years or more. In a contract that requires as many as seven albums to be delivered, the recording artist may be contractually bound to a record company for decades.

In California where many recording agreements are entered into, Section 2855 of the California Labor Code makes personal services agreements unenforceable after seven years. This provision, which benefits actors and others in the entertainment industry, comes with an exception for the recording industry. Under Section 2855(b), should any artist seek to cancel their recording agreement on the basis that it has endured more than seven years, the record company has a statutory right to seek unspecified damages based on any undelivered recordings.[184]

Therefore, recording agreements are typically based on "contract periods," not a term of years. Each contract period is triggered by the artist's delivery of an album of recordings, usually with at least ten "sides" or tracks with a total duration of at least approximately forty minutes. Once delivery takes place, the applicable contract period will run through the later of twelve months from delivery, or the date six months after the album is commercially released by the record company. At

---

183   See *19 Recordings v. Sony Music Entertainment*, 2016 U.S. Dist. LEXIS 133667 (S.D.N.Y. Sept. 28, 2016) (motions for judgment on the pleadings denied). See also: 2016 U.S. Dist. LEXIS 45032 (S.D.N.Y. March 18, 2016) (motion to amend complaint denied); 97 F. Supp. 3d 433 (S.D.N.Y. 2015) (motion to dismiss denied in part and granted in part).

184   In California, Section 2855 of the California Labor Code makes personal services agreements lasting longer than seven years unenforceable, the so-called "Seven year rule." West's Ann. Cal. Labor Code § 2855. See also, *de Haviland v. Warner Bros. Pictures*, 67 Cal. App.2d 225, 153 P.2d 983 (1944). Sound recording agreements however, because they have terms based on delivery of recordings and may last longer than seven years, are the subject of section 2855(b) of the statute, which specifies that should any artist seek to cancel a sound recording agreement based on the agreement exceeding seven years, the artist must first give notice in accordance with Section 1020 of the Code of Civil Procedure, and the record company may then be statutorily entitled to recover unspecified damages for any phonorecords that the artist failed to deliver under the agreement. See also, *MCA Records, Inc. v. Olivia Newton-John*, 90 Cal. App.3d 18, 153 Cal. Rptr. 153 (1979).

that point, the next contract period will begin, assuming the record company has exercised its option for further contract periods and has not dropped the artist.[185]

The definition of what constitutes a deliverable "album" in a recording agreement was disputed between the band "A Day to Remember" and its independent record label in *Woodward v. Victory Records, Inc.*[186] On a motion for a preliminary injunction, the court found that the poorly drafted "deal memo" was vague and ambiguous in the way it described the required delivery of five "albums" as "[a]n Album is a [*sic*] of reproduction, transmission or communication of Recordings, now or hereafter known, manufactured, distributed, transmitted or communicated in any format." The band argued that thirteen released recordings, including some singles, all satisfied the definition, while the label argued that "recognized custom and practice" could only mean "new studio or 'commitment' albums that are delivered in accordance with the eighteen- and twenty-four-month cycle."[187] The court denied injunctive relief, stating that the record label would be entitled to sufficient monetary damages if it prevailed at trial.

The time between contract periods can stretch on for years. The overall period encompassing the creation and release of an album, including the subsequent touring and promotion, is also referred to as an album "cycle," and represents a period of time that may also determine other aspects of the artist's business dealings.[188]

[d]—Delivery and Approval

The record company will seek to reserve the right to approve of the recording budget, participants, repertoire, and final submitted master recording.

[e]—Option Periods

The typical agreement begins with the first album project, which serves as the first contract period. The agreement will specify that the record company will hold a number of options for additional contract periods, at its sole discretion. Options for five or six additional albums are common; however, the option belongs solely to the record company.

---

185   See *Zomba Recording LLC v. Williams*, 15 Misc.3d 1118(A) (Slip Op.), 839 N.Y.S.2d 438, 2007 WL 1063869, at *10 (N.Y. Sup. Feb. 19, 2007) (lack of certitude as regards adherence to notification process for exercising an option can lead to dispute as to whether recording agreement is still in effect).

186   See *Woodward v. Victory Records, Inc.*, 2013 WL 5517926 (N.D. Ill. Oct. 4, 2013).

187   *Id.*, 2013 WL 5517926, at *2.

188   Management agreements may be tied to album cycles.

[f]—Recording Fund and Recoupable Advances

For each contract period and the album to be delivered, the record company will have a total recording fund available. Part of the fund will be spent on the actual recording budget, but to the extent that the recording budget does not consume the entire available fund, the remainder will be paid to the artist as an advance against future royalties. The amount of the recording fund for all option periods is normally specified in the agreement, with a minimum and maximum amount set forth.

In addition, the recording fund amount can be increased by an agreement that it will not be less than two-thirds of the royalties earned on the album delivered in the previous contract period. This provision ensures that any advances paid in the future will reflect the artist's previous success.[189] All advances are recoupable by the record company against future royalties earned by the artist.[190]

---

189   Advances are typically re-negotiated, along with other deal points, in the event the artist proves to be successful. But see, *Noise in the Attic Productions, Inc., v. London Records*, 10 A.D.3d 303, 782 N.Y.S.2d 1 (2004) (new advances based on prior success of recording artists Salt 'N Pepa apparently erroneously posted by record company to royalty account of producer instead of artists). However, increased advances may come at the expense of increased album commitments.

190   In the event releases do not achieve high sales, Artists' royalty accounts can reach considerable deficits. See, e.g., In re Watkins, 210 B.R. 394, 397 (Bankr. N.D. Ga. 1997) (noting in the context of a challenge to a bankruptcy filing by members of the group "TLC" that the group's recording agreement royalty account at one point reflected a negative balance totaling $827,695.12). While royalty account deficits do not need to be paid back in cash, the deficit was one of the overall considerations leading to the artists' decision to file petitions under Chapter 11 of the Bankruptcy Code. For a similar glimpse of the financial difficulties incurred by otherwise well known recording artists, see also, In the Matter of Taylor, 91 B.R. 302 (Bankr. D.N.J. 1988) (member of group Kool and the Gang). Under the Bankruptcy Code, the bankruptcy estate may seek to have recording and other executory agreements rejected in order to obtain a "fresh start." *Id.* at 313. Bankruptcy adjudications involving musicians sometimes provide detailed financial information on complex music industry dealings. See *In re Brown v. Death Row Records*, 219 B.R. 373 (Bankr. E.D. Pa. 1998).

[g]—Release Commitment

Although the agreement may provide a deadline by which the record company must issue a commercial release of the album, the record company is not under any obligation to release the recording. Instead, there may be provisions permitting the artist to terminate the agreement in the event a release does not timely occur. In such event, the artist must first give notice of the intention to terminate, giving the record company an opportunity to cure by releasing the recording. Failure by the artist to proactively give notice of the failure to release may result in a lapse of any such contractual termination right.

Release dates can be the subject of intense planning in order to capitalize on tie-in events, or to strategically gain public attention.[191]

[h]—Name and Likeness, Coupling, Trademarks, and Merchandise

The recording agreement will have provisions for use of the artist's or group's name and likeness for commercial purposes, the artist's right of publicity, including advertising and promoting the recordings.[192] The artist may also want provisions that ensure that any recordings released do in fact appear under the artist's name, in a suitably prominent manner and location, especially with respect to any future compilations or "greatest hits" collections that include other artists.[193]

In the case of releases of an artist's work coupled with sound recordings by other artists, on a compilation, for example, artists can reserve approval over such coupling rights, but courts have held that such coupling approval rights, where authorized, can be enforced only upon a showing of damages arising from the coupling.[194]

Because an artist's celebrity is an important income source, the record company may also seek to:

- Obtain a Web address in the name of the artist;

- Apply for trademarks associated with the artist;

---

191   See *TVT Records v. The Island Def Jam Music Group*, 412 F.3d 82, 86 (2d Cir. 2005) (release date of soloist's new recording allegedly planned to compete with and distract attention from competing sound recordings on other label).

192   See Chapter 6 for a discussion of the right of publicity.

193   In one case for example, a record company released an artist's recordings under the name of a fictitious group associated with a film, a deceptive act likely to cause consumer confusion and to create liability under the Lanham Act. See *Cafferty v. Scotti Brothers Records, Inc.*, 969 F. Supp. 193, 200-202 (S.D.N.Y. 1997).

194   See *Franconero v. Universal Music Corp.*, 542 Fed. Appx. 13 (2d Cir. 2013) (singer Connie Francis originally had a contract that gave her approval rights over coupling, and over the timing of the releases of her recordings).

- Participate in endorsement and sponsorship income that may arise from tours or performances; and

- Create and sell merchandise using the artist's name and likeness.

While such ancillary income areas might legitimately be part of a "360" agreement, as part of a standard recording agreement, such rights should be granted only if there has been a thoughtful negotiation regarding the implications they have on the artist's overall career and financial goals, and whether the record company is willing to make meaningful financial and staffing commitments in exchange for such broad rights.

[i]—Royalties

The initial, and crucial, issue for royalties is whether they are calculated on the Suggested Retail List Price ("SRLP") of the recordings, or on net revenue actually received by the record company, which would constitute much lower wholesale income, typically arising from the record company's published price to dealers ("PPD").

Ideally, royalty rates for an artist at the beginning of his or her career might be 12% to 14% of SRLP during the first and second contract periods, perhaps rising after that by 1% for each subsequent contract period. Since royalty rates, like advances, are typically re-negotiated for successful artists, the agreement may also contain royalty escalations or "bump ups"—for example, increases of half of a percent if the album sells 500,000 copies, and another half of a percent at the level of 1,000,000 copies.[195] There may also be bonus payments if the album appears on selected best-seller charts in Billboard Magazine.

Such royalty rates will likely be tied solely to sales via normal retail channels in the United States in the form of traditional record stores, which is an increasingly less important form of distribution. There will be deductions from that rate of up to 50% less for the many other types of sales, including foreign sales, record clubs, and special promotions.[196] Other royalty deductions might include lower rates for

---

195   See *Gordy Co. v. Mary Jane Girls, Inc.*, 1989 U.S. Dist. LEXIS 14581, 1989 WL 149290 at *37 (S.D.N.Y. Dec. 6, 1989).

196   See *M.T. Industries, Inc. v. Dominion Entertainment, Inc.*, 1991 U.S. Dist. LEXIS 3845, 1991 WL 50979 (S.D.N.Y. March 29, 1991) (whether records were sold at "top line" pricing or reduced pricing reduced royalty from 14% to 10%). See also, *MCA Records, Inc. v. Allison*, 2009 Cal. App. Unpub. LEXIS 4454, 2009 WL 1565037 (Cal. App. June 5, 2009) (Buddy Holly estate dispute with record company, discussing calculation of overseas royalties and use of "uplifts" by record company to estimate foreign sales revenues equivalents to domestic suggested retail list price). *Id.* at *20.

particular configurations, such as "new media" digital downloads. Many CDs are ordered online and shipped to the consumer via e-commerce Web sites and care should be taken to ensure that such online sales of physical phonorecords come within the "normal retail channels" definition in the agreement, and are not subject to a reduced royalty rate.

"Black box" royalties refer to licensing or other income that may be received by the record company in a large lump payment that does not identify specific titles.[197] Although participation in such payments is difficult at best, an artist can attempt to obtain a contractual provision that awards the artist some portion of such black box payments.[198]

In a case involving the royalties for the band Linkin Park, the group's recording agreement allowed the record label to modify the manner in which royalties would be calculated, so long as the change was "pennies neutral," i.e. the change would not have a negative effect on the total dollar amount of royalties paid. Subsequently, the band audited the label, leading to a dispute between the auditor and the band's attorney over whether the change in royalty calculations lead to an increase, or a decrease, in the band's royalties.[199]

[j]—Deductions, "Cross Collateralization," and Other Expenses

Recording agreements may have provisions deducting a "container" or packaging charge from the suggested retail list price on which the royalty percentage is based, up to as much as 25%.[200] They may also have a general deduction contained in a definition such as "net sales," whereby all payments are based on 90% of sales, not 100%.[201] With respect to these two somewhat notorious deductions from royalties, it may be easier to reduce or remove the packaging deduction than to change the

197 See *Gordy Co. v. Mary Jane Girls, Inc.*, 1989 U.S. Dist. LEXIS 14581, 1989 WL 149290 at *44 (S.D.N.Y. Dec. 6, 1989). See *Jobim v. Songs of Universal, Inc.*, 732 F. Supp.2d 407 (2010).

198 One example is through lump sum licensing or other payments from collective licensing organizations in the United States or abroad.

199 See *Hayes v. Hutchinson*, 2013 Cal. App. Unpub. LEXIS 543, 2013 WL 265800 (Cal. App. Jan. 24, 2013).

200 See *MCA Records, Inc. v. Allison*, 2009 Cal. App. Unpub. LEXIS 4454, 2009 WL 1565037 (Cal. App. June 5, 2009) (royalty dispute brought by estate of Buddy Holly where court discussed packaging deductions, noting that deductions up to 25% "did not equal nor was it specifically based on the actual cost to the record company of manufacturing the album jacket, cassette cover, or CD 'jewel box.'" Court also stated that "a 25 percent packaging deduction may have been justified long ago when CD's were first introduced, but it was in questionable good faith over time as the cost of producing CD's decreased dramatically." *Id.* at *19.).

201 Historically, this deduction arose from an allowance for breakage during shipping of the old vinyl "78 rpm" records.

definition of net sales to be 100% of actual sales.[202] In addition, promotional and marketing expenses will also be charged against the artist's royalty account.

The description of what can be so charged should be carefully reviewed and defined as much as possible to exclude normal overhead or accounting costs, and where possible, to be subject to mutual agreement or approvals.

If an agreement covers more than one release, it will state that any advances, or any deductions from royalties that create deficits to the artist's royalty account, can be charged against royalty income from any of the releases. In other words, the potential good royalty income from a successful project that has recouped its advances and costs can be offset by deductions arising from unrecouped advances and expenditures from an earlier or later project that was unsuccessful.

This cross-collateralization can also apply in a larger context, between recording and publishing deals where the two entities are affiliated, or between an old agreement and a new, renegotiated agreement.[203] Because the record company needs the largest possible pool of income from which to recoup its advances to the artist, it may be extremely difficult to limit recoupment to an album-by-album basis, or even to avoid it between old and new agreements. But if at all possible, cross-collateralization should not apply between different income sectors. Publishing royalties should not be offset by unrecouped advances arising from a recording agreement.[204]

[k]—Producer Royalties

The copyrightable elements of a sound recording will usually, though not always, involve "authorship" both on the part of the performers and the record producer.[205] In exchange for assigning the copyright in the recording to the record company or to the artist, the producer is typically entitled to a royalty of 3% or 4%, which typically comes out of and is deducted from the artist's royalty.[206] In addition to the producer's

---

202   See *Thomas v. Lytle*, 104 F. Supp.2d 906, 910 (M.D. Tenn. 2000) (calculating recording royalties based on "ninety percent (90%) of the quantity of product manufactured and distributed for sale by or for the Record Company in the U.S.A. and Canada, and paid for.").

203   See The *Gordy Co. v. Mary Jane Girls, Inc.*, 1989 U.S. Dist. LEXIS 14581, 1989 WL 149290 at *10 (S.D.N.Y. Dec. 6, 1989) (several agreements made over the years between production companies run by Rick James all cross-collateralized although they involved different featured recording artists). See also, *Malmsteen v. Universal Music Group, Inc.*, 940 F. Supp.2d 123, 128 (S.D.N.Y. 2013) (cross-collateralization of audio recording royalties against video costs).

204   See generally, Passman, *All You Need To Know About the Music Business* (8th ed., 2014), widely considered the leading discussion on recording agreement deal points and negotiation.

205   See H.R. Rep. No. 94–1476, 94th Cong., 2d Sess. 56 (1976) (legislative history of the 1976 Copyright Act).

206   The artist's royalty is referred to as "all in" because it includes the producer's share.

work in the recording studio, others may lay claim to a producer credit and royalty, including the venue that hosts the recording of a performance later released by a record label, or a recording studio that does no more than provide the recording facilities.[207]

In addition, the artist must be careful in negotiating his or her own agreement with the producer so that the artist's obligation to pay the producer comports with the artist's own royalty receipt expectations.[208] In their royalty agreement, the producer may expect to be paid royalties from the first record sold, unlike the artist who, despite receiving an advance, will not accumulate any additional cash royalties until the advance has been recouped by the record company. In the event the artist owes money to the producer, the artist can give the record company a "letter of direction" to remit the producer's royalties to the producer. If the record company is willing to do that, they will charge the money as an additional advance to the artist.

Here is a very simplified illustration, based on an agreement where the artist's royalty for sales is 14% all in.[209] It assumes the producer received an advance of $20,000, but will not receive further payments until the artist has recouped the original recording costs:

Artist royalty per album at $1.00

Producer royalty per album at $.40

Recording budget and advance total: $300,000

Producer advance: $20,000

When sales reach 300,000 units, based on the artist's net royalty of $1.00 per album, the artist will have recouped the recording budget and advance. Assuming for this illustration that there are no other deductions the artist is responsible for (for example marketing/video costs or mechanicals "cap" overages), the artist will, starting

---

207 See *Systems XIX, Inc. v. Parker*, 30 F.Supp.2d 1225 (N.D. Cal. 1998) (live concert venue that also had a recording studio and capability of making commercial-quality recordings sued performer and record label for copyright infringement based on claim that venue's live recording of artist, as commercially released, created copyright co-authorship and ownership in venue, which entitled venue to a producer credit and royalty agreement. Summary judgment for venue on copyright claims.).

208 See *Sony Music Entertainment Inc. v. Robison*, 2002 WL 272406 (S.D.N.Y. Feb. 26, 2002) (counterclaim allegation of fraudulent misrepresentation brought by group the Dixie Chicks against their record label with respect to an 8% royalty to be paid to a producer, which amount would be deductible from the group's royalties).

209 The artist will be responsible for paying the producer a 4% royalty.

with the first unit over 300,000 sold, begin to receive $1.00 per unit in cash royalty payments.

However, the producer's accrued and due royalties amount to $120,000 ($.40 x 300,000), less the producer's $20,000 advance, totaling $100,000 owed to the producer by the artist at this point in time when the recording costs have been recouped.[210]

[l]—Sampling

Sampling is the term for using portions of someone else's sound recording in your own recording, thus incurring license obligations to the owners of both the sound recording sampled, and the copyright owners of the underlying musical composition.[211] Courts have held that such samples must be licensed.[212] If the artist includes any samples on their recordings, such usage, because it must be licensed from third parties, may be subject to approval by the record company. It will also be necessary to pay a license fee to the owner of the sample.[213] Such license fees will be the re-

---

210   Given that the artist is only about to start receiving cash royalty payments, they will not have $100,000 to pay the producer in a lump sum. The usual solution, which must be addressed in the agreement, is that the artist may give the record company a letter of direction to pay the producer the $100,000 due. The result is that the artist will increase their debt to the record company by $100,000, and further delay the point at which the artist will be recouped. The alternative would be that the artist has to come up with the $100,000 owed to the producer from other resources (remember that artists can generate income in other areas including live performance, endorsements, and music publishing).

Note also that some label employees, such as those in Artists and Repertoire divisions ("A&R") may be entitled to bonuses based on percentages of sales of the recordings by artists they sign to the label, however such payments are a matter of employment agreements between the employee and the label, and do not come directly out of the artist's income. See *McAnany v. Angel Records, Inc.*, 216 F. Supp.2d 335 (S.D.N.Y. 2002) (breach of contract claim by classical label's Director of Artists and Repertoire whose employment agreement allowed for a royalty of 1% of the retail selling price on all albums released by artists for whom the employee served as either the primary A&R signing contact, or the primary A&R contact, and an additional 3% where the employee also acted as the primary producer of the recording).

211   Sampling became popular in the early days of rap and hip hop when performers would use existing recordings by others as background musical elements.

212   See *Bridgeport Music, Inc. v. Dimension Films*, 383 F.3d 390 (6th Cir. 2004) (In the Sixth Circuit, there is no de minimis defense to an infringement claim based on sampling of a sound recording, even where only a short portion of a sound recording is sampled.). But see, *VMG Salsoul, LLC v. Ciccone*, 2013 U.S. Dist. LEXIS 184127 (C.D. Cal. Nov. 18, 2013) (stating that the Sixth Circuit's "bright line rule" regarding the de minimis defense for sound recording sampling "has not been adopted by the Ninth Circuit"). *Compare, Newton v. Diamond*, 388 F.3d 1190 (9th Cir. 2004) (with respect to underlying musical compositions embodied in a sampled sound recording, the sampling of a three-note sequence was de minimis and not actionable).

213   See *Batiste v. Island Records, Inc.*, 179 F.3d 217 (5th Cir. 1999) (the licensor of music used as a sample received a 40% ownership share in the song and recording that incorporated the sample as well as a $15,000 advance). In

sponsibility of the artist, and will be charged against the royalty account, or at least added to the amount they must recoup.

Sampling may also invoke the need to pay publishing royalties, or mechanicals, to the publisher of the underlying musical composition contained within the sampled sound recording. Those sampling mechanicals will also be the responsibility of the artist.

[m]—Mechanical Royalties: Controlled Compositions

The agreement between the record company and the artist will have several provisions addressing the use of underlying compositions, written either by the artist or by others, on the sound recordings.

Compositions recorded by the artist will be defined as "controlled compositions."[214] Recall that permission to make the first commercial recording of a composition is a right retained by the composer or his music publisher, so the agreement will have a provision granting the record company first recording rights for all controlled compositions, including previously unreleased material.

Next, the agreement will specify that the record company gets a discount on the statutory mechanical royalty license rate, and is obligated to pay only 75% of the rate. This controlled compositions rate will be applied however to any song the artist records.[215] In that case, the third-party publisher may not grant a reduced mechanical rate, and will demand the full 100% of the mechanical royalty rate. The artist is responsible for making up the difference, which will come out of his royalties, or will be chargeable as an additional advance.

---

the case of the music publishing rights, it is not uncommon for the publisher whose work is being sampled extensively to insist on owning most, if not all, of the music publishing rights in the new song. Thus the artist heavily incorporating samples from others may find they do not own the copyright in the resulting composition.

214   See *Universal-MCA Music Publishing v. Bad Boy Entertainment*, 2003 WL 21497318, at *1-*2 (N.Y. Sup. June 18, 2003):

> "A controlled composition clause often included in recording agreements limits the amount of mechanical royalties a record company must pay to the music publisher for compositions contained on records released by the record company to a percentage below the minimum compulsory statutory rate. The rate generally used by record companies is 75% of the compulsory statutory rate. If the total amount due for mechanical royalties for non-controlled compositions included on an album results in an amount in excess of the maximum set by the clause, the record company deducts the excess from the mechanical royalties due to the owner of the controlled compositions, thus limiting the amount of mechanical royalties ultimately due for use of the controlled compositions."

Id., 2003 WL 21497318, at *2 n.2.

215   This is true even if the artist records a "*cover*" version of a song not controlled by the artist or her publisher.

In addition, the agreement will attempt to put a cap on mechanicals generally, stating that for any album released, the record company will pay no more than ten to twelve times the controlled compositions rate. So if the album has more than ten to twelve tracks, or if the album has tracks where the third-party publishers want a 100% mechanical rate, the artist pays the difference.[216] Note also that the licensing costs for any mechanicals that must be paid to third parties as a result of sampling will count towards the cap on mechanical royalties.

Under Section 115(c)(3)(E) of the Copyright Act, for recording agreements entered into after June 22, 1995, mechanical royalties for Digital Phonorecord Deliveries ("DPDs") must be licensed at the full DPD statutory rate, with no "cap." For physical phonorecord formats however, such as CDs, there are no statutory restrictions on controlled compositions clauses.[217]

Here is a simplified example:

First, the calculation of the mechanicals "cap" per album the record company is willing to pay:

Full statutory rate for songs with durations of 5 minutes or less: $.091

75% of that rate for controlled compositions 5 minutes or under: $.06825

Mechanicals cap per album ($.06825 ×10): $.6825

If the artist decides the album will have twelve, instead of ten, songs, the mechanical royalties obligation will be:

Five songs "controlled" by the artist, duration under 5 minutes (5 × 0.6825) $.34125

Two songs "controlled" by the artist with durations of 7 minutes each. The mechanical for each 7-minute song is 7 × $0.175, or $.1225 each, but as controlled compositions the rate is 75% of the full rate or .91875 per song. (2 × $.91875): $.18375

---

216   See *Universal-MCA Music Publishing v. Bad Boy Entertainment*, 2003 WL 21497318 (N.Y. Sup. June 18, 2003) (plaintiffs alleged that defendant who was their co-writer of songs on a successful album, and who was also the featured artist on the album and president of the record label releasing the album, manipulated the controlled composition clause for the album such that the "cap" or limit on mechanical royalties prevented the plaintiffs from receiving any mechanical royalties).

217   See § 4.05[1][a] *supra*.

Five songs that are "covers" of third-party copyrights, and the third parties will only license at the full rate ($5 \times \$.091 = \$.455$): $.455

Total mechanicals due to publishers for the album: $.98

Less allowance in the mechanicals "cap":   ($.6825)

Mechanicals shortfall chargeable to artist per album: $.2975

[n]—Videos and Touring

The agreement may have provisions concerning the production of audiovisual works, in the form of music videos. Music videos are used largely for promotion, although they can generate some income via sales of DVDs or paid downloads. The record company may be willing to absorb half the costs of a video, up to a certain limit, beyond which all the costs would be charged against the artist's royalty account and recoupable by the record company.[218]

[o]—Licensing Approvals

In the event the record company is able to license the master recording for use in film, television, or advertising, the artist will seek approval rights with respect to the content of the usage.[219] Some prohibitions can be written into the agreement, including the prohibition of use in "NC-17" rated films or for advertising for alcohol. The record company may ask for a time limit on any such approvals; if, for example, the artist or his representatives does not reply in ten days, the record company may grant the license.

[p]—Audit Rights

Audit provisions will address a number of procedural and record-keeping aspects including the frequency with which the artist can conduct an audit, how much notice is required, how many past audit periods and what period of past time the audit

---

218   See *Malmsteen v. Universal Music Group, Inc.*, 940 F. Supp.2d 123, 128 (S.D.N.Y. 2013) (50% of video production costs recoupable).

219   See *Franconero v. Universal Music Corp.*, 2003 U.S. Dist. LEXIS 22800, 2003 WL 22990060 (S.D.N.Y. Dec. 19, 2003) (singer Connie Francis sued record label for, inter alia, issuing master licenses for her recordings, without her approval, to films featuring scenes of suicide, prostitution, and rape. On summary judgment of Francis' claims for violation of moral rights under foreign law, intentional infliction of emotional distress, breach of the duty of good faith and fair dealing, and civil rights claims under the New York Civil Rights Law § 51, the right of publicity statute, the court held that Francis did not reserve an approval clause with respect to such licensing in her recording agreement).

can apply to, and provisions requiring the record company to keep complete and accurate books and records of account.[220]

The periods subject to an audit should be, at a minimum, the same as the prevailing statute of limitations on breach of contract claims in the jurisdiction, and should not be arbitrarily limited to shorter periods of time. In addition, there should not be provisions allowing the record company to discard records after a period of time.[221]

The audit clause drafted by the record company may also attempt to prohibit the artist from using an auditor who is already engaged in audits on behalf of other artists.[222] Such provisions may be an attempt by a record company to limit situations where an auditor for an artist discovers general accounting issues that may benefit other artists.

An ideal audit clause will state that in the event any discrepancies in the artist's favor are uncovered, the amounts owing will be remitted immediately and not in the next accounting period. In addition, should the audit uncover an error of 5% or more, the record company will reimburse the artist for the reasonable costs of the audit.

The scope of the audit would include "cross checking" payments and dealings with third parties, such as mechanicals paid to publishers, union fees paid to the American Federation of Musicians ("AFM") based on sales, reserves against returns actually reported by distributors and dealers, licenses to record clubs, and invoices from production plants in order to confirm that those third-party sales and income reports match the reporting made to the artist.[223]

---

220   See *Clinton v. Universal Music Group*, 2011 U.S. Dist. LEXIS 88757, 2011 WL 3501818 (C.D. Cal. Aug. 9, 2011) (royalty dispute over issues including contractual limitations on time within which artist must bring any objections to accounting reports). See also, *Mahoney, p/k/a Eddie Money v. Sony Music Entertainment*, 2013 U.S. Dist. LEXIS 18181, 2013 WL 491526 (S.D.N.Y. Feb. 11, 2013).

221   See *Franconero v. Universal Music Corp.*, N. 55 supra, 2003 U.S. Dist. LEXIS 22800, at *10-*11, 2003 WL 22990060, at *4 (plaintiff was contractually foreclosed from auditing or seeking back royalties beyond the contracted-for review period limited to two years under an "incontestability clause"). See also, *Franconero v. Universal Music Corp.*, 2011 U.S. Dist. LEXIS 15259, 2011 WL 566794 (S.D.N.Y. Feb. 11, 2011) (plaintiff had released record company from obligations including restrictions on "coupling" plaintiff's recordings on compilations with other artists).

222   See *The Gordy Co. v. Mary Jane Girls, Inc.*, 1989 U.S. Dist. LEXIS 14581, at *94-*97, 1989 WL 149290, at *35 (S.D.N.Y. Dec. 6, 1989) (listing areas that come within the scope of a thorough audit, and stating "[b]oth sides recognize the adversarial nature of audits and the ramifications of revealing general ledgers to specialists in the field . . . who represent other artists at other times"). *Id.*, 1989 WL 149290, at *36.

223   *Id.*

Audit results can lead to a host of breach of contract claims and litigation. In one case, the allegations resulting from an audit were that the record company:

- Designated various items as "scrap" but then really resold those items;
- Classified distribution of certain recordings as "promotional" and therefore non royalty bearing, but then really sold the material;
- Entered into licenses with third-parties without plaintiffs' required consent;
- Failed to disclose money received from third-party exploitation such as deals with record clubs like Columbia House and AEI Music Networks, a company that compiles and distributes tape programs to companies for various uses, such as airlines for in-flight music;
- Under-reported the number of units sold;
- Utilized incorrect royalty calculations.[224]

In one case, an audit on behalf of the band Linkin Park led to an unusual result: a dispute between the auditor and the band's attorney over whether a renegotiation of the band's recording agreement resulted in a net improvement or decrease in royalties due to the band.[225]

[q]—Termination, Suspension, Reversion of Rights

The "termination" section in the agreement may give a record company broad rights to suspend its obligations under the agreement, or to terminate its relationship with an artist. Conversely, an artist may have a right to terminate an agreement if the record company fails to release a recording after notice and cure provisions have been observed, but the artist may waive that right if they do not follow the contractual procedures in detail. In the event the artist terminates under such a provision, they will of course no longer have a relationship with the record company, and, in the absence of any reversion provisions, the ownership of any masters recorded to date will likely remain with the record company.[226]

---

224   See *Apple Corps Limited v. Capitol Records, Inc.*, 13 Misc.3d 1211(A), 824 N.Y.S.2d 752, 2006 WL 2726809, at *2 (N.Y. Sup. 2006).

225   See *Hayes v. Hutchinson*, 2013 Cal. App. Unpub. LEXIS 543, 2013 WL 265800 (Cal. App. Jan. 24, 2013).

226   Despite the considerable number of cases brought by recording artists attempting to rescind allegedly oppressive recording agreements or to remedy situations where payments are not received timely or in full, courts are reluctant to grant the remedy of rescission absent a clear showing of fraud or a total long-term failure to pay. See:

Second Circuit: *Nolan v. Sam Fox Publishing Company, Inc.*, 499 F.2d 1394 (2d Cir. 1974) (no rescission where at least some payments had been made).

[r]—Recording Agreement Negotiation

The above list identifies only the "big" issues in a recording agreement. Items such as caps or approvals on marketing expenditures and other costs are important as well. In negotiating a recording agreement for an artist, it is advisable to have points to make on virtually all of the above issues, and to be prepared to juggle them in the hope of reaching an acceptable resolution for both parties. For example, a request for an increase in royalty percentage might be met with a lower advance payment, or a proposal to limit the number of option periods might be achieved only if a concession is made on the packaging deduction.[227]

Here is an illustration of the potential economic impact of recording agreement recoupment and deduction provisions in a scenario where 300,000 units have been sold. It assumes that all retail sales are at normal retail channels at the full royalty rate (remember that sales via record clubs, online sales, and overseas sales are at a reduced royalty rate):

Total advance to artist including recording costs:	$300,000
Retail price of album:	$17.50
Less packaging deduction 20%:	<$3.50>
Royalty base price:	$14.00
Royalty per album at 15% of retail:	$2.10
Less royalty paid producer at 4%	<$.56>
Net artist royalty per album:	$1.54
Gross royalty for 300,000 units sold:	$462,000
Less 10% deduction as defined in "net sales":	<$46,200>

Ninth Circuit: *Peterson v. Highland Music, Inc.*, 140 F.3d 1313 (9th Cir. 1998) (affirming rescission of rights in recording of "Louie Louie" where no royalties had been received for thirty years, and affirming contempt sanctions against defendants who failed to abide by rescission order from district court).

In one case, a recording agreement had a provision whereby after the artist delivered all five of the required albums and the agreement expired, the artist had a right to regain copyright ownership of the masters, provided that the label had recouped all of its advances for all albums within three accountings periods after the expiration of the term. See *Cooper v. Sony Records International*, 2001 U.S. Dist. LEXIS 16436, 2001 WL 1223492 (S.D.N.Y. Oct. 15, 2001) (artists brought action including copyright infringement, breach of contract, and fraud, alleging that label's royalty statements in accurately failed to show recoupment, preventing artists from regaining ownership of masters).

227   See generally, Passman, *All You Need To Know About the Music Business* (8th ed., 2014). See also: Thall, *What They'll Never Tell You About the Music Business* (2002) (a comprehensive overview of music industry practice and custom); Krasilovsky, Shemel, Gross, and Feinstein, *This Business of Music* (10th ed., 2007) (a wide-ranging overview of the entire music industry); Kohn and Kohn, *Kohn on Music Licensing* (4th ed. 2009) (an in depth consideration of music licensing practice and procedure).

Adjusted net royalty for 100,000 albums:	$415,800
Less advance for recording costs:	<$300,000>
Less overage on mechanicals cap as described above ($.2975 × 300,000):[229]	<$89,250>
Less recoupable marketing/video expenses:	<$200,000>
Adjusted unrecouped position of artist:	<$173,450>

After sales of 300,000 units at the full royalty rate, the artist is still not "recouped." Note, however, that if the record company's published price to dealer ("PPD") is $12.00, the record company's gross revenue from the album, before deduction of distribution or any other costs, and before payment of mechanical royalties, would be $3,600,000 ($12 × 300,000).

In this example, because the artist is also a songwriter, the album sales will have generated some music publishing income for the artist, but as part of the artist's entirely separate agreement with the music publisher, as follows:

300,000 units sold, each containing seven tracks composed by artist and paid by record company at controlled compositions rate of 75% of full statutory rate.

Five tracks at five minutes each (5 × 0.6825):	$.34125
Two tracks at seven minutes each (2 × $.91875):	$.18375
Per album mechanicals:	$.525
Total for 300,000 albums:	$157,500
Artist's 75% of mechanicals in a co-publishing agreement:	$118,125

In addition, the artist will have rights income for radio, television, live performance,[229] and Internet performances, and any sync license income. This illustrates the importance of keeping the music publishing revenues completely separate from the recording agreement, so that the artist can earn money from music publishing

---

228   The mechanicals overage is based on all 300,000 units sold. Third party music publishers will not accept accountings based on the record company's 90% of sales "net" calculations.

229   The artist's income from live performances and endorsements is, traditionally, not income in which the record company shares, but is increasingly subject to the terms of a "360 deal."

even where they remain unrecouped, and not receiving royalties, with respect to the recording agreement.

[s]—Other Models for Recording Agreements

The above discussion considers many facets of a traditional, large-scale recording agreement. However, there is nothing preventing parties from using other models. Some independent record labels, for example, offer artists a very simple split of all income, after deducting any recording or manufacturing costs. Where the artist is also the songwriter, such agreements may also include the mechanical royalties as part of the overall split of net income.

Where artists may already have their own master tapes, these simplified agreements would not require any provisions for recoupment of recording expenses. While there may be limited or no advances available, such simplified agreements are increasingly common, especially in an environment where technology has put recording techniques, promotion, and digital distribution directly into the hands of artists.[230]

[t]—A Note on Recording Studios

Recording studios provide a range of services, including space to record, instruments, expert recording equipment and engineering, and the ability to equalize and mix recordings into their final "master" form. Recording studios may also offer musical arrangements for background musicians, and general creative input, all of which can rise to the level of a copyright co-authorship and co-ownership claim based on a producer role in the resulting recordings.[231] In negotiating any agreements with recording studios, the artist or the record company should ensure that the understanding with the studio is clear with respect to copyright, and any producer credits or royalties.

[u]—Quality Control

While the sonic quality of sound recordings offered by record companies is of paramount importance, it is not typically the subject of contractual provisions. In *Zappa v. Rykodisc, Inc.*, the integrity of the sonic quality of the recordings of Frank Zappa

---

230   The artist may want nothing more from a label than basic distribution services and minimal promotion, leaving the artist free to promote themselves via social networking Web sites, performances, merchandising, digital distribution online, and occasional licensing of songs to television programs.

231   See *Systems XIX, Inc. v. Parker*, 30 F. Supp.2d 1225 (N.D. Cal. 1998) (recording studio that also had a live concert venue expected that recordings they made for commercial release would result in a producer credit and royalty).

was the subject of a breach of contract action.[232] Following the death of Frank Zappa in 1993, his estate entered into an agreement with Rykodisc whereby Rykodisc paid $20 million for rights in Zappa's wholly owned catalog of over sixty albums. Among the issues in the case were whether Rkyodisc had acquired only the "final mixes" of the works, or had also acquired the source tracks that could be used to create new versions of the recordings. But the essence of the claims concerned allegations that a contractual clause that prohibited Rykodisc from making any "changes in technical standards . . . which would impact on the integrity of the work as embodied in the . . . final version" gave Zappa's estate control over the media formats used to market the recordings.[233] The case therefore included discussion as to whether albums manufactured from vinyl have superior sound to those digitally mastered for CD replication, and the extent to which compressed digital format MP3 file versions of the recordings available for digital download on Apple's iTunes online service significantly reduced sound quality and therefore violated the "integrity" provision in the agreement between the parties.[234]

[v]—Reserve Accounts

Recording agreements will have a "Reserve account" provision which grants the record company the right to hold an agreed upon percentage of royalties due in reserve for an agreed amount of time (usually covering one or two royalty accounting periods), in case there are returns or other deductions that arise after the royalties are normally payable. In *Clifford v. Concord Music Group, Inc.*, the band Creedence Clearwater Revival disputed several categories of royalty provisions, including a Reserve Account clause which read as follows:

> "Reserve Account: [Label] retains the right, at its sole option, to create and hold a reasonable reserve account against royalties payable hereunder. The reserve account shall be limited to a maximum of twenty-five percent (25%) of royalties earned and shall be used to offset returns. If such reserve account is established by [Label], royalties should be held for not more than six (6) months after what otherwise would be the due date of the payment of royalties as set forth herein."[235]

---

232 See *Zappa v. Rykodisc, Inc.*, 2011 WL 3628897 (S.D.N.Y. Aug. 17, 2011) (granting in part and denying in part the parties' cross motions for summary judgment).

233 Id., 2011 WL 3628897, at *6.

234 Id.

235 See *Clifford v. Concord Music Group, Inc.*, 2012 U.S. Dist. LEXIS 14084, 2012 WL 380744 (N.D. Cal. Feb. 6, 2012).

On a motion to dismiss, the court held that the plaintiffs had adequately stated a claim for the monies held in the reserve account, which totaled $130,000.

[2]—Distinctions Between Featured and Nonfeatured Artists

In addition to featured artists who make recordings pursuant to royalty agreements, there may also be other, non-featured artists and vocalists participating in a recording. These "sidemen" are paid a flat fee, either as union members under wage scales, or as non-union independent contractors. Such distinctions are important because with respect to royalties due performing artists for digital performances of sound recordings on, for example, the Internet and via satellite, SoundExchange, the collecting body for such royalties, makes payments as follows:

- 50% to the copyright owner of the sound recording

- 45% to the featured artists

- 2.5% shall be deposited in an escrow account overseen by an independent administrator jointly chosen by the copyright owners and the AFM for distribution to nonfeatured musicians, whether or not they are AFM members

- 2.5% shall be deposited in an escrow account overseen by an independent administrator jointly chosen by the copyright owners and AFTRA for distribution to nonfeatured vocalists, whether or not they are AFTRA members.[236]

[3]—Production Agreements

In some cases, a producer and an unsigned artist will enter into an agreement aimed at developing the artist's career, typically by producing demonstration ("demo") recordings by the artist and then "shopping" the artist to record labels. While the artist may benefit from the producer's tutelage, guidance, and industry connections, the artist is at a potential disadvantage because there will be a "middleman" between the artist and the record company, and the artist may wind up party to a recording agreement negotiated largely by the producer on their behalf. To the extent possible, any such production agreement should provide the artist with assurances concerning the major deal points in any future agreement with a record company.[237]

---

236   17 U.S.C. § 114(g)(2).

237   See *The Gordy Co. v. Mary Jane Girls, Inc.*, 1989 U.S. Dist. LEXIS 14581, 1989 WL 149290 at *11-*12 (S.D.N.Y. Dec. 6, 1989) (describing generally how singer and producer Rick James created a group called The Mary Jane Girls, set up a corporation in that name, and entered into an agreement with Motown Records whereby Mary Jane Girls, Inc. produced the artists and provided the masters to Motown. The performing artists themselves worked under contract to the Mary Jane Girls corporation and did not have a direct agreement with Motown.).

[4]—"Brick and Mortar" Retailing

During the first decade of this century, several factors combined to change the landscape of retailing in the recorded music industry. First, the onset of online piracy in the form of peer-to-peer file trading software and other technologies drastically cut into sales of physical CDs.[238] Despite attempts by the music industry to stem the tide, it is still difficult to compete with "free."

Second, although the music industry has always been keenly aware that it competes for the consumer's time and money with other forms of entertainment, technology has provided consumers with massive choices online, including the rise of computer games, social networking Web sites, free online video, and many other choices. Purchasing music is but one option among many.

Third, the decrease in the sale of physical CDs changed the retail landscape significantly. Online retailers, with lower overhead, continue to offer a wide selection of titles. Traditional "brick and mortar" retailers that offer a broad variety of CDs in retail locations however, continue to suffer sales declines that have resulted in closure of retail locations.[239]

Instead of the full-line music retailer model selling only CDs with deep catalog selection, a philosophy of leveraging mass market consumer presence with selling the top-selling CDs and DVDs turned out to be a key to success for retailers like Walmart, Target, and BestBuy. These mass merchandisers have become the leading retailers of CD recordings. They have also extended their consumer impact by offering not only online ordering and shipment of physical CDs, but also online digital delivery via downloads, thereby competing with iTunes. The leading retailers have also leveraged their sales leadership into exclusive distribution and release commitments with popular recording artists.[240]

---

238   See generally, *Metro-Goldwyn-Mayer Studios, Inc. v. Grokster, Ltd.*, 545 U.S. 913, 923, 125 S.Ct. 2764, 162 L.Ed.2d 781 (2005) (the probable scope of online copyright infringement of sound recordings is "staggering").

239   Record clubs are another form of direct to consumer retailing of recordings, either independently owned or as an affiliate of record companies. Like book clubs, a record club may offer discounted products to members, as well as subscriptions to new and recommended releases. Record clubs may enter into agreements with record companies allowing the club to manufacture CDs under license. See *Record Club of America, Inc. v. United Artists Records, Inc.*, 696 F. Supp. 940 (S.D.N.Y. 1988) (record club awarded damages for lost sales based on breach and repudiation of contract by record label that failed to timely deliver product).

240   The trade organization representing retailers of recordings is the National Association of Recording Merchandisers ("NARM"). See www.narm.com.

Sales of CDs and other formats are tracked by the market research and monitoring service Nielsen Soundscan,[241] and the resulting sales numbers form the basis for the "charts," lists of the best selling recordings and albums published weekly in Billboard Magazine.

[5]—Digital Distribution and Security Measures

Web sites operated by various companies, most notably Apple's iTunes online music store and amazon.com, are a main conduit for the sale of digital phonorecords. In contrast to albums containing ten or more tracks, digital distribution is based on the retailing of individual tracks. The financial model is typically a cost of $.99 per track, with the retailer retaining 30% and the record company 70%, from which the record company is responsible for paying the mechanical license to the music publisher.[242]

Digital files may be encrypted via digital rights management software ("DRM"). Encrypted files may offer some additional security because the purchaser must have the appropriate software and encryption codes to access the music. On the other hand, there is no universal DRM standard, and it has been argued that the various competing standards impede the progress and development of the online music retailing world. The increasingly popular alternative is to offer files in the universally accepted MP3 format, in the hope that the ease of use will encourage greater consumer interest in buying digital files.

Recent technological developments include users storing their music files online in the "digital cloud," or in storage servers provided by services such as amazon.com and Google.[243]

Security is a major concern for Web sites that sell or stream the digital files. Accordingly, agreements between record companies and online retailers may therefore contain provisions such as "Content Usage Rules and Security Measures," in which the technical specifications and digital security considerations are paramount, and under which the

---

241   Nielsen SoundScan is an information system that tracks sales of music and music video products throughout the United States and Canada. Sales data from point-of-sale cash registers is collected weekly from over 14,000 retail, mass merchant and non-traditional (online stores, venues, etc.) outlets. Weekly data is compiled and made available every Wednesday. Nielsen SoundScan is the sales source for the Billboard music charts. See www.soundscan.com.

242   37 C.F.R. § 255.3; see also, 17 U.S.C. § 115. Note that while the record company has the ability to negotiate the selling price of the digital phonorecord, the music publisher must accept the statutory mechanical rate, currently statutorily capped at $.091 as the compulsory mechanical licensing rate for compositions five minutes or under.

243   See *Capitol Records, Inc. v. MP3Tunes, LLC*, 2011 WL 3667335 (S.D.N.Y. Aug. 22, 2011) (discussing online storage "lockers" for digital music files).

record company can force the removal of the digital files from the retailer's Web site in the event of a security breach.

§4.13   Music Publishing Agreements

Agreements between music publishers and composers and lyricists can be relatively simple: the copyright is conveyed either in perpetuity or for a limited term, and there is a division of royalties based on the type of income received.

There are three main types of music publishing agreements: (1) the basic agreement between a publisher and a writer in which the publisher is the sole publisher and copyright owner of the works; (2) a co-publishing agreement in which two publishing companies jointly own the work; and (3) an administration agreement in which a publisher agrees to act as the exclusive agent and representative of another publishing company.[244] The administrating publisher may perform virtually all of the tasks that arise in a publishing relationship, but will do so for only a percentage of the revenue, without claiming copyright ownership.[245]

To understand these terms, relationships, and types of agreements, it is necessary to review the basic types of income a music publisher deals with, and in particular to understand how performing rights royalties work.[246]

---

244   See § 4.13[3] *infra.*

245   In cases where a songwriter has retained the publishing rights and is successful, it can be a good business proposition for a music publisher to administer that catalog even if the agreement is only for a limited time or territory.

246   Courts have struggled with defining music publishing "terms of art." See *Jasper v. Bovina Music, Inc.,* 314 F.3d 42, 45 n.1 (2d Cir. 2002):

"The parties and the District Court called the first category 'Performance Royalties' and the second category 'Publishing Royalties.' The Court's opinion defined 'Performance Royalties' as 'monies directly generated by record sales and other sound recordings' and 'Publishing Royalties' as 'monies generated by the exploitation of the musical compositions themselves-that is, the words and the music of the songs.' The Court explained that '[i]n the music industry, Publishing Royalties are typically created through the efforts of a musical publishing company or administrator who licenses use of the work to third parties. Such licenses include: (a) mechanical licenses that allow other record companies to use the work ("cover" songs), (b) public performance fees when a song is played on the radio or in a concert, (c) sampling rights that permit other artists to use pieces of the song, and (d) synchronization rights when a musical work is used in a movie, commercial or television show.' We do not think clarity is promoted by using the phrase 'Performance Royalties' to mean income from record sales and at the same time using the phrase 'Publishing Royalties' to include 'public performance fees.'

"We note that although the terms 'performance royalties' and 'publishing royalties' have been used in a few reported appellate opinions, these terms are not terms of art with precise meanings. Indeed, they have not been given consistent meanings. We have said that 'performance royalties' are 'paid by the performer to

[1]—Categories of Music Publishing Income

There is a close correlation between technologies used to exploit music, and the types of income that may arise in music publishing agreements.

[a]—Performing Rights

Performing rights arise from myriad uses, including television and radio broadcasts, Internet webcasts, live concerts, music played at bars, music used by businesses including corporate functions, music on hold phone systems, and many other situations where music is performed in a commercial setting, and fees are collected by performing rights societies ("PRO") such as ASCAP, BMI, and SESAC.

Because PRO's divide the royalties they pay into two equal parts, each share is paid directly to the writer or the publisher, obviating the need for a publisher to account for the writer's performing rights royalties. Agreements typically state that each party will receive that income directly from their performing right society, and each will retain that income.

Even "novice" songwriters will receive performance royalties by joining a PRO. But if they join a PRO solely as a songwriter, they will only receive the writer share of any performance royalties. In order for songwriters to receive publisher share, they must also join the PRO as publishers. Joining a PRO as a publisher does not require that the songwriter actually have an operational music publishing company. It means that the

---

performing rights societies such as [ASCAP], of which the songwriter and publisher are members. . . . ASCAP's practice is to distribute half of the performance royalties to the songwriter ("writer distributions"), and the remaining half to the publisher ("publisher distributions"). . . . [T]he songwriter and publisher may by contract alter the allocation of performance royalties.' *Larry Spier, Inc. v. Bourne Co.*, 953 F.2d 774, 776 (2d Cir. 1992). See *Folkways Music Publishers, Inc. v. Weiss*, 989 F.2d 108, 109 (2d Cir. 1993) ('performance royalties' used to mean payments distributed by performing rights society). By 'performer' we refer not only to the person who sings the song but also to 'radio stations, television stations, restaurants, stores and other entities that "perform" music publicly.' *Woods v. Bourne Co.*, 60 F.3d 978, 984 (2d Cir. 1995). The Ninth Circuit has used 'performance royalties' to refer to the income due a song composer for licensing the synchronization right that permits a song to be recorded on the soundtrack of a movie. See *Fosson v. Palace (Waterland), Ltd.*, 78 F.3d 1448, 1450-51 (9th Cir. 1996). Appellate courts have used the phrase 'publishing royalties' in the context of music to have various meanings. See *Ahern v. Scholz*, 85 F.3d 774, 779, 795 (1st Cir. 1996) (royalties owed by manager of music group to composer of two record albums); *Daily v. Gusto Records, Inc.*, 14 Fed. Appx. 579, 582 (6th Cir. 2001) (unpublished opinion) ('Publishing royalties . . . arise by statute [17 U.S.C. § 115] and compensate the owner of a musical composition for use of the copyrighted material at a set statutory rate.'); see also *Calhoun v. Lillenas Publishing*, 298 F.3d 1228, 1234 (11th Cir. 2002) (intended meaning unclear). The Nimmer treatise categorizes the primary sources of revenue for the owner of a copyright in a musical composition as 'public performance income, mechanical licenses, synchronization licenses, . . . and print publishing revenues.' 6 Nimmer on Copyright § 30.02[F], at 30-102 (2002)."

Id., 314 F.3d 45 at n.1.

songwriter is also the copyright owner of the work, and is asserting their right, as the copyright owner, to act as the publisher and to receive the publisher share of performing rights income.

By asserting copyright ownership of the song, the writer now has, at least on paper, a publishing company, and an expectation that he or she will receive both types of performing rights royalties. This division of performance royalties becomes a key factor for the songwriter in the quest to retain copyright ownership of at least a portion of their works, even after entering into an agreement with a music publisher.

[b]—Mechanicals, Including Ring Tones[247]

Mechanical royalties arise from sales of recordings in both physical and digital formats. Mechanicals also arise from, for example, the increasingly popular use of personalized ring tones, uses in toys, and other technologies that mechanically reproduce a musical composition.

Mechanical income is paid to the publisher by the licensee, remitted either directly to the publisher, or via the collective mechanical licensing entity, the Harry Fox Agency. The publisher will deposit the funds until the next accounting period, at which time they will send a statement of account to the writer, and remit to the writer the contractually agreed-upon royalty share.

[c]—Synchronization[248]

Synchronization income arises from the uses of compositions in film, television, advertising, video games, and other technologies that combine music with visual images. License fees are remitted to the publisher, who typically remits 50% to the writer.[249]

[d]—Grand Rights[250]

It is generally recognized that dramatic works that utilize music, potentially have enhanced value because such works can attract large audiences for extended periods

---

247   See § 4.12[1][m] *supra*, for a full discussion of mechanical royalties.

248   See § 4.06 *supra*, for a full discussion of synchronization rights.

249   Note that the publisher may decide, strategically, to issue a synchronization license at a low fee, in the expectation that the usage, perhaps on television, will result in repeated broadcasts that will generate ancillary income in the form of increased performing rights royalties, or in the form of increased mechanicals income in the event the usage makes the music more popular, resulting in increased sales of recordings.

250   Uses of music in a dramatic performance are commonly referred to as "grand rights," while nondramatic performances are often referred to as "small rights." Performing rights societies do not license grand rights or dramatic performances, limiting their activities to nondramatic uses. Similarly, compulsory mechanical licenses

of time and generate significant revenue. So while the value of a song performed live may be relatively modest and will be reflected in a performing rights royalty, such value pales in comparison to the same song that is part of a hit musical. Courts have held that even in the absence of any scenery or costumes, where most of the selections are performed in sequence and the singers "act" during the concert, the performance is a dramatic performance that must be licensed by the copyright owner and cannot proceed based on blanket small rights performing licenses from a PRO.[251]

Grand rights licenses will vary. To realize their ultimate value, the publisher will seek to obtain a percentage of the gross box office receipts for productions in major venues and subject to audits. In other situations, the licenses will require a flat fee per performance. These fees are payable by the production company to the publisher. The royalties remitted by the publisher to the writer for grand rights are typically 50% of the amount received by the publisher, but in many cases they may be higher.

[e]—Printed Music

Printed music differs from recordings because it can usually be sold only to musicians who read music, and not to the general public. In addition to the needs of professional and amateur musicians, educational institutions and churches consume and purchase considerable amounts of printed music in the form of choral music, instrumental instruction, school band and orchestra arrangements and other materials.[252]

---

are limited to nondramatic works. These licensing arrangements enable the publisher to negotiate a license for grand rights that is in keeping with the enhanced value of such uses. Grand rights also include choreography, i.e., the use of music in a ballet or dance production, and any use where a dramatic story is being told with music.

In the case of opera and ballet grand rights, rental of orchestral materials constitutes another licensing component. See § 4.13[1][h] *infra*. In such cases, the publisher may seek both a grand rights license fee based on a percentage of box office, and a rental fee for the orchestral parts used in each performance.

251   See *Robert Stigwood Group Ltd. v. Sperber*, 457 F.2d 50 (2d Cir. 1972) (concert presentation of musical "Jesus Christ Superstar" was essentially dramatic in nature despite lack of scenery, costumes, or dialogue). See also, *Unichappell Music, Inc. v. Modrock Productions, LLC*, 2015 U.S. Dist. LEXIS 16111 (C.D. Cal. Feb. 10, 2015) (dispute arising from alleged failure to license grand rights for staged musical using songs by The Kinks).

252   Some of the standard printed music formats include sheet music of individual songs; personality folios featuring collections of songs by particular artists or groups; popular songs arranged for concert band, marching band arrangements, and various choral groupings, and teaching methods for piano and for band and orchestral instruments. There is also a market for classical music for all instruments, chamber works, and orchestral works. Thanks to continued efforts to keep music education alive, the market for printed music for education and entertainment is surprisingly robust, amounting to hundreds of millions of dollars per year worldwide. See National Music Publishers' Association 12th Annual Income Survey, available at http://www.nmpa.org/pressroom/surveys/twelvth/NMPA_International_Survey_12th_Edition.pdf.

While some publishers have their own divisions that produce, distribute and sell printed editions and arrangements, many publishers and copyright owners license these activities to specialist companies. The typical royalty for the writer is 10% to 12% of the publisher's printed edition list price. In cases where the publisher licenses the print music operations to a third party, there may be an agreement to split the net income with the author. In some cases, where popular songs are being published, the agreement may specify a specific amount for sales of sheet music for specific songs.[253]

[f]—Digital "Catchall"

It is typical to have a reference to "any other income" arising from technologies now known or hereafter invented, that is split in half. Note that where the phrase "any other income" is not specific enough, courts have limited its scope.[254]

[g]—Permissions, Including Uses of Lyrics

Third parties may seek permission to quote from a musical score in a book, or to reprint song lyrics. While such uses may not appear to be lucrative, a publisher must assess and license all uses of its copyrights.[255]

[h]—Rental of Orchestral Materials

The rental of orchestral materials is unique to classical music publishing, including the world of orchestral "pops" concerts.[256] An orchestral performance cannot occur unless each member of the orchestra, which may be over 100 musicians, has their

---

253   While litigation over printed music may be relatively uncommon, note that singer and songwriter Barry Manilow engaged in extensive litigation concerning print music license rights in his songs. See *Kamakazi Music Corp. v. Robbins Music Corp.*, 522 F. Supp. 125 (S.D.N.Y. 1981). Note that when one considers that printed music is mostly sold through retailers who expect a discount up to 50% or more, the 10% royalty based on list price is the equivalent of 20% of the wholesale price.

254   In one case, it did not apply to income the publisher realized related to United States tax credits arising from taxes paid in other countries. See *Evans v. Famous Music Corp.*, 1 N.Y.3d 452, 775 N.Y.S.2d 757, 807 N.E.2d 869 (2004) (a catchall provision whereby a music publisher would pay the songwriter 50% of all net sums "from any other source or right now known or which may hereafter come into existence" did not apply to monies received by the publisher in the form of foreign tax credits against the publisher's U.S. taxes).

255   With the advent of the Internet and technologies such as karaoke machines, song lyrics have a tremendous value on their own. It is important to protect the copyright by issuing licenses and attempting to control unauthorized infringements.

256   The classical music publishing business, despite the name, is not only involved with the great figures of the distant musical past. There is a considerable amount of music still protected by copyright by composers such as Copland and Stravinsky that is performed every day around the world, and that generates mechanical royalties and performance income for decades.

own printed music "part" from which to perform. Publishers rent sheet music to professional and conservatory orchestras, who then return the music after their performances (orchestras and bands at the high school level typically perform works that are offered at a lower cost). There will be two income streams arising from the public performance of a copyrighted orchestral work: the rental fee charged to the orchestra, and the public performance royalties that will be generated by the performance.

A popular orchestral work can generate impressive sums over time based on rental fees alone. The fees are assessed based on the duration of the work, and the classification of the orchestra based on its size and budget. Rentals can amount to hundreds of dollars for just one live performance and thousands of dollars for a run of several performances.

Rental fees are typically split between the publisher and the composer, with the composer receiving 50%. Public domain orchestral works, such as the symphonies of Beethoven, are not rented, but are available for sale at reasonable prices.

[i]—Agent and Sub-Publisher Fees, Deductions and "At Source" Accounting

Royalties are typically based on monies actually received by the publisher, after deducting any fees[257] or the percentage of income retained by sub-publishers in foreign territories. This can be an area of intense negotiation, as writers may attempt to be paid "at source," or based on the gross collected in foreign territories without deducting the agent's or sub-publisher's commission.[258]

---

257 E.g., the commission retained by the Harry Fox Agency.

258 See *Berns v. EMI Music Publishing, Inc.*, 1999 U.S. Dist. LEXIS 17541, 1999 WL 1029711, at *3 (S.D.N.Y. Nov. 12, 1999):

"Under an 'at source' arrangement, the composer calculates his percentage of royalties from payments received by foreign subpublishers, whereas in a receipts agreement, the writer is entitled to be paid his share of the foreign income received by the original publisher from foreign subpublishing. For example, if $100 was collected by a subpublisher in the UK, and the British subpublisher retained 50% as its fee, remitting the remaining $50 to the American publisher, under a receipts agreement, the composer would take his share (for ex., 50%) from what the American publisher actually retained, yielding him $25. Conversely, if the composer is to be paid 50% of all income receive at the source, then the writer will receive $50."

See also:

Second Circuit: The Gordy Co. v. Mary Jane Girls, Inc., 1989 WL 149290, at *43-*44 (S.D.N.Y. Dec. 6, 1989) (discussing computation of foreign royalties from sub-publishers as being calculated "at source" based on gross revenue in the foreign territory; deduction of fees by subpublishers and how those costs are borne).

In some cases, where the publisher has a wholly owned subsidiary in a foreign territory, it may be possible to limit agency deductions in that particular territory.[259]

In a true "at source" accounting, the record company or publisher will have to completely absorb any agency or sub-publisher fees. In that scenario and based on a 50% artist royalty, if the gross revenue at the source is $100, and the agency fee in that territory is $25, the artist will receive their 50% calculated at source, or $50. The publisher will have to absorb the $25 foreign agency fee, and will retain $25. If the accounting is not "at source,"[260] then the $75 actually received by the publisher will constitute the basis for the 50/50 royalty split, with the publisher and artist each receiving $37.50.

[2]—Co-Publishing Agreements

The term "co-publish" can be used two very different ways: first, as an indication of overall copyright ownership status of a song, where for example there are two songwriters, each of whom has a different music publisher. In this "macro" usage of the term, "co-publisher" means that two music publishing companies own the rights. The second, more "micro," use refers to the type of agreement entered into between a writer and a music publisher.[261]

Sixth Circuit: *B.J. Thomas v. Lytle*, 104 F. Supp.2d 906 (M.D. Tenn. 2000) (extensive analysis of foreign royalties and "at source" accounting issues).

259   See *Jobim v. Songs of Universal, Inc.*, 732 F. Supp.2d 407, 415 (2010) (discussing net receipts vs. at-source accounting for royalties arising from "Girl From Ipanema"). See also:

Ninth Circuit: *Stewart v. Screen Gems-Emi Music, Inc.*, 2015 U.S. Dist. LEXIS 25047 (N.D. Cal. March 2, 2015) (action alleging breach of contract survived motion to dismiss, where defendant publisher's wholly owned overseas affiliates took 50% of overseas revenue "instead of the market rate of 10%").

State Courts:

New York: *Paul M. Ellington v. EMI Music, Inc.*, 2014 N.Y. Slip Op. 07197, Case No. 156 (N.Y. Oct. 23, 2014) (Duke Ellington agreements calling for 50% of foreign royalties "actually received" (a "net receipts" provision) allowed for overseas representatives known as subpublishers to deduct a percentage of revenues for their services, and did not distinguish between affiliated and unaffiliated foreign subpublishers; thus plaintiff could not claim that royalties from territories with affiliated subpublishers should be calculated at source without any agency deduction).

260   Note that where publishers are international in scope and have an ownership interest in the affiliate, they arguably are profiting in a global corporate sense from the $25 fee retained by the agent. Therefore concessions as regards "at source" accounting may be easiest to achieve where the publisher has a wholly owned affiliate in the foreign territories at issue.

261   It is possible to confuse the terminology. For example, where a song has two co-publishers, each of those publishers has an agreement with the co-writer of the song in the form of a co-publishing agreement.

In a typical co-publishing agreement, the writer has already formed his or her own publishing company at least "on paper," usually as a result of registering with a PRO, but does not have an actual business that can perform the functions of a music publishing company. The writer then enters into an agreement with an established publishing company that has promotion, marketing, licensing and accounting resources. In the course of doing so, the writer does not relinquish publishing interests. Instead, the writer shares the publishing ownership with the new publisher. The contract will typically state that the writer grants to the publisher a fifty percent interest in the undivided whole copyright, thus making the parties co-owners of the copyright and co-publishers. In addition, the writer often grants to the publisher exclusive administration rights worldwide, such that the publisher can control all licensing activities on behalf of both co-publishers. The administration rights for the writer's co-ownership may result in the publisher also collecting an administration fee.

In such agreements, not only does the writer receive 50% royalty on all classes of income, but he or she also retains the publishing interest, and splits that with the publisher. The writer receives a total of 75% instead of 50%, consisting of the full writer's royalty, and half of the publisher's share.

In the following chart, "Publisher A" is the established music publishing company. "Publisher B" is the author's own publishing company, which may exist as a d/b/a ("doing business as") and is a member of a PRO.

Standard Publishing Agreement	
All income except performing rights (based on 100% income)	Share
Author royalty	50% of income
Publisher retains	50% of income
Performing Rights (based on 50% author share and 50% publisher share)	
Author share of performing rights directly paid to author by PRO	Entire author share retained by author
Publisher share of performing rights directly paid to publisher by PRO	Entire publisher share retained by publisher

Co-Publishing Agreement	
All income except performing rights (based on 100% income)	Share
Author royalties as author	50% of income

Publisher A retained monies: half to music publisher as co-publisher with author	25% of income
Publisher B retained monies: half to author's publishing company as co-publisher	25% of income
	Author now receives an additional 25% of the income in the form of half the monies normally retained by Publisher. Author's total income as an author and as a co-publisher is now 75% instead of 50%
Performing Rights (based on 50% author share and 50% publisher share)	
Author share of performing rights directly paid to author by PRO	Entire author share, which is 50% of total performing rights
Publisher A: half of the publisher share goes to music publisher as co-publisher	Half the publisher share, which is 25% of total performing rights
Publisher B: half of the publisher share goes to author's own publishing company as co-publisher	Half the publisher share, which is 25% of total performing rights
	Author now receives an additional half of the performing rights income in the form of half the publisher share. Author's total income as an author and as a co-publisher is now 75% instead of 50%

[3]—Music Publishing Administration Agreements

In an administration agreement, a publishing company agrees to perform all the duties of a music publisher in seeking and collecting income, but does not acquire copyright ownership. The grant will be in the form of an exclusive license to the administrating publisher for a limited time. Typical percentages of income retained by the administrating publisher can range from 15% to 25%.

§4.14   Personal Managers and Talent Agents

In the music industry, talent ("booking") agents and personal managers perform different functions. Booking agents in the music industry solicit and procure employment on behalf of their artist clients. Managers advise artists on developing aspects of their talent and careers, including which of those specific engagements to accept.[262]

---

262   While the division of responsibilities between managers and agents is clear in theory, the lines can become blurred between the two functions. The California Supreme Court acknowledges that:

"[t]his division largely exists only in theory. The reality is not nearly so neat. The line dividing the functions of agents, who must be licensed, and of managers, who need not be, is often blurred and sometimes crossed. Agents sometimes counsel and advise; managers sometimes procure work. Indeed, the occasional procurement of employment opportunities may be standard operating procedure for many managers and an

The rights and duties of managers are a matter of contractual agreements between managers and their clients. Managers perform broad advisory functions for which they receive a percentage of the client's overall income. Managers are not generally regulated by state laws, provided their activities do not cross the line into performing the services of an employment agency in violation of state labor and employment regulations and laws.

Agents, however, *are* subject to licensure and regulation under labor and employment laws in the various states, laws designed to protect those seeking employment from exploitation in various forms, including conscionably high commission fees.[263]

California has the most thoroughly developed regulation of talent agencies and resulting administrative and case law via the Talent Agency Act ("TAA"), embodied within section 1700 of the California Labor Code.[264] The TAA is a powerful statutory protection, and sometimes a sword, for artists who can file a petition to the Division of Labor Standards Enforcement alleging a violation of the Act by their agent or manager. Such petitions are adjudicated and ruled on by the Labor Commissioner in a Determination of Controversy.[265]

---

understood goal when not-yet-established talents, lacking access to the few licensed agents in Hollywood, hire managers to promote their careers."

Marathon Entertainment, Inc. v. Blasi, 42 Cal. 4th 974, 70 Cal. Rptr.3d 727, 174 P.3d 741, 743 (2008). New artists may not be in sufficient demand for a licensed talent agency to agree to represent them. The reality may be that such emerging artists have to solicit, and book their own engagements, and in some cases their manager may find themselves involved in soliciting and procuring such employment, even if by doing so, the manager is performing the duties of an agent without the required license.

263   The chapter on film and television contains a more detailed discussion of the functions performed by agents in those industries, and a list of the applicable agent licensing regulations in each state. See Chapter 2. Unlike agents in the motion picture industry who may book work in a wide range of endeavors and also provide management and career advice, talent agents, or "booking agents" in the music industry perform a narrower function: they procure employment for musicians primarily in the form of live concert engagements and television appearances.

New York theatrical employment agencies are governed by the New York General Business Law §§ 170 et seq., and the New York Arts and Cultural Affairs Statutes, §§ 37.01 - 37.11. See also, *Friedkin v. Harry Walker, Inc.*, 90 Misc.2d 680, 395 N.Y.S.2d 611 (1977) (New York's employment agency laws apply to theatrical agents).

264   Cal. Labor Code §§ 1700 et seq. Because of the thorough nature of the TAA, and the body of judicial rulings related to the TAA, most of the comments here will be with reference to the TAA. But a practitioner in a given state should check the regulations that apply in that jurisdiction. See the chart on relevant regulations in each state in Chapter 3.

265   See *Styne v. Stevens*, 26 Cal.4th 42, 109 Cal. Rptr.2d 14, 26 P.3d 343 (2001) (when the Talent Agencies Act is invoked in the course of a contract dispute, the Labor Commissioner has exclusive jurisdiction to determine his jurisdiction over the matter, including whether the contract involved the services of a talent agency as defined in the TAA).

The Labor Commissioner has the power to declare agreements between artists and agents or managers void ab initio in their entirety, or under the doctrine of severability, void as to the specific illegal acts complained of.

In addition, musician labor unions require that their members only use properly licensed, union-approved agents. These "franchised" agents are bound not only by state laws, but also by union regulations regarding issues including the percentages the agents can retain; the duration of contracts; mediation of disputes; and prohibitions against conflicts of interest.[266]

The fees that licensed talent agents can earn in the music industry are limited in two ways: (1) the bookings and resultant fees only apply to live bookings and television appearances; and (2) commissions and fees are limited by statute and union regulations. Managers generally will not want to subject themselves to the limitations on earnings and regulatory requirements that apply to licensed agents. Managers can also more freely take an ownership interest in, or act as, producers for businesses that hire their clients. In so doing, they are not "procuring" employment for their client; instead, they are directly providing employment without acting as an intermediary agent.[267]

Note however, that the TAA has "safe harbor" carveouts that acknowledge some of the special roles managers play in the music industry. Procurement of recording agreements by

---

See *Marathon Entertainment, Inc. v. Blasi*, 42 Cal.4th 974, 70 Cal. Rptr.3d 727, 174 P.3d 741, 743 (2008) (the Talent Agencies Act applied to an unlicensed personal manager who performed the duties of a talent agent, and that the doctrine of severance applied to contracts partially illegal under the TAA) (citing Zelenski, "Talent Agents, Personal Managers, and Their Conflicts in the New Hollywood," 76 So. Cal. L. Rev. 979 (2003); Devlin, "The Talent Agencies Act: Reconciling the Controversies Surrounding Lawyers, Managers, and Agents Participating in California's Entertainment Industry," 28 Pepperdine L. Rev. 381, 386 (2001)). The Commissioner can also require disgorgement of commissions earned in violation of the TAA during the one-year statute of limitations prior to filing of the petition. Appeal can be taken from a Determination of Controversy to the state superior court for trial de novo, with subsequent rights of appeal up to the state supreme court. See TAA, Cal. Labor Code § 1700.44(a); see also, *Buchwald v. Katz*, 8 Cal.3d 493, 500-501, 503 P.2d 1376, 105 Cal. Rptr. 368 (1972).

266   *Marathon v. Blasi*, 174 P.3d at 745. See also, The American Federation of Musicians Booking Agent Agreement, Schedule 1 (table of maximum commissions of 15% for a "steady engagement" of two or more days per week for the same purchaser in the same location, and 20% maximum for Single Miscellaneous Engagements of one day duration). The agreement is available at http://www.afm.org/resources/booking-agent-search. The AFM agreement provides that a musician will always receive at least the union minimum payments for an engagement, thus any fees for engagements booked by an agent will have the commission amount added in addition to the fee for the musician, for example "scale plus 15%."

267   See *Chinn v. Tobin*, Cal. Lab. Comm'r Case No. TAC 17-96, Slip Op. at 7 (March 26, 1997) (the TAA deals with the role an agent plays when acting as an intermediary between the artist and the employer. Managers who have a role in an entity that employs an artist are not acting as an agent/intermediary. The court also stated "[concluding otherwise] would mean that every television or film production company that directly hires an actor would itself need to be licensed.").

managers, for example, is not a violation of the TAA.[268] Nor is a situation where a manager, working together with a licensed agent, negotiates agreements for employment.[269]

If the artist does not object to his or her manager booking live engagements, there may never be enforcement of the state regulations. In California for example, enforcement is predicated on an artist filing a petition with the Department of Industrial Relations Division of Labor Standards Enforcement within the one-year statute of limitations. Should the relationship between the manager and the artist deteriorate, then the artist may indeed bring a petition before the labor commissioner, seeking to have the management agreement voided on the basis of the manager allegedly violating the TAA.

As a result, the manager may find that the client has successfully had the entire agreement declared void *ab initio*, and the manager may also be subject to disgorgement of commissions earned during the one-year limitations period prior to the petition[270] Given that management agreements may require payment of fees to continue after the agreement terminates, voiding of a contract by the Labor Commissioner would also cut off the manager's future income.

Under rulings by the California Supreme Court however, the doctrine of severability may be applied by the Labor Commissioner, who may now declare void only the specific portions of a management agreement that violate the TAA, leaving the rest of the agreement in place and valid.[271]

---

268   Recording contracts are exempted under Cal. Labor Code § 1700.4. Publishing contracts have been held by the Labor Commissioner as not constituting "employment" under the TAA, because licensing of an artist's musical compositions does not involve the artist undertaking an affirmative duty to render present or future services. See *Kilcher v. Vainshtein*, 2001 WL 35678880 at *22-*23 (Cal. Lab. Com. May 30, 2001). But see, Sebert, p/k/a KE$HA, TAC No. 19800 (2013) (disagreeing with *Kilcher v. Vainshtein* and holding that music publishing agreement procurement comes within the TAA).

269   Talent Agencies Act, Cal. Labor Code § 17400.44.

270   Note however the decision in *Kilcher v. Vainshtein*, 2001 WL 35678880 (Cal. Lab. Com. May 30, 2001). Although the court declared the management agreement void ab initio, the court noted that the manager had in fact helped Jewel's career reach considerable heights in other respects, therefore the Labor Commissioner declined to order any disgorgement of the manager's commissions for the year prior to the Petition. See also, *Blanks v. Seyfarth Shaw*, LLP, 171 Cal. App.4th 336, 8 Cal. Rptr.3d 710 (2009) (suit against law firm regarding TAA's one-year statute of limitations).

271   *Marathon v. Blasi*, 42 Cal.4th 974, 70 Cal. Rptr.3d 727, 174 P.3d 741 (2008). The Court in *Marathon v. Blasi* also called for the legislature to consider revisiting the TAA, noting that although the TAA was "adopted with the best of intentions, the Act and guild regulations aimed at protecting artists evidently have resulted in a limited pool of licensed talent agencies and, in combination with high demand for talent agency services, created the right conditions for a black market for unlicensed talent agency services." Id., 70 Cal. Rptr.3d at 756.

For a summary of agreement deal points in management agreements, please see the discussion in Chapter 4 on the Music Industry.

[1]—Personal Management Agreements[272]

The personal manager also serves as a liaison with an artist's other advisors, including the artist's attorney, the booking agent, a publicist, and a business manager.[273] Managers may sometimes act as producers or even music publishers, entering into recording agreements and songwriter agreements with their clients. The manager may then, in turn, enter into agreements with record companies and music publishers, acting as a "middle man."[274]

One of the key issues in personal management agreements is the extent to which the manager's commissions continue after the term expires. As noted earlier, the manager will want a perpetual commission based on agreements entered into or even substantially negotiated during the term, the "deals" that manager helped create. The manager will also seek future fees based on works such as compositions that existed prior to the term or that were created during the term, even if those compositions don't earn any income until after the term expires. The artist, however, will want to limit or phase out the manager's commission in the event the relationship ends.

Reported cases involving disputes between talent and their personal manager demonstrate a variety of business and commission arrangements. In *Columbia Artists Management, LLC v. Alvarez*, a Southern District of New York case, the court held that that even under an oral agreement, a group of opera singers owed a post-termination commission to their former management company for performances arising from engagements obtained prior to the artists and their manager parting ways.[275] In sharp contrast to California's Talent Agency Act, which prohibits unlicensed managers from acting as agents by procuring employment in the form of musical engagements, the New York

---

272   As noted earlier, the role of the manager is to advise and guide the artist in all phases of artistic and career development and goals. In exchange, the manager typically receives a commission amounting to 10% to 20% of gross income received by the artist in all areas, both specific to the music industry, and tangential areas such as endorsements. From the artist's perspective, the manager's commission will ideally not be based on net revenue not including artist expenses, preferably, there will be some limitations or exceptions relating to expenditures by the artist that should not be subject to a commission by the manager, for example the costs incurred for touring or studio time.

273   A business manager provides accounting, tax, investment, and other financial services, including managing any escrow accounts, for example where engagement fees may be paid in to an escrow account before commissions payable to the manager, agent, or attorney are disbursed.

274   This scenario has led to disputes. See *Ahern v. Scholz*, 85 F.3d 774 (1st Cir. 1996) (member of group "Boston" in dispute over royalties and expenses with manager who had signed artist to agreements including management, recording, and songwriting).

275   *Columbia Artists Management, LLC v. Alvarez*, 2011 WL 781179 (S.D.N.Y. March 3, 2011).

court noted, but did not comment on the fact that the management company was not licensed with the State of New York.[276]

A similar result occurred in *Columbia Artists Management, LLC v. Swenson & Burnakus, Inc.*, where the opera singer Ruth Ann Swenson paid her manager ten percent from opera performances and twenty percent from concert performances. Upon terminating the manager and refusing to pay any future commission, the manager sued and was awarded post-termination commissions, notwithstanding the manager's unlicensed status.[277] In stark contrast to the provisions of California's Talent Agency Act, the New York court found that "[p]laintiff's lack of a license did not render the contract unenforceable."[278]

[a]—Term and Territory

The term should be for no more than three years. From the artist's perspective, a two-year term is preferable, with an option for the manager to renew for an additional year, provided the manager meets income benchmarks.

The territory will customarily be "throughout the world."

[b]—Services

This clause is a description of the manager's services, generally including advice and counsel in all matters connected with the artist's professional career. This includes development of the artist's talents, selection of material to perform and with whom, publicity, and the selection of other professionals such as attorneys, agents, and business managers or accountants. There should be a provision that all ultimate decisions and choices are at the artist's sole discretion, or otherwise subject, at a minimum, to the artist's verbal approval.

The artist will exclusively engage the manager and no other manager during the term, but the manager's services are on a non-exclusive basis with respect to the artist.[279]

---

276   *Id.* at *2.

277   *Columbia Artists Management, LLC v. Swenson & Burnakus, Inc.*, 2010 WL 1379737 (S.D.N.Y. March 3, 2010).

278   *Id.* at *1.

279   The manager will reserve the right to provide the same services for other artists. To the extent the artist was, for example, formerly with a musical group that the artist left, and may have obligations to pay a commission to a former manager with respect to those specific activities, the agreement may contain exclusions stating that the new manager has no responsibility to provide any advice with respect to those former activities, and that may also exclude those former activities from commission fees under the new manager.

[c]—Authority of Manager

The extent to which the manager is empowered to make business decisions and to enter into written agreements on behalf of the artist is crucial, and must be subject to careful negotiation. There are benefits to the artist in having the manager make routine decisions and sign routine documents, but there are obvious dangers in allowing a manager to make business decisions or to execute important agreements without the artist's prior approval.

In some cases, the grant of a power of attorney to the manager may be limited in conditional ways. For example, where the artist may be willing to make one-day personal appearances that are limited in scope. In such cases, the agreement can specify that the manager will not execute any such one-day agreements unless (1) the artist is not reasonably available to sign; (2) the artist has approved the material terms of the agreement; and (3) the agreement relates only to "live" personal appearances of no more than one or two days in duration. Other than those exceptions, the artist would retain the right to personally sign all other agreements.

[d]—Artist's Undertakings and Warranties

The agreement may require the artist to state that he or she will diligently devote themselves to their career during the term of the agreement; will refer all offers, communications, and requests to the manager; and will not enter into agreements without first consulting with the manager. The artist may also be asked to warrant that he or she will not engage anyone else to perform similar services or enter into any agreements that interfere with the artist's obligations under the management agreement. The artist may also be asked to warrant that he or she will use only duly licensed talent agents.

[e]—Manager's Commission

In addition to stating the manager's overall commission, this clause of the agreement will have considerable detail concerning the portion of the artist's gross earnings are commissionable. Common exclusions include amounts "advanced" to the artist on paper but never actually received.[280]

Similarly, in the case of a large-scale live performance or tour, expenses such as lighting and sound equipment are typically deducted before figuring the manager's commission. If at all possible, all the expenses should ideally be deducted from the

---

280   For example, in a recording agreement with a $500,000 recording fund advanced to the artist, if $400,000 of that fund is used for production costs, and $50,000 goes towards royalties paid to an independent producer, the artist's actual cash revenue is $50,000, and that would be the commissionable amount.

gross tour revenues to arrive at the true net live concert or tour revenue available to be commissioned, especially where the artist's compensation is based on a percentage of the net revenue.[281]

Non-commissionable items would include, but not be limited to:

- Recording and production costs
- Producer or other royalties
- Costs of a personal appearance tour
- Live performance expenses for sound and lighting, and if possible further expenses relating to live performance
- Royalties or other payments due third-party co-authors of songs
- Any agreed upon exclusions with respect to prior activities, such as income arising from membership in a former band
- If possible, commissions paid to booking agents

The agreement should also address what happens after the current agreement ends. From the artist's perspective, after the agreement ends, there should be a time limit to future commissions, either a simple cut-off date, or a "sunset" provision whereby the commission gradually decreases, for example:

During agreement period:	20%
First year after expiration:	15%
Second year after expiration:	10%

---

281   If the manager insists on their commission being based on the gross tour or live performance income, then it's possible the manager will make more than the artist:

Gross tour income:	$1,000,000
Expenses including agency fee:	$750,000
Artist adjusted gross share:	$250,000
Manager 20% commission based on gross:	$200,000
Artist net share:	$50,000

One solution is a provision in which the manager's commission from live performances or touring will never exceed 50% of the artist's share of net income. In the above example, the artist and manager would each net $125,000. The manager may want a further assurance, for example, that the 50% of artist's net income will never be less than the equivalent of 5% of the gross.

Third year after expiration: 5%

Fourth year and later: 0%

This way, any new manager engaged by the artist can have a corresponding gradual increase in commissions. If things can be so neatly coordinated, the artist never pays more than a 20% commission in total.

Other ways to address post-term commissions is to limit them to a term of years. The manager will, understandably, want to retain the long-term benefits, especially if the artist took years to develop before producing income.

[f]—Expenses

Reasonable and necessary expenses incurred by the manager on behalf of the artist, but not including normal office overhead, can be reimbursable by the artist or charged against their account. Typical controls are, for example, required approval of any expenses over a certain amount.

[g]—Accounting

Most managers will seek the ability to receive all earnings, subtract their commission and expenses, and then disburse the remainder to the artist. It may be more desirable for the artist to hire a business manager and accountant who will be designated to receive all funds and make monthly disbursements. Where the manager has obtained the right to make such hiring decisions and, in fact, engages the business manager, the artist may still want to have controls in place nonetheless, subject to consultation with the artist's attorney.

The agreement will also have provisions acknowledging that should the artist form a business entity for "loan out" agreements, the new entity will be subject to all the terms of the management agreement.[282]

---

282   A "loan out" agreement is where an artist forms a corporation that receives all income on the artist's behalf, and pays a salary and other benefits to the artist. In such cases, agreements are made with the artist's corporation, which corporation promises that the artist will perform the services under the agreement. A "letter of inducement" outlining the arrangements may also be requested by the organization entering into the agreement with the artist's business entity. See also, § 2.06 *supra*.

[h]—"Not an Agent" Notice

Given the possible conflicts of interest if a manager acts as an unlicensed talent agent, management agreements will typically have a notice stating that the manager is not an employment agent, and is not licensed as a talent agency under the Labor Code of the State of California or as a theatrical employment agency under the General Business Law of the State of New York, and does not solicit or procure employment on behalf of the artist.[283]

[2]—Talent Agency Agreements

Many of the provisions of a talent agency agreement are pursuant to state regulatory statutes or the union regulations that grant agents a "franchise" to represent union members.

For example, the licensure application process for agents under the California Talent Agencies Act ("TAA") requires a written application for a license that includes a background character investigation if warranted, a license fee, and the posting of a $50,000 surety bond.[284] The proposed agency contracts and fee schedules must be submitted for approval and to ensure the agreement is not "unfair, unjust, and oppressive to the artist."[285] The agreement must also include the following statement:

> "THIS TALENT AGENCY IS LICENSED BY THE LABOR COMMISSIONER OF THE STATE OF CALIFORNIA. The form of this contract has been approved by the State Labor Commissioner on the __ day of _____, 20__."[286]

Under the TAA, agency agreements must specify the term or duration, and must contain a provision whereby if the artist does not obtain employment or bona fide offers of employment for a period of time in excess of four consecutive months, the agreement may be terminated by either party.[287] The agreement must also refer any controversy between the artist and the agent to the Labor Commissioner. The agent must also file a schedule

---

283   Such notices do not help managers to the extent they actually do perform the services of a booking agent. Under California law, it is the services performed that make a manager subject to the TAA, despite any notices in the agreement. As the California Supreme Court has noted, "[managers] remain exempt from regulation [under the TAA] insofar as they do those things that personal managers do, but they are regulated under the Act to the extent they stray into doing the things that make one a talent agency under the Act." *Marathon v. Blasi*, 70 Cal. Rptr.3d at 727, 737.

284   TAA, Cal. Labor Code §§ 1700 *et seq.*

285   TAA, Cal. Labor Code § 1700.23.

286   Title 8. Cal. Code of Regulations, § 12003.1.

287   Title 8. Cal. Code of Regulations, §§ 12001 *et seq.*

of fees, and set up a trust fund account for receipt of any monies due to the artist, while maintaining all records pertaining not only to the fund, but also to the agent's general books and records of employment history, all of which are subject to state inspection.

Talent agency advertising is regulated as to truthfulness, and the agency may not send any artist to any place where "the health, safety, or welfare of the artist could be adversely affected." Also, no talent agency "shall knowingly permit any persons of bad character, prostitutes, gamblers, intoxicated persons, or procurers to frequent, or be employed in, the place of business of the talent agency."[288] Agencies may not charge a registration fee, and if they charge expenses to procure employment, the expenses must be reimbursed if the employment or the employment fee does not materialize.[289] State regulations may limit the percentage fee the agent can charge to 10% or 15%, and in some cases require that the agent's overall agreement and fee schedule be submitted to the state for prior approval.

The basic provisions of an agency agreement will track the relevant state statutes and union franchise agreements, and in the case of California agencies, the agreement will state that it has been approved by the Labor Commissioner. The main agreement points will be:[290]

- Duration of the agreement

- Exclusivity of representation[291]

- Scope of the entertainment services and industries covered by the agreement

- Commission percentages for various types of engagements, payable only when monies are actually received

- Provisions whereby commissions may be collected on engagements contracted by the agent, but performed after the termination or expiration of the agreement

- Provisions clarifying cases where a performer's agreement may be expanded or renewed yet still subject to a commission as a "substitution" agreement[292]

- Expense provisions

---

288   TAA, Cal. Labor Code § 1700.32-35.

289   TAA, Cal. Labor Code § 1700.40.

290   See the forms accompanying this treatise.

291   The artist may want to reserve the right to use a different agent overseas, for example.

292   Truly "new deals" would not be subject to a continuing commission. See *William Morris Agency, LLC v. Dan O'Shannon* TAC No. 06-05, Slip Op. (Cal. Lab. Com., Sept. 28, 2007) (under Title 8, Cal. Code of Regulations, § 12002, a talent agency is entitled to receive a commission from a replacement or substitution of an agreement it originally procured, but not from a "new deal" that has no connection with the prior agreement).

- Termination provisions in the event no work or offers of work are obtained over four consecutive months or other circumstances

- Trust fund accounts and statements

- Statement that the agent is free to represent other persons

- Procedures and jurisdiction for disputes, referred to either the appropriate state agency, or pursuant to union mandated arbitration

[3]—Career Management Strategies

Some aspiring artists hope to be "discovered" by powerful agents, record labels and concert promoters, perhaps hoping for the "American Idol" type of sudden breakout opportunity early in their career. Others pursue their art by every means at their disposal, including social media, YouTube, and live performance to hone their craft, perhaps with little concern for financial success but hoping to create a fan base that may come to the attention of the industry. Some aspiring artists seek to be supported from the beginning by financiers and create at least the appearance of music industry success in the form of self-produced recordings, videos, and marketing, including professionally designed and maintained web sites and social media presence.

Artists in the third category may enter into agreements with financiers to fund tours, wardrobe, publicity, and recordings, in exchange for a share of future revenues from those activities. Key to such agreements is whether the financier has the following key points:

- Recoupment "off the top" in first position from gross revenues before any deductions, on a most favored nations basis with any agent or manager;

- Recoupment plus a return of 10% to 20%;

- After recoupment, an ongoing share of revenue or defined profits;

- Depending on the level of investment, membership in the artist's or group's business entity and ownership units or shares (which must be formed where there are financiers);

- Information on the artist's management sufficient to determine it is competent, including a business plan, timetable and budget;

- Protection measures for the artist where the artist may be a minor or the artist's family is also serving as management, measures to include ensuring that the artist has majority ownership and control.[293]

---

293 In *Conway v. Licata*, 2015 U.S. Dist. LEXIS 116310 (D. Mass. Aug. 31, 2015), an aspiring singer/songwriter was financed by her wealthy father, who engaged a management company to provide a "rock star" experience in hopes of making his daughter a star. After spending $1.7 million in two years, the parties had a falling out with the father

§4.15   Concert Performance and Touring

Live performance can cover everything from a local bar charging a $5 cover to a multi-million dollar stadium show. For successful artists, live performance can be the most lucrative part of their careers, with gross ticket sales potentially in the range of tens of millions of dollars. But the basic revenue formula is consistent at all levels of the business: income is generated by (1) ticket sales; (2) merchandise such as t-shirts; and (3) concessions.[294]

The economics of live concerts can work several ways. At the lower levels of the business, musicians may pay to "showcase" themselves at a popular club, buying tickets to re-sell or give away. For performers who pay their own touring expenses, breaking even with cover charges can be hard, and such tours are more about developing their talents, learning about audiences, and developing a following. Any merchandise sales are a bonus.[295]

For highly successful musicians, concert promoters will take on the financial responsibility and risk in presenting the performances, and the artists will seek agreements in which they are guaranteed a minimum amount for the performance. In addition, they receive 85% to 90% of the net income, sometimes up to 100% of the ticket revenue with the venue keeping all

---

successfully pursuing a claim against the managers. The factual background portion of the opinion is reproduced below as it provides an astute summary of this unusually extreme "rock star" option, including comments regarding other alternative paths for career development, and serves as a cautionary tale regarding expensive attempts to manufacture music industry success in the absence of public demand for an artist.

294   An additional category of revenue has grown in recent years based on processing and administration fees charged by ticket brokers, such as TicketMaster, who sell tickets on behalf of concert promoters. In addition to the "convenience fees" charged for these tickets, these fees may be shared with promoters and the artists themselves, there is a growing "secondary market" for concert tickets, in which tickets are sold at up to several times face value. While such sales have been conducted in the past by licensed ticket resellers in states that authorize such sales (and by unauthorized ticket scalpers), the concert promoter and the artist would not share in the substantial extra monies generated when fans who can afford to do so pay several times face value for a hard-to-get ticket. The new trend is for the original promoter and ticket broker to set aside tickets for sale at premiums above the advertised price, to control such sales, and to share the increased revenues with artists themselves.

295   In the digital age, virtually all musicians have a Web presence, use social media such as Twitter and Facebook, have tracks available for sale online at iTunes or elsewhere, and will maintain email lists for sending out news of forthcoming live shows. For performers that develop strong followings, they may receive a guaranteed flat fee to perform, and beyond that, a guaranteed minimum fee against a percentage of ticket sales, which can increase the earnings for the performance if ticket sales are strong.

parking and concession revenues, after the promoter deducts expenses, as well as potential additional monies based on ticket sales that exceed the minimum "guarantee."[296]

---

296   See *Rowe Entertainment, Inc. v. The William Morris Agency*, 2005 WL 22833 (S.D.N.Y., Jan. 5, 2005), *aff'd* 167 Fed. Appx. 227 (2d Cir. Dec. 30, 2005), *cert. denied* 549 U.S. 887 (2006). *Rowe* involved an action brought by African-American concert promoters against multiple defendants including talent and booking agencies and concert promoters, alleging Antitrust and Civil Rights violations in the live concert industry. In granting the defendants' motion for summary judgment, the court issued an extensive opinion that includes detailed descriptions of the live concert segment of the music industry, including the various business entities and participants, revenue shares, and types of agreements:

The Live Concert Business

Artists who perform live in concert generally engage booking agencies to procure their engagements. These agencies select and contract with promoters, functioning in particular geographic locations, to present the concerts. Furthermore, a booking agent, acting on behalf of an artist, contacts a concert promoter in order to retain its services to produce a concert at a particular location, on an agreed date. Sometimes two or more promoters co-promote concerts, and share profits and losses. . . . The artist's fee is usually the greater of (a) 85% of net concert revenues (gross revenues less expenses, which include rent, advertising, stage hands, sound, lights, security and the like), or (b) a minimum guaranteed fee. Major artists can command as much as 90% of net concert revenues. A booking agent typically receives between 5 and 10% of an artist's fee. A promoter generally receives the remaining 15% of net revenues, or the amount remaining after the artist's minimum guaranteed fee is paid. The expense amounts are agreed upon and, if they exceed that amount, are born by the promoter. In accounting for the net concert revenues, the promoters are required to show that the agreed upon expenses were incurred in promoting the concert.

Under the contract between the artist and the promoter, the promoter is obligated to rent or otherwise secure the venue where the concert will take place. Venues include small clubs, large clubs, college gyms, auditoriums, outdoor amphitheaters (commonly called "sheds"), large sports arenas and stadiums. Some promoters own or have exclusive booking arrangements with specific venues. If another promoter wishes to promote a concert in such a venue, arrangements can be made with the promoter controlling the venue.

Once the artist or artist's manager and promoter enter into a contract for a performance on a particular date at a particular venue, the promoter advertises the concert, arranges security and performs other tasks to present the concert, including selling tickets to the public, either directly or through ticket sales outlets.

The Role of Booking Agencies and Concert Promoters

In the concert promotion business, the concert promoters are the buyers of the talent or artist, and the booking agencies are the sellers of the talent or artist. The concert promotion business is built on relationships that develop over time among artists, managers, promoters, agents, vendors and radio stations.

An artist's manager generally oversees all aspects of the artist's career and may also engage a booking agent to route and book concert tours for the artist. The booking agent reports to the artist either directly or, often, through the manager.

The artist or the artist's manager may designate the number of concerts, the period during which they would be performed, and the artist's preference for locale, for venue and for promoter, among other aspects. The agent at the booking agency then solicits and obtains offers to present to the artist or artist's manager, among other tasks. The ultimate decision as to whether to enter into a contract with the concert promoter belongs to the artist or the artist's manager.

The concert promoter or co-promoter shares in the profits and losses of the concert. The concert promoter-sometimes referred to as the "lead promoter"-is the entity that acquires the act and contracts with the artist. Generally, the promoter negotiates the terms of the concert with the agent, subject to the approval or direction of the artist or the artist's manager. The promoter is responsible for all financial obligations of the show, including the artist's guarantee, the building deposit, production cost and advertising. This includes the obligation to pay for advertising and all show expenses, regardless of how much money is generated by ticket sales. Due to this obligation, a promoter can end up losing money on any concert, even when a concert was expected to be profitable.

A lead promoter may retain the services of a "co-promoter" to assist the lead promoter with certain promotion tasks inside a particular market. A promoter may be required to have a co-promoter by the artist, the manager, or the booking agent, or a lead promoter may retain a co-promoter because the co-promoter has particular knowledge of the territory in which the concert is performed. Promoters often select co-promoters based on previous relationships. A co-promoter has a financial interest in the show and will share in the profits or losses. A promoter also may retain "street promoters" or "consultants" who typically receive a flat fee for assisting in a local market with such tasks as advertising and poster and flyer distribution. Unlike co-promoters, street promoters and consultants do not share in the promotion risks.

In recent years, some artists or artists' managers have asked booking agencies to solicit bids from concert promoters to produce nationwide tours. A "national tour promoter" is a promoter that procures and promotes a tour across the entire country. In that situation, a concert promoter bids for the entire tour and pays the artist an up-front deposit or guarantee based on the number of concerts to be performed. The promoter also makes other payments based on the success of the individual concerts or the aggregated success of the individual concerts, a collateralized tour. The "national tour promoter" has exclusive rights to the artist's concert performances and may negotiate for specific concerts with "local promoters" instead of the artist or the agent. In some cases, the "local promoter" will pay a guarantee versus a certain percentage of the profits of the concert, and in others, the "local promoter" is paid a flat fee. The artist generally maintains the right to approve each "local promoter" and the terms granted that promoter. Some artists have also chosen to contact a national tour promoter directly without using a booking agency, thereby avoiding the agency's commission.

The Bidding Process

To obtain an act, a promoter must first make an offer. To ensure that they participate in the bidding process, concert promoters " 'have to keep a line of communication with the agencies" ' to know which artists are planning to tour. The most important aspect of promoting is "to be up on the situation about who is coming, what artist is coming out, and to try to be a part of the bidding process."

The evidence shows that the booking agencies are not the only sources of information about artists' plans to go on concert tours. There are a variety of sources which promoters use to learn whether an artist is going on tour, "including rumor, internet websites, television, periodicals, contact with other promoters and booking agents, contacts with record companies and radio [station] executives." If a particular act interests a promoter, the promoter must call the booking agent to express that interest and to inquire about specific dates and the

Where expenses can be held to 75% or less, even a "modest" tour that generates $10 million in

---

artist's availability to perform in certain areas. Additionally, the artists, whose concerts are the subject of the Plaintiffs' complaint, have managers whose names and addresses are available in Pollstar directories. ("Amusement Business" and "Pollstar" publish guides on artists' representation).

The Elements of a Bid

Although a promoter may discuss the terms of his bid over the telephone with a booking agent, the bid must eventually be in writing. An artist or manager will only consider a bid when it is in writing and includes the amount of the guarantee, artist/promoter split and other information that is necessary for the artist or manager to assess the relative value of the bid. This information includes production costs, the cost of the building, participation in any ancillary revenue (such as merchandising or concessions) and projected costs for stagehands, rigging, limousines, catering and advertising. Without this information, the manager will not be able to assess the offer.

The artist's guarantee is the amount of money the promoter agrees to pay the artist for a particular performance. This guarantee is the minimum payment to the artist, who can negotiate a guarantee versus a percentage of the net receipts and, thus, earn more than the guarantee on a successful show. Many major artists rely on the percentage, also referred to as the "back-end split," to receive earnings substantially greater than the guarantee. When promoters determine what guarantee to offer, they consider expected ticket sales and prices, expected expenses for the concert, and the amount the artist generally expects.

After the agent receives a written bid from a promoter, the agent forwards the bid to the artist or the artist's management for consideration. The artist then chooses whether to accept or reject the offer. If the artist rejects the offer, the promoter then decides whether to submit a revised offer attempting to meet the artist's criteria. The artist has the ultimate authority to accept or reject an offer by a concert promoter. The artist may not make the decision itself, but may rely on the artist's manager or the booking agent to choose a promoter. Artists handle decisions with respect to the selection of concert promoters in different ways.

Selecting a Concert Promoter

Artists and artists' managers consider a variety of factors when selecting a concert promoter. Factors include the promoter's (a) experience with a genre of music; (b) relationship with the artist; (c) relationship with the manager; (d) financial wherewithal; (e) relationships within a particular market or region; (f) reputation; (g) production infrastructure; and (h) relationship with the agency. Other factors considered in selecting a co-promoter include familiarity with local area, ability of promoter, length of time in the business and previous shows promoted.

In selecting a concert promoter, the promoter's relationship and track record with the artist are considered. There is a preference for promoters who have worked with the artist in the past. Relationships and past experience with managers is also important in the selection of a concert promoter. When agencies are asked to recommend a promoter, the promoter's relationship with the agency is also relevant. Similarly, when a promoter seeks to retain a co-promoter, the promoter's relationship with the co-promoter can be very important.

A promoter's relationships within a market, e.g., with advertisers, venues or other suppliers, is another consideration in selecting a concert promoter. Important factors include relationships with the local people, and financially, to be able to support and advertise and promote the individual dates.

ticket sales and merchandise, would have a net revenue of $2,500,000, with the artist retaining as much as 90% or $2,250,000 and the promoter retaining 10% or $250,000. Those net artist earnings would be subject to commission fees payable to the artist's manager and agent.[297]

The expenses will include the cost of the venue itself, transportation, lodging, advertising and promotion, all lighting, sound equipment, tour personnel, musicians, stage crew, security, nursing or medical services, catering, insurance, and public performance licensing. Live performance agreements therefore consist of a relatively short employment agreement specifying the time, place, and fee, followed by an extensive schedule, or "rider", that delves into the details and logistics of the tour.

[1]—Concert Performance Agreements

Many of the details of a live performance will be overseen by the artist's tour manager.

[a]—Engagement and Compensation

The date, city, venue will be specified. The compensation will include not only the fee,[298] but also the promoter's obligation to pay for travel and accommodation.[299]

[b]—Merchandising

The venue may charge a "hall fee" for providing staff to sell the merchandise, and the artist will then divide the proceeds with whatever company is managing the

---

In addition to the personal relationships discussed above, the promoter's past experience and reputation in terms of venue, genre and financial stability are also relevant. A promoter's experience and familiarity with a specific genre of music is important in selecting a concert promoter. Additionally, a promoter with familiarity in a specific geographic area or venue is preferred. A promoter's financial capabilities are also crucial. When choosing a promoter, a manager considers, among other things, a promoter's financial ability to be able to support and advertise and promote the individual dates. A promoter cannot rely on ticket sales to cover financial obligations, but rather needs to be able to not only promote the show, but in event of a loss, to sustain that loss without the show being cancelled. In that vein, a good credit history and professional reputation are important to assure an artist and the artist's manager of the promoter's financial stability.

Rowe Entertainment, Inc. v. The William Morris Agency, 2005 WL 22833 at *3-*9 (S.D.N.Y. Jan. 5, 2005). (Internal citations and footnotes omitted.). See also, *It's My Party, Inc. v. Live Nation, Inc.*, 811 F.3d 676 (4th Cir. 2016) (noting artists sometimes offered 100% of the gross ticket sales to appear at a venue).

297   See the above discussion in the Management Agreements section for an illustration of why the artist would not want a manager's 20% commission to be calculated on the gross revenue from live performances. In this example, the manager whose commission was calculated on gross income would receive 20% of $10,000,000, or $2,000,000, while the artist who received 90% of net or $2,250,000, would have to pay the manager's $2,000,000, leaving the artist with $250,000.

298   For example, whether it is a flat fee or a minimum against a percent of net revenue.

299   Additional details are set forth in the rider.

creation, manufacture, and sales of approved merchandise. Merchandise can be a significant revenue source at live performances.

[c]—Sponsorships

If the artist or tour is sponsored, the agreement will address any issues relating to sponsorship, such as tickets provided to the sponsor, advertising banners, *inter alia*.

[d]—Artist Responsibilities

The promoter may want assurances as regards any costs that would normally be paid by the artist, such as salaries for the artist's personal staff, and visas if needed, for example.

[e]—Promoter's Responsibilities

The promoter will be responsible for direct expenses including the rent for the venue and staff, stage, sound, and lighting equipment, catering, public performance license fees, comprehensive liability and bodily injury insurance, advertising, municipal permit costs, if any, stagehands, hotel accommodations, trucking and ground transportation, air travel, and the costs of the opening act.

[f]—Cancellation

The agreement will have to carefully carve out various possible scenarios that could result in cancellation, and the consequences thereof. In addition to a *force majeure* clause, the artist may want an "anticipatory breach" clause if the promoter has financial difficulties. The artist may require escrow payments or other security guaranteeing the promoter's performance of their responsibilities. The artist will also want to have the ability to cancel or reschedule the engagement with sufficient notice, providing that in the event of cancellation the artist returns any monies previously received on deposit.[300] However, where the presenter has relied on the artist's representations and suffers losses because of a cancellation, the presenter may be entitled to damages.[301]

---

300   See *Druyan v. Jagger*, 508 F. Supp.2d 228 (S.D.N.Y. 2007) (dismissing putative class action brought by purchaser of concert ticket who allegedly incurred expenses relating to alleged untimely notification of postponement of concert).

301   See *Elvin Associates v. Aretha Franklin*, 735 F. Supp. 1177 (S.D.N.Y. 1990) (failure of artist to appear in musical production about Mahalia Jackson caused losses to producer who, because no formal agreement had been signed, recovered on grounds of promissory estoppel).

[g]—Audiovisual or Other Recording

Recording is usually banned, unless the artist grants the promoter specific rights to make an audiovisual recording of the performance.[302] The artist may reserve the right to make an audiovisual tape of their performance at the venue, and to use the venue's name in promoting that audiovisual work.

[h]—Box Office and Ticket Audits

The artist will want various rights to electronically audit the sale of tickets, including where tickets were preprinted and not delivered online, the right to obtain a manifest from the printing company to compare the number of tickets printed to the number of tickets reported sold. In the event of discrepancies, the artist will claim the right to be paid as if all tickets were sold, regardless of the actual ticket sales. The artist's tour manager may also obtain the right to enter the box office at any time and to examine the records therein.

[i]—Complimentary Tickets

The number and location of complimentary tickets will be carefully controlled, and the artist may request a list from the promoter identifying all recipients of complimentary tickets. The artist may also wish to control the location of complimentary tickets to ensure, for example, that seats in the front rows are sold to actual fans and not given away as business favors.

[j]—Promoter's Representative

It is essential that the promoter identify a representative who has a copy of the agreement and all riders thereto, and who will be available to the tour manager in person and by phone at all relevant times, with the authority to deal and resolve with any problems or issues that may arise.

---

302 "Bootleg" unauthorized recordings of live concerts are addressed in section § 1101 of the Copyright Act, entitled "Unauthorized fixation and trafficking in sound recordings and music videos." 17 U.S.C. § 1101 Under § 1101, it is an infringement to make unauthorized copies of a live musical performance or to transmit or otherwise communicate to the public the sounds or sounds and images of a live musical performance, or to traffic in any phonorecord of such "bootlegged" recordings. Notably, and unlike most other provisions under copyright law, § 1101 does not preempt state laws concerning bootleg recordings.

[k]—Schedules, Transportation, and Accommodation

Loading times, setup, rehearsals, soundcheck, and show times will all be specified in detail, as will be specifics of travel and hotel accommodations, including types of vehicles, and types of hotel rooms.

[l]— Dressing Rooms and Catering

The rider may have considerable detail regarding, for example, the furnishings in the dressing rooms, availability of toilet and shower facilities, the need for soap, towels, and even some basic garments, catering, telephones, security in the form of locks and keys, and provisions for artist security.

[m]—Ticket Surcharges

Concert promoters may add various ticket surcharges and fees to the price of the actual concert ticket, including facility maintenance fees, parking fees regardless of whether the ticket holder uses the parking facilities, and ticket processing and convenience fees arrived at as part of agreements with third party ticketing services.[303] In some cases, artists may be able to share in this ancillary revenue, and should at least take it into account as they negotiate other deal points.

[2]—Merchandise

Artists will want to retain at least 50% of merchandise revenues, where possible. Recording agreements, however, may grant to the artist's record company the rights in merchandise, subject to the artist receiving a percentage of sales. In such event it is essential that the artist have the record company keep any merchandise revenue in a separate account apart from the artist's royalty account. Otherwise, potential cash income from merchandise sales could be subsumed into the artist's unrecouped royalty account.

§4.16   Unions and Guilds

Where production entities and performing organizations enter into agreements with labor unions and guilds, they become union signatories, and undertake to only hire union member artists. Those engagements, in turn, will be subject to the union's minimum wage scales, including provisions for payments for benefits such as retirement and health insurance, and regulations relating to working conditions and hours. In addition, there will be schedules of "re-use" fees and residuals that must be paid in the future.

---

303   See In re Live Concert Antitrust Litigation, 2012 WL 1021081 (C.D. Cal. March 23, 2012) (ruling on admissibility of expert testimony on issues including live concert ticket pricing and ticket surcharges).

[1]—The American Federation of Musicians (AFM)

The American Federation of Musicians ("AFM") was founded in 1896, and serves more than 250 "locals" in cities throughout North America. The AFM publishes numerous approved agreements, including details of working conditions and wage scales. The AFM basic agreements go into considerable detail concerning minimum (but not maximum) wages and future payments for member health and pension benefits due to AFM.[304]

Production entities will often use "contractors" who engage union musicians, and who are familiar with wage scales and other requirements. The contractor for a film or television or recording project will, under consultation with the producers or composer, hire the musicians, and ensure that the AFM agreements and other record-keeping documents and reporting forms are completed, and where necessary sent to the local union chapter. Specialist accounting firms may also be available to assist with the calculation and issuance of payments under union guidelines.[305]

---

304   For example, the AFM Basic Television and Film Agreement for Independent Producers is 130 pages long. The Sound Recording Labor Agreement is 102 pages long. See *Big Seven Music Corp. v. Lennon*, 554 F.2d 504, 512 (2d Cir. 1977) (noting in the context of calculating damages based on recording royalties that deductions from gross revenues must be made to account for sound recording royalty payments due to AFM).

305   The following AFM documents, including agreements and wage scales, are available on the Web site if the Local 802, the Associated Musicians of the City of New York, at http://www.local802afm.org/frames/fs_wage.htm.

Music Preparation and Copying Agreements

Orchestration Scales

Music Preparation Employer Agreement

Music Preparation Contract Blank

Recording Agreements

Motion Picture & TV Film

Industrial Films Agreement

TV & Video Wage Scales

TV & Video Rules Summary

AFM Television Station I.D.'s

Sound Recording Scale Summary

AFM Low Budget Summary

Television & Radio Commercial Announcements

National Public Radio Agreement Summary

Where engagements and agreements are on a non-union basis, there is typically a provision whereby the artist warrants they, and the engagement, are non-union, and in consequence the performers warrant that they will be responsible for any current or future union or guild dues, fees, or otherwise in connection with the agreement.

[2]—SAG-AFTRA

In the music industry, SAG-AFTRA applies primarily to vocalists performing on television, and occasionally to spoken word artists such as narrators who appear on sound recordings. Instrumental musicians would be covered under AFM.

SAG-AFTRA negotiates and enforces collective bargaining agreements for its members that include minimum (but not maximum) salaries, working conditions and health and retirement benefits, as well as dispute resolution mechanisms.

National Public Television Agreement Summary

New Video Game/Interactive Media Announcement

AFM Experimental Video Game Agreement

Broadway & Off-Broadway Agreements

Broadway Agreement (2003-2007)

Broadway Memorandum of Agreement

Broadway Scale Summary (3/3/08 - 8/31/08)

Commercial Off Broadway Area Standards

Manhattan Theatre Club Agreement

Roundabout Theatre Company Agreement

Non-Profit Off-Broadway Agreement

Radio City Music Hall Agreement

Theatrical Showcase Rules & Regulations

Encores! NY City Center Agreement

Concert Agreements

Single Engagement Classical Wage Scales

Single Engagement Ballet & Opera Wage Scales

Symphony/Ballet/Opera Tour & Run-Out Guidelines

The SAG-AFTRA National Code of Fair Practice for Sound Recordings covers vocalists working on sound recordings in all media as well as books on tape, cast albums, and any other sound recording utilizing vocal performance. The SAG-AFTRA Code not only covers singers, but announcers, actors, comedians, narrators and sound effects artists.[306] Where an SAG-AFTRA member vocalist makes a sound recording that is later licensed for use in television or radio advertising, the SAG-AFTRA member will receive residuals under the SAG-AFTRA scale.[307]

[3]—The American Guild of Musical Artists (AGMA)

The American Guild of Musical Artists ("AGMA"), founded in the 1930s, represents opera and concert singers, production personnel and dancers at principal opera, concert and dance companies throughout the United States.[308] AGMA signatories include some of the leading ballet and opera companies in the United States, and several choral groups affiliated with orchestras.

As with other unions, AGMA agreements establish minimum wages and working conditions, and are extensive. The AGMA agreement with the Metropolitan Opera, for example, is 110 pages.[309]

§4.17   Considerations for Musicians: Co-Ownership and Band Agreements

[1]—Copyright Co-Ownership of Musical Works

Music is a collaborative art, and there are often situations where such collaborations include the creation of copyrightable elements of a work—a portion of melody or harmony in a song contributed by a band member or guest artist or producer. But it may not always be clear when and how such creative collaborations rise to the level of participating in a joint work.

Co-authors of work are also the co-owners, with each enjoying an undivided interest in the whole work. In the absence of any agreement specifying which co-owner may

---

306   Available at http://www.aftra.org/contract/documents/2005_Sound_Recordings_at_a_Glance.pdf.

307   Copies of AFTRA scale payment charts and other agreements are available at www.sagaftra.org.

308   Among the AGMA signatories, for example, are the Dallas Opera, Houston Grand Opera, Joffrey Ballet, Lyric Opera of Chicago, Martha Graham Dance, Merce Cunningham Dance, the Metropolitan Opera, the New York City Ballet, the New York City Opera, the Opera Company of Philadelphia, and the San Francisco Opera.

309   Available at http://www.musicalartists.org/Agreements/MetOpera/MetOperaIndex.htm. Further information, including copies of AGMA agreements with various signatories, is available at www.musicalartists.org.

administer rights, the default position under United States law is that each co-owner may independently grant non-exclusive licenses in the work, subject only to a duty to account to the other co-owners.[310]

Under the Copyright Act, a joint work is "a work prepared by two or more authors with the intention that their contributions be merged into inseparable or interdependent parts of a unitary whole."[311] Thus, the classic songwriting duo of a lyricist and a composer create joint works, with each co-author owning an undivided half interest in the whole.

In the leading case on establishing whether co-authorship exists, *Thomson v. Larson*, the Second Circuit grappled with a co-authorship dispute over the musical "Rent."[312] In that case, a "dramaturg" hired to improve the dramatic flow of the work, claimed, after the death of the show's sole author, that her contributions to the show amounted to co-authorship and co-ownership. In seeking to arrive at a legal test for co-authorship, the court acknowledged that with respect to collaborative works, authors must be protected from overreaching claims of co-authorship in cases where there may be some collaboration, but there is no actual intent to grant co-authorship status.

The *Thomson* test consists of two elements: (1) there must be a copyrightable contribution by each putative co-author, in other words it is not enough to contribute "ideas" or mere editorial amendments; and (2) there must be objective evidence on the part of all parties to create a joint work.[313] Evidence of such intent would include decision making authority; billing and credits; agreements with third parties stating who the author is; and other evidence such as statements made by the author.[314]

Disputes over co-ownership can arise where one party assumes co-authorship and ownership and the other does not, but no express statements are made clarifying the nature of the business relationship. For example, a producer who arranges a song and supervises a recording, and even composes instrumental "hooks," in the absence of a clear statement by the songwriter that such acts did not create any "co-writer" status,

---

310   See *Oddo v. Ries*, 743 F.2d 630 (9th Cir. 1984) (one co-owner cannot sue the other co-owner for copyright infringement, but can bring an action for an accounting under state law). The co-owner's right to unilaterally grant nonexclusive licenses as interpreted by U.S. courts may not be recognized in foreign jurisdictions that apply their own copyright laws.

311   17 U.S.C. § 101.

312   See *Thomson v. Larson*, 147 F.3d 195 (2d Cir. 1998). See also, *Ulloa v. Universal Music*, 303 F. Supp.2d 409 (S.D.N.Y. 2004) (guest at recording session improvised and sang a musical phrase used in the song as commercially released, guest later asserted co-authorship claim in the underlying composition).

313   *Thomson v. Larson*, 147 F.3d 195 (2d Cir. 1998).

314   *Id.*, 147 F.3d at 202-205.

might assume they were a "co-author" and co-owner of the song's copyright, leading to disputes.[315]

Where co-ownership legitimately exists, with respect to non-exclusive licenses granted to third parties, either co-owner may grant such licenses independently, subject to a duty to account to the other co-owner their 50% share of the profits from the license.[316] It also means that a co-owner cannot sue another co-owner for copyright infringement in federal court under the Copyright Act, but can bring an action under state law for an accounting of profits from the co-owner.[317]

[2]—Business Considerations for Groups

Where musicians are members of a band, they are well advised to discuss and agree upon issues such as division of income, ownership of the band's name, ownership of trademarks and copyrights, band members leaving or joining, and how to "vote" on important decisions.[318] Later, if successful, they may wish to form a business entity.[319]

In a dispute between the band Third Eye Blind and a former member who had left the band in its early days, then rejoined the band after it had become established, the former member claimed he was due royalties from recording and touring arising from his former membership in the group.[320] In holding on summary judgment for the defendant band, the court noted that while the band had formed several corporations to govern its

---

315   See, e.g., *BTE v. Bonnecaze*, 43 F. Supp.2d 619 (E.D. La. 1999) (band's drummer who allegedly "worked up" songs by other band member by contributing "ideas and helpful insights" was not a co-author of the musical compositions). See also: *Severe Records, LLC v. Rich*, 658 F.2d 571 (6th Cir. 2011) (co-authorship dispute between former songwriting team); *Corwin v. Quinonez*, 2012 WL 832600 (N.D. Ohio March 12, 2012) (dismissing declaratory judgment complaint for co-ownership of musical compositions).

316   *Oddo v. Ries*, 743 F.2d 630 (9th Cir. 1984). Note that the "profits" may be determined after deduction of related expenses, and do not include unrelated services included in the license.

317   *Id.*

318   See e.g., *Dead Kennedys v. Biafra*, 37 F. Supp.2d 1151 (N.D. Cal. 1999). Although the four band members in the group Dead Kennedys formed a general partnership with equal voting and ownership interests, a dispute nevertheless arose between three of the band members and the defendant, the fourth band member, concerning various ownership and licensing rights.

319   See *Brother Records, Inc., v. Jardine*, 318 F.3d 900 (9th Cir. 2003) (the group The Beach Boys formed a corporation for their intellectual property rights, including trademarks, called Brother Records, Inc., and a corporation for their touring matters and income called Brother Tours, Inc. Four of the original five band members were shareholders and directors of the corporations).

320   See *Fredianelli v. Jenkins*, 2013 U.S. Dist. LEXIS 35757, 2013 WL 1087653 (N.D. Cal. March 14, 2013). See also, *Hayes v. Hutchinson*, 2013 Cal. App. Unpub. LEXIS 543 (Cal. App. Jan. 24, 2013) (rock group Linkin Park had an internal "legal and finance" committee to oversee the business and legal affairs of the band).

affairs, and had submitted to the member draft membership and corporate governance agreements that would grant a share in all revenues, and a corresponding vote in all band decisions, the agreements were never signed thus of no effect.

With respect to the band being a partnership under the law, the court noted that while the new band member was granted a share in revenues while he was in the band, he was excluded from the decision making process, thus did not meet the legal definition of a partner. Also noteworthy is that the court respected the corporate governance that the band had created for financial and decision making purposes, ruling against the member who had not been formally granted corporate shares and a voice in the decision making process. As the court noted, being a band "member" does not necessarily denote ownership.

[a]—Division of Income

Income division may be different in the case of live performances, making sound recordings, and music publishing, depending on the roles of each member of the group. In the case of songwriting, there needs to be clarity on who are the songwriters, and in what situations contributions by band members of riffs or hooks for a song rise to the level of "songwriters."

[b]—Group Name and Trademark Rights

Band names can function as trade names, and as trademarks. In the absence of any written agreements, the name of a musical group usually belongs to the "founding" member(s) or the person who "created" the group and who remains personally involved.[321] Even where a group has agreed to future uses of the group name as a trade

---

321   See:

First Circuit: Bell v. Streetwise Records, Ltd., 640 F. Supp. 575 (D. Mass. 1986).

Second Circuit: Rick v. Buchansky, 609 F. Supp. 1522 (S.D.N.Y. 1985) (where a manager created a group and its name, the manager owned the group name where manager provided continuity in the midst of periodic personnel changes and the manager made important personnel decisions concerning the style and content of the group's act).

Ninth Circuit: Robi v. Reed, 173 F.3d 736 (9th Cir. 1999) (the "person who remains continuously involved with the group and is in a position to control the quality of its services retains the right to use of the mark," also holding that members of a group do not retain rights to use the group's name when they leave the group).

Eleventh Circuit: Commodores Entertainment Corp. v. McClary, 2014 U.S. Dist. LEXIS 147021 (M.D. Fla. Oct. 9, 2014) (granting preliminary injunction against former group member using group name without authorization, and stating:

"When courts are faced with a 'case of joint endeavors' situation—that is, when prior ownership by one of several claimants to a mark cannot be established—they tend to award 'trademark rights to the claimant who controls the nature and quality of the services performed under the mark.' Crystal Entm't, 643 F.3d at 1322 (*citing Robi v.*

name, and have reserved those rights to specific individuals, former band members may still factually refer to their former participation in the band.[322] Even where a

---

Reed, 173 F.3d 736, 740 (9th Cir. 1999). In the context of a band, this is typically the band members who made the band famous. *Id.*; see also, *Bell v. Streetwise Records, Ltd.*, 640 F. Supp. 575, 582 (D. Mass. 1986) (noting that the 'norm in the music industry is that an artist or group generally owns its name' and concluding that the band members, with their 'distinctive personalities and style as performers,' controlled the nature and quality and thus owned the band name mark).

"When members of a band dispute ownership of a mark associated with the band, courts have found that members who remain active and associated with the band have better title to the mark than those who do not. See Robi, 173 F.3d at 740. The Robi court held that a founding member who remained and continuously performed with the band had better rights to the mark and could use the mark 'to the exclusion' of the founding member who had left the band. *Id.* ('[W]hen Robi left the group, he took no rights to the service mark with him. Rather, the mark remained with the original group.').

"In accordance with the decisions of courts in other cases of joint endeavors, the original band members of The Commodores—including Defendant—acquired common law ownership and trademark rights because it was their style and sound that brought recognition to the band name and Marks.4Link to the text of the note Crystal Entm't, 643 F.3d at 1322. However, Defendant no longer has a valid claim to ownership over the Marks. See Robi, 173 F.3d at 740. Rather, the band members who remained after Defendant left in 1984 have prevailing ownership because they 'maintained continuity with the group and [have] been in a position to control the quality of services' of the Marks associated with the band name. See *id.* Defendant has not put forward any evidence to suggest that he maintained quality or control over the Marks associated with The Commodores after he left; rather, it was the other original band members who stayed with the group that continued to control the nature and quality of the Marks, went on to win a Grammy, and further expanded the band's fan base and recognition.5Link to the text of the note (See Doc. 1, ¶¶ 28-33.)"

Id., at *8.

322   See *Kassbaum v. Steppenwolf Productions, Inc.*, 236 F.3d 487 (9th Cir. 2000) (former member of band Steppenwolf who was contractually bound not to use the trade name "Steppenwolf" for musical performances or recordings, was free to factually refer to himself as "former member of Steppenwolf" or "previous member of Steppenwolf"). See also, *Kingsmen v. K-Tel International, Ltd.*, 557 F. Supp. 178 (S.D.N.Y. 1983) (where a former member of the band The Kingsmen re-recorded one of the Kingsmen's songs "Louie Louie" under the trade name The Kingsmen, a likelihood of consumer confusion arose such that a violation of the Lanham Act occurred, however where the same individual re-recorded a song under his own name with the designation "formerly of" there was no likelihood of consumer confusion under the Lanham Act).

See also:

Ninth Circuit: *Reed v. Florida Entertainment Management, Inc.* 108 U.S.P.Q.2d 2004 (9th Cir. Dec. 2, 2013) ("The Platters" trademark).

Federal Circuit: *Willis v. Can't Stop Productions, Inc.*, 497 Fed. Appx. 975 (Fed. Cir. 2012) ("Village People" mark not generic or abandoned by production company owner).

former group member remains as a shareholder or director, use of the group's trademarks requires a license.[323]

Note however that under trademark law, mere creation of a band name does not create potential trademark rights unless the mark is inherently distinctive, or unless the mark is used in commerce such that the mark acquires distinctiveness and secondary meaning in the minds of the relevant consumers.[324] Even a famous group trademark is susceptible to fair use by others In one case for example, a group tried to enjoin a newspaper from conducting a popularity contest that featured the band's name, and the use was held to be a fair use.[325]

[c]—Decision Making

"Voting" on important business and artistic matters should be agreed to by all members of the band, either by majority or unanimous decision. If there is an even number of members of the group, there should be a provision to appoint a tiebreaker vote.

More complex partnership agreements are possible, and the band members should seek legal advice in either event. However, in the case of such a partnership agreement, each band member should ideally have independent counsel.

Recording agreements for groups may have provisions whereby the record company can terminate the agreement if a key band member leaves,[326] as well as provisions that bind the leaving member to the record label. Members must be aware of all their group obligations when entering into any agreement that binds the entire group or individual members.

---

323   See *Brother Records, Inc., v. Jardine*, 318 F.3d 900 (9th Cir. 2003) (former band member who performed on his own using "Beach Boys" mark for his own group, without a license, infringed the trademark owned by the group's corporation).

324   See The Lanham Act, 15 U.S.C.A. § 115(a). See also *Echo Drain v. Newsted*, 307 F. Supp.2d 1116 (C.D. Cal. 2003) (name of funk and groove band "Echo Drain" not likely to be confused with junior user's mark of "Echobrain" for pop rock band. Echo Brain mark was at most suggestive and presumptively weak, and strength of mark was further diluted by other bands' use of word "echo," bands played different types of clubs and catered to different types of customers, the marks looked different and appeared different in the marketplace, there was little evidence of actual confusion and defendants adopted "Echobrain" mark before learning of Echo Drain's existence).

325   See The *New Kids on the Block v. News America Publishing, Inc.*, 971 F.2d 302 (9th Cir. 1992) (use of group's name by newspaper taking reader polls on group's popularity was a fair use).

326   See *The Gordy Co. v. Mary Jane Girls, Inc.*, 1989 WL 149290 at *12 (S.D.N.Y. Dec. 6, 1989) (the parties to an agreement providing the services of a group designated the lead singer as "the only 'key member' whose departure from the group would give Motown various rights and remedies.").

§4.18   YouTube

Google's YouTube service has become one of the world's most popular mediums for the public to enjoy music, the leading "radio" station of the world.

Originally the user-posted content model was based on the Digital Millennium Copyright Act's Safe Harbor provisions for Internet Service Providers. Under the DMCA, copyright owners of music publishing and sound recordings rights were limited to taking down infringing user postings, but did not share in any revenues realized by YouTube from advertising. Reliance on the DMCA proved to be frustrating and led to litigation against YouTube and frustration with the DMCA's outmoded provisions, which never were designed for billions of user postings incorporating unauthorized use of copyrights.

YouTube's business model, while still relying on the DMCA where needed, now includes licensed content via industry wide licensing with artists, songwriters, music publishers and record labels, based on sharing advertising revenue from YouTube's "Adsense" programs, via the YouTube Partner Program which allows users to establish their own "channel" and to monetize their user-generated YouTube content.[327]

For music publishers, revenue arises in two ways: first via YouTube's PRO licenses for public performances on the web site. Second, via YouTube Adsense agreements that provide a percentage of YouTube's advertising revenue for user-posted videos that would normally require a synchronization license from the music publisher.

In such scenarios, publishers do not enter into agreements directly with the end users who incorporate a song into a video, but are paid in the background via their overall consent to YouTube for what amounts to mass synchronization licensing on the service. Publishers may still issue DMCA takedown notices where desired, perhaps for user posted content that is offensive and for which the songwriter prefers their music not be used.

This "background sync licensing" is a recent development, although users cannot be entirely certain that their unauthorized synchronization of a song is authorized, unless they learn that YouTube took down the video pursuant to a notice from a copyright owner. Outside of the YouTube context, such "YouTube blanket sync licenses" may be regarded as unauthorized infringements because copyright owners' consent is limited to the YouTube agreement and Adsense program, inapplicable to other platforms. Creators of user generated content are cautioned not to attempt to monetize such unlicensed creations outside the YouTube platform without securing a license from the original copyright owners of the underlying music, lyrics, and sound recording.

---

327   See YouTube Partner Program Overview, available at https://support.google.com/youtube/answer/72851?hl=e.

For record labels and their artists, YouTube offers exclusive "Channels" via the YouTube Partner Program, with the channel directing Adsense revenue to the artist. Licensing companies have arisen that manage the business relationship on behalf of artists in exchange for a percentage of the revenue, for example FullScreen Media.

Third party digital music services may also offer management services for YouTube, and offer value-add services such as targeted advertising and placements for the client's Multi Channel Network ("MCN").[328]

YouTube also offers record labels a Sound Recording and Audiovisual Content License that provides Adsense revenue in lieu of traditional master licenses for videos, and presumably as some compensation for lost download and streaming revenues (YouTube videos do not qualify for SoundExchange's audio-only digital radio royalties).

Highlights of the YouTube Sound Recording and Audiovisual Content License with the artist or record label ("Provider") include:

- Provider Content License granting Google nonexclusive rights to host the content (sound recordings and videos).

- Art Track Creation License including artist and track information and song lyrics.

- Brand Features License for label trademarks and logos.

- Artwork License for album artwork.

- Audio Matching License for audio track ID services.

- AudioSwap License allowing YouTube users to include tracks in their own videos

- Percentage Rates of ad revenue averaging between 40% and 55%, with some limited user content outlier uses as low as 5% to 10%.

§4.19   Independent Distribution on Streaming Services

Independent recording artists may prefer to retain ownership of their recordings and self-distribute on worldwide streaming services such as Spotify, Apple, etc. This strategy can be successful as streaming becomes increasingly prominent as the consumer choice for music consumption, and distribution of physical media such as CDs is less crucial to success.

---

328   See e.g. http://www.tunecore.com/terms#youtube-sound-recording-revenue (TuneCore agreement for Youtube Sound Recording Revenue).

Several leading digital recording distribution companies specialize in ensuring that independently produced sound recordings are provided to the leading digital streaming services, and may also provide physical media manufacturing options.

Current leading companies include TuneCore, CDBaby, FullScreen Media, Studio71, BandCamp and others. Their business models vary, ranging from a fee charged to their clients, to a percentage of revenue model for digital streams of sound recordings.[329] Some also offer a full suite of music industry services involving music publishing administration, live performance, rights management, and merchandise.

---

329 See e.g. http://www.tunecore.com/terms (TuneCore distribution agreement); http://www.tunecore.com/terms#publishing-administration (TuneCore publishing administration agreement); https://members.cdbaby.com/membercontract.aspx (CD Baby agreement);

CHAPTER 5

Live Theater

---

§5.01   Live Theater

[1]—Unions and Collective Bargaining

Like the motion picture industry, many categories of creative talent on the live stage are members of unions and guilds that set rates of compensation and working conditions via collective bargaining agreements. The leading organizations in live theatre are:

- Actors Equity[1]

- Stage Directors and Choreographers Society ("SDCS")[2]

- The Dramatists Guild (playwrights and authors)[3]

- League of Resident Theatres ("LORT")[4]

- United Scenic Artists Local USA 829[5]

- Theatrical Teamsters Local Union No. 817[6]

For stage directors and choreographers, the SDCS collective bargaining agreements sets out the minimum compensation rates for different types of productions, including Broadway productions and touring productions. The SDCS also provides a short form

---

1   See www.actorsequity.org.

2   See www.sdcweb.org.

3   See www.dramatistsguild.com.

4   See www.lort.org.

5   See http://usa829.org

6   See, e.g. *Leavey v. International Brotherhood Of Teamsters-Theatrical Teamsters Local Union No. 817*, 2015 U.S. Dist. LEXIS 135509 (S.D.N.Y. Oct. 5, 2015) (dispute over hiring of Transportation "Captains" for productions).

contract which incorporates by reference the terms of the full Broadway agreement, and lists basics such as the dates covered by the engagement and the per week fees.

Like all other segments of the entertainment industry, the world of live staged performance, including drama, musicals, and dance, is also subject to disputes and litigation over underlying rights, such as authorship claims, ownership of copyright in choreography, ownership of copyright in fanciful character makeup, and motion picture rights to plays.[7]

[2]—Broadway Theatre Guild Agreements

The hallmark of the leading Broadway theatre guild agreements is that their provisions assiduously protect the artistic and financial rights of authors and creators. Compared to the motion picture industry where profit participation is sometimes regarded as illusory, theatre agreements start from the position that the author has control over the creative process, and that box office receipts are subject to transparent accounting and reporting

---

7 See, e.g.:

Second Circuit: Martha Graham School and *Dance Foundation, Inc. v. Martha Graham Center of Contemporary Dance, Inc.*, 380 F.3d 624 (2d Cir. 2004) (copyright ownership of Martha Graham dance choreography); *Thomson v. Larson*, 147 F.3d 195 (2d Cir. 1998) (co-authorship of musical "Rent"); *Porto v. Guirgis*, 659 F. Supp.2d 597 (S.D.N.Y. 2009) (summary judgment for defendant author of play "The Last Days of Judas Iscariot" on copyright infringement allegations brought by author of novel "Judas on Appeal"); *Einhorn v. Mergatroyd Productions*, 426 F. Supp.2d 189 (S.D.N.Y. 2006) (play director suit alleging copyright infringement, breach of contract, and Lanham Act violations against playwright and producer, motion to dismiss granted in part and denied in part); *Carell v. The Schubert Organization, Inc.*, 104 F. Supp.2d 236 (S.D.N.Y. 2000) (copyright ownership of character makeup design for musical "Cats"); *Mantello v. Hall*, 947 F. Supp. 92 (S.D.N.Y. 1996) (New York stage director claims against Florida production of "Love! Valour! Compassion!" alleging misappropriation of director's "unique direction and staging," with action dismissed on jurisdiction grounds without ruling on merits); *Inge v. Twentieth Century-Fox Film Corp.*, 143 F. Supp. 294 (S.D.N.Y. 1956) (film rights to play "Bus Stop"). See also, *Jacobs v. Felix Bloch Erben Verlag fur Buhne Film und Funk KG*, 160 F. Supp.2d 722 (S.D.N.Y. 2001) (dispute over license rights to produce the musical "Grease" in Germany). See also *Adjmi v. DLT Entm't Ltd.*, 2015 U.S. Dist. LEXIS 43285, 114 U.S.P.Q.2D (BNA) 1784, Copy. L. Rep. (CCH) P30,748 (S.D.N.Y. Mar. 31, 2015) (dramatic stage play "3C" held to make fair use of story elements of television comedy series "Three's Company"); *TCA TV Corp. v. McCollum*, 2015 U.S. Dist. LEXIS 168934, No. 15 Civ. 4325 (S.D.N.Y. Dec. 17, 2015) (use of "Who's on First" routine in a live play fair use). See *also Pai v. Blue Man Group Publishing, LLC*, 2016 N.Y. Misc. LEXIS 3487 (Sup. Ct. N.Y. Sept. 28, 2016) (alleged co-founder of Blue Man Group dispute over profit and royalties, noting the Blue Man Group productions had generated "box office revenues in excess of $1 billion in America and around the world"). *Id.*, at *3.

Fifth Circuit: *Baisden v. I'm Ready Productions, Inc.*, 693 F.3d 491 (5th Cir. 2012) (dispute over DVD home videos of plays produced by defendants based on novels written by plaintiff).

Ninth Circuit: *Corbello v. DeVito*, 2011 U.S. Dist. LEXIS 124779, 2011 WL 5121888 (D. Nev. Oct. 27, 2011) (co-author claims to autobiography upon which musical "Jersey Boys" was based).

on a weekly basis, and that the percentages of revenue due the creative team are ensured by the terms of the Guild's agreements, and are part of the standard weekly accounting process.

The Dramatists Guild, which represents the core creative team including playwrights, authors of the Broadway "book" or story for a musical, lyricists, and composers for theatrical and musical productions.[8] It offers its members an Approved Production Contract ("APC"). In addition, the Guild's services include providing dispute resolution in the form of a Theatrical Conciliation Council, whose members also must be used in the event that any disputes proceed to binding arbitration, ensuring that disputes between authors and producers are adjudicated by knowledgeable members of the theatre world.[9]

In addition to guaranteed payments to authors, the standard agreements provide for royalty participation, either in the form of a share of Net Gross Weekly Box Office Receipts ("NGWBOR," meaning the gross receipts less fixed costs such as credit card charges), or participation in a "royalty pool" based on net revenues remaining each week after deduction of weekly operating costs and investor recoupment.

Below is a summary of the main provisions of the Dramatists Guild APC; the SDCS Broadway Agreement; comments regarding "side letters" also used in the Broadway Theatre world; and a discussion of the Broadway "royalty pool."

[a]—The Dramatists Guild Approved Production Contract

The Dramatists Guild APC is a comprehensive agreement over fifty pages long, between the producer, and the authors of a play or musical, including the "bookwriter" or author of the story, the composer, and the lyricist (collectively the "Author"). All payments to the "author" referred to in the agreement are divided amongst the cre-

---

8   See *Barr v. The Dramatists Guild, Inc. v. The League of New York Theatres and Producers, Inc.*, 573 F. Supp. 555 (1983) (action by the League of New York Theatres and Producers, Inc. against The Dramatists Guild, alleging violation of antitrust laws). The producers argued that the defendants conspired to fix minimum prices for their services, while the counterclaim alleged that the producers conspired to reduce the compensation paid to playwrights. In holding that the Dramatists Guild had the right to maintain a counterclaim against the producers on behalf of its members, the court stated: "[t]he Dramatists Guild satisfies the three elements of the Hunt test. The purpose of the Dramatist Guild is to protect and promote the professional interests of playwrights and to improve the conditions under which their works are created and produced. While individual members could sue in their own right, neither the claim asserted nor the relief requested by the Guild requires their participation in this action."

9   The Stage Directors and Choreographers Society also offers its members several collective bargaining agreements, including the basic "Broadway" agreement which is reproduced in the Appendices for this Chapter.

ative team, which may include the several people noted above. The main contractual sections cover the following:[10]

<u>Initial Grant of Rights</u>: The Author grants the Producer the right to produce the play (or musical) for First Class Performances on the live stage, "in a regular evening bill in a first class theatre in a first class manner, with a first class cast and a first class director." Where the play is not based on any pre-existing material, the author is entitled to additional percentage points. The author reserves all rights in the play, including copyright, and all exploitations not specifically granted in the agreement. Thus, unlike a motion picture agreement, the author's contribution is not a work made for hire but the opposite: the author retains all rights and licenses them to the Producer. The author agrees to perform services including creation of the play, selecting the cast, and consulting with the production crew including the producer, director, scenic, lighting, and costume designers, etc.

<u>Option Periods and Payments</u>: Option periods up to three years until the play is premiered, accompanied by payment of non-returnable option fees.

<u>Advance Payments</u>: Once the work is completed and rehearsals begin, the authors are entitled to advances based on 2% of the show's capitalization, subject to a specific maximum cap.

<u>Royalties</u>: The main variables for royalties are whether the investors have recouped their investment or not at the time of the accounting. Other variables are based on the location and nature of the performance, for example whether it was a "Regular" performance, a "Preview," a "Touring" performance, or an "Out-of-town" performance. The formula is based on Net Gross Weekly Box Office Receipts ("NGWBOR"), and typically the author receives 4.5% of NGWBOR prior to recoupment, and 6% of NGWBOR post-recoupment. There may also be limited scenarios where the author receives a fixed dollar amount. The agreement also covers situations where the Producer may have a financial interest in the theatre presenting the play, requiring that all fees payable to the producer's own theatre be comparable to "arm's length" transactions between third parties.

<u>Royalty Adjustments</u>: This provision considers whether the play is turning a profit based on the "weekly breakeven," weekly profits," and "weekly losses." If the weekly NGWBOR is less than 110% of the weekly breakeven (or sometimes 120%), then the author agrees to adjust their weekly payment to a fixed fee plus a share of the profits, not to exceed the 4.5% or 6% of NGWBOR they would have otherwise been

---

10   The summary discussion of the APC's overall structure is not a substitute for the full approved agreement which contains many different and detailed rights, payment, and royalty terms.

entitled to. In this trade off, the author can still rely on a fixed weekly payment, but may have their royalty share curtailed. Where the play is succeeding more robustly, for example where the production meets an "87% Formula" with ticket sales reaching 87% of seating capacity for an extended period, the author will be entitled to share in the success and have the royalty increase from 4.5% of NGWBOR to 6%. All of these terms reflect the assumption in the Broadway world that there will be transparent accounting on a weekly basis, and the Agreement does require that each week, the Producer must submit to the Dramatists Guild the daily box office statements, signed by the treasurer of the theatre and the Producer, along with the payment due to the author.

Royalty Pool: Exhibit C to the Agreement has an alternative royalty formula for musical plays, a "royalty pool" based on Weekly Net Operating Profit ("WNOP") instead of NGWBOR. See below for a discussion of the "royalty pool."

Production Provisions: The cast and production personnel must be mutually approved by Producer and author. The author has the right to attend all rehearsals, and to be reimbursed for travel and accommodation expenses, as well as appropriate credits and billing. For cast albums, the author receives a 60% royalty and the producer 40%. The producer must pay for the preparation of the musical score (sheet music) materials but may have the right to share in any music publishing rights and revenues. There are detailed provisions regarding what happens if other authors become involved, or if there is a change of author. There are provisions for productions overseas.

Subsidiary Rights: This includes media productions such as television and motion picture, merchandise, stock, amateur, and revival performances. Once the Producer's rights "vest" by virtue of satisfying substantial performance benchmarks, the producer is entitled to share in the subsidiary rights according to several different formulas, such as:

- Media productions: 50% in perpetuity

- Stock and ancillary: 50% for the first 5 years, then 25% for the next five years

- Amateur performances: 25% for 5 years

- Revival performances: 20% for 40 years

- Merchandise: Producer has the exclusive right to license merchandise, with Author receiving a basic royalty of 10% of the gross retail sales not to exceed 50% of the Producer's license fee, with other royalty formulas depending on factors including the location of the merchandise sales, for example in the theatre itself, or elsewhere

Motion Picture Rights: Although it is no longer acknowledged to be an applicable provision, negotiations under the APC for motion picture rights must be conducted by a negotiator provided by the Dramatists Guild, working in cooperation with the author and the author's agent. Payments for the motion picture rights are made to the Guild which forwards the revenues to the author after deducting the Guild's commission. An Exhibit B to the Agreement consists of "Instructions" to the Guild's negotiator regarding motion picture rights, including an admonition to determine whether any portion of the play was financed by a motion picture company, explaining that "[t]he producer who has motion picture backing (by reason of financial, employment or other contractual relations) occupies a dual position. He is both buyer and seller."

Certification: The negotiated agreement must be certified by the Guild, including any changes or modifications. Modifications must be made only where "reasonably necessary" or where they increase the author's percentage, as opposed to lowering it.

Theatrical Conciliation Council: This is a dispute resolution body for authors and producers to submit disputes for resolution. In addition, there are arbitration provisions, requiring that the arbitrators be chosen from members of the Guild's Theatrical Production Arbitration Board.

[b]—The Society of Stage Directors and Choreographers Broadway Agreement

The Broadway Agreement of The Society of Stage Directors and Choreographers ("SDC") covers very similar provisions as compared to the Dramatists Guild Approved Production Contract, however the format is more of an annotated outline with short deal forms than a fully drafted agreement.[11]

For musicals where the services of both a director and choreographer will be required, two formulas for royalties, above and beyond any set weekly fees, are set forth: (1) Royalties based on NGWBOR, with director entitled to a minimum of 0.75% and the choreographer entitled to a minimum of 0.50%; and (2) royalty pools based on WNOP, with the director's minimum is 2.75%, and the choreographer's minimum of 1%.

For dramatic works involving only a director, the NGWBOR minimum is 1.5%, and the WNOP or royalty pool minimum is 3.5% until 125% of recoupment, and 3.85% thereafter.

---

11   See, e.g. SDC-Broadway League Agreement, available at http://sdcweb.org/contracts/agreements/broadway/.

The above is a simplified summary, as there are several other categories of royalty and compensation calculation, including "steps" that apply only where the NGW-BOR is between 110% and 120% of weekly breakeven, and other formulas that provide for a choice between or combination of guaranteed weekly fixed fees and royalties based on percentages of revenue.

The SDC Broadway agreement provides two illustrative examples of how royalty calculations work in practice, quoted below. Note that the assumption is that in the royalty pool based on WNOP, a fixed amount each week is reserved for recoupment of the financiers' investment in the project, commonly referred to as the "amortization" deduction:

Royalties Based on Net Operating Profit

Assume that the contract of a Director of a musical provides for a royalty payment of 3% of the weekly net operating profit and that weekly amortization is $50,000 and that all other terms of the collective bargaining agreement apply.

In week number 10, the net operating profit equals $150,000. Under the Director's contract, after subtracting amortization from net operating profit, the Director is entitled to 3% of $100,000 (or $3,000). However, under the collective bargaining agreement, the Director must receive a minimum of 2.5% of $150,000 (or $3,750). In that week, therefore, the Producer must pay the Director $3,750.

In week number 12, the net operating profit equals $250,000. Under the Director's contract, after subtracting amortization from net operating profit, the Director is entitled to 3% of $200,000 (or $6,000). Under the collective bargaining agreement, the Director would receive a minimum of 2.5% of $250,000 (or $6,250) unless that compensation exceeds the pre-recoupment cap as set forth in Article IV Section (B)(1)(b)(iii) [$4,691; $4,750 as of September 3, 2012; $4,821 as of September 2, 2013; $4,894 as of September 1, 2014]. Thus, because both these amounts exceed the $4,691 ($4,750 as of September 3, 2012; $4,821 as of September 2, 2013; $4,894 as of September 1, 2014) pre-recoupment cap on net operating profit royalties, the director would receive $4,691 in week number 12.

Royalties Based on Percentage of Gross Weekly Box Office Receipts

Assume that the contract of a Director of a musical provides for a royalty payment of 1% of gross weekly box office receipts and that weekly amortization is $200,000 and that all other terms of the collective bargaining agreement apply. In week number 10, the gross weekly box office receipts were $700,000. Under the director's contract, after subtracting weekly amortization from the gross weekly box office receipts, the director is entitled to 1% of $500,000 (or $5,000). However, under the collective bargaining agreement, the director is entitled to a minimum of 0.75% of $700,000 (or $5,250). Therefore, in week number 10, the director must receive $5,250.

In week number 12, the gross weekly box office receipts were $900,000. Under the director's contract, after subtracting weekly amortization from the gross weekly box office receipts, the director is entitled to 1% of $700,000 (or $7,000). Under the collective bargaining agreement, the director must receive at least 0.75% of $900,000 (or $6,750). Therefore, in week number 12, the director would receive $7,000.

[c]—The Royalty Pool

The basic royalty formula for a stage musical is that post-recoupment, two creative teams are entitled to somewhere between 6% and 8% each of Net Gross Weekly Box Office Receipts ("NGWBOR"). One team is the authors (bookwriter, lyricist, composer). The other team consists of the producer, director, and choreographer. In addition, the production entity (the production company, as opposed to the producer as an individual) may be entitled to 1%, in the following hypothetical:

Royalty percentages based on NGWBOR:

- Authors: 6% (or based on 4.5% to authors and 1.5% for underlying rights)
- Producer/Director/Choreographer: 8%
- Production Entity: 1%
- Total: 15% royalties based on NGWBOR

However, instead of basing the percentages on NGWBOR, the royalty pool draws upon weekly net operating profits ("WNOP"), if any, while still maintaining the respective *pro rata* shares of the pool based on the "old" NGWBOR formula. Converting the NGWBOR percentage points to a *pro rata* share of the WNOP yields these percentages:

Pro rata percentage of royalty pool based on WNOP:

- Authors: 40% (same percentage as 6 represents to 15)
- Producer/Director/Choreographer: 53.33% (same percentage as 8 represents to 15)
- Production Entity: 6.66% (same percentage as 1 represents to 15)

- Total: 100% of the royalty pool, with the royalty pool based on weekly net operating profits or "WNOP."

An illustration in dollars assumes a show has $1,000,000 NGWBOR, and $800,000 in weekly operating costs, yielding $200,000 in WNOP.

Under the NGWBOR formula, the authors receive 4.5% pre-recoupment or $45,000. Post-recoupment they receive 6% or $60,000. The authors are thus guaranteed their percentage of NGWBOR, however these payments to the authors will delay recoupment for the investors.

Under the royalty pool WNOP formula, the authors may only receive a flat fee per week until the investors recoup their investment, thus allowing the investors to recoup faster, with the flat fee sometimes determined by multiplying the percentage "points" of NGWBOR times a round number such as $1,000. Once the show is in the post-recoupment phase, the authors begin to receive 40% or the WNOP of $200,000, or $80,000. Any profits lost to the authors during the time when they accepted a flat fee instead of a percentage of the royalty pool are merely deferred until the production has sufficient profits to make the authors whole. However, there may be dollar caps on the royalty pool payments notwithstanding the percentage due to the authors. Investors may also negotiate an extra share of the royalty pool for quicker amortization of their investment, resulting in a fixed weekly amortization deduction from NGWBOR before the WNOP is calculated. The Dramatists Guild has established a minimum of 15.6% of WNOP payable to authors, increasing to 17.8% at recoupment.

Where ticket sales and thus box office receipts are at high levels, the royalties payable under the NGWBOR formula and the WNOP Royalty Pool may "cross," meaning that payments under the royalty pool will exceed payments under the "old" NGWBOR formula. Producers may thus attempt to cap royalty pool payments so they do not provide the talent with a "windfall," or seek the option to change from NGWBOR to royalty pool accounting if it favors the producer.

Current SDCS member minimums are 2.5% of NWOP for the director, increasing to 2.75% of NWOP at 125% recoupment; and 1% of NWOP for choreographers, increasing to 1.1% at 125% of recoupment. A "star" director/choreographer may strike a better deal than the guild minimums, up to 8% to 10% of WNOP plus a share of net profits, or even more in special cases.

The on-stage star of the production may command both a weekly salary as a budget line item in the range of $25,000 to $100,000 per week, plus 5% of WNOP.

[i]—Net Profits After Recoupment

Where a successful production recoups its upfront production startup costs, and if ticket sales continue to more than cover the weekly operating costs, there will be net profits, typically split 50/50 between the production company and the investors, although the largest financiers may also have negotiated to receive a portion of the production company's share.

Here is an example based on a true "hit":

- Production Costs for a Musical: $10 million

- NGWBOR: $1 million per week

- Weekly Operating Costs: $600,000

- NWOP: $400,000

- Royalty Pool: 40% of NWOP = $160,000

- Investors' Pool: The remaining 60% of NWOP or $240,000, applied towards recoupment of the Production costs of $10 million

- In this example, after forty-two weeks the investors will receive $10,080,000, slightly more than the actual recoupment amount. Thereafter, the 60% of NWOP allocated to the investors is the weekly "net profit," not part of the "royalty pool," and split 50/50 between the investors and the producer.

[ii]—Motion Picture Adaptations of Stage Works and Musicals

Underlying rights to a stage musical can arise from a published novel or story, but they can also arise from a motion picture. Motion pictures, in turn, may have been wholly originally created for the screen, or may have themselves been based on an underlying novel, published story, or life story. Adapting a motion picture to the live stage requires a detailed examination of the scope of underlying rights held by the studio that owns the film, and the relevant guild agreements that may govern the new usage.

For example, Article 16A of the Writers' Guild of America Master Bargaining Agreement reserves "separated rights" to a screenplay author, which includes dramatic stage adaptations of the screenplay, provided that the motion picture producer has not exercised those rights within two years after release of the motion picture, or within five years after the original agreement was signed. In the event of any dispute, final determinations as to the exercise of separated rights are made by the WGA.

The studio retains its rights in the screenplay and in the title of the film; thus for purposes of a potential live stage adaptation, the stage producer may need to obtain rights both from the screenplay writer and from the studio. The scope of the rights acquired from the studio may reserve all motion picture rights in the new stage musical, and demand approval rights over creative elements of the stage version.

Should the studio demand the right or option to be an investor as well, the studio will receive both underlying rights royalties and investor rights such as recoupment and net profit participation. Where the studio owns the songs that appeared in the original film as works made for hire, the studio may be the recipient of several of the categories of royalties normally accorded the creative team. Songwriters historically have not had the same "separated rights" protections enjoyed by WGA members, although in more recent years songwriters may retain some co-publishing ownership of their work rather than creating songs on a purely work made for hire basis.

A typical Broadway stage deal includes the concept of "merger" whereby after an agreed-upon number of performances have occurred, the underlying rights are "merged with" and become exclusive to the stage production for all media and formats. In the case of a musical adaptation of a famous film, however, studios may be reluctant to grant any exclusive rights to the stage producer beyond the strict confines of the musical adaptation itself. In addition, there may be thresholds required by the studio—either the number of performances or financial results—which, if not achieved, may lead to "de-merger," or a situation where the stage producer's rights become non-exclusive, and the studio is freed to pursue a different and hopefully more successful adaptation.

Where a motion picture is based on a stage musical or play, there may be a requirement that the film not be released until after a holdback period that allows the stage production to maximize its exclusive ticket sales. And because the world of the stage accords creative and financial rights to authors, film production companies may find that the only way to acquire rights in a hit show is to give the play or musical authors considerable creative approval rights, other than the film directors' reserved "final cut" rights.

[d]—Side Letters

Profit allocations for Broadway productions may be agreed upon in short deal memos or letters of understanding. In litigation before the Southern District of New York between the producers of the Broadway musical "Spider-Man: Turn Off the Dark" and the director and writer Julie Taymor, the public filings included production deal memos noting that the director was to receive the following consideration:

- Directing and collaboration services for the initial Broadway and London productions: $125,000.

- Net profit participation: 2.5% of 100% of net profits.

- Broadway royalties as Director: a minimum guaranteed advance against 6.5% of weekly operating profit pre-recoupment increasing to 7.4274% post-recoupment.

- Broadway royalties as collaborator: a minimum guaranteed weekly advance against 2.5933% of weekly operating profit pre-recoupment increasing to 2.9633% post recoupment.

- Subsidiary rights: One-seventh of the total subsidiary rights participation accorded to all authors of the musical, and 2.5% of merchandise gross retail sales using Taymor's designs.

- Film: Right of first refusal to direct a film version.

- Approvals: Approval rights, not to be unreasonably withheld, for cast and replacement cast; stage manager; scenic designer; costumer designer; puppet designer; sound designer; choreographer; orchestrator and arrangers; conductor; casting agents; music supervisor; lighting designer; assistant director; Broadway theatre; West End (London) theatre; bookwriter/treatment writer.[12]

[3]—Ticket Service Fees

Where ticket sales are the main revenue source, every effort should be made to maintain transparency with respect to "add-ons," such as ticket fees, ticket convenience fees, and the so-called "secondary market" for tickets. Ticket processing fees added to the face value of a ticket by ticketing agencies can generate a substantial amount of revenue. Often, that revenue will be shared between the ticketing agency and the theatre or producer.

The secondary ticket market is where prime location seats are held from sale to the general public, and sold at a premium over the face value, often with the full cooperation of the theatre or producer. Negotiations involving profit sharing in the context of ticket sales for live events should always include the value of per-ticket service fees and the secondary ticket market.

Concession sales are another area that should be included in order to have transparency regarding all forms of revenue generated by a popular production.

---

12   See *Taymor v. 8 Legged Productions, LLC*, Case No. 11 Civ. 8002, Docket No. 23, Ex. 1 (S.D.N.Y. filed Jan. 17, 2012).

CHAPTER 6

Radio

§6.01   Introduction

Like local television stations, radio stations can be independently owned or part of a conglomerate, and they can be affiliated with a network of radio stations.[1] National Public Radio is the radio equivalent of television's Public Broadcasting Service.[2] Like television, radio is broadcast in two basic distribution technologies: over the airwaves "terrestrial" broadcasting, and subscription-based digital radio. Digital radio is usually transmitted via satellite, although it is sometimes carried as a digital signal provided along with cable television services.

Unlike terrestrial radio, which is subject to the FCC broadcast indecency standards,[3] subscription-based satellite radio does not come under the FCC's regulation of broadcast indecency.

Radio syndication is based on the same principle as syndication of a television show: a popular program may be carried nationwide by being programmed, and paid for, by thousands of local stations.

Internet radio may be a station's signal streamed onto the Internet as Webcasting, or programming that originates solely on the Internet.[4]

---

1   See *Prometheus Radio Project v. FCC*, 373 F.3d 372 (3d Cir. 2004) (reviewing FCC revisions of regulations regarding broadcast media ownership, including review of the history of FCC regulation over station ownership in the 1934 Telecommunications Act and The Telecommunications Act of 1996. Held that FCC deregulatory acts permitting broader scope of conglomerate ownership of radio, television, and newspaper print media came within FCC's power to regulate media ownership).

2   See www.npr.org.

3   18 U.S.C. § 1464.

4   See § 4.03[6] *supra* for a discussion of the music licensing requirements triggered by digital and online radio.

§6.02 Radio Formats

According to Arbitron, the media research and ratings survey service for the radio industry, radio broadcasting is divided into fifty-eight radio formats.[5] Those formats are, in turn, the basis of programming offered by radio stations.[6] Formats distinguish a station from the competition in the same radio market.[7] In *Centennial Broadcasting, LLC v. Burns*, the purchaser of a radio station demanded the seller sign a non-compete agreement, in which it promised not to be involved with any radio station in the same Arbitron Metro radio market with a programming format "substantially similar" to any format used by the station.[8] When the seller purchased a competing station with the same format, the buyer successfully obtained an injunction. At issue in the case was whether the defendant was using the same talk radio format, and the parties each had experts testify as to the number of different talk show formats recognized in the industry.[9]

In *Trenton v. Infinity Broadcasting*, the plaintiff claimed that he had created the format for a popular show entitled "Loveline," and unsuccessfully brought suit against the radio station when he was suspended from duty.[10] In *Trenton*, the court determined that the radio program format was a copyright issue, and found that the employer station owned the format as a work made for hire. The state law claims based on property and contract rights were dismissed.[11]

---

5   See www.arbitron.com.

6   See *Children's Broadcasting Corp. v. The Walt Disney Co.*, 357 F.3d 860 (8th Cir. 2004) (plaintiff prevailed on claims including breach of contract and misappropriation of trade secrets relating to format of children's radio programming).

7   This is known as the Arbitron Metro radio market.

8   See *Centennial Broadcasting, LLC v. Burns*, 254 Fed. Appx. 977 (4th Cir. 2007).

9   *Id.* at *3. The defendant's expert identified eleven different talk radio formats. The plaintiff's expert identified five different talk radio formats, including All talk, News/Talk, Full Service Talk, and Specialized Talk. The format of the two stations were described by the expert as "being primarily political and the structure of the two stations as "amazingly similar."

10   *Trenton v. Infinity Broadcasting Corp.*, 865 F. Supp. 1416 (C.D. Cal. 1994).

11   The opinion in *Trenton* gives a valuable description of the process by which a successful new radio show was created over several years, and is quoted below:

I. BACKGROUND FACTS

a) The Parties

Plaintiff James Trenton is a radio announcer/talk show host. He is under contract to defendant Infinity Broadcasting of Los Angeles, Inc. ("Infinity L.A."), owner and operator of defendant radio station KROQ, 106.7 FM, in Burbank, California ("KROQ"). Plaintiff has been suspended indefinitely from broadcasting by his employer since August, 1993. Although suspended, he remains under contract until November, 1994, and continues to draw his regular salary. He has been associated with the station since 1981.

Defendant Infinity Broadcasting Corporation ("Infinity") is the parent corporation of Infinity, L.A. Infinity purchased the station in June, 1986, from Ken Roberts. Defendant Mel Karazin ("Karazin") is President and Chief Executive Officer of Infinity. Defendants Kevin Weatherley ("Weatherley") and Trip Reeb ("Reeb") are employed by Infinity L.A. as, respectively, program director and general manager of KROQ.

b) Plaintiff's Tenure at KROQ

Plaintiff first broadcast on KROQ in May, 1981. Initially, he worked without pay in order to gain experience in the radio business, airing reviews of inexpensive restaurants under the name "Poorman." In September 1982, plaintiff began receiving pay for his on-air segments, which by that time involved various features and promotions. Plaintiff worked without a written employment contract until 1988.

At the commencement of every segment, the hosts and guests were to sing a "mock chorus" in order to "foster a receptive mood in the listening audience and to project the program's attitude of compassion and accessibility." This "chorus" would be comprised of the program name " 'Loveline,' sung with exaggerated emphasis on the syllable 'love' with the pitch beginning high on the syllable 'love' and ending low on the syllable 'line.' "

In January, 1983, plaintiff began broadcasting Loveline on KROQ under the name "Poorman." It initially aired once per week, from 12:00 a.m. to 2:00 a.m. on "Sunday nights." Plaintiff asserts that "[l]isteners received the program enthusiastically, and its popularity grew." Approximately one year later, plaintiff introduced a medical expert co-host, Drew Pinsky, onto the program for the purposes of (1) lending credibility to any medical advice given on the air and (2) enhancing the program's on-air chemistry. In addition to Loveline, plaintiff broadcast several different programs at varying time slots over the next few years, all under the name "Poorman." In approximately late 1985, in response to its increasing popularity, Loveline was placed in an earlier time slot, Sunday nights from 11:00 p.m. to 1:00 a.m. From mid-1986 until February, 1992, the program was broadcast late Sunday nights or early Monday morning., either at that time or in the 10:00 p.m. to midnight or 11:00 p.m. to 2:00 a.m. time slot.

On November 1, 1988, several months after Infinity purchased KROQ, plaintiff signed a three-year employment contract. Plaintiff claims that, at the time of the signing, he (1) believed he was required to sign the contract if he wanted to continue working at the station, (2) did not understand the contract, and (3) did not want to sign the contract. In November 1991, when this contract expired, plaintiff signed another three-year contract.

Meanwhile, Loveline's popularity grew dramatically. By late 1991, it was by far the highest rated program in its time slot, and its audience share, plaintiff claims, was the highest any program had achieved in the Los Angeles market in decades.

In February 1992, station management informed plaintiff that, because of the show's strong performance, Infinity wanted to broadcast Loveline five nights a week during the 10:00 p.m. to midnight time slot. Plaintiff claims he initially hesitated to undertake the new schedule due to concerns about losing the substantial income he had been earning from late evening personal appearances. However, he ultimately agreed to the arrangement after Reeb allegedly told plaintiff that Infinity would: (1) pay off a $25,000 loan plaintiff had taken to start a clothing business; (2) increase his regular compensation to make up for the lost personal appearances; (3) further increase his regular compensation to appropriately reflect any success the program achieved airing five nights per week; (4) give him complete discretion in the number and nature of celebrity guests that would appear on the show; (5) arrange to syndicate Loveline "on plaintiff's behalf" if the show became successful airing five days per week; (6) continue to contract with Pinsky for his services as co-host; and (7) "continue to give plaintiff exclusive recognition for the creation of his 'Loveline Property,' [and] ... continue to acknowledge and honor plaintiff's exclusive right to perform Loveline as the lead host."

Loveline debuted as a Monday–Friday offering on February 9, 1992. The program's success in its new incarnation was swift and resounding, as within one year it had become the number one show in its time slot by a wide margin. By the spring of 1993, Loveline had become the fourth most listened to program in Los Angeles, behind only the three most popular morning programs.

However, Loveline's success did little to improve the increasingly strained relationship between plaintiff and station management. In July, 1989, over two years before Loveline became a Monday-Friday program, KROQ had suspended plaintiff for three days after he invited his listeners to telephone his program and discuss an issue station management allegedly had not wanted discussed on the air. In December, 1992, plaintiff was again suspended, this time for five days, after he mentioned the name "Howard Stern" on the air after being told by station management not to use KROQ's morning competition's name in his program.

Plaintiff was suspended indefinitely following a third incident in February, 1993. During a Loveline broadcast, plaintiff and Pinsky allegedly "choreographed" a dispute, and plaintiff walked off the show "as an artistic and creative decision." Pinsky continued the broadcast, which allegedly generated "intense listener interest" in following segments. Following month-long negotiations between plaintiff, plaintiff's agent and station management regarding the terms of plaintiff's return to the air, plaintiff returned to the airwaves on March 21, 1993.

Plaintiff was suspended, again indefinitely, on August 23, 1993. Plaintiff contends that the suspension was in fact retaliation for the parties' disagreement over the ultimate ownership of the "Loveline Property." Complaint, ¶ 85. On November 1, 1993, KROQ announced a new permanent lead host for Loveline, and since the latest suspension has refused to allow plaintiff to broadcast. Plaintiff remains under contract with Infinity until November 12, 1994, and apparently continues to draw his salary.

c) Plaintiff's Claim

Plaintiff's suit stems from Infinity's (1) suspension of plaintiff from broadcasting and (2) assertion of ownership rights in Loveline. He claims that when he "offered" his program idea to KROQ, he made the offer contingent upon the station's agreeing to give him exclusive recognition as creator and acknowledge and honor his exclusive right to act as lead host. Complaint, ¶ 28. KROQ allegedly accepted plaintiff's offer unconditionally. Complaint, ¶ 29. Plaintiff further avers that when he signed his three-year contracts with Infinity L.A. in 1988 and 1991, he did not intend to convey his rights in the "Loveline Property" and would not have signed the contract if he had thought that by doing so those rights would be affected.

From this set of pled facts, plaintiff brings 20 state law causes of action. Notably, plaintiff's Sixth Cause of Action for copyright infringement is brought as a state law cause of action, and not under federal copyright law. The remaining 19 causes of action may be classified as either (1) claims stemming from defendants' alleged misuse of plaintiff's "property," or (2) breach of contract claims stemming from defendants' suspension of plaintiff and alleged failure to comply with their agreements.

Plaintiff seeks damages totalling $22,175,000, as well as declaratory and injunctive relief regarding (a) his interest in Loveline and (b) his contractual agreements with Infinity. The damages alleged include losses of: (1) $9,000,000 in radio licensing and syndication fees; (2) $4,000,000 in television licensing and syndication fees; (3) $2,000,000 in loss of publicity and advertising; (4) $3,000,000 in damage to plaintiff's reputation; (5)

Format changes by a radio station can also lead to changes in the on-air talent and personalities featured in the programming. This can lead to employment-law based claims, for example age discrimination claims that on-air personalities were terminated when the station switched to a format geared to a younger audience.[12]

§6.03   Considerations Regarding "Live" Radio and On-Air Personalities

Radio personalities, along with their phone-in listeners, fill hours of broadcast time without a script. Such live programming may carry risks. In search of higher ratings, these personalities may make statements that are offensive, either because they may come within the FCC's view of "indecency," or because they are off-putting to listeners or station management for a variety of reasons. The FCC can levy significant fines against stations and the conglomerates owning multiple stations when it finds that a broadcast has violated the FCC's indecency regulations. Ultimately, the FCC can revoke a station's license to broadcast.[13]

In an effort to avoid liability arising from sudden profane outbursts or defamatory statements on the part of on-air talent or their callers, radio stations typically use a so-called "dump button" for live programming, which, with a broadcast delay of several seconds, allows station personnel to mute or "bleep out" offensive statements before they reach the air.[14]

$2,000,000 in performance contracts with television and radio stations; (6) $2,150,000 in wages; and (7) $25,000 in promised funds to pay off plaintiff's business loan.

Id. (Footnotes omitted.)

12   See *DeLoach v. Infinity Broadcasting*, 164 F.3d 398, 400 (7th Cir. 1999) (Disc jockey brought action against radio station under Age Discrimination in Employment Act challenging demotion that occurred in connection with format change. Host of morning drive-time programming had salary drastically reduced when station switched to predominantly syndicated talk radio format, with programs ranging from "the rantings of former Watergate bad guy G. Gordon Liddy to the railings of self-proclaimed "Shock Jock" Howard Stern.)

13   See In the Matter of Clear Channel Broadcasting Licenses, Inc., 19 F.C.C. Rcd. 6773 (F.C.C. April 8, 2004) (defendant radio stations "willfully and repeatedly [aired] program material during two segments of the "Howard Stern Show" on April 9, 2003, that apparently violate the federal restrictions regarding the broadcast of indecent material." The enforcement action levied monetary forfeitures against the stations totaling $495,000, accompanied by a warning from the FCC that "serious, repeated cases of indecency violations could be subject to license revocation" *Id.* at **6.).

14   However, the "dump button" may not always solve issues relating to what on-air personalities say or do in their efforts to increase ratings. See *Lackey v. CBS Radio, Inc.*, 2008 WL 283801 (N.D. Cal. Feb. 1, 2008) (describing "dump button" used to screen out inappropriate content before it was actually broadcast after a several-second delay.).

In *Lackey v. CBS Radio, Inc.*, a radio station in San Francisco attempted to fill the programming gap created when Howard Stern left the CBS radio network to join Sirius Satellite Radio.[15] CBS developed an all-talk radio format and branded it "Free-FM" to emphasize both "free spirited, fun radio" and the availability of content free of charge. The San Francisco affiliate decided to change formats from a Christian format to the "Free-FM" format. The case involved a breach of employment contract claim brought against the station and others by an on-air personality and his two "sidekicks" who were attempting to capture the same audience that Stern enjoyed.[16]

---

15 *Id.* at *1.

16 *Id.* at *1-*3. The opinion gives an insider's view of the radio stations motivations in changing the format, and the issues that arose in the quest to compete. It is essential reading and the background portion of the opinion is reproduced below:

BACKGROUND

This case involves the termination of talk-radio show host John London and his two on-air sidekicks, Dennis Cruz and Chris Townsend. In October 2005, London signed an employment contract with KIFR-FM, a CBS-owned radio station in San Francisco, to host a program called "John London's Inferno." Cruz was the show's producer and London's on-air co-host, and Townsend was the show's "sports guy." KIFR-FM also broadcast a show hosted by Penn Jillette, the self-described "larger, louder half" of the Las Vegas based comedy and magic duo "Penn & Teller." Penn Jillette's show immediately preceded "John London's Inferno." On April 6, 2006, London began his radio show by offering $5,000 to anyone who would kill Penn Jillette, with a bonus of $2,000 if Jillette suffered before he died. The next day, London, Cruz and Townsend were terminated. They filed this action against defendant CBS for breach of contract, alleging that their employment agreements were terminable only for just cause.

By way of background, in December 2004, the infamous radio talk-show host Howard Stern announced that he would leave CBS to join Sirius Satellite Radio at the end of 2005. In response, CBS began to develop a Howard Stern replacement strategy. Led by Rob Barnett, CBS's President of Programming, CBS developed an all-talk radio format and branded it "Free-FM" to emphasize both "free spirited, fun radio" and the availability of content free of charge. The "Free-FM" brand was marketed nationwide, but each individual station was managed locally and was programmed with a mix of shows to suit the local market. The CBS-owned San Francisco radio station KIFR-FM was converted from a Christian format to the "Free-FM" format. As general manager of KIFR-FM, Ken Kohl was in charge of the station's on-air programming and had authority to hire and fire the station's on-air talent.

In May 2005, plaintiffs John London, Dennis Cruz and Chris Townsend produced an audition tape for CBS after learning that CBS was searching for on-air talent to replace Howard Stern and was looking for "all guy all the time. It's booze. It's sex. It's violence. It's sports. The graphic and violent audition tape touched upon such topics as John London threatening to slit CBS's board operator's throat, the gruesome mutilation of two people by monkeys, and an interview with a caller who discussed his plans to eradicate various populations he found to be undesirable. Ken Kohl, manager of the San Francisco KIFR-FM radio station, received a copy of this audition tape. Ken Kohl then contacted London to explore the possibility of London being hired to perform on KIFR-FM. Eventually, Kohl negotiated the terms of London, Cruz and Townsend's employment contracts with London's agent and manager Lisa Miller.

On October 20, 2005, Ken Kohl signed letters with all three plaintiffs to memorialize and "confirm [their] conversation regarding the proposal of compensation and terms" offered by the radio station. All three short-form letters described the plaintiffs' position, salary and benefits and stated that they were being hired for "a Two (2) Year no-cut Agreement terminable by just cause only." Miller and Kohl agreed to this just cause termination clause, but they had no further discussions about its definition or meaning. In all three short-form letters, "the parties agree[d] to negotiate in good faith to execute [long-form agreements] which [would] contain the terms and conditions defined [therein] as well as any other mutually agreed-upon terms and conditions." Although there were negotiations regarding the long-form agreements, none were actually executed.

On November 2, 2005, after the short-form letter agreements were executed and after the show had gone on the air, Cruz and Townsend each signed an employment application requesting biographical information such as age, address, phone number, education, and employment history. The final page of this employment application stated, "I acknowledge that if I am hired by [CBS], my employment will be at will and that my employment and compensation may be terminated at any time, with or without notice, and with or without cause, by me or by [CBS]." These employment applications did not reference the October 20, 2005 short-form letters, nor did they describe in the same detail as the short-form letters, the terms of Cruz and Townsend's employment. Unlike Cruz and Townsend, London did not sign an employment application.

Plaintiffs' radio show "John London's Inferno" was broadcast from late October 2005 through early April 2006 at which time all three plaintiffs were fired. During that time, the show was one of KIFR-FM's most popular programs, and in the 2005–2006 winter Arbitron survey, London had the highest ratings of any KIFR-FM talk show host. The radio show, like the plaintiffs' audition tape, focused on violent, offensive, and confrontational subject matter. For example, London encouraged listeners to go to the station and beat up the stations's program director; he also discussed killing the station manager Ken Kohl by setting him on fire and throwing him off the roof; and he asked a convicted mobster if he wanted "one more job" killing London's ex-wife. Some of London's comments were targeted at Penn Jillette, the Las Vegas based magician who hosted the show broadcast on KIFR-FM immediately before London's show. In January London performed on-air prayers asking God to kill Jillette; in February London said that he would like to kill Jillette personally; and in March London incited Muslim terrorists to kill Jillette. The radio station used "dump buttons" to screen out inappropriate content before it was actually broadcast after a several-second delay. Many violent and confrontational segments were not dumped and none of the segments directed at killing Jillette were ever dumped.

On April 6, 2006 John London began his show with the following "audience promotion": "I'm offering … $5,000 for the person who kills Penn Jillette. Now, I'll add $2,000-that's a total of $7,000-if there is some suffering involved. If it's a clean kill, five grand." London informed his audience that Jillette lived in Las Vegas. As London's on-air sidekicks, Cruz and Townsend added occasional comments and laughter. London's kill-Penn Jillette offer was not dumped by the station screeners.

The next day, April 7, 2006, Rob Barnett, CBS's President of Programming (who was in charge of developing the "Free-FM" talk-radio format to replace the departing Howard Stern), learned about plaintiffs' kill-Penn-Jillette offer and was alarmed by the situation. Barnett testified that he did not recall how he became aware of the situation or who may have informed him. Barnett then contacted various individuals including Ken Kohl, the local station manager; Joel Hollander, CBS's Chairman and CEO; Penn Jillette; and Penn Jillette's manager.

Kohl responded to the situation by speaking with London and London's agent Lisa Miller. Both Kohl and Miller advised London to defuse the situation by apologizing or at least clarifying that his kill-Penn-Jillette

§6.04   On-Air Talent Agreements

On-air radio personalities are represented by SAG-AFTRA.[17] The organization enters into collective bargaining agreements with radio and television stations on behalf of its members.[18]

Employment agreements with on-air talent may include some of the following deal points. Most notable are the provisions setting forth on-air talent's mandatory compliance with FCC regulations.

- <u>Position</u>: Describes the title of the program, and format type of radio host services, and the station, as well as the Designated Market Area ("DMA") as defined by Arbitron and covered by the broadcast signal, and the hours the show is broadcast.

- <u>Duties</u>: Duties will include the program plus live appearances, recording of commercials and other promotional activities, and production of programming, as well as compliance with station policies and procedures, including attending staff meetings. There may be a non-compete provision restricting the host's services outside of the employment agreement.

- <u>Compensation</u>: An annual salary that may include a "Ratings Bonus" based on Arbitron ratings for the program.

- <u>Personal Appearances</u>: There may be additional compensation for personal appearances.

- <u>Syndication</u>: This will address ownership of the syndication rights, and the percentages of syndication revenue that will be accorded the station and the host.

- <u>Termination</u>: Acts that could result in termination will include any acts that jeopardize the station's FCC license or that result in any violation of any rule or regulation of the FCC, including any utterance on the air that is obscene, indecent, or profane as determined by the station or by a court, upon review of a ruling by the FCC.

- <u>Non-Competition</u>: In the DMA, the employee will be prohibited from engaging in direct competition during the term of the agreement, and for a specified period thereafter.

---

offer was not serious. London refused to extend either an apology or a clarification. CEO Joel Hollander responded to the situation by listening to a recording of the broadcast, calling Kohl to ask why London should not be fired, and speaking to CBS's attorneys. After arriving at the conclusion that London's broadcast was "unconscionable," Hollander decided to fire London, Cruz and Townsend. Hollander testified that this decision was his alone. By the end of the day on April 7, 2007, all three plaintiffs were officially terminated. On May 30, 2006, plaintiffs filed this action naming both CBS and Penn Jillette as defendants. *Id.* (Citations omitted.)

17   See § 4.16 *supra* for a discussion of unions.

18   See www.sagaftra.org.

- <u>Name and Likeness</u>: The right of the station to use the host's name and likeness, the right of publicity, for advertising and for any other agreed upon activities or merchandise.

- <u>Payola, Plugola, and Conflicts of Interest</u>: Provisions that the employee will not accept or receive any compensation in connection with any material broadcast, under laws preventing "payola" or other practices where compensation is received in exchange for playing particular songs, for example, or mentioning products.

- <u>Pay or Play</u>: A provision stating that even if the station decides not to use the host's services, they are still obligated to pay the host under the terms of the agreement, and to retain their exclusive rights in the talent's services.

§6.05   Music Licensing in the Terrestrial and Digital Radio Industries

[1]—Governmental and Court Regulation of Mass Media

Radio is a mass medium, with thousands of "over the air" terrestrial radio ("TR") stations as well as Internet, satellite, and mobile based digital radio services ("DR services") making countless songs available to many millions of people every hour of every day, resulting in billions of performances of music each year. Copyright law says music copyright owners of musical compositions (songwriters and their music publishers) must be paid when their songs are performed on traditional terrestrial radio, and in the case of DR services, both the music publishers/songwriters and the recording artists/record labels must be paid.[19] However, there are 15,196 AM/FM terrestrial radio stations in the United States and many more DR services.[20] No copyright owner has the resources or time to conclude licensing agreements with thousands of individual radio services for each song performed.

The solution has been governmental regulation of music licensing on the radio by Congress and the courts, streamlining the process with licensing collectives (Performing Rights Organizations or "PRO") such as ASCAP, BMI, SESAC, and SoundExchange on the "music" side, and the Radio Music Licensing Committee ("RMLC") and the National Association of Broadcasters ("NAB") on the radio side. Licensing rates for these broad collectives are either on a "blanket" license arrangement, with a negotiated fee covering every copyright whether it is played or not, or a per-performance "micro-penny" rate

---

19   17 U.S.C. §§ 106, 114. The provisions in the Copyright Act that regulate digital performance of sound recordings were originally part of two legislative acts passed in 1995 and 1998: The Digital Performance Rights in Sound Recordings Act of 1995, Pub. L. No. 104-39, 109 Stat. 336; and the Digital Millennium Copyright Act, Pub. L. No. 105-304, 112 Stat. 2860 (1998).

20   See FCC News, "Broadcast Station Totals as of December 31, 2012," available at http://transition.fcc.gov/Daily_Releases/Daily_Business/2013/db0111/DOC-318352A1.pdf.

based on reportable digital data on users and performances. Other licensing techniques are used to simplify the process, including annual minimum payments without the requirement of detailed reporting for small and non-profit educational radio services. PROs only license "non-dramatic" performances of songs as typically found on radio, as background music in film and television, and in concerts and many other uses, with "dramatic" uses such as stage musicals licensed directly by the copyright owner.

The PROs only license the public performance right, with other types of music licensing based on making or distributing copies such as mechanical royalties and synchronization licenses handled either by the copyright owner or other types of collectives outside the realm of the non-dramatic public performance right under copyright law.

After its founding in 1914 as the only licensing collective for music publishing performance rights, ASCAP was subject to court challenges on antitrust principles. As a result, there are now three songwriting collectives for public performance licensing, ASCAP, BMI, and SESAC. ASCAP and BMI operate subject to consent decrees supervised by federal courts in the Southern District of New York (the "Rate Court"), designed to prevent licensing monopolies and to ultimately approve license fee rates where the parties are unable to negotiate rates among themselves.[21]

Music publishers and songwriters grant representation rights to the collectives on a non-exclusive basis, and can choose to directly license performances.[22] In the case of digital performances on DR, music publishers have attempted to withdraw their entire catalogs from their PRO limited to digital performances, in order to directly license DR at a freely negotiated rate that is not constrained by the court oversight over ASCAP and BMI's licensing rates. However, the "rate court" that governs ASCAP in the Southern District of New York has held that publishers may not withdraw only a subset of digital rights from the ASCAP repertoire.[23] Where publishers have successfully engaged in direct licensing, courts have held that the PROs must adjust their blanket license rates to compensate for the fact that portions of the PRO's repertoire are licensed directly from some PRO member publishers by the DR service.[24]

[2]—Two Separate Copyrights in Every Song

Every song comprises two entirely separate copyrights: the songwriters are represented by music publishers who own the copyright in the musical compositions; and the musi-

---

21   See, e.g., *United States v. ASCAP*, 2001 WL 158999 (S.D.N.Y. June 11, 2001).

22   See *Buffalo Broadcasting Co., Inc. v. ASCAP*, 744 F.2d 917 (2d Cir. 1984).

23   See *Pandora Media, Inc. v. ASCAP*, 2013 U.S. Dist. LEXIS 133133 (S.D.N.Y. Sept. 17, 2013).

24   See, e.g., *Broadcast Music Inc. v. DMX, Inc.*, 683 F.3d 32 (2d Cir. 2012).

cal performing artists are represented by the record companies that own the copyright in the sound recording. When the music is played on the radio, it is "performed." Copyright law involves other rights such as making copies, publishing, etc., but for radio the copyright category is almost always "public performance."[25]

Congress has decided that, regarding terrestrial radio, the songwriters and publishers have a performance right and must be paid, but performing artists and record labels have no performance rights.[26] In other countries, record labels do have a performance right that covers radio broadcasts of their sound recordings. This is not the case in the United States. Historically, the record labels accepted this status quo in exchange for the promotion value of airplay that drove record sales.

In the digital world of DR services, the "digital audio transmission" right for sound recordings applies, meaning that a DR service must pay a license fee to both the music publisher/songwriter, and the record label/performing artist.[27]

[3]—Terrestrial Radio: Industry-Wide Negotiation of License Fee Rates

The RMLC and ASCAP/BMI negotiate the industry wide rates for songwriters and publishers that every terrestrial radio station must pay. ASCAP and BMI are heavily regulated by federal courts in New York that ultimately can determine license fees when free negotiations fail. Thus, in exchange for having their powerful licensing collectives, music publishers must accept limits on their licensing power imposed by the courts. In effect, through their oversight, the courts "cap" what music publishers can charge for performance rights. The much smaller SESAC is not subject to the same consent decrees and court oversight but licenses on behalf of its members at reportedly similar rates as those charged by ASCAP and BMI. ASCAP, BMI, and SESAC distribute half the license fee royalties they collect to the music publishers, and the other half directly to the songwriters (after deducting a small administrative fee).[28]

Radio licensing by ASCAP and BMI to the commercial radio industry is traditionally based on the mature and profitable terrestrial radio industry business model, which

---

25   See 17 U.S.C. § 106. The public performance right in § 106(4) specifically applies to works other than sound recordings. The limited digital audio transmission right for sound recordings is listed separately in § 106(6).

26   *Id.*

27   See: 17 U.S.C. §§ 106, 114.

28   A fourth PRO was founded in 2013, Global Music Rights, which currently represents less than 1% of the songwriter market share.

generated $17.4 billion dollars in advertising revenue in 2011.[29] Digital online advertising revenue, generated by webcasters affiliated with terrestrial radio stations, generated about $709 million in advertising revenue, which is about four percent of the terrestrial radio industry total ad revenue.

Currently, the commercial radio industry (other rates apply to public radio and educational radio) pays 1.7% or less of that overall revenue for music rights, in a complex formula with lots of exceptions and adjustments that still generates about $175 million per year in terrestrial radio licensing fees. The PROs then have the task of dividing up that revenue among their many songwriter and music publisher members. The fees charged by ASCAP and BMI also include "webcasting," which is where a terrestrial radio station simultaneously streams its signals over the Internet. So if a radio station paid the ASCAP/BMI performance royalty, that blanket license fee also includes the affiliated webcaster Internet stream of the station's programs.

[4]—The Digital Performance Right for Sound Recordings

DR services are treated differently under copyright law. As the world saw the Internet growing in the 1990s, the record industry successfully lobbied Congress for what it had always lacked on terrestrial radio, a performance right. But the sound recording performance right *only* applies to DR. Congress decided that some DR business models would pay the new sound recording performance royalty based on a percentage of revenue, and other DR business models would pay based on a "micro penny" per-performance rate. Gone were the days of terrestrial radio mass media performances where one "spin" could be heard by millions of unidentified people. With DR, it was possible to accurately track exactly which songs were streamed to exactly which listeners. In the brave new world of DR performance licensing for sound recordings, Congress sets various rates, with the current "standard" rate for commercial webcasters at $0.0017 per performance (2016–2020 subject to cost of living increases).

It means that for every 1,000 performances of a sound recording, the license fee paid is $1.70. For every one million performances, the license fee paid to SoundExchange is $1,700. The current rates are for the period 2016 through 2020, with adjustments annually based on the Consumer Price Index. For so-called "Pureplay" services that only offer streamed music, the rate for 2016–2020 will also start at $0.0017. For noncommercial webcasters, the rate is $500 per year unless they exceed a threshold of "aggregate tuning hours" in which case they will pay $0.0017 per stream.

---

29   See "Radio Industry Grows Annual Advertising Revenue," available at http://www.hollywoodreporter.com/news/radio-industry-grows-annual-advertising-revenue-292439.

Unlike the terrestrial radio license fees for songwriters, which were based on a percentage of revenues and allowed for *unlimited number* of performances constrained only by the number of hours in a day, the DR royalties were based on *how many* copyrighted works the DR actually performed. More music equals higher license fees. The licensing collective originally set up by the record industry's trade organization, the RIAA, is called SoundExchange. SoundExchange issues licenses, collects, revenues, and pays out royalties from DR. SoundExchange, distributes 50% of the license amounts to the record label, 45% to the featured artists, and 5% to "sidemen" on the recording (after taking a small administrative fee).

[5]—Types of DR Services: Non-Interactive or Interactive

SoundExchange, the licensing collective for digital performance rights in sound recordings, lists sixteen different categories of services that it licenses.[30] Those categories range from the "pre-existing" services, to commercial webcasters affiliated with terrestrial radio stations, to educational and non-profit small webcasters, and other categories. All of these services essentially act as digital radio, meaning they stream music to listeners based on the service's formulas as to what would be satisfy listeners, often in conjunction with user-determined categories such as "channels" devoted to specific artists. In addition, these services must comply with regulations that limit the user's ability to select a particular song, or to hear multiple songs from the same album in a short time frame.[31]

The rationale is that allowing users to request any song any time on a streaming "Internet radio" service would harm sales of recorded music. Such services are deemed "non-interactive" and thus qualify for the statutory licensing rates for digital performance of sound recordings in Section 114 of the Copyright Act, and in notices published in the Code of Federal Regulations ("CFR").[32]

Interactive DR services that allow a high degree of user control over which sound recordings are streamed do not qualify for the guaranteed or "compulsory" statutory rates for sound recording digital performance and must negotiate licenses directly with the record label copyright owner. Spotify™ is a leading example of a DR service deemed interactive because of the high level of user control over what music is streamed. Thus Spotify's license agreements with the record industry are freely negotiated, confidential and not matters of public record, but reportedly are marginally higher than the non-interactive statutory rates paid by Pandora™ and other non-interactive DRs.

---

30   See generally, www.soundexchange.com

31   See 17 U.S.C. § 114(j)(13) "Sound Recording Performance Complement." See also, 17 U.S.C. § 114(D)(2)(C) limiting advance schedule publication of streamed recordings.

32   See, e.g.: 17 U.S.C. § 114; 37 C.F.R. §§ 360–380.

In 2009, the boundaries between what constitutes a non-interactive service entitled to compulsory licensing of sound recordings at the statutory rate, and an interactive service that must negotiate voluntary licenses with sound recording copyright owners, was examined in *Artista Records, LLC v. Launch Media, Inc.*[33] In that case, the court determined that a DR service that allowed users to select channels based on artists and musical genres, and that used a complex formula to determine what music would be streamed as a result, was not "interactive" because it was in concept similar to the choices consumers make when choosing a terrestrial radio station. Where a listener selects a "jazz" station instead of a "classic rock" or "oldies" station on terrestrial radio, and the station determines what songs will actually be played, the experience remains fundamentally non-interactive.

Currently popular DR services such as Pandora follow the model set forth in the *Launch Media* case, and are able to let users rate songs and choose channels while remaining non-interactive and thus able to take advantage of statutory license rates.

[6]—The "Pureplay Settlement"

The DR industry and the music industry participate in the digital sound recording royalty rate determination process, with the final decision made by the Copyright Office's Copyright Royalty Judges, most recently setting rates for the period 2011-2015.[34]

Beginning in 2002, and again in 2008, some "pureplay"[35] DR noninteractive services and smaller webcasters, concerned with the royalty rates set by the Copyright Royalty Judges, lobbied Congress for relief in the form of the Small Webcaster Settlement Act of 2008, passed in 2009, which allowed Pureplay DRs to negotiate lower rates with SoundExchange as compared to the rates set by the Copyright Royalty Judges.

Under the resulting "Pureplay Settlement" between Pureplay DR services and SoundExchange, the per-performance royalties were cut in half as compared to commercial webcasters, and also had a percentage of revenue component. Currently, for the period 2016 to 2020, the Pureplay royalty rate is $0.0017, the same as nonsubscription commercial webcasters, and subject to annual cost of living adjustments.

---

33   See *Arista Records, LLC v. Launch Media, Inc.*, 578 F.3d 148 (2d Cir. 2009).

34   See 37 C.F.R. § 380.3.

35   Certain digital radio services are designated as "pureplay" because they are entirely online and not affiliated with any terrestrial station and do not currently receive much advertising revenue.

[7]—DR Services and Songwriters

On the songwriting and music publishing side for DR, for those commercial for-profit "Pureplay" services that had no affiliation with a terrestrial station, ASCAP and BMI set up experimental license rates for webcasters, operating within the constraints of court oversight. The DR rates tended to be higher than the 1.7% paid by terrestrial radio, for good reason: the DR industry was not a mature business model with high revenues. While 1.7% might be an acceptable rate for a $17.4 billion dollar industry, it was too low for the business model of a Pureplay DR service, which might forego traditional revenue in the quest for more users, receiving funding via venture capital or the stock market instead of advertising sales.

[8]—The Fee Rate Status Quo

The status quo is currently:

Terrestrial Radio and its Affiliated Webcasters

(1) <u>Sound Recordings</u>: Terrestrial radio pays nothing to publicly perform post-1972 sound recordings. Whether pre-1972 sound recordings have a public performance right under state law is currently being litigated, although some broadcasters have voluntarily entered into license fee agreements.

(2) <u>Musical Compositions</u>: Terrestrial radio pays about 1.7% of revenues to ASCAP/BMI for performances of musical compositions by songwriters, less to SESAC.

(3) <u>Musical Compositions—Webcasting</u>: The 1.7% of revenue paid to songwriters and music publishers also included any internet webcasting services offered by the terrestrial radio station.

(4) <u>Sound Recordings Performed by Affiliated Webcasters</u>: Webcasters affiliated with terrestrial radio stations pay SoundExchange $0.0022 per performance for streaming sound recordings. Small and university webcasters pay SoundExchange an annual fee of $500 provided they do not exceed specified numbers of performances.

Pureplay DR Services

(1) <u>Sound recordings</u>: Under the Pureplay Settlement, Pureplay DR services pay SoundExchange $0.0017 per performance for streaming sound recordings. Pandora pays that rate for users of its free, advertising supported service. Where Pandora has subscribers who pay a monthly subscription fee, Pandora pays a higher rate of $0.0022 per stream.

(2) <u>Musical Compositions via PROs</u>: Pureplay services pay the ASCAP/BMI "experimental" digital blanket license fee rate which is approximately $0.00008 per stream (a thousand streams would generate 8 cents). This rate is "capped" by the courts that oversee ASCAP and BMI. ASCAP's rate court has set a royalty for Pandora of 1.85% of revenue.[36] BMI's rate court has set a royalty for Pandora of 2.5% of revenue.[37]

All of the current rates are the result of industry-wide lobbying of Congress or litigation in the "rate courts" in New York, where both sides have the opportunity to make their case and then must abide by the final decisions of either the Copyright Royalty Judges at the Copyright Office or the judges in the "rate court" that regulates ASCAP and BMI in New York

Interactive Services

In addition to PRO licenses to cover songwriters and music publishers, interactive services (e.g., Spotify) must enter into freely negotiated agreements with copyright owners of sound recordings for digital performances. The statutory sound recording royalties only apply to non-interactive digital services.

In addition, interactive digital radio streaming services must remit "interactive streaming" mechanical royalties to music publishers.

[9]—Legislative Initiatives Regarding Radio and Music Licensing

License fees that govern the use of music on radio are set by the Congress and the courts, subject to hearings and lobbying that put forward the view of all sides, taking into account business models, revenues, comparable licensing, and historical usage.

The recording industry has repeatedly introduced copyright legislation that would create a performance right for sound recordings on terrestrial radio.[38] Strongly opposed by the broadcasting industry, such bills have not passed.[39]

Digital Radio has also been the subject of proposed legislation. Pandora Media, Inc. is the leading Pureplay DR service, with over 200 million users who account for approximately 1.5 billion listening hours per month, using DR technology that allows for

---

36   See In re Petition of Pandora Media, 2014 U.S. Dist. LEXIS 36914, 2014 WL 1088101 (S.D.N.Y. March 18, 2014).

37   See *Broad. Music, Inc. v. Pandora Media, Inc.*, 2015 U.S. Dist. LEXIS 69002 (S.D.N.Y. May 27, 2015).

38   See, e.g. H.R.1836 — 115th Congress (2017-2018) ("The Fair Play Fair Pay Act of 2017").

39   Id.

millions of simultaneous performances.[40] Pandora offers a free advertising-supported service, and a monthly subscription fee service without advertising interruptions. Pandora's business model emphasizes acquisition of users resulting in maximum music performances and maximum value of its publicly traded shares. Pandora's business model has resulted in Pandora spending about half its revenues on music license payments because the more music Pandora performs, the more licensing fees it must pay in the per-performance model that applies.

[10]—Digital Licensing Maneuvers by the Music and Radio Industries

The advent of new digital music industry business models, such as digital radio streaming via Pandora and limited downloads via other types of services, led to several important new digital licensing models with overlapping interests: music publishers license digital mechanicals and digital performing rights simultaneously but through different mechanisms, while coexisting with sound recording digital performance licensing by record companies to the same digital services.

From the perspective of music publishers, their share of the new digital royalties, as compared to the record companies, was tightly constrained by the Copyright Act setting mechanical royalty rates and by the court-governed Consent Decrees that regulate public performance royalties charged by ASCAP and BMI. In an attempt to negotiate "market" rates not subject to regulatory and court restrictions, some large music publishers sought to withdraw from the PROs and privately negotiate with Pandora for only a subset of their overall rights, the so-called "Digital Media" performance rights.

Following rate court decisions that impeded the desire to escape rate court oversight for digital media rights, ASCAP and BMI petitioned the Department of Justice to loosen or amend their respective Consent Decrees. This resulted in a DOJ report that declined to make the requested changes.[41]

[11]—Artist Response

As the Pandora legislative and licensing maneuvers played out, various artists published blogs and articles bemoaning their low royalty fees generated by DR.[42] Some commen-

---

40   See Pandora Media Annual Report, available at http://investor.pandora.com.

41   See Statement of the Department of Justice on the Closing of the Antitrust Division's Review of the ASCAP and BMI Consent Decrees (Aug. 4, 2016), available at https://www.justice.gov/atr/file/882101/download.

42   See "My Song Got Played on Pandora 1 Million Times and All I Got Was $16.89," available at http://thetrichordist.com/2013/06/24/my-song-got-played-on-pandora-1-million-times-and-all-i-got-was-16-89-less-than-what-i-make-from-a-single-t-shirt-sale/. But compare, "Pandora Paid Over $1,300 for 1 Million Plays, Not $16.89," available at http://theunderstatement.com/post/53867665082/pandora-pays-far-more-than-16-dollars

tary was not helpful because it failed to distinguish between songwriting royalties and sound recording royalties, and other commentary was unhelpful because it failed to acknowledge that ASCAP, BMI, and SoundExchange all remit 50% directly to the publisher or record label, then split the remaining 50% between the creators. So if a song has four songwriters, they would each receive 25% of the songwriter share. Thus a songwriter who receives $100 may have received their correct share from an original license fee payment of $800 (distributed $400 to the publisher, and $100 to each of the four songwriters).

Because DR tracks the actual number of performances of a song, in recent years artists are seeing something new on their royalty statements that include DR: precise numbers of performances of their works, and sometimes the numbers seem impressive because they total a million or more. However, one million DR performances or more, while impressive sounding, is not a huge number in United States mass media overall context, and at the moment, under the statutory licensing regulations, does not result in large royalty payments.

[12]—Other Royalty Consequences for Songwriters and Artists

Collective licensing organizations such as ASCAP/BMI/SESAC for songwriters, and SoundExchange for performing artists, deduct a small administration fee for their services, and then make direct payments without any further deductions: half to the publisher/record label, and half to the songwriter/artist. In some cases there is a further 5% deduction from the artist's share paid to "sidemen" on the recordings. But when the collectives handle the licensing, they do not take into account any other contractual agreements that may exist between the songwriter and their publisher, or between the musical artist and their record label.

As noted, there may be situations where licensing is not done through the collectives. Where a DR service is interactive, it does not qualify for the statutory compulsory license rates, and it must license interactive sound recording streaming rights directly from each copyright-owning record label.

In such direct licensing or "voluntary licensing" scenarios, the revenues are all paid directly from the DR service to the copyright owner (music publisher or record label), and are not paid to the PRO or SoundExchange. This means that the songwriter or artist's share of such revenues must first go through their publisher or label, and are now subject to any deductions, recoupment, lower percentage fees or other provisions in the contractual agreement between the songwriter/artist and their music publisher/record label, as well as any accounting or processing delays.

Some publishers and labels may have contracts that simply split such "direct licensing" revenues in the same way as a PRO or SoundExchange would do, while others may have agreements that subject the revenues to recoupment, deductions, lower percentages, etc. In negotiating music publishing and recording agreements, both sides should agree on how such "direct licensing" revenues should be handled.

[13]—The Music Modernization Act of 2018

Several of the complex music industry licensing practices and applicable Copyright Act provisions changed significantly with the passage of the Orrin G. Hatch and Bob Goodlatte Music Modernization Act on October 11, 2018, Pub. L. No. 115-264 ("MMA"). The MMA addressed several areas of the music industry that needed updating as a result of the increasing role of changing digital technologies, especially the popularity of online streaming as the main music delivery technology.

The MMA is divided into three sections summarized as follows, with the highlight being the creation of a new collective licensing organization, the Mechanical Licensing Collective or MLC, for blanket licensing of interactive online streaming royalties payable from digital music services to music publishers, the so-called "streamed mechanicals." As of this writing, the MLC is in the early stages of being organized and will become operational over time, adding a new and important licensing collective to the group including for performing rights ASCAP, BMI, SESAC and GMR, and for digital sound recording non-interactive performing rights SoundExchange.

Title I: Title I of the MMA created the MLC, and changed the streamed mechanical license rate setting process at the Copyright Royalty Board to a "willing buyer willing seller" basis for future licensing rate determinations. It also changed the Department of Justice Consent Decrees for the two regulated PROs, ASCAP and BMI, to replace designated judges in the Southern District of New York with the standard random assignment of judges to each rate court litigation.

Title II: Title II of the MMA, also known as the Classics Protection and Access Act, granted pree-1972 sound recordings partial protections under the Copyright Act. For example, pre-1972 recordings are now including in digital performing rights for sound recordings. However some federal Copyright Act provisions still do not apply to pre-1972 sound recordings, for example termination rights. In practice, this means that digital music service providers will include all pre-1972 sound recordings in their licensing, either via SoundExchange for noninteractive services, or in voluntary private agreements for interactive digital music services.

Title III: Also known as the Allocation for Music Producers Act, Title III confirms that for noninteractive digital sound recording performances administered by SoundExchange, the royalty due to the producer of the recording will be paid by SoundExchange pursuant to a letter of direction instructing SoundExchange to make the payments. Previously, the statute allowed only for payments to the featured artist and to side-musicians, and now producers are statutorily included as well.

CHAPTER 7

Celebrity Rights of Publicity and Privacy

§7.01 Introduction

As a consequence of "rare ability, dumb luck, or a combination thereof,"[1] private individuals in the entertainment industry may achieve some level of celebrity. Fame is often the result of years of hard work and investment,[2] and creates a dynamic between the celebrity and the public that grants the celebrity iconic, symbolic, or even mythic status.[3] One court has noted that "fame and tranquility can never be bedfellows."[4] Indeed, when celebrities venture out in public, they are "fair game" for the photographers who attempt to capture celebrities in an unguarded, embarrassing, personal, or even sensational moment.[5]

---

1 *White v. Samsung Electronics America, Inc.*, 971 F.2d 1395, 1399 (9th Cir. 1992).

2 *Id.* As the California Supreme Court noted,

"[o]ften considerable money, time and energy are needed to develop one's prominence in a particular field. Years of labor may be required before one's skill, reputation, notoriety or virtues are sufficiently developed to permit an economic return through some medium of commercial promotion. For some, the investment may eventually create considerable commercial value in one's identity."

Comedy III Productions, Inc. v. Gary Saderup, Inc., 25 Cal.4th 387, 399, 21 P.3d 797, 106 Cal.Rptr.2d 126 (Cal. 2001).

3 As described by the Tenth Circuit, celebrities play a role in society described as "common points of reference for millions of individuals who may never interact with one another, but who share, by virtue of their participation in a mediated culture, a common experience and a collective memory. Through their pervasive presence in the media, sports and entertainment, celebrities come to symbolize certain ideas and values." *Cardtoons, L.C. v. Major League Baseball Players Ass'n*, 95 F.3d 959, 972 (10th Cir. 1996) (internal citations omitted, and quoting John B. Thompson, *Ideology and Modern Culture: Critical Social Theory in The Era of Mass Communication,* 163 (1990)).

4 See *People v. Pidhajecky*, 20 Misc.3d 1119(A), 867 N.Y.S.2d 19 (Table), 2008 WL 2746722 at *3 (N.Y. City Crim. July 16, 2008) (upholding charges against celebrity stalker).

5 However, some protections based on trespass laws are available to the celebrity; for example, property owners, including commercial establishments such as restaurants, can forbid photography on their premises. Certain states may provide protection against invasive photographic or surveillance methods to obtain images of celebrities when

Ironically, those celebrities who attract the most intense media attention may be the first to file invasion of privacy claims against the media.[6] However, such claims often fail because of the constitutional privilege announced in the string of landmark Supreme Court defamation cases that required a showing of "actual malice" for claims against the press.[7]

---

they are not in fact out and about in public. See Cal. Civ. Code § 1708.8 (stating a cause of action for "constructive invasion of privacy" where the defendant "attempts to capture, in a manner that is offensive to a reasonable person, any type of visual image, sound recording, or other physical impression of the plaintiff engaging in a personal or familial activity under circumstances in which the plaintiff had a reasonable expectation of privacy, through the use of a visual or auditory enhancing device, regardless of whether there is a physical trespass").

See § 5.06 *infra* for a discussion of legal issues relating to celebrity privacy and surveillance, as well as laws regarding celebrity stalkers. See:

California: Cal. Civ. Code § 1708.7.

New York: N.Y. Penal L. § 120.45.

6   The Supreme Court explained that public figures have often sought out their public roles, and also have the special advantage, not available to ordinary citizens, of a public forum in which they can refute any allegedly defamatory statements. The Supreme Court noted that:

"For the most part those who attain this status have assumed roles of especial prominence in the affairs of society. Some occupy positions of such persuasive power and influence that they are deemed public figures for all purposes. More commonly, those classed as public figures have thrust themselves to the forefront of particular public controversies in order to influence the resolution of the issues involved. In either event, they invite attention and comment."

Gertz v. Welch, 418 U.S. 323, 345, 94 S.Ct. 2997, 41 L.Ed.2d 789 (1974).

7   *New York Times Co. v. Sullivan*, 376 U.S. 254, 84 S.Ct. 710, 11 L.Ed.2d 686 (1964) (actual malice standard applies to published statements regarding a public official). See also, *Curtis Publishing Co. v. Butts*, 388 U.S. 130, 87 S.Ct. 1975, 18 L.Ed.2d 1094 (1967) (constitutional privilege announced in *New York Times Co. v. Sullivan* applies to public figures). *Cf., Gertz v. Welch*, 418 U.S. 323, 94 S.Ct. 2997, 41 L.Ed.2d 789 (1974) (discussion of public issue may not be privileged where person defamed is neither a public official nor a public figure). While *New York Times Co. v. Sullivan* applied the "actual malice" standard to defamation claims, courts have held that with respect to celebrity actions against the press, which may include claims for right of publicity and public disclosure of private facts, the same "actual malice" standard applies. Under this standard, any successful privacy action by a celebrity against any media outlet in the United States must prove that the statements were made with a reckless disregard for the truth. This is a higher burden of proof than mere negligence in the context of alleged liability for the tort of publication of private facts. *Curtis Publishing Co. v. Butts*, 388 U.S. 130, 87 S.Ct. 1975, 18 L.Ed. 2d 1094 (1967) (constitutional privilege announced in *New York Times Co. v. Sullivan* applies to public figures); *New York Times Co. v. Sullivan*, 376 U.S. 254, 84 S.Ct. 710, 11 L.Ed.2d 686 (1964) (actual malice standard applies to published statements regarding a public official). See also, *Gertz v. Welch*, 418 U.S. 323, 94 S.Ct. 2997, 41 L.Ed.2d 789 (1974) (discussion of public issue may not be privileged where person defamed is neither a public official nor a public figure). See, e.g., *Eastwood v. NationaTl Enquirer, Inc.*, 123 F.3d 1249 (9th Cir. 1997) (under standard of *New York Times Co. v. Sullivan*, claim for invasion of privacy and misappropriation of name, likeness and personality under Cal. Civ. Code § 3344 and California common law survives "actual malice" analysis); see also, *Hoffman v. Capital Cities/ABC, Inc.*, 255 F.3d 1180 (9th Cir. 2001) (claims for, *inter alia*, misappropriation of name and likeness under California common law

While celebrities are newsworthy, their fame is also valuable. Because the public responds to a celebrity's name or picture,[8] the first step toward selling a product or service is to attract attention. The more popular the celebrity, the greater the name recognition, and the greater the visibility for the product the celebrity endorses.[9] This "marketable celebrity identity value" is a legally recognized property right, most often referred to as the "right of publicity"—a right that, "like copyright, protects a form of intellectual property that society deems to have some social utility."[10]

§7.02   Right of Publicity and Related Rights

[1]—Origins of the Right of Publicity

The first case to coin the term "right of publicity" dates from 1953,[11] and many of the leading decisions that have expanded its scope date back no further than the 1990s. Legal protections exist under two broad areas: (1) common law protections based on theories including privacy torts or the tort of misappropriation of name and likeness; and (2) statutory protections, with some state statutes addressing celebrity rights in considerable detail.[12]

---

and statutory right of publicity against magazine that used altered photo of actor as part of editorial content and not in an advertisement fails under "actual malice" analysis).

8   *Eastwood v. Superior Court*, 149 Cal. App.3d 409, 198 Cal. Rptr. 342, 349 (1984).

9   *White v. Samsung Electronics America, Inc.*, 971 F.2d 1395, 1399 (9th Cir. 1992).

10   *Comedy III Productions, Inc. v. Gary Saderup, Inc.*, 25 Cal. 4th 387, 299, 21 P.3d 797, 106 Cal.Rptr.2d 126 (Cal. 2001).

11   *Haelan Laboratories, Inc. v. Topps Chewing Gum, Inc.*, 202 F.2d 866, 868 (2d Cir. 1953). The seminal events in the development of the right of publicity are:

- Publication of Warren and Brandeis, "The Right to Privacy," 4 Harv. L. Rev. 193 (1890).

- The 1903 enactment of N.Y. Civ. §§ 50 and 51 entitled "Right of Privacy".

- The 1953 Second Circuit decision, *Haelan Laboratories, Inc. v. Topps Chewing Gum, Inc.*, 202 F.2d 866, 868 (2d Cir. 1953) (a right of publicity existed as a property right).

- Publication of two highly influential law review articles by leading scholars: Nimmer, "The Right of Publicity,"19 J. Law & Contemp. Probs. 203 (1954), which advocated for wider adoption of the right of publicity under *Haelen v. Topps*; Prosser, "Privacy," 48 Cal. L. Rev. 383 (1960), which put the common law tort of misappropriation of name and likeness in context among several torts based on invasion of privacy.

- The 1971 passage of the California right of publicity statute.

- The 1977 Supreme Court case, *Zacchini v. Scripps-Howard Broadcasting Co.*, 433 U.S. 562, 97 S.Ct. 2849, 53 L.Ed.2d 965 (1977).

- The 1984 passage of the California post-mortem right of publicity statute.

12   See Cal. Civil Code §§ 3344, 3344.1. See § 6.07[1], infra, discussing legal protections of the right of publicity in the fifty states and the District of Columbia. In some states, both common law and statutory causes of action

[a]—"The Right To Privacy"

The legal concept of a tort encompassing a right to be "left alone," dates back to the seminal Harvard Law Review article written in 1890 by Warren and Brandeis.[13] The article argued passionately for a common-law cause of action for violation of privacy based in tort, and providing for both damages and injunctive relief.[14]

---

exist, while in other states, the right is governed exclusively by either common law or statute. The hallmarks of the right of publicity are:

(1) *State law, not federal*: It is a right that exists at the state level either by application of statutes or the common law.

(2) *Based on tort of misappropriation*: Whether the right is codified as a "right of publicity" statute relating to celebrities or exists at common law, its essence is that it is a tort based on misappropriation of a property right related to name and likeness used for commercial purposes without consent.

(3) *Scope of the right*: It protects an individual's name, image, signature, voice, likeness, and persona used for commercial purposes and advertising, and has been interpreted to include things such as distinctive speaking or singing voices, nicknames, and other images or suggestions that may be enough to evoke a famous personality without actually showing his or her likeness.

(4) *Leading jurisdictions*: The applicable laws in entertainment industry-centric states, such as California and New York, are most often invoked and have generated the bulk of the case law, although there have also been significant cases in other states.

(5) *Property right*: It is a property right that can be licensed and assigned.

(6) *Descendible*: Depending on the state, it may protect the rights of deceased celebrities for varying terms of years. Depending on the state, it is a right that can pass to heirs and legatees.

(7) *Exists separately from copyright and trademark rights*: The right of publicity exists separately from rights that arise under trademark and copyright laws.

(8) *First Amendment and fair use*: When a celebrity's persona is evoked in a context that is not purely commercial speech or advertising, significant First Amendment protections apply to the usage, even in a context where the usage may create revenues for the user.

(9) *Corresponding causes of action*: Where a celebrity enforces his/her right of publicity under state law, he/she may also bring other causes of action under both state and federal laws, such as false endorsement under the Lanham Act, trademark infringement under the Lanham Act (if the celebrity has established trademark usage and rights), misappropriation under state law, unfair competition under state law and under the Lanham Act, and various forms of actions under state law rights of privacy, most notably "false light" claims.

13   Warren and Brandeis, "The Right to Privacy," 4 Harv. L. Rev. 193 (1890).

14   The rationale in the article, based on what were regarded as excesses of the press of the time, warrants an excerpt here:

> "Instantaneous photographs and newspaper enterprise have invaded the sacred precincts of private and domestic life; and numerous mechanical devices threaten to make good the prediction that 'what is whispered in the closet shall be proclaimed from the house-tops.' For years there has been a feeling that the law must afford some remedy for the unauthorized circulation of portraits of private persons; and the evil of invasion of privacy by the newspapers, long keenly felt, has been but recently discussed by an able writer . . . the question

The article proposed the recognition of tort actions, including the awards of injunctions and damages, for violations of the right of privacy, based on analogies to then-existing laws of defamation and copyright protection.

[b]—New York Civil Rights Law Right of Privacy Statute

In 1903, New York enacted a right of privacy law.[15] A provision recognized a personal right of privacy that would allow one to control the use of one's name, portrait or picture for advertising purposes.[16]

[i]—Liability Under New York's "Right of Privacy" Provision

New York's "Right of Privacy" statute states:

- A person, firm or corporation
- that uses for advertising purposes, or for the purposes of trade,
- the name, portrait or picture of any living person
- without having first obtained the written consent of such person,
- or if a minor of his or her parent or guardian,
- is guilty of a misdemeanor.[17]

---

whether our law will recognize and protect the right to privacy in this and in other respects must soon come before our courts for consideration. Of the desirability—"indeed of the necessity"—of some such protection, there can, it is believed, be no doubt. The press is overstepping in every direction the obvious bounds of propriety and of decency. Gossip is no longer the resource of the idle and of the vicious, but has become a trade, which is pursued with industry as well as effrontery. To satisfy a prurient taste the details of sexual relations are spread broadcast in the columns of the daily papers. To occupy the indolent, column upon column is filled with idle gossip, which can only be procured by intrusion upon the domestic circle.

. . .

"It is our purpose to consider whether the existing law affords a principle which can properly be invoked to protect the privacy of the individual; and, if it does, what the nature and extent of such protection is."

Id. at 3-4.

15   N.Y. Civ. Rights L. §§ 50-51.

16   N.Y. Civ. Rights L. § 50. Note that as drafted, the statute is a privacy right to control use of one's name for commercial purposes, but on its face it is not a property right. This interpretation did not come about until 1953, when, for the first time, the court read the statute as constituting a property right. *Haelan Laboratories, Inc. v. Topps Chewing Gum, Inc.*, 202 F.2d 866, 868 (2d Cir. 1953).

17   N.Y. Civ. Rights L. § 50.

[ii]—Damages and Injunctive Relief for Privacy Violations

The statute outlines the scope of actions for injunctions and for damages for violations of the right of privacy, while also containing limitations, including recognition of First Amendment rights to make uses in connection with artistic works.[18]

- Any person whose name, portrait or picture is used within this state for advertising purposes or for the purposes of trade without the written consent first obtained as above provided

- may maintain an equitable action in the supreme court of this state against the person, firm or corporation so using his name, portrait or picture,

- to prevent and restrain the use thereof;

- and may also sue and recover damages for any injuries sustained by reason of such use and if the defendant shall have knowingly used such person's name, portrait or picture in such manner as is forbidden or declared to be unlawful by section fifty of this article,

- the jury, in its discretion, may award exemplary damages.[19]

[iii]—Exceptions

New York's law provides for the following exceptions:

- Lawful articles containing the name or image may be freely sold;

- Photographers may exhibit their work in or about their establishment, including depictions of persons, unless the person depicted objects;

- Use of the name, portrait or picture of any author, composer or artist in connection with his literary, musical or artistic productions which he has sold or disposed of with such name, portrait or picture used in connection therewith.[20]

[c]—Judicial Recognition of the Right of Publicity

In 1953, a case involving a dispute over exclusive rights to a baseball player's photograph used on trading cards, the Court of Appeals for the Second Circuit held that the statutory right of privacy in New York did not merely allow the individual to control use of his name and likeness in an effort "not to have his feelings hurt by such publication," but was a property right that was assignable and licensable like

---

18   N.Y. Civ. Rights L. § 51.

19   *Id.*

20   *Id.*

any other intellectual property right.[21] The opinion was the first to coin the phrase "right of publicity."[22]

[d]—*Zacchini v. Scripps-Howard Broadcasting Co.*

The only Supreme Court case to consider the right of publicity concerned a performer in a human cannonball act who brought an action against a local television company for the unauthorized broadcast of his entire, fifteen-second performance.[23] Zacchini alleged a violation of his right of publicity under Ohio law because the broadcast diminished the number of people who were motivated to purchase tickets to attend his performance. The television station asserted a First Amendment privilege based on news reporting.

In holding for Zacchini and affirming the importance of the right of publicity, even in the face of a First Amendment challenge from the press, the Court recognized the right to "earn a living as an entertainer," and stated:

"[T]he broadcast of a film of petitioner's entire act poses a substantial threat to the economic value of that performance. As the Ohio court recognized, this act is the product of petitioner's own talents and energy, the end result of much time, effort, and expense. Much of its economic value lies in the 'right of exclusive control over the publicity given to his performance; if the public can see the act free on television, it will be less willing to pay to see it at the fair. The effect of a public broadcast

---

21 *Haelan Laboratories, Inc. v. Topps Chewing Gum, Inc.*, 202 F.2d at 868 (license to use likeness of baseball player on trading cards was a property right that could be exclusively assigned and was not merely a personal and non-assignable right not to have his feelings hurt by such a publication).

22 The court stated:

"We think that, in addition to and independent of that right of privacy (which in New York derives from statute), a man has a right in the publicity value of his photograph, i.e. the right to grant the exclusive privilege of publishing his picture, and that such a grant may validly be made 'in gross,' i.e. without an accompanying transfer of a business or of anything else. Whether it be labeled a 'property' right is immaterial; for here, as often elsewhere, the tag 'property' simply symbolizes the fact that courts enforce a claim which has pecuniary worth. This right might be called a 'right of publicity.' For it is common knowledge that many prominent persons (especially actors and ball players), far from having their feelings bruised through public exposure of their likenesses, would feel sorely deprived if they no longer received money for authorizing advertisements, popularizing their countenances, displayed in newspapers, magazines, busses, trains and subways. This right of publicity would usually yield them no money unless it could be made the subject of an exclusive grant which barred any other advertiser from using their pictures."

Id., 202 F.2d at 868.

23 *Zacchini v. Scripps-Howard Broadcasting Co.*, 433 U.S. 562, 97 S.Ct. 2849, 53 L.Ed.2d 965 (1977).

of the performance is similar to preventing petitioner from charging an admission fee.

"...

"Moreover, the broadcast of petitioner's entire performance, unlike the unauthorized use of another's name for purposes of trade or the incidental use of a name or picture by the press, goes to the heart of petitioner's ability to earn a living as an entertainer. Thus, in this case, Ohio has recognized what may be the strongest case for a 'right of publicity' involving, not the appropriation of an entertainer's reputation to enhanced the attractiveness of a commercial product, but the appropriation of the very activity by which the entertainer acquired his reputation in the first place."[24]

Zacchini must be limited to its facts because it involves the appropriation of an entire performance, a case that is perhaps more about a "right of performance" than the right of publicity. However, its affirmation of the right of an entertainer to the fruits of his labors remains for the moment the Supreme Court's "last word" on the right of publicity.

[e]—Right of Publicity as a Distinct Property Right

Haelen's announcement of a new property right generated considerable comment among legal scholars. In 1954, Melville Nimmer, wrote a widely influential law review article entitled "The Right of Publicity."[25] Nimmer surveyed various legal theories that courts had applied with respect to celebrity rights, including privacy torts and unfair competition. In his discussion, Nimmer noted the "community needs" for the growing recognition of celebrity name and likeness as a property right.

"[I]n the *Haelen* case the highly respected Second Circuit of the Federal Courts of Appeals granted to the right of publicity a recognition and status of a qualitatively higher order than had been accorded in any previous case. . . . [W]hether the right of publicity is finally and fully realized by statute or through growth and adaptation of common law principles, eventual recognition of the right seems assured both from the trend of decisions already rendered, and from the more fundamental fact of community needs."[26]

---

24   *Id.*, 433 U.S. at 574.

25   Nimmer, "The Right of Publicity,"19 J. Law & Contemp. Probs. 203 (1954).

26   *Id.* at 222-223.

In 1960, the legal scholar Dean Prosser surveyed the right of privacy as it then existed in the common law in various states, and wrote an article entitled "Privacy."[27] Prosser identified four distinct causes of action arising under privacy jurisprudence:

(1)   intrusion on the plaintiff's seclusion or solitude, or into his private affairs;

(2)   public disclosure of embarrassing private facts about the plaintiff;

(3)   publicity which places the plaintiff in a false light in the public eye;

(4)   appropriation, for the defendant's advantage, of the plaintiff's name or likeness.

In 1977, these distinctions among the types of privacy torts were incorporated into the *Restatement (Second) of Torts*.[28] This tort of appropriation of name or likeness serves as the basis for the common law right of publicity in many jurisdictions. Notably, the tort is characterized as a property right that is misappropriated rather than, as is the case with the other three torts, as an intrusion on a privacy right.[29]

[f]—California Right Of Publicity Statute

California passed its first right of publicity statute in 1971, entitled "Use of another's name, voice, signature, photograph or likeness for advertising or selling or soliciting purposes."[30]

[i]—Infringing Use

The description of the infringing use under the statute includes the requirement that the use be "knowing," which is not part of the common law tort under Cal-

---

27   Prosser, "Privacy," 48 Cal. L. Rev. 383 (1960).

28   *Restatement (Second) of Torts*, § 652C (1977). Prosser's article and the incorporation of his proposals into the *Restatement (Second) of Torts* are often cited in court opinions reviewing the origins of the right of publicity.

29   California's common law right of publicity is based on the elements set forth in Prosser's treatise "Law of Torts":

"A common law cause of action for appropriation of name or likeness may be pleaded by alleging (1) the defendant's use of the plaintiff's identity; (2) the appropriation of plaintiff's name or likeness to defendant's advantage, commercially or otherwise; (3) lack of consent; and (4) resulting injury."

Prosser, *Law of Torts* (4th ed. 1971). See *Eastwood v. Superior Court*, 149 Cal. App.3d 409, 198 Cal. Rptr. 342, 347 (1984).

30   Cal. Civ. Code § 3344.

ifornia law.[31] In addition, the listing of "name, voice, signature, photograph, or likeness" is narrower than "identity" under the common law tort.[32]

[ii]—Damages

Damages under the statute are broadly defined, and include actual damages, profits of the infringer less deductible expenses, and punitive damages. The award of attorneys' fees and costs to the prevailing party is mandatory.[33] The damages are provided for in the statute.[34]

[iii]—Identification

Whether a person depicted is actually identifiable in the infringing use may be a determinative factor. For example, a drawing of a baseball pitcher that did not show his face was construed to be sufficiently identifiable as the plaintiff because of his characteristic pitching stance.[35] The statute states:

---

31   See *White v. Samsung Electronics America, Inc.*, 971 F.2d 1395, 1399 (9th Cir. 1992).

32   *Id.* Liability accrues to any person who:

knowingly uses:
another's name, voice, signature, photograph, or likeness,
in any manner,
on or in products, merchandise, or goods,
or for purposes of advertising or selling, or soliciting purchases of,
products, merchandise, goods or services,
without such person's prior consent,
or, in the case of a minor, the prior consent of his parent or legal guardian.
Cal. Civ. Code § 3344(a).

33   *Kirby v. Sega of America, Inc.*, 144 Cal. App.4th 47, 50 Cal Rptr.3d 607, 618 (2006).

34   Cal. Civ. Code § 3344(b) states:

any damages sustained by the person or persons injured as a result thereof;
in addition, in any action brought under this section, the person who violated the section shall be liable to the injured party or parties in an amount equal to the greater of seven hundred fifty dollars ($750) or the actual damages suffered by him or her as a result of the unauthorized use,
and any profits from the unauthorized use that are attributable to the use and are not taken into account in computing the actual damages.
in establishing such profits, the injured party or parties are required to present proof only of the gross revenue attributable to such use,
and the person who violated this section is required to prove his or her deductible expenses;
punitive damages may also be awarded to the injured party or parties.
The prevailing party in any action under this section shall also be entitled to attorney's fees and costs.

35   *Newcombe v. Coors*, 157 F.3d 686 (9th Cir. 1998).

"A person shall be deemed to be readily identifiable from a photograph when one who views the photograph with the naked eye can reasonably determine that the person depicted in the photograph is the same person who is complaining of its unauthorized use."[36]

[iv]—Exceptions for News

The statute contains exceptions in keeping with First Amendment freedoms of the press and speech in connection with news, public affairs programming, and sports broadcasts.[37]

[g]—California Post-Mortem Right of Publicity Statute

In 1984, the California legislature responded to a state supreme court case brought by the heirs of actor Bela Lugosi, in which the court held that no post-mortem right of publicity existed in California.[38] The legislature expanded the existing right of publicity statute to incorporate a post-mortem application.[39]

[i]—Applies to Deceased Personality

The infringing uses in the areas of products, merchandise, and advertising apply to the use of a "deceased personality's" name, voice, signature, photograph, or

---

36   Cal. Civ. Code § 3344(c).

37   Cal. Civ. Code § 3344(d) states:

- For purposes of this section, a use of a name, voice, signature, photograph, or likeness
- in connection with any news, public affairs, or sports broadcast or account,
- or any political campaign,
- shall not constitute a use for which consent is required under subdivision (a).

38   *Lugosi v. Universal Pictures*, 25 Cal.3d 813, 160 Cal. Rptr. 323, 603 P.2d 425 (1979).

39   Cal. Civ. Code § 3344.1. See: *Shaw Family Archives, Ltd. v. CMG Worldwide, Inc.*, 2007 WL 1413381 (S.D.N.Y. May 7, 2007) and *Milton H. Greene Archives, Inc. v. CMG Worldwide, Inc.*, No. CV 05-2200 MMM (MCx) (D. Cal. filed May 14, 2007), which dealt with the testamentary disposition by Marilyn Monroe of residue of her estate in 1962. The court held she could not convey California statutory right of publicity because the statute providing for post mortem right of publicity in California was not enacted until January 1, 198; thus, the right did not exist at the time of her death and could not be bequeathed. 5. On September 7, 2007 the legislature amended the statute to make post mortem rights effective retroactively. Cal. Civ. Code § 3344.1. See also, *Milton H. Greene Archives, Inc. v. CMG Worldwide, Inc.*, 568 F. Supp.2d 1152, 1158 (C.D. Cal. 2008), *aff'd Milton H. Greene Archives, Inc. v. Marilyn Monroe, LLC*, 2012 WL 3743100 (9th Cir. Aug. 30, 2012) (recognizing that the legislature abrogated earlier holding in the case, but finding that notwithstanding the retroactive effect, Monroe died as a domicile of New York, therefore New York's right of publicity laws applied which does not provide for any post mortem rights). Cal. Civ. Code § 3344.1(o) was enacted in response to issues surrounding the cases involving the estate of Marilyn Monroe, and cures any potential defects in testamentary disposition and chain of title connected with "an action [taken] prior to May 1, 2007."

likeness.[40] The deceased person's property right in the right of publicity can be transferred, assigned or devised by will.[41]

[ii]—Damages

Damages under the statute are broadly defined, including actual damages, profits of the infringer less deductible expenses, and punitive damages. The award of attorney fees and costs to the prevailing party is mandatory.[42]

[iii]—Exceptions

The statute sets out a list of potential noncommercial uses protected under the First Amendment and includes advertisements or commercial announcements of those works, if they constitute entertainment:

---

40   *Id.*

41   Cal. Civ. Code § 3344.1 (b)-(d) states:

- Any person who
- knowingly uses:
- a deceased personality's name, voice, signature, photograph, or likeness,
- in any manner,
- on or in products, merchandise, or goods,
- or for purposes of advertising or selling, or soliciting purchases of,
- products, merchandise, goods or services,
- without prior consent from the persons specified in subdivision (c).

42   *Kirby v. Sega of America, Inc.*, 144 Cal. App.4th 47, 50 Cal. Rptr.3d 607, 618 (2006). The provisions include:

- any damages sustained by the person or persons injured as a result thereof.
- In addition, in any action brought under this section, the person who violated the section shall be liable to the injured party or parties in an amount equal to the greater of seven hundred fifty dollars ($750) or the actual damages suffered by him or her as a result of the unauthorized use,
- and any profits from the unauthorized use that are attributable to the use and are not taken into account in computing the actual damages.
- In establishing such profits, the injured party or parties are required to present proof only of the gross revenue attributable to such use,
- and the person who violated this section is required to prove his or her deductible expenses.
- Punitive damages may also be awarded to the injured party or parties.
- The prevailing party in any action under this section shall also be entitled to attorney's fees and costs.

Cal. Civ. Code § 3344.1(a).

"For purposes of this subdivision, a play, book, magazine, newspaper, musical composition, audiovisual work, radio or television program, single and original work of art, work of political or newsworthy value, or an advertisement or commercial announcement for any of these works, shall not be considered a product, article of merchandise, good, or service if it is fictional or nonfictional entertainment, or a dramatic, literary, or musical work."[43]

The statute also provides an exception to the exception. If a protected entertainment use includes an arguably blatant commercial use, then that commercial use is not excepted, notwithstanding its inclusion in an otherwise protected work.[44]

News reporting is also excepted,[45] and it is a question of fact whether any commercial sponsorship or paid advertising connected with a use that might otherwise be exempt triggers the consent right.[46]

[iv]—Testamentary Disposition and Transferability of the Right; Intestate Succession

The rights established under the California right of publicity statute are freely transferable or descendible by contract, trust, or any other testamentary instrument by any subsequent owner of the deceased personality's rights. The section

---

43   Cal. Civ. Code § 3344.1(a)(2).

44   Cal. Civ. Code § 3344.1(a)(3).

"If a work that is protected under paragraph two includes within it a use in connection with a product, article of merchandise, good, or service, this use shall not be exempt under this subdivision, notwithstanding the unprotected use's inclusion in a work otherwise exempt under this subdivision, if the claimant proves that this use is so directly connected with a product, article of merchandise, good, or service as to constitute an act of advertising, selling, or soliciting purchases of that product, article of merchandise, good, or service by the deceased personality without prior consent from the person or persons specified in subdivision (c)."

45   Cal. Civ. Code § 3344.1(j).

(j) For purposes of this section, a use of a name, voice, signature, photograph, or likeness in connection with any news, public affairs, or sports broadcast or account, or any political campaign, shall not constitute a use for which consent is required under subdivision (a).

46   Cal. Civ. Code § 3344.1(k).

The use of a name, voice, signature, photograph, or likeness in a commercial medium shall not constitute a use for which consent is required under subdivision (a) solely because the material containing the use is commercially sponsored or contains paid advertising. Rather, it shall be a question of fact whether or not the use of the deceased personality's name, voice, signature, photograph, or likeness was so directly connected with the commercial sponsorship or with the paid advertising as to constitute a use for which consent is required under subdivision (a).

also confirms that nothing in the statute affects any agreements entered into by celebrities prior to their death.[47]

The statute provides for a hierarchy of intestate succession in the event the rights were not assigned or there was no will, with spouse, children, parents taking the right in a manner similar to state laws of intestate succession.[48] If however there were no assignments, no will, and no survivors as specified, the right terminates.[49]

Where the testamentary owners of the right of publicity form a business entity to manage the rights, their rights acquired by will must be assigned to the entity to establish a clear chain of title. In *Bruce Lee Enterprises, LLC v. A.V.E.L.A., Inc.*, the heirs of martial arts actor Bruce Lee had acquired his post mortem right of publicity by the laws of intestate succession under California law.[50] In the process of subsequently forming several business entities to manage the estate over the years, the court found that the lack of a writing transferring those rights to the first entity formed a triable issue of fact regarding the rights currently held by the plaintiff business entity.[51]

[v]—Registration of Claims; Searching for Claims

California's right of publicity statute allows a holder of the right to register his or her claim with the Secretary of State on completion of a verified form and payment of a fee.[52] The form must include the name and date of death of the deceased personality, the name and address of the claimant, the basis of the claim, and the rights claimed.[53] Information on such claims is public and can be found on the Web site of the Secretary of State under "Special Filings."[54] The Web page has a simple search function where the name of any celebrity can be entered, and if there is a claim on file, the relevant information will appear.[55]

---

47 Cal. Civ. Code § 3344.1(b).

48 Cal. Civ. Code § 3344.1(c)–(e).

49 *Id.*

50 See *Bruce Lee Enterprises, LLC v. A.V.E.L.A., Inc.*, 2013 WL 822173 (S.D.N.Y. March 6, 2013).

51 Id. at 28–29.

52 Cal. Civ. Code § 3344.1(f)(2)-(4).

53 See Form 407, Registration of Claim as Successor in Interest, available at http://www.sos.ca.gov/business/sf/forms/np-sf-407.pdf. The filing fee is $10.00.

54 See "Special Filings Successor-In-Interest," available at http://www.sos.ca.gov/business/sf/sf_siisearch.htm.

55 For example, a search on "Bob Hope" brings up the following information:

Celebrity Name: Bob Hope

[vi]—Seventy Years Post-Mortem

Under California's right of publicity statute no action shall be brought by reason of any use of a deceased personality's name, voice, signature, photograph, or likeness occurring after the expiration of seventy years after the death of the deceased personality.[56]

[vii]—Deceased Personality Defined

A "deceased personality" is any natural person whose name, voice, signature, photograph, or likeness has commercial value at the time of his or her death, whether or not during the lifetime of that natural person the person used his or her name, voice, signature, photograph, or likeness on or in products, merchandise or goods, or for purposes of advertising or selling, or solicitation of purchase of, products, merchandise, goods, or services.[57] A "deceased personality" includes, without limitation, any such natural person who has died within seventy years prior to January 1, 1985.[58]

[viii]—Identification

The standard as to whether the recognizability of the deceased personality is whether a person can "reasonably determine" that a photograph or video depicts the deceased personality.[59]

Legal Name: Leslie Townes Hope aka Lester T. Hope

File Number: 2003-042

Filing status: active

File date: 10/08/2003

Date of death: 07/27/2003

Transferred by: contract

Name of Claimant: Hope Enterprises, Inc.

Address of Claimant: c/o 10346 Moorpark St., North Hollywood, CA

Percentage interest claimed: 100%

Above percentage claimed in: all types of rights

56   Cal. Civ. Code § 3344.1(g).

57   Cal. Civ. Code § 3344.1(h).

58   *Id.*

59   See § 3344.1(i).

"As used in this section, 'photograph' means any photograph or photographic reproduction, still or moving, or any video tape or live television transmission, of any person, such that the deceased personality is readily identifiable. A deceased personality shall be deemed to be readily identifiable from a photograph when one

[ix]—Secondary Liability for Media

The statute exempts from liability the media that publish an infringing use, such as print media, broadcast media, Web sites, etc., providing they did not have knowledge the use was unauthorized.[60]

[x]—Remedies Cumulative; Jurisdiction

The statute also provides that the remedies are cumulative and in addition to any other remedies provided for by law. The statute applies to acts occurring directly in California. Note however that courts have held that with respect to the deceased personality, that notwithstanding the statute's application to acts occurring directly in California, the law that will be applied is the law of where the celebrity was domiciled at the time of death.[61]

[2]—Jurisdiction, Venue, and Choice of Law

State courts will apply right of publicity law according to the choice of law rules of the forum state.[62] Presuming the local laws are favorable, a plaintiff will typically try to bring an action in his or her home venue and jurisdiction. Where a federal court sits in diversity, it will apply a choice of law analysis of the venue in which the case was brought.[63]

---

who views the photograph with the naked eye can reasonably determine who the person depicted in the photograph is."

60   See § 3344.1(l).

Nothing in this section shall apply to the owners or employees of any medium used for advertising, including, but not limited to, newspapers, magazines, radio and television networks and stations, cable television systems, billboards, and transit ads, by whom any advertisement or solicitation in violation of this section is published or disseminated, unless it is established that the owners or employees had knowledge of the unauthorized use of the deceased personality's name, voice, signature, photograph, or likeness as prohibited by this section.

61   See *Milton H. Greene Archives, Inc. v. CMG Worldwide, Inc.*, 568 F. Supp.2d 1152, 1158 (C.D. Cal. 2008). See also, *Cairns v. Franklin Mint Co.*, 292 F.3d 1139, 1146-1150 (9th Cir. 2002).

62   See, *e.g., Prima v. Darden Restaurants*, 78 F. Supp.2d 337, 344-345 (D.N.J. 2000) (stating with respect to New Jersey choice of law analysis: "The plaintiff's alleged right of publicity is a tort claim. In tort cases, New Jersey has rejected the traditional rule of *lex loci delicti*, pursuant to which the local law of the place where the wrong occurred governed the substantive issues. Instead, New Jersey applies a flexible governmental interest analysis requiring application of the law of the state with the greatest interest in resolving the particular issue. The Court's analysis must be done on an issue-by-issue basis. The issue-by-issue analysis may even result in the Court applying different states' laws to different issues in the same litigation."). (Citations omitted.)

63   See, *e.g. Rogers v. Grimaldi*, 875 F.2d 994, 1002 (2d Cir. 1989) ("[a] federal court sitting in diversity or adjudicating state law claims that are pendent to a federal claim must apply the choice of law rules of the forum state. The New York Court of Appeals has clearly stated that "right of publicity" claims are governed by the substantive law of the plaintiff's domicile because rights of publicity constitute personalty. Rogers is an Oregon domiciliary, and thus Oregon law governs this claim."). (Citations omitted.)

With respect to actions instituted by the estates or assignees of deceased celebrities, California courts will apply the law of the jurisdiction of the deceased celebrity's domicile. Domicile does not necessarily equate with current residence, for "residence is physical, whereas domicile is generally a compound of physical presence plus an intention to make a certain definite place one's permanent abode."[64] Thus the location of a celebrity's death is not dispositive.

Two very high-profile cases in recent years have focused on this issue under the California statute. The Ninth Circuit held that the estate of Princess Diana of Wales could not maintain an action under the California statute, because Diana's post mortem publicity rights were determined by the location of her domicile at the time of her death.[65] Princess Diana's domicile at the time of her death was the United Kingdom, a jurisdiction that does not recognize a post-mortem right of publicity.[66]

Similarly, the Central District of California and the Southern District of New York considered the post-mortem right of publicity held by the estate of actress Marilyn Monroe.[67] Both courts held that despite the fact that Monroe died in Los Angeles, her presence in Los Angeles was temporary and her actual and intended permanent domicile at the time of her death was New York. Thus New York law, which does not provide for a post-mortem right of publicity, governed.[68] Monroe's estate could not maintain a cause of action for right of publicity under California law.[69]

---

64   See *Milton H. Greene Archives, Inc. v. CMG Worldwide, Inc.*, 568 F. Supp.2d 1152, 1158 (C.D. Cal. 2008). See also, *Cairns v. Franklin Mint Co.*, 292 F.3d 1139, 1146-1150 (9th Cir. 2002).

65   *Cairns v. Franklin Mint Co.*, 292 F.3d 1139 (9th Cir. 2002).

66   *Id.*

67   See *Milton H. Greene Archives, Inc. v. CMG Worldwide, Inc.*, 568 F. Supp.2d 1152 (C.D. Cal. 2008); see also, *Shaw Family Archives, Ltd. v. CMG Worldwide, Inc.*, 589 F. Supp.2d 331 (S.D.N.Y. 2008).

68   The *Milton H. Greene Archives, Inc. v. CMG Worldwide, Inc.*, 568 F. Supp.2d 1152 (C.D. Cal. 2008), *aff'd* 2012 WL 3743100 (9th Cir. Aug. 30, 2012); see also, *Shaw Family Archives, Ltd. v. CMG Worldwide, Inc.*, 589 F. Supp.2d 331 (S.D.N.Y. 2008). Note that the court found determinative the fact that Monroe's estate at the time of her death declared in several official documents, including tax documents, that she was a domicile of New York at the time of her death.

69   In the cases involving the post mortem right of publicity held by the estate of actress Marilyn Monroe, one of the issues was whether, prior to the effective date of California's post mortem rights under § 3344.1, a celebrity's will could have devised statutory rights that, at the time of death, did not yet exist. In response to holdings in the cases, in 2007 the California legislature amended § 3344.1 to provide in section 3344.1(p) that'[t]he rights recognized by this section are expressly made retroactive, including to those deceased personalities who died before January 1, 1985.' Monroe died on August 5, 1962. See *Milton H. Greene Archives, Inc. v. CMG Worldwide, Inc.*, 568 F. Supp.2d 1152 (C.D. Cal. 2008), *aff'd* 2012 WL 3743100 (9th Cir. Aug. 30, 2012); see also, *Shaw Family Archives, Ltd. v. CMG Worldwide, Inc.*, 589 F. Supp.2d 331 (S.D.N.Y. 2008).

§7.03   Related State and Federal Causes Of Action

[1]—Lanham Act Claims

[a]—False Endorsement and False Advertising

While there is no federal cause of action for the right of publicity itself, there are claims under federal law via the Lanham Act that can, in certain circumstances, address somewhat comparable issues such as false endorsement, false advertising and trademark infringement. Such claims are often brought in addition to state-based right of publicity claims. In cases where no rights under state law exist, there may still be valid claims under Section 43(a) of the Lanham Act.[70]

False endorsement occurs when a celebrity's identity, his or her "mark," is connected with a product or service in such a way that consumers are likely to be misled about the celebrity's sponsorship or approval of the product or service.[71] Consumer confusion occurs when consumers believe that the products or services offered by the parties are affiliated in some way, or when consumers make an incorrect mental association between the involved commercial products or their producers on the one hand and the celebrity on the other.[72]

---

70   The numerical designation of Section 43(a) refers to the numbering of this provision in the Trademark Act, found at 15 U.S.C. § 1125(a). The Trademark Act, in turn, is commonly referred to as the Lanham Act. The Trademark Act of July 5, 1946, ch 540, § 46, 60 Stat. 444.

71   See:

Second Circuit: Allen v. National Video, Inc., 610 F. Supp. 612 (S.D.N.Y. 1985) (photograph of Woody Allen look-alike in national advertising campaign for video rental club).

Sixth Circuit: ETW Corp. v. Jireh Publishing, Inc., 332 F.3d 915 (6th Cir. 2003); *Landham v. Lewis Galoob Toys, Inc.*, 227 F.3d 619, 626 (6th Cir. 2000) (in false endorsement claim brought by a celebrity the "mark" is the plaintiff's identity).

Ninth Circuit: Wendt v. Host International, Inc., 125 F.3d 806 (9th Cir. 1997) ("Cheers" television program used to advertise chain of airport bars modeled on Cheers set); *Abdul-Jabbar v. General Motors Corp.*, 85 F.3d 407 (9th Cir. 1996) (athlete's name and accomplishments used in television advertisement for Oldsmobile cars); *Waits v. Frito-Lay, Inc.*, 978 F.2d 1093 (9th Cir. 1992) (imitation of singer's unique voice used in radio commercial advertising Dorito Chips); *White v. Samsung Electronics America, Inc.*, 971 F.2d 1395 (9th Cir. 1992) (female robot bearing resemblance to television celebrity); *Bruce Lee Enterprises, LLC v. A.V.E.L.A., Inc.*, 2011 WL 1327137 (S.D.N.Y. March 31, 2011).

72   *Parks v. LaFace Records*, 329 F.3d 437, 446 (6th Cir. 2003) (*citing Cardtoons, L.C. v. Major League Baseball Players Ass'n*, 95 F.3d 959, 966 (10th Cir. 1996)). See also, *Landham v. Lewis Galoob Toys, Inc.*, 227 F.3d 619, 626 (6th Cir. 2000) (actor sued toy company for creating an action figure named after one of his movie characters; court held that in false endorsement claim brought by a celebrity the "mark" is the plaintiff's identity). Note that § 43(a)(1)(A) is the "false endorsement" or "false affiliation" claim provision, while § 43(a)(1)(B) is the "false advertising" component.

As noted in the statute, the test for claims under the Lanham Act is whether the allegedly infringing use is "likely to cause confusion, or to cause mistake, or to deceive." The legal standard thus depends greatly on consumer perception of the use. Therefore, courts in various jurisdictions use a list of factors to aid in determining whether a likelihood of consumer confusion exists sufficient to support Lanham Act claims.

In California, for example, courts use a likelihood of consumer confusion test specially crafted for false endorsement:[73]

1. The level of recognition that the plaintiff has among the segment of the society for whom the defendant's product is intended;

2. The relatedness of the fame or success of the plaintiff to the defendant's product;

3. The similarity of the likeness used by the defendant to the actual plaintiff;

4. Evidence of actual confusion;

5. Marketing channels used;

6. Likely degree of purchaser care;

7. Defendant's intent in selecting the plaintiff; and

8. Likelihood of expansion of the product lines.[74]

In jurisdictions that apply such multi-factor tests to determine whether a likelihood of consumer confusion exists, these factors are not necessarily of equal importance, nor will they apply to every case.[75]

In a case pitting the trust of Albert Einstein against General Motors, the auto manufacturer ran a light-hearted magazine ad superimposing Dr. Einstein's face on someone else's body.[76] The allegations included false endorsement under the Lanham Act.[77]

---

73 *Downing v. Abercrombie & Fitch*, 265 F.3d 994, 1007-1008 (9th Cir. 2001) (basing its test on *AMF Inc. v. Sleekcraft Boats*, 599 F.2d 341 (9th Cir. 1979).

74 *Id.* See *AMF, Inc. v. Sleekcraft Boats*, 599 F.2d 341 (9th Cir. 1979). See also, *Facenda v. N.F.L. Films, Inc.*, 542 F.3d 1007 (3d Cir. 2008) (adapting *Downing v. Abercrombie & Fitch* test for false endorsement).

75 While a federal claim for unfair competition can be contemplated under the Lanham Act, the parties must actually be in competition.

76 See *The Hebrew University of Jerusalem v. General Motors, Inc.*, 2012 WL 907497 (C.D. Cal. March 16, 2012).

77 *Id.*

In applying the Ninth Circuit's eight-factor false endorsement test under *AMF Inc. v. Sleekcraft Boats*, the District Court for the Central District of California noted a lack of evidence of consumer confusion because "[t]he advertisement does not state expressly (or even imply) that Dr. Einstein . . . endorsed the Terrain [the vehicle in the ad], nor would any reasonable reader reach that conclusion. Instead, the Advertisement uses Dr. Einstein's face, superimposed on someone else's body, as a play on People magazine's "Sexiest Man Alive" edition, and to make a light-hearted point about the smart (but "sexy") features of the Terrain."[78]

Focusing on whether the plaintiff's and defendant's "goods" were related under the second *Sleekcraft* test, the court noted:

At most, the Terrain draws its value from Einstein's image only indirectly and remotely; the ad was not for an Einstein product. Einstein is famous largely due to his towering intellect, a point emphasized by the "e=mc2" tattoo sported by the Advertisement's Einstein doppelganger. "So what the Advertisement suggests is that the Terrain vehicle is endowed with "smart (but 'sexy') features." So what? Einstein = smart. Terrain = smart. Ergo, does Einstein = Approval of Terrain? In short, any link between the "hunky" model in the ad, Einstein's image and the vehicle is too weak to create a link between two "goods."[79]

[b]—Trademark Infringement

Celebrities, both alive and deceased, may have trademark rights in their name, logos, and selected images that have been used consistently as source identifiers and identified with particular goods and services. Such rights may exist under common law by virtue of use in commerce, or under federal law by virtue of a federal trademark registration.

If a celebrity asserts a trademark claim either on its own or in conjunction with a right of publicity claim, the celebrity will first have to establish that trademark rights exist. Thus, in a case pitting Presley's estate against a performer who presented "exact copies" of Elvis concerts featuring an Elvis lookalike, the District of New Jersey held that the names ELVIS, ELVIS IN CONCERT, and ELVIS PRESLEY were valid and protectable service marks. They were used not only to identify a particular individual, Elvis Presley, but also used in advertising—such as for performances, concerts, and on records—to identify a service.[80] Under the same analysis, however, the court held that THE KING was not established as a valid service mark, because it was merely a nickname, and the

---

78   *Id.* at *15.

79   *Id.* at *16. In a later ruling, the court held that Einstein's post-mortem right of publicity under New Jersey law had a duration of fifty years and thus the suit, commenced in 2010, was not timely. See *Hebrew Univ. of Jerusalem v. GM LLC*, 903 F. Supp. 2d 932 (C.D. Cal. 2012).

80   *Estate of Elvis Presley v. Russen*, 513 F. Supp. 1339, 1363 (D.N.J. 1981).

Presley estate had offered insufficient evidence to demonstrate that the name was used to identify services.[81]

Courts can reach different conclusions as to whether a celebrity has indeed established trademark rights. For example, the Sixth Circuit found that while Tiger Woods' corporation had duly registered his name as a trademark, Woods could not claim that any and all images of him qualified for trademark protection under the Lanham Act.[82]

Courts have also taken a broader approach to whether a celebrity's name functions as a trademark. Civil rights pioneer and heroine Rosa Parks brought an action alleging that the song by OutKast entitled "Rosa Parks" violated her rights under the Lanham Act and state law claims including right of publicity.[83] Parks' Lanham Act claim was for false advertising under § 43(a). The court stated:

"Rosa Parks clearly has a property interest in her name akin to that of a person holding a trademark. It is beyond question that Parks is a celebrity . . . courts routinely recognize a property right in celebrity identity akin to that of a trademark holder under § 43(a). We find Parks' prior commercial activities and international recognition as a symbol of the civil rights movement endow her with a trademark interest in her name the same as if she were a famous actor or musician. Therefore, even though Rosa Parks' name might not be eligible for registration as a trademark, and even though Defendants were not selling Rosa Parks-brand CD's, a viable cause of action also exists under § 43(a)

---

81 *Id.*, 513 F. Supp. at 1363. The same court held that a lightning bolt logo with the letters "TCB" also rose to the level of a service mark based on various uses, including on the tail of Presley's airplanes. *Id.* With respect to illustrations and photos of Presley "dressed in one of his characteristic jumpsuits and holding a microphone in a singing pose," the court found that the illustration was "likely" to function as a trademark. Having established the existence of enforceable marks under the common law, the court proceeded to conduct the multi-factor likelihood of confusion analysis under New Jersey law (as it existed in 1981), and concluded that a likelihood of confusion existed. *Id.*, 513 F. Supp. at 1370-1371.

82 *ETW Corp. v. Jireh Publishing, Inc.*, 332 F.3d 915, 922 (6th Cir. 2003). The court noted that

"[t]his is an untenable claim. ETW asks us, in effect, to constitute Woods himself as a walking, talking trademark. Images and likenesses of Woods are not protectable as a trademark because they do not perform the trademark function of designation. They do not distinguish and identify the source of goods. They cannot function as a trademark because there are undoubtedly thousands of images and likenesses of Woods taken by countless photographers, and drawn, sketched, or painted by numerous artists, which have been published in many forms of media, and sold and distributed throughout the world. No reasonable person could believe that merely because these photographs or paintings contain Woods' likeness or image, they all originated with Woods."

Id.

83 *Parks v. LaFace Records*, 329 F.3d 437, 446 (6th Cir. 2003).

if consumers falsely believed that Rosa Parks had sponsored or approved the song, or was somehow affiliated with the song or the album.[84]

As an example of how courts determine whether celebrities have established trademark rights in their names or nicknames, note the trademark analysis below from *Moore v. The Weinstein Co.*, a Sixth Circuit case where a member of the "Sam and Dave" soul music duo in the 1960s and 1970s, which performed hit songs including "Soul Man," unsuccessfully asserted trademark rights in the nickname "Soul Man" against a motion picture company that released a film entitled "Soul Men." The court notes whether the plaintiff took steps to claim and protect the mark, and whether the mark is so widely used as to arguably be generic and unprotectable by anyone.[85]

---

84 *Id.*, 329 F.3d at 447. See also:

85 See *Moore v. The Weinstein Co.*, 545 Fed. Appx. 405 (6th Cir. 2013), affg *Moore v. The Weinstein Co.*, 2012 U.S. Dist. LEXIS 72929 at *52-*59, 2012 WL 1884758 at *17-*19 (M.D. Tenn. May 23, 2012) (quote from District Court opinion as affirmed; internal citations omitted).

B. The Marks

Whether the Marks actually constitute protectable trademarks is the subject of vigorous dispute between the parties. The plaintiffs refer to the Marks as 'marks' or 'trademarks,' while the defendants refer to them as the 'Purported Marks.' For ease of reference only, the court will refer to them as the 'Marks.'

The plaintiffs claim to own common law trademarks in the phrases 'Soul Men,' 'Soul Man,' 'The Legendary Soul Man,' 'The Original Soul Man,' and 'The Original Soul Men.' These Marks are unregistered. In 1997, Sam Moore filed an application with the USPTO concerning certain of these Marks, which the USPTO approved. However, because Sam Moore did not file the requisite follow-up Statement of Use, the Marks were not registered.

It is not entirely clear to the court whether any Marks other than 'Soul Man' were subject to Sam Moore's USPTO application. Exhibit 4 to the PRDSUF purports to be Sam Moore's 'trademark application file.' That document appears to contain a signed application only as to the term 'Soul Man.'

The plaintiffs have presented no evidence that they personally spent any money investing in and advertising or promoting the Purported Marks. However, it appears that some third-party promoters advertised performances and appearances by 'The Legendary Soul Man Sam Moore' (or variations thereof), although the plaintiffs have not presented evidence reflecting the total amount of those potential expenditures.

The plaintiffs have never granted a trademark license related to the Marks. However, at least some of Sam Moore's performance agreements include a contract rider setting forth the manner in which Sam Moore is to be billed (as 'The Legendary Soul Man,' for instance). (*See, e.g.*, PRDSUF, Ex. 9 at p. 4, ¶ 5 ('BILLING: SAM MOORE or The Legendary Soul Man Sam Moore'; 'There is to be no deviation from this billing without prior written approval by [Sam Moore's] representative. There is *never* any use allowed for any reason whatsoever to the name 'Sam & Dave' in any marketing, billing, promotion or otherwise to refer and/or describe or advertise Sam Moore.') Sam Moore personally always uses his given name, Sam Moore, in connection with his stage names 'Soul Man', 'The Original Soul Man,' and 'The Legendary Soul Man.' Advertisers and promoters have, at times, referred to Sam Moore by his stage name without reference to his given name.

Similarly, the record contains evidence—including evidence produced by the plaintiffs—that Sam Moore is not always referred to as the 'Soul Man' and that Sam & Dave are not always referred to as the 'Soul Men.' For example, the American Federation of Television and Radio Artists ('AFTRA') awarded Sam Moore a Lifetime Achievement award at the AFTRA Media and Entertainment Excellence Awards ceremony ('AMEE'). In its press release concerning the AMEE awards, AFTRA devotes several paragraphs to Sam Moore without once refer to him as 'The Soul Man' or some related name. Similarly, the record contains multiple references to Sam & Dave as 'Double Dynamite,' rather than as 'Soul Men.' (*See, e.g. id.* at p. 17 (news article).) The cellophane cover of the 2008 documentary regarding Sam & Dave, in which the plaintiffs assert interests in this lawsuit, actually contains a sticker with the phrase 'Double Dynamite' in large capital letters.

The plaintiffs contend that Sam & Dave did not hold themselves out as 'Double Dynamite.' According to the plaintiffs, a third-party promoter simply utilized that term to describe Sam & Dave in promoting a European tour, without input or consent from Sam & Dave. Regardless of the source of the term, it appears that Sam & Dave were also referred as 'Double Dynamite.'

"There are various examples of artistic media that consist or incorporate the terms 'Soul,' 'Soul Man,' 'Soul Men,' and variations thereof. For example:

- There are at least 34 third-party musical albums currently available for sale, the titles for which consist of or incorporate the phrases 'soul men' or 'soul man,' such as 'Soul Man' by Solomon Burke, 'Soul Man' by Bill McGee, 'Soul Men: Their Greatest Hits' (various artists), and 'Soul Men' (various artists).

- Various performing groups (or individual performers) utilize the terms 'Soul Man' or 'Soul Man,' such as 'The Soul–Men' (1960's group), 'The Soul Men' (current group), 'The Soul Men' (another group of the same name), 'Soulmen' (current group), and John 'Soul Man' Castro.

- The Blues Brothers, originally composed of comedic actors Dan Aykroyd and John Belushi, re-recorded the song 'Soul Man' and released two feature films, including the 1998 film Blues Brothers 2000, in which Moore played a backup acting role.

- Several shows have utilized the terms, including: *Soul Man*, a television sitcom starring Dan Aykroyd, and *Stories of a Real Soul Man*, a live show by David Porter, who had co-authored Sam & Dave's 'Soul Man' and 'Hold On I'm Comin'.'

- Many articles have described entertainers other than Sam Moore/Sam & Dave as 'Soul Man' or 'Soul Men,' including: 'Soul Man,' an msnbc.com article regarding Ray Charles; 'Soul Men,' a New York Times article relating to Eugene Record and Luther Vandross; 'Soul Man,' describing R & B singer Sam Cooke; 'Two Soul Men, Reunited for the First Time,' an npr.org article describing former Stax backup recording artists Steve Cropper and Felix Cavaliere; and 'Great Soul Men, Gone too Soon,' a Yahoo! music blog article concerning various artists, such as Dave Ruffin (Temptations), Marvin Gaye, Otis Redding, Quincy Jones, and Michael Jackson.

- At least two feature films have utilized the term 'Soul Man': (1) the 1986 film *Soul Man*, which concerns a white student who darkens his skin color in an attempt to attend Harvard University, for which Sam Moore rerecorded the song 'Soul Man' with Lou Reed and appeared in the film; and (2) the 2007 independent film *Soul Man*.

With respect to the examples listed in the Harvey Declaration, the parties appear to agree that many of the references do not constitute independent trademark uses, except as to the names of performance artists.

[2]—First Amendment Defenses

[a]—Commercial Speech

In applying First Amendment freedom of speech analysis to right of publicity claims, the category of constitutionally based "speech" is a threshold issue, and the extent to which it is deserving of First Amendment protection that abrogates any right of publicity claims. As noted by the Ninth:

> "'Commercial speech' has special meaning in the First Amendment context. Although the boundary between commercial and noncommercial speech has yet to be clearly delineated, the 'core notion of commercial speech' is that it 'does no more than propose a commercial transaction.' Such speech is entitled to a measure of First Amendment protection. Commercial messages, however, do not receive the same level of constitutional protection as other types of protected expression. False or misleading commercial speech is not protected."[86]

The Ninth Circuit held that commercial speech receives a limited amount of protection under the First Amendment and may be freely regulated if it is misleading. Most importantly, the "actual malice" standard of *New York Times Co. v. Sullivan* need not be applied to the statements made.[87] The court went on to note several leading right of publicity cases where "the question of actual malice does not arise," because the challenged use of the celebrity's identity occurs in an advertisement that "does no more than propose a commercial transaction." The court stated that "in all these cases, the defendant used an aspect of the celebrity's identity entirely and directly for

---

Notwithstanding the fact that many entertainers, books, albums, movies, and other media have utilized the term "Soul Man" or "Soul Men," this lawsuit is the only time that Sam Moore has ever made any demands on any third party regarding the use by that third party of the phrase "soul man" or "soul men."

The plaintiffs have not presented any consumer surveys regarding the public's association of the Marks with Sam Moore. The plaintiffs have never received any income for, or related to, the Marks. Furthermore, the plaintiffs have not presented evidence regarding the total amount, if any, that they have spent advertising or otherwise promoting the Marks."

Moore v. The Weinstein Co., 545 Fed. Appx. 405 (6th Cir. 2013), *affg Moore v. The Weinstein Co.*, 2012 U.S. Dist. LEXIS 72929 at *52-*59, 2012 WL 1884758 at *17-*19 (M.D. Tenn. May 23, 2012) (quote from District Court opinion as affirmed; internal citations omitted).

86 *Hoffman v. Capital Cities/ABC*, 255 F.3d 1184 (9th Cir. 2001). (Citations omitted.)

87 *Hoffman*, 255 F.3d at 1185 ("[the]Supreme Court precedent prevents us from importing the actual-malice standard into cases involving false commercial speech."). (Internal quotations omitted.)

the purpose of selling a product. Such uses do not implicate the First Amendment's protection of expressions of editorial opinions."[88]

[b]—Noncommercial Speech

Where courts determine that the alleged right of publicity violation constituted "noncommercial speech," subject to full First Amendment protections, a public figure such as a celebrity can only prevail by showing "actual malice" under the standards established by the Supreme Court.[89]

In applying the actual malice standard to a right of publicity claim, the court must determine whether a defendant acted with "reckless disregard for the truth" or a "high degree of awareness of probable falsity."[90] This requires, first, an identification of the false statement of fact in issue. In a right of publicity case, the "false" statement is the use of the celebrity's persona to imply that the celebrity endorsed the usage.[91]

To show actual malice, the celebrity must demonstrate by clear and convincing evidence that the defendant intended to create the false impression in the minds of the public.[92] Mere negligence is not enough to demonstrate actual malice.[93] "Subjective or actual intent is required . . . there is no actual malice where journalists unknowingly mislead the public."[94] The evidence must clearly and convincingly demonstrate that the defendant knew (or purposefully avoided knowing) that the use would mislead the public into thinking that the celebrity had provided approval and an endorsement.[95]

---

88   *Id.* (citing *Newcombe v. Adolf Coors Co.*, 157 F.3d 686, 691 (9th Cir. 1998) (use of pitcher's image in printed beer advertisement)); *Abdul-Jabbar v. General Motors Corp.*, 85 F.3d 407, 409 (9th Cir. 1996) (use of basketball star's former name in television car commercial); *Waits v. Frito-Lay*, 978 F.2d at 1097-1098 (use of imitation of singer's voice in radio snack-food commercial); *White v. Samsung Electronics America, Inc.*, 971 F.2d 1395, 1396 (9th Cir. 1992) (use of game-show hostess's "identity" in print advertisements for electronic products); *Midler v. Ford Motor Co.*, 849 F.2d 460, 461 (9th Cir. 1988) (use in television car commercial of "sound-alike" rendition of song singer had recorded)).

89   *Hoffman*, 255 F.3d at 1186.

90   *Hoffman*, 255 F.3d at 1186 (*citing Harte-Hanks Communications, Inc. v. Connaughton*, 491 U.S. 657, 667, 109 S.Ct. 2678, 105 L.Ed.2d 562 (1989)).

91   *Id.*

92   *Id.*

93   *Dodds v. American Broadcasting Co.*, 145 F.3d 1053, 1063 (9th Cir. 1998) (*citing Masson v. New Yorker Magazine, Inc.*, 501 U.S. 496, 510, 111 S.Ct. 2419, 115 L.Ed.2d 447 (1991)).

94   *Dodds*, N. 19 *supra*, 145 F.3d at 1064 (quoting *Eastwood*, 123 F.3d at 1256).

95   *Hoffman*, 255 F.3d at 1187.

[3]—Fair Use in Creative and Artistic Works

Creative works also fall into the category of noncommercial speech entitled to First Amendment protections and analysis.[96]

The California Supreme Court considered whether a drawing of the Three Stooges sold on a t-shirt was an expressive work of art entitled to First Amendment deference, or simply a misappropriation of the deceased performers' right of publicity under California law. In crafting a test that would distinguish between First Amendment-protected artistic expression and works that violate the right of publicity, the court pointed out that "what the right of publicity holder possesses is not a right of censorship, but a right to prevent others from misappropriating the economic value generated by the celebrity's fame" through the merchandising of the "name, voice, signature, photograph, or likeness of the celebrity."[97]

In so doing, the court adapted the "transformative use" test, derived from the copyright fair use test applied by the United States Supreme Court,[98] to the right of publicity context. The court stated:

When artistic expression takes the form of a literal depiction or imitation of a celebrity for commercial gain, directly trespassing on the right of publicity without adding significant expression beyond that trespass, the state law interest in protecting the fruits of artistic labor outweighs the expressive interests of the imitative artist. On the other hand, when a work contains significant transformative elements, it is not only especially worthy of First Amendment protection, but it is also less likely to interfere with the economic interest protected by the right of publicity.

* * *

Another way of stating the inquiry is whether the celebrity likeness is one of the "raw materials" from which an original work is synthesized, or whether the depiction of imitation of the celebrity is the very sum and substance of the work in question. We ask, in other words, whether a product containing a celebrity's likeness is so transformed that it has become primarily the defendant's own expression rather than the celebrity's likeness.

Furthermore, in determining whether a work is sufficiently transformative, courts may find useful a subsidiary inquiry, particularly in close cases: does the marketability and

---

96 *Guglielmi v. Spelling-Goldberg Productions*, 25 Cal.3d 860, 868, 603 P.2d 454, 160 Cal. Rptr. 352 (1979) (cited in *Comedy III Productions, Inc. v. Gary Saderup, Inc.*, 25 Cal. 4th 387, 398, 21 P.3d 797, 106 Cal.Rptr.2d 126 (2001)).

97 *Comedy III*, N. 22 *supra*, 25 Cal. 4th at 403.

98 *Campbell v. Acuff-Rose Music, Inc.*, 510 U.S. 569, 579, 114 S.Ct. 1164, 127 L.Ed.2d 500 (1994).

economic value of the challenged work derive primarily from the fame of the celebrity depicted? If this question is answered in the negative, then there would generally be no actionable right of publicity. When the value of the work comes principally from some source other than the fame of the celebrity—from the creativity, skill, and reputation of the artist—it may be presumed that sufficient transformative elements are present to warrant First Amendment protection.[99]

In its opinion, the court noted examples of celebrity portraits that did rise to the level of transformative use, such as the silkscreens of artist Andy Warhol, which

> "have as their subject the images of such celebrities as Marilyn Monroe, Elizabeth Taylor, and Elvis Presley. Through distortion and the careful manipulation of context, Warhol was able to convey a message that went beyond the commercial exploitation of celebrity images and became a form of ironic social comment on the dehumanization of celebrity itself."[100]

The court held that the drawing of the Three Stooges sold on a t-shirt had value that predominantly arose from the celebrity likeness rather than from any transformative use of the likeness. The t-shirt art was therefore a "conventional portrait of a celebrity so as to commercially exploit his or her fame."[101]

[4]—Fair Use Under the Lanham Act

[a]—Classic Fair Use

One defense to Lanham Act claims is fair use. The Ninth Circuit described an important distinction between "classic fair use" and "nominative fair use."[102] Classic fair use occurs where the defendant has used the plaintiff's mark to describe the defendant's own product. In a classic fair use defense, the defendant must prove the following three elements:

(1) defendant's use of the term is not as a trademark or service mark;

(2) defendant uses the term fairly and in good faith; and

(3) defendant uses the term only to describe its goods or services.[103]

---

99   *Comedy III*, N. 22 *supra*, 25 Cal. 4th at 405-406.

100 *Id.*, 25 Cal. 4th at 408-409.

101 *Id.*, 25 Cal. 4th at 408.

102 *Cairns v. Franklin Mint*, 292 F.3d 1139, 1150-1153 (9th Cir. 2002).

103 *Id.*, 292 F.3d at 1150-1151.

The classic fair use defense is available only so long as such use does not lead to customer confusion as to the source of the goods or services. A classic fair use analysis *complements*, but does not replace, the eight-factor likelihood of confusion test used in the Ninth Circuit.[104]

[b]—Nominative Fair Use

Nominative fair use occurs where the defendant has used the plaintiff's mark to describe or comment on the plaintiff's product, even if the defendant's ultimate goal is to describe his own product.[105] Nominative fair use lies outside the strictures of trademark law, because it does not implicate the source-identification function that is the purpose of a trademark.[106] To establish a nominative fair use defense, a defendant must prove the following three elements:

(1) the plaintiff's product or service in question must be one not readily identifiable without use of the trademark;

(2) only so much of the mark or marks may be used as is reasonably necessary to identify the plaintiff's product or service; and

(3) the user must do nothing that would, in conjunction with the mark, suggest sponsorship or endorsement by the trademark holder.[107]

A nominative fair use analysis *replaces* the likelihood of confusion test. Thus in the case in which the estate of Princess Diana alleged that memorabilia infringed her post mortem rights of publicity and under the Lanham Act, the Ninth Circuit conducted a nominative fair use analysis and found no infringement under the Lanham Act.[108]

---

104   *AMC, Inc. v. Sleekcraft Boats*, 599 F.2d 341 (9th Cir. 1979).

105   *Id.* See also:

Second Circuit: Lohan v. Perez, 2013 U.S. Dist. LEXIS 24049, 2013 WL 630100 (E.D.N.Y. Feb. 21, 2013) (use of celebrity's name in a song protected under First Amendment).

Ninth Circuit: New Kids on the Block v. News America Publishing, Inc., 971F.2d 302, 308 (9th Cir. 1992).

106   *Cairns*, 292 F.3d at 1150.

107   *Cairns*, 292 F.3d at 1150 (citing *New Kids v. News America Publishing, Inc.*, 971 F.2d 302, 308 (9th Cir. 1992)).

108   *Cairns*, 292 F.3d at 1154-1155.

[5]—Copyright Preemption

Under the Copyright Act, state law claims are preempted by federal copyright law.[109]

---

109   17 U.S.C. § 301(a). Preemption with respect to other laws

(a) On and after January 1, 1978, all legal or equitable rights that are equivalent to any of the exclusive rights within the general scope of copyright as specified by section 106 in works of authorship that are fixed in a tangible medium of expression and come within the subject matter of copyright as specified by sections 102 and 103, whether created before or after that date and whether published or unpublished, are governed exclusively by this title. Thereafter, no person is entitled to any such right or equivalent right in any such work under the common law or statutes of any State.

(b) Nothing in this title annuls or limits any rights or remedies under the common law or statutes of any State with respect to —

(1) subject matter that does not come within the subject matter of copyright as specified by sections 102 and 103, including works of authorship not fixed in any tangible medium of expression; or

(2) any cause of action arising from undertakings commenced before January 1, 1978;

(3) activities violating legal or equitable rights that are not equivalent to any of the exclusive rights within the general scope of copyright as specified by section 106; or

(4) State and local landmarks, historic preservation, zoning, or building codes, relating to architectural works protected under section 102(a)(8).

(c) With respect to sound recordings fixed before February 15, 1972, any rights or remedies under the common law or statutes of any State shall not be annulled or limited by this title until February 15, 2067. The preemptive provisions of subsection (a) shall apply to any such rights and remedies pertaining to any cause of action arising from undertakings commenced on and after February 15, 2067. Notwithstanding the provisions of section 303, no sound recording fixed before February 15, 1972, shall be subject to copyright under this title before, on, or after February 15, 2067.

(d) Nothing in this title annuls or limits any rights or remedies under any other Federal statute.

(e) The scope of Federal preemption under this section is not affected by the adherence of the United States to the Berne Convention or the satisfaction of obligations of the United States thereunder.

(f)(1) On or after the effective date set forth in section 610(a) of the Visual Artists Rights Act of 1990, all legal or equitable rights that are equivalent to any of the rights conferred by section 106A with respect to works of visual art to which the rights conferred by section 106A apply are governed exclusively by section 106A and section 113(d) and the provisions of this title relating to such sections. Thereafter, no person is entitled to any such right or equivalent right in any work of visual art under the common law or statutes of any State.3

(2) Nothing in paragraph (1) annuls or limits any rights or remedies under the common law or statutes of any State with respect to —

(A) any cause of action from undertakings commenced before the effective date set forth in section 610(a) of the Visual Artists Rights Act of 1990;

(B) activities violating legal or equitable rights that are not equivalent to any of the rights conferred by section 106A with respect to works of visual art; or

Many right of publicity disputes involve copyrighted works—for example, a sound recording that is claimed to violate a singer's right of publicity in the distinctive sound of his voice,[110] or a copyrighted photograph that is claimed to embody a right of publicity infringement.[111]

In the Ninth Circuit, the courts use a two-part test to determine whether a state law claim such as a right of publicity claim is preempted by the Copyright Act.[112] First, the court determines whether the subject matter of the state law claim falls within the subject matter of copyright.[113] Second, assuming that the work is accorded copyright protection, the court must determine whether the rights asserted under state law are equivalent to the exclusive rights of a copyright holder under the Copyright Act.[114]

(C) activities violating legal or equitable rights which extend beyond the life of the author.

110   *Laws v. Sony Music Entertainment, Inc.*, 448 F.3d 1134 (9th Cir. 2006), *cert. denied* 549 U.S. 1252 (2007).

111   *Toney v. L'Oreal USA, Inc.*, 384 F.3d 486 (7th Cir. 2004).

112   See *Laws v. Sony Music Entertainment, Inc.*, 448 F.3d 1134, 1137-1138 (9th Cir. 2006).

113   For this analysis, the court looks to section 102 of the Copyright Act, which describes the types of works subject to copyright protection.17 U.S.C. § 102 states:

§ 102. Subject matter of copyright: In general

(a) Copyright protection subsists, in accordance with this title, in original works of authorship fixed in any tangible medium of expression, now known or later developed, from which they can be perceived, reproduced, or otherwise communicated, either directly or with the aid of a machine or device. Works of authorship include the following categories:

(1) literary works;

(2) musical works, including any accompanying words;

(3) dramatic works, including any accompanying music;

(4) pantomimes and choreographic works;

(5) pictorial, graphic, and sculptural works;

(6) motion pictures and other audiovisual works;

(7) sound recordings; and

(8) architectural works.

(b) In no case does copyright protection for an original work of authorship extend to any idea, procedure, process, system, method of operation, concept, principle, or discovery, regardless of the form in which it is described, explained, illustrated, or embodied in such work.

114   See 17 U.S.C. § 106:

§ 106. Exclusive rights in copyrighted works

A singer alleged that the copyright owners of a recording the plaintiff had made licensed a "sample" of her vocal performance without her permission, and that the resulting use violated the singer's right of publicity.[115] With regard to the first prong of the pre-emption test, the Court had no difficulty finding that the sound recording fell within the definition of protected subject matter. With respect to the second prong, the court compared the "voice imitation" right of publicity cases with the plaintiff's claim.[116] The court noted that the plaintiff was not actually complaining about any imitation of her voice. Instead, she alleged that a true recording of her voice was licensed without her consent. Because the use was licensed, the plaintiff's claims were the equivalent of a copyright infringement claim, and did not have the "extra element" of a claim for right of publicity.[117]

Subject to sections 107 through 122, the owner of copyright under this title has the exclusive rights to do and to authorize any of the following:

(1) to reproduce the copyrighted work in copies or phonorecords;

(2) to prepare derivative works based upon the copyrighted work;

(3) to distribute copies or phonorecords of the copyrighted work to the public by sale or other transfer of ownership, or by rental, lease, or lending;

(4) in the case of literary, musical, dramatic, and choreographic works, pantomimes, and motion pictures and other audiovisual works, to perform the copyrighted work publicly;

(5) in the case of literary, musical, dramatic, and choreographic works, pantomimes, and pictorial, graphic, or sculptural works, including the individual images of a motion picture or other audiovisual work, to display the copyrighted work publicly; and

(6) in the case of sound recordings, to perform the copyrighted work publicly by means of a digital audio transmission.

115   *Laws v. Sony Music Entertainment, Inc.*, 448 F.3d 1134 (9th Cir. 2006), *cert. denied* 549 U.S. 1252 (2007).

116   *Waits v. Frito-Lay, Inc.*, 978 F.2d 1093 (9th Cir. 1992); *Midler v. Ford Motor Co.*, 849 F.2d 460 (9th Cir. 1988).

117   *Id.* The Seventh Circuit reached a similar result. *Toney v. L'Oreal USA, Inc.*, 384 F.3d 486 (7th Cir. 2004). In *Toney*, a model posed for a photo to be used on packaging for hair products. When the photo was later used beyond the scope of the original agreement, the model alleged a violation of her right of publicity. The court held that her claim was preempted under copyright law because she had not asserted that her "likeness" in the photo rose to the level of a celebrity property right. It was merely her likeness captured in a copyrighted photograph, so the gravamen of her claim was that a photo was used without permission, a copyright argument that preempted any right of publicity claims.

In *Baltimore Orioles, Inc. v. Major League Baseball Players Ass'n*, another Seventh Circuit decision, the court affirmed the decision on ownership of copyrights in telecasts, ruling the team owners to be copyright owners because telecasts of baseball games were works made for hire and the owners' copyrights in the telecasts preempted the players' alleged rights of publicity in their performances. *Baltimore Orioles, Inc. v. Major League Baseball Players Ass'n*, 805 F.2d 663 (7th Cir. 1986).

Given that right of publicity claims require additional elements, and that such extra elements would normally defeat copyright preemption, these cases teach that care should be taken in the pleadings and arguments to assert the "extra elements" of a right of publicity claim.

[6]—Common-Law Causes of Action Under Restatement (Second) of Torts and Restatement (Third) of Unfair Competition

In jurisdictions that do not have applicable right of publicity statutes, the common-law jurisprudence may follow section 652C of the Restatement (Second) of Torts, entitled "Appropriation of Name and Likeness." It states in relevant part:

652C Appropriation of Name or Likeness. One who appropriates to his own use or benefit the name or likeness of another is subject to liability to the other for invasion of his privacy.

Comments:

a. The interest protected by the rule stated in this Section is the interest of the individual in the exclusive use of his own identity, in so far as it is represented by his name or likeness, and in so far as the use may be of benefit to him or to others. Although the protection of his personal feelings against mental distress is an important factor leading to a recognition of the rule, the right created by it is in the nature of a property right, for the exercise of which an exclusive license may be given to a third person, which will entitle the licensee to maintain an action to protect it.

b. *How invaded.* The common form of invasion of privacy under the rule here stated is the appropriation and use of the plaintiff's name or likeness to advertise the defendant's business or product, or for some similar commercial purpose. Apart from statute, however, the rule stated is not limited to commercial appropriation. It applies also when the defendant makes use of the plaintiff's name or likeness for his own purposes and benefit, even though the use is not a commercial one, and even though the benefit sought to be obtained is not a pecuniary one. Statutes in some states have, however, limited the liability to commercial uses of the name or likeness.[118]

Some common-law jurisdictions may follow the Restatement (Third) of the Law of Unfair Competition §§ 46-49, which states in relevant part:

§ 46 Appropriation of the Commercial Value of a Person's Identity: the Right of Publicity.

---

118   Restatement (Second) of Torts, § 652C.

One who appropriates the commercial value of a person's identity by using without consent the person's name, likeness, or other indicia of identity for purposes of trade is subject to liability for the relief appropriate under the rules stated in §§ 48 and 49.

§ 47 Use for Purposes of Trade

The name, likeness, and other indicia of a person's identity are used "for purposes of trade" under the rule stated in § 46 if they are used in advertising the user's goods or services, or are placed on merchandise marketed by the user, or are used in connection with services rendered by the user. However, use "for purposes of trade" does not ordinarily include the use of a person's identity in news reporting, commentary, entertainment, works of fiction or nonfiction, or in advertising that is incidental to such uses.

[7]—Liability for Deceptive Advertising Under the Federal Trade Commission Act—"Infomercials"

Celebrity spokespersons and endorsers may incur individual liability for participation in advertisements or for endorsement of products that are found to be deceptive and in violation of Sections 5(a) and 12 of the Federal Trade Commission Act ("FTCA").[119]

Under the FTCA, an individual may be subject to injunctive relief and can even be held personally liable for restitution if the FTC can prove that he or she "participated directly" in the deceptive advertising acts in question or had authority to control them.[120] There is also the potential for "endorser liability." The FTC premises its "endorser" theory of liability on the FTC Guides Concerning Use of Endorsements and Testimonials in Advertising.[121]

According to the FTC Guides, an endorsement is "any advertising message...which message consumers are likely to believe reflects the opinions, beliefs, findings, or experience of a party other than the sponsoring advertiser."[122] The Guides state that "endorsements must always reflect the honest opinions, findings, beliefs, or experience of the endorser, and they may not contain any representations which would be deceptive, or could not be substantiated if made directly by the advertiser.[123]

---

119   15 U.S.C. §§ 45(a) and 52.2.

120   *Garvey,* 383 F.3d at 900.

121   16 C.F.R. § 255.0(b).

122   *Id.*

123   16 C.F.R. § 255.1(a).

In order to prove "participation" liability, the FTC must show that the individual making the endorsement had actual knowledge of the material misrepresentations, was recklessly indifferent to the truth or falsity of a misrepresentation, or had an awareness of a high probability of fraud along with an intentional avoidance of the truth.[124]

In the leading case,[125] a former baseball star became embroiled in litigation and potential personal liability in connection with his endorsements of a weight loss product in a direct-response, long-form television advertisement, or "infomercial."[126] The court found that the defendant's participation in the infomercial and the statements and endorsements he made were based on some reasonable level of due diligence he conducted and his own experience with the product. Therefore, he was not liable, even if the information provided to him by the manufacturer failed to constitute valid substantiation for the claims made in the infomercial, according to governing FTC standards.[127]

What appears to be unspoken in *Garvey* is the fact that consumers are well aware that celebrities who endorse products are paid for that endorsement. Notwithstanding the result in *Garvey*, the mere fact that a celebrity endorser was the subject of an FTC action and had potential personal liability, including restitution, should put celebrities on notice that they have a responsibility to investigate the basis for any claims they are asked to make on behalf of a product, and that they could incur personal liability if such claims are deceptive.[128]

---

124   *Id.*

125   *FTC v. Garvey*, 383 F.3d 891 (9th Cir. 2004).

126   "Direct response" describes the premise that viewers of the advertisement phone in their orders in response to the ad, typically using a toll free "1-800" phone number, rather than the approach used by traditional advertising which creates consumer demand but depends on consumers making the actual purchase later, typically at a retail location. "Long form" advertisements are the commercial productions that air for a full 30 minutes or even a full hour, instead of the usual 30 second or one minute advertisement "short form" format.

127   Subsequently, the FTC filed suit against the manufacturer, alleging that the defendants "undertook deceptive acts or practices and issued false and misleading advertising of a food, drug, device, service, or cosmetic in violation of Sections 5(a) and 12 of the Federal Trade Commission Act, 15 U.S.C. §§ 45(a) and 52.2. *Id.*, 383 F.3d at 895. The FTC sought an injunction, and equitable relief aimed at financially redressing consumers' injuries, and costs. A Stipulated Final Order entered in the case prohibited the manufacturers from making certain representations without reliable scientific evidence, and required them to pay $10 million to the FTC. *Id.*, 383 F.3d at 896.

128   See generally, *A Brief Overview of the Federal Trade Commission's Investigative and Law Enforcement Authority*, available at http://www.ftc.gov/ogc/brfovrvw.shtm. The FTC's Revised Endorsement and Testimonial Guides, which also include guidelines covering interactive and online marketing such as social media and blogging, can be found at 16 C.F.R. 255, and is also available at http://www.ftc.gov/os/2009/10/091005revisedendorsementguides.pdf.

[8]—Food and Drug Administration (FDA) Regulation of Celebrity Drug Advertising

While most of the advertising regulation affecting celebrities occurs via the FTC, in at least one case of social media advertising, the Food and Drug Administration (FDA) issued a Warning Letter to the manufacturer of a drug that was the subject of paid social media advertising by celebrity Kim Kardashian.[129]

The issue was not that the social media post failed to disclose it was sponsored, in fact the text disclosed that Ms. Kardashian was "partnering" with the manufacturer. Instead, the issue was that the post failed to include the lengthy disclaimers and warnings that are required to accompany drug advertising. Here is the original Instagram post—a short time later it reappeared but with lengthy drug warnings included, arguably interfering with the original "personal candid message" intent:

> "OMG. Have you heard about this? As you guys know my #morningsickness has been pretty bad. I tried changing things about my lifestyle, like my diet, but nothing helped, so I talked to my doctor. He prescribed me #Diclegis, and I felt a lot better and most importantly, it's been studied and there was no increased risk to the baby. I'm so excited and happy with my results that I'm partnering with Duchesnay USA to raise awareness about treating morning sickness. If you have morning sickness, be safe and sure to ask your doctor about the pill with the pregnant woman on it and find out more."

§7.04   Leading Right of Publicity Cases

The right of publicity is a still-developing area of the law. The leading cases often have an unusual, highly instructive element or aspect to them. They are not typically based on a straightforward, unauthorized use of a celebrity's name, image, likeness or voice for commercial advertising purposes.

[1]—Contours and Expansion of the Right of Publicity

Nuances in the decisions abound due to differing conceptions of, for example, what constitutes a commercial use or whether the reference to the celebrity actually evoked the celebrity's identity or persona. The body of leading cases is instructive and therefore a summary, grouped into types of uses and sorted by date within each type of use to aid in following the development of the law, is presented below.

---

129   See FDA Warning Letter to Duchesnay, Inc. regarding Kim Kardashian Social Media Post, available at http://www.fda.gov/downloads/Drugs/GuidanceComplianceRegulatoryInformation/EnforcementActivitiesbyFDA/ WarningLettersandNoticeofViolationLetterstoPharmaceuticalCompanies/UCM457961.pdf.

[a]—Evocation of Personas or Nicknames

A televised tobacco advertisement evoked the identity of a well-known racing driver by depicting the driver's readily identifiable car, but not the driver's likeness.[130] The Ninth Circuit found that the driver was "identifiable" because the lower court had:

> "wholly fail[ed] to attribute proper significance to the distinctive decorations appearing on the car. As pointed out earlier, these markings were not only peculiar to the plaintiff's cars but they caused some persons to think the car in question was plaintiff's and to infer that the person driving the car was the plaintiff."[131]

The television entertainer Johnny Carson sued a Michigan company over use of the phrase "Here's Johnny" for portable toilets.[132] The Sixth Circuit found for the plaintiff on the Michigan common-law right of publicity claim, noting that other courts have found that a nickname can serve as an identity.[133]

A printed beer advertisement featured a drawing of an "old time" baseball game.[134] The drawing was based on a 1947 photo that included the plaintiff, whose face was obscured, but whose pitching stance was unique and identifiable. The Ninth Circuit held that even though the pitcher's face was obscured, it was the unique pitching stance that was recognizable.

[b]—Look-Alikes

In *Allen v. National Video, Inc.*,[135] defendants hired a Woody Allen look-alike to pose for photos promoting their video rental stores. In ruling for the plaintiff, the court looked to cases holding that any recognizable likeness, not just an actual photograph of the plaintiff, may qualify as a "portrait or picture" under the New York Civil Rights Law.

---

130 *Motschenbacher v. R.J. Reynolds Tobacco Co.*, 498 F.2d 821 (9th Cir. 1974).

131 *Id.*, 498 F.2d at 827.

132 *Johnny Carson v. Here's Johnny Portable Toilets, Inc.*, 810 F.2d 104 (6th Cir. 1987).

133 *Hirsch v. S.C. Johnson & Son, Inc.*, 90 Wis.2d 379, 280 N.W.2d 129 (1979) (use of the nickname "Crazylegs" for a shaving gel violated the right of publicity of Crazylegs Hirsch).

134 *Newcombe v. Adolf Coors Co.*, 157 F.3d 686 (9th Cir. 1998). See also, *Newton v. Thomason*, 22 F.3d 1455 (9th Cir. 1994) (naming a television character after plaintiff not a violation of right of publicity or trademark rights).

135 *Allen v. National Video, Inc.*, 610 F. Supp. 612 (S.D.N.Y. 1985). See: *Ali v. Playgirl*, 447 F. Supp. 723 (S.D.N.Y. 1978) (clearly recognizable drawing of plaintiff Muhammad Ali portrayed as a boxer in ring, captioned "The Greatest," constitutes "portrait or picture"); *Onassis v. Christian Dior N.Y. Inc.*, 122 Misc.2d 603, 472 N.Y.S.2d 254 (1983) (Jacqueline Kennedy Onassis won an injunction against an advertisement featuring a model who was made up to look like her).

[c]—Sound-Alikes and Sound Recordings

Ford produced a series of advertisements featuring distinctive and famous singers whose songs were played in the background.[136] Well-known singer and actress Bette Midler had declined Ford's invitation to participate in the campaign. Ford then hired one of Midler's backup signers to record a performance that, when broadcast, sounded like Midler's voice. Midler brought an action for violation of her common-law right of publicity.[137] The court held that when voice is a sufficient indication of a celebrity's identity, the right of publicity protects against its imitation for unauthorized commercial purposes.[138]

---

136   *Midler v. Ford Motor Co.*, 849 F.2d 460 (9th Cir. 1988).

137   Bringing a common law action allowed Midler to argue that her "identity" included her unique singing voice.

138   Four years later, singer Tom Waits, who has a distinctively raspy voice, had a policy not to endorse products, brought a claim for infringement. Despite warnings from counsel, the defendant hired a Waits soundalike for an ad. Waits filed suit, the Ninth Circuit affirmed judgment in his favor. *Waits v. Frito-Lay, Inc.*, 978 F.2d 1093 (9th Cir. 1992).

A television advertisement used a vocal imitation of the "swing" singer Louis Prima, performing a song closely affiliated with the plaintiff. Notable in the case is the fact that the musical composition itself had fallen into the public domain. Nevertheless, the defendant was held liable for violating the plaintiff's right of publicity under New Jersey law. *Prima v. Darden Restaurants, Inc.*, 78 F. Supp.2d 337 (D.N.J. 2000). *Compare, Nancy Sinatra v. Goodyear Tire & Rubber Co.*, 435 F.2d 711 (9th Cir. 1970) (Nancy Sinatra had not established any personal trademark rights in her recording of "Boots" song used in commercial under license from copyright owner).

Astrud Oliveira, the singer widely known for her 1964 recording of "The Girl from Ipanema," sued Frito-Lay, which had duly licensed the recording from the copyright owners. In dismissing the plaintiff's trademark claims, the court stated that dismissal was without prejudice to plaintiff's right to re-plead her right of publicity claims under the New York Civil Rights Law. *Oliveira v. Frito-Lay, Inc.*, 251 F.3d 56 (2d Cir. 2001) (noting "a few famous examples" of recordings that, unlike the plaintiff's recording of "Girl from Ipanema," achieved trademark status, including the William Tell Overture for the Lone Ranger; "Sweet Georgia Brown" for the Harlem Globetrotters; and numerous advertising jingles including "See the U.S.A. in Your Chevrolet; "You Deserve a Break Today—at McDonald's;" "Double your pleasure, double your fun with . . . Doublemint Gum;" "Um, Um, good; Um, Um, good; that's what Campbell's soups are, um, um, good;" as well as the theme songs of the "I Love Lucy" show, "The Honeymooners," "Sesame Street," "Mr. Rogers Neighborhood," and "The Sopranos."). *Id.* at n.1.

In *Laws v. Sony Music Entertainment*, plaintiff claimed that her voice and name were misappropriated when a sample of her voice was licensed for use without her authorization. Laws v. Sony Music Entertainment, Inc., 448 F.3d 1134 (9th Cir. 2006). Distinguishing the *Midler* and *Waits* cases, the Ninth Circuit affirmed the lower court's grant of summary judgment on the grounds of copyright preemption, noting that in the instant case, there was no "imitation" of plaintiff's voice, but instead a licensed use of a work of copyright authorship. *Id.* at 1146.

The Third Circuit affirmed a grant of summary judgment to the estate of deceased NFL Films narrator John Facenda. The plaintiff's estate brought a right of publicity claim against the defendant based on the use of a narration sound clip of Facenda's unique booming voice in connection with a program promoting the "Madden NFL 06" video game. The court concluded that although the defendant owned the copyright in the original sound clip, its

[d]—The Expansion Of "Identity"

In *White v. Samsung Electronics America, Inc.*,[139] Samsung planned an ad campaign satirizing a future society where the one reliable constant was the innovation and quality of Samsung electronic products. One of the ads featured a futuristic "Wheel of Fortune" set in which a robot, dressed in a blonde wig and elegant gown, turned the game show letters. Although the robot bore no facial features resembling Ms. White, one of the hosts of the show, she believed it clearly evoked her identity. She sued for violations of her common-law and statutory right of publicity under California law and claims under the Lanham Act, and prevailed on her common-law claim.

In a significant expansion of what constitutes "identity" under the California common law right of publicity, the Court noted that:

> the "*Motschenbacher, Midler,* and *Carson* cases teach the impossibility of treating the right of publicity as guarding only against a laundry list of specific means of appropriating identity. A rule which says that the right of publicity can be infringed only through the use of nine different methods of appropriating identity merely challenges the clever advertising strategist to come up with the tenth . . . the identities of the most popular celebrities are not only the most attractive for advertisers, but also the easiest to evoke without resorting to obvious means such as name, likeness, or voice."[140]

In *Wendt v. Host International, Inc.*,[141] a chain of airport lounges installed life-size animatronic talking puppets sitting at the bar, dressed like and looking like the "Norm" and "Cliff" characters from the "Cheers" television show. Although Paramount Pictures, owners of the copyright in "Cheers," had granted licenses to the defendant for this use, the actors who portrayed the characters claimed that notwithstanding the license the defendant obtained, their right of publicity had been violated.[142]

---

use for product endorsement was beyond the scope of the rights that had been acquired from the plaintiff when he was employed by N.F.L. Films, Inc. to provide voiceovers. Facenda v. N.F.L. Films, Inc., 542 F.3d 1007 (3d Cir. 2008).

139 *White v. Samsung Electronics America, Inc.*, 971 F.2d 1395, 1398 (9th Cir. 1992).

140 Id.

141 *Wendt v. Host International, Inc.*, 50 F.3d 18 (9th Cir. 1995).

142 In holding for the plaintiffs, the court remanded for a determination as to whether the puppets were sufficiently "similar" to the plaintiffs to constitute their likenesses under right of publicity law.

[e]—Imitations of Celebrity Performances

In two cases, Apple Corps, the corporation that, at the time, held the trademark and right of publicity rights to both the group and the individual members of The Beatles, prevailed against live-performance lookalike/soundalike groups based on the Beatles. In *Apple Corps Ltd. v. Leber*,[143] the court held that the producers of the live show "Beatlemania" commercially appropriated the Beatles' persona, good will, and popularity. Despite the additional content consisting of film montages and costume changes that depicted events relating to the 1960s, the court found the production to be "virtually a complete appropriation of the Beatles' 'persona,'" at least in a qualitative sense.

> "The primary purpose of Beatlemania, live on stage, was the commercial exploitation of the Beatles' persona, goodwill and popularity. It's true that the mixed-media presentation was a top-quality performance, organized, put together, and presented by some very highly talented and capable persons, but such only provided the setting for what was a fantasy concert by persons who so accurately imitated the Beatles in concert that the audience, according to contemporary viewers, in great part suspended their disbelief and fell prey to the illusion that they were actually viewing the Beatles in performance."[144]

In 1993, Apple sued a performing group known as "1964 as the Beatles" which toured throughout North America, offering a recreation of a Beatles concert from the years 1964 to 1966.[145] The group imitated the overall appearances, hairstyles, dress, mannerisms, voices, equipment and musical performances of The Beatles.[146]

The right of publicity claim was brought under the Tennessee Personal Rights Protection Act. Under that Act, the court found that the use of the look-alike photos on the simulated "Hard Day's Night" album cover violated the statute. In granting a partial injunction, the court did not enjoin the performance itself, but instead limited the injunction to (1) any use of the names "John," "Paul," "George" and "Ringo"

---

143   *Apple Corps Ltd. v. Leber*, 229 U.S.P.Q. 1015, 1017 (Cal. Sup. 1986).

144   The damages, which were based on a long successful run of "Beatlemania," were assessed at 12.5% of gross income and amounted to over $7.5 million.

145   *Apple Corps Ltd. v. A.D.P.R. Inc.*, 843 F. Supp. 342 (M.D. Tenn. 1993).

146   On stage, the group's members referred to each other as "John," "Paul," "George," and "Ringo," adopt Liverpool accents, and performed only songs that the Beatles recorded or performed. In addition, defendants placed the Beatles' logo on the group's bass drum, with "1964 as" written above the logo in small print. Defendants also marketed merchandise in connection with the show. The defendants also used in advertising an album cover that was closely modeled after the Beatles album cover for "A Hard Day's Night," and which was designed to show how similar the performers appeared to the real Beatles.

(2) any use of any likeness of the Beatles in advertising or promotion; and (3) any use of the name "The Beatles" in advertising or promotion.[147]

[f]—Titles of Movies and Songs

Actress Ginger Rogers brought right of publicity and false endorsement claims over a Federico Fellini film entitled "Ginger and Fred."[148] The plaintiff alleged that the title of the film falsely implied that she endorsed or sponsored the film. The Second Circuit developed what is known as the *Rogers* test: a title will be protected under the First Amendment unless it has "no artistic relevance" to the underlying work or, if there is artistic relevance, the title "explicitly misleads as to the source or the content of the work."[149]

As noted above, the *Rogers* First Amendment test is used by courts not only with respect to titles, but also to trademarks that appear within a film, and to artistic works other than films.[150]

[g]—Motion Picture Advertising

Pinup model Bettie Page sued a video cassette distributor who used her image in advertising for videos of two films in which Page starred in the 1950s.[151] The images were new artworks depicting Page, not stills from the movies themselves. Page alleged violations of California statutory and common-law right of publicity. The court held that the uses were non infringing because they were incidental to the constitutionally protected publication of the videos, stating that "[p]romotional

---

147   *Id.*, 843 F. Supp. at 349-350.

148   *Rogers v. Grimaldi*, 875 F.2d 994 (2d Cir. 1989). The film was the story of an Italian couple who performed in remote venues, and the title was clearly ironic in referring to the glamorous Hollywood duo of Ginger Rogers and Fred Astaire.

149   *Id.*, 875 F.2d at 999. Here, the court affirmed the defense motions for summary judgment granted by the lower court because the movie title did not constitute false advertising, was closely related to the content of the film, and was not a disguised advertisement for sale of goods or services. *Id.* at 1005. See also, *Eastland Music Group, LLV v. Lionsgate Entertainment, Inc.*, 2012 WL 2953188 (N.D. Ill. July 19, 2012) (Movie title "50/50" not a trademark violation of plaintiff's "Phifty-50" mark under *Rogers* test).

Rosa Parks, a heroine of the civil rights movement, successfully brought an action for false endorsement and right of publicity. *Parks v. LaFace Records*, 329 F.3d 437 (6th Cir. 2003). At issue was the title of a song called "Rosa Parks." While the court applied various First Amendment tests in order to acknowledge the importance of free expression in artistic works, it ruled "reasonable persons could conclude that there is no relationship of any kind between Rosa Parks' name and the content of the song."

150   See § 2.12[4][c] *supra*.

151   *Page v. Something Weird Video*, 960 F. Supp. 1438 (C.D. Cal. 1996).

speech may be noncommercial if it advertises an activity itself protected by the First Amendment."[152] Citing *Guglielmi v. Spelling-Goldberg*,[153] the court noted "it would be illogical to allow defendants to exhibit the film but effectively preclude any advance discussion or promotion of their lawful enterprises."[154]

[h]—Parody Comic Books, Caricatures, and Baseball Cards

The producer of parody baseball cards featuring caricatures of Major League players with humorous commentary about their careers prevailed on a declaratory judgment on First Amendment grounds.[155] Musicians Edgar and Johnny Winter sued over grotesque comic book characters that appeared to be loosely based on their names and unique albino appearances.[156] The Supreme Court of California held that the comics constituted fair use under the "transformative use" First Amendment analysis the court had announced in *Comedy III Productions, Inc.*[157]

The Eastern District of Pennsylvania ruled that parody cartoons of wrestling stars printed on t-shirts along with parody WWE slogans constituted a transformative fair use.[158] The court stated, "The graphics are not literal depictions . . . but caricatures of WWE's wrestling characters. Big Dog's use of dogs to poke fun at celebrities and societal norms is an important form of entertainment and expressive commentary that deserves First Amendment protection."[159]

A comic book entitled "Spawn" featured an unsavory character, "Tony Twist," allegedly named after a famous professional hockey player known for his "tough" persona.[160] Although the court acknowledged that the comic character and the real hockey player bore little resemblance towards one another, it applied a test determining that the "predominant use" of the celebrity persona was commercial, and therefore it ran afoul of the Missouri right of publicity. The court did not take into

---

152   *Id.*, 960 F. Supp. At 1443.

153   *Guglielmi v. Spelling-Goldberg Productions*, 25 Cal.3d 860, 160 Cal. Rptr. 352, 360 (1979).

154   *Page v. Something Weird Video*, 960 F. Supp. at 1444.

155   *Cardtoons, L.C. v. Major League Baseball Players Ass'n*, 95 F.3d 959 (10th Cir. 1996).

156   *Winter v. DC Comics*, 30 Cal.4th 881, 69 P.3d 473 (Cal. 2003).

157   *Comedy III Productions, Inc. v. Gary Saderup, Inc.*, 25 Cal.4th 387, 106 Cal. Rptr.2d 126 (2001).

158   *World Wrestling Federation Entertainment, Inc. v. Big Dog Sportswear Holdings, Inc.*, 280 F. Supp.2d 413 (W.D. Pa. 2003).

159   *Id.*, 280 F. Supp.2d at 445.

160   *Doe v. TCI Cablevision*, 110 S.W.3d 363 (Mo. 2003) (*en banc*).

account, as other courts have, the reality that uses protected by the First Amendment may still occur in "for profit" contexts.[161]

[i]—Sports

The Seventh Circuit ruled that the team owners owned the copyright in telecasts of baseball games because they were works made for hire.[162] The owners' copyright of telecasts preempted the players' right of publicity in their performances.

To celebrate a Super Bowl victory, a newspaper distributed posters of football hero Joe Montana without his permission.[163] The court held that Montana's claim for violation of his right of publicity must fail because the poster was newsworthy and was published "relatively contemporaneous[ly]" with the news event.

The Eighth Circuit held that the use of baseball players' names and statistics in a fantasy major league baseball game fell within First Amendment protections.[164]

[j]—Merchandise Catalogs

The fashion retailer Abercrombie & Fitch produced a sales catalog entitled the "Abercrombie & Fitch Quarterly."[165] One catalog had a "surfing" theme, including stories about surfing, and featured a vintage photo of plaintiffs, well-known surfers, alongside advertisements for shirts similar to those depicted in the photograph. The court held that the catalog's combination of sales advertising and editorial content did not immunize the defendant from plaintiff's claims under California's right of publicity and under the Lanham Act.[166]

---

161   For example, the Ninth Circuit ruled in favor of the defendant magazine publisher where the magazine's use of Dustin Hoffman's persona in editorial content was protected speech. *Hoffman v. Capital Cities/ABC*, 255 F.3d 1180 (9th Cir. 2001).

162   *Baltimore Orioles, Inc. v. Major League Baseball Players Ass'n*, 805 F.2d 663 (7th Cir. 1986).

163   *Montana v. San Jose Mercury News*, 34 Cal. App.4th 790, 40 Cal. Rptr.2d 639 (1995). See also:

Second Circuit: Namath v. Sports Illustrated, 48 A.D.2d 487, 371 N.Y.S.2d 10 (1975) (photo of football player Joe Namath was featured on the cover of Sports Illustrated and later used in advertisements to sell subscriptions. No violation of the New York Civil Rights Law occurred because the initial use of the photo was protected news reporting and the later subscription ads were "merely incidental," referring to the contents of the magazine).

Ninth Circuit: Gionfriddo v. Major League Baseball, 94 Cal. App.4th 400, 114 Cal. Rptr.2d 307 (2001) (use of former players' names and statistics constitutionally protected).

164   *C.B.C. Distribution and Marketing, Inc. v. Major League Baseball Advanced Media, L.P.*, 505 F.3d 818 (8th Cir. 2007).

165   *Downing v. Abercrombie & Fitch*, 265 F.3d 994 (9th Cir. 2001).

166   *Id.*, 265 F.3d at 1007-1008.

[k]—Statements and Photos on Magazine Covers

Cher, the well-known singer, granted an interview to a freelance writer for an interview she and the writer intended to be published in a celebrity gossip magazine.[167] The freelance writer, without the singer's knowledge, sold the interview to two less reputable magazines.[168] Cher sued, alleging breach of contract, unfair competition, misappropriation of name and likeness, misappropriation of right to publicity, and violations of the Lanham Act.[169]

With respect to the claim against *Star*, the court found no infringement because the statements could not reasonably be construed as endorsements of *Star*. With respect to *Forum*, the court found liability notwithstanding the standard of "knowing and reckless falsity" required under *Time, Inc. v. Hill*,[170] noting:

> "[i]n view of the fact that Cher had intended to "tell" the rival magazine, *Us*, the very words in the interview, and had not "told" *Forum* anything, the advertising copy was patently false. This kind of mendacity is not protected by the First Amendment, and those defendants responsible for the placement and circulation of the challenged advertising copy must look elsewhere for their protection."[171]

A case before the Ninth Circuit featured the unauthorized use of an actor's photo in a bathing suit on the cover of a sexually oriented magazine. The actor brought claims including common-law and statutory right of publicity, and false light invasion of privacy, alleging that the bare-chested photo of him on the cover along with the salacious headlines gave the false impression that he had posed nude for the magazine. The actor believed that such a false impression not only misappropriated his right of publicity for advertising purposes, but also invaded his privacy by presenting him in a false light to the public.[172] The court ruled that the magazine cover constituted

---

167   *Cher v. Forum International, Ltd.*, 692 F.2d 634 (9th Cir. 1982).

168   *Star* ran the article with cover headers stating "Exclusive Series," followed by "Cher: My life, my husbands and my many, many men." *Forum* ran the article with advertising that used a photo of Cher and statements that "There are certain things that Cher won't tell *People* and would never tell *Us*. She tells *Forum*." The *Forum* ad also stated "So join Cher and *Forum's* hundreds of thousands of other adventurous readers today." *Id.*, 692 F.2d at 638-639.

169   *Id.*

170   *Time, Inc. v. Hill*, 385 U.S. 374, 87 S.Ct. 534, 17 L.Ed.2d 456 (1967).

171   *Cher v. Forum International*, 692 F.2d at 639.

172   *Solano v. Playgirl, Inc.*, 292 F.3d 1078 (9th Cir. 2002). In fact the actor only appeared in one fully-clothed photo inside the magazine.

a misappropriation of the actor's right of publicity, used to boost sales by falsely implying that the actor himself appeared nude inside the magazine.[173]

[l]—Tabloid Newspapers

The actor Clint Eastwood brought defamation claims against the National Enquirer over the publication of an article entitled "Clint Eastwood in Love Triangle."[174] In addition, Eastwood brought common-law and statutory right of publicity claims arising from television advertisements promoting the tabloid by featuring the defamatory article. In applying the "actual malice" standard of *New York Times Co. v. Sullivan* to the right of publicity claims, the court found that the calculated falsehoods were made with *scienter*.[175]

[m]—Editorial Content and Advertising of Editorial Content

The actor brought another case against the tabloid in 1997.[176] The front page of the magazine had touted an "exclusive interview" with the actor. The interview featured quotes from Eastwood on various personal topics including his new baby and his career, when, in fact, Eastwood never had spoken to the Enquirer. The article was a fabrication concocted by a freelance journalist. Eastwood did not claim the article was defamatory, but claimed that, in publishing the story, the Enquirer misappropriated his right of publicity in order to promote their publication.[177] In affirming the lower court verdict and damages award in favor of Eastwood, the court applied the actual malice standard of *New York Times Co. v. Sullivan* to the right of publicity

---

173 In reversing the lower court's grant of summary judgment to the defendant, the Ninth Circuit applied the Sullivan "actual malice" standard, finding that a triable issue of fact existed as to whether the editors knew that their use of plaintiff on the cover would imply that the actor appeared nude inside the magazine. The court ruled that the exception to California's right of publicity statute for news reporting under § 3344(d) did not apply to the acts of the defendant magazine. Id., 297 F.3d at 1088-1089.

174 *Eastwood v. Superior Court*, 149 Cal. App.3d 409, 198 Cal. Rptr. 342, 352 (1984). Eastwood petitioned the Court of Appeal to issue a writ of mandamus to compel the Superior Court to set aside its order sustaining defendant newspaper's demurrer.

175 The court stated, "[T]he deliberate fictionalization of Eastwood's personality constitutes commercial exploitation, and becomes actionable when it is presented to the reader as if true with the requisite scienter." Because Eastwood's complaint had not pled that the article was published with knowledge or in reckless disregard of its falsity, the court granted leave to amend. Id., 198 Cal. Rptr.2d at 352.

176 *Eastwood v. National Enquirer*, 123 F.2d 1249 (9th Cir. 1997).

177 In addition, Eastwood claimed his fans would think him a hypocrite for giving the Enquirer an exclusive interview about his private life, because he was well known for shunning such publicity especially from tabloids, thus his fans would think he was "washed up" as a movie star if he was courting publicity in a sensationalist tabloid. *Id.*, 123 F.3d at 1256.

claims, and found that the tabloid editors "intended to convey the impression – known by them to be false – that Eastwood willfully submitted to an interview by the Enquirer. This intentional conduct satisfies the 'actual malice' standard, permitting a verdict for Eastwood."[178]

In *Dustin Hoffman v. Capital Cities/ABC*,[179] the actor, who had starred in "Tootsie," a film about a cross-dressing actor, sued L.A. Magazine over a story and photo layout on fashion that used the actor's face without permission in an altered "Tootsie"-like pose, showing him in a dress. In analyzing the actor's several claims, including right of publicity and Lanham Act violations, the court determined that the article constituted noncommercial protected speech, and under the standard of *New York Times Co. v. Sullivan* applicable to public figures, the false statement (which was the implication that Hoffman endorsed the article or the magazine) was merely commentary on celebrity and fashion that did not rise to the level of actual malice.[180]

[n]—Computer Games

Right of publicity cases involving video games have involved the distinctively interactive nature of video games, where the game permits users to interact with the virtual world of the game, selecting among other elements the characters, their appearance and mannerisms, the settings, sounds, and plot.[181] In addition, the Su-

---

178   *Id.*

179   See *Dustin Hoffman v. Capital Cities/ABC, Inc.*, 255 F.3d 1180 (9th Cir. 2001).

180   See also, *Stewart v. Rolling Stone LLC*, 181 Cal. App.4th 664, 105 Cal. Rptr.3d 98 (2010) (class action by musicians whose images appeared in "Indie Rock" magazine gatefold layout enclosed by cigarette advertising. Freedom of press barred musicians' claims.).

181   See:

Supreme Court: Brown v. Entertainment Merchants Ass'n, 564 U.S. 786, 131 S.Ct. 2729, 2733, 180 L.Ed.2d 708 (2011) ("Like the protected books, plays, and movies that preceded them, video games communicate ideas—and even social messages—through many familiar literary devices (such as characters, dialogue, plot and music) and through features distinctive to the medium (*such as the player's interaction with the virtual world.*) (Emphasis added.)

Third Circuit: Hart v. Electronic Arts, Inc., 808 F. Supp.2d 757, 785 (D.N.J. 2011) ("EA's artists created a host of physical characteristic options from which the user may choose. For example, EA artists created the several different hairstyles that can be morphed onto the image.").

Seventh Circuit: Dillinger, LLC v. Electronic Arts Inc., 2011 WL 2457678 (S.D. Ind. June 16, 2011) (describing interactive choices made by users including weapons used by characters in "The Godfather" computer game).

See also, Field, *Copyright, Technology, and Time: Perspectives on "Interactive" as a Term of Art in Copyright Law*, 50 J. Copyright Soc'y 1201 (2003).

preme Court has recognized that video games are expressive works fully entitled to protections of the First Amendment.[182]

Thus, plaintiffs alleging right of publicity infringement by video game producers must overcome first amendment defenses based on the depiction of the individual being transformative as a result of the interactive manipulation of the character by the game user. To determine whether a depiction in a game is transformative, courts have used two leading California cases as benchmarks at opposite poles of the spectrum.[183] The case standing for transformative use of a persona, where the plaintiff's persona is only one of the "raw materials" that contribute to a new and fanciful character, is *Winter v. DC Comics*, in which the California Supreme Court held that a comic book's use of two musicians as inspiration for comic book characters was transformative.[184] The case representing the opposite end of the spectrum, with celebrity images used for purely commercial advantage without any transformative elements, for their very "sum and substance," is *Comedy III Productions, Inc. v. Gary Saderup, Inc.*, in which the California Supreme Court found no transformative elements in a drawing showing the Three Stooges sold on t-shirts.[185]

In *Hart v. Electronic Arts*, a 2013 Third Circuit case, a former college football player sued the producer of the interactive game "NCAA Football" based on allegations that the player was depicted in the game.[186] The game allowed users to interactively select many elements, including members of teams, their appearance, uniforms, playing style, and performance. In adopting California's transformative use test, the Third Circuit found that the digitized plaintiff, like the one in *No Doubt*,[187] was presented accurately and not transformatively, thus infringing his right of publicity.

---

182   See *Brown v. Entertainment Merchants Ass'n*, 564 U.S. 786, 131 S.Ct. 2729, 180 L.Ed.2d 708 (2011).

183   See *No Doubt v. Activision Publishing, Inc.*, 192 Cal. App.4th 1018, 1024, 122 Cal. Rptr.3d 37 (2011).

184   See *Winter v. DC Comics*, 30 Cal. 4th 881, 69 P.3d 473 (2003).

185   See *Comedy III Productions, Inc. v. Gary Saderup, Inc.*, 25 Cal.4th 387, 21 P.3d 797, 106 Cal. Rptr.2d 126 (2003). See also, *Hilton v. Hallmark Cards*, 599 F.3d 894 (2010) (greeting card using celebrity face in cartoon-styled scene from her reality television show "Simple Life" was not a parody as a matter of law under analysis of California's anti-SLAPP statute. Court noted that as compared to the *Kirby* case in which the plaintiff's persona was transformed into a new character, the use of the stylized scene from Hilton's television show was not transformative as a matter of law, being closely based on an actual scene from an actual episode).

186   See *Hart v. Electronic Arts, Inc.*, 717 F.3d 141 (3d Cir. 2013). See also, *E.S.S. Entertainment 2000, Inc. v. Rock Star Videos*, 547 F.3d 1095 (9th Cir. 2008) (under a trademark analysis using the test in *Rogers v. Grimaldi*, the use of the name of a Los Angeles strip club had at least some artistic relevance to a video game whose goal was to mimic the look and feel of actual Los Angeles neighborhoods. In holding for the defendant, the court noted that "the game was decidedly not "about" the strip club" and the use was entitled to First Amendment protections).

187   *No Doubt v. Activision Publishing, Inc.*, 192 Cal. App.4th 1018, 122 Cal. Rptr.3d 37 (2011).

Based on the same NCAA Football game, the same result was reached in a case with a different plaintiff in a different jurisdiction, *Keller v. Electronic Arts, Inc.* in the Ninth Circuit, which found insufficient transformative elements in the use of the plaintiff's images in the game.[188]

In *Kirby v. Sega of America*, a singer for a fashion-based pop group alleged that a video game character was modeled on her likeness, including her hair and clothing styling and catch phrases.[189] She brought common-law and statutory right of publicity claims, *inter alia*. The court found evidence that the designers in Japan had never heard of the singer at the time the game was designed, that there were not many actual similarities, and that while there was a question of fact about the significance of any other similarities, the game character was at least a transformative use of plaintiff's persona, and the First Amendment barred plaintiff's claims.[190]

In a case that is a hybrid between transformative interactive use of celebrity persona and contractual agreements granting the right of publicity, the musical group No Doubt entered into an agreement with the producers of the game "Band Hero" that gave the producer the right to depict the band in the game and to have the band perform its songs in the game.[191] The band members participated in a day of pho-

---

188   *Keller v. Electronic Arts, Inc.*, 724 F.3d 1268 (9th Cir. 2013). See also, *Davis v. Elec. Arts, Inc.*, 775 F.3d 1172 (9th Cir. 2015) (former NFL players have right of publicity in electronic game).

189   *Kirby v. Sega of America, Inc.*, 144 Cal. App.4th 47, 50 Cal Rptr.3d 607 (Cal. App. 2006).

190   Notable in the case is the court's award of substantial attorney's fees and costs to the defendant totaling $608,000, based on the provision in § 3344 that "the prevailing party in any action under this section shall . . . be entitled to attorney's fees and costs." *Id.*, 144 Cal. App.4th at 62.

191   *No Doubt v. Activision Publishing, Inc.*, 192 Cal.App. 4th 1018 122 Cal. Rptr.3d 37 (2011). The pertinent language of the agreement between No Doubt and Activision was:

"This Agreement sets out the terms upon which Artist [(No Doubt)] has agreed to grant to Activision certain rights to utilize Artist's name(s), likeness(es), logo(s), and associated trademark(s) and other related intellectual property rights (the 'Licensed Property') and to provide Activision certain production and marketing services in connection with Activision's 'Band Hero' video game (the 'Game')." The Agreement specifically provides that "Artists grant to Activision the non-exclusive, worldwide right and license to use the Licensed Property (including Artist's likeness as provided by or approved by Artist) solely in the one (1) Game for all gaming platforms and formats, on the packaging for the Game, and in advertising, marketing, promotional and PR materials for the Game.' In a section entitled 'Approval Rights,' the Agreement states that 'Artist's likeness as implemented in the Game (the 'Character Likeness'), any use of Artist's name and/or likeness other than in a 'billing block' fashion on the back of the packaging for the Game, and the b-roll and photography or other representation of the Services or of Artist, shall be subject to Artist's prior written approval. [¶] Activision shall submit each of the above (i.e., the Character Likeness, name uses, and b-roll and photography or other representation) to Artist for review and Artist shall have ten (10) business days to either approve or disapprove. . . . [¶] Activision shall not be required to submit for approval uses of previously approved assets, provided such

tography in order to ensure that their depiction in the game was accurate. When the producers released the game with special "unlocking" features that allowed users to manipulate the band's voices and to perform songs by other bands, No Doubt sued for breach of contract, violations of the right of publicity, and other claims.

In holding for the plaintiffs and denying the defendant's first amendment transformative use defense, the court noted that literal depictions of a persona were not transformative. The court compared the *No Doubt* claim to those in *Kirby*, finding that in the *Kirby* case the plaintiff was portrayed as an entirely new character, which may have been "based on" the plaintiff but was nevertheless transformed, and also compared the case to *Hart*, in which user interactivity transformed the plaintiff's persona. The *No Doubt* court instead followed the *Comedy III* and *Keller* line of cases in which the defendants depicted the plaintiffs for the very "sum and substance" of their persona, without creating any "new" or transformative characters either as a result of the creative production process, or as a result of user interactivity.

In *The Romantics v. Activision Publishing, Inc.*,[192] the musical group brought an action against the producers of the video game series "Guitar Hero." The defendant had duly obtained a synchronization license for the song from the copyright owner music publisher. However, instead of licensing the actual recording made famous by the group, the defendant produced its own version of the song, along with a disclaimer. Plaintiffs claimed that the new recording was too much of a "sound-alike" compared to the original recording, and that it infringed a right of publicity plaintiffs had in their performance and sound. In applying Michigan right of publicity common law, the court held that Michigan has never recognized a right of publicity in the sound of a voice, even if distinctive, nor has it recognized a right of publicity in a combination of voices.[193]

---

uses fall within the rights granted herein (e.g., using a previously approved Character Likeness depiction in multiple advertising materials)."

192   *The Romantics v. Activision Publishing, Inc.*, 574 F. Supp.2d 758, 764 (E.D. Mich. 2008).

193   Further, unlike the plaintiffs in *Midler* and *Waits*, plaintiffs presented no evidence that their "sound" was either distinctive or identifiable on its own. Having found that plaintiffs had no right of publicity in the sound of their voices, the court also determined that plaintiff's state law claim was preempted by Section 301 of the Copyright Act, and noted that under Section 114(b), sound-alike recordings do not constitute copyright infringement. *Id.*, 574 F. Supp.2d at 768 (citing 17 U.S.C. § 114(b)). Section 114(b) states in relevant part: "The exclusive rights of the owner of copyright in a sound recording under clauses (1) and (2) of section 106 do not extend to the making or duplication of another sound recording that consists entirely of an independent fixation of other sounds, even though such sounds imitate or simulate those in the copyrighted sound recording."

§7.05   Celebrity Privacy

Those who seek the public eye forfeit some measure of their privacy. The press enjoys a First Amendment privilege to cover and report on the lives of public figures. So long as the reporting does not defame the celebrity under the "actual malice" standard of *New York Times Co. v. Sullivan*,[194] there is often very little a celebrity can do in the United States with respect to a claim for invasion of privacy against the media.[195]

---

194   *New York Times Co. v. Sullivan*, 376 U.S. 254, 84 S.Ct. 710, 11 L.Ed.2d 686 (1964). Some celebrities and others have successfully brought libel actions against publications in overseas jurisdictions where the burden of proof falls on the defendant publisher, and First Amendment protections under *New York Ties Co. v. Sullivan* do not apply. Formerly, such "libel tourism" in overseas forum shopping could result in enforcement actions for damages against journalists and publishers in United States courts, based on libel judgments obtained overseas. Congress responded with an act entitled Securing the Protection of our Enduring and Established Constitutional Heritage Act, known as the "SPEECH Act," which became law on August 10, 2010. See Pub. L. No. 111.223, codified at 28 U.S.C. §§ 4101-4105 (2010). Under the SPEECH Act, state and federal courts are barred from enforcing or recognizing a foreign judgment for defamation unless it can be shown that the foreign judgment is consistent with the United States Constitution and the First Amendment, and also with Section 230 of the Communications Act of 1934 (47 U.S.C. § 230). See also, *Ehrenfeld v. Mahfouz*, 518 F.3d 102 (2d Cir. 2008) (jurisdictional holding in case involving enforcement of foreign libel judgment against American journalist).

195   Celebrities can also attempt to protect their privacy contractually, by requiring employees who have access to intimate personal life details to honor the confidentiality of matters such as family schedule, finances, business affairs and other information relating to the celebrity employer, his or her family, friends, and business associates. Such matters can include verbal statements, documents, phone numbers, e-mail addresses, photographs, videos, purchasing or other habits, and medical care. Employee confidentiality agreements that forbid disclosures of private facts yet do not inhibit the employee from seeking other work in the future have been held enforceable. In *Coady v. Harpo, Inc.*, 308 Ill. App.3d 153, 719 N.E.2d 244 (1999), the employee confidentiality agreement between Oprah Winfrey's production company and former employee who announced intention to write about her experiences was valid and enforceable because, in part, the agreement was reasonable and did not impose any restrictions on employee's ability to work.

> "Defendant does not seek to restrain plaintiff's future career. Plaintiff is free to choose her future occupation, the locale in which she may choose to work, and the time when she can commence her new career. Defendant does not object to plaintiff becoming a journalist, competing with defendant in the same venue and in any locale, including Chicago, and in beginning her new venture immediately. The confidentiality agreement does not restrict commerce and does not restrict plaintiff's ability to work in any chosen career field, at any time. Instead, the 1995 confidentiality agreement restricts plaintiff's ability to disseminate confidential information that she obtained or learned while in defendant's employ. . . . Whether for better or for worse, interest in a celebrity figure and his or her attendant business and personal ventures somehow seems to continue endlessly, even long after death, and often, as in the present case, extends over an international domain." 719 N.E.2d at 250–251.

A celebrity employee confidentiality agreement is included with the forms accompanying this treatise.

Trespass laws may prevent photographers from having access to celebrities in private spaces such as homes and businesses. However, when out in public, celebrities are "fair game." While some public excursions are, of course, calculated publicity exercises or stunts, the press can be invasive in seeking photos and videos in circumstances that most people would consider private.

The photographers who follow celebrities in the hopes of capturing an unguarded or even "sensational" moment for the tabloids are commonly referred to as "paparazzi."[196] For the paparazzi, the more "private" the photograph and the more difficult it was to obtain, the greater its value. Understanding the value of these types of photos, some celebrities have wrested control away from the paparazzi and into carefully controlled "release" of such photos to sell the publication rights for charitable donation purposes.

[1]—Tort Actions for Intrusion into Private Matters

Under the common law of California, the tort of public disclosure of private facts has the following elements:

(1) public disclosure

(2) of a private fact

(3) which would be offensive and objectionable to the reasonable person, and

(4) which is not of legitimate public concern.[197]

The tort of intrusion into private matters has two elements:

(1) intentional intrusion into a private place, conversation or matter,

(2) in a manner highly offensive to a reasonable person.[198]

As public figures who must prove "actual malice" with respect to press accounts of their private life, celebrities may find that legal action based on privacy torts requires significant burdens of proof of actual malice. With respect to photographs, videos, and audio

---

196 The term "paparazzi" is allegedly derived from a photographer character named "Paparazzo" in Federico Fellini's 1960 film "La Dolce Vita." It is generally defined as a freelance photographer who attempts to capture candid photos of celebrities caught off guard.

197 *Taus v. Loftus*, 40 Cal.4th 683, 54 Cal. Rptr.3d 775, 151 P.3d 1185 (2007).

198 Id.

surveillance, neither tort action may adequately addresses the intense level of pursuit of celebrities and the resultant invasion of privacy.

[2]—California's "Anti-Paparazzi Statute"

In response to increasing concern for celebrity safety in the wake of dangers posed by the throngs of paparazzi who chase celebrities, jostling for position, invading the celebrity's "space" and engaging in dangerous traffic chases, the California legislature passed the so-called "Anti-Paparazzi Statute."[199]

[a]—Physical Invasion of Privacy

The statute focuses on visual and audio surveillance of celebrities by providing that the capture of "any type of visual image, sound recording, or other physical impression of the plaintiff engaging in a personal or familial activity" occurs in a way that would be offensive to a "reasonable person." The statute defines such activity in the context of physical trespass as "physical invasion of privacy," defined as when the defendant knowingly enters onto the land of another person without permission or otherwise commits a trespass in order to physically invade the privacy of the plaintiff, with intent.[200]

[b]—Constructive Invasion of Privacy

The statute establishes a "constructive" invasion of privacy when the defendant engages in the same activity under circumstances where the plaintiff had a reasonable expectation of privacy, "through the use of a visual or auditory enhancing device, regardless of whether there is a physical trespass, if this image, sound recording, or other physical impression could not have been achieved without a trespass unless the visual or auditory enhancing device was used."[201]

---

199   Section 1708.8 of the California Civil Code is entitled "Physical or constructive invasion of privacy; damages and equitable remedies; employee-employer relationships; defenses. West's Ann. Cal. Civ. Code § 1708.8. Note that the illegal activities of individuals who invade a celebrity's privacy or act in a threatening manner, such as "stalkers," may come within applicable penal statutes. See e.g., *People v. Soiu*, 2006 WL 1551311 (Cal. App. June 8, 2006) (appeal of an order extending sentence of man who stalked celebrity Gwyneth Paltrow, in violation of Penal Code section 646.9).

200   West's Ann. Cal. Civ. Code § 1708.8(a). See also, *J.P. Turnbull v. American Broadcasting Cos.*, 2004 WL 2924590 (C.D. Cal. Aug. 19, 2004) (defendant's motion for summary judgment on violation of 1§ 708.8 denied where surreptitious video and audio recording of acting workshop participants in private areas and conversations recorded by crew of ABC show "20/20").

201   *Id.* at § 1708.8(d).

[c]—Assault

The statute establishes that an assault committed with the intent to capture any type of visual image, sound recording, or other physical impression of the plaintiff also comes within the penalty provisions of the statute, §§ 1708.8(d), (e), and (h).[202]

[d]—Damages and Disgorgement

Under The statute, a person who commits any acts described in §§ 1708.8(a), (b), and (c) is liable for up to three times the amount of any general and special damages that are proximately caused by the violation, and may also be liable for punitive damages. If the plaintiff proves that the violation was committed for a commercial purpose, the defendant shall also be subject to the disgorgement of any proceeds or other consideration obtained as a result of the violation.[203]

[e]—Further Provisions

The statute has additional provisions relating to vicarious liability for anyone who directs, solicits, actually induces, or actually causes another person to violate the statute, regardless of whether there is an employer-employee relationship.[204] It also confirms that its provisions do not impair or limit lawful activities of law enforcement, and states that it is not a defense to a violation of the statute that no image, recording, or physical impression was actually captured or sold, presumably extending liability to paparazzi who violate the statute, but fail to actually capture a photo.[205]

[3]—Celebrity Stalkers

Individuals who engage in obsessive behavior towards celebrities are often motivated by mental illness or personality disorders.[206] Although the vast majority of stalking victims are private individuals, celebrity stalking by obsessed and unbalanced "fans"

202　*Id.* at § 1708.8(c).

203　Id. at § 1708.8(d).

204　*Id.* at § 1708.8(e).

205　*Id.* at § 1708.8(f).

206　See *People v. E.P.*, 20 Misc.3d 1119(A), 867 N.Y.S.2d 19 (N.Y. City Crim. July 16, 2008) (upholding stalking charges under New York Penal Law § 120.45 against stalker of celebrity producer Lorne Michaels of "Saturday Night Live"). See also, *People v. Carron*, 37 Cal. App.4th 1230, 44 Cal. Rptr.2d 328 (Cal. App. 1995) (detailing psychotic, harassing, and threatening behavior by stalker against model/actor). See also, *Glaser v. Meserve*, 2013 Cal. App. Unpub. LEXIS 2579, 2013 WL 1460339 (Cal. App. 2 Dist. April 11, 2013) (three-year injunction against celebrity stalker).

is increasingly common.[207] The two jurisdictions with a disproportionate number of celebrity residents, New York and California, have penal statutes addressing stalkers.

[a]—New York's Anti-Stalker Statute

New York's anti-stalking statute was enacted in 1999, at which time the legislature noted that:

> "criminal stalking behavior . . . has become more prevalent in New York state in recent years. The unfortunate reality is that stalking victims have been intolerably forced to live in fear of their stalkers . . . who repeatedly follow, phone, write, confront, threaten or otherwise unacceptably intrude upon their victims, often inflict immeasurable emotional and physical harm upon them. Current law does not adequately recognize the damage to public order and individual safety caused by these offenders."[208]

While the correlation between stalking and intimate relationships was foremost on the legislature's agenda, there is no reason to exclude or minimize the impact of stalking that occurs between total strangers, as is most often the case when the target is a celebrity.[209]

The New York statute is succinct.[210] Its provisions encompass the victim's family and acquaintances, and covers behavior likely to cause material harm to physical or

---

207   See e.g., *People v. Soiu*, 2006 Cal. App. Unpub. LEXIS 4962, 2006 WL 1551311 (Cal. App. June 8, 2006) (appeal of an order extending sentence of man who stalked celebrity Gwyneth Paltrow, in violation of Penal Code section 646.9). Other celebrities who have been stalked, most often by self-professed fans, include television personality David Letterman, fashion model and television personality Tyra Banks, soccer star David Beckham, singers Madonna and Janet Jackson, actress Jodi Foster, and, perhaps most famously (and most tragically), musician John Lennon, who was murdered by a stalker.

208   See Donnino, "2004 Main Volume Supp Practice Commentaries," McKinney's Cons Laws of NY, Book 39, Penal Law, Art 120, at 182-183.

209   *People v. Pidhajecky*, 20 Misc.3d 1119(A), 2008 WL 2746722 at *2 (N.Y. City Crim. July 16, 2008).

210   § 120.45 Stalking in the fourth degree. A person is guilty of stalking in the fourth degree when he or she intentionally, and for no legitimate purpose, engages in a course of conduct directed at a specific person, and knows or reasonably should know that such conduct:

1. is likely to cause reasonable fear of material harm to the physical health, safety or property of such person, a member of such person's immediate family or a third party with whom such person is acquainted; or

2. causes material harm to the mental or emotional health of such person, where such conduct consists of following, telephoning or initiating communication or contact with such person, a member of such person's immediate family or a third party with whom such person is acquainted, and the actor was previously clearly informed to cease that conduct; or

emotional health of the victim, including initiating telephone or other communications or contact. It requires that the stalker be clearly informed that such contact must cease.

In interpreting the statute, a New York court found as follows:

- "Course of conduct" means more than "isolated incidents," it means a pattern of conduct composed of a series of acts over a period of time.[211]

- "No legitimate purpose" means the absence of a reason or justification to engage someone, other than to hound, frighten, intimidate or threaten them.[212]

- Actual fear, whether reasonable or not, is not a required element of the offense. The facts need only show that a defendant knows or should reasonably know that his actions are likely to cause reasonable fear.[213]

Note that the New York law is a criminal statute. The stalking victim would need to file a complaint with the police or district attorney. Victims may also pursue a civil restraining order.

[b]—California's Anti-Stalker Statute

Under California's anti-stalker statute, a person is liable for stalking when the plaintiff proves all of the elements of the tort.

[i]—A Pattern of Conduct to Follow, Alarm, or Harass

In order to establish this element, the plaintiff shall be required to support his or her allegations with independent corroborating evidence.[214]

[ii]—Plaintiff's Reasonable Fear for Their Safety

As a result of that pattern of conduct, the plaintiff reasonably feared for his or her safety, or the safety of an immediate family member. For purposes of this paragraph, "immediate family" means a spouse, parent, child, any person related

---

3.   Is likely to cause such person to reasonably fear that his or her employment, business or career is threatened, where such conduct consists of appearing, telephoning or initiating communication or contact at such person's place of employment or business, and the actor was previously clearly informed to cease that conduct. Stalking in the fourth degree is a class B misdemeanor.

211 *Id.*

212 *Id.* Bald threats made by a stalker fit that definition, but so does the type of contact at issue in *Pidhajecky*, where the defendant claimed that his "thoughts" were purloined by Lorne Michaels for use on "Saturday Night Live," a claim that created a likelihood of reasonable fear on the part of the victim.

213 *Id.*

214 See Cal. Civ. Code § 1708.7(a)(1).

by consanguinity or affinity within the second degree, or any person who regularly resides, or, within the six months preceding any portion of the pattern of conduct, regularly resided, in the plaintiff's household.[215]

[iii]—Credible Threats made After a Cease Demand; or Violation of Restraining Order

The third element of the tort can be shown in two ways:

(A) that the defendant made a credible threat against the defendant's safety (or that of an immediate family member) after the defendant on at least one occasion clearly and definitely demanded that the defendant cease and abate his or her pattern of conduct; or

(B) that the defendant violated a restraining order, including, but not limited to, any order issued pursuant to Section 527.6 of the Code of Civil Procedure, prohibiting any act described in subdivision (a) or (b).[216]

---

215   *Id.,* § 1708.7(a)(2).

216   *Id.,* § 1708.7(a)(3). The statute is defined as:

(1) "Pattern of conduct" means conduct composed of a series of acts over a period of time, however short, evidencing a continuity of purpose. Constitutionally protected activity is not included within the meaning of "pattern of conduct."

(2) "Credible threat" means a verbal or written threat, including that communicated by means of an electronic communication device, or a threat implied by a pattern of conduct or a combination of verbal, written, or electronically communicated statements and conduct, made with the intent and apparent ability to carry out the threat so as to cause the person who is the target of the threat to reasonably fear for his or her safety or the safety of his or her immediate family.

(3) "Electronic communication device" includes, but is not limited to, telephones, cellular telephones, computers, video recorders, fax machines, or pagers. "Electronic communication" has the same meaning as the term defined in Subsection 12 of Section 2510 of Title 18 of the United States Code.

(4) "Harass" means a knowing and willful course of conduct directed at a specific person which seriously alarms, annoys, torments, or terrorizes the person, and which serves no legitimate purpose. The course of conduct must be such as would cause a reasonable person to suffer substantial emotional distress, and must actually cause substantial emotional distress to the person.

Id., § 1708.7(b).

[iv]—Damages

The stalker is liable to the victim for damages, including, but not limited to, general damages, special damages, and punitive damages.[217] In addition, the court may grant equitable relief, including, but not limited to, an injunction.[218]

[v]—Rights Cumulative

The rights and remedies provided in the statute are cumulative and supplement any other rights and remedies provided by law.[219]

[vi]—Exceptions for Constitutionally Protected Activity

The statute shall not be construed to impair any constitutionally protected activity, including, but not limited to, speech, protest, and assembly.[220]

[c]—Use of Copyright and Contract Law to Control Adverse Publicity

Celebrities may attempt to control dissemination of personal information by confidentiality agreements, or prevent dissemination of photographs by relying on copyright ownership principles.

In *Vasquez v. Lopez*, a film producer sued singer/actress Jennifer Lopez, alleging that Lopez had improperly interfered with plans to produce a "tell all" film on the subject of Lopez's former marriage.[221] Lopez had previously entered into a confidentiality agreement with her ex-husband, under which he agreed not to disclose information about their former relationship. Despite the confidentiality agreement, the ex-husband made plans to participate in a film based on his relationship with the singer/actress. Lopez sued the ex-husband, was awarded a permanent injunction and damages against the ex-husband and anyone acting in concert with him, and sent a cease and desist letter to the film's producer. The producer in turn sued Lopez, claiming that her actions "destroyed the marketability" of the planned project. Lopez prevailed in the litigation, affirming her strategy to use confidentiality agreements (in this case enforced by the courts) to prevent third parties from violating her privacy.

In *Balsley v. LFP, Inc.*, a television journalist used copyright law to try and prevent publication of embarrassing photos of her, taken years previously, voluntarily par-

---

217   *Id.*, § 1708.7(c).

218   *Id.*, § 1708.7(d).

219   *Id.*, § 1708.7(e).

220   *Id.*, § 1708.7(f).

221   See *Vasquez v. Lopez*, 2012 WL 4336728 (Cal. App. Sept. 24, 2012). See also *Lopez v. Noa*, 2011 WL 3211471 (Cal. App. July 29, 2011) (motion to compel arbitration against ex-husband to enforce confidentiality agreement).

ticipating in a public "wet t shirt" contest.[222] The plaintiff's strategy to try and protect her reputation against photographic evidence of a youthful indiscretion was to purchase the copyright in the only photos of the event, and to sue Hustler magazine when it published the photos as part of a "Hot News Babes" pictorial. Despite the magazine's arguments for fair use and freedom of the press, the plaintiff prevailed. Although the victory on the infringement action resulted in a jury award of $135,000 in damages and $133,812 in attorney's fees, the came too late to stop the publication from occurring, but will presumably be a deterrent against future publication of the photographs.

In *Raanan Katz v. Google Inc. and Irina Chevaldina*, a real estate magnate purchased the copyright in an unflattering photo of him that had been posted on blogs by a dissatisfied former tenant alongside criticism of the plaintiff's business practices and personal ethics. The plaintiff's copyright infringement suit was an attempt to silence the criticism by enjoining any further posting of the photograph, which was taken at a public basketball game and showed the plaintiff momentarily sticking out his tongue. In affirming the lower court's holding of fair use of the photo, the Eighth Circuit noted that the plaintiff was attempting "to utilize copyright as an instrument of censorship against unwanted criticism."[223]

[d]—Statutes Forbidding Posting of Private Photos Online

Smart phones have changed behavior, including the opportunity to capture private moments with a loved one or to create revealing "selfies." At the time such images are created, they are intended for private viewing and not publication. Publication of such private photos may occur as a result of computer hacking by unknown individuals, or intentionally by the former loved one or confidant who may have been sent the photo for private enjoyment. Such posting of private images, intended to shame or embarrass especially after a relationship breakup, is commonly referred to as "revenge porn."

Such photos differ from traditionally invasive paparazzi photography or illegal hidden camera techniques because they are taken by the subjects themselves, initially with full consent. Over twenty states have now passed laws forbidding the posting of such photos without permission.[224]

---

222   *Balsley v. LFP, Inc.*, 2011 U.S. Dist. LEXIS 40152 (N.D. Ohio March 31, 2011).

223   See *Katz v. Google Inc.*, 2015 U.S. App. LEXIS 16546 (11th Cir. Fla. Sept. 17, 2015).

224   See: Alaska Stat. 11.61.120; Arkansas Code 5-26-314; California Penal Code 647(j)(4); Colorado Revised Statutes 18-7-107 and 18-7-108; Section 1335, Title 11 Delaware Code; D.C. Law 20-275; 784.049, Florida Statutes; GA Code16-11-90; Hawaii Revised Statutes 711-1110.9; Idaho Code 18-6609(2)(b); Illinois Criminal Code Sec. 11-23.5; Louisiana R.S. 14:283.2; Maine Sec. 1. 17-A MRSA 511-A; Maryland Code Section 3-809; New Jersey Code. 2C:14-

In California, Penal Code Section 647(j)(4) addresses so-called "revenge porn" online postings and makes them a misdemeanor, even where the subject originally "participates, under circumstances in which the persons agree or understand that the image shall remain private."[225]

§7.06 Celebrity Endorsement Agreements

Those celebrities who choose to monetize their fame by entering into endorsement agreements must exercise extreme caution. However, association with the wrong product or companies can do irreparable damage to the celebrity's image.[226] In addition, such endorsement agreements need to carefully delineate the actual time and services the celebrity will be called upon to provide. Finally, there is always the issue of whether the celebrity is being properly compensated for the use of his or her fame.

Some of the provisions in an endorsement agreement may be similar to non-compete agreements. An endorsement for hair care products might require that a celebrity refrain from endorsing other hair care products, or even the broader field of beauty products during the term of the agreement, but it would leave the celebrity free to endorse non-competing products such as, for example, automobiles.

Other provisions in celebrity endorsement agreements may include a "morals clause" whereby the manufacturer can immediately terminate the agreement if the celebrity engages in any acts or makes any statements that reflect poorly on the manufacturer or the product, or is, e.g., arrested for or convicted of a felony.

9(c); New Mexico Criminal Code (House Bill 142); Nevada NRS, Chapter 200, Sections 2-6; North Carolina General Statutes Section 14-190.5A; Section 12.1-17-07.2 of the North Dakota Century Code; Oregon ORS 161.005; Title 18 Pennsylvania Consolidated Statutes Section 3131; Texas Penal Code 21.16; Utah Code 76-5b-203; Vermont Sec. 2. 13 VSA Sec 2606; Washington Title 9A RCW; Code of Wisconsin 942.09.

225   See Calif. Penal Code §647(j)(4), stating:

"(4) (A) Any person who intentionally distributes the image of the intimate body part or parts of another identifiable person, or an image of the person depicted engaged in an act of sexual intercourse, sodomy, oral copulation, sexual penetration, or an image of masturbation by the person depicted or in which the person depicted participates, under circumstances in which the persons agree or understand that the image shall remain private, the person distributing the image knows or should know that distribution of the image will cause serious emotional distress, and the person depicted suffers that distress."

226   See, e.g., Duke, "The Man Who Made Kathie Lee Cry," Washington Post (July 31, 2005) (discussing investigations into alleged overseas "sweatshops" allegedly using child labor to manufacture clothing endorsed by celebrities and the resulting damage to celebrity reputation), available at http://www.washingtonpost.com/wp-dyn/content/article/2005/07/30/AR2005073001413_pf.html.

In addition, celebrities may demand provisions enabling them to exercise some measure of control over how their images are depicted, including authorization of photographs. Issues regarding copyright and ownership of such photos may also be addressed in the agreement.

Finally, when endorsing a product, a celebrity should be especially cautious about how the product or service reflects upon him or her, and whether it has the potential to damage the celebrity's reputation and public good will. Morever, the celebrity should be aware that he or she could incur liability for participating in advertising that is deemed deceptive under consumer protection laws such as those promulgated by the Federal Trade Commission ("FTC").

The following is a summary of key agreement terms in a celebrity endorsement contract.[227]

[1]—Grant of Right of Publicity

The grant of the right to use the celebrity's identity and persona, including his or her name, likeness, image, voice, and signature will be generally "in connection with the advertisement, promotion and sale of the specified products or services." It is recommended that where a right of publicity statute or comparable statute exists in the celebrity's jurisdiction, the wording of the grant be no less broad than the wording of the statute. For example, if the agreement is for the right of publicity for a celebrity located in Illinois and subject to Illinois law, the language in the Illinois Rights of Publicity Act should be considered as the basis for the grant so that the rights granted are no less than the right specified in the statute. In Illinois for example, the statute defines "identity" as follows:

> "'Identity' means any attribute of an individual that serves to identify that individual to an ordinary, reasonable viewer or listener, including but not limited to (i) name, (ii) signature, (iii) photograph, (iv) image, (v) likeness, or (vi) voice."[228]

[2]—Term

The term of the agreement may also have provisions for renewals, expiration, and termination. Of particular importance is whether the expiration or termination of the agreement is followed by any "black out" period during which the celebrity may not re-enter the market by endorsing a competing brand.

---

227   For samples, see the forms accompanying this text.

228   765 ILCS 1075/5.

[3]—Territory

Territorial restrictions can be crucial to endorsement agreements, especially in situations where a celebrity may be willing to engage in endorsements only in countries outside the United States, or outside the English-speaking world. The rationale for such restrictions may be a perception cultivated by the celebrity that they don't "sell out" by endorsing products, or by endorsing particular kinds of products.[229] Another incentive to carefully craft territorial limitation is to be able to increase endorsement fees by charging larger fees for a larger scope of territories.

[4]—Exclusivity: Products and Media

Exclusivity provisions can apply to the type or category of product, and can also apply to marketing channels. With respect to products, advertisers will demand exclusivity of the celebrity to be so the celebrity can't promote the products of a direct competitor. In addition, an advertiser may want the celebrity's exclusivity for particular modes of advertising, or for specific types of media. Careful lines should be drawn with respect to media limitations. Anything that limits a celebrity's ability to appear in advertising on television or print media or the Internet, for example, should only be considered in the context of an exceptionally attractive offer from the advertiser.

[5]—Personal Services

The "Services" provisions in the agreement may specify a certain number of days per year the celebrity will be available for services, including photography, television and film advertising productions, radio, Internet, personal appearances, consultation concerning product development, and industry meetings. It is crucial that the celebrity consider very specific services, and the exact amount of time they will require, so that the celebrity's prestige and standing is not jeopardized and the duties do not interfere with his or her entertainment industry work.

[6]—Right of Approval

The celebrity may also seek a right to approve all aspects of the advertising in which they appear, including scripts, and generally not allow the manufacturer to control or alter the celebrity's carefully created and maintained image.

---

229   If a celebrity can obtain a lucrative endorsement agreement in, for example, Japan only, he or she may be attempting to maintain a "no endorsements" image in the United States while still financially exploiting his or her celebrity abroad.

[7]—Intellectual Property and Copyright

The agreement should carefully delineate ownership of preexisting intellectual property belonging to the celebrity, such as publicity photos or songs, and set forth provisions for ownership of newly created copyrights and trademarks that may be result from the endorsement activities. With respect to preexisting publicity photos, the celebrity may need to warrant that he or she has all rights necessary from the photographer for the manufacturer to use the photographs.[230] Photographs and television advertisements, for example, created during the term of the agreement will in virtually all cases be copyrights owned by the advertiser. Where the celebrity is a musician, ownership of musical compositions and sound recordings will often lie with their music publisher and record company. Endorsement agreements may have provisions that include licensing those works as part of the advertising campaigns, or at least require the celebrity to cooperate in obtaining those rights.

[8]—Failure to Perform; Morals Clause

The agreement may have provisions suspending the manufacturer's obligations to pay the celebrity, or giving the manufacturer a termination right, arising from the celebrity's failure to perform his or her duties, or arising from any act by the celebrity that may bring the product, the manufacturer, or the celebrity into disrepute. Typical morals clauses have provisions stating that the termination right shall apply where the celebrity is arrested or convicted of a felony, or commits any act of moral turpitude, or engages in behavior or makes statements that do not comport with community standards, or that reflect unfavorably upon the manufacturer, its employees, and its products.

[9]—Trademarks

In addition to the right of publicity, a celebrity may own one or more trademarks or "catch phrases" associated with his or her name.[231] In such cases, the endorsement agreement should have standard trademark license provisions carefully controlling the use of the mark and its associated goodwill, and reserving all rights in the mark to the celebrity such that no use as part of an endorsement inures to the benefit of the advertiser.[232]

---

230   In most cases, the manufacturer will simply hire its own photographer for a photo shoot featuring the celebrity and the product itself.

231   Note that the United States Patent and Trademark Office records show over fifty trademark applications and registrations owned by celebrity Paris Hilton, including "That's Hot", serial number 76615015 in class 25 for clothing; "Heiress", serial number 78977191 in class 3 for cosmetics; "Paris Hilton", registration number 3514355 in class 18 for pet accessories; "Parisized," serial number 77550470 in class 41 for entertainment services, namely personal appearances by a media celebrity; and "Talk to you never", serial number 77550452 in class 25 for clothing. See http://www.uspto.gov.

232   See generally The Lanham Act, 15. U.S.C. §1051 et seq.

[10]—Product Development and Manufacturing

In the event the agreement includes the manufacture of goods bearing the celebrity's image, the agreement will need to provide for celebrity's approval of goods produced, including quality control, safety, and assurances that the manufacturer will comply with all applicable laws and regulations that may apply to the product at issue, include all import and marking requirements.

[11]—Consideration

While many, if not most, celebrity right of publicity agreements are based on fixed compensation established by negotiation, many other factors may apply to the proposed financial dealings. In particular, where the endorsement involves a product, product line, or even an entire company, the celebrity may attempt to achieve meaningful "back end" income, including royalties on products sold during the ad campaign, or bearing the celebrity's name, image, or likeness. In some cases the celebrity will merely lend his or her persona to a business. In other cases, the celebrity may actively participate in the marketing efforts, for example, by designing products bearing his or her name, or by appearing in infomercials or on home shopping networks selling products. Given the many ways that a celebrity's "brand" and services can be utilized, the following are some general items for negotiation with respect to the compensation received.

[12]—Signing Bonus

A signing bonus is not an advance against future payments or royalties, but a pure inducement to sign the agreement. It should be sought in all cases.

[13]—Advances and Guarantees

Advances, or "guarantees," are monies paid in anticipation of future royalties. They are nearly always deductible from those future royalties, but not refundable in the event the sales do not materialize as planned. While a signing bonus may be difficult to achieve because it is virtually a "gift" to the celebrity in addition to all the other compensation paid, an advance makes good sense for both parties. For the celebrity, it is a guarantee that he or she will receive some revenue payable up front for the willingness to work with the manufacturer, regardless of whether sales ever occur.

In addition, an advance shows the manufacturer's commitment to the project. With an advance already paid, the manufacturer has a heightened incentive to vigorously pursue the success of the product, because the only way the manufacturer can recoup the monies paid is through future sales.

One common way to incentivize both parties is to build into the agreement annual increases in the guarantee or advance, based either on a fixed amount, or combining that with guarantee increases based on the previous year's sale and royalties.

[14]—Fixed or Set Fees

Set fees for the celebrity's right of publicity and services payable per annum are another approach. Alternatively, such payments can be at other time intervals during the term of the agreement, and can have automatic increases built in, as well as bonus payments based on sales "plateaus" achieved. In addition to a "general" fee for overall services, there may be itemized fees, such as per-day appearance fees.

[15]—Royalty

A royalty is a percentage of sales paid to the celebrity based on sales of the products being promoted. The royalty "formula" will be based on a carefully defined description of the basis for the royalty calculation. For example, it could be based on an "adjusted gross revenue" that deducts from gross revenue certain expenses and costs incurred by the manufacturer.[233] In some cases the terminology may refer to "Net Revenues" and may define what revenue remains after the above deductions, and others.

Items that may be hotly negotiated include: (1) costs for production of the advertising, including production costs for infomercials, which can be considerable; (2) costs for the media "buy", the air time purchased on broadcast or cable television networks; and (3) an almost unlimited number of proposed deductions from gross revenue. The celebrity's representative must attempt to keep the accounting basis for the royalty as simple and favorable as possible, and, similar to negotiation of agreements in the music and film industries, must be especially wary of vaguely defined categories of deductible expenses such as "marketing" or "fulfillment" costs, as well as items such as legal and accounting costs.

[16]—Royalty Scope

Points for negotiation include whether the royalty only applies to sales that are in some way directly connected with the celebrity's efforts, or whether all sales of a given product will be subject to a royalty on the theory that the celebrity's introduction of, and identification with, the product drives its sales globally. The parties will also need to agree on what period of future time is reasonable for future sales of a product launched by a

---

233   For example: fees charged by a home shopping network that aired an infomercial, processing fees charged by "1-800" call centers and distribution and shipping centers, etc.

celebrity. Certainly, all sales of products that bear a celebrity's name or likeness should be subject to a royalty no matter when they occur.

[17]—Commissions; Payments to Agents or Managers

Note that the celebrity will likely be party to an outside management agreement. The agreement may contain provisions whereby the all of the payments must be made to the manager, and if so, such payments are in full satisfaction of the advertiser's obligations under the agreement. Where a celebrity's management receives not only a percentage of the celebrity's income from the agreement, but also receives a commission from the advertiser themselves, those provisions may also be reflected in the agreement. Either the overall funds paid to the artist may be reduced by an amount contractually paid to the manager, or the manager's additional commission will be factored into deductions from the gross compensation paid to the celebrity.[234]

[18]—Ancillary Sales and Reorders

Additional products or services might be sold by the manufacturer in conjunction with, or after, the initial sale of the royalty-bearing product. Common examples include "up-sales" in which the celebrity's efforts generate a sale for product A, and when the consumer purchases product A they are given the opportunity to purchase product B. Some products are designed to require future orders, and the celebrity should bargain for a share of those additional sales that arise as a result of the endorsement.

[19]—Deceptive Advertising Liability Under the Federal Trade Commission Act

Endorsement agreements should take all possible steps to protect celebrities from personal liability for deceptive advertising or product liability claims. Those protections may take the form of procedures in which the celebrity is informed about the product and the reasonable basis for the claims made about the product; has access to the evidence for substantiation for claims made in the advertising, and personally uses the product so that any endorsement made is based on the celebrity's good faith belief and opinion. The reason for the caution, especially in the area of direct response advertising or "infomercials" that typically include extensive testimonials and endorsements, is that celebrity spokespersons and endorsers may incur individual liability for direct partici-

---

234   See *Wilhelmina Artist Management, LLC v. Knowles*, 8 Misc.3d 1012(A), 801 N.Y.S.2d 782 (Table), 2005 WL 1617178 (N.Y. Sup. June 6, 2005) (upholding management company's contractual right to receive 10% income commission from artist, and additional 20% commission "service charge" from advertiser who engaged artist to endorse products). See also, Moodform Mission v Campbell, 2011 N.Y. Misc. LEXIS 3197 (N.Y. Sup. Ct. June 29, 2011) (contract dispute over fragrance endorsements).

pation in advertisements or for endorsement of products that are found to be deceptive and in violation of Sections 5(a) and 12 of the Federal Trade Commission Act ("FTCA").[235]

[20]—Compliance with Union Rules and Collective Bargaining Agreements

Celebrity actors will be members of SAG-AFTRA, which means that any television and radio advertising production companies must be signatories to the SAG-AFTRA agreements, and abide by those rules.

[21]—Non-Compete Clause

The agreement may have provisions for what happens after the business relationship ends. For example, the agreement may provide for a grace period during which advertising using the celebrity can run its course and cease, or a non-compete specifying an amount of time during which either party may or may not move on to similar projects with others. There may also be provisions confirming that future sales of the product associated with the celebrity may or may not occur after expiration or termination of the agreement, depending on whether the product itself is branded with the celebrity's name, in which event the manufacturer may reserve the right to re-brand the product with the name of a different celebrity. Note that in many jurisdictions, non-compete provisions must be limited in scope, reasonable, and carefully crafted to accord with applicable statutes and legal precedent in order to be enforceable.[236]

[22]—Warranties and Representations: Product Manufacture, Safety, Intellectual Property, and Ethical Considerations

There may be considerable federal and state regulation with respect to product safety, and compliance with, e.g., product labeling under regulations of the Food and Drug Administration ("FDA") and Federal Trade Commission ("FTC"). There may also be regulations relating to the marking of imported goods. In addition, products may implicate several areas of intellectual property including patents, trademarks, copyrights, and trade secrets. The agreement should include warranties and representations that nothing in the products or in the advertising for the products violates the rights of any third parties, and that the products themselves fully comply with all applicable federal, state, and local laws and regulations. In particular, great care should be taken to confirm

---

235   15 U.S.C. §§ 45(a), 52.2.

236   See *Coady v. Harpo, Inc.*, 308 Ill. App.3d 153, 719 N.E.2d 244 (1999) (employee confidentiality agreement between Oprah Winfrey's production company and former employee who announced intention to write about her experiences was valid and enforceable because, in part, agreement was reasonable and did not impose any restrictions on employee's ability to work, noting that "Defendant does not seek to restrain plaintiff's future career). See also, Cal. Bus. & Prof. Code § 16600 prohibiting restraints on engaging in a lawful profession, trade, or business.

that the manufacture of all products is in compliance with the labor, child labor, and safety laws of the country of manufacture and all counties in which the product will be sold, including the United States.[237]

All possible efforts should be made to protect the celebrity financially through indemnification and insurance in the agreement.[238] Given the potential liabilities connected with advertising products, strong indemnification provisions are essential. In addition, the celebrity should confirm that the manufacturer and advertising company have adequate intellectual property and products liability insurance by obtaining a certificate of insurance that also includes the celebrity as a named insured.[239] There may also be provisions granting the advertiser the right to obtain insurance on the celebrity's life or in the event the celebrity is injured or incapacitated and cannot perform his or her duties.

§7.07   Social Media Influencer Agreements

Online social media has created new types of celebrities whose fame is measured in the number of their followers on Facebook, Instagram, Twitter, and other platforms. The ability of a social media celebrity to reach millions of followers with their photos and messages has tremendous advertising value for its ability to directly influence social trends and consumer demand. "Influencers" who endorse products and services via social media videos and messages typically enter into agreements with advertising agencies who represent the brands and products promoted.[240]

Social media influencer agreements are different from traditional celebrity endorsements because the Influencer will want to provide the endorsement in a way that appears to be authentic and part of their bona fide lifestyle. This type of Influencer endorsement is closer to

---

237   Tremendous damage can be done to a celebrity's image in the event it is revealed that the products are manufactured under illegal or unethical circumstances, such as child labor or unsafe or exploitive working conditions overseas.

238   The celebrity may wish to enter into the agreement via a celebrity controlled corporation known as a "loan out" agreement. For a further discussion of such provisions see the discussion of loan out agreements and letters of inducement in Chapter 1, *supra*.

239   Note, however, that with respect to deceptive advertising claims resulting from an FTC action, insurance may not cover such claims because of their potentially fraudulent nature.

240   See, *e.g. Burgin v. NFL*, 2014 U.S. Dist. LEXIS 61935, 2014 WL 1760112 (S.D.N.Y. Apr. 30, 2014) (in denying petition to amend complaint brought by online commentator, court noting that "Plaintiff has not, for example, purported to be an Internet celebrity of the sort that might drive traffic to the site simply because she is included on it. Plaintiff's allegation that she is a "social media influencer, spokesperson[,] and model" is simply not enough." Id. at *11. See also In the Matter of CSGOLOTTO, Inc., FTC Decision and Order No. 162-3184 (Sept. 17, 2017) (finding misrepresentation of independence by social media influencers who promoted a company they owned).

product placement in film and television than traditional advertising: the goal is to make it look as though the Influencer is genuinely integrating the product into their life, and merely "sharing" that information with their followers.

Influencer social media endorsements must still comply with Federal Trade Commission Endorsement Guides, which require "clear and conspicuous" disclaimers alerting consumers to situations where product endorsements are compensated.[241] In practice, Influencers tend to use succinct disclosure hashtags such as "#Sponsor," "#Partner," "#Ad," "#Endorsement."

The FTC has begun to monitor Influencer disclosures by sending warning letters to Influencers providing more detail on what constitutes the "clear and conspicuous" standard. The following quote from FTC warning letters describes some key aspects of adequate Influencer disclosures, noting that in some circumstances the "material connection" between the Influencer and the advertiser could be "already clear from the context:"

> "The FTC's Endorsement Guides state that if there is a "material connection" between an endorser and the marketer of a product – in other words, a connection that might affect the weight or credibility that consumers give the endorsement – that connection should be **clearly and conspicuously disclosed, unless the connection is already clear from the context of the communication containing the endorsement.** Material connections could consist of a business or family relationship, monetary payment, or the provision of free products to the endorser.
>
> The Endorsement Guides apply to marketers and endorsers. If there is a material connection between you and {Marketer}, that connection should be clearly and conspicuously disclosed in your endorsements. **To make a disclosure both "clear" and "conspicuous," you should use unambiguous language and make the disclosure stand out. Consumers should be able to notice the disclosure easily, and not have to look for it.** For example, consumers viewing posts in their Instagram streams on mobile devices typically see only the first three lines of a longer post unless they click "more," and many consumers may not click "more." Therefore, you should disclose any material connection above the "more" button. In addition, where there are multiple tags, hashtags, or links, readers may just skip over them, especially where they appear at the end of a long post." (emphasis added).[242]

---

241   See FTC Endorsement Guidelines, available at https://www.ftc.gov/tips-advice/business-center/guidance/ftcs-endorsement-guides-what-people-are-asking (2017 Edition).

242   See FTC Staff Reminds Influencers and Brands to Clearly Disclose Relationship, available at <https://www.ftc.gov/news-events/press-releases/2017/04/ftc-staff-reminds-influencers-brands-clearly-disclose>.

Influencer agreements may sometimes exhibit a tension between the desire of the Influencer to remain "authentic" in how they endorse products in the natural course of their Instagram photos and tweets, versus the desire of a brand to treat the Influencer more like a traditional celebrity endorsement, perhaps as no more than an online video advertising commercial, which in the social media world runs the risk of looking faked and inauthentic.

Key provisions in Influencer agreements include the following:

Campaign Dates: Social media campaigns may be quite brief, covering a few days or weeks during which the Influencer will post agreed upon deliverables such as photos, videos, and tweets. The parties may negotiate a period of time after the campaign ends during which the social media postings will remain up and available. Influencers will want to limit these residual uses so as not to conflict with future postings for competing products.

Exclusivity: Avoiding exclusivity commitments is a key issue for Influencers who may be offered many short campaigns for competing products. Whether an Influencer grants exclusivity on their channel to a product may depend on whether the advertiser is willing to pay a premium for that exclusivity, because every exclusive endorsement deprives the Influencer of the opportunity to work with other brands in the same channels of trade. Some minimal exclusivity, for example during a short campaign period of a few days, is however common.

Influencer Channels: Specifying the Influencer social media channels that will be used (Facebook, Instagram, Twitter, web site, etc.).

Client Use: This may specify the client's ability to link to the Influencer channels but may or may not include a right for the client to actually post content such as videos on the client's own channels. Influencers may object to their content appearing on a brand's own social media channels, as it may make the Influencer appear to be a traditional "celebrity endorsement" and no more than a low budget video ad.

Media: Often restricted to Influencer channels only, for example no television, print media, radio, etc.

Compensation: Often half upon signing the agreement and half upon campaign completion.

Disclosures: This will specify the disclosures required, ranging from full statements to hashtags such as "#SponsoredContent."

Intellectual Property: Influencers posting on their own social media channels will typically retain all copyright in their work product and control of their trademarks. Retaining copyright ownership of all assets also enables Influencers to control unauthorized future postings, for example demanding that an Influencer video be removed from YouTube after the campaign term ends, a right reserved to copyright owners under the Digital Millennium Copyright Act (DMCA).[243]

<u>Messaging</u>: During the campaign term, the Influencer may agree to use a brand required hashtag ("#Brand") or link to advertiser web sites or sweepstakes.

<u>Platform Disclaimers</u>: Because Influencers rely on third party platforms for their deliverables commitments (Facebook, Instagram, Twitter, etc.) the Influencer may include a disclaimer stating that Influencer is not responsible for any platform failures or unavailability.

<u>Paid Support / Whitelisting</u>: granting the advertiser the right to place paid ads in social media (for example a "Promoted Tweet") supporting the campaign, usually linking back to the influencer's channels.

---

243   See 17 U.S.C. §512.

CHAPTER 8

Cyber Law

§8.01   Introduction

"Cyber law" can include a vast number of laws that affect high tech, computer users, and the online environment, in general. For the purposes of its application to entertainment law, this section will include a concise overview of the Digital Millennium Copyright Act ("DMCA"), the main provision under copyright law specifically addressing online and digital technology, and the Anti-Cybersquatting Consumer Protection Act ("ACPA"), the main provision under the Lanham Act that addresses trademarks in cyberspace. This section will also include an overview of the legal basics regarding Internet domain names: their acquisition, maintenance, and resolution of disputes regarding this valuable online real estate.

§8.02   The Digital Millennium Copyright Act

The Digital Millennium Copyright Act ("DMCA") was passed in 1998, and is encoded in several sections of the Copyright Act, most notably in Section 512, "Limitations on liability relating to material online," and in Section 1201, "Circumvention of copyright protection systems"[1] The DMCA implements treaties signed by the United States under the auspices of the World Intellectual Property Organization ("WIPO").

Section 1201 prohibits technology that circumvents digital rights management protections. For example, motion picture DVDs are encoded with software that prohibits digital copies.

---

1   See 17 U.S.C. §512.

Under Section 1201, copyright owners have prosecuted companies or individuals who use software tools to circumvent those digital copy-control protections.[2]

The legislative intent behind the portion of the DMCA embodied in Section 512 was to encourage the development of the Internet, while protecting on the one hand copyright content owners from rampant online infringement of their works, and on the other hand protecting Internet service providers from secondary copyright infringement liability (under theories of vicarious and contributory copyright infringement) arising from situations where users

---

2   See *Universal City Studios, Inc. v. Reimerdes*, 111 F. Supp.2d 294 (S.D.N.Y. 2000) (anti-circumvention under 17 U.S.C. § 1201(a)(1)); see also, *Universal City Studios, Inc. v. Corley*, 273 F.3d 429 (2d Cir. 2001) (anti-trafficking provisions under 17 U.S.C. §§ 1201(a)(2), 1201(b)(1)). Note that there are limited exemptions from the DMCA anti-circumvention prohibitions issued as rulings by the Copyright Office. See Rulemaking on Exemptions from Prohibition on Circumvention of Technological Measures that Control Access to Copyrighted Works, available at http://www.copyright.gov/1201/. DMCA Section 1202(b) prohibits the digital removal of copyright management information included in a digital file, including the identity of the owner and the copyright notice. See *Murphy v. Millennium Radio Group, LLC*, 650 F.3d 295 (3d Cir. 2011) (removing photographer's name from a digital photo online where the name appeared in a "gutter credit" alongside the photo was a violation of Section 1202(b)).

of their online services committed copyright infringement.[3] The result was the "safe harbor" provisions of the DMCA.[4]

[1]—The Safe Harbor

The Safe Harbor provisions of the DMCA are a shield against copyright infringement liability, including injunctive relief and monetary damages, for Internet Service Providers ("ISP") in several categories, including:

Section 512(a): Transitory network communications;

---

3   The legislative history of the DMCA outlines the issues that Congress was attempting to address, as discussed in this excerpt from the Senate Judiciary Committee Report:

"Due to the ease with which digital works can be copied and distributed worldwide virtually instantaneously, copyright owners will hesitate to make their works readily available on the Internet without reasonable assurance that they will be protected against massive piracy. Legislation implementing the treaties provides this protection and creates the legal platform for launching the global digital on-line marketplace for copyrighted works. It will facilitate making available quickly and conveniently via the Internet the movies, music, software, and literary works that are the fruit of American creative genius. It will also encourage the continued growth of the existing off-line global marketplace for copyrighted works in digital format by setting strong international copyright standards.

"At the same time, without clarification of their liability, service providers may hesitate to make the necessary investment in the expansion of the speed and capacity of the Internet. In the ordinary course of their operations service providers must engage in all kinds of acts that expose them to potential copyright infringement liability. For example, service providers must make innumerable electronic copies by simply transmitting information over the Internet. Certain electronic copies are made in order to host World Wide Web sites. Many service providers engage in directing users to sites in response to inquiries by users or they volunteer sites that users may find attractive. Some of these sites might contain infringing material. In short, by limiting the liability of service providers, the DMCA ensures that the efficiency of the Internet will continue to improve and that the variety and quality of services on the Internet will continue to expand.

"There have been several cases relevant to service provider liability for copyright infringement. Most have approached the issue from the standpoint of contributory and vicarious liability. Rather than embarking upon a wholesale clarification of these doctrines, the Committee decided to leave current law in its evolving state and, instead, to create a series of "safe harbors," for certain common activities of service providers. A service provider which qualifies for a safe harbor, receives the benefit of limited liability."

S. Rep. No. 105-190, 105th Cong., 2d Sess. 8 (May 11, 1998) (quoted in *Viacom International, Inc. v. YouTube, Inc.*, 718 F. Supp.2d 514 (S.D.N.Y. 2010)).

4   Note that although pre-1972 sound recordings are protected under state law and not under the federal Copyright Act, the Second Circuit has held that the DMCA safe harbor applies to pre-1972 sound recordings. See *Capitol Records, LLC v. Vimeo, LLC*, 2016 U.S. App. LEXIS 10884 (2d Cir. June 16, 2016). See also, *UMG Recordings, Inc. v. Escape Media Group, Inc.*, 37 Misc.3d 208, 948 N.Y.S.2d 881 (N.Y. Sup. 2012).

Section 512(b): System caching;

Section 512(c): Information residing on systems or networks at the direction of users;

Section 512(d): Information location tools, such as search engines; and

Section 512(e): Non-profit educational institutions that are not held responsible for the acts of their faculty or students under certain conditions.[5]

[2]—Eligibility for the Safe Harbor

[a]—Reasonably Implemented Policy to Terminate Repeat Offenders

In order to qualify for the Safe Harbor, this immunity is not presumptive, but granted only to service providers that comply with the eligibility requirements under Section 512(i) which require a "policy" that provides for termination of service for repeat infringers:

"(i) Conditions for Eligibility.—

"(1) Accommodation of technology.—The limitations on liability established by this section shall apply to a service provider only if the service provider—

"(A) has adopted and reasonably implemented, and informs subscribers and account holders of the service provider's system or network of, a policy that provides for the termination in appropriate circumstances of subscribers and account holders of the service provider's system or network who are repeat infringers; and

"(B) accommodates and does not interfere with standard technical measures."[6]

The terms "reasonably implemented" and "repeat infringer" are not defined in the DMCA. Courts have held that implementation is reasonable if the service provider (1) has a system for responding to takedown notices, including warnings to users that they must not post infringing content, (2) does not interfere with the copyright

---

5   17 U.S.C. § 512. See also:

Second Circuit: Viacom International, Inc. v. YouTube, Inc., 676 F.3d 19 (2d Cir. 2012), *affirming in part, remanding in part Viacom International, Inc. v. YouTube, Inc.*, 718 F. Supp.2d 514, 525 (S.D.N.Y. 2010).

Ninth Circuit: *UMG Recordings, Inc. v. Shelter Capital Partners LLC and Veoh Networks, Inc.*, 667 F.3d 1022, 1038 (9th Cir. 2011).

6   17 U.S.C. § 512(i).

owners' ability to issue notices, and (3) under "appropriate circumstances" terminates users who repeatedly or blatantly infringe copyrights.[7]

---

7   See *Capitol Records, Inc. v. MP3Tunes, LLC*, 821 F. Supp.2d 627, 637 (S.D.N.Y. 2011):

> "This requirement is a prerequisite for every DMCA safe harbor and is a fundamental safeguard for copyright owners. As described by Judge Posner, '[t]he common element of [the DMCA's] safe harbors is that the service provider must do what it can reasonably be asked to do to prevent use of its service by 'repeat infringers.' In re Aimster Copyright Litig., 334 F.3d 643, 655 (7th Cir. 2003); see also *Columbia Pictures Industries, Inc. v. Fung*, 2009 U.S. Dist. LEXIS 122661, at *67, at *18 (C.D. Cal. Dec. 21, 2009). Other courts have described enforcement of this provision as essential to 'maintain the "strong incentives" for service providers to prevent their services from becoming safe havens or conduits for known repeat copyright infringers.' *Perfect 10 v. Cybernet Ventures*, 213 F. Supp. 2d 1146, 1178 (C.D. Cal. 2002).

"The key terms 'reasonably implemented' and 'repeat infringer' are not defined in the DMCA. Courts have held that implementation is reasonable if the service provider (1) has a system for responding to takedown notices, (2) does not interfere with the copyright owners' ability to issue notices, and (3) under 'appropriate circumstances' terminates users who repeatedly or blatantly infringe copyrights. See *Perfect 10 v. CCBill*, 488 F.3d 1102, 1109-1110 (9th Cir. 2007). The purpose of subsection 512(i) is to deny protection to websites that tolerate users who flagrantly disrespect copyrights. See *Corbis Corp. v. Amazon.com*, 351 F. Supp. 2d 1090, 1100-01 (W.D. Wash. 2004). Thus, service providers that purposefully fail to keep adequate records of the identity and activities of their users and fail to terminate users despite their persistent and flagrant infringement are not eligible for protection under the safe harbor. See CCBill, 488 F.3d at 1110; see also In re Aimster Copyright Litig., 252 F. Supp 2d 634, 659 (N.D. Ill. 2002) (service provider ineligible for safe harbor where users' data was intentionally encrypted, making enforcement of non-infringement policy impossible).

> "On the other hand, service providers have no affirmative duty to police their users. See CCBill, 488 F.3d at 1111. In cases of video and file sharing sites, courts have found reasonable implementation where service providers terminated the accounts of users who had been warned yet continued to upload material that had been the subject of a takedown notice. See, e.g., *UMG Recordings, Inc. v. Veoh Networks, Inc.*, 665 F. Supp. 2d 1099, 1117-18 (CD. Cal. 2009)."

See also:

Second Circuit: Viacom International, Inc. v. YouTube, Inc., 676 F.3d 19 (2d Cir. 2012).

Seventh Circuit: Flava Works, Inc. v. Gunter, 2011 U.S. Dist. LEXIS 82955 (N.D. Ill. July 27, 2011) (denying DMCA safe harbor protection to Web site that failed to act on DMCA take down notices, and whose behavior was "the epitome of willful blindness" to infringing content on the Web site posted by users).

[b]—ISP Must Not Have Actual or "Red Flag" Knowledge or Control of, or Financial Benefit from Infringement

In addition to the ISP repeat infringer policy requirement above, the DMCA includes several other requirements for an ISP to qualify for the safe harbor. With respect to Section 512(c) addressing information posted by users, the statutory eligibility requirements are:

"(c) Information Residing on Systems or Networks At Direction of Users.—

"(1) In general.—A service provider shall not be liable for monetary relief, or, except as provided in subsection (j), for injunctive or other equitable relief, for infringement of copyright by reason of the storage at the direction of a user of material that resides on a system or network controlled or operated by or for the service provider, if the service provider—

"(A)(i) does not have *actual knowledge* that the material or an activity using the material on the system or network is infringing;

"(ii) in the absence of such actual knowledge, *is not aware of facts or circumstances* from which infringing activity is apparent; or

"(iii) upon obtaining such knowledge or awareness, acts expeditiously to remove, or disable access to, the material;

"(B) does not receive a financial benefit directly attributable to the infringing activity, in a case in which the service provider has the right and ability to control such activity; and

"(C) upon notification of claimed infringement as described in paragraph (3), responds expeditiously to remove, or disable access to, the material that is claimed to be infringing or to be the subject of infringing activity."[8]

Whether or not an ISP qualifies for the DMCA safe harbor from copyright infringement liability is crucial to the ISP's business model, which is based on the legislative tradeoff between advancing technology and respecting copyright ownership. Well-known examples of technology-based businesses that depend on their DMCA safe harbor status include the Google search engine (information location tool under Section 512(d)), and YouTube (information residing on systems or networks at the direction of users under Section 512(c)).

---

8   17 U.S.C. § 512(c). (Emphasis added.)

Two Courts of Appeal cases, on opposite coasts in the Ninth and Second circuits, are the leading judicial interpretations of the applicability of the ISP safe harbor under the DMCA. The Ninth Circuit case is *UMG Recordings, Inc. v. Shelter Capital Partners LLC and Veoh Networks, Inc.*[9] It was originally decided in December 2011, and followed shortly by the Second Circuit case, *Viacom International, Inc. v. YouTube, Inc.*, in 2012.[10]

Both courts reached essentially the same conclusions concerning safe harbors under the DMCA, putting the burden of identifying infringements squarely on the shoulders of the copyright owners, holding that notwithstanding general knowledge of infringement on their websites, the ISP defendants in both cases qualified for the DMCA safe harbor so long as they responded to the plaintiff's DMCA notices of actual, specific infringements and otherwise complied with the safe harbor requirements of the DMCA. In both cases, ISPs are not responsible for monitoring for infringement, nor does general awareness that there is infringing activity on their website trigger any responsibility to identify specific infringements or to take action by removing or disabling links to suspected infringements.

But the Second Circuit went a little further than the Ninth Circuit in two respects: (1) the "willful blindness" doctrine could be applied to demonstrate knowledge or awareness of specific instances of infringement under the DMCA;[11] (2) ISPs who induced or encouraged infringement could potentially have liability under the "inducement" doctrine announced by the Supreme Court in *MGM v. Grokster*;[12] and (3) the "actual knowledge" and "awareness" of infringement (the "red flag") standards that can destroy the safe harbor for an ISP unless action is taken, were presented as two separate judicial tests using a combination of subjective and objective standards.[13]

Under the Second Circuit tests, "actual knowledge" of infringement is judged under a subjective standard, meaning that where an ISP believes they have knowledge of a specific infringement and does nothing, they potentially lose the DMCA safe harbor.

---

9   See *UMG Recordings, Inc. v. Shelter Capital Partners LLC and Veoh Networks, Inc.*, 667 F.3d 1022 (9th Cir. 2011), *superseded by UMG Recordings, Inc. v. Shelter Capital Partners LLC and Veoh Networks, Inc.*, 718 F.3d 1006 (9th Cir. 2013).

10   See *Viacom International, Inc. v. YouTube, Inc.*, 676 F.3d 19 (2d Cir. 2012). See also, *EMI Christian Music Group v. MP3Tunes*, LLC, 840 F.3d 69 (2d Cir. 2016).

11   *Viacom International, Inc. v. YouTube, Inc.*, N. 9 *supra*, 676 F.3d at 34-35 ("[a] person is "willfully blind" or engages in "conscious avoidance" amounting to knowledge where the person "was aware of a high probability of the fact in dispute and consciously avoided confirming that fact").

12   *Id.*, 676 F.3d at 38.

13   *Id.*, 676 F.3d at 31-32.

Under the statute, an ISP may not be assumed to have actual knowledge unless and until the copyright owner submits a valid DMCA "takedown" notice to the ISP.[14]

"Awareness of facts or circumstances" of infringement, commonly referred to as "red flag" knowledge, or perhaps helpfully described here as "extreme suspicion of infringement," is judged under an objective standard as would be expected when the standard is the observation of external "facts or circumstances."

The Second Circuit's definition mixes subjective and objective standards as follows: "the red flag provision turns on whether the provider was subjectively aware of facts that would have made the specific infringement "objectively" obvious to a reasonable person."

The dictionary definition of "subjective" is internal mental impressions, and "objective" is defined as observation of external information. It would thus appear that where an ISP believes (the subjective standard) there are facts and circumstances indicating a specific act of infringement, and those facts or circumstances are objectively reasonable (the objective standard), then the ISP has knowledge and must take action by removing or disabling the link to the infringement, without waiting for the copyright owner to submit a DMCA takedown notice, or risk losing the DMCA safe harbor.

The Second Circuit did not provide "real world" examples of how to apply facts to the "red flag/awareness" subjective/objective test. On remand, the District Court affirmed the application of the safe harbor for YouTube, basing its decision largely on findings of fact that "neither side can determine the presence or absence of specific infringements because of the volume of material, [which] merely demonstrates the wisdom of the leg-

---

14   See 17 U.S.C. § 512(c)(3)(B)(i), stating that a valid takedown notice is required in order for an ISP to have knowledge of infringement, but also noting that under some circumstances, where a notice is received that only partially complies, the ISP must attempt to contact the person submitting the defective notice or take reasonable steps to assist in the receipt of a notification that substantially complies with all the requirements:

"Subject to clause (ii), a notification from a copyright owner or from a person authorized to act on behalf of the copyright owner that fails to comply substantially with the provisions of subparagraph (A) shall not be considered under paragraph (1)(A) in determining whether a service provider has actual knowledge or is aware of facts or circumstances from which infringing activity is apparent.

"(ii) In a case in which the notification that is provided to the service provider's designated agent fails to comply substantially with all the provisions of subparagraph (A) but substantially complies with clauses (ii), (iii), and (iv) of subparagraph (A), clause (i) of this subparagraph applies only if the service provider promptly attempts to contact the person making the notification or takes other reasonable steps to assist in the receipt of notification that substantially complies with all the provisions of subparagraph (A)."

islative requirement that it be the owner of the copyright, or his agent, who identifies the infringement by giving the service provider notice."[15]

The District Court on remand also found no showing of willful blindness to specific infringements of the videos clips in the case because of lack of specific notices of infringement, and no right and ability to control infringements because YouTube, among other things, did not preview the clips prior to posting or otherwise exercise control over what was posted by users.[16] The District Court did not actually apply the Second Circuit's somewhat vague "subjective knowledge of infringement as shown by objective facts" test which remains to be further explained, perhaps via another appeal.

In 2013, the Ninth Circuit surprised many by re-issuing its opinion in the *UMG v. Veoh* case, in the process withdrawing its earlier December, 2011 opinion (though not changing the result), rewriting the opinion and adding to it an incorporation of the Second Circuit's standards for willful blindness, inducement, actual knowledge (the subjective standard), and red flag "awareness" (the objective analysis of subjective awareness). Thus the two judicial circuits on the coasts agree on the tests for an ISP's "knowledge" of infringement under the DMCA. As the Ninth Circuit neatly summarized it, "a service provider cannot willfully bury its head in the sand to avoid obtaining . . . specific knowledge."[17]

In a case that is a "bookend" to *UMG v. Veoh* because it reached an opposite result, on March 21, 2013, the Ninth Circuit issued its ruling in *Columbia Pictures Industries, Inc. v. Fung*, which found an ISP *liable* for infringement and *not* qualified for the DMCA safe harbor, in an instructive opinion that is discussed further below in the Section titled "Cases Where the DMCA Safe Harbor Held Not Applicable."[18] As for direct financial benefit and the "right to control" the infringing conduct, courts have held that the standard is not overall financial benefit from the ISPs Web site, or the right to remove infringing postings by users, but direct participation in and financial benefit from the actual act of infringement itself.[19] The Second Circuit has held, however, that the "right to control" does not necessarily have to be tied to specific acts of infringement. Instead, it can be interpreted more broadly, citing to the Supreme Court's copyright "inducement"

---

15   See *Viacom International, Inc. v. YouTube, Inc.*, 940 F. Supp.2d 110, 115 (S.D.N.Y. 2013).

16   *Id.*, 940 F. Supp.2d at 115-122.

17   *UMG Recordings, Inc. v. Shelter Capital Partners LLC and Veoh Networks, Inc.*, 718 F.3d 1106, 1023 (9th Cir. 2013).

18   See *Columbia Pictures Industries, Inc. v. Fung*, 710 F.3d 1020 (9th Cir. 2013).

19   See *UMG Recordings, Inc. v. Veoh Networks, Inc.*, N. 12.4 supra, 718 F.3d 1106.

standard under *MGM v. Grokster*, for example where a service provider exerts substantial influence on the activities of users via "purposeful, culpable expression and conduct."[20]

In *Capitol Records, LLC v. Vimeo, LLC* at the Second Circuit, the court summarized the difficulty in establishing "red flag" knowledge of infringement with this following discourse on the inherent difficulty of members of the ISP workforce making online copyright infringement determinations:

A copyright owner's mere showing that a video posted by a user on the service provider's site includes substantially all of a recording of recognizable copyrighted music, and that an employee of the service provider saw at least some part of the user's material, is insufficient to sustain the copyright owner's burden of proving that the service provider had either actual or red flag knowledge of the infringement. That is so for many reasons.

First, the employee's viewing might have been brief. The fact that an employee viewed enough of a video to post a brief comment, add it to a channel (such as kitten videos) or hit the "like" button, would not show that she had ascertained that its audio track contains all or virtually all of a piece of music.

Second, the insufficiency of some viewing by a service provider's employee to prove the viewer's awareness that a video contains all or virtually all of a song is all the more true in contemplation of the many different business purposes for which the employee might have viewed the video. The purpose of the viewing might include application of technical elements of computer expertise, classification by subject matter, sampling to detect inappropriate obscenity or bigotry, and innumerable other objectives having nothing to do with recognition of infringing music in the soundtrack. Furthermore, the fact that music is "recognizable" (which, in its dictionary definition of "capable of being recognized" would seem to apply to all music that is original and thus distinguishable from other music), or even famous (which is perhaps what the district court meant by "recognizable"), is insufficient to demonstrate that the music was in fact recognized by a hypothetical ordinary individual who has no specialized knowledge of the field of music. Some ordinary people know little or nothing of music. Lovers of one style or category of music may have no familiarity with other categories. For example, 60-year-olds, 40-year-olds, and 20-year-olds, even those who are music lovers, may know and love entirely different bodies of music, so that music intimately familiar to some may be entirely unfamiliar to others.

Furthermore, employees of service providers cannot be assumed to have expertise in the laws of copyright. Even assuming awareness that a user posting contains copyrighted

---

20   See *Viacom International, Inc. v. YouTube, Inc.*, 676 F.3d 19, 28 (2d Cir. 2012) (citing to *Metro-Goldwyn-Mayer Studios, Inc. v. Grokster, Ltd.*, 545 U.S. 913, 125 S.Ct. 2764, 162 L.Ed.2d 781 (2005)).

music, the service provider's employee cannot be expected to know how to distinguish, for example, between infringements and parodies that may qualify as fair use. Nor can every employee of a service provider be automatically expected to know how likely or unlikely it may be that the user who posted the material had authorization to use the copyrighted music. Even an employee who was a copyright expert cannot be expected to know when use of a copyrighted song has been licensed. Additionally, the service provider is under no legal obligation to have its employees investigate to determine the answers to these questions.

It is of course entirely possible that an employee of the service provider who viewed a video did have expertise or knowledge with respect to the market for music and the laws of copyright. The employee may well have known that the work was infringing, or known facts that made this obvious. The copyright owner is entitled to discovery in order to obtain the specific evidence it needs to sustain its burden of showing that the service provider did in fact know of the infringement or of facts that made infringement obvious. But the mere fact that a video contains all or substantially all of a piece of recognizable, or even famous, copyrighted music and was to some extent viewed (or even viewed in its entirety) by some employee of a service provider would be insufficient (without more) to sustain the copyright owner's burden of showing red flag knowledge."[21]

[3]—Take Down Notice

The DMCA contains notification procedures by which copyright owners may contact an Internet service provider ("ISP") to alert it to the existence of infringing materials posted to a Web site hosted by the ISP.[22] The user has a subsequent opportunity to object to the removal of the items via a "counter notification," which requires a statement, under

---

21   *Capitol Records, LLC v. Vimeo, LLC*, 2016 U.S. App. LEXIS 10884 (2d Cir. June 16, 2016) at *47-*54.

22   See 17 U.S.C. § 512(c)(3) Elements of notification. The statutorily required contents of a "take down" notice under Section 512(c)(3) are:

"(3) Elements of notification.—

"(A) To be effective under this subsection, a notification of claimed infringement must be a written communication provided to the designated agent of a service provider that includes substantially the following:

"(i) A physical or electronic signature of a person authorized to act on behalf of the owner of an exclusive right that is allegedly infringed.

"(ii) Identification of the copyrighted work claimed to have been infringed, or, if multiple copyrighted works at a single online site are covered by a single notification, a representative list of such works at that site.

"(iii) Identification of the material that is claimed to be infringing or to be the subject of infringing activity and that is to be removed or access to which is to be disabled, and information reasonably sufficient to permit the service provider to locate the material.

penalty of perjury, that the user has a good faith belief that the material was removed as a result of "mistake or misidentification of the material to be removed."[23]

One court has held that where ISPs offer digital storage in the "Cloud," take down notices with specific locations of infringing files apply not only to the publicly available Web site, but also to users' individual "storage lockers" that mirror the files' locations.[24]

Under §512(c)(3)(A)(v), the copyright owner must have a "good faith belief" that use of the material is unauthorized. In *Lenz v. Universal Music Corp.*, the Ninth Circuit stated that because copyright's fair use doctrine is authorized under the law and not merely an "affirmative defense," the copyright owner sending a DMCA takedown has an affirmative obligation to first consider whether fair use applies.[25] Given the enormous amount of online infringement of music files and the corresponding burden on copyright owners, the court did note that the use of computer algorithms to search out and identify online infringements "appears to be a valid and good faith middle ground for processing a plethora of content while still meeting the DMCA's requirements to somehow consider fair use."[26]

As an example of an algorithm that met this standard, the court noted that if an entire video and audio track were found online, as opposed to short excerpts or some compilation, then that would be an acceptable screening process, requiring a human to review the material as the final step before sending a takedown notice.

Fair use is a notoriously subtle area of the law that demands a four part analysis as well as potential consideration of whether the use is "transformative," thus it remains to be seen whether the above suggested screening process would adequately protect the interests of copyright owners.

"(iv) Information reasonably sufficient to permit the service provider to contact the complaining party, such as an address, telephone number, and, if available, an electronic mail address at which the complaining party may be contacted.

"(v) A statement that the complaining party has a good faith belief that use of the material in the manner complained of is not authorized by the copyright owner, its agent, or the law.

"(vi) A statement that the information in the notification is accurate, and under penalty of perjury, that the complaining party is authorized to act on behalf of the owner of an exclusive right that is allegedly infringed."

23   See 17 U.S.C. § 512(g)(3), Contents of counter notification.

24   See *Capitol Records, Inc. v. MP3 Tunes*, LLC, 821 F. Supp.2d 627 (S.D.N.Y. 2011).

25   See *Lenz v. Universal Music Corp.*, 2015 U.S. App. LEXIS 16308 (9th Cir. Sept. 14, 2015).

26   *Id.*, at *19.

[4]– Designated Agent

An ISP that wishes to have the protections of the DMCA "safe harbor" must designate an agent to receive DMCA notices, and must file a Notice of Designated Agent with the Copyright Office. This filing requires a fee and was formerly done via a paper filing.[27] As of December 31, 2017, each website must first create a DMCA Designated Agent Registration Account, then register the DMCA Designated Agent by using the Copyright Office's online system.[28]

All prior DMCA Designated Agent registrations previously filed via the old "paper" system had to be resubmitted no later than December 31, 2017.[29]

Some Web sites that specialize in posting information provided by users, such as eBay, have their own customized online version of the DMCA notice and take down procedures.[30]

Filing the designated agent form is more than a mere formality. In *Oppenheimer v. Allvoices, Inc.*, the Northern District of California held that no DMCA safe harbor could be invoked by a Web site that had filed its registered agent forms *after* the alleged online infringement began, stating that "Section 512(c)(2) plainly specifies that a registered agent is a predicate, express condition that must be met and that the safe harbor will

---

27 See Interim Designation of Agent to Receive Notification of Claimed Infringement, available at http://www.copyright.gov/onlinesp/agent.pdf. See also, 17 U.S.C. § 512(c)(2), stating:

> "(2) Designated agent.—The limitations on liability established in this subsection apply to a service provider only if the service provider has designated an agent to receive notifications of claimed infringement described in paragraph (3), by making available through its service, including on its website in a location accessible to the public, and by providing to the Copyright Office, substantially the following information:

> "(A) the name, address, phone number, and electronic mail address of the agent.

> "(B) other contact information which the Register of Copyrights may deem appropriate.

> "The Register of Copyrights shall maintain a current directory of agents available to the public for inspection, including through the Internet, in both electronic and hard copy formats, and may require payment of a fee by service providers to cover the costs of maintaining the directory."

28 See U.S. Copyright Office, "DMCA Designated Agent Registration," available at https://www.copyright.gov/rulemaking/onlinesp/NPR/.

29 See U.S. Copyright Office, "DMCA Designated Agent Directory," available at https://www.copyright.gov/dmca-directory/.

30 See eBay, Inc., "Verified Rights Owner Program (VeRO)," available at http://pages.ebay.com/help/policies/programs-vero-ov.html.

apply only if such agent has been designated and identified to the Copyright Office for inclusion in the director of agents."[31]

[5]—Cases Where the DMCA Safe Harbor Held Not Applicable

Internet Service Providers that adhere to the provisions of the DMCA will come within the DMCA safe harbors, as shown in the *UMG v. Veoh* and *Viacom v. YouTube* cases discussed above. However, not all Web-based businesses adhere to the DMCA, or qualify for DMCA safe harbors. Such Web sites fall into roughly three categories.

(1) First are Web sites that do not engage in any Internet Service Provider functions. A website that simply offers its own products online or distributes the products of others and is not a mere ISP transmission "conduit" for third-party users will not qualify. In other words, Web sites that are self-contained businesses and not online "bulletin boards" do not enjoy DMCA protection.

(2) Second are Web sites that, notwithstanding apparent attempts to adhere to the DMCA or at least legal arguments that cite to the DMCA in defense of infringement actions, are pirate sites built on exploitation of copyright infringement.

(3) Finally, there are Web sites that may partly engage in ISP-type activities protected by the DMCA safe harbor, for example allowing users to post content on the site, but simultaneously also engage in non-protected activities that clearly fall outside the definition of an ISP, for example offering direct sales, under the Web site's own name of digital files that may have been obtained from third parties, or manufacturing merchandise based on photos submitted by Web site users. Direct manufacture of infringing physical goods by a defendant, or direct licensing by a defendant as part of their business model, is not excused by any simultaneous online posting of those same infringing items by Web site users.[32]

---

31   *David Oppenheimer v. Allvoices, Inc.*, No. C 14-00499 LB, Slip Op. at 9 (N.D. Cal. June 10, 2014) (citing to *Perfect 10, Inc. v. Yandex N.V.*, 2013 WL 1899851 at *8 (N.D. Cal. May 7, 2013)).

32   See:

Second Circuit: Agence France Presse v. Morel, 934 F. Supp.2d 547 (S.D.N.Y. 2013) (news photo licensing site not eligible for DMCA safe harbor where site directly licensed photos that were obtained from a third party); *Born to Rock Design Incorporated v. Cafepress.com*, 2012 U.S. Dist. LEXIS 129230 (S.D.N.Y. Sept. 7, 2012) (physical manufacture of trademark infringing t-shirts by Web site owners not excused where source of infringing images were postings by Web site users).

Ninth Circuit: Gardner v. Cafepress, Inc., 2014 U.S. Dist. LEXIS 25405, at *13, 2014 WL 794216, at *5 (S.D. Cal. Feb. 26, 2014) (defendant "goes beyond facilitating the sale of products between internet users by directly selling products to online shoppers.... Cafepress has gone beyond operating a service that merely facilitates the exchange of information between internet users").

[a]—Websites That Fail to Meet the Requirements of the DMCA Safe Harbor

Columbia Pictures Industries, Inc. v. Fung is a Ninth Circuit case holding that a Web site did not meet any of the qualifications for the DMCA safe harbor. In *Fung*, an ISP operated a Web site built on encouraging the posting of infringing copies of copyrighted works, including the use of a proprietary bit-torrent tracking software that sought out infringing works.[33] In affirming that the Web site took clear steps to foster copyright infringement and thus not qualify for any DMCA safe harbors, the Ninth Circuit analyzed the possible categories of DMCA safe harbors as follows:

Inducement liability under *Grokster:* The defendant induced infringement by, *inter alia*, responding to requests for help in locating and playing copyrighted materials, including uploading torrent files corresponding to obviously copyrighted material, finding particular copyrighted movies and television shows, getting pirated material to play properly, and burning the infringing content onto DVDs for playback.[34]

No Safe Harbor for transitory digital network communications under Section 512(a): The "tracker" used by the Web site to locate infringing portions of the bit-torrent files gave the website an active role beyond merely providing a neutral transmission platform, therefore the DMCA safe harbor does not apply.[35]

No Safe Harbor for information residing on systems or networks at direction of users under Section 512(c): The defendant stored torrents on the Web site, in addition

---

33   *Columbia Pictures Industries, Inc. v. Fung*, 710 F.3d 1020, (9th Cir. 2013). See also:

Seventh Circuit: In re Aimster Copyright Litigation, 334 F.3d 643, 655 (7th Cir. 2003) ("The common element of safe harbors is that the service provider must do what it can reasonably be asked to do to prevent the use of its service by repeat infringers. Far from doing anything to discourage repeat infringers of the plaintiff's copyrights, Aimster invited them to do so, showed them how they could do so with ease using its system, and by teaching its users how to encrypt their unlawful distribution of copyrighted materials disabled itself from doing anything to prevent infringement."). (Internal citations omitted.)

Ninth Circuit: Perfect 10, Inc. v. Cybernet Ventures, Inc., 213 F. Supp.2d 1146, 1181-1182 (C.D. Cal. 2002) (granting preliminary injunction against defendant website, and not finding defendant eligible for DMCA safe harbor where it participated in the users' infringing activity because it provided users "extensive advice" and "detailed instructions" on content, prescreening submissions and refusing access to users "until they comply with its dictates."). See also *Mavric Photographs, LLC v. LiveJournal, Inc.*, 2017 U.S. App. LEXIS 6028 (9th Cir. Apr. 7, 2017) (no safe harbor where web site team of volunteer moderators led by an employee of the web site reviewed and approved photos prior to posting).

34   *Columbia Pictures Industries, Inc. v. Fung, id.*, 710 F.3d at 1031.

35   *Id.*, 710 F.3d at 1040.

to torrents posted by users; therefore no safe harbor applied for files posted by the defendant.[36]

Actual and red flag knowledge of infringements: The defendant actively encouraged infringement by urging his users to both upland and download particular copyrighted works, thus possessing actual knowledge of specific infringements that disqualify the defendant for the DMCA safe harbor.[37]

Financial benefit and the right and ability to control under Section 512(c)(1)(B): There was a causal relationship between the infringing activity and any financial benefit the defendant reaped because the defendant generated revenue by selling advertising space on the Web site, and the defendant marketed the website to advertisers by pointing to the popular copyrighted movies and television programs available on the site for free. The defendant also exerted control over the infringements via substantial influence on the activities of users.[38]

Information location tools under Section 512(d): No safe harbor under this provision for the same reasons above, including being aware of infringing activity and receiving a direct financial benefit via the advertising that was built on the availability of infringing files.

[b]—Websites That Do Not Qualify as Internet Service Providers

Where Web sites engage in activities that are affirmative uses of a website to sell or license copyrights, they are not "passive" ISPs under the DMCA and do not qualify for any safe harbor. In *Agence France Presse v. Morel*, the plaintiff sought a declaration of non-infringement of photographs posted online without the permission of the photographer.[39] Photo licensing agencies including Getty Images received the images from Agence France Press, then posted the photographers' work on their own Web sites, offering to license the images to their customers, thus the photos were not posted by "users" of an ISP acting as a mere "conduit," but were posted on a commercial website for the purpose of further licensing, a simple commercial offering not covered by any DMCA safe harbor. As the court noted, "licensing copyrighted material online more closely resembles the mere sale of goods (albeit, in this

---

36   *Id.*, 710 F.3d at 1042.

37   *Id.*, 710 F.3d at 1043.

38   *Id.*, 710 F.3d at 1044.

39   See *Agence France Presse v. Morel*, 934 F. Supp.2d 547 (S.D.N.Y. 2013).

case, intellectual property) than facilitating users' activities online. . . . Getty's role extends beyond merely providing a file-hosting service to AFP. . . . Getty itself acted as a licensor of the Photos-at-issue."[40]

[6]—Voluntary Cooperation and New Technological Measures in Addition to the DMCA

The notice and take down provisions of the DMCA are based on specific infringing digital files in specific locations, a "one file at a time" approach that does not take into account the speed at which digital files can proliferate and be copied online in today "viral" online environment. Digital technology has advanced since the DMCA was enacted in 1998, especially in the area of digital fingerprinting tools that can identify digital versions of copyrighted works by their unique digital "signature."

Some ISPs have taken advantage of such technologies to more effectively monitor user postings of infringing content. In the District Court opinion in *Viacom International, Inc. v. YouTube, Inc.*, the court noted that YouTube had a "Claim Your Content" system using the Audible Magic software, "a fingerprinting tool which removed an offending video automatically if it matched some portion of a reference video submitted by a copyright owner who had designated this service. It also removed a video if the rights-holder operated a manual function after viewing the infringing video to be removed"[41]

In addition to using digital fingerprinting technology to identify and remove infringing files posted by users, the same technology can be used to "monetize" such postings, with the permission of the copyright owner, by placing online advertising on the same page as the content, and sharing the ad revenue between the ISP and the copyright owner. In one such example, YouTube and the National Music Publishers Association ("NMPA") have a program entitled the "YouTube Licensing Offer" under which copyright owner music publishers receive a share of YouTube ad revenue generated by user postings of videos that include the publishers' copyrighted songs.[42]

In addition to monetizing user generated postings online, some ISPs have instigated a voluntary enforcement program with copyright owners whereby the ISP monitors its service for evidence of infringement. As part of a "graduated response," the ISP sends as many as six separate notices to the user, prior to any decision to terminate service.

---

40   *Id.*, 934 F. Supp.2d at 566-568.

41   See *Viacom International, Inc. v. YouTube, Inc.*, 718 F. Supp.2d 514, 528 (S.D.N.Y. 2010), *affirmed in part, vacated in part, remanded by Viacom International, Inc. v. YouTube, Inc.*, 676 F.3d 19 (2d Cir. 2012).

42   See http://www.youtubelicenseoffer.com.

The program includes privacy protections for the users, as well as the opportunity for the user to respond to any notices.[43]

[7]—Secondary Liability for Online Trademark Infringement

As noted above, copyright law's Digital Millennium Copyright Act ("DMCA") was intended to encourage the growth of the Internet by shielding Internet Service Providers ("ISPs") from secondary liability for copyright infringements committed online by the ISP's customers, providing that the ISP complied with the DMCA requirements.

But what is status of an ISP or Web site that hosts advertising and sales of goods that constitute trademark infringement? Without the clear "safe harbor" afforded to copyrighted works by the DMCA, does a web site have secondary liability for contributory trademark infringement if its users advertise and sell infringing merchandise bearing unauthorized and pirated logos and brand names?

In *Tiffany (NJ) Inc. v. eBay, Inc.*, the Second Circuit addressed the question of contributory trademark infringement online.[44] Tiffany, the jewelry brand, alleged that the online auction site eBay facilitated the sale of counterfeit Tiffany merchandise, which was being auctioned alongside genuine Tiffany products.

While eBay's use of the Tiffany mark to describe genuine Tiffany products was deemed fair use, Tiffany maintained that eBay engaged in "willful blindness" with respect to the use of the Tiffany brand and trademarks in connection with the sale of counterfeit merchandise.[45]

As a general matter, the court agreed that an ISP is not permitted to engage in willful blindness because "willful blindness is equivalent to actual knowledge for purposes of the Lanham Act."[46] However, the court held that when eBay was given specific information on counterfeit merchandise, it acted upon the information sufficiently to avoid secondary liability.[47]

Citing to the Supreme Court case on secondary liability for trademark infringement, *Inwood Laboratories, Inc. v. Ives Laboratories, Inc.*, the Second Circuit stated the two-part

---

43   See www.copyrightinformation.org/alerts.

44   See *Tiffany (NJ) Inc. v. eBay, Inc.*, 600 F.3d 93 (2d Cir. 2010).

45   *Id.*, 600 F.3d at 102-103 (fair use); 600 F.3d 109-110 (willful blindness).

46   *Id.*, 600 F.3d at 110 (quoting from *Hard Rock Café Licensing Corp. v. Concession Services, Inc.*, 955 F. 2d 1143, 1149 (7th Cir. 1992)).

47   *Id.*, 600 F.3d at 106.

test as applicable to service providers.[48] First, if the service provider "intentionally induces another to infringe a trademark," and second, if the service provider "continues to supply its [service] to one whom it knows or has reason to know is engaging in trademark infringement."[49]

In applying the test to eBay, the court found that once eBay was notified of a claimed trademark infringement by the trademark owner, its practice was "promptly to remove the challenged listing from its website, warn sellers and buyers, cancel fees it earned from that listing, and direct buyers not to consummate the sale of the disputed item." The court therefore declined to hold eBay contributorily liable for the infringing conduct of those sellers.[50]

While the holding in *Tiffany v. eBay* puts ISPs on notice of their obligations to take action in order to avoid contributory trademark infringement liability, not every online merchandise website is as diligent as eBay's response described by the court. Unless and until Congress adds a DMCA-like provision to the Lanham Act that makes ISP obligations clear in the trademark context, trademark owners are well advised to aggressively pursue their rights against merchandise websites that mistakenly believe they automatically have DMCA-like safe harbors, without the corresponding duty to act against infringers as described by the court, including:

- Provide an efficient DMCA-like "notice" system for trademark owners

- Remove the challenged listing(s) promptly;

- Warn sellers and buyers prominently and effectively;

- Direct buyers not to consummate the sale;

- Cancel any commission fees, or preferably disgorge them to the rightful owner of the trademark

Failure to meet the above standards articulated in *Tiffany v. eBay* arguably creates secondary trademark liability for ISPs. One aspect conspicuously missing from the acts performed by eBay as described by the court is disclosure to the trademark owner of

---

48 *Id.*, 600 F.3d at 104-109 (*citing Inwood Laboratories, Inc. v. Ives Laboratories, Inc.*, 456 U.S. 844, 854, 102 S.Ct. 2182, 72 L.Ed.2d 606 (1982) ("if a manufacturer or distributor intentionally induces another to infringe a trademark, or it if continues to supply its product to one whom it knows or has reason to know is engaging in trademark infringement, the manufacturer or distributor is contributorily responsible for any harm done as a result of the deceit.")).

49 *Tiffany (NJ) Inc. v. eBay, Inc.*, 600 F.3d 93, 106 (2d Cir. 2010).

50 *Id.* See *Born to Rock Design Incorporated v. Cafepress.com*, 2012 WL 3954518 (S.D.N.Y. Sept. 7, 2012) (Web site that manufactured shirts found liable for trademark infringement. Defendant attempts to cite online context as a defense described by court as "facetious" and "irrelevant" where "the alleged infringer physically places the mark on goods that it sells to its customers.").

the identity of the allegedly infringing seller, for purveyors of counterfeit merchandise rarely provide their identity or viable contact information. Perhaps Congress will consider legislation that codifies the holding in *Tiffany v. eBay*, and that goes a step further by including an obligation for the ISP to decline its services to commercial retail online vendors who conceal their identity from the public.

§8.03   Anti-Cybersquatting Consumer Protection Act

Registration of domain names is a "first-to-file" process without review of any potential intellectual property claims to the name in question. In the early days of the Internet, some "first to file" registrants legitimately scooped up potentially valuable, but generic, domain names. Some examples include business.com, or travel.com. There were no trademark rights infringed by the acquisition of a generic word as a domain name.

In other cases, individuals registered domain names that were clearly using, derived from, or identical to established company names and trademarks, then attempted to sell those domain names to what would normally be considered the "rightful owner." In a seminal Ninth Circuit case, the domain name, "www.panavision.com," was registered by an individual who then attempted to sell it to Panavision International, L.P. at an inflated price.[51] Instead of paying the individual for the domain name, Panavision sued, prevailing on claims under the Federal Trademark Dilution Act[52] and the California anti-dilution statute.[53]

Panavision addressed the new technology of domain names, Web sites using the domain names, and the creation of a domain registry system that had no oversight regarding those words that could be registered and by whom. In response, Congress enacted the Anti-Cybersquatting Consumer Protection Act ("ACPA") to prevent cybersquatting, the bad faith, abusive registration and use of others' distinctive trademarks as Internet domain names, with the intent to profit from the goodwill associated with those trademarks.[54] To successfully assert a claim under the ACPA, a plaintiff must demonstrate that; (1) its marks were distinctive at the time the domain name was registered; (2) the infringing domain names complained of are identical to or confusingly similar to plaintiff's mark; and (3) that the defendant has a bad faith intent to profit from that mark.[55] In cases under the ACPA, bad faith and an intent

---

51   See *Panavision International L.P. v. Toeppen*, 141 F.3d 1316 (9th Cir. 1998).

52   See 15 U.S.C. § 1125(c).

53   See Cal. Bus. & Prof. Code § 14330.

54   See *Sporty's Farm, L.L.C. v. Sportsman's Market, Inc.*, 202 F.3d 489, 495 (2d Cir. 2000) (cited in *The New York City Triathlon, LLC v. NYC Triathlon Club, Inc.*, 704 F. Supp.2d 305 (S.D.N.Y. 2010). The ACPA is encoded as Section 1125(d) of Title 15 (Section 43(d) of the Lanham Act).

55   See 15 U.S.C. § 1125(d)(1).

to profit can be determined by the court using nine non-exclusive factors set forth in the statute.[56]

Under the ACPA, a court may order the forfeiture or cancellation of the domain name or the transfer of the domain name to the owner of the mark.[57] The ACPA also allows plaintiffs to pursue statutory damages:

> Statutory damages for violation of section 1125 (d)(1)
>
> In a case involving a violation of section 1125 (d)(1) of this title, the plaintiff may elect, at any time before final judgment is rendered by the trial court, to recover, instead of actual damages and profits, an award of statutory damages in the amount of not less than $1,000 and not more than $100,000 per domain name, as the court considers just.[58]

---

56   The nine factors enumerated in the ACPA are:

(1) the rights of the person, if any, in the domain name;

(2) the extent to which the domain name consists of the legal name of the person;

(3) the person's prior use, if any, of the domain name in connection with the bona fide offering of any goods or services;

(4) the person's bona fide noncommercial or fair use of the mark in a site accessible under the domain name;

(5) the person's intent to divert consumers from the mark owner's online location to a site accessible under the domain name that could harm the goodwill represented by the mark, either for commercial gain or with the intent to tarnish or disparage the mark, by creating a likelihood of confusion as to the source, sponsorship, affiliation, or endorsement of the site;

(6) the person's offer to transfer, sell, or otherwise assign the domain name to the mark owner or any third party for financial gain;

(7) the person's provision of material and misleading false contact information when applying for the registration of the domain name;

(8) the person's registration or acquisition of multiple domain names which the person knows are identical or confusingly similar to marks of others that are distinctive at the time of registration of such domain names; and

(9) the extent to which the mark incorporated in the person's domain name registration is or is not distinctive and famous within the meaning of subsection (c)(1) of section 43.

15 U.S.C. § 1125(d)(1)(B)(i)(I)-(IX). See also, *Bosley Medical Institute, Inc. v. Kremer*, 403 F.3d 672 (9th Cir 2005).

57   See 15 U.S.C. § 1125(d)(1)(C).

58   See 15 U.S.C. § 1117(d). See also, *Citigroup, Inc., v. Chen Bao Shui*, 611 F. Supp.2d 507 (E.D. Va. 2009) (awarding maximum statutory damages of $100,000).

Note that Web sites legitimately created for the purposes of criticism and commentary may refer to a company or its mark as part of the domain name under First Amendment principles, providing there is no likelihood of consumer confusion created by the use.[59] Thus a Web site called "ballysucks.com", designed by a disgruntled former employee as a forum to criticize the Bally Company was not liable for trademark infringement on First Amendment principles. However the parody Web site called "peta.org" infringed the rights of the organization, People for the Ethical Treatment of Animals ("PETA"), because the comedic nature of the Web site was not immediately apparent from the domain name itself.[60]

§8.04   Domain Names

[1]—Domain Name Registration

[a]—ICANN

Web site domain names, also known as Uniform Resource Locators ("URLs"), are administered by a central source, the Internet Corporation for Assigned Names and Numbers ("ICANN"). ICANN is a nonprofit organization that globally coordinates Internet addresses. ICANN does not host Web sites or have any responsibility for the content of the Internet. Its only role is to coordinate the "addresses" so there is a unified, worldwide system.

[b]—Domain Registries

ICANN works with registries to manage Top Level Domains ("TLD"), which are the familiar extensions added to domain names, such as ".com," ".org," ".gov," and ".net". Each country in the world has a TLD.

[c]—Registrars

ICANN accredits registrars, individual companies that sell domain names. The policy aims to create the greatest diversity in the market by having hundreds of domain name registrars competing with each other, based on service and pricing and other

---

59   See *Bally Total Fitness Holding Corp., v. Faber*, 29 F. Supp.2d 1161 (1998) ("Bally sucks" Web site used to criticize plaintiff's company protected by First Amendment). As noted by the court, "The explosion of the Internet is not without its growing pains. It is an efficient means for business to disseminate information, but it also affords critics of those businesses an equally efficient means of disseminating commentary. Here, trademark infringement and trademark dilution do not provide a remedy for Bally." *Id.* at 1168.

60   See *People for the Ethical Treatment of Animals v. Doughney*, 263 F.3d 359 (4th Cir. 2001).

factors. All ICANN accredited registrars must abide by the Uniform Domain-Name Dispute-Resolution Policy ("UDRP").

[d]—The Registrant

The registrant is purchaser of a domain name. Domain names may be acquired for varying lengths of time. After the registration expires, the domain name becomes available for purchase. In registering a domain name through an ICANN accredited registrar, the registrant agrees to be subject to the UDRP's mandatory domain name dispute resolution procedures.

[e]—The Host Server

Web sites available via a domain name must be housed on a Web host server, a computer connected to the World Wide Web that holds the data that comprises the Web site. Thus obtaining a domain name is only part of the process of creating a Web site. In addition, the owner must enter into an agreement with a Web host, and the files comprising the Web site must be transmitted to the host server. Some registrars offer Web hosting services as well.

[f]—Whois

The availability of domain names can be researched online, using the "Whois" search protocol offered by many providers. A Whois search will result in information on whether a domain name is registered, and who the owner of record is. In some cases, the owner of the domain name may not make their identity available online.

[2]—The Uniform Domain Name Dispute Resolution Policy (UDRP)

All ICANN accredited registrars must follow the Uniform Domain Name Dispute Resolution Policy ("UDRP").[61] Under the policy, most types of trademark-based domain name disputes must be resolved by agreement, court action, or arbitration before a registrar will cancel, suspend, or transfer a domain name. Disputes alleged to have arisen from abusive registrations of domain names may be addressed by expedited administrative proceedings that the holder of trademark rights initiates by filing a complaint with an approved dispute-resolution service provider.

To implement the procedures mandated by the UDRP, ICANN has approved arbitration centers authorized to resolve domain name disputes. The two primary approved

---

61   See http://www.icann.org/en/udrp/udrp.htm.

arbitration centers are the World Intellectual Property Organization ("WIPO"), and the National Arbitration Forum ("NAF"). ICANN has approved other providers.[62]

Under the UDRP, a registrant is required to submit to a proceeding as follows:

> a. Applicable Disputes. You are required to submit to a mandatory administrative proceeding in the event that a third party (a "complainant") asserts to the applicable Provider, in compliance with the Rules of Procedure, that

> (i) your domain name is identical or confusingly similar to a trademark or service mark in which the complainant has rights; and

> (ii) you have no rights or legitimate interests in respect of the domain name; and

> (iii) your domain name has been registered and is being used in bad faith.

> In the administrative proceeding, the complainant must prove that each of these three elements is present.[63]

The UDRP procedures are an alternative to an action under the ACPA. Under the UDRP, the remedy is cancellation of the domain name or transfer to the plaintiff; the ACPA provides for statutory damages, as well. However, an action under the ACPA requires litigation in federal court, while an action under the UDRP is typically less expensive and quicker. Under the UDRP, the action may consist of only a complaint, a response, and a decision by a panel.[64] A searchable, online database of WIPO decisions under the UDRP is available to the public.[65]

§8.05   Public Licenses: Open Source Software

Public licenses, often referred to as "open source" licenses, are used by artists, authors, educators, software developers, and scientists who wish to create collaborative projects and to dedicate certain works to the public.[66] For example, public licenses support the GNU/Linux operating system, the Perl programming language, the Apache Web server programs, the

---

62   See http://www.icann.org/en/dndr/udrp/approved-providers.htm.

63   See Uniform Domain Name Dispute Resolution Policy, ¶ 4, available at http://www.icann.org/en/dndr/udrp/policy.htm.

64   See WIPO Guide to the UDRP, available at http://www.wipo.int/amc/en/domains/guide/.

65   See http://www.wipo.int/amc/en/domains/search/.

66   See *Jacobsen v. Katzer*, 535 F.3d 1373, 1378-1379 (Fed. Cir. 2008). *Jacobsen v. Katzer* included patent law issues, as well as the copyright law open source issues, which is why the case was appealed to the Federal Circuit, the more common forum for patent law appeals.

Firefox Web browser, and the collaborative Web-based encyclopedia *Wikipedia*.[67] By inviting the software programming community to make improvements to a program by announcing its "open source" status, the original creators of the program may still seek to exercise some level of control over how the resulting altered and improved programs may be commercially exploited by "downstream" programmers.

In a leading case on open source software, the creators of a software program that controlled model train sets made their operating program source code available online, via download, on an open source basis.[68] They included an "Artistic License" statement within the source code, which granted a broad non-exclusive license to downstream programmers to "use and distribute the [code] in a more-or-less customary fashion, plus the right to make reasonable accommodations."[69] When the defendants incorporated the plaintiff's software code in a new commercial product, under a new name, and failed to comply with the above terms and conditions of the open source license, the plaintiffs sued for copyright infringement.

The defendants argued that they could only be sued for breach of contract, not copyright infringement, because the non-exclusive license served as a defense to infringement.[70] In holding for the plaintiff, the court stated that "[c]opyright holders who engage in open source licensing have the right to control the modification and distribution of copyrighted materi-

---

67 *Id.*

68 *Id.*

69 *Id.*, 535 F.3d at 1376. The "Artistic License" included the following terms and conditions, which were intended to preserve the integrity of the original program by requiring any changes to be clearly labeled, limiting commercial exploitation of future open source versions, requiring attribution of authorship, and requiring anyone who wants to exceed the scope of the license to contact the original copyright owner:

The Artistic License grants users the right to copy, modify, and distribute the software:

provided that [the user] insert a prominent notice in each changed file stating how and when [the user] changed that file, and provided that [the user] do at least ONE of the following:

(a) place [the user's] modifications in the Public Domain or otherwise make them Freely Available, such as by posting said modifications to Usenet or an equivalent medium, or placing the modifications on a major archive site such as ftp.uu.net, or by allowing the Copyright Holder to include [the user's] modifications in the Standard Version of the Package.

(b) use the modified Package only within [the user's] corporation or organization.

(c) rename any non-standard executables so the names do not conflict with the standard executables, which must also be provided, and provide a separate manual page for each nonstandard executable that clearly documents how it differs from the Standard Version, or

 (d) make other distribution arrangements with the Copyright Holder.

Id., 535 F.3d at 1380.

70 *Id.*, 535 F.3d at 1379-1380.

al," noting that the open source user is authorized to make modifications and to distribute the materials "provided that the user follows the restrictive terms of the Artistic License." According to the terms of the license, it was "outside the scope . . . to modify and distribute the copyrighted materials without copyright notices, and a tracking of modifications from the original computer file."[71]

Thus, there are economic rights being preserved in open source software licensing. The original copyright owner of the software code enjoys the benefits of the improvements made by others, while ultimately retaining control over the process by requiring documentation of changes made, and controlling commercial exploitation of the results. As noted by the *Jacobsen v. Katzer* court,

> the attribution and modification transparency requirements directly serve to drive traffic to the open source incubation page and to inform downstream users of the project, which is a significant economic goal of the copyright holder that the law will enforce. Through this controlled spread of information, the copyright holder gains creative collaborators to the open source project; by requiring that changes made by downstream users be visible to the copyright holder and others, the copyright holder learns about the uses for his software and gains others' knowledge that can be used to advance future software releases."[72]

---

71   *Id.*, 535 F.3d at 1382.

72   *Id.*

This balancing act between inviting alterations to the copyrighted software code from the public, and retaining ultimate control via imbedded non-exclusive licenses within the program was further described by the court:

> The lack of money changing hands in open source licensing should not be presumed to mean that there is no economic consideration, however. There are substantial benefits, including economic benefits, to the creation and distribution of copyrighted works under public licenses. For example, program creators may generate market share for their programs by providing certain components free of charge. Similarly, a programmer or company may increase its national or international reputation by incubating open source projects. Improvement to a product can come rapidly and free of charge from an expert not even known to the copyright holder.[73]

---

73   See id., 535 F.3d at 1379. See also, *Planetary Motion, Inc. v. Techsplosion, Inc.*, 261 F.3d 1188, 1200 (11th Cir. 2001) (program creator "derived value from the distribution [under a public license] because he was able to improve his Software based on suggestions sent by end-users.... It is logical that as the Software improved, more end-users used his Software, thereby increasing [the programmer's] recognition in his profession and the likelihood that the Software would be improved even further.")..

Index of Cases

M

About the Author

COREY FIELD. Corey Field represents clients in all facets of the entertainment industry including film, television, music publishing, music recording, live concerts, book and magazine publishing, social media, internet and high technology, celebrity rights, agents, managers, and software. His clients range from some of the largest entities in the entertainment industry, to new and emerging companies, celebrities and athletes, the estates of novelists and public figures, high technology and software enterprises, nonprofit arts and cultural organizations, composers, writers, performing and dance groups, and entrepreneurs.

Prior to practicing law, Mr. Field was an executive in the international music publishing industry, and is a trained musician with a doctorate in music. He is active nationwide as a speaker, author, television commentator, and board member. From 2010 to 2012, he served as the President of The Copyright Society of the U.S.A. (New York); and currently serves on the board of leading nonprofit arts and entertainment industry organizations including as a Trustee of the BMI Foundation; a Trustee of the Kurt Weill Foundation for Music; a member of the Classical Radio KUSC Advisory Board; and is on the Grammy Foundation's Entertainment Law Initiative Advisory Committee. He formerly served as Treasurer of the American Music Center (New York), as a Governor of the Philadelphia Chapter of the Recording Academy, as a Trustee of the Marlboro Music School and Festival (Vermont), and as a board member of the Music Publishers' Association of the United States.

His writings on entertainment and copyright law have been published in scholarly journals including the *Journal of The Copyright Society of the U.S.A.; the UCLA Entertainment Law Review; The Delaware Journal of Corporate Law; the Journal of Intellectual Property Law; Entertainment and Sports Lawyer; and the Entertainment, Publishing, and the Arts Handbook.* Mr. Field served as an Adjunct Professor at the USC Gould School of Law where he taught courses including, Entertainment Law, Entertainment Law in Practice, and Music Law in Practice. He was formerly an instructor for UCLA Extension where he taught Copyright Law in the Entertainment Industry. He is a guest speaker and panelist for law schools, legal organizations, and entertainment industry associations nationwide, and recently conducted a course on film and copyright law in Beijing, China, for leading Chinese entertainment industry companies, on behalf of the USC School of Cinematic Arts. Mr. Field currently also serves as Outside Counsel for the Sundance Film Festival and Sundance Institute.

Mr. Field's work as an attorney on behalf of his clients has been recognized by inclusion in *The Best Lawyers in America* in the field of entertainment and copyright law and as a Southern California Super Lawyer in the field of Entertainment and Sports Law. He is a member of the California, New York, and Pennsylvania bars and holds a B.A. in Music from the University of California at Santa Barbara; a Ph.D (D.Phil.) in Music Composition from the University of York, England, and a J.D. *cum laude* from Widener University School of Law where he attended while working full time in the music industry and was a staff member of the law review *The Delaware Journal of Corporate Law*. He is the author of several published and recorded musical compositions and articles on music, and is the editor of *The Musician's Guide to Symphonic Music*. Corey formerly practiced in the Los Angeles office of a national law firm, and is the founder of Corey Field Law Group, P.C., a boutique specializing in entertainment, media, copyright and trademark law (www.coreyfieldlaw.com).

CPSIA information can be obtained
at www.ICGtesting.com
Printed in the USA
LVHW061347211222
735644LV00001B/2

9 781793 514738